The Murder of Helen Jewett

The Murder of Helen Jewett

THE LIFE AND DEATH OF A PROSTITUTE IN NINETEENTH–CENTURY NEW YORK

Patricia Cline Cohen

ALFRED A. KNOPF NEW YORK 1998

WWW.RANDOMHOUSE.COM

LIBRARY OF CONGRESS CATALOGING-IN-PUBLICATION DATA
COHEN, PATRICIA CLINE.
THE MURDER OF HELEN JEWETT : THE LIFE AND DEATH OF A PROSTITUTE IN
NINETEENTH-CENTURY NEW YORK / PATRICIA CLINE COHEN. — 1ST ED.
P.   CM.
ISBN 0-679-41291-3
1. JEWETT, HELEN, D. 1836.   2. PROSTITUTES—NEW YORK (STATE)—
NEW YORK—BIOGRAPHY.   3. PROSTITUTION—NEW YORK (STATE)—NEW YORK—
HISTORY—19TH CENTURY.   4. MURDER—NEW YORK (STATE)—NEW YORK—
HISTORY—19TH CENTURY.   5. UNITED STATES—MORAL CONDITIONS.
I. TITLE.
HQ146.N7C65   1998
306.74'2'09747—DC21   98-14561   CIP

MANUFACTURED IN THE UNITED STATES OF AMERICA
PUBLISHED AUGUST 11, 1998
SECOND PRINTING, SEPTEMBER 1998

For my sister,

Mary Weavers Cline,

whose love of old New York inspired my own

CONTENTS

The Murder of Helen Jewett

Snow in April

A PRIL 9 OF 1836 was an unseasonably cold Saturday night in
New York City, coming at the end of the coldest and longest winter of the early nineteenth century. Just a few days earlier, a late
storm dropped snow all over the northeast and mid-Atlantic states, but
now a sudden thaw seemed to be in the making, signaling the late arrival
of spring. The Hudson River, extending along the west side of Manhattan
Island and north into upstate New York, had been frozen since mid-
December; in February New Yorkers could walk to Hoboken on the ice.
That particular Saturday in April, the ninth, was the first day since winter began that steamboats ventured to depart from Albany to churn their
way through the icy waters down to the metropolis. The slight warming
brought a drizzle to the city that night, and the moon, in its last quarter,
rose at 3:11 in the morning. The streets of lower Manhattan were cold,
dark, and wet.[1]

Sometime in the early morning hours of Sunday, April 10, Rosina
Townsend awoke in the first-floor front bedroom of a house she leased on
the south side of Thomas Street in downtown Manhattan, just three

OVERLEAF: *New York City, 1840. The inset circle, bisected by Broadway, shows City Hall (19), the post office in the rotunda (22), the Police
Court building (23), the Park Theatre (14), the College of Physicians and
Surgeons (18), and the New York Hospital (26). Bridewell had been torn
down by 1840; it stood between the R and the K in "PARK." Rosina
Townsend's brothel was on the south side of Thomas Street,
midway between Chapel and Hudson.*

blocks above Chambers Street and three blocks west of Broadway. She was roused, she maintained, by a knock at her bedroom door; a man asked to be let out the locked front entry. Rosina recalled exclaiming, without leaving her bed, "Get your woman to let you out," which was her general rule at this house on Thomas Street, a successful, well-ordered brothel. Each of the nine young women who lived in the house knew that Rosina always locked the door around midnight and knew further that the lock required a key both inside and out. Some customers came and went during the evening hours, while others stayed the night. In the event that a late-night customer had to leave before morning, the house rule ensured that each departing man would be escorted to the door, which minimized problems of mischief or theft. But no female inmate came for the key after the man's request, and Rosina maintained that she quickly dropped back to sleep. The disturbance was so minimal that her bed companion did not wake up at all.[2]

Soon after, Rosina awoke again, this time to a loud knocking from the outside of the street door; it also awoke her bedmate. On this occasion she checked the clock on the mantel over the fireplace in her room, which indicated it was now three in the morning. The knock signaled a regular customer who had arranged to arrive late for an engagement with Elizabeth Salters, whose room was on the front east side of the second floor. (Salters confirmed this late arrival of a friend at the trial.) Rosina checked the man's identity by peeking through her bedroom window at the front steps outside; she then lighted a lamp in her room and let him into the house. As he disappeared upstairs, she reported that she encountered her first real clue that something was amiss. Through the door at the back of the hallway, she spotted a globe lamp sitting on a marble-topped table in the parlor at the back of the house; it was out of place, and it was lighted. Only two such lamps with the distinctive round glass font fitted on a square metal base existed in her house. Each was normally kept in a second-floor bedroom.

Rosina entered the parlor and next noticed that the door to the backyard was ajar. This was a door that did not require a key but instead locked with a bar that could be removed by anyone inside the house. The backyard, some sixty feet deep, contained a garden and trees, tables, a cistern, and an outdoor privy; it was fully enclosed by a continuous fence that varied in height from eight to twelve feet. Where a neighbor's stable backed up to her fence, Rosina had pickets installed over its top to prevent unauthorized entry. Brothel keepers in New York City found it wise to be security conscious. Three years earlier the Thomas Street brothel had been stormed by three ruffians who managed to clamber over the fence into the yard and who entered the house shouting profanities at Rosina's boarders and guests.[3]

Rosina concluded that a resident or guest had gone out back, possibly to use the privy, but this was a bit odd and certainly not routine, given the inclement weather and the availability of chamber pots in every room. She returned to her room and sat down, dozing for about ten minutes. But the open door and the absence of any sound of returning footsteps made her uneasy. She went back to the parlor, took up the out-of-place lamp, and called "Who's there?" out the back door several times. She next barred the door and then climbed the stairs to see which of the two possible rooms was missing its lamp.

On the second floor Rosina first tried the door of the back east bedroom, occupied by Maria Stevens. It was locked from the inside, just as would be expected when Maria had an overnight guest. She then tried the back west bedroom door, the door to Helen Jewett's room, and found it unlatched. When she pushed open the door, smoke billowed out. Rosina's first thought was that Helen and her guest would surely suffocate in there. In fright, she pounded on the door of Caroline Stewart's room, a front west room directly above Rosina's. Caroline and her companion for the night raced into the hall, and in short order the cry of "Fire!" had awakened the entire house.

For the next several minutes, pandemonium prevailed. Rosina recalled going down to her own bedroom window to shout "Fire!" into the street. The call was heard by a watchman stationed at a sentry post about sixty feet away, at the corner of Thomas and Chapel (now named West Broadway, two blocks west of Broadway). He came running, joined quickly by a second watchman whose post was three short blocks away at Franklin and Chapel. In the meantime, Rosina and Maria Stevens braved the smoke to try to rescue Helen and her overnight guest. What they found sent them out of the room in horror. The bed was smoldering rather than blazing; Helen was dead, her nightclothes reduced to ashes and one side of her body charred a crusty brown. More shocking still, three bloody gashes marked her brow, and blood had pooled on the pillow beneath her body. Helen Jewett had been murdered, and her companion of the previous evening was nowhere in sight.

What had begun as a routine evening at a business establishment in New York had taken a turn into a grisly criminal event that within the week would be publicized all over the country, via a network of rapid newspaper exchanges. Rosina Townsend, thirty-nine, had enjoyed a certain confined and local reputation in her line of work, but she now suddenly found herself a public woman of quite another sort, a public woman whose name carried instant recognition for years to come. Her melodramatic account of her newsworthy moment, the discovery of Jewett's body, became a set story that she was obliged to tell—indeed, according to one reporter, was especially eager to tell—repeatedly over the next several days and weeks. On at least five occasions, her narrative of her actions on the night of April 9–10 was taken down, by a newspaperman (once) or a court recorder (four times, under oath), and while she sometimes omitted or added minor details, in all the tellings her account was essentially consistent. But a story, after all, is what it was: a first-person narrative of how she remembered discovering the corpse, a memory obscured first by the veil of sleep and then of smoke and sheer panic. In the ensuing trial, Rosina became the classic star witness for the prosecution of Jewett's accused murderer, and indeed the only witness who could place him in Jewett's bedroom at a time contradicted by his alibi. Her credibility was fiercely contested in court by defense attorneys, who planted doubts, attacked her immoral and "polluted" character, and worked hard to foster suspicion that Rosina herself might well be the murderer.

Within minutes of Rosina's shout of alarm, four watchmen arrived at the house. Finding very nervous men in the hall, coats missing and cuffs unfastened, one of the watchmen wrongly surmised that he had been called to break up a fistfight. The fire quickly commanded their entire attention, and, helped by some of the women, they doused Helen's bed with water from the backyard cistern, using pitchers and pots that came to hand. One of them found a handkerchief marked with a man's name under a bed pillow and pocketed it as potential evidence.[4] Rosina, fairly well agitated, recalled that her own bedmate ordered her to "compose herself," as he had apparently already done, for as soon as the front door was unlatched to allow the watchmen to enter, he and the other overnight customers of the brothel melted away as quickly as they could, some in a state of partial undress. By the time a watchman ordered that no one could leave the premises, all the men had vanished, and so had one woman from the third floor, who slipped out carrying a hat and a bandbox as though she did not intend to return anytime soon.

New York City watchmen in 1836 were little more than a citizens' security force consisting of laboring men moonlighting for extra money. Stationed at sentry posts every few blocks, they kept an eye out for fires and by their presence discouraged burglaries and robberies. The city had no professional police force, but a small number of men had full-time employment as police and watch officers.[5] One such was George Noble, the assistant captain of the watch, who was on duty at a sentry station at City Hall Park when word came of the murder. Noble, accompanied by two or three additional watchmen, converged on 41 Thomas Street at about four in the morning. Another professional policeman was Dennis Brink, constable of the Fifth Ward, a ten-year veteran of police work who lived two blocks north on Leonard Street. He arrived a half hour later, having been summoned by a watchman. Brink and Noble directed the watchmen to search the backyard for clues, on the reasonable theory that the murderer had escaped through the back door. No clues were found in the dark, but at daybreak someone spotted a hatchet on the ground near the southwest back fence, wet and caked with earth.[6] A watchman then jumped the fence into the rear yard of a house fronting on Hudson Street and discovered a long cloak. It lay about fifteen feet from the fence, rather too far to make it likely that someone could have thrown it there from the Thomas Street yard. Brink and Noble theorized that the killer fled over the fence and dropped the cloak in flight. There being no exit from that yard to the street, they presumed the killer scaled several more fences to escape via an alley onto Duane Street or Chapel Street.

Brink and Noble questioned the women of the Thomas Street brothel about the victim and the guests of the house the night before. Rosina Townsend identified the dead girl as Helen Jewett, age twenty-three, from Hallowell, Maine. (Police, newspaper writers, and witnesses all used "Helen" and "Ellen" interchangeably throughout the case; probably the girl's own friends were not aware which name she preferred, unless they had seen her signature, where she clearly put an H. It must be that both were voiced exactly the same in 1830s New York.) Rosina then provided a chronology of the prior evening, arranging in sequence events that in the moment must have seemed to her routine and unmemorable. Every Saturday night Helen was usually visited by a young man known as Bill Easy, but on April 9 she had requested that Mrs. Townsend bar Bill Easy's entrance because she expected someone else. Rosina described admitting a young man known as Frank Rivers to see Helen between nine and ten in the evening. Although he had held a cloak up to cover his face, Mrs. Townsend had checked his voice, stature, and what she could see of his face to make sure the man was not the unwelcome Bill Easy. Rivers went right up to Helen's room, and he was still there at eleven, when Helen called for a bottle of champagne. Rosina carried the champagne up, along with two glasses, and made the essential observation of Frank Rivers—more precisely, the back of his head—lounging in Helen's bed, reading by candlelight. No one had seen Rivers leave, and no one else had arrived to see Helen. The clear presumption was that Frank Rivers was the man to find. Someone in the house supplied Rivers's business address, on Maiden Lane near Pearl Street, and policemen Brink and Noble went there and learned the suspect's real name was Richard P. Robinson, a young clerk who lived in a boardinghouse at 42 Dey Street, about a half mile south of the brothel, where they arrived at about seven.

The house on Dey Street was operated by Mrs. Rodman Moulton; its site, near Greenwich Street, is now under the large cement plaza just east of the World Trade Center towers. (Mr. Rodman Moulton lived there too, along with at least one son the age of the boarders; but in all the court documents, the boarders called it Mrs. Moulton's house, reflecting the common understanding that it was a woman's responsibility to manage the board-and-keep arrangements.) Like the Thomas Street house, Mrs. Moulton's had many bedrooms, but it was much more crowded, with two or three young men to each room. The tenants were in their late teens and early twenties; most of them, like boardinghouse men all over the city, were not native New Yorkers but came from towns and villages in New England and upstate New York. They were generally from the middle and upper ranks of their rural societies, boys who could be spared from the farm and who desired training for a commercial or professional career beyond what their small towns could offer. Richard Robinson's Connecticut father owned many parcels of land and served eight terms in the state legislature, an indication of his solid social and economic standing in the village of Durham, seventeen miles from New Haven. Bill Easy, whose real name was George P. Marston, was the son of a lawyer and judge in Newburyport, Massachusetts. Young men like Robinson and Marston came to Gotham to learn the business of business, clerking in various shops and mercantile establishments.[7] By day they penned letters, measured cloth, swept out stores, sold to customers, or perhaps kept the books, learning the cashier's trade. At night they were on their own, unsupervised young men ready to take in the amusements of the metropolis to the extent permitted by their pocketbooks.

Ten or fifteen years earlier, such young men typically would have followed the centuries-old custom of apprenticeship and lived with their employers—more accurately, masters—in a familial relationship. The location of work *was* the home, and indeed for many artisans and small shopkeepers, so it remained. But in the 1820s and 1830s, the more prosperous merchants in cities like New York departed from this practice.[8] Urban omnibuses enabled them to move their families several miles away from their stores, into the new residential districts of the city. Mercantile clerks were on their own now, renting rooms in the many freestanding boardinghouses west of Broadway or sometimes living in rooms above the stores. (There was evidently someone living at or near Robinson's Maiden Lane business address, who at six-thirty in the morning could direct officers Brink and Noble to 42 Dey Street.) The new living arrangements allowed for a masculine youth culture to form virtually on its own, with little guidance from adults. Merchants did not totally abandon their charges, however: a philanthropic group of businessmen backed an Apprentice's Library, founded in 1820, which circulated moralistic self-help books to the clerks and offered a lecture series on topics such as "The Importance of Industrious Habits to Young Men." Cloth merchant Joseph Hoxie, Robinson's employer, was an active member of this group. Perhaps he hoped that such an organization could substitute for his not standing in loco parentis for his three young employees. It was a hope ill founded.[9]

The Moultons' boardinghouse made no pretense of familial support or supervision. Meals were not provided, leaving the young men to their irregular habits of meals purchased at oyster bars and small cafés. They came and went at will; each resident had his own key to the front door. Robinson shared a first-floor front bedroom on Dey Street with James Tew from Rhode Island, who clerked for a Williams Street clothier.

Officers Noble and Brink first spoke to a servant girl who answered the door at Mrs. Moulton's on this early Sunday morning. (Having a servant in no way implied that Mrs. Moulton's house was a luxury establishment. Maintaining a boardinghouse of young men plainly required the labor of more than one woman.) The girl then knocked on Robinson and Tew's room, awakening Tew; Robinson appeared to be deep in sleep. Noble and Brink entered the room and announced they were policemen looking for Robinson. Tew shook him awake, and Robinson quickly got up and pulled on his trousers. At that point Brink noticed that one pant leg had a whitewash or paint stain on it. They asked Robinson to accompany them to the Police Office, located in a building on Chambers Street behind the City Hall in the park. Tew volunteered to come along too, to keep his friend company. While Tew dressed, Brink asked Robinson if he owned a dark cloth cloak, and the young man replied that he did not: his cloak was made of "camblet," a luxurious soft fabric made of wool and silk, and it was hanging in his room. Robinson put on a double-breasted frock coat for this sudden Sunday morning trip.

Both Brink and Noble later testified that Robinson seemed curiously unalarmed and calm during this first encounter. Only when the carriage bypassed the Police Office, continuing north on Broadway, did he show some small trace of concern. Robinson's color changed, Brink testified, when he learned they were headed for the brothel on Thomas Street. Still, he remained impassive and unexcited, even when informed of the death of Helen Jewett. When Brink finally told him he was being arrested for her murder, he flatly denied the charge.

By the time Robinson was ushered into the house on Thomas Street, the parlor held the eight remaining women residents; seven watchmen;

the city coroner, William Schureman; and the highest-ranking police mag-istrate of the city, Oliver Lownds. Two neighboring brothel keepers, Mary Berry and Mary Gallagher, arrived soon after. Mrs. Gallagher, whose brothel was around the corner at 120 Chapel Street, asked Robinson "what induced him to commit so cruel and barbarous an act," and he replied, "Do you think I would blast my brilliant prospects by so ridicu-lous an act—I am a young man of only nineteen years of age yesterday, with most brilliant prospects." Besides, he added, "there is another man's handkerchief under the pillow with his name in full upon it; I am not afraid that I shall be convicted." This was true; George P. Marston's name was definitely linked to the crime scene via the distinctively marked silk handkerchief. Mrs. Gallagher, who had never met Robinson before, was impressed and evidently took pity on him, for she put her arm around his neck and said, "God grant that you may prove innocent for the sake of your poor mother." She asked if he had seen the body yet and predicted his heart would break to see Helen "burnt almost to a crisp" and her head "split open." Robinson complained that the police would not yet let him see her, but just then Brink stepped in and cautioned Mrs. Gallagher not to talk to the suspect. Brink reminded her that no one, the police included, could ask him anything that might cause him to incriminate himself.[10]

Robinson was not spared the horror of viewing the crime scene. Early American criminal legal practice had at one time set great store on the ritual moment of placing a murder suspect in direct confrontation with the victim's body; if the suspect touched the corpse, and the corpse bled fresh blood, it was taken as a powerful sign of guilt in seventeenth-century New England. The all-seeing eye of God provided such signs to leave no doubt as to guilt.[11] New Yorkers in the 1830s retained a vestige of the earlier ritual, but now they watched the suspect instead of the corpse. Robinson was taken up to Jewett's room and confronted with the bloody and charred body. The officers scrutinizing his reaction were amazed to note his composure and impassivity.[12] He continued to insist he was inno-cent, having been at home after eleven the night before.

Around nine, two doctors summoned by the coroner, Dr. David L. Rogers of nearby Chambers Street and Dr. James B. Kassam from Walker Street, arrived to perform an autopsy. Dr. Rogers was a surgeon and "an expert anatomist," notably famous for his willingness to perform the highly dangerous ovariotomy.[13] Rogers and Kassam moved Jewett's body out of the bed to the floor of the room. They first examined the fore-head wounds and determined that they were sufficient to have caused instant death. They next made a lengthwise incision from neck to lower abdomen and sliced into several organs. They pronounced her lungs clear and healthy, her chest cavity filled with "a considerable quantity of blood," her stomach half full of partially digested food, and her uterus "unimpregnated but labouring under an old disease." Basing his opinion on the position of the young woman's body in bed and the peaceful expression on her face, Dr. Rogers concluded that the young woman had died "without a struggle" from an unexpected blow to the head; the charring of her flesh came after death.[14]

Coroner Schureman next rounded up twelve men to form a coroner's jury, plucking them from the crowd beginning to gather in the street; this was the customary procedure in any case of death from doubtful cause. The jury heard ten witnesses from the assemblage on the premises of the brothel. Rosina Townsend gave her first account under oath of how she had admitted Robinson to the house the preceding evening between nine and ten and how she discovered the body at about three. Next Elizabeth Salters and Emma French, residents of the house, testified to seeing Robinson arrive on Saturday evening and go upstairs with Helen. Mary Berry, the brothel keeper from around the corner at 128 Duane Street, where Helen had recently lived, identified Robinson as the young man who under the name of Frank Rivers had visited Helen regularly since 1835. Two watchmen described finding the hatchet and cloak, and Dennis Brink described the arrest. Dr. Rogers read his autopsy report into the record.

One of the last witnesses was James Tew, Robinson's roommate. He was still hanging around the crime scene, no doubt forbidden to leave by Coroner Schureman and probably now very sorry he had volunteered to accompany his friend. When asked to tell what he knew of Robinson's movements, he produced a version of the previous evening's events that was remarkably vague and elastic. He and the accused took tea together at the boardinghouse, Tew said, until 7:30, and then went for a walk. They parted company near the American Museum on Broadway at about 8:30. Tew admitted he was at the Thomas Street house himself sometime between 9:30 and 10:30, but he stayed downstairs and talked to a young woman for only a few minutes. He could hardly avoid admitting this, since the young woman was Elizabeth Salters, present at the inquest. Tew went home by 10:30 that Saturday night and was asleep by 11:15, he testified. Robinson came in later and was in bed when Tew awoke somewhere around 1 (as he guessed) and reportedly then inquired of Robinson what time he had come in; his bedmate replied half past eleven.

Tew was able to stick by his story of his roommate's comings and goings right through the trial. He never claimed to have consulted a clock or watch for any of these times—the room was too dark, he said, and in an odd way that worked to make him a more credible witness, for a lying witness surely would have nailed down the time. But in other respects Tew fell short of credibility, for he also claimed that it was his understanding that Robinson had known Helen only for three weeks. Several of the women there knew that was untrue. His worst moment came when he was shown the cloak that had been found out back. Tew tried to equivocate: "Witness said he dont know the Cloak but has seen the prisner wear a Cloth Cloak Similar to the one shown him.—As near like it as one Cloth Cloak is like another.[15] One newspaper reported the next day that this amounted to an identification of the cloak as Robinson's, sputtered out with "much agitation" by Tew, now fully realizing the predicament of his roommate.[16]

The coroner's jury quickly concluded that "It is the opinion of this Jury from the Evidence before them that the Said Helen Jewett came to her death by a blow or blows inflicted on the head, with a hatchett by the hand of Richard P. Robinson."[17]

Robinson was soon carted off to Bridewell, an old city jail dating from the mid-eighteenth century, located on Broadway just west of City Hall. Many hundreds of captured American soldiers had frozen and starved in Bridewell during the Revolutionary War, when the British held New York City. Now the dilapidated jail, on the verge of being torn down, was used only as a debtors' prison and a holding cell for suspects awaiting indictment. By midday Sunday, several newspapers had learned of the crime, and reporters converged on Bridewell to watch for the suspect. The *Herald* related that he arrived at the jail with "his countenance clear, calm, and unruffled, and on being put into his cell, his last request was for some segars to smoke."[18]

The citizens of the jury disbanded, and the doctors and police officers departed, but still the brothel teemed with spectators. Rosina Townsend held forth in the parlor, retelling her story to a gathering of young men. Outside, a large crowd of men and boys lined up to file through the house and view the corpse, shepherded by watch officers. (One of the onlookers was William Van Ness, a neighborhood porter, who joined the throng out of curiosity and then realized as he viewed Jewett's body that she had at times hired him to deliver letters.)[19] By four o'clock, as twilight approached, the remaining police guards cut off the spectacle seekers but admitted the editor of the *New York Herald*, James Gordon Bennett, for a private tour. "He is an editor—he is on public duty," the guard explained to the crowd as he opened the door to let Bennett enter.[20]

Bennett, a crusty forty-one-year-old Scotsman, was in many ways the most enterprising of the more than half-dozen newspaper editors of the city. In the first "Visit to the Scene," he described his entry to the house, through the crowd and past the guard, in tones of self-importance. He briefly scanned the lower floor and observed Rosina Townsend and the young men in the parlor. "This room was elegantly furnished with mirrors, splendid paintings, sofas, ottomans, and every variety of costly furniture," Bennett reported. A policeman led him to the second floor, and the editor became the eyes of all New Yorkers, now able to visualize this den of sexual iniquity in all its ghastly, bloody horror. "What a sight burst upon me! There stood an elegant double mahogany bed, all covered with burnt pieces of linen, blankets, pillows black as cinders." The body of Helen Jewett, still on the floor, was covered by a linen sheet, which the policeman pulled back. "I could scarcely look at it for a second or two," wrote Bennett.

> Slowly I began to discover the lineaments of the corpse, as one would the beauties of a statue of marble. It was the most remarkable sight I ever beheld—I never have, and never expect to see such another. "My God," exclaimed I, "how like a statue! I can scarcely conceive that form to be a corpse." Not a vein was to be seen. The body looked as white—as full—as polished as the pure Parian marble. The perfect figure—the exquisite limbs—the fine face—the full arms—the beautiful bust—all—all surpassing in every respect the Venus de Medicis. . . . For a few moments I was lost in admiration at this extraordinary sight—a beautiful female corpse—that surpassed the finest statue of antiquity.[21]

Bennett did not fail to linger over the "dreadful bloody gashes" on her brow and the strangely beautiful, burned skin, "bronzed like an antique statue." Her face was calm, and one arm draped over her breasts while the other, raised, encircled her head. Bennett managed to package violence, gore, sexuality, and beauty into a riveting and grotesquely erotic vision. To keep this rapturous vision of a dead Venus so pure, he shrewdly neglected the autopsy incisions made seven hours earlier, which surely disfigured the dead girl's chest and abdomen. Her "beautiful bust" had been slit down the middle and probably peeled back to enable Dr. Rogers to reach her lungs, and no amount of skilled repair work could have concealed that laceration. Bennett's rhetorical strategy favored a sexualized corpse over a mutilated one. He chose to present Jewett as a work of art perpetrated by her murderer, with head wounds and singed skin, rather than a postmortem dissection at the hands of anatomists.

Bennett surveyed Helen's room and pronounced it "wild and extravagant." She had a "small library" of books, by such writers as Lord Byron, Sir Walter Scott, and Edward Bulwer-Lytton, as well as recent copies of several highbrow literary periodicals such as the *Knickerbocker*, a New

York monthly. A picture of Lord Byron hung on one wall, and "theatrical fancy sketches" used to advertise actors in drama productions were pinned over the mantel. The dead girl kept an album or scrapbook where she copied down poems and other literary passages. A worktable was strewn with pens, ink, and expensive writing paper. Jewett was a letter writer, and a trunk in her room yielded over ninety letters both from and to her that were impounded by the police as potential evidence in the murder. (Bennett hoped to be able to print them in the *Herald*, but police magistrate Oliver Lownds prohibited it; Bennett managed to publish only one.) To find books, paper, letters, and pictures of literary celebrities in a brothel bedroom evoked surprise in Bennett. This had been a girl with not only beauty but talent and wit, wrote Bennett. "She was a remarkable character, and has come to a remarkable end."[22]

Bennett visited 41 Thomas Street again on Tuesday, April 12. He went in the company of a young man already familiar with the brothel, the two intending to grill Rosina Townsend about the crime. The lead paragraph of the *Herald* story describing this visit introduced Bennett's growing doubts about Robinson's guilt, but his reasoning surely strained his readers' credulity: "The tragedy of Ellen Jewett, still continues to agitate the public mind. Not the slightest pause has taken place. Who is the murderer? It cannot be possible that Robinson was the person! How could a young man perpetrate so brutal an act? Is it not more like the work of a woman? Are not the whole train of circumstances within the ingenuity of a female, abandoned and desperate?"[23] Women more brutal than men—could Bennett expect his readers to accept that? Perhaps yes, if he put the twist of class on it. Robinson was a young man with respectable family origins, while the women of Thomas Street were friendless and wretched. In desperation one of them might sink to murder for private gain, Bennett insinuated. Helen Jewett had owned considerable money and jewels; where had they disappeared to? he wondered aloud.

Bennett's companion, a young lawyer named William Wilder, talked further to Rosina Townsend, who "sat on the sofa, talking—talking—talking, of Ellen—Ellen—Ellen" and recounting her tale of the night of the murder. Meanwhile, Bennett wandered through the house and reported on more props of sin, in addition to the mirrors and rich sofas he had previously described. He revisited Helen's bedroom; the body was gone, buried the day before, on Monday morning, and the room now was a chaotic mess from the police search. Under a boot he found a well-read copy of *Lalla Rookh*, an epic poem first published in 1817 by the English poet Thomas Moore, the romantic plot of which involves a Persian princess journeying to her prearranged marriage who falls in love with a servant in her caravan, only to find at journey's end that the servant is none other than her prince in disguise. A volume of poems by Fitz-Greene Halleck, a popular New York poet and member of the Knickerbocker circle of literary lights in the 1820s, had every page cut as evidence of its having been read thoroughly. Under a velvet dress the inquisitive editor uncovered copies of *Don Juan* and *Beppo* by Lord Byron with passages underscored. Bennett even rifled around in the bloodied bedsheets and found a London edition of a recent book by Lady Blessington, *Flowers of Loveliness*, apparently unharmed by the fire. Lady Blessington was a romantic writer who had recently produced a literary biography of Lord Byron. Her own life suggested a model for Helen's. Starting out as a servant girl, Lady Blessington capitalized on her ambition, beauty, and a determination to flaunt traditional morality to gain entry to the leading literary circles of Britain and a title in the process. Helen Jewett's taste in reading gave New Yorkers a sense of her personality: romantic, literary, running to the heart-stirring love story that crosses class lines. Bennett also added two weekly literary periodicals, the *New-York Mirror* and the *Albion*, along with the monthly *Ladies' Companion*, to the list of Helen's subscription reading he had noted in his first tour of the room.[24]

In the parlor downstairs Bennett paused to contemplate a painting in one corner, depicting a kneeling white woman about to be dispatched by two Indians wielding tomahawks. Bennett managed to turn even this item into a clue for his growing suspicion that a woman in the house could have committed the murder. "What a remarkable type—or hint—or foregone conclusion of the awful tragedy perpetrated up stairs. If a woman who had borrowed money or jewels of Ellen—if a rival in the same line of life, wanted to make away with such a troublesome competitor, would not that picture, perpetually hanging there—visible at all hours—suggest to female vengeance or female design—the very act that was perpetrated?" The picture suggested to Bennett that thoughts of raising an ax to a woman's head were never far from the mind of anyone who lived in this house.[25]

April 10, the day of Helen Jewett's murder, had dawned sunny and bright, still cold but with a promise that the long grip of winter was finally broken. By nightfall, Richard P. Robinson was in jail, confidently smoking "segars"; Rosina Townsend was talking up a storm about her moment of fame; and newspaper editors—James Gordon Bennett being the most inventive and industrious of the lot—were well launched on a heated, competitive rush to publish up-to-the-minute exclusive news on the crime. A young woman's intimate life, a life that intersected with many men probably not keen to have that connection be known, was about to be disseminated in newspapers in New York and elsewhere around the country. Who was the girl, and how had she met this terrible end? Who had a motive to kill her? Was Robinson really the only suspect? By nightfall of April 10, editors and policemen were asking themselves these questions, which would spill over into the columns of the papers in the weeks to come. All these questions clouded the certainty of the morning's coroner's jury. The promise of an end to winter's grip proved illusive as well: on April 13, six more inches of snow fell on the city, and spring held off until May.[26]

CHAPTER TWO

Sensational News

NEWSPAPERS IN NEW YORK did not publish on Sundays. Nonetheless news of the crime spread quickly by word of mouth, drawing large crowds not only to the brothel but also to Bridewell, outside the window of Robinson's cell. Over the next week, city newspapers covering the story saw their circulation leap upward by many thousands of copies, imparting such an urgency to this local event that newspapers up and down the East Coast picked up the story and gave it great play in their columns too, in a departure from the usual journalistic practice of ignoring unseemly crime. From its initial moments, the Jewett murder struck a chord of some kind, one that resonated even for readers unfamiliar with New York City and the world of prostitution. A variety of factors drove public interest in Jewett's murder to unprecedented heights, making it one of the most highly sensationalized crimes of its era.

One simple reason for the attention was the rarity of such an event. Deliberate murder was surprisingly infrequent in the 1830s. New York City, with its 270,000 inhabitants, had only seven official homicides in all of 1835, and in 1836 only two capital murder cases reached trial.[1] Such a low murder rate did not make New York City a safe place to live, however. Nonlethal but brutal violence was endemic, and the Police Office files bulged with dozens of assault-and-battery complaints brought daily by citizens against other citizens; the number in the mid-1830s had rapidly risen to an annual figure of over ten thousand warrants.[2] Dead bodies of questionable origins regularly turned up every couple of days: Coroner Schureman ran a busy office rounding up citizen juries to hold perfunctory cause-of-death inquests on bodies fished out of the East and North

Rivers, on newborn infants found dead in alleys, or on corpses of starved or frozen indigents.[3] Routine deaths attracted little notice. But premeditated murder delivered by hatchet blows to the head was far from routine. A gruesome murder held the power to shock, startle, and alarm; it disrupted daily life even in a fast-growing and increasingly impersonal city.

That Jewett was a well-known courtesan further enhanced public interest. Many men, perhaps several hundreds, young and old, knew her personally or knew of her. The Thomas Street brothel drew in a middle- and upper-class clientele of lawyers, merchants, and their understudies, the clerks. The victim, then, was in a sense a prominent New Yorker, certainly more prominent than most women could ever expect—or fear—to be, known by reputation to a slice of the masculine mercantile world of the city. Jewett's personal relationships with a few key men in the newspaper business ensured that her death would not suffer neglect in the newspapers. The mayor of New York, Cornelius W. Lawrence, dignified the crime scene with his presence Sunday afternoon, demonstrating that high city officials cared about Jewett's death.[4] Lawrence, forty-five, was merchant, banker, and mayor from 1834 to 1837, and his visit to the brothel came literally on the eve of the annual election that returned him to office; polling took place April 11, 12, and 13. A decade later the mayor was revealed to be a brothel habitué himself, so perhaps his official interest in inspecting the crime scene was amplified by a private interest as well.[5] "Ellen Jewett was well known to every pedestrian in Broadway," the editor of the *Herald* claimed, in its April 12 edition. "Last summer she was famous for parading Wall Street in an elegant green dress, and generally with a letter in her hand. She used to look at the brokers with great boldness of demeanour, [and] had a peculiar walk, something in the style of an Englishwoman."[6] If in life she was remarkable and remarked upon, for being bold, eccentric, beautiful, and connected to the mercantile elite of the city, in death she became an instant celebrity.

Even people who had never seen nor heard of Jewett were fascinated by her murder, for it afforded an opportunity to contemplate the forbidden, the taboo life behind the velvet curtain of her brothel. Sexuality infused this crime, inspiring both attraction and repulsion. Just in the preceding six years, prostitution had become a matter of grave concern to a variety of local moral reform activist groups whose insistent message was that sexual licentiousness was surging out of control. While the existence of widespread prostitution was no secret to urbanites, until the Jewett murder polite society largely ignored the moral reformers' entreaties and sometimes condemned them for raising indelicate topics. Jewett's murder suddenly put a human face on prostitution. Large questions about the spread of prostitution (or contagion, the moral reformers said) could now be

The Real Helen Jewett, *a postmortem lithograph by Alfred M. Hoffy, printed in late May 1836. The artist represents a confident Jewett, equipped with letter, parasol, and handkerchief, echoing the* Herald's *description of her daily outings to the post office. Her fancy dress and hat and her tiny hands and feet were taken to be desirable signs of feminine beauty.*

framed around specific life stories. What circumstances brought a young woman to 41 Thomas? Were such women victims of men, or their victimizers? The murder provided an opportunity to talk and write about power relations between men and women. The subject was sex, an intimate topic normally beyond the frontiers of polite and public discussion. Under the guise of "news," literary and artistic depictions of the corpse itself—beautiful, naked, dead—presented material for erotic contemplation.

The unlikely person of the accused transfixed yet more public attention on the Jewett murder. Richard P. Robinson seemed a disquieting suspect, so young and apparently so respectable, coming as he did from a family of local consequence in Connecticut. His sixty-three-year-old father farmed land in Durham, Connecticut, northeast of New Haven along the Boston–to–New York stage road. He represented Durham for eight one-year terms in the Connecticut state legislature in the 1820s and 1830s (including one term in 1837, which suggests that the notoriety of his son seems not to have tarnished his standing with the voters in Durham).[7] To be sure, Durham was a small village, containing 1,116 inhabitants in 1830; with only about 150 householders (roughly equivalent to the number of voters), it was not really a major distinction to get elected. The elder Robinson was a big fish in a very small pond. Young Richard was the eighth child and first son in a family that eventually numbered twelve children born over a thirty-five-year span of time, a feat that required two successive wives.

On the surface, young Richard P. Robinson appeared indistinguishable from thousands of other similarly situated young clerks. Were they all secretly leading disreputable lives? Could he—could they all—be capable of committing a horrendous murder? Circumstantial evidence seemed to powerfully implicate Robinson, but newspapers and the public were baffled in their effort to understand how such a quiet, mild-mannered youth could commit this crime. The most typical murderer in the collective experience of New Yorkers was the violent blackguard with a history of committing aggressive beatings and drubbings. The rare premeditated murders could only be committed by "fiends" and "monsters," words that put a killer outside human society. Robinson's life before April 9 did not match those labels; indeed, friends and employers called him an "exemplary" young clerk. The only jarring element in his presentation of self for the public was that he appeared to be strangely unruffled by his serious plight.

One of the newspapers, the *Transcript*, summarized all these ingredients of the public "excitement" in its edition of Tuesday, April 12:

> It is not to be wondered at that such an excitement does exist as was manifested in every part of the city yesterday, in relation to this dreadful and almost unparalleled atrocity. The high respectability of the family and connexions of the unfortunate young man who is charged with the aggravated crime; his heretofore exemplary and excellent character and conduct; his youth; the superior accomplishments, beauty, and attractions of the poor murdered girl, compared with those ordinarily possessed by the common herd of unfortunates; the deliberate, premeditated, ferocious character of the assassination; and the desperate means which were resorted to, to prevent exposure and detection; all combine to invest the catastrophe with an interest and a horror that have rarely, if ever, been connected with the occurrence of any homicide, however heart-rending and awful, in any country.[8]

Another paper, the *Sun*, echoed that assessment on Wednesday. Robinson, the paper editorialized,

> still appears perfectly calm and unmoved, and wholy maintains his innocence of the horrible crime with which he stands accused. The excitement throughout the city in relation to this melancholy business continues unabated. The cold-blooded, deliberate and savage manner in which the unfortunate girl was massacred—her well-

known reputation for beauty, intelligence, accomplishments, and gentility of appearance—the youth of her supposed murderer, and the high reputation in which he was held by all his friends and acquaintances—his general mildness of disposition and correct deportment—all these circumstances tend to increase rather than diminish the agitation of the public mind.[9]

Newspapers like the *Sun* and the *Transcript* transformed the Jewett murder from a local affair to a nationwide sensation. The *Sun*, founded in September 1833, pioneered the concept of a penny paper reporting on lively human interest stories. By April of 1836, there were three additional penny papers competing in this new market, fine-tuning a formula based on humor, sensation, and crime reporting to attract a wide readership. The papers were small four-page affairs, on the order of twelve by eighteen inches or smaller, and were sold by individual copy in the streets by newsboys or by weekly subscription. The *Transcript* (started in April 1834), the *Herald* (launched in May 1835), and the *Ladies Morning Star* (first issued twelve days after the murder), together with the *Sun*, were all poised to grab the Jewett murder case and milk it for all its revenue-generating possibilities. As unusual and disturbing as the crime was, with its enthralling, bloodied victim and its improbable perpetrator, still without the competition of the press, interest in the case would probably have sputtered out in a short time. Instead, the upstart penny press whipped up public interest, sustained a high level of enthusiasm over many months, and spread a sense of urgency about this particular crime to daily and weekly papers all around the country.[10]

New York City already had more than a half-dozen daily newspapers of the six-cent variety that attended to political and economic news—the *Evening Post*, the *Commercial Advertiser*, the *Morning Courier and New York Enquirer*, the *Evening Star*, the *New York Times*, the *Journal of Commerce*, the *Mercantile Advertiser*, the *New York Gazette*, and the *Daily Advertiser*. Crime reportage did not fall into their definition of news. Instead, these large-format dailies printed ship arrivals and departures, speeches of favored politicians, exhaustive coverage of debates on bank and railroad charters in Albany, congressional news from Washington, and columns of business and legal notices. They were sometimes called blanket sheets because of their size (as much as two by three feet per page) and potential function (four by three feet when opened out, enough to take a snooze under—the 100 percent cotton rag paper could even withstand a rainstorm without disintegrating). Their presumptive readers were men of the business classes and of public affairs who could spread the large papers over their store counters or big desks and soak up news of commercial and political significance. In contrast, the smaller penny papers could be held in the hands and read on the street, or in a crowded tenement, a saloon, or even a privy. Subscribers to the big papers paid weekly or monthly rates for a paper delivered to their business establishment; there was no way to buy individual copies on the streets. These papers rarely covered local news at all, on the assumption that what happened locally was already known to readers.

Several of these six-cent newspapers ran regular court columns summarizing the activities of the Police Court and the Court of General Sessions, but this news was reported in the spirit of legal notice rather than in the distinctive whimsical and facetious style of the penny papers. About the most sensational accounts these papers generally carried were reports of transportation disasters, of which there were an increasing and distressing number as the race to move ever faster heated up in the 1830s. Stagecoach upsets, derailed trains, and steamboat explosions qualified as classic "news"—information coming from far away and carrying significant economic implications—while at the same time they supplied a touch of the macabre, chilling, and thrilling. Once the Jewett murder story gained momentum in the penny papers, the more traditional papers found themselves struggling to square their sense of journalistic ethics and conventions about what constituted legitimate "news" against a story that had become the talk of the town. To varying degrees, each started to attend to the story, some apologizing to readers for the sordidness of it all. The *Evening Post* of June 8, for example, called it "disgusting" and "disagreeable," covering it only to satisfy a "public excitement."

Although the penny papers all differed from the bigger papers in size, price, and style of coverage, they were far from identical. Each bore the stamp of its editor; each consequently took a distinctive position, different from its competitors, on the Jewett murder. The papers have often been lumped together as vehicles for an emerging working-class consciousness, or at least an anti-elite, irreverent view of current affairs, but the actual allegiances and reader responses were far more complicated than such a simple generalization allows. Each clamoring for attention to its own version of the Jewett case, the papers of the penny press framed much of the meaning of the story for readers not only in New York but around the country. The three newspapermen who figured most prominently in the Jewett story—and differed dramatically in their views—were Benjamin H. Day of the *Sun*, James Gordon Bennett of the *Herald*, and William H. Attree, who worked for the *Transcript*, the *Courier and Enquirer*, and the *Herald* in succession.

In stepping into the Jewett murder so decisively, the penny papers of New York were breaking new ground for daily journalism and pulling the reluctant traditional papers after them. Yet there was a different model for the penny papers; crime found its way into print elsewhere. Since the eighteenth century, some American printers had been producing small pamphlets containing ministers' execution sermons for capital crimes, often with some brief account of the crimes or confession speeches from the criminals appended. Initially, such pamphlets garnered respectable interest, presumably because of their moral and religious utility and not because of any morbid fascination with criminals' dying moments. Murder presented an opportunity for ministers to define transgressive evil and to urge their congregations to contemplate the fate of sinful persons; the focus was on the criminal's soul rather than the foul deed or the victim. Starting in the 1770s, crime pamphlets became more elaborate, sometimes reporting on the murder story as it had unfolded at trial, or indeed creating an independent narration that artfully rearranged a strictly chronological rendering and fastened on the horrible or the shocking aspects of murder. As printing presses multiplied in the early nineteenth century, a popular literature of crime emerged in the form of sixteen- and twenty-four-page octavo pamphlets, no longer shaped by ministers but by journalists, printers, and lawyers. Trial reports and accounts of crimes increasingly directed attention to the victims, to the dramatic moment of murder, to the shocking discovery of the mangled body, or to the supposedly twisted motives of the monstrous killer. Morbid fascination with murder found frank acknowledgment. Bloody imagery was deployed and played up to titillate, excite, and awe readers. Overtly erotic themes were not often added to the mix until the 1830s, when several landmark cases transfixed the reading population with stories of female victims in sexual relationships with their murderers.[11] Jewett's murder was a leading example of the popular genre: a prostitute, murdered with a hatchet in her brothel bed, deepened the connections between titillating eroticism and titillating horror.

That her murder in 1836 came precisely at a moment of supreme rivalry among a group of editors of penny newspapers in New York only strengthened the association between sex and murder. Already accustomed to covering minor crimes in regular Police Office columns, the penny papers leaped on the Jewett case, framing their storytelling in the conventions borrowed from the popular pamphlet literature on fatal crimes. But the daily publication schedule of newspapers significantly altered the genre. The editors could not tell completed stories, as did the crime pamphlet writers who knew from the outset the identity of their villains. The Jewett murder had to be shaped into a story for readers within hours after the killing, before anything could be conjectured about Robinson's motive. That alone forced a fine-grained focus on Helen Jewett and her life as a prostitute right from the start. An aesthetic of erotic murder was in the making, one that centered the story on the victim, and the Jewett case played a major role in shaping its central conventions.

A second important departure from the crime pamphlet literature quickly became apparent. In covering the story as it broke, the penny papers inserted themselves between the crime and the audience, mediating between the principals in the case and a public that, ultimately, would stand in judgment over the accused—either as jury in the court proceedings or in the court of public opinion, after the trial. Unprecedented, extensive pretrial publicity forced newspaper editors for the first time to consider the possibility that what they printed might have an effect on impending judicial proceedings. Canons of objectivity in news reporting were not fully established for the press in general, much less for the humorous, entertainment-oriented penny press. Should the press have access to evidence uncovered by the police? Could editors develop their own leads, uncover their own evidence? How could authentic evidence be distinguished from fabrication in the press? What was to prevent editors from simply making up material to entertain or to win a competitive edge over other papers? Should editors declare their opinions on the guilt or innocence of the accused? After the trial, could they second-guess judges and juries and criticize the outcome? In a battle between circulation figures and the integrity of the justice system, which would win?

In the first week after the murder, the newspapers clashed sharply over the question of Robinson's guilt. To many, the slightly built and seemingly personable nineteen-year-old appeared incapable of such a crime, and Robinson encouraged that view by dropping notes out his jail window at Bridewell to the crowds below, saying "Not guilty!" and calling out, "I am innocent, and I shall prove it tomorrow" and "it will all turn out right; see if it don't, now."[12] The *Sun* at first emphasized that Robinson "is a young man of excellent general character, fine, manly appearance, and most respectable connexions, not yet twenty years of age, and was much esteemed by his employer, Mr. Hoxie, and many others whom we yesterday heard say they had known him long and intimately."[13]

The endorsement of Joseph Hoxie carried a lot of weight. Hoxie, forty, was a New York merchant well known for his benevolent, educational, and political work. After a Rhode Island childhood, he came to New York City as a youth in 1812 and in the 1820s directed a private school for boys in the Fourth Ward, gaining experience caring for the intellectual and moral souls of adolescents. In the 1830s Hoxie opened a cloth-merchandising store on Maiden Lane and started joining business clubs like the General Society of Mechanics and Tradesmen and the New England Society, a social club composed of transplanted Yankee merchants. He also joined the New York City Temperance Society and became active in local and statewide Whig politics. In 1834 he stood for election to the city's Board of Aldermen for the Seventh Ward, losing by a small margin of only 23 votes. He ran again in 1836, and the three-day-long poll was in progress on the very days that Jewett's murder was monopolizing headlines. Amazingly, though Hoxie's name appeared in print as Robinson's employer, he was never identified in the murder covereage as a current candidate. Hoxie lost, but by only 34 votes out of 2,500 cast in his ward, which suggests that the arrest of his clerk for murder had little negative impact on Hoxie's bid for office. In 1837, Hoxie ran again and won by more than 500 votes.[14]

Hoxie, educator of boys, supporter of the General Society's lecturer program for youth, and advocate of reform and temperance, was precisely the sort of employer who championed moral uplift for apprentices and clerks. His fervent support of Richard Robinson (carried to the point of sitting next to him at the trial in June) was taken as a strong character endorsement of the young man. Although the papers did not say so, Hoxie was in fact related to Robinson's family. James Robinson, first cousin to Richard but a man of Hoxie's age, had been Hoxie's business partner in the early years of the Maiden Lane store and had married Hoxie's sister Hannah. It was probably through this cousin that Richard P. Robinson landed his clerking job initially. A web of family relations characterized many New York businesses in the 1830s, a common hiring practice in an economy that did not yet credential its young with licenses and degrees to certify skill or knowledge. Knowing someone's family served as a proxy for knowing his job qualifications. Hoxie employed as bookkeeper a twenty-year-old son of James, along with another nephew, an eighteen-year-old clerk named Joseph Hoxie. A third clerk, Newton Gilbert, and a store porter, James Wells, rounded out the Hoxie establishment. Family loyalty between Hoxie and Robinson would be put to the test in the months to come.

The editors of both the *Sun* and the *Transcript* marveled that one so young and unblemished as Robinson could be a killer, but their bafflement was vanquished by the weight of circumstantial evidence—his visit to the brothel, the cloak, and the hatchet. "Everything which has as yet transpired in relation to this strange and unnatural case, goes so strong against the unfortunate young man, that it seems impossible a loop can be found whereon to hang a doubt that the life of Miss Jewett was taken by any other hand than his."[15] By the end of the first week of news coverage, the *Sun* editor even published brief excerpts from a journal alleged to belong to Robinson that cast grave doubts on his moral character. The journal, it said, had "done him most essential injury in the minds of his best friends and the police authorities"—and, it need hardly have added, now in the minds of the readers of the *Sun*. Equally damaging was the *Sun*'s reassessment of Robinson's physical appearance. "The striking emaciation of his frame, and unnatural glaring of his eyes . . . give evidence . . . of the fearful war that agitates his bosom."[16]

In contrast, James Gordon Bennett of the *Herald* reminded readers of the need to presume innocence until guilt was proven in court. Were there other potential suspects? Bennett had hinted at several in his columns describing his tour of the brothel: perhaps a girl in the house jealous of Jewett's beauty, success, and expensive jewels, which he alleged were now missing. Or Rosina Townsend, who possibly was deeply in debt to Jewett. On April 15, the day the *Sun* went public with extracts from a diary said to be Robinson's, Bennett printed an anonymous letter purporting to be from the real killer, not a prostitute but a man and rival for Helen's affections who described how he hid under the bed and wielded the ax while both Helen and Robinson slept, the plan being to frame the young clerk for the foul deed. (The letter neglected to explain how Robinson supposedly managed to sleep through the crime and not see the perpetrator.) But now remorse had set in, and the tormented self-confessed murderer was writing to clear Robinson's name even as he obscured his own and fled the city.[17] The *Sun* and the *Transcript* scorned Bennett's printed letter as a preposterous fake, charging Bennett had paid someone fifty dollars to write it. Bennett never mentioned the letter again, a tacit admission that it was bogus. After the first week of intensive coverage, Bennett no longer championed the innocence of Robinson, which suggests that his early move was simply calculated to differentiate the *Herald* from the other penny papers in the interest of boosting circulation. If so, it worked. Within a week Bennett's paper was selling out print runs of between 10,000 to 15,000 copies.[18] The *Sun*'s circulation rose as well, and on April 21 its editor noted that it had secured 1,300 new subscriptions for home delivery of the *Sun* just in the past two weeks. The more staid New York dailies that limited their coverage to the official news of the case found that their sales remained stable, at the premurder low level of 1,000 to 2,000 copies per day.

A more pointed and lively disagreement in the press involved the question of Helen Jewett's identity. Who exactly was this young woman? How had she come to be a prostitute? Where was her family? Was she really the accomplished and talented person she was reported to be? The police authorities evinced no interest in delving into her background or locating her family. She was dead, and their task, narrowly construed, was to bring her murderer to the bar of justice. Having arrested Robinson, they felt no need to learn anything more about the victim. But the enterprising editors of the penny press leaped on the unknown and conflicting stories of her origins to construct a profile of Jewett the prostitute and Jewett the murder victim. In part, their goal was to make Helen Jewett into a sympathetic and worthy victim, so that the public would care about bringing her murderer to justice. That different versions of her story lay ready to be discovered only deepened the inherent mystery of her life and death. The penny papers made the most of these differences, each claiming its version was the only authentic and uniquely accurate report.

Citing a "respectable source," the *Sun* asserted in its paper of Tuesday, April 12, that the dead girl was really Ellen Spaulding, the legitimate daughter of a Major General Spaulding of Maine. The detail of the father's military rank signaled a substantial family standing. Ellen, said the *Sun*'s informant, attended a boarding school (another mark of privilege) where she gained proficiency in music and learned to speak French and Italian fluently. A bank cashier seduced her at school, however, dooming the accomplished girl to a quick descent into prostitution. The villain was thus the cashier: "She abandoned herself to her late degraded course of life in consequence of his [the seducer's] heartless perfidy."[19]

In contrast, the *Transcript*'s more compelling and detailed account of Helen's youth rang with authenticity because it came practically verbatim from the girl herself. The *Transcript* editors rummaged back through old editions of the paper to a column printed in June 1834, when Helen Jewett had appeared in the New York Police Court to press assault charges against a young man. The *Transcript* reprinted its 1834 story virtually complete on Tuesday, April 12. Jewett went to court to complain about a son of a Pearl Street merchant who, she claimed, indecorously kicked her while she was bending over in the stairway of the Park Theatre to pick up a ten-dollar bill she had dropped. He then ran off laughing. The *Transcript*'s court reporter, William H. Attree, eagerly sought out Jewett's life story and printed it as proof "of the misery resulting from the villainous artifices of those whose sole aim in life, seems to be the seduction of a young and innocent girl."

Helen Jewett told Attree that she had been born in Massachusetts and orphaned at an early age. A guardian charged with her care sent her to a boarding school outside Boston, where the son of a "respectable merchant" met her, "engaged her affections," seduced her, and spirited her off to Boston to live in sin. Her guardian rescued her and instituted legal proceedings against the young rake, who was so dishonorable that he fled the city. Helen stayed with the guardian for a while, but felt such shame at her ruin that she finally left the respectable guardian's home for New York City. Reported Attree,

His unfortunate victim, although kindly treated by her guardian, was but too soon aware, that to regain her former standing in society, was impossible; and in order to escape from scenes, that only served to remind her, with a soul-harrowing power, of what she was, and what she had been, she came to New York, alone and unprotected.

As in the *Sun*'s shorter Ellen Spaulding version, the *Transcript*'s report seemed to endorse the idea that losing female virginity inevitably spelled a woman's doom. Helen herself, the source of the story, apparently offered no challenge or reproach to this unforgiving social practice. The *Transcript* concluded its account with notice of Jewett's two previous appearances before the Police Court, once to lodge a complaint against a British naval officer who ripped up several of her dresses in an angry brothel dispute, and the other when she was arrested in a sweep of a house of prostitution on Duane Street. "Her quiet and genteel deportment procured her dismissal" in the latter incident. Thundered Attree, the court reporter, in his sermon on Helen's behalf, "Could her betrayer now see the once fascinating and innocent inmate of the boarding school from which he seduced her, reduced to the condition we have described, he would, if human, need no further punishment than the remorse which would then gnaw his inmost soul." The seducer was the wretch, and she was the innocent victim; but nonetheless, a severe stigma attached to the woman who had fallen from virtue. Respectability was beyond retrieval for such a woman; at least, such was the story concocted for public consumption in the *Transcript* in 1834 by Helen Jewett, aided by William Attree.[20]

A third and rather different account of Jewett's identity was published in the *Herald* on April 12, the same day that the *Sun* and *Transcript* printed their background stories. The victim, Bennett announced, was really named Dorcas Dorrance, a poor orphan from Augusta, Maine. She was taken into the family of Judge Western of that town, who made her a playmate of his daughters and gave her a fine education at the Cony Female Academy. In the summer of 1829, she was sixteen and lovely, but also fascinating, passionate, even wild. She lost her "honor and ornament" to a cashier from an Augusta bank named "H—— Sp——y." (The letters punctuated by dashes suggested specificity and yet mystery too; more important, the contrivance protected against lawsuit.) After quarreling with the judge, Bennett wrote, she left the Western family, moved to Portland, and commenced the life of prostitution under the name Maria B. Benson. Next came Boston, where she lived under the name of Helen Mar, and then New York, where as "Helen Jewett" she lived and worked in the most fashionable brothels.

Bennett indicated no sources for his story, but his reportage of the previous day had made clear that he ranged well beyond his office, beyond the Police Court and the rest of officialdom, to capture information for his stories. The *Transcript* got its background story from its own files; the *Sun* likely picked up its Spaulding story from someone at the Police Office, since that is where it got all its other news of the crime. James Gordon Bennett, however, was the one newspaperman who broke with custom and visited the scene of the crime himself, and not once but twice.[21] No other paper dispatched reporters to the scene. Under the traditional routines of journalism, even among the penny papers, editors for the most part were content to let news come to them; they passively received and printed official documents, politicians' written speeches, or courtroom testimony they heard as spectators. They might publish about events they observed, if they were newsworthy events, but there was as yet no practice of investigative reporting. Bennett changed that, by innovatively tracking news, interviewing witnesses, peeking into drawers in Helen Jewett's bedroom, and launching inquiries into her life story. Bennett was the reporter as gumshoe, shadowing the police to search the crime scene for unnoticed clues.[22] Somewhere in this process, someone—a housemate at the brothel or maybe a client of Jewett's—told him the Dorcas Dorrance story.

All three versions of the Jewett background quickly entered circulation, first appearing as bits and pieces in the city's six-cent papers—the *Courier and Enquirer*, the *Evening Post*, the *Evening Star*, and even the weekly sporting newspaper, the *Spirit of the Times*. From there they spread quickly to points north (Boston and Portland), to points south (Baltimore and Washington), and to points as far west as Columbus, Ohio, and Natchez, Mississippi, where papers reprinted the confusing multiple accounts verbatim. Rapid improvements in roads, stagecoach lines, and post office conveyance of mail in the 1830s had facilitated a fairly dependable system of newspaper exchanges, so that even tiny weekly papers like the *Oxford Democrat* of Paris, Maine, could count on receiving and selectively republishing news items from New York City newspapers within a fortnight of the event. Out-of-town newspapers often protested a moral squeamishness even as they dedicated space to the murder. The *Natchez Daily Courier* pronounced the story "revolting" but then reprinted conflicting articles from the penny papers. The *Columbus Ohio State Journal* at first refused to reprint the New York news on Jewett, claiming that such reports only "gratify the vitiated and depraved taste of the community" and "excite and inflame those passions, which but too frequently prove an overmatch for human reason." But by mid-May the Ohio paper had capitulated to public interest, covering the news yet all the while producing a running commentary on how terrible it was to lift up a dead prostitute and glamorize her life: "The press is endeavoring to give her an apotheosis!"[23]

The conflicting versions of Jewett's life created puzzlement and confusion. The *Philadelphia Gazette* finally dismissed all the stories as fabrications. "It has become really amusing to read the attractive fictions in which the life and character of the wretched ELLEN JEWETT have been dressed by the penny prints." Here was a beautiful girl who could play the guitar, harp, and piano, and speak Italian, French, and Spanish; "next we will probably hear she knew the Augustan classics." Her "physical charms" have been compared to "Italian marbles" and her ancestry attributed to eminent generals or majors or merchants. In fact, the *Philadelphia Gazette* declared with satisfaction, her true story has now emerged, courtesy of the *Boston Post*.[24]

The *Boston Post* of April 16 wrote:

THE MURDER OF MISS JEWETT. The New York papers are full of fictions about this girl. One describes her as surpassingly beautiful—another as remarkably refined, fascinating, and accomplished. The *Star* makes her the daughter of a Major-General Spaulding in Maine, while, by the way, there is no such man in that State, and says that her heartless seducer was a cashier of a bank, who perpetrated his high offence while the unsuspecting Miss Spaulding was at a boarding school &c. Now the true history of this unfortunate wretch is simply this: She was the child of poor and destitute parents, who resided in, or near Augusta, Me., by the name of Dawen—her name was Dorcas—at the age of four or five years she was taken as servant into the family of Judge Weston of Augusta, where she remained until she was eighteen years old. While in this family, she was treated with great kindness, received a common school education, and every effort was made to instill into her mind those high moral principles which could alone secure her happiness and respectability. At an early period she betrayed rather uncommon mental capacity, but an obtuseness of moral perception which excited the apprehensions of those in whose charge she was. Such however, was the strict discipline she was subjected to when with the Judge's family, that her conduct, as far as their knowledge extended, was unexceptionable, although she often declared that nothing should restrain her from following an abandoned mode of life the moment she should be eighteen, for then she would be her own mistress, and freed from restraint; and she fulfilled her determination. Upon reaching that age, she left the family that had so long protected her, and was soon degraded—not by a cashier, as the *Star* says, but by a young man of her acquaintance and own standing. About three months after this, she went to Portland, and entered a house of ill fame, under the name of Maria Stanley; after remaining there a short time she proceeded to Boston, and found similar lodgings here, which she occupied, five or six months calling herself Helen Mar; from this city she proceeded to New York, where she called herself Ellen Jewett, and there ended her miserable career, after a residence of about four years, in the shocking manner which has before been described. She possessed a naturally depraved and reckless disposition—was a great thief from her youth up, as we are informed by one who knew her in Augusta, and who has furnished us with the above particulars relative to her. If she acquired the rare accomplishments attributed to her, it must have been while she was in New York, which, from her mode of life, is not very probable. Her personal beauty, we are informed, was not at all extraordinary—her figure was short and full, and her face rather prepossessing. She is described as having been shrewd and very artful and as having contributed as largely to the ruin of young men as any female of her character in the same space of time.[25]

So here was an independent version, quite negative, of Jewett's background, printed in a Boston newspaper that for the preceding three days had contented itself with reprinting the columns of the *Sun*, the *Herald*, and the *New York Evening Star*. Its great specificity seemed to confer on it a higher degree of credibility than the other versions of Jewett's life, and it too traveled and gained currency on a circuit of wide reprintings in newspapers around the country. The *Post* described its informant as "one who knew her in Augusta, and who has furnished us with the above particulars relative to her." The *Post* did not point it out, but obviously its informant was someone who had also followed Jewett's career after Augusta, through six years of aliases and prostitution locations.

When the *Boston Post* article reached New York, Bennett reprinted it directly and completely in his *Herald* of April 19, without any editorial commentary whatsoever—a very unusual silence, for him. (The *Transcript* had acquired the *Post* article first and reprinted it on April 18; the *Sun* never reprinted it at all.) Perhaps Bennett stayed mum because he hoped before long to be able to ferret out and to lay before his readers the true identity and childhood of the mystery victim. On April 14, just after his second visit to Rosina Townsend's brothel, Bennett set in motion plans to contact Judge "Western" in Augusta, to ask him directly about Helen Jewett. He was awaiting an answer to a letter.

CHAPTER THREE

A Self-Made Woman

JUDGE NATHAN WESTON was not at home in Augusta in mid-April of 1836. His duties as chief justice of the Maine State Supreme Court required him to travel around the state to hear cases and appeals, and in the week following the murder of Helen Jewett he was in Portland, starting the spring circuit of his court.[1] At fifty-three, the judge was remarkably young for one at the pinnacle of his profession. Since age twenty-nine, he had worn judicial robes, first as the presiding judge of a Circuit Court. He was promoted to associate justice of the Maine Supreme Court when he was thirty-eight, in 1820, the year Maine broke off from Massachusetts to become a separate state, and since 1834 he had served as chief justice. In his entire judicial career, he reportedly never missed a single day of work at the bench, owing to uncommonly good health and a general steadiness of character. Augusta's historian and Weston's fellow lawyer James North, who knew the judge for twenty-five years, described him as a man who "possesses a mind of no ordinary vigor and capacity, great power of investigation, application and analysis, with an unusually retentive memory."[2]

Usually his wife did not accompany him on his judicial trips, but on this particular jaunt to Portland, Mrs. Paulina Cony Weston had come along. Thus the two were together when they learned of Helen Jewett's murder. The news was first published on page 3 of the April 14 *Eastern Argus*, Portland's main paper, available in the judge's hotel lobby or at the courthouse. Like most urban four-page dailies, the *Eastern Argus* carried advertisements on the front and back pages, reserving the inside two pages for news and editorials. The item in the Thursday paper was a

LEFT: *Mrs. Paulina Cony Weston.* RIGHT: *Judge Nathan Weston.*
The portrait of Judge Weston hangs in the Kennebec County Courthouse
in Augusta, Maine, in the courtroom he presided over in the 1830s.

reprint from the *New York Commercial Advertiser*, describing the "Horrid
Murder and Arson" of Ellen Jewett, said to be from Hallowell, Maine (as
Rosina Townsend had told police), and the arrest of her paramour,
Richard P. Robinson. Hallowell was a mere two miles south of the judge's
home in Augusta, where resided a Jewett family well known to the judge.
Jesse Jewett, the Kennebec County deputy sheriff in 1836, ran the
county jail next door to Judge Weston's courthouse. Weston may have at
first wondered if the victim was related to the sheriff.

Except for the information that the dead girl came from Hallowell,
there was nothing about the item printed on the fourteenth to tip off the
Westons to their personal connection to the case—unless they somehow
knew the last in a string of aliases that their onetime servant girl had
appropriated for herself. Friday's edition of the *Eastern Argus*, however,
told them everything, reprinting lengthy extracts of James Gordon Bennett's articles from the *New York Herald* of Monday and Tuesday describing in engrossing detail the beautiful prostitute's corpse. The unusual
eyewitness report of the grisly crime scene and the arrest of Robinson
made for dramatic reading, even for a judge. But imagine Weston's surprise as he read on to find Bennett's account of the Maine childhood of

the young murder victim. Helen Jewett was identified as Dorcas Dorrance, who had lived in Augusta before succumbing to seduction and embracing prostitution, going first to Portland under the name of Maria Stanley, on to Boston as Helen Mar, until finally becoming Helen Jewett in New York City. Judge Weston would have been thickheaded indeed if he did not now recognize as the victim his onetime servant Dorcas Doyen, whom he had last heard of (or so he later said) as Maria Stanley in Portland. Judge and Mrs. Weston had to recognize that someone who once resided in the bosom of their family had died a violent death.

Very soon the judge would also learn that the *Eastern Argus*, as well as the other major Portland paper, the *Daily Advertiser*, which also featured in its April 15 issue a shortened form of Bennett's "Visit to the Scene," discreetly omitted a key sentence in the *New York Herald*'s coverage, the one in which editor Bennett had named Judge "Western" of Augusta as the kindly guardian of Dorcas Dorrance. The Portland editors could easily recognize Nathan Weston here; the *Argus*'s editor, Ira Berry, had himself lived in Augusta between 1832 and 1834, when he was the publisher of the *Augusta Age*, and he surely knew Judge Weston personally. He probably figured there was no point in dragging into the public prints the name of a revered and distinguished Maine citizen, especially one so prominent in the state's Democratic Party. (In the 1820s Judge Weston had seriously contemplated running for governor; the *Eastern Argus* was financed by Van Buren Democrats.)

Other newspapers in towns around the Northeast had no reason to recognize or to protect the Judge Western of Bennett's story, so it was only a matter of time before the Portland papers too would have to acknowledge the Weston family's connection to the case. On April 15, the judge and his wife could feel sorrow for the sad end of young Dorcas without feeling themselves to be exposed, but before a week had passed they recognized that many difficult questions would soon be put to them by friends, acquaintances, and newspaper editors, who could easily decipher Judge "Western" of Augusta. And before long the *Boston Post* story of April 19, with its unmistakable account of the Weston household, would make the rounds. They could not avoid being publicly implicated in a distasteful murder story.

This realization was forcefully brought home to them by the arrival of a letter from New York City, signed by William Wilder, the young lawyer and friend of James Gordon Bennett. When Bennett printed the story of the Maine girlhood of "Dorcas Dorrance" in the *Herald* two days after the murder, he obviously drew his information from New York sources near at hand, perhaps from Wilder, the man at his side on his second visit to Townsend's house, and a man identified by the *Sun* as a frequent visitor to the brothel.³ The first story in the *Herald* was thus Helen's own, subject to her strategic embroideries as well as the varying memories of her acquaintances. With two other New York papers printing radically different versions of her background, Wilder and Bennett decided to try to sleuth out and verify the information they had at hand, and on Thursday, April 14, Wilder had sent off his inquiry to Judge Western at Augusta.

Mail stages traveled quickly in the 1830s; a letter from New York City to Augusta took no more than three or four days. When Wilder's letter arrived, probably on Monday the eighteenth, the Weston household contained five of the six Weston children, one of whom forwarded the letter to their parents in Portland.⁴ The judge and his wife had by now had five days since the *Eastern Argus* news story appeared to collect their thoughts, so when the opportunity arose to get their guarded version of Helen Jewett's childhood into print, they were ready. It does not seem to have occurred to the judge that he should inform his sons or coordinate his response with them.

Weston sent one copy of his reply, dated Wednesday, April 20, to Wilder in New York and a second to the editor of the *Eastern Argus*, whose friendship and support he knew he could count on. The *Argus* printed it in full in its April 22 edition, scooping the *Herald* by almost a week. In this way the judge protected himself against the possibility that his letter might be distorted and misrepresented by the disreputable penny press of New York City. But as it happened, Bennett was delighted to print the entire Weston letter in the *Herald* of April 28, because he felt it basically substantiated his initial "Dorcas Dorrance" version and thus bolstered his own reportorial credibility. He invited readers to inspect the original at the *Herald*'s office as proof that he had not altered it.

Judge Weston framed his letter around the key elements already embedded in the *Herald*'s Dorrance story, elaborating or differentiating where necessary on her parentage, education, accomplishments, and her fall from virtue. His letter was authoritative yet circumspect:

Sir: Yours of the 14th inst. after having gone to my residence in Augusta, has been forwarded to me at this city, where I am holding a court. I have noticed the account of the murder recently perpetrated in New York, in which the victim was a female, known by the name of Ellen Jewett. From some intimations in the papers, relative to her history, I am induced to believe that her true name might have been Dorcas Doyen, and that she once resided in my family. Dorcas was the daughter of a mechanic who, from intemperate habits, has been for many years very poor. After the death of her mother, who I believe was a good woman, she was, at the request of her father, received into my family as a servant girl, in the spring of 1826, she having been thirteen years of age the preceding fall. In that capacity, she continued with us until she was eighteen years old. She was, I believe, very faithful in the performance of what was required of her. She was sent at times to the common schools, where she made great proficiency. She was remarkable for quickness of apprehension, which was more particularly noticed at the Sunday schools, where she was a constant attendant; and had cultivated a taste for reading, in which she was permitted to indulge. No improper conduct of hers had ever been noticed by any member of my family. Some little time before she left us, rumors to her disadvantage had reached the ears of Mrs. Weston, which she was led from the protestation of the girl, to believe untrue. At length reports to her prejudice became so general, that we could not believe them unfounded—and they have been but too well confirmed by her subsequent character. By whom seduced I do not know. She was visited by no young man at our house, to the knowledge either of Mrs. Weston or myself.—She left us in the fall of 1830, passing where she went, as we were given to understand, by the name of Maria Stanley. She has been recognized in the streets of New York by persons who had known her in Augusta—and I have reason to belive [sic] that she has misrepresented the condition in which she resided in my family. The profligate life to which she abandoned herself, has been followed by a very tragic end. Both are to be deeply deplored; and I very sincerely hope that the catastrophe, cruel as it was, may not be without its moral uses. I am sir your ob't servant, Nathan Weston.[5]

In printing this letter, a triumphant Bennett boasted with some overstatement that "every material fact we have published of this unfortunate creature is thus clearly substantiated by the highest legal authority in Maine."[6] Western was really Weston, Dorcas Dorrance was Dorcas Doyen; her age, humble birth, and partial orphan status were confirmed. Bennett had indeed demonstrated his first report was more accurate than the *Sun*'s or the *Transcript*'s.

The judge acknowledged that Dorcas had remarkable talents and proficiencies for schoolwork, reading, and religious studies, although he attributed her education to the common schools rather than the elite Cony Academy named by the *New York Herald*. A large bequest from the judge's father-in-law, Dr. Daniel Cony, had established this private school for girls in 1815, and Judge Weston's two daughters, Catharine and

Louisa, had attended.[7] The judge was at pains to correct the impression that Dorcas had enjoyed the same privilege as his own daughters. But it is remarkable that he sent Dorcas, supposedly a live-in servant in his home, to any school at all. She was an adolescent during the five years she resided with the Westons, an age when a servant girl's basic education usually would have been concluded and her time devoted fully to cleaning, cooking, and washing. Yet the judge had allowed her time off for studies, and he further confessed to indulging her interest and taste in reading. Something was out of the ordinary in this girl's relationship with the Weston family.

Judge Weston's letter became somewhat elliptical when it came to describing Dorcas's descent from virtue. His task was a delicate one: to explain how a high-priced prostitute, a devotee of debauchery murdered in the capital city of vice, could have emerged from under his and his wife's moral tutelage. The judge insisted that Dorcas's conduct under his roof had been entirely proper; no men had visited her—to his knowledge, he hedged. He chose circumlocutions like "rumors to her disadvantage" and "reports to her prejudice," finally sliding into the word "seduced" only in one place in the entire letter: "By whom seduced I do not know." That one key sentence omitted Dorcas from both subject and object and draped the seducer in mystery, leaving only the "I" of the judge himself declaring his ignorance. When the girl could no longer deny the rumors, she left the Weston home, he said. Here was another claim that obscured more than it revealed. What was the substance of the rumors? Why could she no longer deny them—what evidence had come to light that gave them credence? And why exactly did she leave his home? Judge Weston carefully omitted to say whether he threw her out or whether she struck out on her own. In contrast, the dramatic focus of all the other narratives of Jewett's early life was the inevitable disaster of seduction, where either internal guilt and shame, or rejection by the respectable, forced a victim into a downward path to vicious crime. The judge instead opted for a reflexive verb to describe her entry into prostitution: it was a career to which "she abandoned herself." Weston completely avoided the usual clichés: he did not characterize her as the innocent victim of some evil man's passions, forced into a path of vice by a heartless world and its double standard. Neither did he paint her as an immoral temptress. His cautiously crafted statement deflected blame altogether.

On the whole, Judge Weston sounded basically sympathetic toward the girl. He had fostered and admired her talents and seemingly chose to believe her initial declarations of innocence, yet he was also resolute about her now-confirmed moral failings. In striking a tone of cool and distant regret, Weston succeeded in conveying the impression that the unfortunate Dorcas was, after all, just a house servant of some years past and of no more particular concern to him.

Newspapers everywhere seized on the judge's letter as the final word on the mystery of Dorcas's origins. By the first week in May, papers around the country reprinted Weston's letter in its entirety, capping off several weeks' worth of clashing narratives, each claiming superior credibility.[8] In addition to the four newspaper versions of her early life already in circulation, a pamphlet literature had sprung into being, providing three more variant accounts of Jewett's life.[9]

Different as these stories were, they all had three elements in common: they all placed Jewett's birth in northern New England, all furnished her with a kindly guardian, and all recognized her to be uncommonly bright. And nearly every story contained a sprinkling of details that corresponded to real events or people in her life. A letter in a Boston paper from someone claiming to be a personal friend of the Weston family noted that the stories contained "nine parts of falsehood to one part of truth; though it must be admitted, that the one part of truth has been ingeniously interwoven."[10] The odd mixtures of accurate details in the multiple fictions suggest that the source for each story had ultimately been Dorcas Doyen herself. Taken together, the several versions of her childhood and fall from grace may not reveal very much about the actual circumstances of her early life, but they do give a glimpse of the playful and duplicitous character of a young woman who reinvented herself to enhance her prospects. As a prostitute who had adopted at least four different aliases, Jewett was under no compunction to tell a "true" version of her life to anyone; she took liberties to invent and lie, as it suited her. The move from Maine to New York allowed her to fabricate a life, mapped loosely over her actual past, with a confidence that no one would attempt to verify it. Jewett's propensity to embroider was confirmed by one pamphlet author who claimed to know her personally, who commented, "The great discrepancies which appear in the accounts of her, which have been published, respecting her true name, arise from her own misrepresentations."[11] The editors of the *Augusta Age*—who had their own personal interest in further entangling the plot—were sure that "many of the accounts in the New York papers of her character and circumstances while here, are altogether wrong, and were probably furnished by the miserable girl to some of her acquaintances in order to afford some excuse for her conduct."[12]

For example, the *Sun*'s brief story identifying a Major Spaulding in Maine as the alleged father of Ellen Spaulding had to have originated in a Jewett fabrication, because of the conjunction of two elements: the bank

cashier and the name "Spaulding." The *Boston Post* article of April 18
disingenuously dismissed the entire story as false because there was no
Major Spaulding in Maine. True enough about the military title, but there
was a large Spaulding family with branches in Augusta and Hallowell.
Harlow Spaulding was a cashier of an Augusta bank in 1836; his initials,
"H.Sp.," matched those of the *Herald*'s encoded villain. Dorcas could well
have had a romance in Maine with Spaulding, the bank cashier. And later
in her career perhaps she tried out his last name as her own, in a fantasy
of possessing the old beloved again. A New York housemate or client not
fully apprised of the details might then report that Helen Jewett's real
name was Ellen Spaulding, implying a father named Spaulding. The
additional embroidered elements of the *Sun*'s story included the boarding
school stint and the assertions that Helen was highly accomplished, fluent
in French and Italian, and a capable musician, qualities that betokened
gentility. Jewett effectively deployed these claims to class status to further her masquerade, secure in her knowledge that daily routines in a
New York City brothel would rarely if ever require her to display her foreign language competency.

The *Transcript*'s story presents an even more vivid example of Jewett's
imaginative disguise. The crime reporter William Attree approached Jewett during her Police Court appearance in 1834 (when she had been kicked
on the theater stairs), asked her directly about her background, and
printed the story of the pitiful seduced girl at the Boston boarding school.
This version had the hallmarks of a factual account because of its immedi-
acy: the reporter heard it firsthand and had the opportunity to ask questions of her. Nevertheless, almost nothing in the story belongs to Helen's
past. Attree was a streetwise reporter whose usual style was to ridicule in
print (and not interview) the unfortunates who appeared before the court.
But this twenty-year-old prostitute captivated him, and he approached
her, swallowed her classic story, and printed it with righteous indignation
as if it were fully authentic. Helen puffed out a tale of the innocent orphan
thrown on the world, the wily merchant's son who seduced her under false
promises, the well-intentioned but heartbroken guardian, the soiled victim
who voluntarily flees, now alone and unprotected, knowing that rehabilita-
tion of true virtue is completely impossible.[13]

Did Attree realize there was no early orphanhood in her past, no
Boston boarding school, no rescuing and forgiving guardian? Probably
not, at least when he first met Helen. Letters from Attree, found in
Helen's room after her death by the police, substantiate his belief in her
seduction story. They also reveal how far Attree himself deviated from the
moral values his column on Helen seemed to champion. Far from seeing
her as a miserable, pitiable creature, Attree became an enraptured client.

In one letter he gushed warmly about the pleasures of lying on her bosom and praised her "rich lips" and "full bust." He then asked, "Did you see the account I gave of you in my paper? How I have served up the immaculate rascal!" "Rascal" was not nearly as harsh a pejorative as the "heartless seducer" and "betrayer" Attree had castigated in print. Calling him an "immaculate rascal"—the oxymoronic phrase perversely suggested this rascal was somehow impeccable and stainless, the opposite of a "dirty rascal"—further complicates the question of Attree's attitude toward male seducers. Attree came clean in two final sentences, completing his about-face and demonstrating that he privately envied the man. "What a prize the villain had who seduced you at the Boarding School," he wrote Helen. "How I should liked to have been in his place!"[14]

Attree's frank and robust admission was exactly the response to her story Jewett expected. It reinforced Helen's sense of what men, even hard-boiled newspapermen, preferred in the way of sexual scripts. Her self-presentation as an innocent victim of a man's lust worked to enhance her sexual appeal, but not at all because her clients might expect to feel compassion for victims. Despite all the language in the *Transcript*'s printed story about the "unfortunate victim" mired in her life of "misery," there was no real play for pity here. The seduction story's subtext engaged a male fantasy that placed masculine desire at the core of sexual interaction and endowed it with the magical potency to unlock a slumbering female sexuality. The boarding school girl was innocent and naive, unawakened sexually until the first man led her astray. Such a scenario positioned Jewett as a passive participant in sexual surrender. It removed agency from her actions and absolved her from responsibility for losing her virginity. Since nineteenth-century American society attached a powerful stigma to women who were sexually autonomous, Jewett, a successful prostitute, framed a public image to underplay her autonomy. In absolving herself, she seemed to place the blame on the evil seducer, following the conventions of domestic fictions of the day. Yet blaming men was hardly good for business either. The real message of her story was that men have the power to awaken a woman's desires. Male readers of Attree's police column clearly found it pleasant to fantasize about violating the virginal status of a trusting girl and transforming her in the process.

To keep the story convincing, Jewett was able to mix in just enough details drawn from her Augusta connections. It was probably not hard for her to fancy Judge Weston in the role of guardian instead of employer, since he allowed her to read and provided her with schooling.[15] Nor did she have to fabricate wholly the boarding school near Boston. Several young women of the Weston-Cony clan in Augusta had attended Mr.

Joseph Emerson's well-respected academy for young women in Saugus, just north of Boston, in the mid-1820s, and in her almost five years of family service Dorcas probably heard something about this school.[16] As for the evil merchant's son, Helen had only to think of the event that had brought her to Police Court that day: the merchant's son who so rudely accosted her, now cast as a worthy villain in her free promotional advertisement in the *Transcript*.

The *Herald*'s version of "Dorcas Dorrance" came the closest of all three newspaper versions to Helen Jewett's actual early life, but still it was embellished with misrepresentations that reveal the twists Jewett added to her life story in order to gain client interest. A close reading zeros in on the subtle distortions and restores Jewett to the center of the story, as subject rather than as the object Bennett thought he was describing. Wrote Bennett in his April 12 issue of the *Herald*:

> Her private history is most remarkable—her character equally so. She is a native of Augusta in the State of Maine, and her real name is DORCAS DORRANCE, but in New York she has generally passed under the name of Ellen Jewitt—in Boston as Helen Mar. She was an orphan—her father and mother, poor people, having died when she was in her infancy.

The error of "Dorrance" for "Doyen" sounds like the kind of garbling "Doyen" could easily undergo when passed on by Helen to someone who had no particular reason to remember it until Helen was murdered and the editor Bennett came around asking questions. Helen's self-described status as a poor orphan suggests she wished to eradicate the Doyen family from her past altogether, a move strengthened by her adoption of aliases that expunged the name. "Helen Mar" and "Helen Jewett" may have been remembered by Bennett's informant because "Jewett" was her current name, and Mar was a character from a popular Scottish historical romance novel of the day.[17] Judge Weston said in his letter that he had heard she went by the name "Maria Stanley," and other articles or pamphlets about the girl dredged up the names "Maria Benson" and "Ellen Spaulding." It was common practice in the 1830s for a prostitute to work under an assumed name, but Helen had an unusually long string of them.

As Judge Weston noted, Dorcas was not really an orphan at all, since her father was still alive; the law recognized only paternal death as the grounds for legal orphanhood. Her mother had died some years before, and by 1826, when Weston took her in, John Doyen had been married for three years to his second wife. Dorcas's stepmother was a woman just thirteen years older than the girl and sixteen years younger than her husband.[18] Dorcas was a stepdaughter in a reconstituted family, not a friend-less orphan as she contended.

Bennett's story continued:

> In Augusta, Maine, lived a highly respectable gentleman, Judge
> Western, by name. Some of the female members of his family pity-
> ing the bereaved condition of young Dorcas invited her to live at
> the Judge's house. At that time Dorcas was young, beautiful, inno-
> cent, modest, and ingenuous. Her good qualities and sprightly
> temper won the good feelings of the Judge's family. She became a
> *chere-amie* of his daughters—a companion and a playmate.

Judge Weston, in his letter, had insisted she was a servant; Helen boldly represented herself as playmate and friend of the girls of the fam-ily, with nary a mention of domestic service. The judge had two daugh-ters; Catharine, the elder, was fifteen when Helen moved in; Louisa, the younger daughter, was only two and a half in the spring of 1826, hardly old enough to be a playmate, much less capable of persuading her father to open his doors in generosity. Perhaps, however, Helen meant to suggest that Mrs. Weston was part of the ranks of pitying "female members" of the Weston household who invited her to live there.

> At an early age, and just as her mind was budding, she was sent to
> a Female Academy, at Coney, we believe it is called, over the Ken-
> nebeck river. At school her intellectual powers shone forth with
> great and remarkable brilliancy—but not more so than her form,
> appearance, and looks. She was the pride of her teachers—she was
> beloved of her school mates—she was obliging, good-tempered,
> intellectual and refined.

In short, a remarkable student. Bennett got one small detail right, which again shows the voice of Jewett herself in constructing this story: the Cony Academy was across the river from the Weston home. Unfortu-nately, the Cony Academy no longer exists, nor are there any remaining records of its scholars. The judge unequivocally denied that she had been sent there, and instead said she had a common school education. It is hard to imagine that he would lie about her schooling in a public letter, since many Augustans would easily know whether or not she had really been a Cony student.

Yet it was not so unthinkable that she might have been. Daniel Cony, Mrs. Weston's father, had set up the school with an explicit and generous endowment precisely to provide scholarships for orphaned, indigent girls, who would attend along with the daughters of the well-to-do of Maine.[19] It would not have been an extravagant notion to send her there, especially if she was unusually bright and her employer (or guardian?) was already allowing her some time off for schooling. Judge Weston himself sat on the five-man board of trustees for the school, which administered the indigent scholarship fund. In short, for a girl like Dorcas, attending such a school would not have been an impossible dream. Helen evidently convinced New Yorkers like the lawyer Wilder that she was the product of such a refined private girls' school, an important clue to her capacity to manifest lady-like gentility and learning. The Cony Academy offered its female students an ambitious curriculum. An advertisement in an 1828 Augusta newspaper specified courses in "orthography, reading and writing, arithmetic, grammar, rhetoric and composition, geography, History and Chronology, Natural History, Natural Philosophy and Astronomy, use of the globes, Drawing Maps, and also Drawing, penciling, and painting, and a variety of needlework." If required, French and Latin could also be taught by Mrs. Dillingham and Miss Aldrich, the two multitalented sisters who ran the school. A new boardinghouse had been built for out-of-town students in 1828, and the preceptresses promised that "particular attention will be paid to the morals and manners of those misses who may be separated from their parents or guardians; and every exertion will be made for the improvement of all, who may be placed under their care."[20] The Cony Academy well understood the necessity of vigilance in safeguarding the morals of girls living away from home, where even the cozy community of Augusta (population about four thousand in 1830) might pose a threat.

> After having continued at the Academy for some time, Dorcas, during the summer of 1829, went to spend the vacation at a distant relative's at Norridgewock, a town on Kennebeck river, about 28 miles above Augusta. Dorcas was then sixteen years of age— and one of the most lovely, interesting, black eyed girls, that ever appeared in that place.

Actually, Dorcas was fifteen that summer.[21] Both the judge and the New York informants consistently and independently advanced her age by a year, giving rise to the suspicion that Helen herself had always padded her age since she was eleven or twelve. The highly specific destination of Norridgewock (indeed, precisely twenty-eight miles by direct back roads north of Augusta) presents a puzzle. Jewett did have paternal grandparents, aunts and uncles, and cousins spread out in several towns perhaps ten miles around Norridgewock.[22] But no Doyens or other close relatives lived in that particular town. So why would this sentence be part of her own self-narration of her seduction story, as told to someone like William Wilder? One hint is contained in the calculated vagueness of the phrase "distant relative," embedded in a story fragment with so many other exact particularities—the town name, the river site, the twenty-eight miles, the vacation trip. Perhaps Jewett was repeating a lie she first told for the Westons' consumption: that she was going to visit distant relatives in Norridgewock. Could she have been visiting someone else, a principal in the seduction tale?

> In intellectual accomplishments, particularly the art of conversation, interspersed with brilliant wit and repartee, she was unsurpassed. Yet even at this young age, she occasionally gave indications of a wild, imaginative mind—without fixed principles—or a knowledge of the true point of honor in morals. Her passions began to control her life. Her education only gave additional power to her fascinations.

These claims about Jewett's consummate conversational powers and "imaginative mind" would obviously not be part of her self-told tale but represent the assessment made by Bennett's informant, who had known her personally in New York. Probably the informant then pushed that characterization back six or seven years into her midteens to imagine the shoals on which such a witty and passionate young woman might founder and come to grief, unconstrained by fixed principles and firm morals.

> In this town, in the course of visiting, she became acquainted with a young man, by the name of H—— Sp——y, a fine youth, elegant and educated, since said to be a Cashier in one of the banks in Augusta. After a short acquaintance with him, all was gone that constitutes the honor and ornament of the female character.

No family surname in Norridgewock fits the rubric "Sp——y," but there was a large Spaulding family in that town. As the New York *Sun*'s version of Helen's background had suggested, "Spaulding" was a name with meaning in Helen's past, and an 1848 version of the Jewett story revised the initials of the bank cashier to "Sp——g."[23] Asher Spaulding moved with his bride to Norridgewock from Massachusetts in the 1790s. Their fourth child, Harlow Spaulding, was twenty-six years old in 1829 and unmarried.[24] By 1827, he had moved to Augusta and had opened a bookstore on Water Street, a few minutes' walk from the Westons' house. In 1829–30 he published an Augusta newspaper, the *Maine Patriot and State Gazette*. From 1833 to about 1838 he was the cashier in the newly chartered Freeman's Bank.[25] In 1829, Spaulding no longer lived in Norridgewock, but no doubt he still visited his parents there. The initials Bennett reported, along with the banking and Norridgewock connection, would surely have made every Augustan who saw a copy of Bennett's essay leap to suspect young Harlow Spaulding instantly.

Bennett concluded the story of Dorcas's Augusta life:

> She returned after a short season to Augusta. Her situation soon became known in the Judge's family. A quarrel ensued. She left her protector, after having in a moment of passion lost all the rules of virtue and morality.
>
> After having recovered from her first lapse from the path of virtue, she retreated to Portland, took the name of Maria B. Benson, and became a regular Aspasia among the young men, lawyers, and merchants. In this town, she gave out that her family name was Benson, and that she had several connections of that name, at a short distance.

In terming Jewett an "Aspasia," Bennett put a glamorous gloss on being a prostitute. Aspasia, as any reader with a modicum of classical training would have known, was the mistress of Pericles, noted for her philosophical talents as well as for holding a salon in fifth century B.C. Athens. An Aspasia, then, was a talented courtesan who catered to an elite clientele. Bennett did not invent the term; for decades, learned women with unconventional sex lives—or, rather, the few such who came to public notice, like Madame Germaine de Staël of France—were typically called Aspasias. As with his several references to the world of art (the Venus de Medici, made of Parian marble), Bennett never assumed that readers of his penny press were uncultured.

Like Weston, Bennett was silent about whether the Westons threw Dorcas out or whether she defiantly left. If Bennett did not know, Weston did, and chose not to say. Bennett seems to have missed her first alias in the trade, "Maria Stanley," but he knew three others—"Maria Benson," "Helen Mar," and "Ellen" or "Helen Jewett." The judge knew about "Maria Stanley," as he reported in his April 20 letter to the *Eastern Argus*.

Curiously, however, the *Argus* had already printed the name "Maria Stanley" in its April 15 news story, which was supposedly extracted from the *Herald*—which did not mention "Stanley." How had the *Argus* been able independently to supply her first Portland alias? Someone who worked for the *Argus* must have known, and that person was likely Ira Berry, the paper's editor. During his two-year stint in Augusta in 1832 to

1834, he had been a business associate of both Harlow Spaulding and George Robinson, close friends of the Weston sons. If these young men still talked about Dorcas Doyen, two years after her departure from Augusta, Berry was there to hear them. Berry had lived in Portland from 1831 to 1832, when Dorcas lived there as Maria Stanley and then Maria Benson.[26] So either from male gossip of Augusta about a recently departed but still memorable fallen woman, or perhaps from personal knowledge acquired in Portland, Berry could have known that Dorcas was Maria Stanley. When the *Herald* story arrived by mail at the *Argus* office, it was probably he who edited out all the references implicating the Weston family and then added his own information on her local name, so that Portland readers in the know would realize whose death they were reading about.

Where Dorcas's aliases came from can only be conjectured. Clearly she chose them herself and maintained a certain consistency in opting for "Maria" twice, and "Helen"/"Ellen" at least twice. For surnames she sometimes chose familiar families of central Maine: many Stanleys lived in the region around Farmington, where Dorcas Doyen's father lived, and a few in Augusta too; Hallowell was home to the Jewetts and to a Benson family as well. But none of these families seems to link up to Dorcas's life in any demonstrable way. She did not choose names from her own family tree, nor did she choose names connected to the Westons or other leading families of the Westons' social set. She might have picked "Jewett" as a humorous gibe at the county deputy sheriff, Jesse Jewett; "Helen Mar" was clearly a literary reference.

What Bennett meant by a *recovery* from "her first lapse" in virtue is puzzling, since respectable citizens of the 1830s supposedly considered female sexual virtue to be irrecoverable once breached. Most likely Bennett meant that Dorcas lost her head to a first love but somehow came to her senses and put it behind her, only to find that the judge's family could not, forcing Dorcas to take up prostitution in Portland. Certainly Bennett did not mean anything as corporeal as a recovery from a pregnancy. Maine law, which Judge Weston well knew, required unwed mothers to name the child's father, who was then obliged to appear in court to post bond for child support. A concealed pregnancy with delivery in secret was a serious crime, drawing three months in jail or a $100 fine for a mother; the death of a child born in secret carried a sentence of five years at hard labor. Intended as a powerful deterrent to infanticide, such laws propelled bastard births into public notice. No matter how much Judge Weston might have wished to keep his servant's sexual sins secret, a pregnancy would have been near impossible to keep under wraps and away from the meddling of town authorities vigilant to determine paternity.[27]

As close as Bennett's story came to Judge Weston's, its general slant impugned the virtue and morality of prominent Maine citizens. Certainly the Westons themselves were vulnerable to the charge that, at the least, they had failed sufficiently to supervise Dorcas's behavior, and the small coterie of bank cashiers, four in number in Augusta (one per bank), must have been uneasily eyeing each other. Although the *Eastern Argus* of Portland had judiciously pruned the cashier's initials out of Bennett's story, out of reluctance to point fingers and implicate local bigwigs, a rival paper, the *Portland Courier*, was not so circumspect. Unbeholden to any political party, the *Courier* quickly realized the sales possibilities in spicy scandalmongering. The *Courier*, like the *Herald* in New York, favored humorous human interest stories, and its editor, Seba Smith, would soon be famous in journalism circles for his invented character Major Jack Downing, whose down-home countrified commentaries on Washington politics ridiculed and deflated pompous politicians. Bennett's features on the Jewett murder were perfect material for the *Courier*, and Seba Smith eagerly reprinted them.[28]

Smith took the liberty of embellishing one of them, possibly for the sheer fun of causing trouble. In reprinting the *Herald*'s "Dorcas Dorrance" story, someone in the *Courier* office substituted the initials "H****e B****e" instead of H—— Sp——y for the seducing bank cashier, carefully counting out the precise number of asterisks to represent suppressed letters. The *Argus* denounced Smith for this terrible slander perpetrated by the *Courier*, printing a letter of complaint that charged that the switch of initials was a deliberate smear against "a very respected citizen of Augusta." "The Satanic malevolence of the wretch!" sputtered the letter writer, identified only as "M***."[29]

To explain this letter of "M***" to its readers, the *Argus* now finally had to restore and publish the story of H—— Sp——y, bank cashier, which Ira Berry had earlier sensitively edited out. To lessen the damage, Berry naturally added his assurance that "neither of these accurately represent the name of any cashier of a bank in Augusta," which was technically true, due to Bennett's error of printing a *y* for a *g*. "But the latter," Berry added, referring to "H****e B****e," "does accurately represent the name of a highly respectable citizen of Augusta;—and the alteration must have been made designedly." Berry did not reveal who H.B. might be, of course. The *Argus* editor reported that he confronted the *Courier* editor only to be told that a lowly typesetter had made a simple mistake of setting, at random, the wrong letters. This seemed highly improbable, "a flimsy excuse," inasmuch as the initials "H****e B****e" so unambiguously identified a prominent Augusta resident. Of course the *Argus* did not say so, but the *Courier* could only have meant the thirty-year-old bachelor Horace Bridge, son of the recently deceased James Bridge, who had been one of the best-known attorneys in the entire state and the second-richest man in Augusta.[30]

The *Courier* thus succeeded in provoking Berry of the *Argus* into printing more of the background story than he had originally intended; Harlow Spaulding was now at risk for exposure, because one of the largest circulation papers in Maine had finally printed "H—— Sp——y" identified as an Augusta bank cashier. But very possibly Seba Smith's real target was the newspaper editors of Augusta, who not unexpectedly might prove shy about taking up the story of the murder of Helen Jewett. If Ira Berry in Portland felt protective of Judge Weston, then Augusta editors who saw the judge frequently and face-to-face would have even more reason to try to squelch the story. And as it turned out, it was not merely deference to a leading citizen that governed the actions of the Augusta papers.

Two newspapers operated in Augusta in 1836. One was a weekly Whig newspaper, the *Kennebec Journal*, edited by Luther Severance, a career journalist who was trained on the *Philadelphia Aurora* and the *National Intelligencer* in Washington, D.C. Severance came to Augusta in 1824 at the behest of Adams men in town (that wing of the National Republican Party that favored John Quincy Adams) and started printing the *Kennebec Journal* in 1825. In 1836, the editor was thirty-nine, married, and active in state politics, taking a seat in the state legislature once it came to Augusta. Severance was very much a political man, and his paper by and large steered clear of frilly features and calamity stories, devoting its columns instead to the standard fare of long speeches by Whig politicians.[31] The Jewett murder was startling enough to draw his attention, however, because it involved a local personage. In his edition dated April 20, Severance reprinted first the story from the *New York Commercial Advertiser* describing the discovery of the body and the arrest of Robinson and then also the *Herald*'s "Visit to the Scene" essay. He omitted all of Bennett's background information, only copying from the *Advertiser* the line about Jewett's being a girl from Hallowell. He then added his own final paragraph to clarify for Augusta readers exactly who the victim was:

> This "Ellen Jewett" we understand is a native of this town. Her real name is Dorcas Doyen. She was from her childhood in one of the most respectable families in this town, as a domestic, where she was treated with great kindness, and had unusual advantages of education for one in her situation of life, which she improved so far as to enable her to pass well among strangers. We are told that in New York she passed for quite a literary character, although all her

associations, since she left here, have been with the profligate. Her example should be a warning to those who would, like her, disregard the instruction of the good, and deviate from the path of virtue.[32]

Severance went easy on the Westons; despite Whig-Democratic differences, he did not use the Jewett murder to discredit a leading local Democrat. He had learned about Dorcas's unusual education from someone; his information on her literary pretensions was likely deduced from the New York newspapers. The town of Augusta must have been buzzing with gossip, but Luther Severance did not intend to add a stick of fuel to the fire or engage in any character assassination, preferring instead to teach a moral.

The other local newspaper was the *Augusta Age*, a weekly that came out on Wednesdays, and its coverage of the Jewett case was much more opinionated. The *Age* had begun publication in 1831, when the state capital came to town. Jacksonian Democrats felt the need of a strong counterbalance to Luther Severance's Whig paper, and Ira Berry and another former editor of the *Portland Argus*, Frank Smith, were lured to Augusta to start the *Age*. They did not start from zero, however; they bought out the stock, press, and premises of the weekly *Maine Patriot and State Gazette*, which had folded just six months earlier, the paper that Harlow Spaulding had owned between 1829 and 1831. Berry and Smith absorbed the *Patriot*, adding political news to the old paper's format of light features.[33] Readers continued to find humorous articles on how to pick a marriage partner, the influence of reading novels on moral character (argued in the positive), and news of seduction and breach of promise cases from other papers.

In contrast to the *Kennebec Journal*, run by the mature Severance, the *Age* and its predecessor the *Patriot* were youthful enterprises, and the young men who in succession ran them were fledgling members of Augusta's professional elite. Of the eleven men associated with the *Patriot* and the *Age* between 1827 (when the *Patriot* was started) and 1836, the year of the Jewett murder, seven were young bachelors who started working for the paper in their late teens or twenties (four had been under age twenty-two) and who left it within a year or two, to get on with intended careers in law, politics, or banking. Four had attended Bowdoin College, thirty-five miles to the south in Brunswick. Five of them were law students or lawyers, and two of them eventually went on to serve in the U.S. Congress.[34]

The editors of the *Age* in 1836 were two rather young men named George Robinson and William R. Smith. Both were born in 1813, the same year as Dorcas Doyen. Robinson had edited the paper for a while in 1832, when he was nineteen, under Ira Berry's ownership; he then left the paper for two years and devoted himself to training for the bar under Reuel Williams, Judge Weston's brother-in-law. He resumed his editorial work in 1835, when he and William Smith purchased the paper. Sometime in 1835 or 1836, Robinson and Smith accepted assistant editorial service from another young law student in Augusta fresh out of Bowdoin College (class of '34), George Melville Weston, third son of Judge Weston and not quite twenty years old in the spring of 1836. This was the team on duty at the *Augusta Age*—Robinson, Smith, and young Weston—when the news of the murder of Helen Jewett arrived in Augusta.

The *Age* plunged right in: no need to pussyfoot around, not when it had a version of events rendering local families blameless. In its issue of April 20, the *Age* reviewed the basic facts of the "Horrid Murder and Arson" as presented by the *New York Mercantile Advertiser*, the *Morning Courier and New York Enquirer*, and the *New York Herald*. The *Herald* said she was Dorcas Dorrance from Augusta, the *Age* reported, but now they crisply set the story straight, according to their own lights: "The real name of the victim is doubtless *Dorcas Doyen*—she left here in the fall of 1830." The editors knew this date independently of the judge's letter, since their story appeared on April 20, the same day the judge was writing his response in Portland. These three young men, who had ranged in age from fifteen to eighteen back in the fall of 1830, either remembered, or knew where to find out, the season and year of Dorcas's departure from town.

> Many of the accounts in the New York papers of her character and circumstances while here, are altogether wrong, and were probably furnished by the miserable girl to some of her acquaintances in order to afford some excuse for her conduct and impose upon her associates. As to her ever having been "seduced," it is a thing out of the question. The course which she passed was entirely voluntary on her part. Such is said to have been her character in this respect that she sought infamy rather than yielded to temptation.[35]

Dorcas actively sought sexual adventure; no victim here, no innocent yielding to sexual temptation and surrender, as William Attree, the New York crime reporter, preferred to believe. It appears that George Robinson, William Smith, and George Weston, young men all, thought they knew a thing or two about Dorcas's character that appeared to have eluded Judge Weston. Weston's letter professed to puzzlement about who her seducer might likely have been—"no improper conduct of hers had ever been noticed by my family," the judge asserted, and it was the ponderous weight of rumor alone that had forced him and Mrs. Weston to conclude that all was not right with Dorcas.[36] The young men of Augusta apparently were much more certain that she had exhibited willfully improper conduct.

The *Age* declined to reprint the *Herald* background essay on Dorcas, having pronounced it "altogether wrong" in the opening paragraph. But in case any of its readers had seen the *Herald* piece in the Portland or Boston paper, the editors hastened to set out a disclaimer about the bank cashier story by declaring with great blustering authority that "we need not add that the story of her visit to Norridgewock and her acquaintance there with a respectable gentleman of this town . . . is an entire fabrication."[37] It is easy to imagine Harlow Spaulding, armed with the damning April 19 issue of the *Eastern Argus* (the one that finally published the initials "H.S." and "H.B.," candidates for the villainous bank cashier), acquired fresh off the daily stage from Portland, striding up Water Street from his bookstore to visit his old *Patriot* publishing office. There he finds the three-man staff of the *Age* plotting their strategy for covering the Jewett murder in its April 20 issue. Reprint nothing from the *Herald*, one argues, for that will give it credence and further circulation; yet, beseeches Harlow, can you not single out and condemn this one item about H.S., the bank cashier, without actually printing the initials or the occupation? Good idea, comes the reply; and so it was done, exactly thus. Yet perhaps the editors of the *Age* were too clever by half: by asserting that the story of Dorcas's acquaintance in Norridgewock with a respectable gentleman of Augusta was a fabrication, they were implicitly admitting that H—— Sp——y, bank cashier, was a recognizable person.

To supplant the *Herald* version of Dorcas's youth, the April 20 *Age* reprinted in full the previous Saturday's article from the *Boston Post* (April 16; reproduced in chapter 2). The editors prefaced it with the claim that the *Post* story was "substantially correct," needing only one amendment, relating to Dorcas's age when the Westons hired her. Since it was common practice for newspapers in the 1830s to reprint entire articles from other papers rather than to write fresh ones, readers would see nothing unusual in the *Age*'s doing so in this case. Reprinting put a little extra distance between Dorcas Doyen and her Augusta connections. A Boston source was invoked, not a local one. (Yet that Boston source was, according to the *Post*, "someone who knew her in Augusta.") The amendment the *Age* offered relative to Dorcas's age did establish that the editors had independent information on the story of Dorcas Doyen.

The *Post* story placed Dorcas "Dawen" with the Westons from age four or five. (Here the *Age* "corrected" this to fourteen; even George Robinson and William Smith mistook her true age, which was twelve in the spring of 1826, when she joined the Westons. They assumed she was a year older than they were, when in fact she was the same age.) The *Post* was the first paper to get the name "Weston" right, another clue that the Boston informant was an Augustan insider. Dorcas had been treated well, the *Post* story admitted, and was provided with a common school education, in recognition of her "uncommon mental capacity"—further confirmation of her unusual intelligence and the judge's generosity in schooling a servant girl. But this informant had seen evidence of "an obtuseness of moral perception" that made her guardians apprehensive and concerned; evidently Judge Weston may not have been so oblivious and distant a paternal figure as he represented himself to be.

The judge had raised her with appropriate strictness, the *Post* informant reported, but young Dorcas was impatient to be eighteen and "freed from restraint." Clearly the informant for the *Post* agreed with the editors of the *Age* that Dorcas took active charge of her own sexuality. But whom did she pick for her first prey? It was a man of her own standing, said the *Post*; as if it were an inappropriate term for consensual sex among the lower classes, the word "seduction" was nowhere used. She reached eighteen, she willfully "left the family that had so long protected her," and only then did she degrade herself with this lowly man. The Weston family thus played no role at all in her descent from virtue, according to the *Post*, for she was no longer under their care. Three months later she was in a Portland brothel, calling herself Maria Stanley; so this informant also knew of her first alias, the alias editor Bennett had missed.

To complete the attack on Helen Jewett, the *Post* wrapped up the article damning her character, looks, and accomplishments. To call her "shrewd and very artful," "a great thief," and of "a naturally depraved and reckless disposition" further removed the Westons from blame by making it seem that Dorcas was simply born bad. Indeed, one might pity the poor Westons, saddled with a troubled and delinquent child. Her departure at age eighteen came probably not a moment too soon. And what of her beauty, trumpeted by the New York papers? Her figure was "short and full," her face "not extraordinary." The inference here was that no one should assume that this girl attracted men on the basis of her looks; instead, the reader was meant to conclude, she probably had to throw herself at men. Depicting her as unattractive helped submerge the thought that the respectable young men of Augusta (such as the males of the Weston family) might be impudently eyeing her and feeding her sense of power over men.

The *Augusta Age* editors endorsed this version of Dorcas with authority. Young George Weston had certainly known Dorcas personally, and very likely George Robinson and William Smith had as well. But of course they did not openly acknowledge this connection in their paper. Anyone in Augusta would have known anyway, but readers from afar (like Bennett in New York) were spared the useful knowledge that a Weston family member helped prepare the *Age*'s coverage.

Who then was the *Boston Post*'s informant for the April 16 story, so quickly conveyed to the *Age*'s editors? Clearly the information did not come from someone on the *Post*'s staff, for it marked a radical departure from what the paper had been printing about the crime in the preceding few days. The first brief notice of the murder had appeared on Wednesday, April 13, in keeping with the usual two-day travel time for mail between New York and Boston. On Thursday the *Post* reprinted the *New York Herald*'s "Visit to the Scene" essay, and on Friday they were deep into reprinting speculations from the *New York Sun* and the *Herald* about the dead girl's background, offering both the Spaulding and Dorcas Dorrance stories to their readers. So the Saturday denunciation of the New York "fictions" broke sharply from their own previous coverage; it had to have been sparked by the Augusta informant who crossed their threshold sometime on Friday to lodge his complaint.[38]

Two young men from Augusta had motive and opportunity. The oldest son of Judge Weston, Nathan Weston Jr., was rooming with his cousin Joseph Williams at Harvard, where they both were studying law. At age twenty-three, Nathan Jr. was an indifferent student struggling to keep his head above water in his class of fifty-two students at the Cambridge campus. His aunt and Joseph's mother, Sarah Cony Williams, wrote them a cheerful note on April 16, 1836, containing family gossip from Augusta and exuding happiness that "you both can have so great a privilege as you now are enjoying in that School," which she hoped would have a "salutary effect" on Nathan.[39] Evidently Sarah Williams did not read the Portland papers, or at least not in a timely fashion, for it is clear that at this point she had heard no news at all of the death of Dorcas Doyen, which did not make the Augusta papers until April 20.

But young Weston and Williams in Boston had access to the news as early as April 13, and they probably anxiously acquired several Boston papers each day to follow the progress of the case. When the April 15 *Post* revealed the name "Judge Western," the time had come to denounce the New York coverage and meet head-on the insinuations that the Westons had somehow created and nurtured an extraordinary prostitute. Of the two cousins, it seems more likely that Joseph Williams was the one who visited the *Post*'s office. Although he was a year younger than Nathan (at twenty-two, six months younger than Dorcas), Joseph was the surer of the two, more confident and self-possessed, and he was already playing the protector over his slower and clumsier cousin.[40] Also the informant was just slightly off in two details that a resident of the Weston household would have gotten right: he spelled "Doyen" as "Dawen," and he said she had been a servant with the Westons since age four or five.

A second paper in Boston, the *Daily Advocate*, not only implicated the Westons by name but also suggested a far more serious charge, which earned it a quick visit from an Augusta informant, probably cousin Joe again. On April 14, the *Advocate* printed its first story describing the crime and arrest of Robinson, a direct reprint from the *New York Mercantile Advertiser*. On Friday, April 15, the *Advocate* sketched in the Augusta background, summarizing (not directly reprinting) some New York papers. She was "brought up in the family of an eminent Judge of the Maine Supreme Court"—no name given, but the occupation certainly narrowed the field—and her great beauty and dangerously romantic heart (indicated by her admiration for Byron) "proved her ruin—she was seduced by a son of the Judge."

Here was a damning statement in print that surely made Nathan Weston and Joseph Williams redouble their efforts to contain the damage. The next day, Saturday morning, the *Advocate* inserted a small notice: "We are requested to state that our correspondent [from the New York papers] is mistaken as to Ellen Jewett having been ruined by a son of a distinguished Judge. The sons of that gentlemen were all at college at that time, and of course could not have committed the act. We state this in justice to the highly respectable family referred to."

Not content with this short notice, the Augusta informant to the *Advocate* persuaded the editor, Benjamin F. Hallett, to carry a long letter in the paper of Monday, April 18. Note that the writer managed to avoid mentioning the Westons by name, and that Dorcas's age on entering service was now corrected.

There seems to be considerable excitement created, on account of the murder of a girl who, in New-York, went under the name of Ellen Jewett; and that excitement has been increased by false accounts of her early situation and education.

An attempt is made to throw a peculiar interest about the transaction, by representing her as having come from respectable parents; as an orphan, bro't up in the family of a distinguished Judge, in Maine, as one of the children, and as having received the education of a lady. Then comes an account of her seduction by one of the sons. Knowing the true state of the facts, and being a friend of the family, I feel bound to give them as they are. A more glaring misrepresentation could not well have been made—nine parts of falsehood to one part of truth; though it must be admitted, that the one part of truth has been ingeniously interwoven.—And first, as to the respectability of her parents. So far from having been respectable, they, or at least the father, are notoriously otherwise. Next, as to her being an orphan. Her real mother is dead, but her mother-in-law and father are still alive.—Then as to her situation in the family alluded to. It is true, that she lived in the family, I think from the age of twelve to eighteen, but not as a companion of the daughters. She lived there as a domestic. As to her education, it was no better than that of any other domestic in the country, or rather, I should say, her opportunities of education were no better. As to her having attended the Corry Female Academy, it is not true. Finally, as to her seduction by one of the sons. This is more serious, inasmuch as this contains a charge affecting the *living*. It is almost needless to add, that this statement, like the rest, is a sheer fabrication. At the probable time of her alleged seduction, the sons were all too young to have committed the act, with the exception of one, who was at college. Whether she was seduced at all, is very problematical. It is much more likely, from her known temperament, that she was the seducer, instead of the seduced.— After this exposé, every tittle of which can be substantiated, publishers will be cautious how they promulgate any report derogatory to the character of the family in question.[41]

The whole letter has a kind of neophyte-lawyer cast, from the point-by-point refutation of key inaccuracies to the final veiled warning of legal consequences to publishers who persisted in printing falsehoods. Jewett's father is "notoriously" unrespectable; a stepmother is living; she was no orphan or companion but a mere domestic servant. The letter introduced an interesting evasion on the subject of Jewett's education. The writer first wrote that her education was not exceptional, but then he made a fine adjustment: her "opportunities of education" were not exceptional, meaning that she did not attend the local girls' academy (here called "Corry," a mistake best explained as a typesetter's error in reading the manuscript cursive word "Cony," since no true Augusta informant would have gotten the name wrong and no other newspaper had called it Corry). The tiny adjustment signaled that the writer was not comfortable asserting that she had possessed only a low level of mental training or acuity. After all, a servant girl who read the five-volume novel *The Scottish Chiefs* and who picked a character in it, Helen Mar, to be her alter ego was no typical uneducated Maine servant girl.

More experienced legal minds might have found a way of blaming Dorcas without repeating the allegation of seduction by a son of the judge. But this writer did repeat the charge, giving it even further currency than it might otherwise have enjoyed.[42] In fall of 1830, when the seventeen-year-old Dorcas Doyen left Augusta, the four Weston sons were aged seventeen, fifteen, fourteen, and eight. Nathan, who turned seventeen in February of 1830, started college that fall at Bowdoin, a day's stage ride to the south; trips home would not have been difficult. And why assume that the "seduction" occurred that fall? Daniel, fifteen, and George, fourteen, were on the young side, but cannot be entirely ruled out from having "committed the act"—here the writer craftily suggests that just one act, leading to total ruination of the girl, is at issue. The informant's strongest claim rested only on his assessment of the girl's true temperament: she was sexually assertive and therefore more likely to have been the aggressor, not a victim of seduction. Cousin Joe and Nathan, sixteen and seventeen respectively in the fall of 1829, and therefore both old enough to have "committed the act," must have been made of stern stuff to resist a sexually aggressive young temptress living with Nathan's family.

None of the existing half-dozen letters in the Williams family papers written that spring mentions the Jewett murder case; nor do two letters Paulina Cony Weston sent to an old neighbor who now lived in Philadelphia. The women in town wrote small-town gossip to the boys away at school, and the boys wrote back less often and just as vacantly. Mrs. Weston's June 2 letter to her Philadelphia friend began with the vague and disingenuous observation "I don't know as any thing very special has occurred in the neighborhood, since you left." (The trial for Jewett's murder would open the very next day in New York.) The rest of her letter was a hodgepodge of aimless gossip and minute facts concocted to fill the letter's preordained space without saying much of anything personal: who was confined with child, how many scholars had started in the high school, how the building of the dam on the Kennebec River was progressing. Was this purposeful omission by the mothers and aunts of these boys? The sensational murder of a girl who had lived at the Westons for five years hardly seems too trivial to mention. More likely, it was far too painful and too dangerous to commit to paper.[43]

The *Post* and *Advocate* articles planted by Joseph and Nathan had circulated just days before Judge Weston's authoritative statement of April 20 made the rounds. The *Philadelphia Public Ledger* compared the *Post* article with the judge's letter and concluded that Weston's letter completely refuted the *Post*'s allegations. The *Post* article cast Jewett as an immoral thief, but the judge's letter said the girl's mother was a "good woman": "No girl," declared the *Ledger*, "brought up to the age of thirteen by a mother 'who was a good woman,' as Judge Weston describes, would have been a willing votary to vice." Having a good mother simply precluded the possibility. The *Ledger* continued, "Who was her seducer, the Judge does not know. One of the New York papers says he was a son of the Judge; another that he was a cashier of a Bank in Augusta. —That he was a respectable scoundrel we cannot doubt, and it is probable that the statement of the Boston *Post*, which Judge Weston has so thoroughly stamped [contradicted], was published at the suggestion of her seducer. If the villain can be ferreted out, he ought to be exposed."[44] In surmising that the *Post*'s informant was someone feeling defensive and even guilty, the *Ledger* was right on target.

The *Boston Post* article condemned by the Philadelphia paper was reprinted approvingly not only in the *Augusta Age* but in the other leading papers in Maine as well. Ira Berry inserted it in the *Portland Eastern Argus* on April 18. The *Oxford Democrat* of Paris, Maine, put it in its April 26 issue. Down in New York City, James Gordon Bennett, whose mail brought him copies of the Maine newspapers, remarked on the New England enthusiasm for the *Post* article. Bennett read the attacks on Dorcas Doyen's character as the uncomfortable squirming of uneasy editors trying to protect the rich and powerful men of Maine who had really been responsible for Dorcas's ruin. His sources in New York confirmed that she was considered to be fascinating, intelligent, and beautiful; to claim she was not was a transparent lie. The true culprits, said Bennett, were "the cashiers, or colonels, or majors, or generals, or great men of the state of Maine [who] destroyed the virtue of Ellen—and now want to destroy her intellectual character, in order to diminish the enormity of their own guilt." Bennett singled out the "political hacks" of the *Augusta Age* who were trying to "diminish their own wickedness of having been the cause of her original fall." Bennett's intuitions were powerful, considering he had no way of knowing exactly who the editors of the *Age* were.[45]

Judge Weston's letter, however, printed and reprinted extensively at the end of April and the beginning of May, did not appear to Bennett to be part of a suspicious Maine cover-up. The judge allowed that Helen was smart and attractive, a key difference from the mean-spirited stories in the *Post* and the *Age*. Bennett accepted the judge's letter because it confirmed much of his own investigative reporting, for which he was grateful. It was also impressively vague about the circumstances of her fall from grace. Judge Weston's judicious (but also tendentious) response said all he needed to, and nothing more, to get the Weston family name out of the newspapers.

The conflicting newspaper stories about Helen Jewett that circulated after her death created mystery and tension, which contributed greatly to the media frenzy around the case. The sharply contrasting interpretations of her character allowed members of the reading public to imagine her in different ways, as it pleased them, either as a once-innocent victim worthy of shocked sympathy or as a bad girl, a sexual predator even, who got what was coming to her. That the kernel of each of the stories originated in some way with Jewett herself provides a remarkable glimpse of her, even though her intent in each particular version was to masquerade. The total effect suggests a young woman who could appear romantic, wistful, and tragic but who also was quite able to be clever, deceitful, and manipulative.

A lot was at stake in these conflicting portrayals, joined within weeks by several more slightly altered versions of her life story issued by pamphleteers. Judge Weston and his sons were motivated to rescue their family from blame or suspicion, and so they minimized her claim to sympathy by serving up an unsavory view of her character. New York friends and acquaintances pressed hard to elevate Jewett into a worthy victim, someone whose death should be mourned and whose murderer should be spared nothing of what the law ordains for first-degree murderers. In many ways, the supporters of Helen Jewett had the harder task: to make the public accept a prostitute as an admirable and virtuous heroine.

CHAPTER FOUR

New York's Sex Trade

TO EVOKE EMPATHY FOR a career prostitute was, on the face of it, a daunting task. A prostitute could not lay claim to public sympathy as though she were an unblemished daughter. Prostitutes trafficked in sex outside of marriage, something that ministers, moralists, indeed anyone with a claim to respectability, even worldly newspapermen like William Attree and James Gordon Bennett, felt compelled to condemn when they wrote or spoke about it in public. No one dared argue, not openly, anyway, that illicit sex was anything other than sinful and dangerous. Yet it is equally clear that prostitution flourished openly in 1830s New York, barely challenged by law and frankly tolerated by the city's leading citizens. Despite the strictures of traditional morality, approval of prostitution was in fact implicit and widespread, so long as nobody had to go on record defending it. New York City was fast earning a reputation for being the number-two city in America for sexual vice, second only to New Orleans.

Not just in sex commerce but in all kinds of commerce, New York City surged ahead in the 1830s to become the premier urban center of America, surpassing Boston, Philadelphia, and Baltimore in size, population, and mercantile activity. The root cause of the dramatic change was the completion of the Erie Canal in 1825, which transformed the city into the Atlantic-coast outlet for a vast agricultural hinterland stretching inland to the Great Lakes and beyond via rivers into the vast interior of the Old Northwest Territory. People, goods, and money flowed in and out of the city in a continual stream of activity—among them, Helen Jewett, age nineteen, who moved there from Boston in 1832.

In the 1830s, commercial and residential structures thickly covered the blocks from the southernmost tip of Manhattan Island up to Greenwich Village. Back in 1815, before the Erie Canal was begun, the city's northern boundary of settlement stopped not far from City Hall Park, a triangular wedge of land enclosed by Broadway on the west, Chatham Street and Park Row along the east, and Chambers Street on the north. The elegant white-marble facade of City Hall, built in 1812, faced south onto the park green and beyond to the expensive residences and churches that lined Broadway; its back side was constructed of a cheaper grade of gray freestone, betraying the architect's naive assumption that the significant part of the city would always lie to the south of the park, centered along the mile down Broadway to Battery Park at the island's end.

Twenty years later, that assumption was completely obsolete. A massive rebuilding and expansion of the city had been launched. In the 1830s, many structures were less than a decade old, and year by year in the 1830s hundreds more were being constructed. In 1835, 1,259 new buildings went up, and in just the first eight months of 1836 (a year of intense economic activity and speculation that ended in the Panic of 1837), the number was 1,621.[1] The vast majority of the buildings were two- and three-story private residences; for example, the elegant brick row houses that yet today line the north side of Washington Square Park in the Village date from the early 1830s. North of the Village, from Union Square up to the mid-Twenties, streets were laid out and named on maps, but the blocks they defined were near empty, awaiting the anticipated development about to sweep over them. Bellevue, the city's almshouse and prison (where Richard Robinson stayed in the weeks between his arraignment and the trial), opened in 1831 on an isolated spot on the edge of the East River at Twenty-sixth Street. A decade later, it was surrounded by new residential structures.

Fifteen ferry and steamboat slips, all south of Canal Street, provided gates of entry to the city for passengers who arrived and departed by the thousands every day on the five dozen steamboats advertised in an 1837 mercantile directory. An additional ninety wharves crowded both the east and the west shores of Manhattan, serving intercoastal and trans-Atlantic commercial shipping lines. Coaches owned by six long-distance stage lines entered the city from the north, coming down the Bloomingdale Road and then Broadway to deposit passengers in the very heart of the city. In 1835, over 270,000 people—around 25,000 to 30,000 persons per square mile—inhabited the island of Manhattan, an amazing 35 percent increase in just five years.

Jewett upon arrival was already an experienced prostitute, or "girl on the town," the euphemism of choice in the 1830s to refer to a prostitute.

She was not alone in her trade. The heavy traffic of unattached people into the city—young men seeking clerkships, young women coming for domestic service, businessmen arriving on annual buying trips—created fruitful ground for a market in commercial sex. Statistics of women's occupations are notoriously hard to pry from the early-nineteenth-century censuses, where only the head of the household (usually a male head) had his name inscribed and where occupation was not noted for individuals. City directories remain the best source of occupational data, but not surprisingly, official New York directories did not list brothels or identify workers in the sex trade. But there were enough such women to stir up some alarm about their prevalence. The perception that prostitution was on the rise—maybe greatly on the rise—prompted several individuals and groups to attempt to gauge the severity of what they thought of as a serious social problem.[2]

The most alarmist estimate, made in 1831 by the Reverend John McDowall of the newly formed New York Magdalen Society, put the figure at ten thousand.[3] McDowall's followers and fellow activists, called moral reformers in the 1830s, stuck by that estimate throughout a turbulent decade of agitation over sexual sin that pitted reformers against others far more sanguine about prostitution. A sharp rebuke to McDowall's estimate appeared in an anonymous pamphlet published in 1831, which computed that ten thousand prostitutes amounted to one out of every three New York females age fifteen to forty-five, a number too large to be credible, the author claimed. (The author's figuring was off, however; probably a more reasonable figure for women fifteen to forty-five was in the vicinity of seventy-five thousand, so ten thousand prostitutes constituted one in seven women.) He further complained that McDowall's exaggeration caused real harm to virtuous society; statistics could be dangerous. Foolish men, upon hearing these figures,

> may reasonably calculate that as so great a proportion of females, of a suitable age, are of this character, and as they have more leisure to walk in the streets than those who are more virtuous, it is fair to presume that a majority of those who walk the streets are of this number. To accost a female in the streets, therefore, on this subject, the chance is in his favor; and should he make a mistake, it will be over looked, he may think, as the thing has now become so common. Many a virtuous female, therefore, may, and probably *will*, be insulted in the street in consequence of this very Report.[4]

McDowall's shockingly large number prompted the grand jury of the city to undertake its own estimate. It directed the City Watch officers to canvass each ward in late summer of 1831, and the aggregate result was a more reassuring finding of 1,438.[5] This effort was not a household census, however, but rather a summation of the best estimates of each ward officer, probably ruminating on a mental map of the known brothels of his district. It represents a lower bound for a number that would continue to grow in the 1830s, a certainty based on the city's rapid population growth alone. No doubt the true number lay somewhere between the two contending estimates of 1,500 and 10,000; certainly it was heading upward rapidly in the 1830s.

The sharp dispute over numbers signals the contested terrain that was prostitution in the 1830s. McDowall's Magdalen Society sparked at least three more benevolent organizations in the 1830s that were devoted to exposing sexual sin and/or reforming prostitutes. The several hundreds of moral reformers initiated a moral crusade through pamphlets, speeches, and reform newspapers. Their opponents, restrained by polite convention from arguing in favor of prostitution, tried to discredit the moral reformers by charging *them* with immorality, as if reformers obsessed with licentiousness were the real culprits in spreading sexual sin.

Such a simple thing as terminology indicates something of the city's ambivalent attitude toward prostitution. The phrase "girl on the town" (or sometimes "girl of the town") was nicely ambiguous and fit well with a rapidly growing city where so many people were new and their characters could not always be read from their faces or their clothes. Uncertainty marked social interchanges on the streets. In contrast, Paris in the 1830s developed a rich and precise vocabulary differentiating more than a half-dozen kinds of prostitutes, each of whom recognizably fit a particular slot in a well-defined social hierarchy of *les filles publiques: grisette, lorette, lionne, biche, cocotte, grande cocotte, grande horizontale.*[6] London too had a long list of terms for the sexually loose woman, most of them used interchangeably rather than taxonomically and carrying a connotation of either disorder or dirt: "prostitute," "whore," "harlot," "strumpet," "trull," "hussy," "trollop," "slut." But New Yorkers preferred indistinct and even polite designations, using mainly "prostitute" as the general case, or "courtesan," "cyprian" (a romantic and bookish term referring to the island of Cyprus, shrine of Aphrodite, the goddess of love), "the frail sisterhood," and "girl on the town" in almost all printed usages. Verbal usage might of course have been more earthy, more English, more suggestive of disease or dirt, but it has left few tracks in print for historians to follow. "Loathsome" or "polluted" as adjectives to modify "prostitute" or "woman" were the most scornful characterizations used in print.

"Girl on the town" was a euphemism that coyly avoided naming the behavior that defined such women, linking them instead to urban geography, not sexual practices or uncleanness. In use in England since the early 1700s, the phrase signified an association with the dissolute, debauched life: "men of the town" were rakes; "girls of the town" were prostitutes. The word "town" anchored the concept in location, a town site where dissolute men and women congregated together, away from the protective custody of families and masters.[7] In America, only the feminine phrase came into widespread use. Without its masculine counterpart to keep it pegged strictly to libertine dissipation, the phrase underwent a subtle shift in meaning. A girl on the town, or of the town, was a girl who lived independently of a family and earned money by selling sex; a loose woman, to be sure, but also a woman unattached and unrestrained. The verb form to "go on the town" conveyed a sense of agency or choice on the part of the woman, who in leaving a father or master's control was claiming a certain breezy freedom of her own. But along with autonomy came certain risks and certainly opprobrium: a girl on the town was on the streets, in public view, a public woman. Freed from dependency on a particular man, she instead depended on a wider masculine public, the male inhabitants of the town, to supply her with a livelihood.

New York City put few barriers in the way of such public women. Strictly speaking, prostitution was not illegal. No statute law in New York in the 1830s prohibited selling sex for money. If such a transaction took place off the streets, in a private place, with no evident disorder, the law could not touch it. When regulated at all, prostitution was curbed through broadly interpreted state laws outlawing vagrancy and disorderly conduct. Keeping a house of ill fame was also actionable, if another citizen lodged a complaint. In New York in the 1830s, police applied these laws with considerable tolerance.[8]

So in the eyes of the authorities, it was not so much selling sex for money as the *way* in which this was done that constituted the real offense: women on the loose, women out of place, women behaving in an offensive or disorderly way in public, were what attracted the attention of the law. These same laws of course covered men's disorderly public behavior; they were not gendered as written in the statute books. But the kind of behavior that got a man arrested as a vagrant or for disorderly conduct was in practice very different from what triggered a woman's arrest. As is clear from the dry log of Police Office records and the humorous reporting of the same events in the penny press columns, both sexes could be picked up for being drunk, for living on the streets, or for behaving bizarrely in public; but mostly men were. Women charged with vagrancy or disorderly conduct usually were prostitutes. In contrast, men walking the streets looking to buy sex were never arrested for either offense.

No language in the law required that the woman be caught in an act of solicitation. An arresting officer had a great deal of discretion, especially in the vagrancy charge, which did not even require a citizen complainant. Under it, a woman could be arrested simply for being out in public, unescorted by a male, looking suspiciously like a streetwalker. Being unescorted was not illegal, and respectable women could and did stroll on city streets alone without fear of arrest. And being a prostitute was not in itself illegal. Instead, some ineffable combination of the two might—or might not—cause a police officer to question and challenge a woman's right to be where she was at a given time. In practice, vagrancy proved an elastic concept, most elastic in the moment of encounter on the street between an officer and a woman of doubtful character.

When a woman was actually arrested for vagrancy, she appeared in court, heard the charges, faced conviction without witnesses or evidence entered in record, and then went to jail and/or paid bail. Jail sentences could be imposed for up to six months. At both the point of arrest and point of bail, prostitutes like Jewett from the district west of Broadway stood a far better chance of evading incarceration than did women who worked the streets of the area around Five Points in the Sixth Ward. One historian who has analyzed the New York arrest records from a slightly later period, the 1850s, found that the Sixth Ward, known as the Bowery, produced many more vagrancy arrests of women than any other ward in the city.[9] In the Bowery, a working-class tenement district east of Broadway and City Hall Park and centered on the notorious Five Points and Bowery Street, streetwalkers abounded, servicing their customers in semipublic spaces—down alleys, in back rooms of taverns, in crowded apartments. Police concentrated their attention on this kind of sexual traffic; they regarded streetwalking by a poorer class of girls a more serious affront to public morals than the brothel-based prostitution of the west side of lower Manhattan.

A charge of disorderly conduct was the other legal mechanism for intimidating and controlling prostitutes. This charge had to be initiated by a citizen's specific complaint, and once the complainant troubled to visit a Police Office to swear out a warrant against a woman, the police were obliged to arrest her and hold a court appearance where the defendant had the right to be confronted by her accuser. As with vagrancy, a conviction on disorderly conduct entailed fines and a maximum six-month jail sentence. Helen Jewett was never arrested for vagrancy, and only once for disorderly conduct, very early in her New York career.

The perceived increase in prostitution in the 1830s triggered a few attempts to tinker with the laws governing it. The city's Common Council first tried to increase penalties for disorderly conduct in 1833; and the state vagrancy law in that same year increased the maximum sentence from two to six months. In 1834 and again in 1835 some aldermen proposed licensing houses of prostitution. Better to control and regulate than to ignore, they reasoned, but the proposals failed in passage because of the official approval that licensing implied.[10] The simple fact remained that prostitution was increasing in both visibility and quantity. Yet there was evidently little political will either to restrain the sex trade or to crack down on it, beyond the complaints individual citizens brought to the attention of authorities. In effect, the pliant state laws permitted a large measure of local control. Behavior not tolerated on the streets of Syracuse, Troy, or Ithaca flourished on the streets of certain wards in New York. Lax enforcement represented acceptance and tolerance of commercial sex in the metropolis.

Travelers from upstate towns like Syracuse, Troy, or Ithaca found the New York City sex trade to be novel—shocking to some, no doubt, but deeply attractive to others. New York's large and growing population swelled every day with the addition of thousands of country merchants traveling to the big city to place orders and procure credit in the state's largest commercial center. Out-of-town buyers were the targets of "drumming," in which city merchants offered inducements to capture the custom of the country merchants. To "drum up" business, local merchants deputized clerks to frequent the hotels, link up with the visitors, and show them a good time, in the hope of making them obliging customers. Tours of brothels were said to be one of the more alluring perquisites in these package deals. Supplying or recommending sexual entertainment enhanced male sociability and helped to cement business relationships between strangers. A writer in a moral reform newspaper described the business practice: customers were invited "to champagne parties, to the theatre, and to houses of infamy, with the offer to bear all the expense. This is done to create in the mind of the country merchant a feeling of obligation to make his purchases at *your* store, where he is expected to repay in the price of his goods the money expended in drumming up his custom."[11]

Editor James Gordon Bennett of the *Herald* linked Helen Jewett to the drumming trade, calling her "the goddess of a large race of merchants, dealers, clerks, and their instruments" who offered her services to men from far-off states like Ohio and Missouri.[12] Drumming could as well happen without the involvement of the wholesale merchants, simply as a direct method of generating patronage for brothels and gambling houses. The common mark in both scenarios was the country merchant in town on business:

A traveler arrives in the steamboat and takes lodgings in Broadway. He is soon politely accosted by a *gentleman*, who has taken pains to be seated by his side at the dinner table, and whose object is to ascertain whether he is a stranger to the city, and can be easily *fleeced*. If a stranger, an offer is made to show him the city, accompany him to places of amusement and introduce him to some choice female friends. Wives and sisters in the country little suspect the deep laid schemes that are laid to ensnare their husbands and brothers, as they visit the city.[13]

Drummers commonly took their guests to the theater, long an arena of vice as well as spectacle. The world of actors had for over a century in Europe and America never been entirely clear of the suspicious cloud of illicit sexuality, but early-nineteenth-century American theater managers took the association between the stage and immorality one step farther by reserving special seating sections solely for prostitutes. Admitted at a cheaper price (twenty-five cents, or even free at times, in contrast to one dollar charged for box seats), the women enhanced a theater's ability to attract male customers.

The two most prominent theaters in Jewett's period in New York were the Park Theatre, on Park Row near City Hall, and the Bowery, located on the west side of Bowery Street, a half block below Canal. The Park was a somewhat tonier establishment, but both drew audiences from the city's cultivated elite as well as more ordinary customers. (Not until the late 1840s did audience segmentation take hold, at which time the Bowery became more of a working-class theater.)[14] Other theaters of the mid-1830s included the Richmond Hill Theatre, the Italian Opera House (soon renamed the National Theatre), and the Franklin. All of these establishments welcomed respectable women only if accompanied by men. Custom limited them to box seats, which formed the first tier above the all-male pit, the ground-floor area of seats. A larger proportion of women audience members consisted of disreputable women. They came alone or in groups, entering through special side doors and stairways that led up to the notorious "third tier," the highest gallery far above the stage. From their opulent perch, they enjoyed the evening's entertainments, visited with their friends in the trade, and met customers old and new. Openly designating this semipublic space a rendezvous for negotiating commercial sex conferred powerful tacit approval on prostitution. Women on the town were not confined solely to the top balcony: when escorted by men, well-dressed prostitutes could claim front-door entry, space in the lobby, and seats in the first and second tiers.[15]

Unlike theatergoers today, audiences of the 1830s did not sit in a darkened, hushed hall, quietly attending to the business onstage. House-lights stayed up during performances, to permit audience members to interact with each other and even with the actors on the stage. An evening's show typically lasted four or five hours, with a double bill of plays and entr'actes of music or acrobatics. No one expected the audience to pay attention throughout. The casual, interactive ambience permitted male spectators to roam around and visit the third tier to arrange for later trysts.[16]

Both the Park and the Bowery were plush establishments, equipped with expensive upholstered seats, gaslit chandeliers, elaborate painted woodwork, ladies' lounge rooms with attendants, and a bar serving food in the basement. More basic requirements were met by outhouses. The Bowery, for example, maintained a privy with four separate apartments outside on the Elizabeth Street side of the building near the prostitutes' special entrance, "so arranged that the females may go into theirs with-out being seen by the men." Four privies could hardly have met the needs of a nightly audience of three thousand.[17] Everything about the theater appointments, then, warned that outward forms of restraint and self-control were imperative. The disruptive potential latent within a highly masculinized and pleasure-seeking social space was tempered by luxuri-ous surroundings associated with genteel behavior.

The moral reformers regarded the theater as a highly dangerous place, a threat to morals. But for the disreputable women who attended, it was actually a uniquely safe space in which to advertise their availability, conduct business, and enjoy an evening out. No police harassed them there, and the chances of physical assault and violence were minimized by being in a large crowd that accepted their presence. Helen Jewett visited the theater often, sometimes several times a week.

The brothels that housed prostitutes of the theatergoing and drum-ming set in the 1830s were mostly clustered by twos and threes in the blocks of the Fifth Ward, west of Broadway from Chambers Street up to Canal. By the later 1830s, the trade was beginning to make significant inroads into the Eighth Ward above Canal, along Mercer, Greene, and Wooster Streets. A second dense concentration of brothels centered in the Sixth Ward, east of Broadway, stretching over to Bowery Street and down to Five Points, but these were distinctly less elegant establishments, shar-ing blocks with crowded tenements along Centre, Orange, and Mulberry Streets.[18] The various houses where Helen Jewett lived were all in the Fifth Ward, intermingled with residences of some of the city's leading families.

Expensive commercial sex required a prosperous and dignified location. Jewett lived at brothels on Leonard, Chapel, Duane, and Thomas Streets, houses that stood side by side with other private residences, churches, and schools. The general area was just two or three blocks west of Broadway, where large stores and four- and five-story hotels (like the newly built Astor House) were beginning to edge out the huge older residences that had once made Broadway a very fashionable private address. Massive public buildings nearby proclaimed the area as the city's cultural and political center. The New York Female Hospital occupied a large double block between the Thomas Street brothel and Broadway. Despite the misery within, the hospital presented a grand stone edifice of monumental proportions. A five-minute walk to the south, City Hall Park, a triangle of garden and trees, marked the civic center of the city. The palatial City Hall, complete with exterior Corinthian columns and rotunda, contained a grand marble circular stairway leading to high-vaulted courtrooms. The Park Theatre with its gray-columned front also faced City Hall Park and received audiences numbering up to 2,400 each night. Just a half block south across from the point of the park sat the American Museum, a cultural amusement center exhibiting unusual natural history curios. Peale's Museum on Broadway, St. Paul's Episcopal Church, the nearby College of Physicians and Surgeons on Barclay Street, and Columbia University a block west of Broadway rounded out the major cultural institutions in the vicinity.

The history of Jewett's first brothel residence, a row house at 55 Leonard Street (on the north side between Church and Chapel), illustrates the integration of prostitution into reputable neighborhoods. The structure sat amid substantial three- and four-story private residences, row houses built in the Federal style in the 1810s and 1820s, joined by cultural and religious institutions and several discreet brothels. Across the street at number 48 lived one of New York's few full-time police officers, Dennis Brink, the man who arrested Richard Robinson the day of the murder; number 50, right next door to Brink, was a brothel. Six contiguous lots next to number 55 had recently been the grounds of a sugar refinery; in 1833, the Italian Opera House, with 1,200 seats, was erected on the site, on the northwest corner of Church and Leonard. A Zion Methodist church with a black congregation occupied the southwest corner of that intersection. A short half block away, between Church and Broadway, stood number 73 Leonard, the city residence of Edward P. Livingston, a member of the famed Hudson River Livingston family, known for its fortune, influence, and political activity. This Livingston had been mayor of New York, a member of the U.S. House and Senate, and, most recently, secretary of state under President Andrew Jackson.

Another half block from Livingston's house, around the corner on Broadway, was the home of Cornelius Lawrence, mayor of the city at the time of the Jewett murder. The neighborhood was definitely not decrepit or faded.

Number 55 Leonard, where Jewett lived, had quite recently been the home of William Dunlap, a prominent New York dramatist, writer, theater manager, miniatures painter, and prolific chronicler of the New York art world, who had rented the town house along with his brother, an attorney, for sixteen years before he moved out in 1832 on May 1, the traditional moving day of all leased housing in New York. The owner, John C. Van Allen, rented it to a brothel madam named Ann Welden as soon as the Dunlaps' lease ran out. Since Van Allen, a coach maker, lived across the street at number 54, he must not have thought a brothel at number 55 would adversely affect the neighborhood. Brothels on this block easily coexisted with the policeman's residence, the church, and the opera house. Leonard Street residents in the 1830s would have regarded the opera house, not the brothel, the greater threat to public safety, for theaters were often sites of serious fires. Sure enough, the opera house burned to the ground in September 1839, taking with it a school and three churches and damaging part of 55 Leonard, at the rear of the theater.[19]

Eight weeks after William Dunlap vacated the house, a cholera epidemic hit New York. Grateful for his new higher and drier lodgings in Greenwich Village, Dunlap reflected on the fate of his previous house in his diary: "In the house I left three or four cases of cholera are reported and two deaths," wrote Dunlap. He had probably seen the daily bills of mortality listing all new cases and deaths by street address, issued by the New York Board of Health. The Leonard Street area occupied low, marshy grounds, he explained, but equally pertinent in Dunlap's view was the moral character of the diseased: "One thing is plain, the greater number of victims are the vicious the dirty the depraved."[20] It was a terrible, wrenching, but speedy epidemic, lasting less than two months but killing about half of all who contracted the disease, and killing them very quickly, in a matter of a day or two from first onset of symptoms. All New Yorkers who could leave the city took flight; street traffic diminished, businesses shut down. Chances are Jewett did not yet occupy rooms at 55 Leonard, or anywhere in New York yet. New York was a place to flee, not a desirable destination in those warm months of 1832.[21]

In September, about six weeks after the epidemic abated, the city tax assessor made his annual round to record property values. The new mistress of the premises at number 55 had pulled together a fancy establishment, concealing all signs of the scourge and deaths of July. Ann Welden was listed on the September 1832 tax assessment as the primary resident of the house. An 1849 novella treatment of the Jewett murder case characterized Welden as a two-hundred-pound woman with "exuberant flesh" and "a bountiful face," living in a house of "splendor" with a twenty-five-year-old idle paramour.[22] The bulking weight of the madam and the foppish young man might have been literary embellishments, but the claim of splendor was accurate enough. Welden's personal property—furniture, carpets, drapes, clothes, artwork, books—was assessed for two thousand dollars, twice that of the well-to-do Dunlap brothers' assessment of one thousand dollars the year before. (A more typical personal property assessment in the neighborhood fell in the range of two hundred to four hundred dollars.) Among her possessions, Welden kept on the premises a multivolume Bible illustrated with plates and a complete edition of Shakespeare.[23] Clearly the madam had spruced the place up and added furnishings double the value of what Dunlap, an established cultural figure, had kept in the same space. The house itself was assessed at five thousand dollars.[24]

Welden's high tax assessment suggests that her decor matched the elegance later found in the same house and described in detail in an 1848 exposé of the New York underworld. The author of the exposé visited number 55 Leonard and admired its first-floor parlor featuring Brussels carpeting, a fancy chandelier, and plush divans, sofas, and ottomans all upholstered in crimson velvet. The message conveyed by the furniture was that the occupants of this house indulged in aristocratic yet also sensuous luxury. Crimson was the color of kings, velvet a cloth once restricted by sumptuary laws to the knighted classes, and residual meanings still inhered in the choice of fabric.[25] Such surroundings subtly encouraged the clients to feel rich and act rich, even when they were not. Large elegant mirrors hung on the downstairs walls, communicating the idea that the women who lived here must be beautiful and vain enough to take delight in their constant reflection.[26] The male clients too might well find added satisfaction in catching glimpses of themselves at play with beautiful young women. In a parlor full of playactors, going by stage names, gesturing with stage gestures, counterfeiting the motions of initial desire, the mirrors provided a self-reflective audience for the gathered performers. (Unfortunately, the 1848 exposé did not describe any of the private rooms of 55 Leonard.) For nearly thirty years, this house operated as a brothel, under several successive madams. Welden built the business location from its infancy until 1836.[27] The proprietor in 1839 called herself Ellen Jewell, a trade name obviously meant to reap advantage from Jewett's burst of celebrity three years earlier.[28] In 1842, the current madam, Julia Brown, purchased the property herself and became both owner and mistress for a number of years.[29] Published guides of brothels in the early 1840s rated "Princess Julia's" house one of the very best in the city.[30]

Lax laws and even laxer law enforcement, "drumming" business practices arising from the competitive national market, theaters accommodating prostitutes and clients, and reputable, tolerant neighborhoods were all evidence of how legal, business, and cultural institutions of antebellum New York City gave their tacit approval to commercial sex. As much as vocal groups of moral reformers publicized their opposition to the sin of licentiousness and worked hard to convince others it was a serious social problem, many other New Yorkers shrugged at prostitution, maintained an unofficial policy of leniency, and on occasion turned the tables and accused the moral reformers of being the real cause and source of sexual license.

In this highly charged and ambivalent context, the scores of seemingly senseless brothel attacks that afflicted New York in the 1830s take on a certain intelligibility. Starting in the 1790s and peaking in the 1830s, rowdy male assailants posed the most serious threat of danger to prostitutes. What these rioters understood was that the traditional guardians of social morality and order (clergy, police) would neither attack nor defend prostitution in any truly effective way. The path was open, then, for some citizens to strike out on their own, perhaps to deputize themselves to uphold community morals or, more insidiously, to use such justification to engage in campaigns of terror against women acknowledged to be bad.

After a few isolated riots in the 1790s, bully attacks escalated in the years up to 1825, averaging about twenty incidents in each five-year interval, according to the historian Paul Gilje. The numbers then jumped sharply, with sixty-three riots or attacks in the period 1825 to 1829. Investigating New York brothel riots between 1830 and 1860, Timothy Gilfoyle found that nearly 60 percent of the total number of riots occurred in the 1830s, the peak decade for disorder attributed to prostitution. Gilje and Gilfoyle derive their figures from police records, so these incidents only included attacks that were reported to the authorities, usually by the aggrieved women themselves.[31]

In the 1830s, Fifth Ward brothels, in the blocks between Church and Chapel Streets, increasingly became targets of ruffians. An event typically included forced entry, verbal intimidation, and property damage. When three men came over the back fence at 41 Thomas Street in 1833, Rosina Townsend and her girls were relatively lucky; the assailants limited themselves to shouting obscenities.[32] Julia Brown, who ran a brothel at 64 Chapel Street, had an unhappier time. In March 1834 two men burst in, refused to leave when asked, and then beat up Brown and broke some furniture. Two weeks later a neighbor entered a complaint about her disorderly house, describing how a gang had gathered outside Brown's door at eleven at night and stoned her house, breaking windows. And at the end of April, five men "intruded themselves into her house," threatened to beat her, and behaved in "a rude and offensive manner."[33]

Most of the police assault-and-battery warrants are brief and contain stock phrases about intrusions and unspecified "offensive" conduct. The police scribe filling out the paperwork undoubtedly was condensing accounts from women complainants into a formulaic legal document. Occasionally a fuller surviving deposition gives a flavor of the men's goals and motives in accosting prostitutes. One from March 1836, only five weeks before Jewett's murder, details an attack by a gang on Eliza Ludlow's house on Greene Street, just above Canal. Members of the Bowery-based Chichester Gang, composed mainly of men from the butchering trade, were in the Police Office newspaper columns often in the early months of 1836 for their acts of mayhem, vandalism, and terror; the newspapers took to identifying them as a "gang" when the same group of men turned up in a series of incidents. They definitely were not regular Fifth Ward brothel customers. According to Eliza Ludlow's sworn affidavit, John Chichester and three other men came to her door and requested something to drink, which Ludlow refused. The men stormed in, swore, and threatened her until, to placate them, she produced some brandy, which they drank and splashed over the furniture. Next they smashed the glasses in the fireplace and demanded fresh drinks of porter, again spilling it about. They then went downstairs to the basement (the location of the kitchen and dining room of the house) and roughed up some women there. In an upstairs room, Chichester pulled hot coals from the fireplace with a poker, allowing them to burn the rug for some minutes before stamping them out. The men threw a bench at one young woman, smashing it on the wall, while threatening to beat her brains out and telling another they planned to throw her out the window. In another room they strewed ashes around and dumped water on them to intensify the mess. More was going on here than a drunken rampage by bullies: the whole affair was also a carefully calculated, drawn-out insult. Ludlow feared for her life, she testified, which was what the men intended.[34] But strikingly, nothing in the deposition indicates that any woman was seriously hurt or sexually attacked. The men waged a campaign of terror and scorn, forcing the women to serve them, spilling the drinks, playing with fire, and smashing furniture.

The rioters were not "robbers" come to a brothel to steal what richer men came to buy. They were contemptuous vandals, there to remind the women of the ultimate power men have over them by sheer physical force and intimidation. Through such violent actions, these men reassured themselves that gender hierarchies trumped hierarchies of class. Of course they would never have contemplated busting up a household of merchants' wives and daughters—there were clearly limits to the precedence of gender privilege over class privilege. But prostitutes who served the mercantile classes, who pretended to the elegance and erudition of the upper classes but whose own origins were rather less exalted—these were the front-line targets of the terrorist gangs, who struck repeatedly in the 1830s. Misogyny reinforced by class animosity: the ruffians' actions demonstrated contempt for the expensive and therefore out-of-reach prostitutes, and by extension resentment of the male clerks and merchants who patronized them.[35]

Gang attacks on refined brothels were most common in the 1830s, at a time when prostitution enjoyed a fairly protected relationship with the police authorities. When official tolerance for the sex trade began to erode, in the 1840s and beyond, the gang attacks lessened. The Police Reform Act of 1845 signaled a major departure from old practice, putting a much larger and newly professionalized police force on the city streets to discourage solicitation by girls of the town. Prostitutes initiated fewer appearances as complainants in the Police Court, finding their credibility and standing to take legal action increasingly challenged. An 1850 commentator on the trade declared that now the women's "oaths are seldom regarded in a court of justice, scarcely even in a police court." One after another, theaters barred prostitutes from their premises in the 1840s, first by hiring knowledgeable security guards to screen them out and then by requiring all women spectators at evening performances to have male escorts. Probably in reaction to the decline of police protection, New York prostitutes increasingly turned to male pimps to help handle unruly customers. By the 1850s, the era of tacit acceptance of prostitution was clearly over, even as the practice of prostitution continued unabated.[36]

Helen Jewett launched her career in New York in the freer 1830s, at a time and place surprisingly unpunitive about nonmarital sexual activity. From her perspective, prostitution as practiced in the Fifth Ward offered the advantages of good money and independent living. Prostitutes at this high end of the trade resided in swank and roomy houses in comfortable neighborhoods. They negotiated public space—streets, theaters, eateries—with minimal fear and no need of male escorts or pimps. Jewett had joined a business controlled by women, not men. The police barely restrained them, and the court system treated them like ordinary citizens and permitted the likes of Eliza Ludlow and Julia Brown to bring legal action against rowdy intruders. Brothel bullies provided the single most serious source of fear and threat of violence, but even there, shrewd madams who vigilantly guarded their doors and fenced their yards could reduce the prospect of terrorism.

In part, the New York newspapers became excited about Helen Jewett's murder because it was so unexpected; prostitutes in the 1830s enjoyed a relatively protected status and the actual chance of winding up murdered was extremely low. Friends and patrons who had admired Jewett were angered by her death and took to the prints, both newspapers and pamphlets, to portray her as an attractive victim worthy of public sympathy. Rather than transforming Jewett into an innocent paragon of virtue, however, in a bid for conventional sympathy for a conventional good girl, the authors instead focused on Jewett's accomplishments as a both sensitive and sensible, self-possessed young woman.

Outside New York, that portrait proved to be a harder sell, or at least a controversial one. Negative press on Jewett had already been ventured by the self-protective, self-interested Weston family. The Westons' view found reinforcement in newspapers disinclined to be tolerant of prostitution, whose editors expressed astonishment at the New York press's efforts to glamorize Jewett. The *Ohio State Journal* in Columbus sputtered about this "wretched woman" turned into "a heroine of romance" and invested with "rare accomplishments, lofty feelings, and extraordinary qualities." Worse still, the Ohio paper continued, "a literary gentleman" had announced plans to write a memoir of Jewett, a book that the editors were sure could only lead to the corruption of innocent but thrilled readers whose eyes would be opened and then attracted to the "pollution" of brothel life.[37]

While no well-known literary figure in fact produced a memoir of Jewett's life in 1836, a spate of short pamphlets soon issued forth, most of them propounding versions of the worthy victim tale.

• CHAPTER FIVE •

Acclaim for a Woman of Spunk

T HE MOST ELABORATE ATTEMPTS to make Helen Jew-
ett a worthy murder victim appeared in a set of small pamphlets
published within two to four weeks of the crime. None of the
anonymous authors offered a defense of prostitution; that would have
been too great a breach of propriety. Rather, they focused on the character of Jewett herself, making her out to be a noble and spirited young
woman who somehow miraculously transcended the inevitable degradation of her occupation. One pamphlet also accented illuminating moments
in Jewett's career, which, when corroborated with and augmented by
other fragments of information from the newspapers and police reports,
reveal much about her practice of prostitution in New York City and in
particular her spunkiness in the face of various dangers.

A small number of copies of three pamphlets have survived in
twentieth-century library collections: *Authentic Biography of the Late
Helen Jewett, a Girl of the Town, by a Gentleman Fully Acquainted with
Her History* (New York); *The Life of Ellen Jewett; Illustrative of Her
Adventures with Very Important Incidents, from Her Seduction to the
Period of Her Murder, Together with Various Extracts from Her Journal,
Correspondence, and Poetical Effusions* (New York); and *A Sketch of the
Life of Miss Ellen Jewett, Who Was Murdered in the City of New York, on
Saturday Evening, April 9, 1836, with a Portrait Copied from Her Minia-
ture* (Boston).[1] Three other titles were published and advertised in the
spring of 1836 with no copies known to survive.[2] For an ephemeral popular literature hastily produced for an eager but very time-limited market,
it is amazing that copies survive at all.

Jewett's friends had already made considerable progress elevating her status through their connections with the penny press in New York. As different as the stories were in the *Sun*, the *Transcript*, and the *Herald*, they all represented Jewett as an unfortunate victim of seduction who succumbed to prostitution due to forces beyond her control. Personal friendships no doubt played a big role in this, as in the case of the young lawyer William Wilder, who toured 41 Thomas with James Gordon Bennett, or the *Transcript* court reporter William H. Attree, who had been smitten by Jewett in 1834.[3]

The pamphlets expanded on Jewett's childhood and seduction, and while none of their accounts was accurate, two of them took their material from the stories Helen had told friends and so more fully reveal her flair for self-invention. (The third, the *Sketch*, published in Boston, was a total and complete fabrication designed to cash in on the Jewett-mania.) One of them, the *Authentic Biography*, is of particular interest because internal evidence suggests its author knew Helen well during her New York days. Written by "a gentleman fully acquainted with her history," the *Authentic Biography* announced its purpose in a brief preface:

> Public curiosity has been much abused by the numerous misrepresentations respecting the adventures and character of the late Helen Jewett. The object of this publication is to satisfy the public curiosity upon this subject, and rescue the character of an unfortunate girl from the odium which has been attempted to be cast upon it. It is true, she was a girl of the town; but she was far removed from the degraded, ignorant, vicious beings generally known as such; and the misrepresentations in a Boston paper, in which she is designated as a common thief, a girl naturally depraved from her childhood, deserve the severest reprobation of every honest member of the community.[4]

Ordinary prostitutes were vicious and degraded, but not Jewett, this author insisted; his goal was to demolish the Weston-inspired article in the *Boston Post* that had been circulated nationally. One-third of the sixteen-page pamphlet recounted her background in Maine in a variant story from the three renditions in the penny papers. Another third presented revealing vignettes of her life in New York showing her to be charming, witty, spirited, authoritative, imperious even, and certainly unafraid of and undeferential to men. The final section of the pamphlet, mostly lifted from the *Sun*, recounted Rosina Townsend's discovery of the body along with some added speculation about motive in this inexplicable and sensational crime.

The girl's history introduced interesting variations on the Maine orphan story. Her real birth name, the author insisted, was Maria Benson (a name reported as only a pseudonym by the *Herald*); she was born in Hallowell, Maine, in January 1812. (This advanced Jewett's real age by twenty-one months.) Maria's father, cheated in the lumber business by a dishonest partner named Caleb Talbot, died when Maria was one. Her beautiful widowed mother took up schoolteaching to support her daughter and instructed her as well. By age five, Maria "had made more progress in the usual studies, than the generality of children at twice her age." The child's beauty and brightness gained her the mentorship of Judge "Western" and his family, who sent her to "a select school" in Augusta, "at which she made the most astonishing progress in her studies." Unfortunately, the mother then died, and the "Western" family took her in, treating her "in every respect as a member."

In the summer of 1826, the pamphlet continued, the judge sent Maria and his daughter to a boarding school in Portland, Maine. "It was her fifteenth year, although in appearance she was somewhat older." The school was short on dormitory rooms and so boarded some girls out, and in this unprotected environment she met a young law student named Lemuel Lawton, who attended her constantly at church and at social gatherings, took her for walks and rides, and flattered her. The clever Lawton "directed her taste for reading into new channels." Lord Byron's *Don Juan* finally and fatally weakened her: "Its vivid images of the grossest licentiousness, half veiled in the charm of the poetry, worked upon her active imagination, excited her naturally ardent temperament, unsettled the principles of virtue, and disposed her, in an evil hour, to fall a prey to her seducer's arts." After a year of bookish tutelage, Lawton finally administered a "medical preparation" to remove Maria's last shred of resistance. "These facts speak strongly, considering her extreme youth, for her natural strength of mind," the pamphlet writer reasoned. In no time the unfortunate girl became pregnant and in shame ran off to Boston with her seducer. Judge Western implored her to return home, but she wrote him back (in a letter the pamphlet author assured his readers he had actually seen), "I was dead to virtue—I am now dead to society, and it is my most earnest wish that I may soon be dead to nature." The infant died, the scoundrel took off for Alabama, and Jewett had no choice but to settle into her ordained life of prostitution. "How deeply it is to be regretted that a girl of her extraordinary mental powers should not have had the watchful guardianship of a mother, at a time when the passions are bursting forth in their full strength," the author lamented. "Had she been saved from the first false step, no one who knew her will hesitate to believe, that with her clear, sound judgment, brilliant and glowing imagination, and her quick yet profound sensibility, she might have made an American *De Stael*."

As in the story Jewett told Attree, the *Authentic Biography*'s version of the girl's seduction excused the girl from nearly all responsibility. The Boston boarding school named in the 1834 *Transcript* column was relocated to Portland, and the scoundrel this time was a law student, not a merchant's son (or a bank cashier, as in the *Herald*'s version). But it was essentially the same story, the kind Jewett found good for a prostitute's business: a charming rake could sexually awaken a beautiful, bright, and virtuous girl. Lawton was slow and deliberate, warming Maria's passions and building her desire through his strategic deployment of injurious books. Once ruined, Maria could not go back to the respectable Western family; dishonor was permanent, even though the judge tried to retrieve her. A sensitive woman like Jewett *especially* realized her moral debasement and nobly declined to try to pass as a good woman again, even when given the opportunity. And for this gesture of sacrifice, so splendidly feminine in its renunciation of self, the "gentleman" author of the *Authentic Biography* admired her all the more! Helen Jewett clearly knew how to craft a seduction story to gain admiration from men.[5]

The reason to credit Jewett with this Portland seduction story is that it so closely resembled the stories told to Attree and to James Gordon Bennett's informant on Dorcas Dorrance, even as it departed from those in factual particulars. Several fixed points anchor them: the elevated age, the orphan status, the precociously educated mind, the kindly and forgiving judge, the ardent young man in training for a professional job, the intimacy and dangers of shared reading. The pamphlet titled *The Life of Ellen Jewett* also featured these plot points, stretching the Attree story of the Boston seduction out to fifty-two pages of small print. The author of this version both admired and pitied Jewett and was far more inclined to describe her as a "polluted" and "degraded wretch," suggesting that its author was not of like mind with Attree or the *Authentic Biography* author on the evils of prostitution. But running underneath all the versions is the voice of Jewett, concocting her autobiography to suit her circumstances.

Comparing Jewett to Madame Germaine de Staël was a lofty claim indeed, but not totally groundless. De Staël was a formidable Frenchwoman, intellectually and romantically active during the French Revolution, up to the 1820s. Her unconventional life—essayist, novelist, lover of a half dozen of the leading men of her day—was precisely the sort of career the ambitious Jewett could dream of, supported by stories of her own exceptional mental acuity and given life by demonstrations of her forceful personality.[6]

The *Authentic Biography* next outlined Jewett's life in New York City and gave examples of her forcefulness in action. The author listed her early residences, at brothels run by Mrs. Post, Ann Welden, and Rosina Townsend; the newspapers had only mentioned Townsend. She also lived with men as a "regular kept mistress," and she communicated with lovers via letters, two of which the pamphlet printed in full. And then the author recounted five incidents in which Jewett bested cloddish men by using "her powers of bitter, biting sarcasm." One of these incidents can be corroborated in three other sources, so it is not unreasonable to presume that the other four vignettes also had some basis in Jewett's life. Which is not to say that these events happened as reported in this pamphlet: almost nothing in Jewett's self-generated stories can be taken as literal truth. Her penchant for self-dramatization is perhaps the truest thing about them.

Rowdies who invaded brothels presented one form of threat to women like Jewett; another more insidious threat might arise from men admitted to the premises who then failed to play their role as gentlemen. Getting rid of them delicately and without provoking an ugly reaction took skill and tact. The author of the *Authentic Biography* claimed that despite her youthful age Helen acted as an assistant to Ann Welden at number 55 Leonard Street, where her duties included reprimanding boorish guests in the parlor. To one "poor devil" who uttered offensive witticisms, she reportedly snapped, "Your conversation is as silly as it is disgusting. There is the door, Sir, and I beg you to do me the favor never to call here again, as you will save me the trouble of ordering the servant to kick you into the street."[7] Whether or not she said these words, the point is that the pamphlet author believed her capable of saying them. Giving orders to men was consistent with her general character.

This story meshed with another one illustrating her command over men. Again according to the *Authentic Biography*, she once subdued with considerable courage a man brandishing a pistol:

Without being in the least agitated, she instantly struck the pistol from his hand, and with her bright eyes flashing fire, in tones calm and clear, indicative of the strongest contempt, she said to him, "You poor contemptible libel upon manhood! You have done what would disgrace the meanest coward that walks the street. You must see therefore, the necessity of making an immediate apology for such brutal condnct [*sic*]." Her opponent declared he would do no such thing. "Then," said Helen, "You must see the necessity I am under of pulling your nose." Suiting the action to the word, she took the gentleman's proboscis in her fingers, and tweaked it in no gentle style.[8]

Nose tweaking may sound faintly ridiculous to modern ears, capping a paragraph that sounds like nothing so much as a scene from a cheap adventure thriller of the period, down to the cliché of the bright flashing eyes. But pulling the nose was in fact a well-known, highly dramatic, and effective gesture of contempt in the 1830s, part of the repertoire of insults available to men (and only men) who accounted themselves too dignified for fisticuffs. When decisively accomplished, it amounted to an unauthorized invasion of personal space and a commanding and painful affront. The son of President John Q. Adams had his nose tweaked by an angry journalist under the U.S. Capitol dome in 1827; President Andrew Jackson's nose was once grabbed and twisted by an irate citizen.[9] Apocryphal or not, this Jewett story furthered a public construction of a fearless and feisty woman who could insult and emasculate men when the occasion required. She not only disarmed her antagonist by knocking his pistol aside, she impugned his masculinity both explicitly and symbolically. The story illustrates one way of dealing with ungentlemanly behavior in the parlor. But it only worked if the man in question could lay claim to being a gentleman subject to the conventions of honor.

The dangers to prostitutes illustrated by this story were real enough, even if Jewett's response was melodramatically invented. Difficult, unpleasant, or potentially violent encounters with men might emerge of a sudden. There always had to be a measure of uncertainty about men in this playacting world who presented false credentials as nice fellows. Out-of-town men, arriving under the auspices of the drummers, posed a special risk, for they might take advantage of freedom and anonymity to behave in ways they felt they could not be held accountable for. A prostitute had to be able to size up a client swiftly, take her measure of him, and decide how close to let him come. Safety in a brothel depended on sound appraisal of potential clients at the theater and on the street and on careful gatekeeping at the front door, which was always kept locked, as well as on winnowing out men already admitted to the parlor whose behavior began to turn worrisome.

Another story of Jewett's courage in confronting an ill-behaved man also dates from her time at Ann Welden's house. Jewett told the story of Captain Burke and the cutup dresses several times, to the author of the *Authentic Biography* and also to William Attree, who put it in his 1834 *Transcript* column. It also appeared in the fifty-two-page pamphlet (*The Life of Ellen Jewett*), and again, in even more detail, in an 1849 novella on the murder case by George Wilkes. Jewett told Attree the salient facts: one evening at the brothel a British officer named Burke presented in payment for wine a three-dollar bill that she challenged as counterfeit. The ensuing dispute so enraged Burke that he "cut to pieces several of her dresses." The next day Jewett went to the Police Office to swear out a warrant against Burke. When Burke was hauled into court, he brought a friend, a Colonel Morris, who vouched for Burke's respectability and upheld his claim that he did not know the bill was counterfeit. (In Wilkes's 1849 version, the colonel claimed his friend had had too much wine when he cut the dresses.) Burke was then made to pay Jewett one hundred dollars for the dresses, and she withdrew her complaint.[10] When the *New-York Transcript* resurrected this early column and reprinted it, in the wake of Jewett's death, the editors faithfully included the anecdote but with one omission: they snipped out the half-sentence reference naming Colonel Morris.[11] (Morris was very likely George Morris, the prominent young editor of the *New-York Mirror*, a literary weekly Helen subscribed to in 1836, known to all his friends as General Morris.)[12]

The *Authentic Biography* pamphlet pumped up Jewett's role in the drama to show again how she could upbraid a man—a military man, no less, in the daunting setting of an official court proceeding.

She appeared, upon one occasion, before the Police, to make a charge against a man by the name of Burk, an officer in the British army, who, out of revenge, had cut and destroyed her dresses. She walked into him at the examination in great style. "You," she said, "pretend to be an officer in the British army! What a calumny upon his Majesty's service. You, an officer! It is impossible. The men holding his Majesty's commissions have generally some pretensions to the character of gentlemen."[13]

The author was no doubt retelling the story as Jewett preferred to tell it, conjuring a picture of an outspoken young woman holding her own in a courtroom, smartly dressing down a British officer. The story has an air of retrospective triumph, of what Jewett wished she had said in court and what she probably told friends back at Ann Welden's that she had said.

A fourth story in the *Authentic Biography* had Helen rebuking a "dandified jackass" who was "attempting to do the amiable to Helen in the most extravagant style"—in other words, pressing sexual attentions on her. She made a cutting remark, not reported, to which he replied, "Now really, Miss Helen, it is too bad in you to be so hard upon me." "You are right," returned Helen; "it is wrong in me to be hard upon so soft a subject—we never use diamonds to carve geese." Calling a man soft in a brothel setting was probably an effective way to insult or discourage him.

The final vignette in the *Authentic Biography* consisted of a dialogue between Jewett and an attorney identified only as F.J. supposedly uttered during a court appearance when Jewett was a witness for a brothel keeper. The lawyer inquired about the nature of the business of the house; did men visit, and why did they come? A hostile witness, Jewett finally replied, "I believe there is no one better qualified than yourself to answer that question, as I have observed you frequently among our visitors; will you be so kind as to save me the trouble of answering the questions, and communicate to the Court your own experience upon the subject."[14] The story again speaks to her outspokenness, her willingness to expose hypocrisy and embarrass men who would normally count on deference from women well below their station in life. Whether or not she fired such a snappy reply to a lawyer in court cannot ever be known. But she did appear in the Court of General Sessions at least once, when her brothel keeper Mary Berry was charged with keeping a disorderly house, in April 1835. The district attorney who prosecuted that case was Ogden Hoffman, so this was not F.J. A year later Hoffman headed the defense team for Richard P. Robinson.

These five vignettes in the *Authentic Biography* produced a portrait of a woman who was hardly a victim. She had fallen prey to the law student Lemuel Lawton, but even there, her resistance lasted a year and still required some medical potion to clinch it. The episodes of spunk portrayed her as her friends in New York knew her to be: a clever and haughty young woman, able to stand up to men who ranked far above her in social status—lawyers, military officers, and the generality of traveling merchants and jackasses who found their way to expensive New York brothels.

Two final incidents of Jewett's audacity appear in other records but were not part of the *Authentic Biography*'s list. Jewett filed charges in Police Court in 1834 the morning after a young man kicked her in the Park Theatre; this was the day she entranced reporter Attree with her story of seduction. According to Jewett, she was going up the stairs of the theater to the second tier when she dropped a ten-dollar bill; as she bent over to pick it up, John Laverty accosted her, kicked her, laughed at her, and then ran off with a male friend. Jewett knew who the young man was and entered a formal complaint against him the next morning. Attree's news item spared John Laverty no embarrassment, identifying him in print as the son of the wealthy Henry Laverty of the firm Laverty and Gantley on Pearl Street.

Jewett refused to let men get away with abuse. Not many New Yorkers, male or female, would have reported such an incident to the police as an assault. A man might have answered such an insult with a challenge to fight or duel; a female victim might have relied on a male protector to defend her honor with a threat or a punch. But Jewett was on her own and therefore chose to use the police as her protectors and avengers. That some New Yorkers saw a kick in the rear as trivial, especially if directed at a woman of ill repute, was demonstrated by the *New York Sun*, which made light of the whole event:

> *Insult with intent to kiss:*—A lady of the third tier of boxes in the Park Theatre named Helen, a perfect representative, no doubt, of her who caused the Trojan War, lodged a complaint at the police office, against one of her admirers named Laraty [*sic*], who, conceiving himself to be a second Paris, indelicately assaulted the fair Helen by throwing his arms around her neck and endeavoring to perpetrate a kiss in the public lobby of the establishment. This the fair Helen resented with becoming spirit, and gave the rude assailant an appropriate rebuke for his indelicacy towards her. This was modest and commendable, and we are pleased to find that the ladies of the third tier dare to assert their rights, and entertain so high a respect for their own character and standing, as to resent every assault calculated to cast contempt upon their virtue.[15]

Did the *Sun* reporter misunderstand the charge as a kiss instead of a kick? Or was this a willful misrendering of the incident, suggesting that kicking and kissing were all the same, harassments fully permissible to men wanting to tease or bully prostitutes? Perhaps Laverty made an unwanted advance and then, rebuffed, followed with the indecorous kick. The *Sun*'s version pays less attention to Helen and Laraty (her surname omitted, his conveniently distorted and thus somewhat disguised) than to the surprising idea that a prostitute might defend her own honor by seeking remedy from a court. Prostitutes went to court all the time, to report serious assaults and thefts; at issue here was whether an unwanted kiss or a boot in the rear justified going to the police. The *Sun* story does at least confirm the Attree account in its broadest stroke: Helen did swear out a warrant against Laverty for an assault in the Park Theatre in 1834, even though no warrant remains in the boxes of Police Office records stored in the New York Municipal Archives. Most likely Laverty's father managed to have the complaint withdrawn and removed from the record, just as Captain Burke had done with the aid of Colonel Morris.

A second and more serious incident led Helen to file charges in the Police Court in 1835 against one John Boyd, a barber who lived on Barclay Street who was associated with the Chichester Gang, the same group that stomped into Eliza Ludlow's brothel and a dozen others in the mid-1830s. Boyd testified that he and his friend John Spencer went to 128

Duane Street, "a notorious house of prostitution," on February 25, 1835. Jewett was living there at the time, under the management of Mary Berry and her partner, Frank Berry. Boyd sought his wife, after being "privately informed" that she was enticed to frequent the house by Mary Berry. From the door he caught a glimpse of his wife as she ran downstairs, but Mary and Frank Berry barred his entry and insisted the wife was not there. When Boyd persisted, he said, the Berrys and Helen Jewett seized him, tore his clothes, and ejected him from the house. Only the aid of Spencer saved him from serious injury.

Or so Boyd testified on March 13, defending himself against an assault complaint swiftly filed by Helen Jewett. Of five people involved in this February altercation, only Jewett rushed to the Police Office to file a complaint on the very day it happened. Probably it took her just a few minutes to get there: the Police Office occupied a first-floor room in an old three-story brick building on Chambers Street, behind the City Hall, just two short blocks from the Duane Street brothel. The structure was built as city almshouse around 1800; in 1815 it was leased to the American Academy of Fine Arts and the New-York Historical Society; and in 1831 it reverted to city use as the Police Office and the Court of General Sessions. The successive uses of this building—from almshouse to art museum to lower courtrooms—suggest that the first-floor Police Court was probably a large but fairly ordinary room, a room where Jewett and other prostitutes evidently felt comfortable taking their complaints. (In contrast, the grand marbled and pillared courtrooms located in the City Hall implicitly commanded awe from citizens.)

Jewett's warrant contained no specific allegations on the printed police form beyond a standard assault-and-battery charge. When the case was heard before a judge, on March 13, her version of events was reported in the Police Office column of the *Transcript*, certainly written by her reporter friend William H. Attree. "Barber-ossa brought to his bearings" ran the satirical heading, implying that the raging barber was at fault. According to the *Transcript*, Boyd's wife made a living for both of them as a hairdresser for prostitutes. (This amounted to a gratuitous dig at Boyd's masculinity: his wife supported him.) In a "drunken or crazy fit," Boyd went to the brothel shouting loudly for her. The wife, aided by sympathetic prostitutes, slipped out the back door, "whereupon, he fell afoul of an unoffending female, and tore her dress, threatening to cowskin her, but was ultimately put out of the place." (Attree declined to put Helen Jewett's name in the paper, but the assault warrant makes it clear she was the "unoffending female" in question.) Boyd was portrayed in print as a drunken lout, his friend Spencer as an insolent goon. But the judge hearing the case chose to believe Boyd and Spencer, dismissing Jewett's

An assault-and-battery warrant sworn out by Helen Jewett against John Boyd, 1835. Her signature at the bottom clearly shows the H in "Helen."

assault charge and indicting the Berrys for keeping a disorderly house. The *Transcript* printed a cautious retraction the next day: "We have been informed that the case of Mr. Boyd, the barber, was somewhat misrepresented in yesterday's police report" for possibly "he was the injured party and that petty malice and envy have prompted the present prosecutions against him."[16] Boyd convinced the judge he was the injured party, injured because he could not regain "possession of his wife" (who did not come home until late at night, according to his deposition) and because both Frank Berry and Helen Jewett assaulted him, he claimed. Boyd's assault case and the disorderly house charge appear on the docket of the Court of General Sessions in April 1834, but there is no record of the disposition of either case.

The Duane Street brothel had seen violence the day before Boyd knocked on the door, in an incident possibly indirectly related. On February 24, a man named Benjamin Ferris caused trouble, leading Mary Berry and another girl of the house, Mary Daton, to swear out assault-and-battery warrants against him. In his usual light style, Attree wrote in the *Transcript*: "She [Daton] was going out to a party, and had her hair dressed—he came to the house, and put his cap on her head, and disturbed her head gear. She threw the cap on the ground, and he struck her."[17] He also struck Mrs. Berry. The *Sun*'s Police Office column also made light of the event: Ferris was arrested for beating Mary Berry and Mary Daton, "lady prostitutes" at 128 Duane Street, "whose sanctuary he had invaded for purposes best known to himself, and there getting into a row, very gallantly pummeled the fair ones until they delivered him over to the watch man." But Ferris did not appear in morning Police Court; he "perhaps overslept," the *Sun* joked. "So much for trying to break crockery ware which cuts one's fingers sometimes."[18] Ferris didn't oversleep; a small note attached to Mary Berry's complaint warrant in the police files reveals that Ferris's family connections to a police justice released him. The clerk of the court wrote the watch captain: "A young man by the name of Ferris (a cousin of our friend of the 6th) is in your watch house. If you can receive bail to appear in the morning I should feel obliged. I don't know him but have heard the particulars from a friend."

The Berry-Ferris altercation started over mussed hair, so possibly Mrs. Boyd had been called to the house on February 25 to restore Mary Daton's coiffure. In any event, this brothel had seen police action twice in two days, a very unusual frequency. Jewett and the Berrys were probably nervous when Boyd and Spencer, known bullies, came knocking at their door.

The incident with John Boyd and John Spencer was probably the closest Helen Jewett came to getting in serious trouble with violent men—until her murder. Boyd was something of a hothead; he appeared in the Police Office and General Sessions Court records at least four other times from 1834 to 1836 on various assault charges.[19] His most chilling attack on record occurred in New Jersey: Boyd stalked William Attree and knifed him in the face. His motive was revenge for a humorous column Attree wrote about Spencer in May 1835, in which Attree reported that Spencer cowered in a privy in a futile attempt to hide from police. Boyd trailed Attree and a young lady on the Hoboken ferry and shadowed them into Sybil's Cave, a popular romantic spot carved into the New Jersey palisades. When the couple went inside the cave to sip water from the spring there, the ruffian jumped Attree, knocked him down, and stabbed him viciously in the face with a dirk. The woman's screams brought help, and several men carried Attree to a nearby public house and summoned medical aid. His condition was reported to be grave, but within three weeks he had recovered. He thereafter wore a brace of pistols to be ready for self-defense. Boyd was arrested and held on $3,500 bail.[20] Luckily for Jewett, Boyd did not brandish a weapon when he accosted her at Mary Berry's brothel; he was clearly capable of cutting flesh as well as fabric.

In all the various stories of Jewett's challenges to men, the constant theme was her brazenness and her strong sense of herself as a woman who could challenge men and demand justice. To the author of the *Authentic Biography*, this made her an admirable character. But to most of the rest of the literate public, the ideal of virtuous womanhood brought quite different attributes to mind: acquiescence, submission, piety, self sacrifice. And Helen Jewett had none of those.

CHAPTER SIX

The Brothel Business

HELEN JEWETT LIVED in New York City for four years. Most of the time, she lived and worked in a succession of brothels in the Fifth Ward, but periodically she took private rooms paid for by some wealthy client for whom she was a "kept mistress." This chapter and the next move beyond what her enthusiastic supporters alleged about her character and image in their published tributes, in an attempt to piece together everything that can be learned about her actual life as a highly paid prostitute. City directories, censuses, tax assessment records, old maps, deed books and property conveyance records, arrest warrants, and finally her private letters provide the material for grounding her story in the day-to-day life of the city.

Jewett probably arrived in New York from Boston after the cholera epidemic of July 1832 had subsided—for it would have been foolish for anyone to move into the center of a terrifying epidemic during those summer months. Probably by fall 1832, and certainly by January 1833, she was living at Ann Welden's new but sizable establishment at 55 Leonard Street, large enough to accommodate fourteen women in separate bedrooms. Jewett's first and only arrest of record for disorderly conduct occurred that January, when she and Ann Welden had to appear in Police Court on complaint of a Bowery Street butcher named Eliphalet Wheeler. The butcher's role in the complaint is puzzling; according to the city directory, Wheeler lived on Bowery Street near Hester, just under a mile north and east of the Leonard Street brothel, and he practiced his trade at the meat markets on Fulton, about a mile to the south. Complainants in disorderly conduct cases were typically not clients but offended neighbors, but it is hard to see how Wheeler's workaday orbit brought him into contact with the two women. Possibly the women had been attending the Bowery Theatre, a little south of Wheeler's house, and had committed their offense of "disorder" on his home turf. The official record is thin, consisting only of a single log entry in the watch docket books; no surviving warrant elaborates on the butcher's complaint. In any event, the women spent several days in custody in Bridewell, the old and crumbling holding jail just west of the City Hall, and then were released on bail, five hundred dollars for Welden and three hundred dollars for Jewett; both sums exceeded the allowed fine for a conviction. The watch docket fails to record who paid the bail, which strongly suggests that the women themselves came up with the money; it was an extremely large amount for the day. From available records it appears that the case never went to a court hearing. Very likely the two forfeited their bonds on a promise of good behavior in lieu of conviction, fine, or jail sentence.[1]

This was how the law usually worked. It better resembled a city-run shakedown than a punitive judgment meant to discourage prostitution. The police and courts did not really expect Jewett and Welden to stop practicing their trade, a sound inference because the women soon appeared in the same courts as complainants in prostitution-related cases. Welden, for example, brought assault-and-battery charges against three men who invaded her house in May 1833 and became offensive and rowdy. Again in October 1833, she brought charges against a man who forced his way in and struck her.[2] The nature of the business at 55 Leonard Street would not have been a mystery to the Police Court judges, especially in view of Welden's arrest the preceding January. Clearly the legal authorities were not particularly interested in shutting down brothel keepers, only responding when a citizen complained about disorderly activities. Welden and other madams could feel confident about asserting their rights as citizens to take their own complaints about threatening and violent bullies to the Police Office.

Jewett also brought an assault-and-battery complaint to court in April 1833, just three months after her fine for disorderly conduct. Her assailant, she said, was Ann Welden, none other than her erstwhile madam, who scratched her "in the face several times and otherwise ill treated deponent." Jewett's new address on the warrant was 72 Chapel, a brothel located one lot above the northwest corner of Duane and Chapel; an eyewitness she brought to court to support the complaint was another woman from 72 Chapel. Apparently Welden, still running her house on Leonard, paid a visit to Jewett at her new residence and attacked her there, for reasons unknown. Perhaps trouble between them had driven Jewett to leave and seek new lodgings; or perhaps Jewett's decision to relocate, which no doubt meant some loss of business at 55 Leonard, made Welden angry. Welden was released in three days, on one hundred dollars bail. Surprisingly, the court log book notes that the bail was paid by the deponent, that is, Jewett herself, and a regular bail bondsman. That Jewett helped make Welden's bail suggests that the young woman had second thoughts about pursuing a legal case against her onetime madam. Whatever they had fought over, it was apparently quickly put to rest. Jewett's generosity also shows that, young as she was, she had ready access to a not inconsiderable sum of money (some fraction of the one hundred dollars bail). The Police Court records show no further action on the case.[3]

The brothel at 72 Chapel was smaller and less resplendent than 55 Leonard. Its owner, Thomas Platt, paid taxes on a $3,600 assessment, and the madam, Eliza Lawrence, had just $500 in personal property. (Platt's respectable enterprise was the firm of Platt and Duncan, Importers, on Fletcher Street, near Pearl Street and Maiden Lane in the heart of the downtown business district.) How long Jewett stayed here in 1833 is unknown. In his 1849 novel, author George Wilkes located her for part of 1833 in private rooms leased in a house on Mercer Street near Broome, where she lived as a "kept woman" under the care of an English commercial agent.[4] But Wilkes missed the Chapel Street residence, attested to by Police Court records. The "gentleman" author of the *Authentic Biography* also skipped over several of her known addresses, moving her from Ann Welden's directly into an arrangement as the kept mistress of a wealthy southern man identified only as "Mr. C******."[5]

Such liaisons were probably short-lived, lasting only a matter of months or even weeks. The *Biography*'s author indicated as much, when he wrote, "It would be useless, and in fact impossible, to particularize her numerous paramours with whom she lived as a regular kept mistress."[6] As a method of making a living from sex, working as a kept woman differed markedly from brothel-based prostitution. Such a status required deeper personal involvement with a client, indeed a kind of commitment on the part of both parties. The client committed to ongoing financial support in the form of food, housing, maid service, and theater tickets on a level that greatly exceeded what a fee-for-service arrangement would cost. Only a client with considerable and, equally important, concealable discretionary income (invisible to business partners, or to a wife) could manage such a transaction. Significantly, the two clients so obscurely alluded to in the Wilkes and "gentleman" stories were non–New Yorkers (an English agent, a southern gentleman), men in a position to set up a temporary home away from home, far from inquisitive family and friends. For her part, Jewett committed to a somewhat more solitary life, living apart from other female friends and somewhat less able to maintain (and derive income from) relationships with other men. And both parties to the transaction, in choosing to live together however temporarily, were affirming that the relationship had an emotional dimension, that it consisted of something more than sex for pay. A man presumably spent more hours a day with his kept mistress than he would with a brothel prostitute. In return for his financial support, she was to give her feelings and body to a relationship unmediated by any third party. (In a brothel, Jewett could and on occasion did instruct the madam to bar entry to particular men.) And yet, this was an arrangement that could be terminated swiftly, perhaps in a matter of weeks, which suggests that neither party would become too dependent on the other, either emotionally or economically. Jewett could always return to a brothel and support herself quite adequately. She was free to share her heart and her body with a paramour for only as long as she wished.

According to the "gentleman" pamphleteer, Jewett did not entirely relinquish attentions from other men during her kept-woman periods. "It cannot be said that she was perfectly faithful to her different keepers," he wrote, which implied that a woman who agreed to such a bargain usually was expected to be faithful for the duration of the arrangement. "She most generally had some one upon whom she betowed [bestowed] her favor *par amours*." (This was a pamphlet rushed into print, as its many typographic errors attest.) In other words, even as a kept woman Helen sustained relationships with certain other men and "would spare no pains to secure for a while the object of her desires." The "gentleman" writer of this pamphlet had, two pages earlier, praised Helen, née Maria Benson, for maintaining her virginity for an entire year while the evil young Portland law student plied her with medical and literary aphrodisiacs. But in short order, Jewett had matured into a forceful young woman who took the lead in seducing certain attractive men, according to the "gentleman." As evidence of Helen's ardent pursuit of a man not her keeper, the writer offered two letters she allegedly wrote, during her residence with "Mr. C******," to a physician she came to know in the course of his business practice, which included house calls on brothels:[7]

My Dear Sir—

Allow me to say dear, for I assure you you are so to me. I think of nothing but you. You alone of all the creatures of your sex by whom I am surrounded, have evinced the least spark of real sympathy with my feelings, the least pity for my faults and misfortunes. You I think are willing to belive [*sic*] that a woman may cast away "the immediate jewel of her soul," without becoming wholly depraved, or entirely losing the feelings and characteristics of her sex. Think, then, how anxious I must be for your society, and if you have the least spark of compassion for me come and see me as often as you can. You do not know what a pleasure your acquaintance is to me; I shall always look upon it as the brightest spot in the latter years of my existence—a single oasis in the vast desert of wretchedness, shame, guilt, blighted prospects and perverted powers which I am compelled to call my life. Come and see me as soon as you can; I shall expect you every evening.

Yours, truly, and forever, if you please, HELEN.

And the second letter:

Dear T——,

What is the matter with you? are you getting tired of me? What can be the reason that you have not been to see me for six whole days—almost a week—perhaps you don't know that six days are almost a week. I assure you they are, and a long one too in love's almanac. I am almost disposed to punish you for your negligence. I have half a mind to bore you with a whole ocean of sentiment about my own love and misery, and your selfishness and coldness—but I forbear. I'll spare you till next time. Come up and see me this evening. Don Alonzo [a soubriquet for her keeper] has gone to Philadelphia. He wanted to take me with him. I was very much tempted to go but I thought of you and refused. Evince your gratitude, and let me behold the light of your countenance once more. *Adieu jusque les moments delicieux.* HELEN.

The first letter strikes several themes repeated in other letters found in Helen Jewett's room after the murder: that this client is unique because he can see past her degradation to offer her sympathy and compassion; that her life is wretched and blighted and she desperately needs a true friend; that she is still worth a lot and still has feminine (i.e., delicate) "feelings and characteristics."[8] (The unstated assumption was that a fully depraved prostitute would have somehow forfeited her womanly feelings of reserve and delicacy.) The story Helen told to William H. Attree of the *Transcript* had the similar purpose of drawing him into her confidence and flattering him into assuming the role of vindicator of the noble-hearted but ruined woman. And it had worked then, even with the canny Attree: he championed her in print, lavished her with sympathy and compassion, and then in private became a devoted client, obviously enamored of her physical charms. To the "doctor," too, she promised in her earnest closing to be his "forever, if you please." The author of this fervent letter evidently did not fear appearing melodramatic.

The second letter adopted an altogether different tone, impudent and even petulant. The relationship has progressed past the modestly self-deprecating opening moves of the first letter. The Jewett of the second letter exhibits a sexual authority here, in declaring her desire for the doctor openly, commanding his presence at her lodgings, and rearranging her life with her keeper to make such a visit possible. The pretext of the letter is that a six-day hiatus is unbearably long for Jewett, in love and miserable about it, while the doctor is playfully painted as a cold and heartless fellow who may be in need of punishment for his neglect of her. In truth the doctor may have been just as ardent and interested in this lively relationship as the young woman claimed to be, but her letter flattered him by supporting a masculine notion that a man should not be so dependent on a woman. It also flattered him by its frank sexual assertiveness; she let him know that she found him desirable. The closing line in French tantalized with sexy promise: "Goodbye until the delicious moments." Even then, French was the language of illicit sex; in antebellum New York, French lunar pills brought on "blocked" menstrual flows, Madame Restelle was the city's foremost abortionist, Dr. Mauriceau the pseudonymous author of an 1840s sex manual. Maybe Jewett had studied French after all, amid the boiling tubs of laundry at the Westons' in Augusta.

Calculated flattery was exactly what Jewett needed to put forth in order to draw in this doctor. What is of course missing from these letters is any allusion to the exterior framework that actually supported the relationship. The doctor was, after all, Jewett's paying client; perhaps he was slow to visit because of what it would cost him, or because of his need to conceal his activities from a wife. What these letters really demonstrate is a shrewd business acumen: a prostitute reeling in a promising customer and manipulating him into spending more money on her services.

No respectable young maiden of the 1830s could have written such forward and erotically charged letters to a beloved without running considerable risk of casting doubt on her sexual purity. In the normal course of courtship, men did not receive letters like these. This might explain why the recipient took pains and possibly risks to preserve them, yielding them up to the "gentleman" three years later only for the noble mission of trying to defend Jewett from the *Boston Post*'s charge that she was low and common.

But were these letters truly products of Helen Jewett's pen? The evidence strongly suggests they were. They markedly resemble her other letters to clients, letters that were not published anywhere in 1836 but that did have some degree of unauthorized circulation as a result of leaks in the Police Office to favored newspaper editors. A clever writer could have adopted elements of her style—the calculated flattery, the florid prose, the sexual assertiveness—and concocted the whole episode. Certainly other aspects of this *Authentic Biography* (namely everything pertaining to Jewett's life before 1832) were fabrications. But they were fabrications done up by Jewett herself (the Portland school, the law student, the generous judge) and palmed off on someone who met her around 1833 or 1834, when these letters to the doctor were supposedly written. Perhaps the strongest argument against the letters being wholly contrived stems from their being used so naively in the "gentleman's" pamphlet. The author presented them as genuine evidence of Jewett's clever mind and her provocative sexual initiative, characteristics which he expected would gain sympathy for her from the men for whom he wrote. He clearly intended to foster a portrayal of the dead prostitute as a quite bright but unfortunate girl, who still had managed to salvage some self-respect and win love and validation from such men of standing as the doctor. He read the letters precisely as Jewett had intended the doctor to read them. Both doctor and "gentleman" were blind to their correspondent's shrewd business motives.

One possible—and certainly interesting—candidate for doctor-lover was David L. Rogers, age thirty-seven in 1836 and a surgeon of rising reputation who maintained an office and a house on Chambers Street. He had treated Rosina Townsend for various maladies as early as 1828 when she was entering the trade, so others among the women of 41 Thomas may have been patients as well.[9] Later famous for his pioneering surgical work on ovaries and hernias, Dr. Rogers at this point was developing expert anatomist skills through occasional autopsy work supplemented with dissections of bodies stolen from graveyards. (Legal dissections were rare, being limited by New York law to executed criminals, victims of duels, and unclaimed paupers. Rogers and his mentor, Dr. Valentine Mott of the College of Physicians and Surgeons on Barclay Street, were skilled at orchestrating body snatchings—lifting fresh corpses from graves in the dead of night, a common sort of theft in antebellum America wherever a medical school was near, as was the case in lower Manhattan.)[10] It was Dr. Rogers, accustomed as he was to nighttime work, who was called in the very early hours of April 10, 1836, to attend Jewett's body, probably because he was Townsend's doctor, because he lived close by—Chambers was just three short blocks south of 41 Thomas Street—and because he had special competence as an anatomist. Once there, the coroner deputized him to perform the autopsy on Jewett's body, which, if he had once been her lover, must have been a rather disconcerting experience.

For most of her time in New York City, Helen Jewett did not work as a kept woman. From 1834 to 1836, she conducted her work from brothels. She met clients at the theater, in her parlor, by referral, and on the street. That she avoided arrest for vagrancy means that she had mastered the art of selective concealment in public. A woman who was smart, attractive, verbally adept, and experienced at playacting with men, she evidently learned how to negotiate or ward off encounters with authorities very effectively. Jewett was not demure, but she could disguise her identity as a prostitute when it suited her. The *New York Herald* had described her as a public figure who walked a bold walk and returned bold stares at Wall Street brokers as she strode down Broadway on her frequent trips to the post office in her legendary green silk dress. She did on occasion pick up clients on busy daytime streets, as happened, for example, on the afternoon of her murder when she met a young man on Broadway in front of A. T. Stewart's large department store and arranged for him to follow her, prudently at a little distance, back to her room. She successfully deployed the strategically bestowed bold stare, the flirtatious smile that targeted a potential customer but left other men, and certainly policemen, none the wiser about her occupation. Her deportment far more than her clothes signaled her availability. She could turn her glance on or off and thereby avoid undesirable clients, as well as the police, and exercise considerable control over her work.

Her dress alone—splendid dress is how it was described at the trial[11]—did not mark her as a prostitute, even her trademark green silk outfit. Silk dresses with ribbons and bows were high fashion among the daughters of mercantile New Yorkers, and even such provocative features as low décolletage, tiny waists, and flounced sleeves were not spurned by the virtuous. Complaints about respectable women wearing silks and low necklines in daytime in public substantiate that fancy dress worn on the street indeed was a cultural marker for sexual availability. And it appears virtuous girls were the ones encroaching on the boundary, making it open and ambiguous.[12]

A chief distinction about Jewett's wardrobe was not so much the rich fabric and stylish display of any one outfit, which could be duplicated by a respectable wealthy woman, but the sheer number of outfits she possessed. At the trial, George Marston (a regular client who had patronized Jewett under the nickname Bill Easy) was cross-examined about her wardrobe and jewelry and testified that she had a large variety of valuable dresses, which she sometimes wore plain, without ornamentation, but at other times, when she was fully dressed, were dazzlingly bejeweled. Marston reported that she owned at least six rings, two of emerald; he had seen her wearing "more than one ring on every finger." Earrings, belt buckles set with precious gems, and a gold watch chain were further parts of self-decoration. "Ellen was one of the most splendidly dressed women that went to the third tier of the theatre," Marston said, indicating that theater attendance called for full formal dress.[13]

Drawing men's eyes on the street or at the theater was the public part of prostitution, which Jewett conducted with decorum. She then took her clients to her brothel, either to the parlor to socialize or to her room for more intimate contact. She lived at three addresses over the last two years of her life, all of them a short distance west of Broadway and to the north of City Hall.

For nine months in 1834, Jewett lived at 41 Thomas Street under Rosina Townsend's management and returned there three weeks before her death. Between those two stays she lived at 128 Duane Street, from fall 1834 to January 1836, in a place known by insiders as the Philadelphia House, run by Mary Berry, a woman of English birth who grandly styled herself the Duchess de Berri. After fourteen months with Mrs. Berry, Helen moved to number 3 Franklin Street, run by a Mrs. Cunningham, but relocated to Thomas Street in March 1836.

In all of these houses, Jewett could still control her work fairly tightly. She was not obliged to sell her sexual services to any and all men who might find their way to her front door. She maintained an exclusive clientele, typically seeing only one or two clients a day, and this was the general pattern for the women at 41 Thomas Street. Rosina Townsend testified at the trial that about a hundred men per week patronized her house. With ten working women, that averaged out to ten clients a week per woman. In Jewett's circle of clients, a few visited regularly, perhaps more than once a week, so that a hundred patrons a week for the house might really amount to 125 patron-visits per week. Still, even figuring in a significant traffic in repeat customers, the number is strikingly small.

The women did not need to expand their client base because they charged high rates and derived quite comfortable incomes from the limited numbers of men they saw. Members of the grand jury that indicted Robinson seem to have taken an especially keen interest in asking about the basic terms and conditions of the girls' employment. In response to questioning, inmates of 41 Thomas explained that the typical charge to a customer was three to five dollars "at a time"—a phrase not further elaborated in the court recorder's transcript. On the expense side, each girl paid Townsend twelve dollars a week for room and board; there is no evidence suggesting that the madam took any cut of each fee a girl collected.[14] At 41 Thomas, Jewett also hired her own maid, a young black woman named Sarah Dunscombe, who came to her room twice daily, in the morning between eight and nine to clean up and do washing, and in the late afternoon from around five to seven, to help Jewett dress, bring up the wood, build the fire, and fetch pitchers of water. (Jewett had employed her at the house on Franklin Street, too, in early 1836.)[15] The business was organized, then, loosely on the model of a boardinghouse, with each girl an independent operator building her own clientele and engaging in sex work in the same room that was her private living space. The madam made her profits from the high lodging charge and by supplying wine and food in the parlor.

Both of these figures, $5 for sex and $12 for lodging, were high prices, even taking into account that the spring of 1836 was a period of very rapid inflation that would soon collapse into the Panic of 1837, a major economic recession marked by waves of bank failures and business bankruptcies. In 1836, a typical price for room and board at a regular boardinghouse was on the order of $2 a week. A charge of $12 approached the cost of a week's stay in a well-appointed room with full meals at the newly built swank Astor House Hotel on Broadway. A box ticket at the Park Theatre was $1 (but the third tier only 25 cents); a good hotel or restaurant meal 12 to 31 cents. Ten dollars was the cost of a stagecoach ticket for a multiday long-distance trip, for example, from Philadelphia to Pittsburgh, exclusive of meals.[16] A young man clerking in a mercantile house might earn at most $4 per week (an entry-level job), while a highly skilled journeyman at his prime in the busy building trades could earn $10 to $12 a week.[17] Prostitutes like Jewett earned a lot more. With an average of just ten clients a week, a young woman could earn $50, or $38 after deducting for lodging and food. Clothes, theater tickets, hairdressers, and private maid service were other regular business expenses. (Helen's jewelry, in contrast, was her form of savings.) Altogether, it was possible for a prostitute to clear something on the order of $1,500 to $2,000 a year at 41 Thomas.

The wonder is that young clerks on beginners' salaries could afford such expensive sexual services. Established men of the mercantile and professional classes could manage the fee, and probably a good proportion of the clients came from those ranks. Out-of-town merchants brought to the brothel via the drummer custom had their bills picked up by local mercantile houses as a business expense. A highly favored client, like Robinson or for a time George Marston, might find his fee per time waived, in honor of the deeper emotional ties of the relationship, but he was still expected to give the woman money. In such a moment, the favored client was in the position of the man picking up the tab for the kept-woman arrangement in that his payments were not pegged to specific services she performed. A postscript in one of Marston's letters made oblique reference to such a payment: "Do not be angry that I enclose the piece of paper accompanying this. It is all I have or it should be more."[18] Marston evidently adopted the conceit of pretending his bank note was a superfluous gesture that might make Jewett angry. (Or maybe Marston was more realistic than that: the bank note was inadequate, he realized, and it would therefore make Jewett angry.)

For the clerks who paid each time, three dollars to five dollars was surely a stretch. Many of the young men came to the parlor merely to socialize, spacing out their expensive visits to the upstairs rooms. Socializing, perhaps as much as sex, accounted for a lot of the brothel attraction for young clerks. A moral reform article highly critical of the social conditions that led clerks into brothels blamed merchants and their wives for shamefully neglecting their young clerks. Unsupervised and lacking the smile of a fond mother or sister, clerks ventured out into the throngs of the evening streets and fell in with more experienced boys who introduced them to theaters and then "genteel brothels" where they met "the beautiful, intelligent, and accomplished daughters of merchants, lawyers, and ministers." (The reformers apparently accepted such girls' own stories of high-status family background.) These talented women offered music, cards, and conversation to lonely boys; the solution was for respectable families to receive the clerks at home and keep them socializing with the virtuous.[19]

On the evening before Jewett's murder, obviously the most well-documented night at 41 Thomas Street, James Tew and Rodman Moulton, youths who both lived at the Dey Street house with Robinson, illustrated the reformers' concern. Walking up Broadway with time on their hands, but probably little money, they stopped in at 41 Thomas to talk with Elizabeth Salters and then left.[20]

Parlor talk was free; food and drinks were not. At 41 Thomas Street, there was another potential parlor expense. According to editor Bennett of the *Herald,* Townsend had a set of house rules that forbade kissing or sitting in men's laps in the parlor, under penalty of twenty-five- and fifty-cent fines imposed on the clients. Bennett claimed this was a rule "establishing order and decorum," but any reader with the slightest degree of worldliness could easily understand this as an amusing game in which clients bought a foretaste of sexual favors at a bargain price and the madam skimmed extra money. The upstairs activities were very expensive, because the women were selling more than just ten or fifteen minutes' worth of sex. Very often, a customer spent the night, or a good part of it. On April 9, 1836, six men were tucked away in prostitutes' beds, expecting to remain the entire night.

Rosina Townsend had a decade's worth of experience living in and running brothels. When under oath, she gave her name as Rosanna Brown; her parents lived up the Hudson River near Castleton, just south of Albany, she said, where she married, probably in the early 1820s. Deserted in Cincinnati, Ohio, by a husband who took off with another woman, Rosina returned to her parents' house for a month before moving to New York City in fall 1825. In less than six months, she had entered the trade of prostitution, having first tried sewing and servant work to earn a living. At the trial she testified that she had worked as a chambermaid for a Mr. Henry Beekman on Greenwich Street, which was possibly her first experience mixing with the well-to-do. (The wealthy Henry Beekman, a South Street merchant and member of the politically prominent old-Dutch Beekman family, lived at 60 Greenwich Street.) Her stay at the Beekmans' was short, lasting only a few weeks in 1826 and ending when she was installed in a house of assignation, she reported. The fact that Rosina chose to lift up that one work experience from among others she doubtless had in those first six months suggests that it had special significance in her own telling of her career. Either it represented a real turning point for her, or it was a splendid opportunity to embarrass from the witness stand a well-known family as the whole city hung on Rosina's every word. In the weeks at the assignation house, she probably was living in a kept-woman situation. By April 1826, she was ensconced in a brothel, her typical work site from then forward. In 1828 she ran a brothel at 28 Anthony Street (now called Worth), and in 1829 she moved to 41 Thomas Street.[21]

The house Rosina managed sat in the middle of a short block of Thomas Street just before it ended at Hudson Street. The entire extent of the street was only two blocks, running from Hudson up to the back of the New York Hospital. (Thomas now runs all the way to Broadway.) Even more than Leonard Street, Thomas Street was quite residentially mixed and crowded. In the 1830 census, the forty separate addresses on the two blocks housed 567 people, 115 of whom were blacks. The races were intermingled at many addresses, sometimes as a consequence of three or more families sharing one structure, or possibly of white households with black servants. Extreme residential segregation by race was not yet a routine feature of urban life, but these particular blocks around and just north of Thomas constituted one of the more heavily concentrated black areas in the lower wards.[22] The house at 41 Thomas Street as captured in the 1830 federal census consisted of five white women (two aged fifteen to nineteen and three aged twenty to thirty) and two black women (one aged ten to twenty-four, the other twenty-four to thirty-six).[23] Rosina

Townsend's name appeared as the head of household; the two black women might have been live-in servants (unlike Sarah Dunscombe, the day servant who came in twice daily to attend Helen in 1836), or they might have been prostitutes in an interracial brothel.

The interracial dealings in the neighborhood can be glimpsed in one indictment filed in the district attorney's office. In June 1835 a black woman named Ann Williams was arrested for possession of stolen goods. Williams had four bolts of silk, each worth $32.50, reportedly taken from a nearby yard-goods store on Broadway owned by Horatio Humphreys. She approached Tabitha Hill, a black woman residing at 18 Thomas Street, who bought one bolt and then resold twenty-three yards of it to Rosina Townsend in the next block for twelve dollars. Hill judged well that her neighborhood's prostitutes would find it attractive to buy a luxury fabric, would be able to afford it, and could accomplish the purchase without meddling husbands or fathers to raise a challenge about the provenance of the silk.[24]

Number 41 Thomas was the westernmost of three narrow Federal-style row houses, each three stories high and fronting less than seventeen feet along the street. All three houses were owned by John R. Livingston, an aged and wealthy businessman, brother of prominent New York politician Robert R. Livingston and Edward Livingston, so recently President Jackson's secretary of state.[25] John R. Livingston had acquired two of the Thomas Street lots in 1802 and the third in 1816, at a time when he was buying up considerable property in lower Manhattan. In 1808 a house was built on the eastern lot, number 39, and in 1825 two more houses were constructed, at number 39½ and number 41.[26] The two new ones were evidently built to be brothels, for that was their use right from the start. The older existing house also joined the business that year, and from 1825 onward, annual tax assessment lists show women as householders at all three addresses. In 1833, the two structures built in 1825 were combined into one house, renumbered 41, and placed under Rosina Townsend's management, and this was where Helen lived for much of 1834. The consolidation resulted in a much grander establishment boasting two symmetrically placed staircases that met at a shared landing just before the second floor and then continued up to the third floor, the whole central vertical space illuminated by two large skylights in the roof. The double house now afforded a good-sized backyard, thirty-three feet wide and sixty feet deep, entered through a piazza or covered porch running the width of the back. The yard in the rear contained a well-landscaped garden, with arbors and benches amid evergreens and flower beds. Where before there had been two medium-sized parlors in the back, each about sixteen by sixteen, now the old wall was knocked out to create a large double parlor, still dividable by folding doors that could be pulled across the space, to accommodate smaller parties desiring more privacy. The wall one floor up which once divided the two houses now merely separated one bedroom from the next. In 1836, Helen Jewett's bed lined that thick, dense, lath-and-brick wall, built to withstand fires, and so rendering the noise of lovemaking, arguing, blows, possibly even screams far less audible in the room that adjoined it.[27]

John R. Livingston's ownership of the Thomas Street brothel was not publicly acknowledged at the time of the murder, yet it was not unknown to neighbors on Thomas Street. One short-lived New York publication, the *Journal of Public Morals,* issued by a male moral reform organization, called for exposure of the owner in its June 1, 1836, issue. Who could own such a terrible place, they asked, "so genteel in its exteriour" but in reality "one of the gateways to death and hell"? This was a rhetorical question, meant merely to frighten the owner, perhaps, and position the moral reformers as righteous exposers of evil in high places—the very job they hesitated to do. They could easily have answered their own question by checking the city's real estate conveyance records in City Hall, or inquiring among Thomas Street neighbors, but they did neither. Their reluctance to implicate respectable and prominent businessmen even extended to the rental agent handling Livingston's property when the house was vacated in May 1836. How else to explain their conscious decision to suppress the name of the agent in their report of the vandalism the rental sign had been subjected to. "THIS HOUSE TO LET, inquire of ————," the paper reported, in telling of the sign posted high over the door at number 41. Their apparent news here was that the sign had to be moved out of reach because several previous signs posted next to the door, in the usual place, had been repeatedly torn down by souvenir seekers. The real news embedded in this item, however, was that even moral reformers could not bring themselves to point a finger of blame and actually name the respectable property owners and agents who made money from prostitution.

Neither could James Gordon Bennett. The *Herald*'s editor frequently hinted that he had hot or privileged insider information he was about to release, but somehow it never saw print. Three days after the murder, Bennett slyly hinted that the house is "knowingly let out for such purposes by one of our most respectable and pious citizens."[28] And certainly neighbors on Thomas Street knew who the owner was. In 1830, a group of them from across the street filed disorderly conduct charges against the three women running the establishments at 39, 39½, and 41, complaining especially about the display of naked bodies in the windows. The neighbors named Livingston as the "agent" of the madams, a word which implied he was connected to their business practices far more closely than just an indifferent landlord might be. The complainants expressed the hope that the police would go after him rather than the women in the windows, whose places "may be filled in twenty minutes." Livingston "lets these houses with a knowledge of their infamous purposes," they charged.[29] Livingston owned property all around these blocks, on Thomas, on Chapel, on Anthony and Orange (now Baxter) Streets. From the 1820s to the 1840s, most of these properties, numbering thirty or more, were brothels. For example, one block to the north, on the corner of Chapel and Anthony, Livingston owned three more side-by-side brothels at 24, 26, and 28 Anthony (now the southwest corner lots along Worth at West Broadway). Mary Berry started her madam career in number 26 back in 1830, when she was calling herself Mary Francisco, or Mary Cisco, and Rosina Townsend lived for a time at number 28 before moving to 41 Thomas.

In the mid-1830s, John R. Livingston was an elderly man, close to eighty. Possibly he was a vigorous eighty, since he lived to be ninety-six, dying in 1851. As he had for decades, he divided his time between his country manor along the Hudson River, near Red Hook in Dutchess County, and his town house in the city, which in the 1830s was a house on Duane just west of Hudson Street, perhaps a three-minute walk at a leisurely old-man's pace from the triple Thomas Street properties. Livingston was accounted a respectable man, from his very distinguished family connections and his wealth, some inherited but most of it the product of incessant real estate wheeling and dealing, not only in New York City but in large tracts of western New York State land. His inherited fortune rested on the several thousand acres of land he owned in Dutchess and Columbia Counties, on the east side of the Hudson River, farmed by tenants under a quasi-feudal system set up in the seventeenth century, complete with feudal dues of goods and service owed the landlord.[30] Livingston never sought a public career as had his brothers Robert and Edward. At his peak of public respect, Livingston was invited to be one of five equestrian honor guards flanking the coach carrying George Washington down Broadway to his presidential inauguration in 1789.[31] Yet he had a more checkered past than his place in the presidential guard suggests. His propensity to cut deals to make money sometimes sacrificed the nicer points of honor and patriotism. During the Revolutionary War, when he was yet young, the pursuit of shipping deals with British merchants earned him criticism from his less flexible patriotic friends.[32] Worse still, Livingston teamed up in 1778 with Benedict Arnold, then a Continental Army officer secretly selling out to the British. Arnold and Livingston schemed to set up a kind of protection racket promising several Loyalist merchants in British-held New York City that they would protect their property when the American forces retook the city, in exchange for two-thirds of the protected goods. They expected to make a killing when peace returned and prices shot up on the open market. When Arnold's separate, treasonous plan to let the British capture West Point came to light in 1780, Livingston rushed around issuing affidavits putting a distance between himself and Arnold by swearing that he had merely offered to buy on credit (that is, no cash up front) the Loyalist goods in New York.[33]

All his life John Livingston took risks and forged opportunities to make money. In the early 1780s, he bought up large quantities of depreciated public securities issued by the confederation government in the hope that his brother Robert, then active in the Continental Congress and soon to be a delegate to the 1787 Constitutional Convention in Philadelphia, would find a way to pump full value back into the near-worthless paper. Try to become president of the Continental Congress, John early wrote to Robert, "it will be productive of great advantages to your friends."[34] The new Constitution was all John hoped in its guarantee of full repayment of the federal public securities. In the early nineteenth century, he and Robert joined with Robert Fulton to make the first operational passenger steamboat in the country; John's task was to squeeze out competitors and try to seal their company's monopoly on the Hudson River.[35]

In short, John R. Livingston spent a lifetime figuring out how to maximize his profits and investments with little or no regard for the moral implications of his moneymaking schemes. Renting urban properties to prostitutes clearly was a highly profitable enterprise, and for thirty years he was the single largest owner of brothels in the city. Did he visit his establishments, collect his rents in person? Did agents or possibly his sons handle any of this business for him? None of this can be settled at this remove; the only large collection of John Livingston's papers, at the New-York Historical Society, covers the years of the 1790s to 1820, ending just at the time when the prostitution rentals started to feature prominently in his investment strategy.[36]

One final clue speaks to Livingston's personal involvement with prostitution at 41 Thomas Street. Several paintings decorated the walls of Rosina Townsend's parlor, along with the huge, expensive mirrors.[37] When James Gordon Bennett paid his second visit to Rosina's house, he noted elegant paintings and described one for his readers: "It represented a beautiful female, in disorder and on her knees, before two savages, one of them lifting up a tomahawk to give her a blow on the head." The painting he saw was evidently not familiar to him, but to any dedicated member of the New York art community, his description would have called to mind John Vanderlyn's *The Death of Jane McCrea*. Executed in 1804 in Paris, Vanderlyn's painting had been owned since 1805 by the New York Academy of Art. Exhibition catalogs document that the painting was on view in the 1810s and 1820s at the Academy's exhibition rooms on Chambers Street behind City Hall. It apparently went into storage around 1831, when the Academy vacated Chambers Street; and in 1842, when the by-then-defunct Academy auctioned off its holdings, the McCrea painting was sold in a large group of paintings to a Hartford, Connecticut, art dealer. There is no record of where the painting was in the mid-1830s; it was never listed in an exhibition catalog for the Academy after 1827. John R. Livingston, along with his brothers Robert R. and Edward, were all charter members of the Academy; for a decade, Robert had been its president. Robert, John, and John's wife had all sat for portraits by Vanderlyn, so they were personally familiar with the artist. John's New York town house was three blocks west and two blocks north of the Chambers Street exhibition hall. Perhaps the picture Bennett described was indeed the famous Vanderlyn painting, carried off by John when the Academy closed in 1831 and placed in the Thomas Street brothel.[38]

Editor Bennett was of course struck by the phenomenal coincidence of finding such a picture on the scene of a terrible ax murder. Vanderlyn depicted a highly sexualized Jane McCrea about to be dispatched to a bloody death. On the left, a powerfully built Indian is poised to bring a hatchet downward with full force on the head of his victim. The woman's cleavage and full breast overflow her neckline, exposing a nipple, a voluminous, palpable thigh strains against the tight fabric of her dress, and a pink sash around her waist unfurls its loose end right over her pubic region, visually defining her sex between her open legs. The female figure has long flowing hair worn loose down her back and in the grasp, not of a lover who might wish to touch such golden hair, but of a ferocious Indian on the right, who in moments will be using his tomahawk to scalp the woman. The painting depicted a well-known Revolutionary-era story of the scalping of Jane McCrea, an event of 1777 that had acquired legendary proportions by the early nineteenth century.[39]

To Bennett the picture clearly meant that thoughts of raising a hatchet to a woman's head were never far from the mind of anyone who visited this parlor. By the end of the first week after the murder, Bennett was busily constructing alternate hypotheses to the indictment of Robinson, both to take the heat off the nineteen-year-old clerk and to boost a sense of mystery and suspense about the crime, which of course was good for selling papers. He seized on the painting as a possible inspiration for the murder: depictions of violence somehow beget actual violence, he

LEFT: *John R. Livingston,*
in a portrait by John
Vanderlyn, 1802.
BELOW: The Death of Jane
McCrea, *by John Vanderlyn.*

asked his readers to believe. A picture of virile Indians about to kill a sex-ualized woman, Bennett improbably argued, could somehow inspire the murder of a prostitute by a jealous rival.[40]

In asking his readers to contemplate the meaning of this picture on the parlor wall of 41 Thomas, Bennett raised some interesting questions. Someone—John R. Livingston or Rosina Townsend—had decided it was appropriate to hang it on the wall in the most public room of the house, the room where genteel clients both familiar and new gathered to drink and chat with the young prostitutes, where banter and flirtation led to pairing off in the seclusion of upstairs rooms. Mirrors on the walls ampli-fied the moves of the shy to embolden them and encouraged the more experienced who knew how to lean forward with interest, how to laugh engagingly, how to negotiate a price for sex. Rich surroundings of deep carpets and soft sofas established a style and a tone, and original art-works extended the sense of a high-priced and visually stimulating brothel. In such a setting, a painting of a lethal attack on a woman seems incongruous.

A more likely candidate for Rosina's parlor wall was Vanderlyn's full-length nude picture of *Ariadne Asleep on the Isle of Naxos,* which was actu-ally for sale in New York in 1835; Vanderlyn complained about having a hard time finding a buyer. Here was a picture to set men thinking of sex: in an outdoor setting, a life-size shapely nude woman, eyes closed, reclines languidly on a red cape, arms tucked back behind her head to offer no resistance to the viewer and to expose fully her neck, breasts, abdomen, and legs, with a diaphanous wisp of a drape barely covering her genital region. In 1809, the year Vanderlyn began this painting, he wrote to a friend that he hoped his provocative picture would at least draw a crowd to his public exhibitions. "The subject may not be chaste enough for the more chaste and modest Americans, at least to be displayed in the house of any private individual, to either the company of the parlor or drawing room, but on that account it may attract a greater crowd if exhibited pub-lickly," Vanderlyn astutely figured.[41] *Ariadne* was shown several times in the 1820s and 1830s, and the artist finally sold it in 1835 to a New York engraver, Asher Durand, who reproduced the voluptuous nude in small posters which also, strangely, failed to find much of a market.[42] (Maybe Durand's price was too high, or he was selling in the wrong stores, for the 1830s art market encompassed a strong pornographic segment of litho-graphs that enjoyed high sales in New York.) The price of the *Ariadne* was quite possibly lower than that of a well-framed mirror of the same size—large mirrors were *very* expensive—but Livingston did not buy it. Perhaps its large dimensions ruled it out: a canvas sixty-eight and a half inches high by eighty-seven inches long could not easily be accommodated on the wall of a private house. Yet the double parlor of 41 Thomas Street, thirty-three feet across the back of the property, surely had some wall space big enough. Or perhaps the painting simply spoke too directly to the business of the brothel, and Livingston and Townsend wanted to establish a more discreet and subdued atmosphere. Later in the nineteenth century, full-length nudes turned up most frequently behind the bar in saloons. Rosina's brothel aimed to emulate an elegant mansion, not a raucous saloon.

To a money-conscious businessman like John R. Livingston, borrowing *The Death of Jane McCrea* was a better deal than buying the *Ariadne*. It was a conveniently small picture, on the order of three feet by two feet, and it did show a beautiful woman in tantalizing nakedness amid near-naked men with torsos like Greek gods. Perhaps a person blind to the terror on Jane McCrea's face could have thought that the depiction of so much naked flesh was just the thing to dress up a brothel wall. Yet perhaps whoever provided the picture was not entirely sure of the appropriateness of the choice: the painting was hung in a dark corner of the parlor, Bennett reported.[43] Maybe this was Rosina Townsend's effort to mute Livingston's choice of decoration.

But exactly how would male guests read this picture? And what about the female inmates, girls like Helen Jewett, who saw it in their work environment day after day? The legend of McCrea, well known in the 1830s, offers some insight into contemporary ways to read the picture. Rendered in poetry since the 1790s, the McCrea story took off in the 1820s and 1830s, when McCrea's grave became something of a shrine and tourists stole chips of her tombstone. By 1837, when William Dunlap (once the renter of 55 Leonard Street) popularized it in a public school history textbook for all New York children to read, the McCrea story was a classic.[44] Jane McCrea, daughter of an American family, fell in love with a young Tory American who joined the British army under Burgoyne's command during the campaign leading to the battle of Saratoga in 1777. Jane eloped to join him, guided by Indians sent by the British to escort her. But she was killed on the short journey; shot in the cross fire of war, claimed the British, or murdered by savage Mohawks, ran the American legend. In the immediate moment, the American war leaders played her up as a martyr to the cause, to inspire soldiers to defeat Burgoyne and his thuggish Indian allies in defense of American womanhood. But in the long run, Jane McCrea was a problematic martyr, a young woman disobeying her family and running off to a Tory lover, a traitor to the cause, in the name of foolish love. In the half-dozen poems and stories that memorialized her, and in the several artistic depictions of her plight, the point of focus was always on her bloody, terrible death. The true deeper meaning of the legend was that women who claim independence and freedom of choice in lovers should expect the possibility of an untimely and bloody end.[45]

Most of the women who worked at 41 Thomas Street had made exactly such a choice: to leave a disapproving family to follow a man, or men in generality, who behaved in ways the girls' families would not like. Such men were sexual seducers rather than political traitors, but the enticing of a naive or apolitical girl away from the path of righteous virtue is common to both stories. Vanderlyn's painting shows McCrea's lover, a small figure far off in the distance who is helpless to save her—he cannot possibly run fast enough to get there in time. Male lovers cannot save you, the picture said, they are puny and not there when you need them. Such a woman can only rely on herself. And Vanderlyn's Jane is trying her best. One hand strongly grips an Indian's wrist as if she will try to throw him off balance, while her eyes implore pity to stay the hand of the man about to deliver the murderous blow. But her fate is clear. This cannot have been a comforting picture for women like Jewett to see every day.

But of course brothel decoration is really there for the customers, not the workers. To the young men's eyes, this was a picture of an attractive damsel in deep distress. As small as the faraway lover is, the figure at least provides inspiration for a fantasy of rescue. The distressed damsel is vulnerable to these strong attackers, who may just as likely rape her, in view of her naked breast and tumbling hair, as kill her. The threatening weapons might only be employed to scare and subdue her, not decapitate her; or so a man anticipating sexual satisfaction upstairs might reasonably conclude. If rape is the real intended crime, then there is in fact time for the tiny lover to run to the scene, to come upon (and maybe watch) a rape in progress, and ultimately to save the grateful maiden. The painting encourages voyeuristic fantasies cloaked in noble motives. Alternatively, men viewing the picture might identify with the Indians themselves, with their powerful muscles and attractive neoclassical bodies. Seen in this frame, the painting then is about sexual power, about men (in the plural) having total dominion over a woman, perhaps to kill her but more likely to have their way with her. In these two interpretative strategies, Vanderlyn's painting might well be a satisfying visual aid to men in the specific context of a brothel parlor. They might enjoy imagining that they could rescue an unfortunate girl from death, or a fate worse than death, turning their visit to the brothel into an act of charity and benevolence. Helen Jewett certainly encouraged some of her clients, like the doctor or William Attree, to think of her this way. Or, drawing on darker subterranean themes in the psyche, male viewers of the picture might contemplate the fantasy of exercising total sexual power through threat of violence.

Powerful fantasies contrasted sharply with the actual circumstances of the customers. In reality men in a brothel parlor, especially newcomers green to the transactions of commercial sex, were far more likely to be entertaining unsettling thoughts that they would have liked to push away. They might be worrying about an unaware wife or fiancée; they might be struggling to remember the false name they have presented as their own. Many must have been uneasy about the expense of the evening, wondering how much this experience would cost them, wondering if their nervousness would keep them from performing sexually with the young women. From the customer's point of view, the sexually experienced and authoritative women in a brothel like 41 Thomas Street held a lot more high cards against the men than a gathering of respectable women in a respectable parlor. The prostitutes could throw men out; they could laugh or intimidate them into impotence; they could overcharge or otherwise cheat them. The painting of Jane McCrea gave them something else to think about.

Upstairs in her own room at 41 Thomas, Jewett put on the wall a small picture of Lord Byron, a literary favorite of hers. If the picture of the epicene poet sent any message at all to clients, it probably was a simple one: a refined language of love and poetry is spoken here. Or a step farther: a man admired by Helen Jewett does not have to have rippling muscles and he-man bulk; the sexually androgynous Byronic look is what is preferred. Downy-cheeked youths of nineteen or twenty would have taken comfort. Helen Jewett and her housemates could easily ignore the fate of Jane McCrea, even though it was on the wall in front of them every day. It was just a brothel prop, a decoration meant to shore up jittery customers.

CHAPTER SEVEN

Epistolary Enticement

W HEN HELEN JEWETT met Richard P. Robinson in 1835, she had been supporting herself at her trade for nearly five years and by all accounts was proficient and successful at it. Her occasional relocations to new brothels around New York's Fifth Ward expanded her network of women friends, and the Duane Street house where she lived the longest, from October 1834 to sometime in January 1836, was an especially sociable and prominent enterprise. Its madam, the Duchess de Berri, maintained an informal connection to a brothel in Philadelphia, and Helen and other prostitutes exchanged visits and clients with that establishment in the City of Brotherly Love. Many of the letters found in Jewett's room after her murder date from the year she lived at the Duchess's house (although some are earlier), and these letters open windows on her manner of engaging with clients and woman friends. It seems to have been a happy time for her.

Robinson came into her life halfway through the year, in June, and the two began an intense relationship that, their letters suggest, had many emotional highs and lows. Their correspondence needs to be evaluated in the context of other letters she received. How much of the romantic banter exchanged with Robinson was actually unique to their relationship? Except for the two she wrote to the doctor, none of Jewett's letters to other men survives. But much can be inferred from the twenty-five extant letters she received from clients. Whether as a business practice, personal inclination, or possibly both, she fostered emotionally intimate, romantic relationships with many men.

The Duchess's brothel, at 128 Duane Street, occupied the south side of the block between Chapel and Church, along with six or seven other narrow, three-story Federal-style row houses. The immediate neighborhood had that same mixture of uses found throughout the Fifth Ward. To the east toward Broadway was a brewery. To the west there was an African Primary School, one of four in the city, to educate the black children of the ward, many of whom lived in the blocks above Duane on Thomas and Anthony Streets.[1] And one block farther west, on Duane just across Hudson near a small triangular park, sat the town house of the wealthy and aged John R. Livingston.

A nameplate next to the front door of the Duane Street brothel stated simply MRS. BERRY, presumably enough for visitors in the know.[2] The property owner of record was Thomas Blakely; three men of that name lived elsewhere in New York City. Because of its ties to the Philadelphia brothel, Mrs. Berry's house was sometimes known as the Philadelphia House.

Mary Berry moved there in late 1832 or 1833, bringing with her two thousand dollars' worth of personal property—probably the brothel madam's customary heavy investment in carpets, drapes, plush divans, wooden bedsteads, and large and costly mirrors. (The previous occupant of 128 Duane, a Miss Myers, had only a modest five hundred dollars' worth of movables to be taxed.)[3] Mary Berry also brought with her a gambling man named Frank Berry, once described as "a man of good appearance and consumate in his arts."[4] Police Office warrants always identified Mrs. Berry as a spinster, a legal (and probably accurate) label that held her fully accountable for all her actions and financial transactions. (Not until 1848 could married women in the state of New York own any property or sue and be sued in their own names.)[5] Frank Berry had been her partner for several years, back in a less elegant brothel on Anthony Street, but it seems unlikely they were ever legally married, even though she had taken his name. Nevertheless, Longworth's *City Directory* listed the property at 128 Duane Street as the home of Francis Berry, tailor. Evidently when Thomas Longworth walked the blocks of Manhattan to update his biennial directories, he ignored the doorplate and inscribed the man of the house as the only householder of record, just as he had done in 1831, when Frank and Mary lived at 26 Anthony Street in a row of three Livingston-owned brothels. To find Longworth representing Frank in his directory as a tailor heading a family must have seemed a good joke to Mary Berry and the other women of the house. Such a deception required him to disregard what must have been strikingly obvious about the opulent household of mostly young women with a woman's name on the doorplate. The 1830 census of the Fifth Ward, conducted by Longworth as enumerator, reveals that he did know the real business of Mary Berry's house. There he recorded 26 Anthony Street as headed by Mary Francisco (that is, Mary Cisco, later Mary Berry), and he classed the inhabitants as one white male in his twenties, six white females, only one of whom was over thirty (Mary herself), and two black females. Yet when Longworth prepared his own city directory of 1831, this household too became sanitized to that of Francis Berry, tailor. Actually, Frank was probably the only inhabitant of number 26 who was not working for a living.[6]

Mary Berry's duchess act held up for quite a while. An admiring squib published in an 1842 racy men's newspaper, the *Flash*, praised her unfaded beauty and her classy establishment:

> Her table is excellent, her boarders are ladies, her furniture is splendid. In her manner to her visiters [*sic*], she merits the noble title she has acquired—the Duchess—for if not a Duchess, she is the next thing to it. We wish her all possible success, and recommend gentlemen who wish to look upon splendor and magnificence, to visit her house.[7]

A rival racy newspaper, the *Sunday Flash*, in 1841 ran an informative feature article on Mary Berry that was much less flattering. Titled "Life and Exploits of La Duchess de Berry," the article promised it contained only authenticated facts, not rumors. (The three editors of the *Sunday Flash* published only pseudonyms on the masthead, but George Wilkes, who later wrote a novelization of the Jewett case, was one of the three, and this sort of claim was a consistent pattern in his journalistic career.[8] And in this case, the handful of checkable facts in the story do check out.) The *Sunday Flash* asserted that Mary Berry was born Mary Cisco in London, the daughter of a common thief who booted her out when she lost her virginity at age eighteen. Soon after, Mary came to America for a fresh start. "About ten years ago, the present Duchess de Berry, then plain Mary Cisco, commonly called Moll Cisco, rented one of three little crasy [*sic*] yellow wooden houses in Anthony street, next to Chapel, now occupied by negro harlots, thieves, and burners. Moll Cisco's house, however, was the best of the three, and its proprietress managed to drive a pretty brisk trade in the seafaring line."

Soon, continued the *Sunday Flash*, she hitched up with Frank Berry, described as a good-looking "lummux" and a petty thief. She fired her kitchen help and set Frank to work doing brothel chores—making breakfast for the women, building the fires, and delivering wine to the rooms in the evening. When the Berrys had saved up money for new furniture, they moved to the Duane Street house. "Her house became the fashionable resort for all Philadelphia female visitors, and was in consequence called the Philadelphia Bazaar," the *Sunday Flash* reported. (Either this was a slip of the pen or a typesetter's error, or else the writer knew Mary Berry's house very well, for women from the Philadelphia brothel did visit.) On Duane Street, Mary Cisco Berry appropriated her noble title along with, said the *Sunday Flash*, insufferable "airs of nobility." Pretty soon she also got rid of Frank and replaced him with a new bodyguard, one Charles M. Locke, who later left for Texas. (Police Office records confirm that a bookkeeper named Charles M. Locke swore out assault warrants on Francis Berry in August and September 1835.)[9] By 1841, the *Sunday Flash* alleged, the Duchess was fifty-seven, toothless, hairless, and in consort with a Negro lover—all unlikely slurs in keeping with this racy newspaper's savage ridicule of Mary Berry and her way of life.

Among Fifth Ward brothels, the Philadelphia House was somewhat unusual for having a man on the premises full-time. Frank did more than housework for the brothel; he also engaged in drumming for customers. A court case in late 1835 revealed his methods: Berry frequented places of public amusements to pick up some "green" young man. After drinking with the mark, he would suggest a walk, steer the man to the Duane Street brothel, and then leave him there at the mercy of the evils of cards and dice, liquor, and "fully developed female blandishments." Frank made the penny papers' police columns because one man, a visitor from Saugerties who lost three hundred dollars in an evening swindle, was so bold as to go to the police to swear out a warrant against Berry. Berry appeared and confidently offered the man only a third of his money back, the other two hundred dollars being his price for allowing the man to avoid the newspaper exposure of a Police Court case.[10]

Having a man on-site brought the women of Duane Street some extra protection. On one of the few occasions when Helen Jewett got into a physical altercation with a man, the incident with the angry barber John Boyd, Frank Berry was on hand to assist her. But such events were rare for Jewett. In her letters, her clients presented themselves as respectful, even adoring, men.

An undated letter from a fellow named "J." shows how Jewett carefully managed the beginnings of a relationship. "I am highly gratified at the promptitude, with which you have responded to my desire to form your acquaintance, the more so, because if I am to believe you, (and as yet I have no reason to doubt your sincerity) it is a favor which has not been granted to all who have sought it." J.'s experience, then, was that Jewett regally granted permission for men to approach her and in doing so let them think that she was quite selective in granting her favors. J. framed his letter with politeness and deference, but notice the wary parenthetical clause offering a hint of a challenge to Jewett's veracity: you say you are selective, he implies, and "as yet" your sincerity seems honest.

J. was right to be on guard. The world of commercial sex called forth dissimulation and playacting far more often than sincerity: men and women with faked names and faked pasts engaged in often-faked emotions and pleasures, paid for with depreciating or even counterfeit bank notes. But J., having gained privileged access to her, also could not risk offending Jewett. His purpose in writing was to explain that a fall from a carriage prevented him from attending her right away, and a doctor had confined him to bed and forbidden "all excitement." Impatient to see Helen, he urged her to write him, something he knows she can do well because he has her first elegant note. "Tell me what impression I have made upon you. Anything so that you write," he begged, with a note of desperation. And then something closer to a command in the final line: "Do not disappoint me I pray you."[11]

Although they had just met and J. was presenting himself as a humble supplicant seeking Helen's permission to court her, still by the end of the letter J. was insisting that she inaugurate the romance by letter since he is bedridden. What he specifically wants to hear is what Jewett finds attractive about him—what about him has caused her to accept his addresses. In early courtship moves with a virtuous, respectable woman, J. would probably not have made such demands, out of a reasonable apprehension of scaring her off. Two people in the delicate first stages of romance, when an initial mutual appraisal is under way, are likely to be afflicted with doubts and fears: how could this person whom I desire really like me? But J. here insists that Helen tell him; he wants to hear what has gained him favor with this discerning woman.

None of this is really surprising. J. after all is about to become a favored but still a paying client of Jewett's. We should expect that the sexual exchange at the heart of prostitution would differ from noncommercial sexual exchanges subject only to the customs of courtship and marriage. In agreeing to pay for her romantic interest, J. feels he has earned the right to be bolder and insist on what he wants, which at the outset is to be assured of his own attractiveness to her, to have his ego bolstered.

What did commodified sex, wrapped in the romantic conventions of middle-class courtship, mean to Jewett and her clients? It does not appear that these men were buying sex as a way of avoiding time-consuming or inconvenient emotional obligations to women, as is sometimes the appeal of prostitution. Jewett's terms of conducting business required her clients to court and flatter her, write love letters, and bring gifts. This was not exactly obligation-free sex. If men merely wanted to experience quick sexual release, in a society that generally discouraged and penalized free sexual expression among unmarried people, they could purchase it much more cheaply from streetwalkers over in Five Points or in taverns near the wharves. Jewett's clients were choosing to spend far more in order to acquire a bundle of romantic illusions. Their purchase brought them an alternative intimate relationship, unburdened by the strictures and restraints of bourgeois courtship and free of the renunciations and monotony of lifelong marriage. For Jewett, prostitution was surely a way of making a living, but it may also have been a way of exercising power over men, or of meeting needs for emotional intimacy and self-validation. Her insistence on commitment and on the trappings of romance was not in the least inconsistent with her charging a fee for sex. She screened her clients, which allowed her to pick only those with some appeal for her, men she liked being with. In that context, getting paid surely enhanced her pleasure in and dedication to her work.

Two letters to Helen from a man named Edward give one version of the epistolary intimacies beyond sex that Helen extended to clients. Written nine days apart, the extremely polite and graceful letters reflect Edward's assessment of the strength of their affections and also bring a close to their relationship, a close Edward thinks Helen has been signaling.[12]

> Dear Helen: I have not time this morning to answer, at length, the letter which you put into my hands, an evening or two since, and in which you were pleased to lavish upon me compliments as undeserved as they were unlooked for, from you. I fear I shall never be able to think you serious when you pay a compliment to my personal appearance, it is so much against my own judgment, although the besetting sin of vanity might make me wish to believe you.

Helen's letter, delivered in person, apparently flattered Edward for his attractive looks—the very thing J. had insisted Helen write him about. As part of her sex work, Helen takes it upon herself to flatter men about their bodies and appearance. Furthermore, it sounds as though Helen has flattered Edward this way more than once, and Edward, while professing modesty, actually manages to accept her compliment gracefully. Helen is cajoling him, either by custom or because she has hard news to deliver. The fact that her note is hand delivered raises several questions: Is this their customary way of communicating? Is this perhaps a relationship largely conducted via letters? Or has she committed thoughts to paper in this instance because she cannot trust that her words would all be aired or heard in a conversation? Or are they meeting in public, hence the need for a written document unobtrusively slipped from one hand to another? Apparently the location of the letter exchange was not the theater, because Edward writes:

> You say you cannot see me, nay, not even recognize me in the theatre, and conclude, by saying, in your own peculiar manner, that you have sought my society from the best of motives, and now relinquish me with regret. In this sentence you have paid me a great and undeserved compliment, but in the ready manner with which you say you relinquish me, I think you have shown that any preference which you expressed for me was not very deep seated. Woman seldom yields without a struggle. I do not mention this because I expected it would be otherwise, but only to show you that I was right in my opinion.

So Helen's was a Dear John letter. And yet it is not clear who is actually initiating the break. The line about yielding without struggle implies that it is Edward who wants to break things off, and Helen is yielding all too readily, a sign to him that her "preference" for him was not very substantial:

> You may recollect that I once said to you, "when your friend returns you will discard me, even from your memory;" and see how truly I prophesied. I do not mention this in the way of complaint. God forbid that I should place any obstacle in the way either of your interest or inclination.

Edward sees himself as giving way to a man with firmer claims to Helen's heart. He is the one who is yielding, easily and without a fight, generously not wishing to block Helen's free choice of men. There is no sign of jealousy here, only regret, no sign of Edward's urging her to love him still, which would not be unexpected in a more ordinary love relationship undergoing a breakup. The closing line of the letter underscores this remarkably civil and gentlemanly concession: "I wish you more happiness in the company of your friend than you could possibly receive in the society of . . . Edward." Consider, though, that Helen is a prostitute with a circle of clients; why must Edward quit Helen's company altogether and cede place to the old friend? One clue might lie in these sentences, which hint at some emotional or physical disability Edward suffers:

One word in conclusion, in reply to your remark, that your feelings have been met with coldness. In this, Helen, you do me positive injustice. If I have not allowed those feelings to appear, it has been from reasons which I have more than once hinted to you. Namely. That I could not be to you the friend, which, perhaps, you anticipated. Could I have been so, you would never have received a refusal to accompany you home. But enough of that, for it is as unpleasant to hear as to relate.

Edward has strong feelings for her, but he has suppressed them and has declined to go home with her, possibly out of concern for his sexual performance. His subject-changing "enough of that" at least suggests such a reading. What seems most remarkable, if this is a reference to impotence, is that the ever-polite Edward frames his disability in terms of not being good enough for the (sexual) happiness of Helen. Edward writes as if they both expect a prostitute-client relationship will bring some kind of sexual fulfillment to both of them. Even if his real reason for not going to her house is at bottom a disappointment and embarrassment over his inability to achieve sexual gratification, in this letter he nevertheless delicately casts his concern as one of his inability to provide mutually satisfying sex. Notice, too, the information that it is Helen who in the past has invited him home, probably from an encounter at the theater; she has taken the lead in this relationship, instead of taking the demure feminine role of waiting to be asked. And he has declined.

A second letter from Edward nine days later makes it clear that he is bent on extricating himself from the relationship. Jewett has written him in the meantime, and he apologizes for being so slow to respond. After hemming and hawing about how much he enjoys discussion and argument with her because she has abundant "good sense," he comes to the point:

Had not this correspondence better be discontinued for the present at least. Start not at the proposal; it is with reluctance that I speak of it, but you are with your young friend, and . . . your attachment for him must increase, while for me, it must lessen. . . . No doubt, Helen, that you think well of me, respect me as a gentleman, and would no doubt be gratified with my occasional visits, but as you well remarked I am too much a man of the world to flatter myself that a woman's heart is gained because her tongue speaks me fair.

Helen's intervening letter must have professed respect for the gentlemanly Edward and a wish to continue seeing him. But Edward now throws back in Helen's face her aphorism that a sophisticated man will realize that mere "fair" words from a woman do not mean that her heart is truly engaged. Edward's challenge to her was fully justified, and Helen knew it, because she used this line with other clients, in an effort to hook them into believing in her sincere protestations of love. Evidence that this was a calculated strategy on her part comes in a letter she wrote Richard P. Robinson very early in their relationship, where she deployed the same adage she apparently proposed to Edward:

> It is unnecessary for me again to repeat to you "that I find much pleasure in accomplishing anything which may be productive of happiness to you," for all my efforts can never make suitable return for the generous disinterested course of conduct, which tells me more plainly than words that solicitude for my happiness seems interwoven with every feeling of your nature. You have too much good sense to flatter yourself that a woman's heart is gained because her tongue speaks you fair. You will not the more readily believe I love you madly, fondly love, because in all my letters I so frequently repeat the assertion.[13]

A guileless young clerk smitten by Helen's beauty and newly admitted to her inner circle would find this seemingly sincere and confiding remark about her love, shown in ways beyond mere words, and his superior ability to discern it, an exciting passage indeed. Edward, however, seems to have been an older and more worldly man, able more decisively to cut things off with Helen by quoting back to her her own remark.

Edward's second letter alluded to another delicate subject:

> During our last interview your partial refusal on a certain matter, convinced me that I reigned in your bosom with no very deep seated preference. It spoke volumes in favor of your feelings for your friend, and your regard for your word, but very little for your partiality for me. Pardon me for alluding to the circumstance even in this remote manner. Straws, they say, show which way the wind blows, so from this little circumstance I am obliged to draw conclusions which prevent me from believing you entirely, when you profess ardent attachment.

Did Jewett refuse him something sexual? Or some other token of affection? Whatever she did not do Edward interpreted as a mark of preference for her other man. Edward was not a man easily manipulated, it is clear; he was observant and alert to nonverbal cues. The romantic diction of their exchange makes it easy to forget that Jewett was a prostitute selling sexual services and Edward a customer. Her plan was to make each customer feel especially beloved. Certainly each knows that she sees and sleeps with other men, but some allow themselves to take seriously her profession of particular affection for them. So has Edward in the past, but now he feels he is slipping in her affection because another special friend had returned. Even as he slips out of her grasp and refuses to play her game anymore, he still imagines that the larger game has a certain reality to it: if Helen no longer is partial to him, it is because she is more partial to another.

Even though Edward is breaking off the relationship, at the end of the first letter he declares "I shall still call at the house to enquire of your well being" and in the second he names the time he will call. So while they have agreed to ignore each other at the theater and not to have private visits, Edward feels free to come to her door or parlor to inquire after her, as if he were making a house call in respectable society, to pay his respects and see about her "well-being." Jewett's parlor thus resembles a parlor in polite society, but one with two kinds of transactions in process. Some men stopped by as visitors, to chat with friends, have a drink, exchange news, and maybe dally with the women; others came to initiate appointments in private rooms. Coming to the parlor did not obligate one to make expensive visits upstairs.

Finally, Edward expressed concern about the fate of his letters: "Helen, if you have one latent spark remaining of kindness, you will let no one see this, but destroy it immediately," he wrote in the letter alluding to his possible impotence. In the second, he said, "Do not betray my confidence by showing these letters to any one." Some two years later, both letters were carefully preserved in the trunk in her room at 41 Thomas Street, hauled to the Police Office by detective Oliver Lownds, read by all the attorneys in the case, and then deposited in the city's hall of records. Whoever Edward was, he must have been a worried man after the murder in April 1836, when the newspapers described the contents of Jewett's confiscated trunk. His two letters remained undisclosed until 1849 when George Wilkes published them in the *National Police Gazette*.[14]

A letter from a third correspondent, T.C., illustrates more of the game playing Jewett fostered. T.C. explains that he left town for Albany without saying goodbye because "I knew you could control me as you pleased" and thus would somehow delay his leaving. T.C. apparently liked to invest Helen with power over him; at another point he says, "Think of me, Nell, and remember you have wrongfully abused me; but I forgive you and am resolved to forget it." He writes because "a line from him who actually loves you will not be unacceptable," and he asks for "an answer for unhappy me." T.C. is rather toadying, not a style of conduct that would please Helen, for she has in fact scorned him—"a SNOT as you called me"—but despite that, T.C. offers to send her money anytime she asks, if she is sick or needy. The real reason T.C. didn't come to see her before he left town may have been that he was unsure she would receive him, and this letter serves to disguise his fear of rejection, to dress it up smartly and perhaps set their relationship back on a more agreeable course. The offer to support her if needy (which Jewett certainly was not) at once reminds her of women's vulnerability and men's usual dominant, protective role as economic providers. T.C. is trying—too hard—to recover from being a "SNOT" in her eyes. (His capitalizing the word betrays how much the insult stung him.) He closes his note "devotedly," and then a curious postscript follows:

> P.S. My friend P. will see you and state my feelings towards you. Pray do not make yourself too common, excuse me for so saying, but my reason is, that I was told you were any one's for five dollars, I will not believe it. Write me at Montreal speedily, Ever yours, Henry.

Was T.C. really Henry, suddenly dropping his cognomen? Did he fear that Helen was not so selective after all? Three to five dollars was the going rate at the brothel at 41 Thomas Street, according to the depositions given by the female inmates at the grand jury hearings after the murder, and a five-dollar charge represented a very substantial sum of money. Such a price would screen out many men, but each of Jewett's clients wanted to believe he had a claim to her beyond price. Knowing she slept with other men, each wished to believe he belonged to a very narrow circle. Henry is suddenly worried that if Jewett accepts anyone who can pay her fee, she will become distressingly common. But another purpose entirely might be advanced by such a bogus concern: if Henry and T.C. are the same person, perhaps this postscript was intended to insinuate T.C. back into more exclusive company, to override his dismissal as a "SNOT."[15]

Each fancying he is particularly beloved, Jewett's clients respond with effusive love letters and gifts. A short note signed "Cambaceres" accompanied a gift book (a large-format literary miscellany, usually nicely illustrated) which he purchased for Jewett in late 1835:

> My Dear Helen—Stopping a few moments in a book store in Broadway to see a friend, I noticed a new publication called the "Magnolia." Thinking it a very pretty thing, and knowing your taste for reading, I bought it, and requested my friend for a sheet

of paper to write a note to a lady, requesting her acceptance of the book . . . [which] will confer upon the donor more satisfaction than the receiver can possibly derive from it.[16]

A Frederick writes to say that a friend embarking for Paris will bring Helen on his behalf a French present of whatever she may desire. He also asks her to return a novel he has loaned her, *Norman Leslie* (written by Theodore Fay, an editor of the *New-York Mirror*). A literary man signing himself "J.J.A.S." enters a subscription to the *Boston Pearl* for Helen, "being aware that you as well as myself are amatures [*sic*] of literature."[17] Several letters refer to the exchange of miniature portraits and rings as well, as tokens of special affection.

Helen's letters themselves constituted gifts to selected clients, bolstering her reputation for literary talent. George P. Marston was extravagant in his praise:

I read the beautiful letter you sent me from Philadelphia on Sunday, and read it over and over again with great pleasure. You must not expect my letters to be equal to yours, in any respect whatever, for I am wholly incompetent to answer letters so far superior to any I can write. You seem to think I shall soon find others whom I shall like as I do you. But that is impossible, for I well know there is no other like you.[18]

J. had requested a letter to start his relationship, and Edward and Helen apparently had a cerebral romance conducted through letters. John and Ben from Saco, Maine, self-described as "two unlucky dogs 'what' cannot forget Gotham," wrote to say they had sent Helen several letters and wish to hear back; Ben—clearly far less elegant a wordsmith than Edward—"is in a duced pucker to hear from her whom he deems the most fascinating of her sex." Charles Chandler wrote a long, rambling letter from his uncle's in Salem, New York, prompted by a mutual friend, Harvey, who informed him Helen would like a letter from him. "If I had not your promise [to reply] I should write without the expectation of an answer, knowing that this epistle will be hardly worth a perusal, much less an answer, but as I have your promise that is sufficient, and allow me to say that the moments spent in penning these few lines for your perusal, will never be regretted by your friend Charley." Chandler next quoted verses from *Lalla Rookh*, the book-length Persian poem he fondly remembered they had read together in New York; evidently reading romantic poetry with her clients in the privacy of her room was another of Helen's business practices. After praising Helen for her sincerity—"Helen, you are the first one in your circumstances with whom I have ever been acquainted, who has not always displayed more or less deception"— Chandler directs her to write him at Salem, where he will be staying several more weeks.[19]

Helen Jewett used letters not merely to keep in touch with clients but also to fashion herself as a literary romantic, someone high above the degradation and dullness that men expected to find in a prostitute. Marveling at her refined sentiments and her talent for graceful expression, her clients would find her all the more alluring. In one note Richard Robinson informed Helen about a Mr. G. who had recently received a letter from Helen. "Mr. G. will be down to see you this evening. I heard him and others talking of your letter. I don't think that he yet is convinced that you wrote it, but thinks it a hoax."[20] Apparently some men were surprised to learn that a prostitute could mimic gentility so well. Writing, then as now, reveals a good deal about the education, intelligence, self-assurance, and social class of the writer. Mr. G. might well have thought that Helen Jewett copied her letter from some writing manual or school text of the day.[21]

A frequent exchange of letters with men required several things in addition to Helen's literary skill. She needed an assured private means of conveying letters that would not risk compromising the recipient. The United States Post Office was well established by the 1830s, offering regular and reliable service between major cities. Post roads and mail stages carried personal mail at about the same speed or faster than a determined traveler could cover the same distance. Postage was quite expensive, however, based on the distance a letter traveled and the number of sheets it contained. Letters lacked envelopes in the 1830s; instead, the sender carefully folded the sheets and sealed them with wax. While this provided some degree of security, a nosy postmaster might in theory be able to decipher words by holding the letter up to light. There was as yet no home delivery, so family members could not perform the same operation. In Salem, New York, Charles Chandler surely picked up his own mail personally, if he expected a letter from Helen. He could thus avoid the risk of having his uncle intercept a gilt-edged letter, an event that surely would be very difficult or embarrassing to explain away.

Until December of 1835, New York City's federal post office was on Wall Street, located inside the imposing and highly masculine Merchant's Exchange Building. From the Fifth Ward brothel district Helen had to walk a mile each way daily to send and retrieve her mail. Editor Bennett of the *Herald* had noted her routine promenade when he wrote that "last summer [1835] she was famous for parading Wall street in an elegant green dress, and generally with a letter in her hand."[22] Her trip amounted to an invasion of male space, among the Wall Street brokers and merchants who normally crowded the Merchant's Exchange. Post offices in general were known as masculine preserves where respectable women were reluctant to go, and by the 1830s many big-city mail facilities had begun to provide a separate window for women only to pick up mail, a small accommodation to alleviate fears about women mixing with the hurly-burly of men conducting business. The *New York Evening Post* argued in 1835 that having the post office on Wall Street "virtually excluded" women customers.[23] But not Helen Jewett, who went there near daily.

The chance to rectify—somewhat—the unfriendly atmosphere for respectable women arrived in December of 1835, when New York's Great Fire of December 16 and 17 burned nearly six hundred buildings in the First Ward, including the Merchant's Exchange. The city designated an elegant rotunda building on Chambers Street, just to the east of City Hall, for the new temporary postal headquarters. This structure had been built in 1818 as an exhibition hall for the artist John Vanderlyn's large panoramic paintings. (Vanderlyn failed to make a success of the museum, and when his lease expired in 1829, the city reclaimed the building.)[24] The art exhibition hall was not overtly marked as a masculine space, although the mail patrons still continued to be overwhelmingly male. For Jewett, the new location was not only much closer to her house, it was also right next door to the Police Office on Chambers Street, another sadly familiar destination of hers. Immediately to the southwest, looming over the rotunda, were the vast courtrooms on the second floor of City Hall, including the room where Helen Jewett's murder trial would open to overflowing crowds in June 1836.

In either location, Wall Street or the rotunda, postal service was not always to Helen's liking. In a note to Robinson, Helen complained about missing letters: "A gentleman told me last night, that he had written me twice, and neither of his letters have I received, and this morning I blew up the post office without finding them." The Maine correspondents John and Ben inquired whether Helen had received their two earlier letters and, if not, advised her "you must blow up the postoffice."[25] To "blow up" here appears to be slang for making an angry fuss about poor service, an unladylike behavior that surely drew attention to her. The mere fact of her regular attendance already flaunted the customs of the post office, so how much more she was violating gender norms by lodging complaints about service. Perhaps it was not the hurly-burly of men alone that made the post office an uncomfortable place for respectable women to patronize.

Jewett used the post office as a local mail drop as well. A letter signed "Pupil H." asked Helen to "just drop me a line what night I shall see you, put it in the office on Saturday."[26] Beyond the addressee's name, Helen might add further information to specify the recipient (for example, "101 Maiden Lane," Robinson's work address at Hoxie's store). But still the fear of discovery was ever present. On one occasion, Helen complained that Robinson did not come to her as she had requested, and after three days of waiting, she began to worry that her letters had gone astray: "The two letters of which I speak were enclosed in a wrapper, and dropt in the office a few minutes before three, directed to you, 101 Maiden lane; and if you have not read them I fear the worst."[27] The fear could only be that someone known to them was intercepting their mail, perhaps Robinson's employer Joseph Hoxie himself, if he was suspicious of his clerk's extracurricular activities. To allay such fears, Richard Robinson secured a post office box at the Chambers Street rotunda: "Whenever you send me a letter through the Postoffice, direct Box 1628, which I think will not be intercepted."[28] In a letter to Jewett in early 1836, Robinson announced he would leave it at the post office, "but the Postoffice department is managed so bunglingly, I don't suppose you will get it under a week."[29]

Helen also hired street porters to carry her letters distances up to a mile or so, and some of her letters came to her the same way. Porters were not entirely reliable either, but when they were, they had the virtue of being very fast. In one note to Robinson sent by porter she indicated that she expected "an answer before dark" that day; in another she wrote that she expected an answer "by the bearer of this," probably the quickest way to secure a reply.[30] Robinson once hired a porter who failed to deliver, and in this instance he seemed to be less fearful of the consequences of interception: "I have as yet heard nothing about your letter, neither do I expect to again, as you say, doubtless someone has benefitted themselves by it ere this. I walked up in Broadway this morning to see if I could discover anything of the man I gave it to, but I could not; well, never mind, I hope it will do him good whoever has got it; I had a great deal rather you had got it, however."[31]

Using porters was a common practice for written communication in New York City, but it could be risky if a porter failed to be discreet. One porter, called to testify at the trial, described his confusion on taking a letter to Robinson when he did not realize the need for discretion. The porter went into Hoxie's store on Maiden Lane and asked for Richard P. Robinson:

> As I went in at the door, a young man passed me. I found out by inquiry at the store that it was him who had just gone out. I went into the street and spoke to him in front of the store. I told him that I had a letter for him, which I was directed to give to him. I

An illustration from George Wilkes's National Police Gazette, *1849, showing Helen and Bill Easy in their early acquaintance.*

don't know that I told him who the letter was from. I think I showed him the letter, but am not certain. He told me to pass through the store, and leave the letter on a bureau—I thought he went in the privy. I went through the store into the yard, but thinking the conduct of Mr. Robinson very strange, I did not leave the letter, and I passed through the store and went and did a job with my cart. On returning to my stand, at the corner of Maiden lane and Pearl street, he came up to me, and asked me what I had done with the letter. I told him that I still had it in my possession, because I was expressly directed to give it to him. I did give it to him, and he gave me two shillings.[32]

The danger was discovery: that a young man's employer might learn of the nefarious carryings-on of his young clerk. A gilt-edged letter of romantic yearnings could fall into the wrong hands. The risk to reputation was greater still if a prostitute called on a clerk at his store. George Marston once had a fright upon hearing from another employee in his store that a young woman who had come in to buy stationery had inquired after him. He assumed it was Helen and wrote immediately to chastise her: "I hope when you enquired of the clerk for me, that none of the bosses were near. I must confess I was not a little surprised that you should mention my name at all, for instance, if it had been D. Felt himself that you asked, I should have been blown slick as a whistle." David Felt, forty-three, owned the paper goods and stationery store at 245 Pearl Street where Marston worked, as well as several paper manufacturing factories in Brooklyn. Felt was not a man to wink at immoralities. A small-town New Englander by birth, and a Puritan descendant, Felt was once characterized as "an austere man." He eventually left New York City's vice-ridden streets and founded a temperance village in 1845—Feltville, in Union County, New Jersey—to provide an environment free of the "temptations and sorrows of city life."[33] Marston was right to fear being "blown," or found out. Marston took some reassurance from knowing that the clerk who waited on his visitor "has been in the store but a few days, is just from Scotland, and is devilish green"—meaning that the newcomer had not yet learned to recognize the subtle differences between virtuous women and prostitutes in New York City. "What is more," Marston continued, he "is religious, and I think likely enough would blow me if he suspected the truth. I hope you will never ask for me again in that manner, for you must be aware that a discovery would be a serious evil to me."[34]

For all the care they took to keep letters from going astray, in some circumstances Jewett and some of her select clients deliberately breached privacy. Jewett sometimes wrote a letter to one man but first sent it to another for his perusal, instructing him to leave the letter in the post office for its recipient. The surviving correspondence suggests she mainly did this with Robinson, sharing letters to Mr. Gilbert (probably Newton Gilbert, Robinson's coworker at Hoxie's store)—but of course her letters to other men are not available. In one letter to Robinson, she reviewed the practice, since the letter had somehow become lost: "On Wednesday last I wrote you a letter, and took the liberty of enclosing one to Mr. G., which I had written him, that you might have the pleasure of reading it first, after which you were to seal and put it in the [post] office for me."[35] Another letter revealed much the same thing: "My dear Frank—I enclose you Gilbert's letter, and you may have the pleasure of reading it, after which you will seal it and drop it in the office."[36] In a much later letter, Robinson reminded her of her practice of sending letters to Gilbert enclosed in letters to him.[37] Evidence suggesting that this practice went beyond the favored Robinson and the hapless Gilbert shows up in her letters from George Marston and William Attree. At some point Marston became the favored first recipient of letters addressed to Robinson: "The letter to Richard I put in the office myself as soon as I could," Marston wrote her.[38] A letter from Louisville sent by *Transcript* reporter William Attree refers to an enclosed letter meant for Mr. P. in Cincinnati, but Attree seems not to have been aware of his full privileges in acting as Helen's conduit: "The enclosure to Mr. P. I shall destroy unopened, as I shall not return by Cincinnati."[39] The final recipient probably had no idea that his letters from Helen were amusing someone else first. But Helen clearly expected her special favorites to enjoy reading her love letters to another man; they occasioned no jealousy, nor were they expected to.

The civility shown by Edward, by Marston, by Robinson, and by others about Helen's multiple romantic relationships would have been surprising in respectable society, where flirtation, romance, and courtship were steps along the way toward pairing off in monogamous relationships. But a prostitute's clientele could not expect an exclusive right to her love. Helen flattered her clients into thinking they held a special place in her heart, but that heart had more than one such place, and the men knew it. Indeed, they were more than willing to give way, as Edward had done, and to promote their friends to Helen. Young Marston was especially eager to impress his friends with Helen—and impress Helen with his important friends:

> How do you like my tall friend Mr. Cook? I hope you feel a better disposition towards him than to Harry [George's boarding house-mate]. He is a very fine man. In fact I never knew a person in my life, whom I like better than Mr. Cook. If you knew him as well as I do, you would not only love, but you would also respect him. He has just called to see me, and says he intends to go with me at the Bowery [Theatre] this evening, and I expect he will wish you to go home with him. If so I should wish you to comply with his request. I would rather forego the pleasure of your company myself than be the cause of disappointment to him.[40]

Mr. Cook was apparently very important to the nineteen-year-old Marston. Harry, on the other hand, was a clerk and one of five boys who shared a room at Marston's boardinghouse on Cliff Street. Harry did not pass muster with Helen, and Marston was determined not to feel slighted by Helen's rejection. Indeed, he cleverly managed to turn it around and suggest he was a generous soul for forgiving Helen her choosiness:

> The dislike you feel for my friend Harry does not in the slightest degree affect my feelings towards you, unless it is to render you still more attractive in my eyes. For I like you for your candidness. I did not introduce him to you expecting he would be idolized, and if it has been his misfortune to have fallen below par in your esti-

mation, it is all the same to me. Every one has their own taste. I can say one thing with feeling, that he will never know or experience the exquisite delight that I have in your society.[41]

Marston was happy to share his exquisite delight with Mr. Cook, however. A client who signed his letter "Stanhope" sent his apologies for having to miss an appointment with Helen and recommended a friend in his place. "I am glad, however, in this absence of ability [to keep the appointment], and not inclination, that I can offer a legitimate excuse and a proper friend, who insists upon usurping, what I would not forego even for friendship under other circumstances, and who I am glad I can consistently give way to, hoping, as I do, for pardon, and assured as I am of his perfect gentleness."[42]

Marston's desire to share Helen with Mr. Cook was more than an expression of generosity or camaraderie. The elaborate rituals of yielding place and the intense curiosity about each other's performance suggest that for these young men, heterosexuality had a homosocial dimension. Sexual experience was mediated via a network of male friends as well as between heterosexual partners. In offering Helen to Cook, Marston was saying: Look at the prized woman I sleep with, have sex with her, and thus learn something of how I experience sex. Their eagerness to imagine friends having sex with Helen and Helen's sharing of their letters suggest the culture of sexuality in this circle of young men had homoerotic dimensions.

Jealousy played no manifest role in this culture. The men made friendships via Helen. Robinson and Marston met through Helen, but soon they were meeting together by themselves for meals and drinks of porter.[43] Robinson's fellow boarders joked among themselves about the fact that several of them visited Helen.[44] A man named "Bob" from Cincinnati asked Helen to tell Frank (Robinson's brothel pseudonym) to look him up if he ever came west.[45]

Unfortunately for Marston, Mr. Cook did not fare so well with Helen, either because he was too diffident or because Helen brushed him off. In what may have been a sequel to his first letter about Mr. Cook, W.E. (William Easy, Marston's brothel pseudonym) tried to repair the damage and again interest Helen in his friend by making extravagant claims of Mr. Cook's infatuation:

My friend Cook was disappointed in not seeing you home from the theatre last evening, though I don't see as he can blame you any for going with another person. You certainly waited long enough for him to acquaint you with his intentions, and I thought we gave him hints enough to that effect. By saying he ought not to lay any blame on you; I don't mean to infer that he does, for that is impossible. I don't believe he could be angry with you if he tried, he loves you too well. Perhaps you are not aware but I think I am a better judge in this case, as I have been longer acquainted with him. I know that since he has become acquainted with you, his habits are entirely changed. He is a different person altogether. When I introduced him to you, I little expected he would so soon become infatuated. Whether his feelings towards you are reciprocated is no business of mine. I was not jealous of him, but I do hope he will never have your miniature in his bosom.[46]

Marston here takes the role of procurer: "we" tried to get Cook to come forward and assert his intentions to ask to go home with Helen. (This scene appears a sharp contrast to Edward's experience, in which Helen took the initiative in asking him home. Mr. Cook was simply not so interesting to her, or perhaps she had a better alternative that evening.) Marston asserts that Cook is a changed man, due to his powerful infatuation for Helen. Love has transformed him; Marston obviously thinks this will play to Helen's habit of asserting power over men through romantic game playing. The final two sentences reveal Marston's ambivalence. In the first, he claims not to wonder whether Helen reciprocates Cook's passion. Despite ostensibly working so hard on Cook's behalf, however, in the last sentence Marston also expresses the hope that Cook will never merit receiving Helen's portrait miniature, the most treasured gift she could bestow. Marston does not want to be displaced where it really matters to him, in the exchange of tokens that signify a deeper and more intimate commitment than mere sexual union.

Marston carried his romantic fantasy about Helen a step farther than the other men who corresponded with her. He not only gave her gifts, he received in return gifts representing traditional female domestic arts. Helen made him a pincushion, "a splendid article," he declared; "it shall stand upon my dressing table as long as one piece of it is left." (In the 1830s and for some years after, straight pins did all the work of fastening seams, securing closures, and pinning in detachable collars and cuffs in men's and women's clothes, so that men as well as women had need of pincushions. Even infants' diapers were closed with large straight pins. The safety pin was not invented until the 1850s.) Marston showed the pincushion to the other boarders on Cliff Street, a set of people that included some women. "I showed it to our boarders, at the tea table, last evening, and every one were loud in their praise of it, especially the ladies. They little thought where it came from." Marston enjoyed his little secret to the extent of imagining that if the ladies had asked him who made the pin-cushion, he would brag about his friend, who though "unfortunate in some respects was, in all others, as far superior to them; as—my language fails me." George did not hesitate to press his requests for female needle service: in one letter he enclosed strings representing the dimensions of a table in his room, so that Helen could make him a tablecloth. Expensive fabric was not necessary, he said, common would do, for its real value to him would be Helen's hand in making it.[47] Her sewing was invested with high personal meaning for him.

Not mentioned in any of the letters was the handkerchief, with Marston's initials or name on it, found under her pillow at the time of the murder. At the trial, Marston explained its provenance:

> I took it [the handkerchief] there [to her room] for several days before her death for her to mark my name upon it. When I took it there, she asked me if the colors were fast, I mean if they would not fade. I told her that I bought it for a first rate English handker-chief. . . . After marking my handkerchief, Ellen washed it, and the colors washed out. She bought me another one and marked it and kept the one that I bought, as she said, for a duster.

But he was not asked to produce the second handkerchief as evidence. Marston was pleased to have Helen do needlework for him as a wife would for a husband—or a servant for a master. On cross-examination at trial, the defense attorney asked him a series of questions meant to elicit a fuller picture of Helen's sewing services. Given the chance, Marston now was quick to suggest that what he received was not unusual, that she sewed for other people as well. "As far as I know, Ellen Jewett was very fond of being employed at her needle; she was fond of obliging persons. Previous to marking the handkerchief I have spoken of, she made some shirts for me. I don't know that she ever mended any. Independent of sewing things for me, I believe she did similar favors for other persons. I have seen other clothes there. I have left things with her to be mended and fixed by her."[48] Under the pressure of cross-examination, Marston's ear-lier delight with Jewett's sewing, prized so highly as her special sign of affection for him, now was transformed into (and disguised as) a routine service such as any seamstress might provide for a price in the open mar-ket. The attorney neglected to ask Marston if he paid for Jewett's needle-work. Did she do it for free, another variation on the theme of romance, a gesture connoting love and affection? Or did she charge, regarding the work as a job for payment, as any hired seamstress might? The answer probably lies somewhere in the middle: Marston (and others) gave her ample money, and her job in return was to act as if she were a friend and lover, mending shirts as an act of love.

Helen Jewett preferred her prostitution all rigged up with romance. Through the exchange of gifts and gilt-edged letters of flirtation and promise, she flattered her clients and made them feel special. She displayed literary talent in her prose and some claim to erudition in her reading, but mainly she showed considerable deftness in handling the men who sought her company. She met them at theaters and invited some to her house and a more select group up to her room. She convinced them she was a young woman of wit and refinement, not yet jaded or coarsened by her profession. Only one letter in the entire set—Henry's plaintive worry that she might be anyone's for five dollars—alludes to the financial underpinnings of her business. Instead, all the writers maintained the fiction that matters of the heart were the heart of the relationship.

Helen cultivated relationships that gave inexperienced young men an accelerated course of study in the rituals of bourgeois courtship—learning to read and write love letters, to seek favor by means of gifts, to bend two heads over one poetry book, to defer gallantly to women, to flirt, and more. Presumably they also engaged in sex with her, but sex is rarely even alluded to in the correspondence and then only very obliquely. But beyond sex and a playacted romance, what Helen's clients found was a sexually assertive woman who would take the initiative, flatter and seduce them, play the coquette, comment on their bodies and charms, and assume a sexual authority that these young men could not expect to find among respectable women in Jacksonian America. Such authority was apparently deeply attractive to them, and yet at the same time it violated the tenets of what a good woman should be like. Helen resolved that contradiction by presenting her clients with a narrative of her life blaming her fall from virtue on a gentleman rake. This allowed the clients to believe that she was a once virtuous and refined girl awakened to sexuality by a bad but lucky man, now enabled by her superior education and perhaps by her selective gentle clientele to avoid the degradation of indiscriminate sex. As Marston said in his pincushion letter, Helen was an "unfortunate" girl (a word implying bad luck) but still far superior to the ladies of his boardinghouse.

Helen's clients paid to see her, but she chose them; she, not they, set the terms of the relationships and called them handsome—or a snot—on her own terms. Prostitution as Jewett practiced it involved something of a reversal of roles. In courtship in polite society, men were always supposed to take the lead, do the choosing and asking, and take full responsibility.

The men may have been engaging in an apprentice courtship, but they would not likely wind up marrying a bride who much resembled Helen Jewett.

At Jewett's brothel, sex was not merely a commodity for sale. Instead of emotion-free sex, Jewett saturated her sexual relationships with rituals of masculinity and femininity, and of love, romance, and intimacy. The exchange of money in these relationships discouraged anyone from thinking Jewett's love was exclusive. Everyone recognized that she made her living this way, commanded good fees, and expected to be paid. That she performed for cash undoubtedly made Helen all the more alluring to some men. Consider Marston, so eager to imagine his friends spending a night with Helen, which they could do if they paid and if she accepted them. Men pretended to court her or be infatuated with her in order to secure her acceptance (for example, Cook), but in reality, their payment of money discharged their obligation to be truly committed to her. Both parties to the bargain, Jewett and each client, could be playactors, and the money payment at the heart of it—unspoken but of paramount importance—gave each a measure of power and control in the drama they played out.

CHAPTER EIGHT

A Servant Girl in Maine

I N SEPTEMBER OF 1827 a woman traveler in Maine called at the house of Judge Nathan Weston in Augusta:

> When I knocked at the door of judge Western, it was opened by a little girl of about eleven years old, who saluted with inimitable sweetness, and with a graceful wave of her hand, invited me to take a seat on the sofa. I knew her to be a servant, which surprised me the more. Stepping back as she opened the door, with an air of the most accomplished lady—I forgot to ask for the Judge, but began to question the little girl respecting herself.[1]

Most unfortunately, the woman traveler did not record any of the details of her conversation with little Dorcas Doyen, who was then thirteen, not eleven as the traveler guessed. But the stranger did coax out of Mrs. Weston a boast for having raised such an accomplished young charge, and in her short stay in town she managed to capture and convey a remarkably rich sense of the town's social atmosphere. As in any American town of the 1820s, a set of customs both honored gender and class, and left room at the margins for playfulness. Both formal custom and play were imprinted on the servant girl in the very years when she was transforming herself from Dorcas into Maria Stanley. To reach 1827, that point in the story when the infamous Mrs. Anne Royall, the woman traveler, came to town, we must first move back to the earliest years of

Maine's history to situate the Westons and the Doyens in the migrant stream that poured into this northernmost area of settlement.

Twenty to thirty years before 1813, the year of Dorcas Doyen's birth, the fathers of Judge Nathan Weston and of the shoemaker John Doyen had trekked to the Maine frontier and established their families in Kennebec River towns, overlapping for a short while in Augusta. Doyen and Weston had both been born in the early 1780s, but they shared nothing else in common. The Maine frontier was no social leveler. Some settlers arrived with more capital, skills, and advantages than others. Class mattered, and class differences for these two families only grew over time. The most abundant records document the upper-class Augusta families—the Westons, the Williamses, the Conys, the Bridges, whose monopoly of wealth, power, and land created records assuring them a place in public and private archives. The Doyens, in contrast, left faint but still legible footprints—usually planted just one step ahead of their creditors or the law.

Judge Weston's father, also named Nathan, moved up to the Maine country from Reading, Massachusetts, in 1766, after the end of the French and Indian War. (Maine was a noncontiguous part of Massachusetts until 1820.) The senior Weston, then twenty-six, established a trading store and lumber business at the lower end of the Kennebec River and brought goods in from the Massachusetts coast on his own thirty-ton sloop, which gave him the right to be called Captain. In 1778 he moved twenty-five miles farther north up the river to the lower part of Hallowell, then a tiny village (population under six hundred) nestled on the side of a steep hill rising west from the water.[2]

The Kennebec was a large, broad river navigable as far north as Hallowell, at least when it was free of ice. In the winter, the river became a different sort of highway, a frozen roadbed clear of the inconvenience of tree stumps and bramble. Hallowell offered good prospects for a sloop-owning businessman, for the countryside stretching away from the river was beginning to attract a steady stream of migrants, mostly farmers from the crowded towns of Massachusetts and lower New Hampshire who were looking for inexpensive land. A well-stocked store promised quickly to become a godsend for pioneers who did not want to rough it in the wilds any more than absolutely necessary.

Two miles north of Captain Weston's store was the only other major general store of central Maine, the outfit run by James Howard and his sons. The Howards also owned sloops and occupied the buildings inside Fort Western, on the east side of the Kennebec, a timbered fortification left over from the French and Indian War. James Howard had been the fort's commander during the war, and after the peace of 1763, he stayed

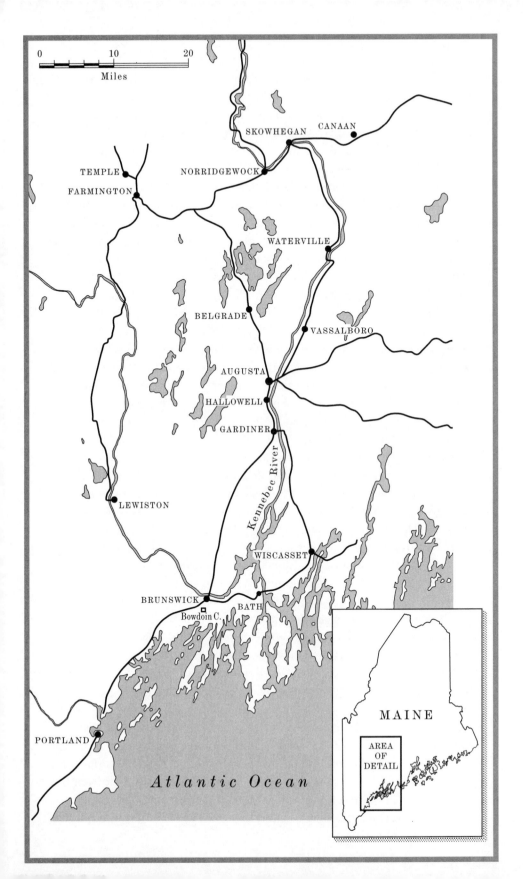

on and turned it into the first store of the region.[3] Now, with the population increasing all around the countryside, there was certainly business enough for two general stores in the region. The area around the fort was also part of the township of Hallowell; it remained one town with two population centers several miles apart until 1797, when the northern settlement broke away to become the town of Augusta.[4]

The thousands of acres centered along the Kennebec Valley had originally been owned by a small group of wealthy Massachusetts men, the Plymouth Proprietors, who claimed their title from a very early (and conveniently vague) seventeenth-century grant awarding all of central Maine to the same religious devotees who settled Plymouth Colony in Massachusetts, under the leadership of William Bradford. Bradford's Pilgrims called the Maine territory New Plymouth, and a few of them, John Alden and Miles Standish among them, had actually settled temporarily at the site of the future Augusta and built a trading company outpost at the river's edge as early as 1628. A single cold Maine winter drove them back to the original Plymouth settlement. Now, 150 years later, the pressure of growth in Massachusetts was finally drawing settlers to the Kennebec countryside. With the French threat removed by the Peace of Paris in 1763, the Plymouth Proprietors, no longer Pilgrims but instead wealthy Boston investors like Thomas and John Hancock, Sylvester Gardiner, Gershom Flagg, and James Bowdoin, who had bought out the descendants of the Pilgrims, mapped their domain, and began selling it.[5]

A second wave of settlers who flooded north at the end of the Revolutionary War overwhelmed this orderly progress of land sales. The new settlers, the Doyens among them, were lured by the hope of very cheap lands as reward for wartime soldiering. They helped Captain Weston and the Howard family prosper. They would also soon provide plenty of work for lawyers, hired by the Boston proprietors to straighten out the jumble of land titles that ensued, as land purchasers confronted squatters and disputed their claims to ownership.[6]

In 1781 Captain Weston moved his household, his store, and his sloop two miles upriver to the settlement at Fort Western. Within a few years, he had moved to the west side of the Kennebec River and had purchased a large strip of land extending from the river a mile inland, along the south side of Winthrop Street. He built a wharf for his sloop and erected a store adjoined by a potash manufactory on Water Street, which quickly supplanted the east side of the river as the central business district of the town. For a while he maintained his residence at a house also down on Water Street, but later he moved to a larger house a block back from the river on Winthrop Street, halfway up the hill rising steeply from the river. Weston's land dealings alone assured his moderate fortunes in the town, for the intersection of Water and Winthrop lay at the heart of nineteenth-century Augusta.[7]

Soon Weston adorned his economic standing with political office, in the party of the Jeffersonian Republicans. In 1799 and again in 1801 he represented Augusta in the Massachusetts General Court (the state's legislature), and he also served as a town selectman in 1803. Finally he earned the title of the "Honorable" Nathan Weston, after his election to the Massachusetts state senate and a term of service on the Executive Council of the government.

Captain Weston was widowed twice, in early manhood, before he found the widow Mrs. Elizabeth Bancroft Cheever from Salem, Massachusetts, a bride as hearty as himself. They married in 1781, the year they moved to the fort. This third Mrs. Weston was a devout, Calvinistic Puritan who read the entire Bible on an annual cycle. She revered books in general and read secular works voraciously, leading her four children (all sons) in family reading and book-centered conversation.[8] Longevity blessed them both; Mrs. Weston lived to be eighty-five, and the captain lived to be ninety-two, dying a year apart in the early 1830s. Their oldest child, Nathan Weston, was born in 1782.[9]

His father's high social standing secured the younger Nathan many advantages. He attended Hallowell Academy in the late 1790s, when the school first opened. The academy offered a classical curriculum of Latin and Greek to about forty adolescent boys from all over central Maine, most of whom would expect to go on to college. In its early years, it was the only private academy east of Exeter, New Hampshire, which underscores Hallowell's ambition to make itself the cultural center of Maine. Weston then advanced to Dartmouth College in New Hampshire, where he graduated in 1803 with great proficiency in the classics and an academic record that qualified him for an invitation to Phi Beta Kappa, a recently formed collegiate honor society. He next went to Boston and studied law for three years in the office of the United States district attorney for Massachusetts, the wealthy and energetically sociable George Blake. Doubtless his father's political connections in Boston smoothed the path into this prestigious legal apprenticeship. From Blake, Weston adopted the practice of reading Blackstone's *Commentaries* annually—his mother's Bible cycle transmuted.

In 1806, Weston was admitted to the bar and moved back to Augusta. For three years he practiced law in New Gloucester, fifteen miles inland from Portland, but in 1810 he returned to Augusta with his recent bride, Paulina Cony, one of the four daughters of the wealthy Daniel Cony, an Augusta doctor and judge of the Probate Court. There, their first child, Catharine, was born.

Augusta's legal community in 1810 already numbered over a half-dozen lawyers. The most lucrative trade, handling land litigation for the Plymouth Proprietors, was sewn up tightly by James Bridge, a Harvard graduate, in partnership with Reuel Williams. Williams was one genuine case of a man rising from humble origins into Augusta's elite. His father had been a tanner, and at age fourteen young Reuel earned favorable notice from the lawyer Bridge for his punctual daily duty as toll collector on the bridge across the Kennebec River, linking Fort Western with the Water Street business district. Impressed with his diligence and native intelligence, Bridge paid for Williams to attend the Hallowell Academy and then took him into his office to read real estate law. When Reuel Williams passed the bar, James Bridge made him full partner in his firm. By 1810, both were very rich men. (Bridge became even richer after opening the Augusta Bank in 1814, of which he was president for many years.) Young Reuel's acceptance into the highest level of Augusta society was confirmed in 1807 when he married Sarah Cony, an older sister of Paulina Cony.[10]

Nathan Weston began his law practice in Augusta with no prospects for breaking into the real estate practice dominated by Bridge and Williams. But within a year, an unusual opportunity came his way when the governor of Massachusetts, Elbridge Gerry, picked Weston, then twenty-nine, to be the chief justice of the newly established Second Circuit Court for the district of Maine.[11] With this boost to his career, Weston embarked on building a home and family to match his new station. His first house, at the corner of Court and State, was big enough to serve as a hotel called the Mansion House when the judge sold it in 1817.[12] The judge and his wife busily filled this house (and a subsequent one) with children. Catharine's birth in 1810 was followed three years later with the birth of son Nathan, in February 1813. Next came Daniel in 1815, George in 1816, Paulina in 1818, Charles in 1822, and Louisa in 1823. All survived to adulthood except baby Paulina, who died at age two.

Nathan's wife, Paulina Cony Weston, came from another prominent Augusta family. Her father, Daniel Cony, was a judge of the Probate Court in Augusta, and for a while he also presided over the Court of Common Pleas, but he had not been formally trained in law. Cony was a physician, a profession he pursued from his first arrival in town as a young man in 1778. (He occasionally shared patients with Martha Ballard, the well-known Hallowell midwife.)[13] Town magistracies came his way in the 1780s and 1790s when Hallowell was a burgeoning town of over a thousand and Cony was approaching his forties. He served as clerk of the town in 1785 and as one of Hallowell's three selectmen in 1786 and again in 1789. By the 1790s he was chosen moderator for the town meeting, a prestigious and demanding office he garnered yearly for thirteen years. He was elected to the Massachusetts General Court, as representative, senator, and counselor, and was chosen by the state legislature to cast a vote for George Washington in the electoral college for the presidential election of 1792. Cony's political network thus extended far beyond the woods of central Maine, to the urbane capital city of Boston. In the early 1800s when his four daughters were all approaching marriageable age, he tried to capitalize on his political connections by presenting the girls in a formal debut to the wider world of eligible and prominent men at a party in Boston. If he sought a marital link to the state capital, he failed, for all four of the girls married local Maine men. But if his ultimate hope was to foster a political dynasty, he did in a measure succeed. One son-in-law became a high court judge (Weston) and another (Reuel Williams) became a United States senator. Two of his grandsons became governors of Maine, and a great-grandson became chief justice of the U.S. Supreme Court.[14]

Cony's reputation for public service and leadership no doubt smoothed his way into the various local judgeships he held until his eccentricities indicated the advisability of retirement in the 1820s. By that decade he was padding around Augusta still dressed in the knee breeches and cocked hat of the 1770s. He even attended church wearing clothes that the current generation considered informal morning dress, but that no doubt seemed fine to the old gentleman. His 1770s costumes fittingly honored what he considered to be one of the great moments in American history, the battle of Saratoga, where he had rendered medical services. Cony annually celebrated the surrender of the British general Burgoyne, while his fellow townsmen saved their toasts and speechifying for the more conventional holiday, the Fourth of July.

For all his eccentricities, Augustans were fond of Dr. Cony. He had played a major role establishing Hallowell Academy for boys in the 1790s, contributing money and greasing the wheels down in Boston for a charter for the school. He was also a trustee of Bowdoin, the first college established in Maine. In the 1810s he developed the advanced notion that an academy education ought to be available to girls as well, not an altogether strange idea for a father who had raised four daughters and worked hard to marry them off to educated young men. In 1815 he began building a structure at the corner of Bangor and Cony Streets, a block from his own home, without telling anyone what it was for. Townsmen and relatives spent months guessing what old Cony was up to; he evidently enjoyed keeping folks in suspense. First his building appeared to be a large house, but when he erected a bell tower on it, betting switched to a church. Only when the desks arrived did he announce his liberal endowment establishing the Cony Academy to advance female education. Dr. Cony appointed five younger men as trustees for the school, including three of his sons-in-law: Nathan Weston, Reuel Williams, and Samuel Cony. A lawyer and a minister rounded out the board, an agency whose duties included certifying the acceptability of worthy "orphans and other females" who could attend the school free, their tuition generously covered by income from ten shares of bank stock Cony had purchased in the Augusta Bank. (Dr. Cony sat on the board of directors for this bank; its president was James Bridge.)[15] Had Nathan Weston wished, he could probably have sent Dorcas Doyen to the Cony Academy free of charge, her fees paid by the endowment from the stock shares.

Dorcas would surely have qualified as indigent. The Doyens' experience in Maine was a far cry from that of the Westons, the Bridges, and the Conys. Dorcas's grandfather, Jacob Doyen, and his brother Samuel came to Maine from the village of Pembroke, New Hampshire, sometime in the 1780s. They had neither the trade nor professional skills of Dr. Cony and James Bridge, nor the capital that had enabled Captain Weston to acquire a sloop. Close to thirty when they migrated to Maine, Jacob and Samuel had served in the Continental Army during their late teens. In lieu of pay, they had been promised free land at the frontier, a pledge made by a Continental Congress unable to meet its military payroll in cash. In the 1780s and 1790s, thousands of Yankee veterans like the Doyens turned northward, to frontier Maine, in hopes that the new government might be persuaded to make good on that promise.

Pembroke, the town the Doyens left behind, was barely a crossroads in southern New Hampshire, despite sixty years of settlement. Francis Doyen and his wife, the grandparents of Jacob and Samuel, had been the very first settlers of the town in 1728; they spent that winter in a rudely constructed cabin not far from the Merrimack River, and when the other new grantees joined them in the spring, they were somewhat surprised to find them still alive.[16] Being a town proprietor, one of the original grantees given land by the colonial government, usually promised prosperity, but the hard-luck Doyens failed to capitalize on the advantage of being present at the creation. About thirty men made up the list of town grantees, and this group decided who got what lands and how much. The usual method of land division, replicated in newly founded towns all over New England in the seventeenth and eighteenth centuries, eschewed creating an economic democracy in favor of dividing up the land according to some mutually agreed-upon sense of social status. The "better sorts" always got the most and best land, and the lesser-ranked men got much smaller portions—but usually still substantial enough to settle full farms on several subsequent generations of descendants. Under this system driven by prestige and social status, Francis Doyen got a plot only a half mile by a half mile, or about 160 acres, the site of his cabin.[17] He was low man in the hierarchy of Pembroke's first settlers.

This earliest Doyen in America already had established a reputation for being difficult, and perhaps that soured his fortunes with the other Pembroke grantees. Doyen was the son of Huguenot refugees who had fled Paris after the Revocation of the Edict of Nantes in 1685. The Huguenots were French Protestants, and when the Catholic king abolished their right to worship, hundreds of thousands fled the country in a matter of months to avoid violent persecution. The Doyen family joined a substantial Huguenot émigré settlement in Dublin, and Francis was born there some fifteen or twenty years later. Around 1720 he and another young Huguenot lad named Jacob Shute fled again, this time for the far less noble purpose of escaping from an unpleasant apprenticeship to a Dublin stocking weaver. The two boys stowed away in a ship bound for Massachusetts, secreted in the hold until their hungry stomachs drove them above decks. With no money to pay for their passage, they had to sell themselves into indentured servitude when they landed in America. A captain paid their passage in exchange for service until age twenty-one, and according to tradition in the Shute family, the captain asked young Dawen (as it was spelled in this account) "if he would be a good boy and work well, provided he would pay his passage?" and Dawen obsequiously replied "Yes, the Lord bless him," while young Shute bristled and chafed at the prospects of renewed servitude. "On trial, however, Shute proved an industrious, faithful hand, while Dawen was indolent and deceitful"— so went the story handed down for more than a century among Shute descendants, who lived one township away from the Doyens in eighteenth-century New Hampshire.[18]

After settling in Pembroke, Francis fathered at least two sons, and the elder, Jacob, redeemed the family name enough to marry the daughter of a "gentleman" of Concord (self-described in his will), just a short distance up the Merrimack River. (When the gentleman died, in 1769, he left only four Spanish dollars to Rebecca Doyen, hardly enough to have a dramatic impact on the lives of Jacob, Rebecca, and their six children.)[19] For fifty years in the eighteenth century, the Doyens left almost no tracks in New Hampshire public records. The family took the patriot side in the Revolutionary War. In his midforties, Jacob Doyen was one of three men of the Pembroke "Committee of Public Safety," a vigilante group that strongarmed suspected Loyalists and reluctant revolutionaries.[20] His first son, Jacob (born in 1759), and possibly Samuel as well (born 1764), joined the Continental Army two years into the war, in March 1777. This younger Jacob Doyen was Dorcas Doyen's grandfather.

Having enlisted when he was barely eighteen, the younger Jacob served for three years and experienced fully the long-distance travel, squalid living conditions, and interminable waiting of eighteenth-century army life. He saw action in three major engagements. Doyen fought at the battle of Saratoga in New York (October 1777), where he subsequently claimed he took a bullet in the breast. Two months later his unit joined the encampment at Valley Forge in Pennsylvania, enduring the famous starving time of the winter of 1778. The following June the soldiers moved quickly up through New Jersey and fought the British at the battle of Monmouth. They next inched through Connecticut and built winter quarters near Danbury. The campaign of 1779 was Jacob Doyen's hardest and bloodiest service. His regiment traveled west to the Wyoming Valley of Pennsylvania and joined others under the command of General John Sullivan of New Hampshire, who took his army into Indian country on a search-and-destroy mission. The Americans' deadly raids on Iroquois villages in the Finger Lakes region of New York produced terror-inducing retaliation from Indian ambushes. Doyen survived several grueling months of privation and horror, so different from the more formal and limited battles with the British, and was mustered out of the army in March 1780 at age twenty-one.[21] The veteran returned home, married, and started a family, his first child born in 1784.

But Jacob and his brother Samuel could count on little support or help from their father. Sometime in the mid-1780s, both of them went north to Maine, and a third brother later followed. When the elder Doyen died, in Pembroke in 1799, his estate was worth very little once his creditors got their shares and the estate administrator gouged it for probate expenses. By then his landholdings had dwindled to only twenty-one acres, which had to be sold to raise cash.[22] Going to wide-open Maine must have seemed like the only way up and out to the sons of Jacob and Rebecca.[23]

The first traces of the Doyens in the legal records of the district of Maine underscore the perpetuation of their essentially marginal status on the northern frontier. Samuel Doyen had staked out land in Vassalboro, a town of about a thousand inhabitants just to the north of Hallowell. He appeared only once in early Vassalboro's town records, when he was chosen for the annual office of hog reeve in 1787, along with three other young men. The ancient duty of the hog reeve was to fetch wandering pigs back to their masters, but in practice, New England towns, not reckoning wandering pigs as a major source of public disorder, typically awarded the title to newly married young men. "Hog reeve" thus was a humorous honorific marking the men's passage from wandering single males to captured husbands; variant possibilities for working the pig into the metaphor were probably the essence of the humor. Samuel Doyen, age twenty-three, was most likely a newlywed in 1787 (although the surviving marriage records of the town do not list his name). Four decades' worth of annual reports on town meetings and elections to office in this small village fail to yield another instance of a Doyen entrusted with an office more lofty than that of hog reeve. Since each year a substantial proportion of townsmen were named to dozens of offices, honorific or dutiful, the Doyens' absence from the record marked marginality, or their townsmen's low regard for them.[24]

The 1790 census for the district of Maine included Samuel Doin, heading a household of five members, but the census taker mistakenly placed him in Hallowell instead of Vassalboro, perhaps because he lived right on the border between the two. No Doyen appears on any of Hallowell's tax assessment lists for the late 1780s through the 1790s, where owning as much as one pig would earn status as a "ratable poll" in Hallowell. The tax rolls even listed a few "nonratable polls," men who owned nothing and who escaped even the basic head tax levied on men over age sixteen. Clearly Hallowell did not consider Doyen a resident, since he was not included on its tax rolls. However, Samuel Doyen *wanted* to live in Hallowell, that much is clear, and by February 1792 he and his wife and children had made their presence known to the selectmen. The town, however, did not want them to settle there and issued a warrant ordering them to depart:

> To Samuel Doyen of Vassalborough, in Lincoln County, yeoman, who has lately come into this Town for the purpose of abiding therein without the town's consent . . . that he depart the limits thereof with his wife and children within 15 days.[25]

New England towns for generations had reserved the right to pass judgment on who could join a community. "Warning out" was a time-honored method of ensuring homogeneity and peacefulness by forbidding undesirables to stay, even to visit. Warning out was not lightly or frequently practiced; minimal standards for community membership prevailed with enough freedom so that New England towns still each had their usual share of town drunks, crabby scolds, and abusive husbands. Warning out was reserved mainly for recently arrived indigents, outsiders without prospects whom the town reasonably feared would become a charge on the respectable citizens. A longtime citizen of a town who fell into poverty would typically be supported by the town and not turned out, his remaining assets handed over to a guardian to safeguard while the distressed person struggled to get back on his feet.[26] In contrast, warning out was a gatekeeping function exercised against newcomers from whom the town leaders sensed danger or failure. It was resorted to more often in the early decades of a town's growth, at a time when an emerging elite had consolidated its power enough to be able to make authoritative discriminations, yet before the time when a settled and large town could afford to absorb an unpromising settler or two. Two decades into its settlement, Hallowell in the 1790s was at precisely that stage of development.

From 1791 to 1792, the town had warned out twelve undesirables; twenty-two years later the town clerk carefully copied the warrants into the Hallowell town records, which suggests that these were the only set of warrants ever issued, making that year a very unfriendly one in the history of the town. Ten of the warrants were addressed to men with families, and two named single women. The men were variously described as transient persons or laborers; only two, a shoemaker and a baker, had trades. Samuel Doyen, age twenty-eight, was the only one described as having the relatively elevated status of "yeoman," meaning that he led town authorities to think he owned farming land somewhere. (Property tax records for Vassalboro fail to substantiate his claim.) One of the family men warned out was Edmund Fortis of Virginia, "a Negro Man" with wife and children. While all the official warning-out documents are silent about why the town acted, in the case of Fortis some retrospective evidence is available. A few years later, Fortis was convicted of a capital crime in his new town, Vassalboro, which evidently was a town more generous than Hallowell in accepting as neighbors people who were different or risky. In his gallows statement, Fortis confessed to lifelong habits of drinking, stealing, and gaming. Citizens of Hallowell turned out in large numbers to observe the rare public hanging and probably congratulated themselves for their foresight in warning out Fortis.[27] They were not so successful in ridding themselves of the Doyens, however.

One of the two single women warned out was identified as a "transient person" and was ordered to leave along "with any child she has"; Hallowell was determined not to support unwed mothers who came from afar. The other single woman, warned out on February 20, 1792, the same day as Samuel Doyen as it happened, was named Dorcas Spaulding. It is startling to see this pairing of warrants against Doyen and Spaulding, for this woman's name prefigures the imaginings of the Dorcas Doyen born twenty years later, who confided (falsely) to New York friends that her real surname was Spaulding. But the appearance of this Dorcas Spaulding seems to be nothing more than coincidence. She does not seem to have been related in any way to the large Spaulding family of Norridgewock whose descendants included the bank cashier Harlow Spaulding.[28] No child is mentioned in her warrant; yet warning out a single woman who was not an unwed mother was rather unusual. Most homeless unattached women, if they were of reasonably good character, could find families willing to trade room and board for women's work and could soon find husbands. Dorcas Spaulding, judged in the same moment as Samuel Doyen to be a poor prospect for permanent residence, must have been a woman of questionable repute, or else a woman strongly determined not to become someone's servant. (Possibly she was the unnamed woman once recalled by Judge Nathan Weston who behaved bizarrely in the 1790s: calling herself the Queen of Sheba, a deeply tanned woman with uncovered head seated herself with the judges at court and insisted this was "her rightful place"; the sheriff had to evict her from court.)[29] Whether Dorcas Spaulding was strong-minded or simply mad, her expulsion from Hallowell and its relation to Samuel Doyen's, on the same day, present a puzzle whose solution lies beyond us. Whatever her shortcomings in the eyes of Hallowell selectmen, Dorcas Spaulding appears to have recovered from her warning out. Seven years later and still a single woman, now of the town of Winslow, she successfully sued a Norridgewock man for non-payment of a debt amounting to $21, a fairly large sum of money in 1799.[30]

Presumably Samuel Doyen and his family abided Hallowell's decision and left town. Doyens reappear in the public records of Maine in 1800, when the brothers Samuel and Jacob were listed in the census for Vassalboro. The comprehensive state tax assessment of 1798 failed to list either of them anywhere in the Maine district, either as landowners or renters; Samuel's description of himself as a yeoman in the warning out of 1792 bespeaks a talent for charlatanry. In August 1800 both brothers were named in a suit for nonpayment of a $34 debt, entered by William Howard, the merchant at the Fort Western store. Howard pursued many such suits, listed one after another with great regularity at the tail end of each quarterly sitting of the Court of Common Pleas. For the Howards, it was a routine part of the cost of doing business with hardscrabble farmers of Maine, who purchased goods on credit in a largely barter economy. Inevitably, some like the Doyens failed to pay. Howard asked for $60 damages in addition to the recovery of the debt with interest. The Doyens failed even to show up, so lost on default, and the judges—Daniel Cony being one—just as predictably denied the exorbitant claim to damages and awarded Howard $34 plus court costs.[31] Maybe William Howard got damages awarded just often enough to cover some of his routine losses. How did he plan on collecting from the Doyens? The next step would presumably have been to send the sheriff to impound Doyen property. But if the Doyens had none, or could render themselves invisible as they did whenever the tax collector came around, the brothers probably eluded this debt altogether.

In 1804, Jacob Doyen was party to another case before Judge Cony. This time he was named as an inhabitant of Strong, so evidently he had left Vassalboro sometime in the previous three years and moved forty miles north and west, to this small village north of Farmington. In a rare show of audacity, Doyen brought action appealing a judgment against him in a small-debt case heard before a justice of the peace. But Doyen failed to show up, and the original judgment against him for $12 was confirmed. The other party was a Hallowell man, Stephen Smith, which shows that the net linking debtors and creditors stretched all over Kennebec County.[32]

Meanwhile, back in Vassalboro, brother Samuel was successfully untangling his legal claim to his land, perhaps also going up against the lawyers Bridge and Williams to boot. Two conveyance records of 1804 document the sale of Doyen's land on the border between Vassalboro and Augusta, land that apparently was part of the larger picture of endless litigation between the Plymouth Proprietors and poor farmers. Doyen sold one hundred acres for $270, being "the same [land] which the commissioners to settle the disputes between the Plymouth Company and the settlers or the commissioners to quiet the settlers in their possessions awarded to me." As soon as Samuel had clear title, he sold the property within the month.[33] He then disappeared from view, that is from the Maine record books, until 1823, when he was known to be living near his brother Jacob in the town of Canaan.[34]

After Jacob failed to appear in the 1804 debt case, he moved to the village of Temple, situated in hilly, thin-soiled terrain above the Sandy River Valley. Sheep grazing and two sawmills were the best this mountainous country had to offer in the way of commercial activity. Jacob probably eked out a bare subsistence as one of the poorest inhabitants in a very poor rural community, whose population numbered under five hundred.[35] A town map showing all landowners in Temple in 1807 includes no Doyens, so Jacob was still either renting or squatting on someone else's land.[36]

Jacob the drifter spent the longest stretch of his adult life in Temple. He and his wife, Mercy, finally felt rooted enough to report to the town clerk the names and birth dates of all their living children. Over a twenty-two-year period, they had had nine, seven of whom survived to adulthood. The oldest was John, born in 1784 (probably when the family was still in New Hampshire), and after a space of a decade (when presumably the two nonsurviving births took place) six more children followed, all sons but one.[37] Jacob Doyen had a male labor force ready to hand, but he had also created a large, new generation of Doyens whose birthright in the world would be just about nothing.

John Doyen, the oldest, was Dorcas Doyen's father. He spent his infancy in New Hampshire and his later childhood in Vassalboro. By 1806, at age twenty-two, he had married and started a family with his first wife, Sally, in Farmington, a few miles south of Temple. He earned a living as a cordwainer, that is, a shoemaker. Evidently he took no part in raising sheep, for the Farmington town records do not include a mark for any Doyen in their log of sheep graziers' brands. John and Sally's first child was a daughter, Nancy, born in Farmington in September 1807. A second child, David Tuck Doyen, appeared in September of 1810, also in Farmington. John and Sally then moved to Temple, joining his parents Jacob and Mercy; both households are entered in the 1810 census (as "Dawan"). There, the third and last recorded child of John and Sally Doyen, Dorcas, was born on October 18, 1813.[38]

"Dorcas" was an infrequently used New Testament name that had been added to the New England name pool by Puritans who had found that families of a dozen and more required extended naming practices well beyond the typical English "Richard," "John," "Mary," and "Alice."[39] The New Testament Dorcas was an early Christian who performed charitable work and sewing for poor widows. The name evoked and signified female self-sacrifice and obligation; many women's church-based charity groups of the early nineteenth century were known as Dorcas Societies. In Acts 9:36–42, the biblical Dorcas secured her place in Christian history by being raised from the dead by Peter in the first miracle performed by a disciple. No doubt John and Sally chose their baby's name as an exemplar of self-sacrificing womanhood, not because of any premonition she might benefit from resurrection. For her part, as soon as she could, Dorcas abandoned the name her parents had given her, later insisting that Maria Benson was her natal name.

Except for John Doyen's brief mustering into the militia in 1813 when he spent four splendid days in an artillery unit that never left Farmington, much less got to the coast of Maine to engage the British enemy, nothing more is known about John and Sally's first fifteen years of marriage.[40] There is no record of further children born after Dorcas in 1813, which could mean there were none, or, more likely, that the couple had left the Farmington-Temple region.

In 1820, the cordwainer John Dawen appears in the Augusta census, heading a household of eleven people. Possibly John figured the market for shoes would be better in a thriving town than in a backwater village, and having spent his adolescence there, he was familiar with the Augusta-

Vassalboro region. Four members of his household were boys age ten and under, so it would appear that David Tuck Doyen acquired some new brothers after Dorcas was born. (There is no record of any Doyen births, however, in the Augusta vital records. Registering births was required by law, but it also required a small fee paid to the clerk. True to form, the Doyens seem to have skirted such legal niceties when possible. The three births in Temple were entered into the town records, but Temple was such a tiny place that it would have been hard to avoid notice.)[41] Two young men in their late teens or early twenties (census category sixteen to twenty-six) also had joined the Augusta household; they might have been apprentice cordwainers working with John, who was then thirty-six. Dorcas was living in this household as well; the census tally mark recorded one female under age ten. So by age seven, and possibly several years earlier, Dorcas was living in Augusta.

Her father, John, returned to Temple by 1822, where he figured in an exceedingly odd land deal. In September of that year, he bought a small piece of property (2.7 acres) along a millstream for $15, his first appearance as purchaser in the conveyance records of Maine, and six days later he sold it to one Albert A. Dillingham, for $145, nearly ten times the price he had just paid for it. Moreover, a few months earlier he had mortgaged a mere acre of property in Temple to the same Dillingham, for the extraordinary amount of $100.[42] (How John came to own this second piece of property is not clear; probably his father, Jacob, had given it to him without officially deeding it over when he moved to Canaan between 1819 and 1820.) Using real property as security for a loan was not unusual; the conveyance records of Maine are full of documents that look like deeds, where an owner "sells" land to the "buyer" with a stated purchase price which is equivalent to the loaned sum, with a rider stipulating that the transfer of ownership is null and void if the owner pays the loan back by a certain date. What is unusual here was the ratio of loan to land. Unimproved backcountry land in Maine rarely sold for above $4 per acre, whereas the Dillingham loan was $100 for the acre.[43] For some reason, Albert Dillingham was willing to buy a remote and tiny piece of land from a shoemaker for an extremely inflated price, and also loan him $100 in addition, with only an acre of land as security. Doyen was no real estate shark; these three transactions are his only entries into Maine property records, although he lived to be at least in his midsixties, appearing in the 1850 census for Avon (a village carved out of a northern piece of Temple), still a shoemaker, and probably still occupying this same acre of property used as security for the loan from Dillingham.

Clearly John Doyen and Albert Dillingham must have had some sort of personal connection that would account for this extraordinary set of transactions. Dillingham was a young man of twenty-two, born and raised in Augusta. Most likely, the connection between the two men was forged in Augusta in the years around 1820. They differed greatly in both age and social status, however, which would have limited their opportunities for friendship. Dillingham came from a family much higher up Augusta's social scale. His father, Pitt Dillingham, was a merchant and innkeeper as well as deputy sheriff and jailer for Kennebec County, and he occupied town offices of trust throughout the decade of the 1810s (moderator of the town meeting, selectman, and legislator in the Massachusetts General Court).[44]

Was Dorcas Doyen in some way involved in the Doyen-Dillingham connection and the curiously imbalanced land dealings? The census puts her in Augusta in 1820, and she began working for the Westons there in 1826. Every account of her at the time of her death identified her as a native of Augusta or Hallowell; maybe she never returned to Temple with her father in 1822 but stayed on in Augusta as a servant or "help," thus fostering the illusion among people who had known her in the Weston household that she had always lived in town. In 1822, when her father enjoyed his windfall profit from the land deal with Dillingham, Dorcas was nine years old, a young but not uncommon age for girls to begin household apprenticeships.[45]

Orphan girls were at especially high risk for being bound out into domestic service. Dorcas was not, strictly speaking, an orphan, since her father was still alive, but sometime between 1820 and 1823 her mother, Sally, died, depriving her of traditional female training as well as of a mother's love and care. Her father returned north to Farmington and married a younger woman.[46] Losing a mother often propelled girls as young as nine into domestic service. For example, a woman in Reuel Williams's family counted it a triumph that she placed two sisters, age nine and eleven, whose seamstress mother was dying, with a mother and daughter living in adjoining homes in Boston. The Boston mistresses "wanted little girls" and had pledged to keep them until they reached age eighteen.[47] Orphan girls in this way avoided the almshouse (or the streets) and acquired a surrogate family to raise them and train them in domestic duties. Mistresses acquired household help, for even nine-year-olds could carry wood, wash dishes, and help with the laundry. There was also a substantial degree of noblesse oblige in such arrangements, for the mistress who pledged a long employment took the risk of having to keep a bad or problematic servant-child who could not be easily dismissed. Often no money changed hands when orphans were bound to mistresses; food, lodging, and training were the central benefits to the young girls, plus the promise of secure placement until age eighteen. Such arrangements were thus ambiguous: a child so placed was not really a servant, working for wages and free to leave, but neither was she an adopted daughter, enjoying the same entitlements as the biological children of the family. Instead she was a kind of foster child, earning her keep and gaining her training through household service. Mistresses had no intention of subverting class boundaries; by disciplining young girls to heavy household labor, they elevated their own status as women who did not work. Nevertheless, they gave unfortunate young girls an opportunity to observe closely the life of a lady of leisure. In the servant phase of her career, Dorcas Doyen proved an apt student of the ways of the upper classes.

Albert Dillingham was not yet married, nor were any of his three brothers and four sisters, who ranged in age from nine to twenty-eight. So Dorcas might have gone into service in this large family. Pitt Dillingham had buried his first wife in 1818 and had just taken a new wife in 1821, young Hannah Aldrich, preceptress of the Cony Academy. Responsible for seven stepchildren and a new baby of her own within the first year of marriage, the new Mrs. Dillingham no doubt had her hands full. (Pregnancy proved no bar to the young wife's employment, for a Williams family letter of the spring of 1822 noted that Mrs. Dillingham had just opened her school, even though she was "fat as a seal.")[48] The baby did not survive infancy, and Mrs. Dillingham, aided by her sister, continued to work full-time at the helm of the Cony Academy.[49] Given her large family and high status, she undoubtedly employed household help; her unusual position as a married woman with a full-time teaching job guarantees that she would have had several female servants. At nine, Dorcas would have been just the right age to begin such work.

If Dorcas lived with the Dillinghams, Albert Dillingham's vastly inflated payment for the millstream property and his generous loan to John Doyen may have been a courtesy or even in part compensation to John in return for his daughter's good services in the Dillingham family. In the late twentieth century, foster parents are paid for taking in homeless children because children now count as economic burdens. But in the early nineteenth century, any child, but especially a bright and talented youngster, added productive labor to the household. An internship with the Dillinghams would help explain how Dorcas could pass for a girl with a genteel education. Boasting the largest private library in town in the 1820s, the Dillingham house would have been paradise to a book-hungry young girl.[50] The household tutelage of the preceptress of the Cony Academy may have been the mother of Dorcas's inventing herself, years later, as a student there.

In 1823, when Dorcas was nearly ten, her father married Lydia Dutton, a twenty-three-year-old woman from Farmington. By the time the census snapped their picture in 1830, John and Lydia had a household in Farmington with four children under the age of ten, plus two teenage boys (the older one possibly David, Dorcas's older brother). Lydia, for many years the only female in the household, no doubt could have used Dorcas's help. A decision to put the girl out at service and struggle along without her help at home suggests the trade-offs that a family of modest means had to make about the labor of its teenage daughters. There was no one to fill in for her; Nancy, the oldest daughter from John's first marriage, in her midteens when her father remarried, had vacated the household by 1830. Yet despite the lack of older female help, the family was willing to put Dorcas out at service. Maybe Dorcas had already been committed to the Dillinghams when her mother died, so there was no retrieving her. Or perhaps antagonism between stepmother and daughter entered into the decision—or the obverse: father and daughter who could no longer live under one roof. Possibly putting her in service was a straightforward calculation meant to maximize the value of the girl's labor. Either the family, or even Dorcas herself, might have imagined that by exposing her to the finer side of life, service to an important Augusta family might somehow enlarge her own prospects.

Whatever the pathway, Dorcas had joined the Weston household in Augusta in the spring of 1826, and they had agreed to keep her until she reached eighteen.[51] Such a promise meant that this was no casual servant hiring; the Westons were taking on an obligation of several years. Dorcas evidently had the standing of a foster child, earning her bread and keep and probably getting no wages. Perhaps it was her virtual orphan status that dictated these terms, or the fact that her father and stepmother, living thirty-five miles away, could not look after her themselves. She was thirteen that fall, and already developed enough in mind and body to pass for fourteen.

But how did the Westons come to know Dorcas? One surmise is that they got her from the Dillinghams, who lived a few short blocks away, at the corner of State and Winthrop. The labor market for more casual female help ran very informally in towns like Augusta. The female gossip networks of the town easily circulated information about who needed help and who needed work. Some local girls on short-term hire might occasionally live at home while rendering service, but more commonly girls worked and slept under their employer's roof and visited home only by permission. Mrs. Weston's sister Sarah Williams congratulated a newly married daughter on her prospects for a particularly promising servant girl: "It is a great recommendation, I think of any one to stay so long in a place as you say this girl has and I hope she will prove a good one to you, but if she is not more than middling don't forget you are as well off as half of the

folks. I have had many more poor girls than good ones in keeping-house."
Mrs. Williams had just acquired "a small girl of 14 who I expect to keep
the winter at least" who had been living for a year with a family she knew
in Pittstown, a good example of how the labor market worked by relying
on word of mouth and personal recommendations.[52] Once in a very great
while, the town's newspapers might run an advertisement for domestic
help, but this was very unusual. The *Maine Patriot* in Augusta carried
this notice in 1828:

> Wanted: An industrious Capable GIRL, to do the work in a fam-
> ily—one that is willing to rise early, and devote her whole time to
> work, will hear of a good place by enquiring at this office. One of
> the above description will receive *good* wages—no others need
> apply.[53]

Perhaps the Westons simply consulted the Dillinghams and hired Dorcas away from them. If Dorcas was in Farmington with John and Lydia
up to 1826, it is a little harder to explain how she could have been hired
into service by a family in distant Augusta. News of a job with the Westons might easily have spread through the kinship networks extending
between the two towns. (Mrs. Weston had several families of second
cousins living in that town, and one Weston son, Daniel, was known to
stay with those Farmington relatives in the 1820s.)[54]

As it happened, the paths of the Westons and Doyens had indeed
crossed before 1826. The one solid piece of evidence putting Judge
Nathan Weston in a room face-to-face with a Doyen specifies two
moments, first in 1818 and again in 1820. Jacob Doyen, Dorcas's grandfather, the Revolutionary War veteran, was entitled to a pension from the
United States government under the first pension act of 1818. For thirty-
five years, the government had resisted pensions for soldiers, fearing the
formation of a lazy pensioner class. But by 1818 the old soldiers were
advancing in years and dwindling in number; Jacob Doyen was then fifty-
nine. Concern for indigent and aged patriots who had sacrificed in the
cause finally overtook fears of creating a group dependent on government,
and the newspapers carried notices of the new congressional action establishing pensions based on economic need. Veterans were instructed to
appear before a judge to swear to their service records and to explain their
economic circumstances to substantiate need. Jacob Doyen, then living in
Temple, appeared before Judge Weston on one of his circuits through
Farmington in mid-March and described under oath his record of service
in the Continental Army. A witness confirmed his testimony, and he also
procured a letter from his old regimental commander. Doyen also swore

that he was now indigent, the other requirement for receiving funds. A pension was issued starting in 1819.

In 1820, the government again required pensioners to restate their claim and elaborate more completely on their financial status, so in June of that year Jacob Doyen—now identified as a carpenter from Canaan—again appeared before Judge Weston. The elderly Doyen swore he was penniless and wholly dependent on his pension for support. His total declared property amounted to one swine and minimal clothing and bedding. He claimed to have no house, no land, no family "residing with me," and debts totaling $1,500. Judge Weston countersigned the document, and Jacob's pension continued.[55]

These pension documents not only substantiate that Dorcas's grandfather had encountered Judge Weston, they also reveal what a slippery old codger Doyen was. The census for 1820 caught a rather different picture of the senior Doyen's household in that same summer. Doyen had indeed moved to Canaan, but the census recorded a full house of six members headed by Jacob Doyen, three males and three females, with two persons identified as employed, one in agriculture and the other in manufacturing (the carpenter).[56] The rest of Doyen's pension record consists of two lengthy and competing petitions filed in 1843 and 1853, by women both laying claim to widows' pensions. The earlier one was filed by Mercy Doyen, who testified to her 1783 marriage date and bolstered her claim by presenting a certified record from the Temple town clerk listing the birth dates of the children they had together. Mercy said that Jacob died in April 1830, and she quickly remarried (at the age of sixty-five!) in October of that same year. Widowed a second time, she was now in 1843 seeking to gain Jacob's pension rights. In 1853 a second widow came forward with a bevy of witnesses, testifying that in March 1820 Jacob Doyen, the very same Revolutionary veteran, had married Mary Griggs in Cornville, a town about twelve miles by road northwest of Canaan. Mary was fifty-three at the time, Jacob sixty-one. Witnesses testified to the cohabitation of the couple, and Mary further reported that Jacob became a pauper and separated from her in 1828, dying a year later on April 15, 1829, in the town of Belgrade. Ironically, Judge Nathan Weston lent his own credibility to this second claim, by noting that the justice of the peace who submitted Mary Griggs Doyen's papers and witness's statements (she being too aged and infirm to come to court herself) was known to him as the president of the Maine state senate; "the fullest confidence may be placed on his statements," wrote Weston in an endorsement in 1853. It would appear that Jacob Doyen had an unorthodox family life in his latter years. He abandoned his first wife (probably just before 1820), married a second without bothering to divorce the first, and lied about both of them on his 1820 pension claim when he swore he was single and destitute. The 1820 census household listed as Jacob Doyen's in Canaan contained his first wife and their semiadult children, probably maintaining face in front of the census enumerator at their door by reporting that Jacob still lived there. And probably Mercy took up with her future and second husband around the time that Jacob left, when she was fifty-five; a sixty-five-year-old woman with no estate was an extremely unlikely candidate for bride.[57]

Dozens of indigent veterans appeared before Weston, and perhaps he never connected the girl who later served his family with the aged and guileful Jacob Doyen. Still, central Maine (the judge's circuit) in the 1820s was a relatively small territory. Kennebec County numbered around fifty thousand people, spread out in two to three dozen villages, each with a thousand or two in population, all looking to Augusta as the area's political and economic hub. An ordinary backwoods family might well have recognized the Weston name and appreciated his high standing as a judge. An opportunity to go into service in his household would have been seen as a lucky break for a girl like Dorcas.

When the thirteen-year-old Dorcas joined the Westons in the spring of 1826, the family consisted of two daughters, Catharine (sixteen) and Louisa (three), and four sons, Nathan (thirteen), Daniel (eleven), George (ten), and Charles (four). The judge and his wife, Paulina, lived near the original Kennebec County Court House, at the corner of State and Court.

In the fall of 1827, the traveling busybody Mrs. Anne Royall came through Augusta and, following her usual custom, gained the acquaintance of all the leading families in town in the short space of a few days. Mrs. Royall, an irascible but shrewd woman in her late fifties, had devoted the better part of the 1820s to roaming the major thoroughfares of the country, from Alabama to Maine, writing chatty books that evaluated in minute detail the places she went, the people she met, and the treatment she received. On every trip she appeared to be fully engaged with drumming up subscription sales for her most current book, but at the same time she was alert to material for her next, taking extensive notes and perhaps even writing the chapters as she traveled. The trilogy describing her travels of 1826 to 1828 carried the somewhat ominous title *The Black Book*. Woe to the folks who were rude to Mrs. Royall, for they ran the risk of being soon identified in print as boors, morons, jackasses, or—her favorite insult—"contemptible puppies." An uncommonly large number of people treated her unkindly (not altogether a surprise, given her penchant for speaking utterly frankly to strangers), so she had plenty of grist for her mill.

During her trip to Maine in that September and October, newspaper editors often announced her arrival in town and said a few words—kind or mocking—about her enterprise. The *Portland Eastern Argus* reported, a month after she passed through, that they at last had learned the historical reference that gave her the working title for the series. In the reign of Henry VIII, the paper said, "a black book" recorded the "scandalous enormities" alleged to be occurring in monasteries and religious houses, in order to speed their dissolution, thus giving rise to the idiomatic warning, "I'll set you down in my black book."[58] In similar fashion, Mrs. Royall inflated the foibles of Americans into enormities, especially as she found them among the rich, the arrogant, the pious, or the pretentious.

Thanks to Anne Royall, we have an extraordinary eyewitness description of Augusta when Dorcas worked at the Westons'. Mrs. Royall took a boat up the Kennebec, and her first stop was Hallowell, whose citizens treated her with warmth and courtesy. Their many kindnesses and good manners over her two-week visit were a sharp contrast to Augusta, her next stop, whose citizens "are a long ways behind the citizens of Hallowell, in urbanity and good breeding—no comparison." The only truly worthy family in Augusta, Mrs. Royall gushed, was that of Judge "Western":

> Judge Western and his family alone, would secure the reputation of any place which might have the honor of his residence. The judge is of low stature, but very dignified; he said he was forty years of age; I would suppose him at once, not more than twenty-five—he is the youngest-looking man of his age in America. . . . In his manner he is frank, polite and easy as the evening gale, and at the same time the most commanding and dignified man in the United States, and I would suppose among the most learned judges; there is something in the tone of his voice originally pleasing; and take him on any ground, he is altogether one of our first men; he is a long way ahead of any judge I have met with north of Washington City.[59]

Mrs. Western seemed "quite as affable and interesting" as her husband, and their daughter, whom Anne Royall mistakenly named Miss Sarah B. Western, was described as "a small aerial nymph, handsome and accomplished as her parents." (Sarah B. Williams was Catharine Weston's cousin, whom Royall also met.) Royall's fullest praise for the Weston household, however, was lavished on the amazing young servant she met there, who could be none other than Dorcas Doyen:

> But of all the families I saw, [I was] most astonished at a little girl in the capacity of a servant. I generally (and doubtless others, do too,) form my opinion of the master and mistress of a house by the servant who opens the door. If I find the servant civil and polite, the

master is certain to be so. But if I find the servant insolent, I never fail to find a thorough proud v——n [vixen], in the house. . . . When I knocked at the door of judge Western, it was opened by a little girl of about eleven years old, who saluted with inimitable sweetness, and with a graceful wave of her hand, invited me to take a seat on the sofa.[60]

To summarize her conversation with the child, Royall resorted to a line of poetry: "A lamb, a dove so mild." Evidently Dorcas appeared docile as well as sweet and graceful to the older woman.

What an easy matter it must be, I thought, to be polite when this child has become so perfect in the art. After exchanging salutations with the family, I could not forbear a remark upon the little girl— expressing my astonishment at her graceful manners, when Miss [probably a misprint for "Mrs."; Mrs. Royall was rather a slapdash author] W. informed me, she was a poor orphan child, whom she took and raised. This is saying enough for Mrs. Western. This deed had more goodness in it, than all the bible and tract societies ever performed in their lives.[61]

So Mrs. Weston was taking full credit for inculcating gentle manners and a sweet disposition in this poor orphan girl! To say that she "raised" the girl suggests more than a year of cultivation; yet the Westons much later were very clear about stating the date of Dorcas's 1826 entry into their home. Mrs. Weston could easily have exaggerated her own role in transforming her charge, simply in order to impress the guest. Or it is possible Mrs. Weston had known Dorcas before 1826 (at the Dillinghams', perhaps) and had taken an interest in her care. Dorcas's previous condition of pitiable orphanhood must have been painted in especially bleak colors to have made Mrs. Royall think that hiring her as a servant was a form of rescue work and extraordinary Christian charity.[62] Whatever the truth of her remarks, Mrs. Weston won for herself and her husband the only favorable mention Mrs. Royall could bring herself to bestow on an inhabitant of the sorry little town of Augusta.

The young men of the town irked Mrs. Royall, and two in particular earned four scathing pages from her. Apparently the sweet, graceful Dorcas was coming of age in a town that tolerated impudent youth. Mrs. Royall met these two in the public room of the inn where she was staying, on State Street close by the courthouse. (This was either the Cushnoc House at State and Winthrop, once owned by Pitt Dillingham, or the Mansion House at State and Court, once the home of Judge and Mrs.

Weston.) The County Court was in session, so the inn was filled with
lawyers and others there on court business. In the midst of this crowd,
"two silly fopish [*sic*]" young but grown men intruded and indelicately
approached too near her. They

> would pick up my books, open them, look in them, look at each
> other, and grin with a wink at the company, and look at me awry.
> Not satisfied with this, they began to ask me a number of imperti-
> nent questions. . . . Their taking hold first of my subscription, and
> then my books, was insufferably rude, as they were not introduced,
> and had no intention of purchasing. But their language and sneers
> full in my face, and their affrontery in intruding so near my per-
> son, in the presence of a numerous company, was insolent.[63]

Mrs. Royall did not record how she responded to this insolent behavior,
but "it may be supposed, they met with that sort of treatment [from Roy-
all] their impudence deserved." The woman then left the tavern and went
to a house to try to sell her books, but the young men shadowed her there.
Next she went down the steep hill to a bookstore on Water Street (most
likely Harlow Spaulding's bookstore), and again the men pursued her.
She asked the bookstore owner to call a constable for her, whereupon the
pranksters took off. She decided to return to the tavern but had only gone
a short distance up Winthrop Street when she caught sight of the two
again, lingering in a doorway and watching her. Mrs. Royall marched
straight into a nearby newspaper office (no doubt Luther Severance's
paper, the *Kennebec Journal*, housed in a building on Winthrop just off
Water Street) and demanded protection. The editor, very surprised,
assured her that those two young men came from the best families in
town; one was named "B*****," son of the banker, and the other was
"G***," whose father was "one of the first gentlemen of Maine." (Royall
here followed the familiar dodge of many newspaper editors, using carefully counted asterisks to disguise minimally the names of people she castigated in print, to protect her from libel suits.) Mrs. Royall, no fool, was
not one to accept class standing as a guarantor of gentlemanly behavior.
She insisted that the editor accompany her downstairs to the paper's
reading room, where she was certain the young men were now hiding.
Sure enough, they were lying in wait for her in a corner, and the embarrassed editor sent a young boy to escort her back to the inn.

    We have of course met "B*****" before, as an asterisked butt of a
joke published by the *Portland Courier* in 1836 to link a leading young
man of Augusta with a dead prostitute. Horatio (also known as Horace)
Bridge and Franklin Gage, twenty-one and twenty respectively in the fall

of 1827, were recent graduates of Bowdoin College. Both were preparing for careers in the professions—Bridge in law, Gage in medicine. Within a year they would open their practices, sharing office space on Water Street in Augusta.[64] Their fathers were indeed among the leading men of the town: James Bridge, lawyer and banker, and Joshua Gage, erstwhile member of the House of Representatives in Washington. Mrs. Royall interpreted the young men's rudeness to her as an instance of general disrespect for women. About Bridge she said, "He ought to have been taught practically from his infancy, that respect for women is alone the characteristic of a gentleman, and let him have whatever advantage he may, without a proper respect for the sex, he is a brute."[65] Gage seemed to her to be beyond useful rebuke; he was an "insignificant p——y [puppy]" with a little, pointed face, a "sickly white" complexion, and a ridiculous flat cap.[66]

Obviously the men were not displaying the customary courtesies and deference expected by Mrs. Royall. But neither was she in the habit of playing the submissive female. Wherever she traveled, she encountered men who made fun of her, tricked her, or were rude to her, and as skillfully as she read their gestures of dominance (for example, standing too close, touching her belongings without permission), she never connected these actions with her own self-presentation as an outspoken woman who did not behave deferentially to men. She preferred to think such men were rude to all women, instead of understanding their actions as measures to put an out-of-place woman in her place.

Young Bridge and Gage chose to insult and alarm the older woman with a juvenile strategy of a menacing hide-and-seek. They were openly expressing an aversion to Mrs. Royall that some of the mature men of the town also shared but dealt with by avoiding her. Mrs. Royall tried to visit the Gage residence (before she knew that the young sickly faced fop was a Gage) and walked there with Judge Weston, who also had business with Joshua Gage. The senior Gage had made his money in mercantile activity in Maine and had occupied many local and state political offices, capping his career with a two-year term in the House of Representatives. Judge Weston squired her to the Gage parlor and went to seek the host. Mrs. Royall next caught out of the corner of her eye the two men tiptoeing down the stairs, and then "G. walked out at the back door, and the Judge walked softly out at the front door, doubtless ashamed to deliver so mean a report of his neighbor." After sitting awhile longer, she was told by a servant that Mr. G. was not at home. True to form, she challenged this information. " 'He cannot be far off,' I said, 'I saw him go out just now.' Is it any wonder those people's children are so mean, with such examples as this?"[67]

Mrs. Royall was also determined to meet Reuel Williams, by this time the richest man in town. (The only other Augustan who approached Williams in taxable wealth was his law partner and patron, James Bridge.)[68] She called at the Williams home and met his wife (sister to Paulina Cony Weston) and daughters. (There was no mention of his son, Joseph Williams, who a decade later would be roommates at the Harvard law school with his cousin, the third Nathan Weston.) The daughters said their father worked late every night, so she dropped him a note at his office, asking for a bit of his time. He sent back "a trifling excuse in writing—thinking, doubtless, his wonderful condescension in scribbling a pitiful excuse, was an equivalent equal to an interview." Williams, she decided, was "mean enough to play at hide and seek with me. Why did he not act like a man?—Why did he not call on me, as other gentlemen did?—" Soon enough, however, she ran into him at the bank (Judge Bridge's bank):

He made his bow, and said a word, now and then, I felt somewhat disappointed, I expected to have seen either one of your keen, intelligent, wisdom-fraught men; I expected to have seen a countenance of placed sageness, indicative of deep thought, and glowing with Unitarian kindness; I expected at least to see a gentleman— instead of all this, I found a great bold swaggering, conceited, rough, black-complexioned man, with a whistling air, in manners and appearance like a Kentucky bully.[69]

Mrs. Royall had traveled extensively in Kentucky and Tennessee, meeting what she considered to be Kentucky bullies in the flesh countless times, so she felt certain of her own assessment of Williams's character. Reuel Williams may have been the richest man in Augusta, and he would soon sit for six years in the United States Senate. But his rude treatment of Mrs. Royall caused her estimation of him to plummet.

Reuel Williams's fourteen-room mansion on Cony Street, on the east side of the river, was the grandest house in all Augusta. When Mrs. Royall paid her call, Catharine Weston was also there with her cousins, playing the piano. Williams family letters of the 1820s and 1830s tell of multifamily Thanksgiving dinners, with servants of all families in attendance to help with preparations, so Dorcas Doyen likely visited the house occasionally during her years as ward of the Westons.[70] The house rivaled any wealthy merchant's house in Boston or Salem, and its particular noteworthy feature was an octagon parlor at its south end. The parlor's walls were papered with an elaborate French wall covering in a tropical motif depicting South Sea natives preparing to greet Captain Cook; *Les voyages de*

Captaine Cook was the title given the paper by its designer. Assuredly, Mrs. Royall was not shown the octagon parlor by the Williams women during her visit, for had she seen it she would have taken delight and spared no sputter of astonishment in blasting it in her book, given her low opinion of Reuel Williams. The large landscape panels depicted scores of bare-breasted and bare-legged women exposed to midthigh in togas more classical than Tahitian. The women all sport feather headdresses and dance in triads with scarves in front of seated men, or point boldly (the better to give their breasts lift and definition) to English ships on the horizon, presumably bearing the famous Captain James Cook. (Without the designer's title, it would be hard to know this was a great moment in history about to happen.) While it is true that Captain Cook's voyages to Tahiti, Fiji, and Hawaii in the 1770s captured the imaginations of colonizing Europeans and Americans and created a rage for books, memoirs, and artistic depictions of the courageous Cook meeting the exotic South Seas natives, still this particular depiction backed up a step in time and invited viewers to contemplate the nearly nude beauties awaiting Cook rather than the courageous white men themselves in the act of cross-cultural contact.[71] (And it still can be contemplated: when the Williams mansion was razed in 1947, the unusual wallpaper was removed and reinstalled in the Asa Stebbins House in Historic Deerfield in western Massachusetts.)

Reuel Williams entertained President James K. Polk and his secretary of state, James Buchanan, in this parlor in 1847, which clearly shows that the wallpaper passed muster as respectable decoration.[72] The panorama of exotic female nakedness seems an odd choice for the parlor of an upwardly mobile town leader. But its unself-conscious use demonstrates something of the mores of this provincial town, where female breasts and legs could be acknowledged so long as they were subordinated to grander themes. The block-print paper gained respectability by being art—daring art, to be sure, in the often timid sexual climate of American bourgeois culture in the 1820s—and by memorializing the exploits of a Western hero. Its message about the triumph of the dominating and colonizing West spoke louder—just barely—than its invitation to think about sexually available native women. The men who saw the wallpaper—senators, presidents, important lawyers—could no doubt conclude that the adventure of exploration around the world was very attractive and exciting. They could think thoughts of Western mastery and conquest and of sensuous indulgence at the same time. The Williams women lived with the wallpaper too; all we can say for sure is that they chose not to show it to Mrs. Anne Royall in 1827. For a servant girl like Dorcas, the naked women provided fanciful information and perhaps even grounds for a fantasy of other cultures and other sexualities, where beautiful young women danced for men and showed their bodies without a hint of embarrassment.[73]

Mrs. Royall's candid assessment of the leaders of Augusta society illuminates the social milieu Dorcas observed and absorbed when she lived with the Westons from 1826 to 1830. The young people of the town who came from families of means—the Westons, the Williamses, the Bridges, and the Gages—did not stand much on ceremonial politeness to strangers and were not averse to taunting with cruel humor an eccentric woman. They were not backwoods boors, nor were they prissy prudes. They came from ambitious and confident families, secure of their leadership in society. The community they built substantiated their claim to self-assurance. They had transformed Augusta from a frontier fort in the forest to a cultivated town of four thousand inhabitants in less than four decades. (Nearby Hallowell added another four thousand, making this spot on the Kennebec River the most populated location in Maine after Portland, a port city.) Spacious and well-built homes—a goodly part of them still standing today—covered the many blocks spreading out from State and Winthrop Streets. The banks, law practices, newspaper offices, and bookstores that lined four busy blocks along Water Street provided culture, information, and legal and financial services to the five counties that formed the heart of central Maine. Two elite private academies enrolled the young of both sexes from these families, and two dozen common schools served the rest of the population, including at least one bright servant girl. Dorcas Doyen was a servant in this town, but one given special privileges (an education, books and time to read them, food, and servant quarters more comfortable than a poor shoemaker's daughter could expect) that probably encouraged the ambitious child to identify with the wealthy families she served.

The Augusta elite were so sure of themselves that in 1823 they mounted a campaign to get the state capital removed from Portland to their city. From his seat in the state legislature, Reuel Williams himself led the effort. Augusta was certainly more centrally located than the southern seacoast city, and it could also lay claim to a level of civility and gentility, as well as an alert legal and journalistic community, well able to support the pomp and ceremony of state government. In 1827 Williams's campaign succeeded, and in 1832 the governor and legislature took up residence in Augusta. A classical statehouse designed by Charles Bulfinch of Boston commanded a stretch of land called Weston's Hill, sweeping up from the Kennebec River to State Street. Much of that land had been bought up in small parcels by Judge Weston in the early 1820s, and the final decision to locate the capitol building on the site made the judge a wealthy man.[74] The acerbic Mrs. Royall harrumphed about Augusta's pretensions to civic celebrity—"I am sorry the citizens are not more worthy the distinction" of hosting the government—but obviously her sentiments were not widely shared.[75] Augustans thought of themselves as the social equals of anyone down in Portland or Boston; one young Augustan, a daughter of Reuel Williams, visited New York City in 1832 and wrote home to brag that "the Kennebeckers are equal to any body's folks."[76]

Anne Royall of course did not think so. When in 1828 *The Black Book* broadcast its vituperative characterizations of Augustans, one local newspaper (the *Maine Patriot*) marked the event by reprinting a Maryland newspaper's rather subdued review of the work: "In her sketches of individual characters she seems to have been guided pretty much by feelings excited by their treatment towards her; and we need not add, that she has drawn a hideous portrait of many; these, we think, will not sit for a second likeness."[77] By early December, Harlow Spaulding's Water Street bookstore advertised the three-volume set for sale, and no doubt many Augustans hurried in to pick up copies, eager to see what the sharp-tongued Mrs. Royall had to say about them.[78]

Dorcas Doyen surely read Mrs. Royall's book. Spaulding's bookstore was a mere five-minute walk from the Weston house; could Spaulding have resisted leafing through the new book in his stock to see what Mrs. Royall had to say about Augusta? Would he have neglected to tell Dorcas of Mrs. Royall's flattering sketch of her? The Westons, the only Augusta family treated favorably in the book, might even have purchased a copy of the set. The avid girl reader, in poring over the laudatory passage about the refined servant girl at the Weston house, would have found her ability to play the lady confirmed. But more significant than her praise for good manners, Royall bestowed upon Dorcas her first brush with fame. She appeared in Royall's book as a very minor character, to be sure, but a first tiny taste of celebrity might have turned the head of any servant girl. Dorcas Doyen, the girl who read books to imagine a world beyond the pantry and laundry room, had now become a character in a book. The experience was bound to unleash ambitions—inappropriate ambitions for a poor shoemaker's daughter in Maine of the 1820s.

CHAPTER NINE

Reading and Imagination

D ORCAS D O Y E N made the most of her five-year servant's apprenticeship with the Westons. She joined them in worship at Reverend Benjamin Tappan's First Congregational Church and proved a prodigious study at Sunday school. She was indulged with the run of the Westons' private library and enjoyed walking along the Kennebec River with an older mentor and talking about books. She spent at least part of each year attending school, and she wrote and received letters at the local post office. She took stagecoach trips up the river to visit relatives in Norridgewock and perhaps to other towns as well.

She learned to "play the lady" well enough to impress the carping Anne Royall, and from her nominally marginal status as servant girl in the Weston house, she observed the comings and goings of the provincial elite as they strove to enact genteel and polite behaviors in the rising capital city of Maine. The young men went off to Bowdoin, Dartmouth, or Harvard and then returned to take their places beside their fathers in town, in their shops, newspaper rooms, and law offices. Even their evenings were dedicated to honing their leadership and social talents in debating societies like the Nucleus Club, the Franklin Debating Society, the Augusta Union Society, and the Augusta Lyceum.[1]

The young ladies of these families—the Williamses, the Fullers, the Bridges, the Westons—went off to girls' academies in Portland and Boston, or locally at the Cony, where they perfected their skills in reading, writing, French, and needlework. Back home in Augusta, they took piano lessons and played for family gatherings and parties. They spent evenings together sewing leghorn bonnets and party dresses, or watching young men play chess on the evenings when the debating clubs did not meet. The pleasant task of arranging private parties, cotillion balls at the Mansion House, and summer steamship excursions on the Kennebec River fell to the women of Augusta's social elite. The youthful social scene facilitated romantic matches, and the Williams family letters are full of news of the local pairings off through courtships and marriages.[2]

The Weston family staged one wedding during Dorcas's term with them: in the spring of 1830, twenty-year-old Catharine (Cassy), the eldest Weston child, married Frederick Fuller, a young attorney and son of another Augusta judge, Henry Fuller, a Dartmouth classmate of Nathan Weston's. Even though Dorcas Doyen had spent five years under the same roof as Cassy, her servant status would probably have relegated her to a supporting service role in the affair, since it took place at the Fullers' large house on Pleasant Street on a Monday afternoon. If it had been a church wedding, the girl might have attended as a guest, since she attended services with the Westons.[3]

As a servant, Dorcas had a hand in making all these lavish social events happen—preparing food, ironing party clothing and table linens, and cleaning up afterward. Her daily and weekly duties encompassed cooking, sweeping, and laundry, the least pleasant and most arduous household task of the period.[4] But somewhere in this chore-filled life she found (or was granted) time to pursue studies and read books.

By the 1820s, the so-called reading revolution was well under way in America. The spread of elementary education and common schools raised literacy rates dramatically between 1800 and 1830. Historically, rates for females had always lagged behind those of males, but in the early nineteenth century New England girls began catching up. Innovations in producing books and periodicals and sending them into the far reaches of the country meant that, by the 1820s, books had become familiar commodities. The vast spread of literacy found favor in a republican country that entrusted political power to the will of the majority. Public education, financed by tax dollars, propelled literacy rates and presumably made for a better-informed electorate. What remained controversial, however, was the particular value or danger associated with reading fictional works.

Lively disputes over the place of the novel in everyday life still energized debating society meetings and gave rise to newspaper essays. Opponents of novel reading worried that domestic and sentimental novels gave young people, girls especially, unrealistic or downright wrong ideas. Moral philosophy, religion, and history all elevated the mind and soul, but novels allegedly engaged the passions and plunged readers into a fictive world of romance and emotion. A commencement speaker at a young girls' academy in 1818 expressed the fear that female readers of fiction would acquire a "morbid restlessness for something new and interesting in life which the readers of fictitious works so constantly desire." Novels fed an expectation of pleasure, clearly not what most young women should expect, the naysayers implied; novel readers would ever be dissatisfied with dreary, ordinary life. They would learn to *feel* too much and be indelicately aroused to passions they should not indulge. At the very least, novels were condemned as being a simple waste of time, an addictive habit that cut into time better spent on housework and other duties.[5]

Evidently the Westons did not share this view, for the judge himself had introduced his explanation of Dorcas's unusual reading by stressing that she had not been negligent in her duties: "She was, I believe, very faithful in the performance of what was required of her. She was sent at times to the common schools, where she made great proficiency. She was remarkable for quickness of apprehension . . . , and had cultivated a taste for reading, in which she was permitted to indulge."[6]

What did Dorcas read? A bookstore down on Water Street advertised its latest titles in the *Maine Patriot and Gazette* every couple of weeks. Harlow Spaulding—the "H.Sp." of the *New York Herald*'s account of Jewett's seduction—owned the store and chose the stock of books; he also maintained a lending library of recent titles, probably for a small fee. Other enticing entertainments enhanced the appeal of his store: two advertisements in 1827 and 1828 proclaimed the availability of musical instruments such as bugles, flutes, and violins; embossed writing papers; pens and penknives; wallets; visiting cards; cologne water; backgammon game boards; and playing cards and dice, all accouterments of a life of leisure and gentility.[7] Spaulding was twenty-five (and unmarried) when he ran these particular ads; his youthful success in the book business probably owed something to the fact that his brother, Calvin Spaulding, senior to Harlow by six years, ran a book-and-stationery store two miles down the road in Hallowell. (Hallowell was perhaps in advance of its twin city, Augusta, for it boasted three bookstores in the late 1820s.) The book titles Harlow Spaulding presented to Augustans represent the kind of reading readily available to families like the Westons, and by extension to Dorcas Doyen.

Most of his advertised stock consisted of very recently published books from 1827 to 1829, many of them novels, travel books, or collections of essays, and most of them quite ephemeral. Spaulding placed no ads for religious, moralistic, or philosophical works. He offered current titles by the popular authors Washington Irving (*The Life and Voyages of Christopher Columbus*) and Sir Walter Scott (*Tales of a Grandfather*). Spaulding stocked exotic adventure titles such as *Life in India; The Adventures of Hajji Baba of Ispahan; Northern Regions, A Relation of Uncle Richard's*

Voyage for the Discovery of the Northwest Passage; *Tales of the Wild and Wonderful*; *The Conquest of Grenada*; and *The Spy Unmasked, or, The Memoir of Enoch Crosby*. There were collections of essays such as *Whims and Oddities*, by Thomas Hood; *Death's Doings*, by Richard Dangley; and *Sketches*, by Nathaniel P. Willis, a first book from a young American on the verge of a celebrated career in American letters. The notorious Anne Royall's *Black Book* trilogy was available at his store; Augustans might well have bought the books just to destroy them, but for Spaulding a sale was a sale.[8] Novels could be purchased or borrowed from Spaulding's circulating library, whose authors included Edward Bulwer-Lytton (*The Disowned*), Charles Sealsfield (*Tokeah; or The White Rose*), James Boaden (*Man of Two Lives*), Truesay Cosio (*The Castilian*), and the Scottish sister writing team of Jane and Anna Maria Porter (*Coming Out; or The Field of the Forty Footsteps*). The poetic, passionate fiction of Lord Byron was available as well, in a compendium volume called *The Beauties of Lord Byron*. Only one title appears to be of the genre of advice literature: *Domestic Duties, or Instructions to Young Married Ladies*, by Frances Byerly Parkes, in an 1829 edition. The title of another book about marriage sounds suspiciously like a spoof rather than a moralistic conduct book: *Sailors and Saints, or, Matrimonial Manoeuvers*, by William N. Glascock, a noted British author who wrote naval books.

In one ad, Spaulding featured four plays; all were by foreign playwrights, but each had recently been staged in New York City, at the Bowery Theatre or the Chatham Street Theatre. Within four years, Dorcas would be a near-nightly patron of New York theaters, seeing plays she could well have read in Augusta. In such ways did reading bridge the great cultural gulf between Gotham and the northern frontier town on the Kennebec.[9]

All thirty-six titles in Spaulding's advertisements were books fresh off the press. Most came from just two or three London publishing houses, with a small scattering from establishments in Boston, New York, or Philadelphia. None of them was a local product, although two printers in Hallowell produced religious tracts and school textbooks.[10] Spaulding was clearly enmeshed in a larger network of book distribution, enabling him to acquire very recent works quite quickly.

One example of this remarkable speed was a new first novel by a young, anonymous author, titled *Fanshawe*, which was published in Boston in October 1828 and was advertised as being in Spaulding's store in the November 29 issue of the *Maine Patriot*. But perhaps a local connection explains why this particular book so quickly made its way to Augusta. *Fanshawe* was the first novel of Nathaniel Hawthorne of Salem, Massachusetts. Hawthorne had just graduated from Bowdoin, where he met several young Augustans and in particular cemented a deep and life-long friendship with Horatio Bridge—the same young man who had offended Mrs. Anne Royall on her visit to Augusta, the same man whose initials the *Portland Courier* later substituted for Harlow Spaulding's as the bank teller who seduced Helen Jewett. Bridge acted as a kind of liter-ary agent and financial angel to Hawthorne in his earliest years as an author, and doubtless it was he who lodged some copies of the novel with bookseller Spaulding and asked him to sell them on consignment. So Dor-cas Doyen could have found *Fanshawe* on the shelves of Spaulding's shop. This romantic melodrama, set on a college campus remarkably like Bow-doin, tells the story of Ellen Langton, a beautiful girl who lives with a guardian because her father has been away at sea for years. Three young men round out the principal characters, two of whom are a thinly dis-guised Hawthorne and his friend Bridge. Tedious conventional devices drive the plot—a rake, a near rape in a cave, threats to reputation, a happy marriage at the end. Hawthorne, soon realizing that the book fell below his own literary standards, quickly disavowed the work, trying his best to destroy all copies of *Fanshawe* and remove it from circulation.[11] But it was just the sort of romantic tale that Dorcas Doyen most enjoyed.

Dorcas's alias "Helen Mar," briefly adopted in 1832, offers a clue to her tastes in fiction. Jane Porter's novel *The Scottish Chiefs*, a hefty five-volume work, offered a heart-thumping account of the thirteenth-century defense of Scotland by William Wallace and other noble clan leaders against English aggression, helped on by the brave, heroic Helen Mar, a young girl whose passions are engaged by the patriotic struggle for justice and freedom. Helen is described as both beautiful *and* strong-minded, able to command troops when the occasion requires; at other times she experiences ladylike faints, trembling limbs, and a heaving bosom, but one "heaving in the snowy whiteness of virgin purity." She is an altogether admirable character, in contrast to the wicked stepmother Joanna Mar, whose rapidly beating heart, flushed face, and insatiable eyes give away her quite inappropriate, adulterous—and unrequited—passion for the hero, William Wallace, who is heroically oblivious to Joanna's unsubtle boldness.[12] Sixteen American editions of *The Scottish Chiefs* were printed between 1809, its English publication date, and the early 1830s, when Dorcas Doyen most likely read it. Harlow Spaulding surely sold it, for he advertised a more recent title by Porter.[13] So popular was it that two ves-sels were named the *Helen Mar,* one a Maine-based schooner and the other a side-wheel steamboat built in 1832. "Helen Mar" proved to be an unlucky name in 1836. In April the girl who had borne the alias was mur-dered. In early May, the schooner sank in a storm off the North Carolina coast; in June the steamboat exploded and burned on the Ohio River.[14]

The Scottish Chiefs and its near relations, the historical fictions of Sir Walter Scott, commanded widespread attention, but they were exactly the sort of books that antifiction moralists condemned either for being a waste of time or for filling girls' heads with impossibly romantic ideals of love and heroism. Dorcas Doyen read *The Scottish Chiefs* and imagined an alter ego in Helen Mar (and significantly not in the forward and seductive Joanna). But commanding patriotic armies and being rescued and beloved by a heroic leader were far afield from the everyday life of the real Dorcas Doyen, who washed dishes and ironed linens in a Maine household.

Still, the Weston family let her read. During her New York years, Dorcas recalled to mind a companion from these days in Augusta, a man who spent time with her talking about the books she had read. In a letter to Richard P. Robinson early in their association, she expressed her love for him by recalling this earlier relationship: "I have met very few persons who could share in all my feelings so largely as ———, who was my earliest companion. When I walked, read, or conversed with him, I whispered to my heart, if I could find one like him how much I should love him."[15] When this letter was finally published, in the *National Police Gazette* of 1849, the editor deleted the man's name, possibly because thirteen years after the murder he might still be alive in Maine, with a reputation to defend (and lawyers to help him do it). But from the way Dorcas described this friendship verging on love, at least on her part, it is clear that the man in question was someone who was out of reach as a lover, since she whispered to her heart that she hoped to find someone *like* him—she could not dream of full intimacy with him. Perhaps the gulf of class between the servant girl and her kindly interlocutor precluded realizing her fantasy of legal connection to him; or possibly he was a married man. In any event, it was her mental bond to him—conversations, shared reading—that made him the idealized lover, or so she wrote to Robinson. It is easy to imagine how book talk could slide into flirtation, allowing a man and woman to have an earnest conversation about romance, love, and even sexual emotions, safely displaced onto the characters of a novel. Either through the guise of instructing her, or—more dangerous yet— through the guise of listening to *her* opinions about books, the amiable reading partner of Dorcas's youth worked his seductive ways on her. The experience set her to yearning for a lover who could share her feelings and ideas, who would take her literary interests and opinions seriously.

In her New York years, Dorcas subscribed to at least four genteel literary journals published in New York: the *Knickerbocker*, the *Ladies' Companion*, the *New-York Mirror*, and the *Albion*, titles editor Bennett of the *New York Herald* found on her bedside table or tucked in among her clothes.[16] The *Knickerbocker* and the *Mirror* carried short stories, about-the-town commentaries on masculine styles and activities, reviews of plays and novels, poetry, and historical sketches. The work of a newly established literary elite, they represented a taste in reading Dorcas acquired on her own, in New York City. For most of these journals had begun publication in the 1830s; in the 1820s nothing similar could have found its way into the Weston household. But others among the books found on her New York bedside table reflected tastes Dorcas acquired in Maine, with its pretensions to literary urbanity. Bennett spotted books by Byron and Scott, as well as the popular *Lalla Rookh*, Thomas Moore's book-length poem subtitled "An Oriental Romance." Works by Byron and Scott were readily available at Spaulding's bookstore, and Moore's romantic poem about a Persian princess was being passed around the Weston and Williams girl cousins in 1826, when Sarah Williams (daughter of Reuel Williams) wrote to her Aunt Helen from boarding school in Massachusetts the tidings that sister "Paulina is now in the bed reading Lallah [*sic*] Rookh, don't you admire it excessively, I do."[17]

Scott's novels were evidently particular favorites in the Weston family. Nathan, the oldest Weston son, chose to write a defense of Scott for his commencement address topic at Bowdoin in 1833. (Every Bowdoin student with passably decent marks had to give a short commencement address; the exercises might thus include as many as thirty speakers, and the event typically drew a large public audience.)[18] Scott's novels, young Nathan wrote, exhibited a "brilliancy of prose" and a "power of interesting the heart" that were essential qualities in all good novels.[19] Cassy, the oldest Weston daughter, had a suitor who wrote her about their mutual interest in Scott. As with Dorcas, book talk substituted for more direct statement of romantic feelings; the suitor piously reminded Cassy that even "particularly moral people approve of Scott's novels, because so much of history is therein interwoven," but he followed this sentence immediately with a joking "ahem!" as if the two of them both understood very well that Scott's appeal was not really his history lessons at all.[20] The two other Weston sons at Bowdoin also prepared commencement addresses on the value of sentiment and emotion in creative works. Daniel's speech was titled "The Influence of Natural Scenery upon the Character of National Music," which he illustrated with reference to Scottish music and its relationship to the "wild and irregular" landscapes of the Highlander country, which beneficially "excite emotion." And George, graduating from college at the tender age of eighteen, prepared his talk on the supernatural in fiction, in which he defended imaginative fiction and the power of the "marvellous" in romances. It gives, he wrote with an adolescent attempt at eloquence, "a soul to the moaning breeze and a spirit to the dark forests." Imagination and the supernatural produce "the love-tinged fables of the Persians" (possibly a reference to *Lalla Rookh*), evidently a preferable state of mind, according to young George, compared with the dull "practical and everyday realities of life."[21]

It is hard to tell whether sentiments like these were a hallmark of a Bowdoin education in the 1820s and 1830s—Henry Wadsworth Longfellow, Nathaniel Hawthorne, and Franklin Pierce were Bowdoin graduates of the period—or whether what we are seeing here is a distinctive Weston family predilection for imaginative affect. Clearly the family did not share the prejudice against novel reading or fear its overexcitation of the emotional faculties; excitement and feeling in and of themselves were highly prized by them. The Westons' youngest child, Louisa, drafted her own novel in the early 1840s when she was nineteen and sent it to Ralph Waldo Emerson, with whom she had been corresponding for two years. A respectful Emerson returned the manuscript and wrote in his diary: "This morning sent L.M.W.'s manuscript with some regret that my wild flowers must ever go back. Their value is as a relief from literature, these unhackneyed fresh draughts from the sources of sentiment and thought, far, far, from the shop and market, or the aim at effect." (In another diary passage Emerson bracketed her with Nathaniel Hawthorne as unaffected writers whose creativity was unsullied by commercial forces.)[22] Emerson shared Louisa's manuscript with Caroline Sturgis, a good friend from his Transcendentalist literary circle, who immediately appreciated the naive but highly evocative tenor of Louisa's work:

> I like those writings of Louisa's because they are so natural. They are exclamations and not sentences to other thoughts. There is much more fancy shimmering of sunlight upon flowers, glancing of fireflies through the night, but it is because the tenderness of her feelings makes her love all images that can be associated with them. The delicacy and purity of feeling often gives force to her expression, but she has no grasp of thought, no sequence, no melody.[23]

The Weston children, then, were all strong on feeling, if less than fully competent at constructing workmanlike narratives or arguments in their college addresses or novels. To Dorcas Doyen they were kindred spirits who could nurture her enthusiasm for romantic, imaginative literature. (The one child whose reading habits remain unknown was Charles, who eschewed college, became a midshipman in the navy, and in 1842 at the age of twenty was court-martialed for seditious and contemptuous behavior. The impetuous Charles said, "I will have your heart's blood" to his captain and then challenged him to a duel the next day, a challenge that landed him in confinement belowdecks for a month. He also called the ship's lieutenant "a God damned son of a bitch" and then jumped ship as soon as he could.[24] There is no record that Charles enjoyed reading about Scottish medieval swordplay, but it would appear that he had a well-developed flair for the dramatic.)

Another form of reading available to Dorcas during her Augusta years was the local newspapers. The *Maine Patriot and Gazette*, owned for a while by Harlow Spaulding and at other times by that series of rather young men, offered lighter fare than Luther Severance's *Kennebec Journal*. It was a Democratic paper, more likely than the Whig *Kennebec Journal* to find its way into the Weston home. In its brief five-year publication run (1827 to 1831), it frequently carried amusing essays and small news items on love, courtship, marriage, and the relations between the sexes in general. (In contrast, Severance's straitlaced political paper generally hewed to an orthodox Whig Party line.)

The very first issue of the *Patriot and Gazette*, for example, carried an original article titled "The Influence of Novels and Romances on the Morals." Evidently the young men editing the paper judged this to be a deeply interesting topic that would catch the eye of the Augusta public: the pros and cons of novel reading were a newsworthy subject in this town. The author argued that novels, and especially historical fictions, were eminently suitable reading because it was possible to learn "profitable lessons" from characterizations of fictional people, both the good like the chivalrous Richard I and the bad—for example, the "licentious profligacy of Charles II." (Those who condemned novel reading would never agree that a character study of a licentious and profligate man, however historical or fully fleshed out, could provide wholesome or instructive reading.) Novels "vivify the imagination . . . they tend to raise the spirits" and present "human nature in its liveliest colours," all features to be admired. Of course, some novels were admitted to be "pernicious" in their effect—Fielding, Rochester, and Smollett were singled out as perhaps dangerous. But Richardson, Scott, and Irving got the seal of approval as being both educational and simply good to read.[25] The use of authors' last names alone shows that the Maine newspaper expected its Augusta readers to be familiar with the works in question, even as they acknowledged that controversy existed over the propriety of reading them.

Over the months, the weekly *Patriot* embellished its columns with small articles on personal advice for navigating the world of relationships between the sexes, probably reflecting the preoccupations of the youthful male editor. A November 1827 article on matrimony declared that the happiest marriages occurred when "the contracting parties are of a condition nearly equal; so that when the first ardours of love are abated by time, neither can assume a superiority, or think it a condescention [*sic*] to have acceded to the nuptial alliance."[26] The servant Dorcas would not have found this advice encouraging; a girl with designs on someone in her employer's class might have read it as a rebuke or a timely reminder to a young man in danger of taking such a girl too seriously. Two articles reprinted from other literary gazettes championed the importance of strong romantic feelings: one was titled "The Sweets of Matrimony" and the other "The Dream of Love," which warned that passion for a lady love can strike even the most sane and reasonable of men.[27] A third article, reprinted from a Philadelphia journal, solemnly made the case that violent passion was too transitory a basis for marriage, a false emotion that in half of all couples doomed a marriage to misery. Instead, men and women alike should seek "respectability of character [and] . . . purity of morals" as essential qualities in a mate, prizing genuine affection over "headstrong and uncontrollable excitement."[28] That such excitement existed was of course never in doubt.

On the side of passion, an article in the May 7, 1828, issue, flagged as "original to the Patriot," engaged in an idealized reverie about early romance:

> Who is there that has forgotten, who ever can forget the first avowal of mutual passion between him and the woman of his chosen love? . . . The look of fond abandonment at last unchecked; the tone of tenderness no longer dissembled . . . the voice of enthralling love. . . . Alas! tis but for a time we start from that trance of sweet thought, and the desolate truth strikes upon our heart in agony! . . . once gone it is gone forever . . . who would not forfeit *all* for the joys of that hour to remember.[29]

The editor at that moment was twenty-year-old Aurelius Chandler, so if these were his words, his enthralling—and evidently reciprocated—rush of love, gained and then lost, was essentially a teenage boy's experience.[30] Readers of the article were meant to understand that mutual passion, declared and enacted between male and female, was a normative state of early love—everyone experiences this, who can forget it, and would one not give anything to have such a delicious moment back again?

Columns of the *Patriot* instructed and judged women's true womanliness. An item titled "Conversational Intercourse of the Sexes" asserted that women who talked to men were much more interesting and less trivial than women who restricted their socializing to other women. Likewise, men who spent time with women were less rude, pedantic, or sullen than they otherwise would be.[31] An item from a July 1828 issue asserted that the ideal woman combined the strong good sense of a man with a delicate, refined nature; she should have no affectations and should always seek her happiness in life through a man.[32] A year later, the ideal woman was portrayed as a tender, cheerful, graceful domestic creature, not one of those "petticoated philosophers, blustering heroines or virago queens."[33] To find a phrase like "virago queen" part of the active vocabulary of young Augustans suggests an uneasy vigilance over the question of sex differences. The word "virago," from the Latin *vir* (meaning man, as in "virile"), denoted a woman who was manlike in courage, intellect, and forcefulness. The mythical Amazons were the classic virago queens. The *Patriot* clearly meant to condemn such creatures, but in introducing the vocabulary, the paper also acknowledged that such women could in fact exist; there was a word for them. For some young women, surely, to learn of virago queens was to expand the limits of the possible.

For all its youthful breeziness, the *Patriot* adhered to traditional standards. In a list of "matrimonial maxims," printed in February 1828, the editors insisted that women must always submit to their husbands. But the *Patriot* amplified the rule, as though it needed extra bolstering with legalistic or practical justifications. Women must submit because it is, after all, what they promised at the wedding ceremony; and if they challenge their husbands, the men will look weak in the eyes of the world, a bad business for both of them. Therefore, the real kernel of advice to a wife was: overlook his faults, smooth over problems, and avoid disputes.[34] This was hardly a ringing statement of natural male superiority.

The *Patriot*'s youthful focus on courtship and marriage articles could have helped a young girl from the Maine backcountry understand the mores and expectations for courting behavior among young men and women of the Augusta elite. The *Patriot* approved of women's outrageously wide shoulders and blousy sleeves of fashionable dress; it took its readers on a tour or "Peep into the Seraglio," the harem of the sultans. The paper made a bid for laughs with slightly suggestive stories, like one about a misunderstanding between a Frenchman and an American girl over the phrase "be easy," taken for "baiser" (to kiss) by the man, or another titled "Flirtation," with characters named Edmund Weston and Helen Clapp. They even referred to a poem about "Black Sal, or Dusky Sally," the alleged slave paramour of Thomas Jefferson of forty years before—and this in a Democratic paper, the party claiming to be heir to the party of Jefferson.[35] The paper reflected a playful 1820s sensibility about courtship, friendship, and romance: suggestive but not ribald, upholding good morals but without being prudish in the least.

Even direct curiosity about sex could be tastefully handled, the paper demonstrated. In August 1828 the *Patriot* advertised a traveling lecture show that would teach young Augustans the fundamentals of sex and reproduction. Dr. Williams's "anatomical preparations in wax" of the human body could be seen at the Masonic Hall on Water Street from eight in the morning until four in the afternoon—seen by men only, that is. There was a Mrs. Williams too, and she presented the wax figures to a ladies-only audience, between four and seven in the evening. Admission for this diverting and edifying entertainment was twenty-five cents.[36] Dorcas, then age fourteen, thus had a source of sex education to supplement whatever Mrs. Weston did or did not teach her. An entirely different sort of entertaining waxworks exhibit toured through Augusta a few years later, in 1833, bringing lifelike representations of famous murderers, pirates, dwarfs, and Siamese twins. Dorcas was no longer in Augusta then, but she had easy access to a similar or identical show at Barnum's American Museum a few blocks from her living quarters in Manhattan; waxworks shows were gaining in popularity rapidly in the 1830s, satisfying a taste to bring the public safely face-to-face with freaks, criminals, and victims. Augustans attending this particular event were invited to contemplate unfortunate celebrities, little guessing, of course, that Dorcas Doyen herself in short order would be represented by a wax figure, a famous victim, in a similar exhibit.[37]

Newspapers of the 1820s and 1830s, including the *Patriot*, routinely covered one other form of news about sex: court cases over breach of promise suits, culled from other newspapers in distant jurisdictions. (Civil suits over seduction were much less common but no less interesting to readers.) Such news items were usually just small snippets of a story, a column inch or two, telling the two most essential points—how the fellow deserted the girl and how much she recovered in the way of damages. For example, in February 1829 the *Patriot* ran an item from a Boston paper about a Wayne County, New York, girl, pregnant and jilted on her wedding day. The jury awarded her $500, somewhat on the low side for successful suits.[38] From such stories, uncommonly enacted in the courts but widely reprinted in the press, young men and women in the throes of courtship learned about the substantial costs of transgressive behavior. Pregnant brides could wind up deserted; grooms on the lam could be out anywhere from $500 to $1,500.[39]

In September 1828 the *Patriot* carried a small notice of a New York City civil action for breach of promise, involving a clerk who courted his landlady's daughter for seven years and then suddenly married another. The jury awarded the aggrieved girl $1,500. A much fuller account of the same story appeared in the Hallowell paper, the *American Advocate*, which was published by Calvin Spaulding, Harlow's older brother. If Dor-

cas shopped for books in Harlow's store, she might have happened on the
juicy details of this human interest story. The *Advocate* reported that the
clerk was seventeen, the girl fifteen, when the courtship began. Seven
years later the clerk had married another, and his lawyer argued on his
behalf that any man can be a victim of the "uncontrollable nature of true
love"; when "passion touches his breast . . . he does not look into Blackstone." The lawyer was William Price, one of Richard Robinson's lawyers
in 1836, when he would again defend a New York clerk charged with an
offense against a lover. In the 1828 trial, Price took the line that a young
man was entitled to marital passion and happiness, and that having suddenly found it with a new woman, he was right to abandon the old love—
in fact, to marry the first girl knowing he did not love her would have been
a disservice to her. The lawyer for the young woman countered by saying
that Lawyer Price, a bachelor, had no understanding of marriage; when
the defendant put a ring on the plaintiff's finger and whispered in her ear
(what, it apparently mattered not), clearly a pledge of marriage had been
made. He appealed to the men of the jury, all married, to consider the
obligations of engagement; the plaintiff had even tended the defendant in
illness, a gesture of service presumably denoting an expected return.
Thus a circumstantial promise of marriage was confirmed, and the jury
found for the young woman. How the young clerk, now twenty-four, managed to come up with the enormous $1,500 fine is nowhere part of the
record. The presiding judge in the case was Josiah O. Hoffman, father of
lawyer Ogden Hoffman, who would soon work with Price to defend
Richard Robinson.[40] "So, young men, take warning!" admonished the
American Advocate. Dorcas, too, had a forewarning—of fickle clerks, of a
legal system adjudicating matters of the heart, and of Price and Hoffman, so soon to be involved in her own disastrously failed romance.

Reading was all around young Dorcas Doyen. Augusta had two newspapers, Hallowell one, and other papers entered the town biweekly from
Portland and points south via the stage. An Augusta bookstore operated
by an agreeable young bachelor stocked up-to-the-minute publications
and rented books as well; two miles away in Hallowell, three more bookstores proffered their goods. Families in town like the Westons and
Dillinghams prided themselves on their own private libraries; the Westons
in particular were partial to the writings of the new romantic movement.
A servant girl of uncommon mental talent indulged by a family that valued romantic reading: antinovel moralists would have identified this as a
recipe for certain disaster.

A leading antinovel moralist of the 1830s named John Todd, a Massachusetts minister of the orthodox Congregationalist faith, spelled out the
pollutions and contaminations brought on by novel reading in his best-

selling advice book for the young, *The Student's Manual*. The Reverend
Todd's book, issued in twenty-four editions in the two decades after its
first publication in 1835, devoted a chapter to "Reading" with the subtitle
"Beware of Bad Books." Reading was both solitary and stimulating; its
close affinity with the evil of masturbation lurked just beneath the surface
of Todd's book. Reading could be ruinous, the Reverend insisted. Byron
especially was "putrid," and other authors were so bad and dangerous
that Todd declined to name them, for fear of giving them greater currency. Authors he was willing to risk naming—Byron, Moore, Bulwer,
Scott, Cooper, and even Hume and Paine—might have literary merit, he
conceded, but they were even more insidiously dangerous because of their
veneer of art. Stick to history and astronomy, Todd counseled. As for the
ever-popular Sir Walter Scott, Todd rejected him as a menacing literary
magician. "There is danger in putting yourself in his power."[41]

A review of the Reverend Todd's book that highlighted his strong opinions on the dangers of novel reading ran on the same page in a male moral
reform publication in June 1836 that also presented an analysis of the life
and death of Helen Jewett. Her problem, the editors declared with assurance backed by the Reverend Todd, stemmed precisely from early and
unwise reading:

> Among the means employed to corrupt her mind were the popular
> novels of the day, and especially the works of Byron. The vivid
> images of gross licentiousness, half-veiled in the charms of poetry
> and fiction, thus presented to her mind, and operating on a warm
> imagination, completely unsettled the principles of virtue.

This female of "uncommon talent" wasted her mind on the "pernicious
works of Bulwer" and the worst destroyer of all, Lord Byron, whose portrait "hung conspicuously in her chamber." The moral of the Helen Jewett story was clear: "Avoid the perusal of novels . . . it is impossible to read
them without injury."[42]

Another moral reform publication of July 1, 1836, used the theme of
"the corruption of the press" (exhibited in the coverage of Robinson's
murder trial) as a springboard for indicting bad reading in general.
Novels were singled out because they "seduce the heart through the
senses . . . pollute it through the medium of imagination":

> The youthful reader puts herself in the place of the heroine, she is
> absorbed in *her* pains and pleasures, identifies *her* feelings with her
> own, and comes from this ideal world, into every-day scenes of life,
> with dissatisfaction and disgust at their insipidity.

The "feverish excitement" of a novel contrasted favorably with "the boredom of life"; fictional seducers became fascinating and their victims sympathetic and attractive. What could one expect but that readers of novels would aspire to imitate the life they read about, to render their own less tedious?[43]

Moralists predicted that unwise reading led girls like Jewett astray. What, then, of a novel *about* Jewett that attended to her reading habits? One appeared in 1849, an embellished racy serial of love and death that had first been published in weekly installments for over a year, from 1848 to 1849, in the *National Police Gazette*. Editor George Wilkes spun out the story one chapter at a time, basing it loosely on the facts of the Jewett murder. He interpreted Judge Weston's report of the studious girl's reading habits through the lens of the alarmist Reverend Todd: reading was very dangerous, Wilkes seemed to agree. Alone in the judge's library, Jewett's latent ardency was stirred to life:

> Then it was that her young blood, only warm before, became alert and fervid; then that the glance of her large black eye, from the mere sparkle of thoughtless cheerfulness, became soft and languishing with voluptuous meditation. The romances of Richardson inspired her with sentiment; the heroines of Scott aroused and flattered her imagination; while the strains of Byron, the mysterious noble, who had just then become famous in this country by his history as well as by his verses, fevered her veins and made her pillow the confidant of yearnings, which had they received fruition, would have rendered her ineligible to have hunted in the train of Dian.[44]

There is delicious, heavy irony here. Wilkes seemed to be articulating and supporting the antinovelists' fears that reading leads to inappropriate yearnings and even feverish activity in bed. Yet he was, of course, their very nightmare. Wilkes earned his living writing racy literature in the 1840s; the *Sunday Flash*, with its tours and ratings of New York brothels, benefited from his talents. The *Police Gazette* was in fact one of his most respectable literary outlets. Wilkes not only understood the moralists' concerns about the sexual consequences of certain kinds of reading, he happily reproduced the effect in a passage that made Dorcas's eroticism palpable. By disguising his lure as a moralistic warning against the evils of romantic reading, Wilkes seduced his readers down exactly the same dangerous path.[45]

CHAPTER TEN

Tracing Seduction

ALL AROUND HER—in the *Patriot* columns, in the books she read, in the doings of the Weston/Williams/Fuller clans, Dorcas Doyen could observe flirtation and romance among the elite group of Augusta. There were frolics and cotillion balls at the Mansion House, with sixty to one hundred young people in attendance, and steamboat rides organized to take groups to the annual Bowdoin commencement. Young women wrote each other teasing letters about the men, and on occasion a brave man sent a valentine to a lady. One bachelor wrote his female cousin about the "fair damsels" and many parties of Portland, where he found it "pleasant to give loose to my feelings": "There are ladies here that come up very well to my mark and I am not aware that I should be a great sufferer in transferring to this place a share of my high regard I have hitherto entertained for the Augusta fair."[1] This was a mannerly, playful, sociable set, certainly, that Dorcas had come to live with.

But she was a servant girl, by station consigned to the shadows and not entitled to mingle with the employer class on an equal footing. Men might notice her; her looks, her charm, her cleverness, would not have been easily overlooked. Whether the intemperate shoemaker's daughter could translate men's notice into a form of class mobility, a marriage upward into the highest ranks of Augusta society, remained to be seen. The Weston sons in their various newspaper accounts after her death insisted that her sexual connections in town were with a man of her "own standing," clearly an inferior standing compared with their own. But that was an after-the-fact (and quite self-serving) judgment they rendered about her market for admirers. In the moment, Dorcas might have rated her own possibilities and ambitions a good deal higher. A girl blessed with brains, beauty, and bearing was not completely mistaken to believe that Jacksonian America, with all its brash admiration of self-made men, might also hold the promise of upward ascent for a girl whose human capital made up for lack of family background and connections. If a servant at the Westons could not marry a Weston son, she might ponder moving to a different town, taking up work as a milliner or teacher, and attracting a young man of comfortable background into a serious and respectful interest in her.

But when a servant, she stayed in the shadows. The women of the Williams and Weston families mentioned household help in their letters only in reference to the tasks of housework: "You are fortunate indeed to have Mary for help—she is so clever," wrote Sarah Williams to her newly married daughter, upon learning that Mary was cleaning all the windows. Good work was praised, bad work complained of, but rarely was anything personal ever said about any of the help. Of course, these were the women of the family talking, the ones who supervised the tasks of housework.

For one young man's view of Augusta servant girls, we are fortunate to have a record penned by an introspective man of letters, the thirty-three-year-old bachelor and budding author Nathaniel Hawthorne. Hawthorne visited his college chum Horatio Bridge in the summer of 1837 and spent a month living at the twenty-room Bridge family mansion about a mile north of Augusta's center. Horatio's father and mother were recently deceased, and his other brothers and sisters were off starting families of their own. Horatio rattled around in the mansion and rented a small section of it to a young family who in exchange provided necessary female labor, in the form of their own hired "help," to wash his clothes, make beds, and do light housekeeping for him. Nancy was her name, "the pretty, dark-eyed maid servant," Hawthorne noted in his journal, two weeks later repeating nearly the same phrase as if the words captured her perfectly: "a pretty, black-eyed intelligent servant-girl." He was much taken with her, but, being a shy man, he kept his distance. His notebook entry managed to impart subtle erotic overtones to her performance of the laundry; indeed, he imagined that her every move was somehow a deliberately seductive exhibition performed for the benefit of voyeuristic men:

> She comes daily to make the beds in our part of the house; and exchanges a good morning with me, in a pleasant voice, and with a glance and smile—somewhat shy, because we are not well

acquainted, yet capable of being made conversible. She washes
once a week, and may be seen standing over her tub, with her
handkerchief somewhat displaced from her white bosom, because it
is hot. Often, she stands with her bare arms in the water talking
with Mrs. Harriman [the renter]; or looks through the window,
perhaps at Bridge or somebody else crossing the yard—rather
thoughtfully, but soon smiling or laughing. Then goeth she for a
pail of water. In the afternoon, very probably, she dresses herself in
silks, looking not only pretty but ladylike, and strolls round the
house, not unconscious that some gentleman may be staring at her
from behind our green blinds. After supper, she walks to the village. Morning and evening, she goes a milking—and thus passes
her life, cheerfully, usefully, virtuously, with hopes, doubtless, of a
husband and children.[2]

Hawthorne imagined Nancy parading in silks, playing the lady, ever conscious of her effect on the young men and smiling warmly to think of her
appeal. What is far more likely is that Hawthorne was anxiously fixated
on his own appeal, cautiously testing his sexual magnetism with a girl who
by station had little choice but to be deferential and polite, in other words
someone who would not overwhelm him in his extreme shyness with
women.[3] One wonders what Nancy really thought of Horatio Bridge and
Nathaniel Hawthorne, as she stood over the hot laundry tub with her
sleeves pushed up that July afternoon. Here were two unmarried men, in
their early thirties, whiling away their time that summer month in taverns, swimming holes, and cross-country rambles, picking raspberries,
tending and then killing some orphan baby birds, peeping through window shades, drinking steadily (claret, brandy, and sherry), and then writing about their adventures in notebooks late into the night.

The story of Nancy illuminates one style of cross-class flirtation in
Augusta, where a servant girl was subjected to a young man's experimen-
tation with his charms and where deference required that she take it in
good humor. Similarly placed, Dorcas would have taken it in good humor
and maybe done a little flirting of her own. She could toy with men—her
letters show that—and her perfect imitation of ladyhood that so startled
Anne Royall in 1827 shows she could put on airs. She might have been
more than a match for the shy bachelor Hawthorne, had they ever met.

Bridge certainly knew Dorcas. Their paths would have crossed at the
Reverend Tappan's Congregational church, at social events at the Westons', or at Spaulding's bookstore on Water Street. Bridge mentioned her
in a letter to Hawthorne in May of 1836, a month after her murder: "My

morals have improved exceedingly in the past year; your advice in a former letter was very efficient in this improvement, and Helen J——'s fate
has confirmed me."[4] (Bridge assumed Hawthorne was familiar with Jewett, either through reading newspaper accounts of her death or because
the two men had talked about her when they had recently been together in
Boston.) Jewett's fate, to be scandalously and brutally dead, helped
Bridge maintain his resolve to be moral; to be overtly sexual, to be a prostitute or to visit prostitutes, carried a huge penalty.

Dorcas did meet someone, on intimate terms. Later Judge Weston
obliquely portrayed her fall from grace in a few quick strokes in his letter
to editor Bennett:

> No improper conduct of hers had ever been noticed by my family.
> Some little time before she left us [in fall of 1830], rumors to her
> disadvantage had reached the ears of Mrs. Weston, which she was
> led, from the protestation of the girl, to believe untrue. At length
> reports to her prejudice became so general, that we could not
> believe them unfounded; and they have been but too well confirmed
> by her subsequent character. By whom seduced I do not know. She
> was visited by no young man at our house, to the knowledge either
> of Mrs. Weston or myself.[5]

The several young men who edited the *Augusta Age* in 1836, it will be
recalled from chapter 3, were not so generous in their assessment of her
character. They declared she was determined to be mistress of her own
fate at age eighteen and chose quite deliberately and willfully to set out on
the path to destruction. Both accounts agree, however, that Dorcas lost
her virginity and her respectability no later than the fall of 1830 and left
the Weston home soon after.

Dorcas, born in October 1813, had just turned seventeen in the fall of
1830. Judge Weston elevated her age by a year in his letter to the *Herald*,
and accounts of her death in New York City did too, suggesting that she
herself usually added a year to her age. The discrepancy matters, because
a servant girl in her circumstances, one who traded adolescent service for
multiyear care and protection in a kind of foster family, terminated her
agreement at age eighteen, the customary age of majority for girls in the
nineteenth century. If the Doyens and the Westons had the usual arrangement, Dorcas was not free to leave their employ—and supervision—until
fall of 1831, when she turned eighteen. If an underage girl left her
employer it would normally be to return to her parents' house. By
padding her age, Dorcas Doyen left the Westons early. She also altered

the set of legal options open to her or to the Westons to make trouble about her seduction. If she were known to be under eighteen and therefore still in service, the Westons would have had legal standing to sue her seducer—providing his identity was known to them.

Seduction suits were an old and, until the 1820s, a largely underutilized feature of English common law. Under strict application of the law, fathers, masters, or guardians of seduced women could bring a tort action under trespass law to recover damages for loss of service. The key idea was loss of service and attendant damage to a man's property in a woman: a seduction allegedly undermined ability to perform duties to parent or master. Pregnancy was not essential to the action, but it did increase both the credibility of the plaintiff's case (in proving the sexual intercourse had taken place) and the prospect of recovering demonstrable expenses and damages. Under the traditional grounds for suit, the complicity of the girl in the intercourse was immaterial, oddly enough; this was a legal dispute between men. If a father or master encouraged a romance, say, by permitting bundling to occur—night courting in a bed alone—then it was difficult to persuade a judge to award damages.[6]

Seduction suits surged in popularity in the early nineteenth century. In the years between 1815 and 1830, courts increasingly entertained cases of jilted brides and desolate or pregnant lovers and began to award fairly hefty damages, typically from five hundred dollars to two thousand dollars. Judges often remarked in their opinions that they were departing from the old fictions of lost service and were really compensating women and their families for loss of reputation, emotional damage, and lowered marriage chances. Women were now construed to be the victims of seduction, not complicit participants.[7]

Judge Weston certainly knew seduction law, because he had sat in judgment on several cases appealed to the Maine State Supreme Court, and he was squarely part of the new trend in using the law to repair emotional pain. In April 1826, he ruled on a case where the contested question was who had standing to sue: a father whose house the girl had left some five years before or her uncle, to whom she was indentured but whose service she left by mutual consent of all parties to go live with a grandfather, where she was seduced by the defendant. In his judicial opinion, Weston wrote that

> the loss of service is merely a fiction of law; the real ground of the action being the disgrace of the family, and the injury to their feelings. It is a rule founded in common sense, as well as in strict justice, that fictions of law shall not be permitted to work injustice. . . .
> And it seems unnecessary, and even absurd, to require proof of any

service to the father, since this often forms no part whatever of the ground of damages, which are frequently the largest where the least service is proved.

To say that the damages were largest where the service was least betrays a class bias—a seduced rich girl suffers more damage—but the judge at least agreed that the father of a servant girl should enjoy the same legal remedy as the father of a girl away at boarding school:

> The actual damage is precisely the same as if the daughter were an indented apprentice; and if the action lies in the one case, why not in the other? The father is entitled to this action because he is the protector and guardian of the morals and virtue of his child. And if he has, for a time, relinquished his right to her services, are his obligations and his affections suspended? Must he be supposed insensible to circumstances so deeply affecting his own happiness and the peace of his family? Shall this action be given to a person of elevated rank, whose daughter was absent for the purposes of education; and be denied to one of a grade less elevated, whose child was removed from him to be instructed in subjects pertaining to humble life; but to whom an unblemished reputation and virtuous character were equally dear?[8]

In the spring of 1826, precisely the time that Dorcas Doyen entered service in his family, Judge Weston had given close thought to the ramifications of seduction suits. Following his own reasoning, when Dorcas was seduced in 1830, he as her master had legal standing to sue, but he would also agree that her father had standing as well, since the Doyen family had been disgraced. In his own experience, of course, the Weston family was also disgraced; they had raised this girl from the age of thirteen, and it was their responsibility to keep her from sinful ways. Instead of invoking any of these legal arguments, however, the judge simply let her leave—or threw her out. If he truly thought she had just turned eighteen that October, instead of seventeen, and if he imagined that the seduction happened after her birthday on October 18, then he would have been entirely in keeping with the law to simply let her go. But in fact, Dorcas Doyen turned only seventeen that October, and possibly her initiation into sex came before her birthday, when she was sixteen. To claim she was eighteen was a powerfully convenient fiction, both for Weston, who wanted to be rid of a problem child, and for Dorcas, who was perhaps eager to escape and gain independence.

So who was Dorcas Doyen's seducer? Was there one man, or more?

What kinds of reports reached the Westons that could be "general" and therefore credible?

Fingered by the *New York Herald*, Harlow Spaulding was the first candidate impugned in print. Editor Bennett printed only the initials, but the *New York Sun* linked the name "Spaulding" with Helen Jewett, lengthening the shadow of suspicion on Harlow. The *Herald* identified him as a bank cashier, a job Spaulding did not assume until the 1833 chartering of the Freeman's Bank, three years after Helen had left Augusta. Evidently she kept in touch with someone in Augusta as late as 1833. She spoke of Harlow Spaulding to her New York friends, she implicated him in her seduction, and she followed news of his career for several years.

Spaulding scarcely welcomed being identified in print as the seducer of the murdered prostitute. We have already speculated about his conspiring with the *Augusta Age* editors to prevent the spread of the *Herald* story about him in Maine. Someone from Augusta wrote a letter to two other New York papers several days before the murder story was printed in Augusta papers. The letter, dated April 18, 1836, went to the *New York Courier and Enquirer* and the *New York Commercial Advertiser*, which printed it on April 25. The letter referred to *Herald* stories reprinted in the Boston papers and begged to set the record straight in New York about the maligned bank cashier, "one of our most respectable citizens."

> The story of her seduction at Norridgewock, and by the gentleman alluded to, is a complete fabrication without one particle of foundation; and justice to that gentleman requires that it be so distinctly understood in your city. Here his character is too well known for a story of that kind to do him any injury.[9]

The suppression of the H.Sp. story in the Augusta papers demonstrates that the editors there were not at all confident that the story would crumble on first reading. But a swagger helps deflect suspicions, so the letter to New York exuded confidence that the Spaulding story was impossible to credit. No doubt the letter was written by a Weston son, an associate on the *Age,* or Spaulding himself.

Spaulding could well have been her seducer. He was single, and he worked very near to the Weston house. He sold books, and Dorcas was a bookworm. Perhaps Harlow was Dorcas's romantic reading companion, guiding her choices and discussing her reactions to various books. Since he was unmarried, he was presumably available to her for love and/or courtship, and he was not so rich and wellborn that a legal union with a smart, beautiful servant girl serving a highly placed family would have been totally out of the question, unless he coveted a marriage that would elevate his own class standing. Harlow Spaulding did not live alone, so an illicit sexual liaison would have been limited to semiprivate spaces afforded by the back room of the store, in wooded glens, or under the cover of night on a warm summer or fall evening—in short, in the traditional risky spaces that lovers manage to find.[10] In any event, all that can be said for certain is that Helen Jewett kept abreast of Spaulding's employment in Augusta for at least three years after she left town, and, for whatever reason, she did name him as her first lover to some of her New York friends.

Between 1833 and 1837, Spaulding stayed in Augusta, cashiering at one bank, buying stock in another, and appearing as grantor or grantee in twenty or thirty land deals around Kennebec County between 1830 and 1837, many of them agreements using land as collateral for loans. The last of the deals came in April 1837, when Spaulding and three partners bought land in the town of Clinton, north of Augusta. The cashier ended his job at the Freeman's Bank in mid-December 1837. Thereafter, Harlow Spaulding entirely disappears from the Maine records; he was nowhere in Maine (or elsewhere in New England or New York) in the 1840 or 1850 federal census. A large Spaulding family genealogy printed in 1872 listed Harlow in his family group, with the notation that at this late date (he would have been sixty-eight) he was still unmarried and resided at the Brooklyn Navy Yard. His brother Calvin and several other siblings stayed on in Augusta, but Harlow apparently left town and never returned.[11]

Another candidate for the Jewett despoiler is Frederick A. Fuller, but the evidence here is entirely circumstantial. Fuller was a lawyer in Augusta, age twenty-four in 1830 and eldest son of the judge of probate for Kennebec County. He lived a few blocks from the Westons, and he courted their daughter, Catharine, marrying her in May of 1830 in a big family wedding held in Judge Fuller's spacious house on Pleasant Street, a house that two years later he sold to Nathan Weston. In late summer of 1830, the newlyweds Fred and Cassy appeared in the 1830 census for Augusta about fifteen households away from Judge Fuller's, the two of them living together along with a black female age twenty-four to thirty-six. (The federal census in these early decades only listed the name of the head of the household and then the other occupants by sex, race, and broad age groupings.) Here was a sign of affluence indeed, to have a black adult woman as a servant instead of a mere white girl as "help." Augusta had only 37 black residents in 1830, out of a town population of 3,980. Of those 37, only 7 were adult women. Two families totaling 8 blacks happened to live right next door to Judge Weston in the census: Jacob and Levi Foye were the two heads of the households, and perhaps it was a Foye relation who went to live with Cassy and Fred.

A first baby arrived in April of 1831 and a second in February 1833, both sons. But then, within three months of the second baby's birth, Catharine entered a petition with the Supreme Judicial Court for a divorce from Fred, on the grounds that he had committed adultery. Her petition claimed Frederick had, "on the first day of July 1830 and at various other times between that day and the first day of February last, at Augusta foresaid and at Sidney in said county of Kennebec and at various other places in the state of Maine committed the crime of adultery with various persons to your libellant unknown."[12] A warrant was issued to the sheriff of Penobscot County to find Fred and get him to court in June; apparently Cassy picked a moment when he was out of town to consult her lawyer (who was also her uncle, Reuel Williams). Fred returned to appear in court and denied the charge "in the manner and form" alleged; he asked for a trial, but the court overruled him and granted Cassy the divorce.

Placing Fred's adultery on specific dates in named locations could mean that Cassy was actually knowledgeable about his activities, or perhaps the law required her to be specific about time and place. The date July 1, 1830, was a mere two months after their marriage; theirs was a very short honeymoon. (A Williams cousin wrote to her sister on September 8, 1830, that Catharine and her mother visited her, and "Frederick came and took coffee—I was glad to see him at Mr. F's church on Sunday afternoon with Catharine." This cryptic reference with its very slight note of concern might mean that women of the family were already alert to irregularities in Fred's behavior.)[13] Nothing suggests that Fuller's early paramour might have been Dorcas Doyen except that in the last half of 1830 Dorcas was gathering her fast reputation in town, and Fred was betraying his marriage vows. Allegedly he continued his philandering ways into 1831 to 1833, with "various persons" unknown as his sexual partners over those years and around the state. Dorcas had left Augusta, but through 1831 she lived in Portland, only a day's travel to the south.

All of this is immensely speculative; at the very least we can say that the Weston family had its hands full of sexual improprieties in the latter half of 1830 and beyond. Anxiety over Fred's adulterous behavior might have made them momentarily blind to the activities of other dependents on the margins of the family; equally likely, the discovery of a sexually active servant might have been all the more explosive in a family already in turmoil over the infidelities of a son-in-law. And if the two had been lovers, it would help explain the Westons' determined impassivity upon learning of Jewett's murder.

A note from Catharine to her mother during her difficult times with Fred shows that she was not totally devastated by the breakup of her marriage.

Dear Ma, You must not feel at all bad for me—the storms and cares of this short life are soon over and if we are depending upon another and better inheritance which fadeth not away and not upon earth and the things of this world we can bear them with patience. It was an unexpected shock but I *do* feel that God who is a present help in trouble can and *does* support me.[14]

She got custody of the children, and her parents raised them, while she rented a room in a house two doors down the street and earned money giving piano lessons. She had a few suitors and then remarried in 1844, when she was thirty-four, and moved to Wisconsin, leaving the children still with the judge and his wife. Fred also remarried, five years after the divorce, and lived in Orono, Maine.[15]

That any Weston family papers of these troubled years exist at all is a lucky happenstance owing to the later public fame of Melville Weston Fuller, the second son of Catharine and Fred. Following family tradition, Fuller became a lawyer. He eventually won appointment to the chief justiceship of the United States Supreme Court, a position he held from 1888 to 1910. The Fuller Papers in the Chicago Historical Society contain anxious letters Catharine and Paulina wrote Melville as he matured into young manhood, stressing the paramount importance of avoiding drink and sexual sin. Their admonitions especially targeted the hazardous atmosphere of college. Paulina Weston, his grandmother, repeatedly addressed him as "Dear Baby" when he was at Bowdoin and advised "be a good boy—let no one entice you to do wrong—stand your ground and do right and you will come off victorious and have an approving conscience." Another time she wrote, "Don't let the students inveigle you into any mischief. If there is any thing disorderly going on, go directly to your room."[16] In an undated letter, the grandmother wrote "try hard to be a good boy— Oh, if you can get through College, without any trouble, how thankful I shall be." Cassy warned him, "Don't taste one drop of liquor," and gave him pointed advice about premarital chastity: "Keep yourself unspotted from the world and *deserve* to have a *wife*—you know very well *what I mean*— . . . the vicious don't enjoy a wife as the virtuous do and the path of virtue is the path of happiness in this life."[17] The two Weston women perhaps had reason to fear the dangerous shoals of college life.

A third possible candidate as the Augusta seducer was the eldest Weston son, Nathan Jr. He was the same age as Dorcas, and at least one newspaper, the *Boston Advocate*, had reported the suspicion that one of the judge's sons might have been the culprit—followed by that quick retraction claiming the sons were away at college.[18] But this was something less than an airtight alibi for each of the boys. It is true that Nathan, Daniel, and George (ages seventeen, fifteen, and fourteen in the fall of 1830) attended Bowdoin College, and with graduation dates of 1833 and 1834 we can presume they were all on campus the fall of 1830. (The fourth son, Charles, was only eight.) Bowdoin had three quarters in the academic year, with the fall quarter running from late October until December, so there was time aplenty in September and early October for an autumnal fall from grace. But why assume the sexual relationship was limited to that fall, and not the spring or summer before? And with Bowdoin only a day away, surely occasional visits home were not hard to arrange.

Daniel and George were perhaps on the young side for Dorcas, but Nathan is a plausible suspect. He did like reading Scott, if his valedictory address was genuine at all, so he had that much in common with Dorcas. After Bowdoin, Nathan studied law, indifferently, at Harvard with his cousin and was admitted to the bar in Augusta in 1836. In May of that same year, one of his girl cousins wrote to a relative about some young woman who liked Nathan, "but he does not care a straw for any lady"— surely an unusual attitude for a member of his Augusta social set. Possibly remorse over Jewett's murder a month before had dulled his romantic interests.[19] His cousin Joseph Williams conveyed news of Nathan from Harvard to their family in Augusta in a letter in May of 1836, because, he said, "I believe Nathan has not written home lately." Joseph assured them that the twenty-two-year-old was finally working hard: Nathan's weakness, "a passion for being fashionable," finally worked in his favor because at Harvard the fashion was "to study with zeal," so Nathan could be both fashionable and studious. Joseph, a future state senator and governor of Maine, was really sharp; he knew how to shade his report to bring comfort to the mothers and aunts of this clan, surely worried about Nathan, without putting into writing any unseemly topics, like prostitutes, sex, and murder.[20] (The *absence* of any mention of Helen Jewett in these letters is the real giveaway: she had lived with the Westons for five years and now she was dead, murdered, headline news all over the eastern seaboard. And Joe writes home about Nathan's improved study habits.)

In 1837 Nathan moved to Orono, in Penobscot County (where Fred Fuller had moved). He married a young Orono girl in 1838, but there seems to have been some rift in his family, since five months after the wedding, his mother wrote to a friend that she had still not met his bride (although his sister Catharine had); Orono is only seventy miles from

Augusta.[21] In the early 1850s, Cassy wrote about Nathan to her son Melville, in a sentence that directly followed her characteristic admonition to avoid alcohol: "Your Uncle Nathan does not do well—oh, Melly it is hard to break old habits—far easier not to form them."[22] It is hard to escape the impression that Nathan was a disappointment to his family.

A fourth candidate for Dorcas's lover is someone whose existence can only barely be verified. In the 1849 serialized version of the murder that appeared in the *National Police Gazette*, the New York writer George Wilkes narrated a story of young love and seduction for Dorcas involving a boy close to her own age named Sumner. There are only two reasons to pause a moment over Wilkes's story. First, although Wilkes probably did not personally know Helen Jewett, he claimed to have two fresh sources of information: interviews with old friends of hers in the brothel world and a scrapbook found in her room which he had borrowed from the police files.

> This story of the lover is not, as some will be ready to suspect, the production of the imagination of the writer. It is related in a series of epistles which Dorcas Doyen, when shame made her heiress of another name, directed to a friend. Their original draft, or copies, were found transcribed in a large scrap-book, taken from the trunk at the time of her murder. In the reproduction of this portion of its contents, nothing is altered but the style. These letters were probably written during her career in Boston, as they are signed "Helen Mar." They are, without doubt, accurate records, as far as they go, of her earliest attachment.[23]

In 1836, the scrapbook was said to contain poems and notes, but no commentator at the time mentioned anything about copies of letters signed "Helen Mar." Just as conceivably, Wilkes made up the Sumner story and conveniently ascribed it to the missing scrapbook—that was perfectly his style. However, the second reason to reconsider for a moment is that in the tiny town of Temple, Dorcas Doyen's birthplace (with a population of 615 in 1820), a boy named Sumner True was born in 1813.

The year Jewett was killed, George Wilkes was a sixteen-year-old New York City street tough. The son of an obscure cabinetmaker who lived just off Leonard Street east of Broadway, he was probably too poor to afford to visit Fifth Ward brothels, and especially brothels of the sort Jewett lived in. Wilkes grew up quickly on these streets; an articulate wit and a talent for sarcastic social criticism set him apart from other bullies of the urban underworld, perhaps not in his sentiments and views, but in his fluency with the written word. In 1841, at age twenty-one, he undertook a newspaper-editing venture with two somewhat older but shady business associates. With them, Wilkes edited a succession of racy underground papers—the *New York Flash*, the *Whip*, the *Subterranean*, *New York As It Is*—and finally landed in the Tombs, New York's brand-new jail, built to resemble an Egyptian palace, on conviction for libel. He served a month (and wrote a pamphlet about the low-life characters he encountered there), and then not surprisingly, in view of his outrage over his conviction, next took up the study of law and called himself an attorney for a short while. But in 1846 he returned to his true vocation, sensationalist journalism, and started the *National Police Gazette*. His years covering the brothel beat for the racy papers finally gave him the entrée to the world of exclusive prostitution that his earlier poverty had denied him. From 1848 to 1849 he published a yearlong serial in the *National Police Gazette*, rendering Jewett's life into a narrative which drew on the conventions of the urban mystery novels, seduction tales, and partaking too of the hot-blooded stories favored by the racy underground press he had helped to originate and shape. (It was republished as a paperback book in 1849.)

Wilkes devoted five installments to Dorcas Doyen's Maine life. He portrayed her as a naive but ardent young girl whose father, an intemperate widower, unwisely neglected the growing friendship between his eleven-year-old daughter and the rustic neighbor boy named Sumner. Soon their friendship went too far, and Sumner was sent away to sea, on a whaling voyage. Her father next approached Judge Weston to ask if he would take her in "as an assistant in his family." The judge complied, wrote Wilkes, out of concern for "the unhappy prospects of the child, if allowed to remain under the example of her parent."

In Wilkes's story, Sumner returned from sea when Dorcas was sixteen, and the old romance rushed into more dangerous channels, helped along by a Negro woman named Nancy, who let them use her cottage for their trysts, for a fee. Here Wilkes moved full speed into the lush descriptions of sexual awakening on a ripe-for-romance young girl:

> There are women who are driven into sin by the very necessities of their natures. To such as these, when they fall into soft transgression, we must accord some lenient allowance, and measure their lapses with a rule which will balance their temptations against their powers of restraint. The spark which will set fire to tow, will make no sensible impression upon flint. The warmth which melts the quicksilver, and makes it overflow the zenith, will not start a globule to the surface of a vase of water. The touch which fevers the impatient pulse, and sends it bounding to the verge of ecstasy, will fall without a thrill on tempered veins. Had the lovely Dorcas been

the flint, or the limpid element to which we have alluded, our philosophy would not have been put to these justifying contrasts.

But, alas, she was not, and when the arms of her old playfellow
clasped her waist, and held her close as he expressed a still warmer
welcome on her lips, she summoned no prudery for her defence, but
let the hot flash of passion shrivel all resisting sense, and record its
triumph in a languid sigh.[24]

Wilkes's assertion that a naturally passionate woman driven to sin
deserves more forgiveness than a reserved prude probably reflects a
shrewd assessment of what his own (mainly male) readers of the *Police
Gazette* most wanted to hear. It gave men permission to go the limit and
beyond with a sexually excitable woman.

Wilkes has Sumner leave town, fleeing a shipowner whose ship he had
jumped. The fictional Dorcas, now fully awakened to her sexual powers,
continued to use Nancy as a go-between for letters in her flirtations with
other young men of Augusta. Her next serious lover, however, was
"Sp——g," a handsome cashier from a Portland bank, who visited
Augusta, met Dorcas in church, and soon began to see her at Nancy's
cottage.

We need not follow the fallen girl through the passages of this
amour, nor trace the various stages of her lascivious declension.
Her digressions from propriety continued and increased, until they
at length became so flagrant, that the town was filled with rumors
of her shame. These rumors, at length, forced themselves upon the
ears of the kind family which had done so much for her, and trembling with consciousness of guilt, she was summoned to answer in
her defence. Her tears and protestations gained her an acquittal
for a time, but subsequent disclosures, which were soon afterwards
brought forward, confirmed all previous reports of her inconti-
nence, and with a rebuke which cost her sorrowful reprovers more
agony perhaps, than it inflicted on herself, she was turned from the
hospitable roof which had so long protected her, to find a shelter in
that hollow world whose vanities and vices, she had so weakly chosen for her counsellors.[25]

This passage by Wilkes is nothing more than an ornate rewriting of
the judge's letter of April 20, 1836, with trembles, tears, and agony added
for effect. It seems very unlikely that Wilkes actually had an independent
source of information for the Sumner story. (If he had, there would have

been more new information about Dorcas as well.) He certainly stretched to make it appear as if he had new evidence, however. A chapter-long sub-plot follows Sumner on his sea voyage to the Philippines in a ship called the *Cyrus*, where Sumner falls into a brawl, gets involved in the killing of a Jesuit, lands in jail, and is bailed out by the American consul. It is precisely at this point in the story, when the fantastic yet specific details begin to sound most like a popular adventure fiction, that Wilkes inserted the footnote testifying to the scrapbook of letters supporting every detail, as if to allay a reader's creeping doubt. But mainly he was just enlivening a story with vivid particulars. A search of the manuscript records of the American consulate in the Philippines shows that the appointed consul on duty in the 1820s left his post for the years from 1825 to 1829 for health reasons, and no one took his place.[26] Clearly Wilkes invented that aspect of the story.

Nothing of this Sumner story can be authenticated, except that Sumner True did grow up near Dorcas Doyen. (And the families were acquainted, probably well acquainted. It was Sumner's maternal uncle who sold Dorcas's father the small piece of land for $15 that Doyen sold to Albert Dillingham within a week for $145.)[27] Unlike the fictional Sumner, who died—in Wilkes's version—in a fight with another of Helen's lovers in Portland, Sumner True appears to have had a very uneventful life. He was born in Temple, he appears in the 1850 census for that town with a wife and infant son, and he was buried there in 1862, when he was forty-eight. Oddly, he never left a trace in any of the census or land conveyance records of Maine before 1850. Possibly he was out of the state for much of his young adult life—roaming the high seas, conversing with prostitutes, dreaming (here, like Wilkes, we claim the liberty of imagination) of the beautiful playmate who had captured his heart back in the village of Temple. Or maybe he was just a poor Maine renter.

But maybe it was Dorcas, instead, whose imagination ran free and created Wilkes's story line. Maybe she remembered Sumner True as a first crush and confided him to her scrapbook. The added touch of black Nancy had a plausible ring to it; Cassy and Fred had their black servant woman, the Westons had the black Foye families next door, and the Williams daughters off at boarding school spoke of "black Jerusha" bringing them supplies and letters from Augusta.[28] And apparently there was a black man in Augusta who worked at Barker's Mansion House on State Street who functioned as a procurer; on his 1837 visit with Bridge, Hawthorne witnessed a sad exchange between this "negro, whom they call 'the doctor,' a crafty-looking fellow, one of whose occupations is that of pimp," and a bedraggled stranger seeking his estranged wife who had become "one of a knot of whores."[29] Maybe Dorcas embroidered these elements into a creative rewriting of her early history inscribed in her scrapbook. Wilkes perhaps borrowed it, then, just as he had also in fact borrowed the set of letters and the murder weapon from the police archives.

A final candidate for the seducer of Dorcas Doyen is Judge Weston himself. No one at the time ever suggested such a thing; besmirching honorable and highly placed judges could be a risky and libelous business. New York editor James Gordon Bennett condemned the bigwigs of Maine, but he notably omitted judges and lawyers in his list of possible Jewett seducers: "The cashiers, or colonels, or majors, or generals, or great men of the state of Maine destroyed the virtue of Ellen," he railed in his April 25 article blasting the Maine newspaper coverage of the crime. But why assume that a judge, simply because of his exalted station in life, was incapable of falling into the conceit of imagining that an attractive servant girl would be eager to please him. (Indeed, one Portland newspaperman had run an article two weeks before the Jewett murder specifically detailing the alleged sexual sins of some highly placed but unnamed Maine judges.)[30] Consider, then, the evidence on Judge Weston, which is admittedly slender, beyond the simple fact that she lived in his house and worked for him.[31]

Dorcas's first love built the relationship on the reading and discussion of books; it was Judge Weston who let her rummage in his library, and he was known particularly as "a great reader" and a man "of easy conversational talent."[32] He was a playful and young-at-heart man. He told Anne Royall he was forty when she met him in 1827, when in fact he was forty-five; and she remarked in her book that "I would suppose him at once not more than twenty-five—he is the youngest-looking man his age in America." Mrs. Royall first saw him holding court in Wiscasset, Maine, a week or so before her visit to the Weston house in Augusta. He was hearing a case involving a man charged with turning his deranged wife out-of-doors and taking in another woman. Mrs. Royall thought Judge Weston "was cool, keen and dignified," "though young." She was impressed with his concern for the wronged and deserted wife (although, just as likely, his real sympathies were with the actual plaintiffs in the case, the overseers of the poor for the town now responsible for the care and feeding of the abandoned wife). "Judge Western is low of stature, very young for a judge, his countenance naturally bright, open and benevolent, his gestures free and natural, as a judge, he commands great attention—his voice is soft and musical, and above all speakers he has the happiest felicity of expression, few states can boast a more able judge." Mrs. Royall formed snap judgments that usually stuck, so when Weston a week later took her to Congressman Gage's house in Augusta and then tiptoed out the door to avoid her as she sat alone in the parlor, even then the testy woman continued to hold a good opinion of him.[33]

Judge Weston seems to have stuck by Dorcas even when the first reports of her immorality were bruited about town, choosing to disbelieve them at first. Perhaps he was fond of her and felt protective; or perhaps it was in his own interest to ignore or deny the rumors as long as possible. Even though she was under the age of majority by a year, and his contracted servant, the judge chose not to take any legal action against the man who had seduced her, although he was perfectly within his rights to do so. He knew the law and had applied it in court, yet he did not even counsel Dorcas to pursue a breach of promise or seduction case. Surely he could have helped her a great deal with such legal remedies; sympathetic, wronged young women could collect rather munificent sums. If, however, the man was someone Dorcas should have known absolutely would not marry her, say because he was already married, then her chances for successful suit were small indeed. Or if the guilty man was someone the judge felt a greater obligation to protect—a son, a son-in-law, or himself—then it becomes understandable that he would set aside legal remedies and simply let the girl leave, or discharge her.

Unfortunately, very little can be learned about Dorcas Doyen in the year and a half after she left the Westons and before she arrived in New York City. The youthful editors of the *Augusta Age* seemed to know the most about her career in these years: she went to Portland three months after leaving the Westons, they said, and lived in a house of ill fame under the name of Maria Stanley. A "short time later" she moved on to Boston, where she lived five or six months as Helen Mar, and from thence she journeyed to New York City. Evidently, they cared enough (and had the means) to keep track of the girl's travels and abodes. The only documentary evidence that supports any part of this story is a notice in the post office's monthly unclaimed letters column that appeared in the *Portland Eastern Argus*. In February 1832, two letters addressed to Dorcas Doyen had not been picked up.[34] Dorcas's appearance in the Portland paper's list means that she probably left for Boston shortly before that date. It also establishes that she maintained a correspondence with a person or persons who knew her under her birth name.

Where Dorcas Doyen lived in Augusta those three months after the fall of 1830 is a mystery. There might well have been someone like the fictional black Nancy willing to take her into her cottage. Or perhaps her lover sheltered her for a time; but four of the five candidates lived with families, and it is probably not too much to assume that those families would not be warm to the idea of helping Dorcas in her hour of need. (The fifth suspect, Sumner, can't even be placed in Augusta with any confidence.) In Portland and Boston there were plenty of places a girl newly arrived in a city could go—houses of ill fame—but Augusta seems to have had no acknowledged brothels. There were women who sold sex; Hawthorne's encounter with the black "doctor" of the Mansion House incident in 1837 shows that a sex market operated, to a degree, in this town. On that occasion, the black man led the inquiring estranged husband off to the "haunt" of his erstwhile wife, so such women had "haunts"; maybe one of them was willing to harbor Dorcas for three months.[35]

In Portland Dorcas became Maria Stanley and joined in brothel life immediately.[36] George Wilkes's serialized story filled in many details of Dorcas's career in Portland and Boston, but there is no reason to credit anything he wrote.[37] The real story of Dorcas Doyen from 1830 to 1831 cannot be recovered. Portland's brothels were clustered on two streets on Munjoy Hill just to the north of downtown, and presumably she found her way to these quickly. (Munjoy took its name from a British settler of the seventeenth century, but in the 1830s it was often called Mount Joy Hill, in humorous honor to the brothels lining Larch and North Streets.)[38] Portland in the late 1820s was not a joyful place to be a prostitute, however. On three occasions in 1825 alone rioters threatened prostitutes and pulled down some of their houses; the culprits were said to be "idle roaring boys and raw Irishmen," and in one struggle guns were fired and a man in the street was killed.[39] By the late 1820s male violence was getting to be more generalized, threatening any women out on the streets. The *Eastern Argus* editorialized about the nasty "corner boys" in 1827, "full grown boys" who collected into menacing groups in the evening, singing obscene songs and using profane language. For the "safety, convenience, and feelings of the female community," the paper implored that some authority must be found to restrain the young men, since the customary restraint, "a sense of shame, or regard for his own character," obviously was no longer doing the job.[40]

In 1830, just before Dorcas arrived, newspaper articles continued to complain about street violence and added a new note of concern about the swelling brothel population. The *Portland Daily Courier* carried a series of articles about unofficial and official raids on brothels, about disorderly women promenading openly, and an unusual letter from a girl on Mount Joy Hill defending her choice of occupation.[41] Augusta banks and stores carried the Portland papers for casual readers, so it is entirely likely that Dorcas knew of the public contestations over brothel life in Portland before she ever left Augusta, in that fall of 1830.

Perhaps the flurry of newspaper stories attracted her to life in Portland, giving her a sense of alternatives in life. Prostitution was one; the other option was to start over someplace new, perhaps in a town where distant relatives lived, and claim both freedom from continued servanthood and respectability. Jewett took the route to prostitution.

None of the pamphlet and newspaper accounts of Jewett's descent into prostitution considered her career a freely made choice. The unquestioned assumption was that a ruined girl had no alternative; there was simply no recovery from loss of virtue. One postmurder Jewett pamphlet spelled out with precision the ironbound convention that would force an intelligent, sensitive woman to embrace prostitution over return to family. (This speech, put in the mouth of Jewett and delivered to her grieving parents, came from a wholly fictional pamphlet published in Boston in 1836.)

> You may wish me to return to my home, repent and be happy; that I can never do—such is my sensibility of feeling that it seems as though I would rather sink into my grave with all the guilt upon my head! In such a case my former friends would slight and neglect me, my invidious enemies would triumph in my ruin; the neighboring tea-tables would resound my disgrace. I should be the scorn of my own sex. The virtuous would shun my company as a dangerous infection; the eyes of modesty would be averted at my approach; and the cheeks of innocency redden with a blush.—Men of honor would treat me with neglect, and libertines with saucy freedom.[42]

This fiction reflected the presumption that sexual initiation resulting from seduction carried lifelong consequences, including gossip and scorn from women and neglect or, far worse, insolence and presumption from men. The fallen woman was contaminated, like an infected person, and the virtuous could never be safe near her again. Recovery from the taint was impossible because men would somehow know, sense her stain, and forever target her as a loose woman. Although these words came from a fictionalized account of Jewett, they articulated the dynamics of social ostracism that were supposed to operate, to separate the female moral leper from innocent womanhood.

But why? *Why* did some presume that the loss of virginity thoroughly disgraced an unmarried woman? To ask this question is to challenge a cultural assumption so powerful in the 1830s that no one writing about Dorcas/Helen in 1836 ever paused to question it. The language of theft, of ruin, of loss of jewels and treasure, explicitly conveyed the conviction that a woman's value was permanently destroyed by a single instance of unchaste behavior.

This had not always been so, as recently as thirty years before in Augusta. Premarital sex was surprisingly commonplace in the years up to about 1800. Across New England, and indeed in rural old England as well, the proportion of brides pregnant on their marriage day topped up in the range of 30 to 40 percent.[43] (Premarital pregnancies provide a lower-bound measure of fornicating couples, of course, since these data only capture the instances of intercourse that resulted in pregnancy.) Augusta-Hallowell was the home of midwife Martha Ballard, who from 1785 to 1812 delivered 814 babies in her twenty-seven-year career, 106 of them to first-time mothers. Out of the 106 first births, 38 percent were children conceived out of wedlock. Historian Laurel Ulrich, whose biography of Martha Ballard explores the contours of sex and marriage in late-eighteenth-century Augusta, found that half the town's selectmen in those years experienced prenuptial pregnancies among their children.[44] But three-quarters of the illicit pregnancies were soon regularized by marriage vows, and legal actions, if any, were mainly confined to a small number of bastardy suits.[45]

Late-eighteenth-century Augusta was no freethinking society where young people could follow their hearts and desires without fear of consequences—far from it. A long tradition of Puritanism in New England assured that, for the unmarried, chastity was the preferred state, and fornication remained defined as a sin, even as the penalties for it underwent gradual relaxation. Virginity and monogamy formed the cornerstones of patriarchal society, deemed desirable in early America for the order they imposed on inheritance patterns, on dependable care of the young, and on protection of women from male violence. The sexual regulation of women was valued for the way it ordered the social relations of the sexes. But somehow, in a small but significant way, some element of the traditional courtship and marriage system was slightly askew for a time, so that the customary sequence of marriage followed by sexual initiation was momentarily reversed for over a third of all courting couples. The sin of fornication did not pass unnoticed, but neither did it exact from women enormous legal, religious, economic, or emotional penalties. A courting couple who engaged in intimacies and became pregnant fairly routinely got married. The cohesion of the community and specifically the power of older generations over young men were still strong enough to enforce an outcome that minimized single motherhood and the associated expenses that might fall to the community. And even for young women who bore bastards, public penalties and shaming techniques were slight in the late eighteenth century. It was not uncommon for an unwed mother to make a reasonably good marriage to another man a few years later.[46]

This was no epidemic of adolescent pregnancy; the couples were typically at the point of making a marriage decision, being indistinguishable in their age and station in life from other marrying couples whose first child came a more respectable nine months after the wedding. Perhaps young women were granting greater liberties to their young men, secure in the knowledge that marriage would surely follow, if not completely voluntarily, then by the pressure of the community. Granting premarital intimacies could be advantageous for a woman, in fact, as a way to demonstrate powerfully her commitment to a courting man. A young woman probably had to time her consent with shrewd calculation: to yield too soon might send the wrong message and increase the risk of single-motherhood. On their part, young men optimistic about their prospects in life for supporting a family might be more accepting of the risks of pregnancy in asking for sexual favors. The economic climate of the late eighteenth century in towns like Augusta supported an encouraging view of family formation and support. Virginity was being forsaken, but since most couples wound up marrying each other soon thereafter, the regulation of women's sexuality was really not threatened, and patriarchy was undisturbed. The minimization of church discipline for fornication seemed to give at least tacit consent to the sexually expressive courting behaviors of youth.[47]

By the 1820s, this tolerant attitude toward female virginity had been reversed, and the New England premarital pregnancy rate had plummeted. Not one of the nineteenth-century sons or daughters in the dozen most prominent families of Augusta had a first child less than nine months after marriage.[48] Sexual expressiveness in courtship still seems to have been allowed; the articles in the *Maine Patriot* wrote indulgently of romance and passionate feelings. Nevertheless, young women more successfully avoided the risks of premarital pregnancy. Any young woman's strategy for landing a marriage partner now had to take into account the remarkable mobility of the male population brought about by the commercial and transportation advances of the 1820s. A man who was granted sexual liberties too quickly, before his heart was fully captured, might simply leave town and thereby avoid the community pressures to marry.[49]

But how does a community raise up barriers to long-accepted habits? One way was to emphasize that dire punishments would befall sexual sinners. (Running Dorcas Doyen out of town in 1830, for example, furthered that goal.) Stories and novels featuring seduction plots gained renewed popularity in the early nineteenth century, featuring women victims who typically suffered from madness or death after lustful men ruined them.[50] In a case of life imitating art, seduction suits in court reinforced the message; large sums of money measured a woman's ruination. Both law cases and seduction fictions accorded an increased value to female virginity. Underlying both was an assumption that women's sexual desires were not nearly as strong as men's; a belief in women's general "passionlessness" took hold. Seduction happened because of male lust and female innocence; women's lower sexual energy effectively diminished their responsibility for sex.

The illogical part in this formulation was that the presumed innocent victim, the passionless woman, bore the brunt of the social punishment. But at the same time, it was an effective formulation: it gave the party thought to be least likely to succumb to sexual temptation the extra motivation to put the brakes on any illicit behavior. The outcome of irreparable damage to a woman's reputation and prospects powerfully discouraged her from agreeing to illicit sex.

Historians have charted this sea change in attitudes about female sexual desire in arenas beyond seduction law. Historian Nancy Cott has traced these ideas from English evangelicals whose message took hold in the United States in the years after 1800, arguing that "passionlessness" was attractive to women precisely because it awarded them the high moral ground in relationships with men. Strengthening women's bargaining power in the terrain of consensual sex, passionlessness not only reduced the bastardy rate but also contributed to the early decline in the marital fertility rate that so dramatically fell between 1800 and 1900.[51] What has been less often remarked, however, is that positing a lowered sexual desire in women recast sex as a wholly masculine prerogative, an activity that enhanced male mastery and power. This helps explain why many people not influenced by moral evangelism could also subscribe to the new cultural ideal. As Dorcas Doyen so effectively demonstrated with her self-told tale of seduction, the treasure of female virginity and slumbering sexual desire could be immensely attractive to many men as well.

CHAPTER ELEVEN

Adolescent Clerks

SEDUCTION FICTIONS as well as seduction lawsuits of the early nineteenth century centered on women's struggles to retain virginity against the entreaties of manipulative men. The culture was steeped in the conviction that chaste and respectable women experienced negligible sexual desire and could easily become the unwitting victims of lustful men. Rarely was male sexual interest itself called into question or rendered problematic. Some moralists challenged and condemned exploitative styles of masculine sexuality, but they conducted no campaigns on behalf of diminished male desire. However, acknowledging the existence of male sexual energy did not mean that parents condoned its expression in unmarried youth. Desire was one thing; sexual activity quite another. (Even among the married, sexual restraint was held up as a valued goal.) A new apprehensiveness over prostitution's effect on men accompanied and paralleled the panic over the seduction of respectable women. Just as women of supposedly negligible sexual appetite could be duped by bad men, so virile but innocent young men could easily be led astray by bad women. A middle-class ideal of male virtue and control took shape in precisely the years of the rising tide of prostitution, and a spate of advice books in the 1830s took specific aim at young men living away from home.

There was little need in this culture to resort to deep psychological portraits to explain a male's lapse from virtue. Temptation abounded, and male chastity advocates sought not to deny the power of sex but to portray it as overwhelmingly dangerous. The advice books sound prudish to our ears, but they actually grew out of a realistic assessment of the enticements facing men. Written mainly by ministers, doctors, and health reformers, the books vigorously promoted the maintenance of chastity and warned of "the monstrous tide of depravity and dissipation" awaiting youth in the city.[1] William A. Alcott, physician and schoolteacher, wrote more than a half dozen moral-advice books in the 1830s on right living, including *The Young Man's Guide* (1834), which warned that "the whole race of young men in our cities, of the present generation, will be ruined" because of prostitution, which led to "disease and premature death."[2] Health and diet reformer Sylvester Graham toured major cities between 1832 and 1837 delivering his "Lecture to Young Men on Chastity," which was finally published in 1834, passing through ten more editions throughout the 1830s and 1840s. Graham, Alcott, and others knew that big cities posed sexual dangers precisely because unsupervised youth there confronted a highly visible traffic in illicit sex.

The understanding that male sexual temptation was omnipresent helps explain why the newspapers paid very little attention to Richard P. Robinson in the weeks immediately after the murder. In fact, all the young men whose names surfaced at the trial or in accounts of the Jewett murder were ignored, as if their involvement in the world of illicit sex commanded little interest, posed no problems, and piqued no curiosity in the public. The relative silence about the details of Robinson's life is especially striking. Helen Jewett, the mystery girl, commanded center stage, feeding public fascination with questions about her reputed early innocence, her sexuality, her complicity in sin, and her contested position as a victim worthy of public sympathy. Perhaps the spotlight stayed on Jewett because newspaper writers were men, and their presumed readership was also male. Also, and perhaps more to the point, Jewett did not have a vigilant family or a lawyer on retainer to defend her reputation, erect barriers around her past, and keep her out of the newspapers. The protective circle the lawyerly Westons drew around themselves excluded their former servant. Robinson instantly hired a top-notch New York attorney, Ogden Hoffman, who kept his client's profile as low as he could.

The newspapers were remarkably uninterested in delving into Robinson's past. This was quite in keeping with the prevailing journalistic practice of acquiring facts from official sources rather than by investigative reporting. Yet investigating Jewett seemed warranted by the many puzzling and contradictory stories about her background.

The *Herald* lavished column after column on Jewett, but of her accused killer said only that "Robinson is a native of one of the Eastern States, aged 19, and remarkably handsome, and has been for some time past in the employ of Joseph Hoxie, 101 Maiden-lane."[3] The *Transcript* at first misreported his name as "Francis P. Robinson," son of a man of the same name from Durham, Connecticut, a confusion probably arising from Robinson's brothel alias, "Frank." Within a day it had the name right, but that paper never specified his employer, his workplace, his job, or his age, instead preferring general assertions about "the high respectability of the family and connexions."[4] The *Sun* was scarcely less reticent. Robinson, it reported, "is a young man of excellent general character, fine, manly appearance, and most respectable connexions, not yet twenty years of age, and was much esteemed by his employer, Mr. Hoxie, and many others whom we yesterday heard say they had known him long and intimately. We understood he was from Maine."[5]

Emphasizing Robinson's respectability accomplished two things. First, as shorthand for his class position, it also conveyed assumptions about his moral character. And second, it highlighted the mystery of the crime (and thus sold papers), because of the presumed incongruity of a person of reputable character committing a murder. The notion that the young man was respectable and had "respectable connexions" was established—or, rather, asserted—by his employer. Joseph Hoxie vouched for him, and to many that was enough.

Outside New York, where Hoxie's name carried no weight, it was easier to challenge the assumption that Robinson's respectable family connections elevated his character. The *Philadelphia Ledger*, for instance, was a newspaper founded by artisan printers disdainful of wealth. A penny paper on the model of the *Sun* and the *Transcript*, the *Ledger* noted in connection with Robinson's arrest that the word "respectable" had become debased in modern usage. Nowadays, the paper editorialized, "respectable" really simply meant "wealthy": in the marriage market, for example, parents who said they desired a respectable man for their daughter really only meant a husband with money. No longer were there moral connotations in the word, because the wealthy were generally no longer moral, the editors wrote; sons of rich or comfortable families were especially prone to immorality, having the idle time, the money, and the lack of ambition to get into serious trouble. "American youth are corrupt, deplorably corrupt," said the *Ledger*, "and we find the causes in a false standard of respectability, want of early moral education, want of proper occupation, and vicious example."[6]

In reality, Hoxie was not at all wealthy, nor was Robinson's Connecticut family; but neither were they poor or struggling. The clerk's family background was similar to that of thousands of other young men of the New England countryside who had come to New York City to make their fortune. The Robinson family had lived in Durham for over 150 years; the American progenitor came to Hartford in 1640 in the first wave of Puritan migration into the Connecticut River Valley, and the second generation moved on to found Durham. The village remained small all those years, drawing on farming, shoemaking, and tavern keeping for its economic base. In 1830 the U.S. Census counted only 1,116 inhabitants, which was 14 fewer than in the 1810 census. Small and stagnant as it was, it was not an out-of-the-way backwater. Durham sat on the main stage road between Boston and New York, and in the early nineteenth century the immediate stretch of road through town was a privately owned toll road, the New Haven Turnpike. Many stagecoaches and freight wagons passed through daily, and all stopped in Durham because it was a toll collection point; as many as a half dozen stagecoaches might be lined up all at once near the hotel at the town's center, to pay the toll, refresh the passengers, and change horses.[7] Durham's children could plainly see it was an easy place to leave, which is exactly what most of them did when they reached young adulthood.

Robinson's father, also named Richard, was sixty-three in 1836. He owned substantial property in and around the town. The family house stood about a half mile west of the turnpike on the old Quarry Hill Road (now called the Wallingford Road), on the bank of the Coginchaug River at the edge of the Durham Meadows. The elder Robinson was a farmer, but he probably earned more money buying and selling land and negotiating loans than he did from raising crops and livestock; conveyance records for Durham show that over the course of his adult life he engaged in sixty-six sales and ninety-nine purchases of local land parcels.[8] (Some of these apparent purchases were undoubtedly loans Robinson made, secured by property deeded to Robinson for the life of the loan, a common financial practice in New England.) His eight terms in the Connecticut state legislature further demonstrate his substantial standing with his neighbors.[9]

Young Richard was the eighth child and first son in his family; four more children followed him. The elder Robinson had six daughters with his first wife, Tabitha, who died in 1811, and then three daughters and three sons with a wife two decades younger than he. Richard was the second-born in the new family set. His mother, Cynthia Parmelee, came from the adjacent town of Killingworth. One of her brothers had just a few years before married the eldest daughter of the senior Richard Robinson, and yet another Parmelee married the third oldest in 1819.[10] The families were thus closely intertwined, and Cynthia must have been more peer than stepmother to her stepdaughters, two of whom were also her sisters-in-law. All that the New York papers ever reported about Robinson's parents was that they were aged and gravely ill with grief on account of his trouble. His mother never came to New York to visit him during his incarceration, although she sent him letters.[11] Attending the trial appears to have been men's business; his father came, along with an older sister's husband, most likely the man who was brother to Cynthia Parmelee Robinson.

Little can be learned of Richard's childhood. Perhaps there really was not much of high interest for the New York papers to sleuth out, had they even been so inclined. Durham's nineteenth-century town historian, William Fowler, recalled that wrestling was a popular boys' sport in his youth, and the town champ was "sometimes laid on his back by a young Robinson," of whom there were several—Richard, his younger brothers, and an assortment of cousins. This scrap of information suggests that Robinson family boys had gained a reputation for being physically vigorous and fully part of the "boy culture" of the antebellum Northeast—a stage of middle childhood where boys escaped the domestic hearth and gave vent to aggressive yet still friendly impulses.[12] Six common schools met Durham's needs to educate its youth in basic skills. Each consisted of a one-room building accommodating seventy or eighty male pupils of all ages during the winter session. (Girls attended the summer sessions.) The students sat at plank benches and writing desks and struggled to learn the rudiments of reading, spelling, grammar, and arithmetic with goose-quill pens. At about age twelve, the brightest boys then graduated to the Academy on the town's central green, presided over by teachers Benjamin Coe and Gaylord Newton.[13] Richard P. Robinson likely attended the Academy, since he had learned enough Latin to add flourishes in that ancient language to his letters to Helen Jewett. But he did not stay past age fourteen, when most boys finished schooling and began an apprenticeship.

Still, like Helen Jewett, Robinson had access to books in Durham. Durham's greatest claim to fame was having one of the first public libraries in the entire country. Founded in 1733, just two years after Benjamin Franklin had started Philadelphia's first subscription library, it was a matter of great communal pride.[14] Self-education further prospered with the founding of a local lyceum society in the late 1820s, affording members a chance to hold debates and develop skills in public declamation. The first debate, held in 1829 when Richard Robinson was twelve, took up the burning political topic of Indian removal, an ambitious plan proposed by the newly elected Andrew Jackson to relocate eastern Indians to lands west of the Mississippi River.[15] Durham may have been a tiny village, but its male citizens were very much a part of the larger world of Jacksonian-era politics.

Ministers of New England Congregational churches provided another route to education by providing intellectual and moral training for the youth of a town. Very often the minister kept a Sabbath school and also tutored college-bound boys in Greek and Latin. But Durham had a long and very unhappy relationship with its minister. It seems highly unlikely that the Reverend David Smith provided any moral or spiritual mentoring to young Richard in his formative years.

Smith was a rigid enforcer of church discipline; he brooked no mercy when it came to Sabbath violations, once excommunicating a farmer for hurriedly harvesting his fall crop when a severe Sunday storm threatened to ruin it entirely. The Robinson family came in for more trouble than most. In 1801 Reverend Smith took complaints against James and Amy Robinson, then in their late sixties and the grandparents of Richard P. Robinson. More unspecified complaints against them surfaced in 1802, and Smith's disciplinary committee "withdrew their watch and care over them as Christian brethren," or, in other words, expelled them from the church. (Over three extremely troubled years, 1804 to 1806, Reverend Smith expelled 18 people from his church. In such a small town—approximately 150 households—18 expulsions indicate a serious fracturing of the covenanted community.) Tabitha Robinson, the first wife of Richard P.'s father, was charged with a "breach of the covenant" in 1805; and when she died in 1811, at age thirty-four, Smith entered the cryptic notation "d—nk—d" next to her name in his register of deaths. The notation appeared against two or three decedents' names each year; in one place the word "drunk" appeared, and in another, "hard drinker."[16] Smith not only kept vital statistics in his register, as did most New England ministers, he also entered the data to construct moral statistics from the permanent church record.

The Reverend Smith "was not afraid of making enemies," according to an unusually blunt local informant who contributed recollections to an 1884 county history; "there were threats, and, it was thought, actual danger, of personal violence."[17] (The informant did not specify whether the threats of violence emanated from or were directed at the Reverend Smith. Even so, to have reported this much about the minister registered an extraordinary departure from the usual bland, filiopietistic stories of early town history that are the hallmark of the late-nineteenth-century county histories.)

For thirty-three years Smith hung on to his pulpit, intimidating some townspeople and probably angering them all. Two small rival religious societies, one Methodist and the other Episcopalian, began meeting in the 1800s to 1810s. Composed of castoffs from Reverend Smith's Congregational church, neither was large enough to afford a minister. For over thirty years, the embittered and mean-spirited Reverend Smith battled his congregation, until in 1832 the members finally got the courage to dismiss him. Smith nursed his grievances, kept his records of moral lapses, and bitterly contested his dismissal. Clearly he was not the sort of minister to steady a rambunctious youth or prepare the juvenile seedbed of Richard Robinson's soul for a spiritual awakening.

This sorry background of religious strife explains a tantalizing tidbit of information reported in July of 1836 by the *Illuminator,* a moral reform newspaper published in Boston. Soon after the Jewett murder, a passenger who stopped in Durham while traveling on the Boston stage line to New York boldly inquired about the Robinsons' religious standing and reported back to the *Illuminator* that the family was said to be complete infidels back two generations, and that Richard had never been sent to Sabbath school.[18] To a moral reformer, this explained all; it suggested an irresponsibly irreligious family that neglected the fundamental moral training of youth. The Durham source—perhaps toll keeper, liveryman, hotel owner, or barmaid—had found a way to explain to inquisitive passersby the town's infamous bad boy. Perhaps the source was close to the truth. But the gossiper neglected to add that the same might have been said of any number of disaffected Durham families, turned from the path of active Congregationalism by the embittered Reverend Smith.

The press sought out none of these meager details about Robinson's hometown and youth. (The one exception, the *Illuminator*'s brief snippet, was submitted by a reader who learned of it by happenstance and who understood its evangelical newsworthiness.) Even the father's service in the Connecticut state legislature was not noted in New York. The minimal treatment of Robinson in the New York papers perhaps was partly due to deference to Joseph Hoxie, rising local politician, or shrewd news management by the lawyer Ogden Hoffman, but mainly it arose from the fact that newspapers did not generally undertake investigative reporting on their own.

The young men boarding at Mrs. Moulton's or employed at Hoxie's store were not named in the paper until they testified at trial, and even then nothing was said about them as individuals. Neither were they interviewed nor their opinions sought. This was true even for George P. Marston (Bill Easy), Robinson's chief rival for Helen Jewett's affections, whose handkerchief was found under her pillow. Not only did the New York papers ignore him, his hometown paper in Newburyport, Massachusetts, ran the full transcript of the trial over a week's time in early June, printing young Marston's testimony verbatim, without ever pointing out that the George P. Marston giving testimony was a local youth clerking in New York. Did the editor of the *Newburyport Daily Herald* simply not realize there was a very considerable local angle? Not a chance: Newburyport was a small-sized town, population seven thousand, with a tight and entrenched local elite which included the Marstons at the center. The paper devoted much space to the trial, day after day well after the trial ended, both reprinting other papers' commentary and—significantly—engaging in considerable original analysis of its own. Likely the editor shielded the local family out of deference even as he answered a special hunger in town to keep abreast of the story, precisely because a local family was involved. It was simply not newsworthy, or seemly, somehow, for newspapers to enlighten readers about the motivations and behaviors of the respectable young men implicated in this crime.

The family of Judge Stephen Marston, young George's father, lived in a very large three-story Federal-style house at 33 Green Street in Newburyport, a small port city north of Boston. A Vermont native, the judge had graduated from Dartmouth in 1811, read law in Salem under the famous Daniel A. White, married White's daughter, and set up a practice in Newburyport. His oldest son, George Phillips, was born in 1818; three more sons and a daughter quickly followed. Stephen Marston was one of only six lawyers in town, and his local prominence was manifested in his continued reelection to eight annual terms in the Massachusetts General Court, the state's legislative body, during the 1820s. He also served as town selectman for three years and as judge of the Newburyport Police Court, a position he held from 1833 to 1855. During the 1830s Marston engaged in several high-risk business ventures: he was co-owner of at least seven ships, a trustee for a savings institution, president of the Newburyport Bank, and president of the Newburyport Steam Cotton Company, a textile factory built near the town's wharf. None of these businesses fared well in the anxious economy of the mid-1830s, and the bank and the cotton factory went into receivership in the recessionary years after the Panic of 1837.[19]

Money troubles plagued the Marston family enough to keep the two oldest sons from going to college, but not enough to drive them from their splendid house. Adolescent mischief making also plagued them. In August 1834, George, age sixteen, and two other boys were arrested for setting fire to a one-story schoolhouse on Green Street, up the block from the Marston home. After a trial in the Court of Common Pleas, two (including George) were found not guilty by a jury, and the third had charges dropped. In this instance the Newburyport paper did not engage in self-censorship out of deference to the family, probably because everyone in town knew who they were; the trial generated great interest, the paper reported, and "sympathies" from many people "of both sexes." Names of the three boys at trial were printed by first initial and last name; their respectable parents were not named, sparing them out-of-town publicity. The paper editorialized that the boys were let off because of their good characters and families and because the damage was minimal. "Few believe they possessed motives in common with the midnight incendiary," said the editor; two desks were burned, but the night was wet and rainy and the building far from others, meaning the danger was slight. Even if they had been convicted, he continued, the perception of their act as a "thoughtless freak of youth" would have spared them the maximum punishment. Nevertheless, the editor issued a solemn warning about a local male youth culture needing more supervision:

> The very young men of this town have been in the habit of meeting at clubs, which have not been the best associations for youth of warm tempers, inexperienced minds, and characters not established. To the danger of these and other sources of evil, we hope, however, that their eyes are now opened.[20]

Three weeks earlier, just after the fire, the paper had run another editorial on the "Dangers of Young Men." This article echoed a local sermon expressing adult disapproval of a male youth culture surging out of control—just what the schoolhouse arson exemplified. The Reverend Dr. Beecher warned that "hot blood, unchecked imaginations, inexperience of life transport [a youth] to the midst of dangers"; "thoughtless and cruel" behavior caused parents terrible shame.[21]

At this juncture a cousin visited the Marston family and reported to her sister: "I found them in trouble at Uncle Marston's, in consequence of George's trial which was then pending, for having been engaged in setting fire to an old schoolhouse—which was rather a development of folly on his part, than of vicious propensities. But it bore distressingly on his father and mother, and I do not know when I have been happier than I was after I left, to learn he was acquitted."[22]

If Judge Marston had ever planned to send George to college, he now abruptly set him on another course. In late 1834, he shipped him as a crew member on one of his vessels, a freighter bound for New Orleans, telling the captain to show him "no special consideration."[23] The voyage proved disagreeable to George, as Judge Marston probably intended. Upon his return, George found work as a clerk in New York City and was in residence there by April 1835. At the same time, his brother Stephen, at fifteen a year younger than George, was placed in a dry-goods store in Boston, even though he had been studying Latin and Greek in anticipation of college. The parents now settled their hopes for college and a professional career on their third son, William, 14.[24] They still held up George and Stephen as good examples for William. The older brothers were steady and happy young men, their mother wrote William at boarding school. Her letter brimmed with motherly advice—avoid sugar, brush your teeth, study, be punctual and obedient. She fervently hoped

William's behavior would equal George's, whose New York landlady had reported that "he is one of the best she ever had."[25]

Unfortunately, William did not live up to his parents' expectations. He entered Dartmouth in 1841; college records reveal that he was excused from tuition on account of "poverty," so the family fortunes had sunk low indeed. He absented himself for a term in his second year and was readmitted on probation. In the fall of his third year, according to the college's disciplinary records, he and three other boys were fined five dollars each for vandalizing Franklin Hall. Judge Marston was informed "of his misdemeanors."[26] About this time, the judge wrote to George:

> Oh, George, what will become of him: He is a poor, wretched, wandering cripple and what can he do? God help him. I have done every thing I could and tried in all ways possible to have him go through college and be a man. He had good talents—but I fear he is now ruined for sure!! It may, however, and I can but hope it will lead him to a proper sense of his situation. It will either *save* him or *send him headlong to destruction*.[27]

But worse was to come for William. In 1845 he left Dartmouth for good, he wrote George, because "I got into a confounded scrape for having a *woman* in my room and before the Faculty had time to invite me to a *tete a tete* I mizzled." William felt especially bad for disappointing his father, but he also reflected on the ways that he and his brother were similar: "There seems hitherto to have been much similitude in our fortunes. We have both of us been 'unlucky Devils' and the rascally imps of darkness have delighted to *track* us."[28]

Blaming "imps of darkness" for their scrapes with women was surely a convenient way for the Marston boys to evade responsibility. But George fell into far deeper trouble in New York in 1836. His mother was very ill that summer, and she died July 30, at age fifty-two. A letter from the same cousin who had visited during the schoolhouse fire incident conveyed the Marstons' distress. (The ellipses in the letter reflect editorial decisions made by Marston descendants who compiled a laudatory family history, one that failed to mention the Jewett murder.)

> Springfield, July 13th, 1836. My dear Uncle, I thank you for writing me in this hour of your calamity, for it shows me that you do but estimate my interest in you and your family as it deserves. I have felt that you must be deeply afflicted, even before I knew that Aunt was so very ill, and since I received your letter I have thought of her and yourself continually. . . . It sometimes seems as if trials

were accumulated upon us to show us at certain seasons of our life that "surely our help is in Jehovah." I pray that both you and she may be enabled to cast all your care upon Him, feeling intimately assured by His own spirit that He "careth for you." That "whom He loveth He chasteneth."[29]

This Springfield relative had been worrying about the family's deep affliction even before learning that the mother was mortally ill. News of Marston's testimony at Robinson's trial had probably reached her before the judge's letter. One of the most alarming editorials appeared in the daily *Boston Advocate*, which wrote right at the end of Robinson's trial, "We deem it more than probable that the 'Bill Easy' who is named in the evidence as the usual Saturday night visitor of Miss Jewett, was the *real* murderer."[30] The consoling cousin mustered her sympathy to remind the Marstons that God chastens those he loves.

George Marston did not sound especially chastened in an oddly upbeat letter he wrote his father from New York in mid-August 1836, just two weeks after his mother's death. George touched on only three topics: the impressive business credentials of the young man carrying the letter for him, the news of a failure of a firm in Buffalo that did business with his firm, and his own health. "I have enjoyed perfect health since my return. I don't know the reason, but I was more unwell when home than I had been before since my first living in New York. How do you get along now? Does Aunt Charlotte stay with you yet? I hope your health is good and all the rest. Give my love to all the children and family. Your respectful and affec. son Geo. P. Marston."[31] Not a word about his mother's death, and certainly not a word about what it might be like to return to work after playing a feature role two months earlier in the biggest murder trial of the year. He confessed to being clueless about why he would be so unwell at home in Newburyport and yet in perfect health in New York. Young Marston seems to have had thick armor against strong emotion and an unusual ability to distance himself from unhappy events. He also had had a year of practice writing letters home that kept his mother in the dark about his adventures with Jewett; maybe the habit of writing false good cheer was simply hard to break.

Even in his relationship with Helen Jewett, George Marston evinced signs of being something of a dolt. He deeply admired Jewett and professed love for her; he exclaimed over her handiwork and exulted over other men denied admission to her inner circle. But he had a hard time reading her moods and catching her signals. Two undated letters illustrate his struggle to negotiate deeper emotional waters than he was accustomed to. The first one also contained the paragraphs on Harry and Mr.

Cook (quoted in chapter 7), so George was veering between dismissing Helen's ill humor toward him and gladly offering her other partners. He seems to have attributed Helen's depression solely to her troubles with Robinson, and he repeats—but does not hear—her warning that she is on the verge of discarding him completely.

> Monday evening
>
> Dearest Helen—You say in your last letter, that you write to beg my pardon for any expressions, which your *ill humor*, as you termed it, arising from disappointment and hopes long defered, might have caused you to utter calculated to wound my feelings.
>
> I was not aware that you had used any expressions of that sort, and was rather surprised at your asking my pardon. I know that I'm a dull and stupid fellow, and that I have a *blockhead*. That accounts I suppose for my not having observed your *ill humor* on Thursday evening.
>
> But though *that* escaped my notice, my thick and stupid head observed with pain that you were unhappy, and it guessed the cause. Helen! if I *could* but restore that man to your affections, if I *could* but remove the cause of your unhappiness; if I *could* but dispel the mist and uncertainty in which you are envolved; in one word if I *could* but make you happy, I should ever experience the liveliest joy, in knowing that my endeavors to render myself of some service to you, had not been wholly fruitless, and that I had been the humble cause of many happy hours. . . .
>
> I knew you was not serious when you told me that Thursday night, might be the last one which I should pass with you, for I won't believe that you could tell me *that*, and not manifest any feeling of regret at all on parting. The deprivation of your society would be a serious loss to me and one that *could not be repaired.*[32]

A second letter must have taken some courage and effort for him to write. His act of writing gains him a little higher standing than that of blockhead; after all, a self-described blockhead at least realizes his deficiencies. While the letter itself shows some degree of self-awareness, the event he describes reveals his total confusion about Jewett and his inability to comprehend her:

> Monday evening.
>
> Dear Nelly—Need I say your conduct to me this evening surprised me much. I little thought when you stood by me so long, and suffered me to keep my arm so long around your waist, that the

very next hour would see you angry with me. What under Heaven was the reason of your most inexplicable and mysterious conduct towards me, when about leaving the theatre? Have I done anything to merit such treatment from you? Has any one been endeavoring to lower me in your estimation or have you seen some one you liked so *much* better than me, that you entirely forgot you had me to bid good night. From the time I left you talking with Mary Morgan, I had been walking fore and aft, free from all unhappy thoughts. I at last saw a friend go down stairs whom I wished to see, and immediately followed him down, walking past you. I came up again in about five minutes, just in time to see you going down the opposite side. Is it possible, thought I, she can be going home without bidding me good night? but I discovered [discarded] the idea, as soon as it occurred to me, and thought you had only stepped down on the stairs a moment to speak to some friend, but after waiting a few moments and seeing nothing of you, I followed you down and met you at the door when you immediately came up, and commenced *reprimanding* me as I thought. Indeed, I know not one word you *did* say, for I was so perfectly astonished in the first place, to see you going home without appearing even to think of me, and then when I met you at the door to find out that you was angry with me, I knew not what to make of it. There were many people looking at us, and I knew it. *That* entry was too public a place for any explanation, therefore I went upstairs, expecting, if you *cared* anything about it one way or the other, that you would shortly follow me up—but I saw nothing of you after.

Please write me and let me know how I have offended, and if you consider me still your friend and welcome to your house. The most prominent bump in my character must be one relative to intruding where I am not wanted, for I would cut off my arm sooner than go more than once where I knew I was not wanted. Ever your sincere friend, W.E.[33]

These are not letters Marston would willingly have shared with parents. He was only seventeen and several months into a relationship with a woman light-years ahead of him in her ability to manage both feelings and people. Insofar as he concealed his activities at brothels and theaters from his parents, his employer, David Felt, his landlady, Mrs. Morrison, and the women at his residence who admired his pincushion, he was leading a double life. But in another sense, this life in the shadows was not really completely different from his respectable world: Marston was the same dimwit in either place. His naïveté prevented him from being fully transformed into a worldly rake or debauched libertine through his association with Jewett. Despite the strident warnings of the William Alcotts and Sylvester Grahams of the 1830s, young men like Marston and Robinson probably saw no reason to suppose that visiting the Thomas Street brothel would bring on the alarmist sequence of depravity, disease, and death predicted by the moral reformers.

One man of Helen Jewett's intimate acquaintance came far closer to fitting the fearful stereotype of degeneracy antiprostitution activists bandied about. But William H. Attree made few claims to moral rectitude in the first place, and the sin that brought on his premature death was too much drink, not illicit sex. When Attree met Jewett in 1834, on the occasion of her police complaint over being kicked at the theater, he had only been in the country for about two years. Born in Brighton, England, he immigrated to New York in about 1832. His 1849 obituary in the *Herald* (probably written by James Gordon Bennett) praised highly his retentive memory and writing skills, but also said "the greatest enemy he had was himself" due to his "morbid craving for stimulants."[34] A scathing 1841 profile of him in the *Sunday Flash*, one of the city's racy papers, called him "Oily Attree" and claimed he fled England on a jailbreak, socialized with blacks in New York, engaged in journalistic blackmail, never bathed, and drank so excessively that his nose permanently turned bright red.[35] Attree did figure in a handful of Police Court cases, often libel suits involving other newspapermen. (In one in 1835, he offered an excuse for his excessive drinking: "The printing business . . . more than any other, exhausts the physical powers of a man, as well as his mental energies," which then leads a printer to seek "artificial stimulus to recruit his powers" at the end of each week.)[36] The knifing he suffered in Hoboken at the hands of the barber John Boyd was the worst of several altercations he got into.

But when it came to Helen Jewett, the rough and coarse Attree turned mannerly and even a bit romantic. He wrote her two letters while traveling in the winter of 1835 to 1836. In the first, written from Louisville, he went on for several sentences about her name: "Ellen," he preferred to write, not "Helen," because of a beautiful and noble character, "above the usual run of common mortals," in Sir Walter Scott's *Lady of the Lake*. (Helen of Troy, from another book he presumed both had read when "young and in our prime," was not a name that befit Helen Jewett, Attree wrote, because the mythic Helen had "cuckolded her husband.") He compared Jewett to a swan

that is compelled to pass, in the course of its career, through and across some devilish dirty and impure stream (as well as very many translucent ones), yet the instant she is freed from immediate contact with them, she simply "shakes her feathers," stretches her noble pinions, and her plumage resumes its pristine purity and beauty.

Helen had taken care of some business for him in his absence, and he thanked her for it: "Accept the pure and fervent thanks of a deep-thinking, intensely feeling heart, for the numerous acts of kindness which your letter tells me that you have conferred upon me; when I read that part of it relating to the commissions which I gave you to do. I felt real mean for troubling you with such trumpery." He next asked about the "movements of Frank and B[ill]," so apparently he was in the habit of hearing gossip about these two young men from her. Attree wished that Helen could have accompanied him to make his journey "completely delightful." "On my soul, Ellen, I never knew but two women whose society I thought worthy of accepting on a journey. Jane Price was the one, and yourself is the second. You must believe me, for I cannot remember to have ever behaved so like a scoundrel or a barber's clerk as to have flattered you."[37]

In his second letter, written in late January from Texas, Attree described meeting a young American girl also named Ellen, traveling alone because her brother had been killed in "the taking of San Antonio." The girl fell ill, and he nursed her with medicines he acquired from his brother in Louisville. He planned to deliver her to New Orleans, and "may the God who made me, curse me if I harm her." "God bless you Ellen," he continued to Helen Jewett, "I long to see and talk to you, for I have seen such sights—but yet I have not yet transgressed with an Indian girl, no, nor with any other kind since I left New York, but this is not virtue, for I wish oh, how I wish I had you with me this very night."[38]

These two had known each other for nearly two years, and it sounds as if they had a lighthearted and firm friendship combined with a sexual relationship that still sparked, at least on his side. She entertained him (and privileged him) with tales of Frank and Bill, and she obliged him by running errands. He valued qualities that would make her a good traveling companion. Given the hardships of antebellum travel, these had to include an easygoing, patient, generally resilient frame of mind. (Attree reported to her he was overturned four times in mail stages on his way to Louisville.) And he still persisted in seeing her as he had back in 1834: beautiful and "pristine," her "soul unpolluted," like the swan, not in the least contaminated by the "dirty" streams she had to cross.

The worldly Attree and the callow Marston both enjoyed romantic friendships with Helen Jewett. They accepted her unconventional sex life and did not insist on one-and-only love in return from her. She made each feel special enough to make some claim to her heart, and at the same time each welcomed without a hint of jealousy her reports on other men. Marston's snit in the theater stemmed more from his sudden fear that Jewett was inexplicably ignoring him, and not from jealous anger. In their eyes, she was a good woman—generous to friends, skilled with needle and pen, blessed with the temperament for adventurous traveling, and in general fun and interesting to be with. On their end of the game, they found it advantageous to promise exclusive allegiance to her. Marston on several occasions professed his sincere dedication to Helen, and even "Oily" Attree felt it useful to write that he had not slept with anyone on his trip to Texas, not even an Indian. Helen favored devoted admirers.

Nothing about these unconventional romances conformed to the fears of the reformers who blasted seduction and prostitution as the sins of the age. Neither Marston nor Attree was a treacherous man, learning from Jewett the wily arts of seducing decent womanhood; nor were they innocent lads dragged down to destruction and disease. They paid her court— as well as money—and in return they got friendship, love, and sex, all things that they valued and enjoyed. If the culture around them insisted that prostitutes were polluted hags, and sexualized women were unnatural and suspect, they simply made an exception for Helen Jewett.

Richard P. Robinson joined Helen's circle on the same terms as Marston, Attree, and many others. But, it turned out, he was not so able or willing to sustain his assigned role.

CHAPTER TWELVE

Love Letters and Lies

I N THE BEGINNING of their relationship, Helen Jewett wrote
Richard Robinson letters of effusive compliments and seemingly
intimate self-disclosure—her usual game with clients. They met in
June 1835, and until August, her letters were full of the stuff of intense
romance: idealization of the other, confessions of private sorrows, teasing
jokes. The couple had a falling-out sometime in August, when Jewett's
letters betrayed genuine hurt and anger—the first clue that perhaps her
earlier letters conveyed more real feeling than she usually allowed herself
to attach to clients. November and December were also rocky months; the
connection faltered and actually broke off for a time. But then it resumed
in January 1836 and continued until April. The letters, forty-three from
Jewett, fifteen from Robinson, are the best evidence of the tenor and
course of their liaison.

Surprisingly, lawyers at the murder trial showed little interest in
establishing the emotional texture of their relationship. Witnesses who
could have described it—George Marston, Robinson's roommate James
Tew, his coworkers in Hoxie's store, or any of the several prostitutes who
testified—were not asked about it when on the stand. Instead, the attorneys focused narrowly on events the week and night of the murder. When
the police found the letters in her dresser and trunk, they recognized their
possible relevance, and so police magistrate Oliver Lownds took the set of
ninety letters home to read. Police also found a diary in Robinson's room.
Parts of some letters and the diary were read aloud at the restricted grand
jury proceedings, but the scribe's sketchy notes do not indicate which

ones. The district attorney tried to introduce the diary and Robinson's letters at the trial in June, but uncooperative witnesses hesitated to identify the handwriting as the clerk's. Four letters in particular seemed important to the prosecution, but the judge ruled for the defense and admitted only one, dated November 14, 1835.

The police apparently shared a few of the letters with editor James Gordon Bennett, who printed one (from William Attree) in the *Herald* on April 13. Bennett described the whole set as written in a handwriting "uncommonly beautiful—a neat running hand." Jewett's high-grade stationery featured edges variously colored green, blue, yellow, or gold.[1] Two men of the theater also acquired and spread knowledge of the letters. The managers of both the Bowery and the Park Theatres, Thomas S. Hamblin and Henry B. Harrison, somehow gained the privilege of attending the closed grand jury proceedings and heard some of the letters read there.[2] Soon after Bennett reported that "the most secret passages of all the letters and journal are quoted by many theatrical gentlemen of our town." And the letters surely made for dramatic reading: "I love you Frank—ah! you know how I love you! but do you want to know how much I can hate you? Take care, I will show you." This volatile mixture of passion and fury was recited by actors during rehearsal at the Bowery Theatre, according to Bennett, as though it were "a scene from Shakespeare."[3]

For the next dozen years, the letters gathered dust in the district attorney's files. Then George Wilkes, editor of the *National Police Gazette*, obtained them (as well as the murder weapon) when he wrote his multipart serial on Helen Jewett published over many months from 1848 to 1849. In his highly fictionalized rendering of the story, Wilkes sought to breathe life into the Jewett-Robinson romance, supply a motive, and make her murder comprehensible. But like the police magistrate and the district attorney before him, Wilkes had a hard time turning the letters to his purposes. Only a few recounted actual events, and most were undated. Several hinted at lovers' quarrels but were murky about the causes. As love letters, their chief purpose was to convey emotional states. They supplemented conversations between the lovers, instead of substituting for talk, making them even more opaque to decipher. Wilkes did not fully know what to make of them, so he reprinted a few key ones in his serialized story and then set the rest aside—until a hungry public demanded to see the actual letters themselves. The unfinished business of the Jewett case—a concern that sense had not yet been made of the murder, that evidence had been suppressed at trial—propelled many New Yorkers to urge George Wilkes to make all the letters public. So he used five issues of the weekly *Police Gazette* to run all the letters, put in as reasonable an order as he could guess at. He even mistakenly printed several over again, a clear sign that he was not fabricating them. Finally he displayed them, along with the murder weapon, in the window of the *Police Gazette*'s office on Nassau Street, and crowds reportedly showed up to gaze at them.[4] The originals of the letters are no longer in the district attorney files; all that remains is a list of them, logged in 1836. Wilkes likely threw them out after printing them, instead of returning them. (Thus they contain occasional errors not in the originals but introduced by the printing process.) The hatchet has likewise disappeared.

But of course the letters are far more revealing than George Wilkes realized. Rosina Townsend explained why forty-three written by Jewett were found among her own things. The brothel keeper reported that Jewett told her in the week before the murder that she and Frank Rivers were breaking up again, and they had agreed to return each other's letters. Apparently Jewett had not yet—or not entirely—carried out her side of the bargain, so that some fifteen of Robinson's letters were found among hers. Returning letters and gifts at the end of a love affair is a common way to speed closure, to mutually divest of symbols of affection, to recuperate and erase professions of devotion and attachment. In the case of an illicit relationship, a return of letters might also effectively prevent blackmail. With such a prospect in mind, Robinson had once already asked Helen to return or destroy his letters.[5]

Putting the letters in order poses a challenge. Only nine bear complete dates, while two others give weekday and calendrical number, which narrows the possibilities. A few refer to the season or weather; brief references to earlier letters allow some to be put in sequence. Some letters refer to theatrical events, and these can be checked against George C. D. Odell's four-volume reference book, *Annals of the New York Stage*, an exhaustive chronicle of the playbills at every New York theater in the 1820s to 1840s. And finally, the most formulaic letters by Jewett clearly date from the early days of her friendship with Robinson.

The earliest is dated June 17, 1835:

My dear Friend—When I made you a promise that I would write, you, perhaps did not expect I would, as the ladies are not apt to keep their promises when there is nothing in a tangible shape to make them binding. I shall indeed deserve censure should I be remiss in anything which would be productive of the slightest gratification to you, who have so faithfully performed the most trivial promises you ever made to me. You were truly kind to write me on

Monday morning, when your feelings must have been of a very painful nature, owing to the intelligence of your brother's illness. I sincerely hope he may recover, for you who are so kind and good do not deserve to be afflicted, and when I see you I really trust I may learn that he is convalescent.

I called upon Clara as you wished and made your apology which was perfectly satisfactory; but she would be happy to see you upon your return. To-night is Chapman's farewell benefit at the Park. I have an engagement to go with Clara; and if you get in town and my letter in season, you will have arrived most opportunely, for then we may expect the pleasure of your company. However, if you do not, of course I shall see you immediately on your return, and you do not know how much I want to see you. Believe me, I think your acquaintance a very valuable acquisition, and should dispense with your visits with much reluctance and regret; and shall never voluntarily do anything which may render me unworthy your confidence and esteem. Affectionately, H.

P.S.—I had a little private chat with the manager of a certain theatre since you have been gone; which, however, I intend to explain and obtain entire absolution for.   H.[6]

Jewett opens with her familiar gambit about writing as a promise she now keeps, even without some "tangible" sign from him to bind her promise as a proper lady might require. (Her tutelage in a lawyer's household is evident here in her application of legal give-and-take to the world of emotions.) This is her first letter to Robinson, whom she has recently met, but he has already written to her, apparently to explain a sudden trip home on account of family illness. They have already had "visits" together, and they also have a friend in common, Clara (Clara Hazard, a prostitute friend of Jewett's from Philadelphia). Throughout, Jewett maintains a polite yet still personal stance, expressing concern for the brother's illness and the hope of seeing him with Clara at the theater that night. And then comes the commanding line buried in the politeness: "you do not know how much I want to see you." Her postscript introduces a playful suggestion of jealousy, that a chat with a potential rival will require "absolution"—a sentence that conveys both a reminder that she has other men friends and a strategic concession that Richard has a claim on her now, in the form of power to grant absolution. (Thomas Hamblin, the enormously successful manager of the Bowery Theatre, had several long-term relationships with prostitutes and actresses, and on at least one occasion Jewett wrote him to praise his performance in the lead role of

Othello. Along with Harrison of the Park Theatre, Hamblin had gained admission to the grand jury proceeding.)[7]

On June 20, a few days later, she wrote Robinson again:

> I know not my Dear Frank what your idea of this chequered life may be, but to me the current of existence would be but a black and sluggish stream, if love did not guild [*sic*] its surface and impel its tide. I anticipate a further acquaintance with you will throw an additional charm over my time, and make the sands of life run more gaily than before. There is so much sweetness in that voice, so much intelligence in that eye, and so much luxuriance in that form, I cannot fail to love you. The pleasure I feel in your presence and your smile, speak of hours and nights of joy; I long to see you, to hear your conversation animate your features once again, but I must defer that pleasure until your next visit. I must now bid you an affectionate adieu. Helen.[8]

Again, a trademark Jewett letter: her unfortunate life can be refreshed if not restored by his special love. She longs to see her Dear Frank, anticipating "hours and nights of joy"—her joy, her pleasure. This sexually assertive Jewett praises his physical qualities, voice, eye, form; all this echoes her letters to other new clients. She wants to persuade him of his magnetic effect, to flatter him for his own sexual attractiveness, and to tell him he alone can lift her spirits from the inevitable sadness of her "chequered life."

Another formula letter from the early phase of late June or early July went to Robinson at his address on Maiden Lane. Jewett was still heavy on the compliments, but to avoid arousing doubts about her sincerity, she introduced her clever remark that he is too smart to be taken in by words alone. (She had used this before on Edward, nearly word for word.) In this letter she also recalls the reading companion of her youth and his importance in her memory (or fantasy) as her ideal man, a standard that young Robinson is now invited to believe he has met.

> To Mr. Richard P. Robinson, 101 Maiden Lane.
>
> My Dearest Richard—You wish me to write you but when you are with me I say so much that I have not now any ideas, and when you receive this it will fall so far short of your expectations that you will not immediately solicit another.
>
> It is unnecessary for me again to repeat to you "that I find much pleasure in accomplishing anything, which may be productive of happiness to you," for all my efforts can never make suitable

return for the generous disinterested course of conduct, which tells me more plainly than words that solicitude for my happiness seems interwoven with every feeling of your nature. You have too much good sense to flatter yourself that a woman's heart is gained because her tongue speaks you fair.

You will not the more readily believe I love you madly, fondly love, because in all my letters I so frequently repeat the assertion. You, my dearest R., will recollect saying to me when you were last with me, that you were perhaps the happiest being I had ever met. I had often observed that such was the case, and it gives me pleasure because you deserve it. You are one of those happy persons gifted with so pleasing a disposition that you seem born for the purpose of commanding love. Your graceful ease of manner renders you welcome in any society, you are so obliging that you always interest yourself in what others are saying to you; indeed you forget yourself in order to oblige others; you flatter no one; affect nothing; consequently please every one; because nature has ordained that you should be pleasing, and I, but for reasons which you are already apprised of, should be the happiest woman in existence, to possess so large a share of your regard as I am convinced I do. I have met very few persons who could share in all my feelings so largely as ———, who was my earliest companion. When I walked, read, or conversed with him, I whispered to my heart, if I could find one like him how much I should love him. These are my earliest impressions; latterly there has been in me a romantic feeling that wished for, but quite despaired of ever finding a beau ideal, until I met you. I felt if devoted love or deep tenderness could make my heart happy, I was capable of imparting it, yet with all these ideas I did not entertain the thought that there could be found a living being who could love me, and now that I feel quite assured of being beloved by the only one whom I value, I feel no scruple of pride in acknowledging it. Your thoughts have now become the breath of my existence, you are entwined inseperably [*sic*] with my dearest feelings, and you repay me in all the sincerity of a heart generous, virtuous and uncontaminated by the views of those bad and vicious persons who I have heretofore met. The greatest kindness you have ever conferred upon me is permitting me to have your miniature. It is ever before me, and as the representative of one so dear to me, I prize it.

    As affections tribute, friendship offering, whose
    Silent eloquence, more rich than words,
    Tells of the givers faith, and truth in absence

LEFT: *Cover from* Sketch of the Life of Miss Ellen Jewett *(Boston, 1836), said to be taken from her miniature portrait.* RIGHT: *Profile of Richard P. Robinson, said to be taken from his miniature, printed by the* National Police Gazette, *February 10, 1849.*

And says, "forget me not."

I last night saw the person whom you are desirous of meeting, tried to induce him to go to the play to-night but he refused. I wish you would drop in there tonight, as I am going quite early. In my selfishness I could say to you "do not forget me for a moment," and believe me, as in truth, I am,   Devotedly yours, Helen.[9]

Helen describes Richard as happy, generous, easy of manner, completely forgetting himself to oblige others, and uncontaminated by the vicious; clearly this is a letter written before she knew him well. A few months later, she would not make the mistake of thinking he could be cajoled into believing such things. But in late June, she could not only declare her love for him, she was confident of his love for her and had no scruple about asserting it. This ploy probably effectively captivated such inexperienced young men as Robinson appeared to be. At this early moment in the relationship, she had already made a prize of his portrait miniature, a gift that carried very significant meaning in the prephotography era. Miniatures were expensive (on the order of twenty-five dollars to forty dollars), unique, and, when made for one's beloved, thought to be a window into the giver's heart. As small ornaments they were meant to be worn on one's person, as a locket, brooch, or tiepin. Wearing someone's miniature announced serious commitment, a wish to have that person ever present. Robinson's miniature depicted a youthful lad with "ruddy features" and "bronze clustering ringlets" framing his forehead.[10]

Jewett's elegant letter closes with a rather pretentious attempt at poetry and then wraps up with a sentence that reveals Robinson's own manipulative proclivities: he has asked Jewett to arrange a meeting for him with someone he wishes to get to know, and she is trying to oblige.

Several other short letters must come from this early period. In one she thanks him profusely for a "splendid present": "I have already received too many obligations at your hands, and you have never now-a-days anything for me to do by which I can requite you," likely a reference to sewing and other practical offerings meant to match his gifts. Jewett situates their relationship in the realm of freely given gifts and acts of kindness and service, a pattern of exchange far removed from sex for money. A postscript adds: "For the reason I mentioned, do not forget my green ring." Apparently she has given him a personal and valuable token, but for some good reason not indicating a diminished regard for him, she needs to have it back.[11] Helen wrote Robinson another note in late June, this time from Philadelphia, where she had traveled to visit Clara for a few days. (The two cities were six hours apart by train; she went on a Saturday and returned on Tuesday.) She professed to miss him and wrote "I do not think I shall feel happy here, besides, when night comes I cannot see Frank."

Only one of Robinson's letters dates from this early phase, written on the Sunday of her June trip to Philadelphia. Considering they had known each other less than a month, it is an extraordinary document. His writing veers from reverie and jest to moody darkness, as though he is testing whether he can reveal his innermost thoughts to her:

[To Miss Helen Jewett] New York, Sunday June.
    Dearest Nelly,—I have but one sheet of ragged paper to figure on before me. Here I sit, now almost noon, just out of bed, fresh from heavenly dreams of you. Nell, how pleasant it is to dream, be where you will and as hungry as you will, how supremely happy one is in a little world of our own creation. At best we but live one little hour, strut at our own conceit and die. How unhappy must those persons be who cannot enjoy life *as it is*, seize pleasure as it comes floating on like a noble ship, bound for yonder distant port with all sails set. Come will ye embark?—then on we go, gayly, hand in hand, scorning all petty and trivial troubles, eagerly gazing on *our rising* sun, till the warmth of its beams (i.e. love) causes our sparkling blood to o'erflow and mingle in holy delight, as mind and

soul perchance some storms arise, but our good bark conscious of its valuable burden, labors and yields momentarily to the breezes of Heaven, but like a fond girl, after the storm is past, is ten times more fond of its lover and burthen. At last we arrive at our journey's end, but not without marks of old age and trials, beloved by all. But Nell, I never expect to see that number of years. Although I am seemingly so happy and cheerful with all around, I am not without my bitter moments of dismal misery, when I loathed all, myself and everything on earth. Ah! many's the time when alone at dead of night, on my knees, with my arms outstretched to Heaven, and heart sick, I've called on my heavenly father to take me away, and I would bless all, bless every thing, friends and enemies—the storm passes away, again I am happy, contented and cheerful.

Nelly don't forget that to-day is Sunday and I am just giving you a copy of my sermon; to be sure it is short, but as you say, "don't you know that I like short sermons." But lately I get so little sleep that I am becoming fond of long church service, for there I can sleep, and the girls (now govern your jealousy) dare not disturb me. *You know* I always talk when I begin to awake, and once I asked the minister as he was in the full tide of his sermon, how many yards that piece of goods had in, that he had been measuring for the last half hour, for which the modest damsels beside me pinched and run pins in half length, as if they were harpooning a whale.

Of course you have told me in your letter which it may be you are writing about this time, all about your travels through the strange city, and how *Clara* is. I hope your spirits are in a higher key than when you left, and if Clara don't *mend* you, she shan't have that torn corner of this letter which I have kissed for her. Tell her that, and tell her that it is *Frank's* wish that she boards you till next Saturday. Nell, I am in *one point* your physician, (doctor) and you must obey me. Did Cashier come to see you after I left? Yours, Frank.[12]

Dismal misery, self-loathing, and midnight terrors that pass like a storm suddenly give way to the self-mockery of Sunday sermonizing and jokes about falling asleep in church with girls all around. The final two sentences show how Robinson matched Helen's forceful personality with his own. He asserts the right to order her about like a physician to a patient, and insists on knowing about a client they call Cashier. This sounds like the kind of homosocial bantering men like Marston engaged in, but subsequent letters make clear that Cashier was someone Robinson avoided, disliked, and certainly kept his eye on. On several occasions he extracted what apparently was business information about Cashier from Helen. From the earliest stages of their relationship, these several small comments about other men suggest that Robinson was using Helen as a go-between for his own purposes.

Despite Robinson's confession of dark moods, Helen for a time continued to praise his "amiable disposition"; if he had faults, she wrote in a letter dated July 24, 1835, they were hard to detect. Her conduct, more than her words, she reiterated, expressed her love for him. Jewett's constant invocation of obligation, kindness, and service as the currency of the relationship obscured the reality of the cash transaction at the heart of prostitution. Maybe she thought emotional obligation gave her more leverage in a relationship, or maybe this was her form of denial about her line of work. The final paragraph in this letter alluded to her recent court case with the Berrys, arising out of the incident with John Boyd, which was tried on July 13 and would have been in the Police Office columns of the papers shortly thereafter:

My Dearest Richard—You will recollect I promised to write you as soon as my hand would permit, and this being the first time that I have felt able to remove the dressing, with how much alacrity do I employ it in writing to one to whom I am under so many obligations and can never make any adequate return, but to be the gentle amiable good girl you in your kindness would wish me.

I have often wished I possessed your amiable disposition, it is one which will through life recommend you to the notice of the sensible and refined, beside which you have such a happy faculty of rendering yourself agreeable, witty and amusing, that whatever society you may come in contact, you cannot fail to please.

I feel that you are unlike all other persons whom I have known, that you are too good to be happy with one who is deficient, which a woman ought to possess, who is so fortunate as to call you friend. If you have faults, they are so small I should (like those who would observe spots on the sun) be obliged to examine you through a piece of smoked glass, with the closest scrutiny, to detect them.

I have often told you that I love you, (which perhaps a woman should blush to do) but it is not that I have told you so that I would have you believe it, but in all my conduct I would evince the devotion I feel for you, and I have often wished I had never been educated, but like those I every day meet, I could not read my name in *print*, but somethings which I was taught at an early age, and have never had occasion to make use off [*sic*], have contributed to your gratification, and if I feel any gratitude to my instructress, it is when I can be of service to my dear Richard, and I shall never intentionably [*sic*] neglect anything which can be productive of the slightest pleasure to you. You must pardon me now, for it has required an effort to write thus far, my hand is so painful. Wishing you all happiness, I remain yours truly, Helen.[13]

While she seems on the surface to be regretting her education, because she must confront newspaper reports of herself, really she is bragging about her educational superiority over other girls in the trade. An early "instructress" (Mrs. Dillingham of the Cony Academy?) has taught her things she never needed to draw on until she met Richard, things that now provide him with gratification, meaning perhaps her skill in elegant writing or in reading aloud. Here is the instrumental use of female education—the pleasing of men by putting cultivated talents in their service. As was typical in her client letters, Helen boldly announced her love and then protested that such a declaration required a blush as well—an erotic melding of assertiveness with a more acceptable feminine reticence.

A happy portion of the letters likely date from July and early August. Helen sounded more spontaneous, less calculating; the sense of romance and attraction was still strong, but she generally skipped saluting his virtuous character. One short note jokes about their active sex life:

My dear Richard.—Do you feel today as if you had been floored last night, or not; for my part, I feel literally *used up*, and mean to enjoy to its fullest extent, a state of single blessedness for at least—for at least—for at least—well never mind. I shall go to the Park tonight, and shall hope to have the pleasure of seeing you there early, if not do call upon me before. I wish you could have seen me an hour after you left my room. His Grace the Duke, the Captain, Louisa and myself cracked nearly a dozen bottles of champagne; however, this must be uninteresting to you, and having little time to say the much I would say—sum it up in four words, may God bless you.   Ever yours, Helen.[14]

She is telling him that their extended bout of lovemaking has left her "used up," but her next words remind him that "single blessedness" does not obtain for long in a brothel. She casually, but provocatively, lets him know that she joined a drinking party after he left; the "Duke" was Frank Berry, the "Captain" some other regular customer of the house, and a lot of champagne was drunk. To call this "uninteresting" suggests that Robinson does not usually try to pry into other aspects of her brothel life—or alternatively, he does, and she is really teasing him.

In another letter, she returns to her stance of elaborate deference. She wishes he would stay a night with her, but she concedes, not quite convincingly, that he is right to decline and that her happiness is less important than his determination not to stay. Undercutting her deferential tone is the barb embedded in the closing, where she reminds him again of her alternatives:

> Well, my dearest Frank, I promised to write you, but I have been extremely busy with a lady, a friend of mine, who has been ill—the only apology I can make you for not writing more than a note. At six I shall expect a note from you, and, in that note, the pleasing intelligence you partially promised me. It is indeed hard that you cannot for one night, at least, manage to remain with me. I urge you, because I am fond of you; but when I reflect, I am sure it is wrong, and all you say and do is best and wisest, and I deserve your censure for wishing you first to deviate for my happiness; and I will not again solicit you when you tell me you *cannot*. How cheerfully I should extend this to a long letter, but the parlor is full of persons, and I am called off from writing to the only person on earth whom *writing* is a pleasure—and for what am I called?   Ever yours, Helen.
>
> P.S.—Monday I promise you one of my longest letters.[15]

Had he never yet spent a whole night with her? That seems unlikely, but still possible. Robinson was not accountable to his boardinghouse keeper for his evenings and nights, so it is hard to understand why he would say he "cannot" stay. Perhaps he could not afford an entire night; possibly he had business or pleasure elsewhere to attend to; or maybe he was worried that an attack of night misery would strike when with her. The letter nicely illuminates Jewett's acute balance between feminine deference and imperious assertions of her own desires. And it ends with a veiled reference to a parlor full of other customers ready to purchase intimacy with her.

Robinson answered her a few days later. His letter began with compliments so eloquently put that they sound artificial, as if they dated from very early in the relationship. But he then launched into a long apology for ill-tempered and shameful behavior:

> My Dear Helen—Your letter was received on Sunday. Your apology for not answering my letter sooner was fully sufficient for an excuse. Indeed, such employment (that of assisting a sick friend) would be a sufficient apology for a much more heinous offence than

that of neglecting to answer a letter, and I am rejoiced to know that you are willing and *do* spend so much of time and money in endeavoring to promote the comfort and happiness of those around you. Yes, Helen I acknowledge *that* is one reason why I take such an interest in you. 'Tis not your beauty only that makes me love you—*no*, it is your *goodness*. You have a heart which can beat for the distress of another, and a generous hand ever ready to assist the unfortunate. These are qualities very rare among your class of unfortunates—qualities which (as far as my knowledge extends) you, and you alone, possess. . . . So you have concluded not to attempt to undeceive me in my opinions of you. You are right, for you *could not* alter my opinions of you by *writing*. I shall be judged by your actions and conduct, not by what you say, for I know that you would not do yourself justice. You close your letter by saying, but alas, let it go by; we will try to shut our eyes to the past and hope for something better in the future.

Helen, I must now again, beg your pardon, for my most ungenerous and ungentlemanlike conduct last night. You have always treated me well, *too* well, and why I should thus requite you, I myself know not. True it is, that I have treated you most shamefully, without the slightest cause whatever, and I fear it will take a long time to regain that place in your affections, (that is if I ever possessed any) which I last night so madly, foolishly threw away. The cause of my stubbornness and ill-nature, I cannot acquaint you with, for I know it not myself. But *believe* me when I say, that *you*, nor *anything* relative to *you*, were the cause. I know I was acting wrong, in trifling with feelings such as yours, but yet, I could not help it. When you told me you were unhappy and wished me not to act so foolishly, I felt for you, and pitied you, yet *I* could not have spoken a pleasant word, if *I* would. But it is done, and the only way in which I can atone to you is, in future, to be more a *gentleman*, and more, myself, for it was not Geo. who staid with you last night, it was Bill E——y.   Good bye Nell, Your affectionate friend, Frank.[16]

The final lines of this letter are very puzzling. Robinson (Frank) promises to be more of a gentleman, indeed, more himself, but the connection to a visit of Bill Easy (George Marston) is quite unclear. Marston knew Jewett for about eight months, so they were new acquaintances in August when this letter was probably written. Possibly Robinson was betraying jealousy here. Rosina Townsend reported at the trial that Helen once asked her to study Robinson's face intently "and say whether he or Bill Easy was the handsomest," so Jewett was not above encouraging a little rivalry between the two.[17]

In early August the couple had their first real rupture. Helen learned that Robinson had betrayed her with another woman. Four of her letters, probably written over a two-week period, outline the progression of her suspicion, anger, disappointment, and effort to reconcile. (The letters are undated, except for weekday and hour.) The first note hints at jealousy, but she apologizes and dismisses it as a foible of womankind:

I resume my pen to you with much pleasure as I have now half an hour which I hope I shall be able to call my own, if I am not called upon to do something to oblige the ladies. You must pardon me for the *ungenerous* remarks I might have made the last night you remained with me, but really I could not help it. It is indeed a misfortune that *jealousy* should have been so lavishly used among the ingredients of my composition. It has often made me unhappy and I have vainly tried to cover it. There are very few men who *understand* the feelings of poor women. We are often obliged to smile and hide with a cold exterior, the feelings which sometimes nearly cause our hearts to break. Women only can understand woman's heart. We cannot, dare not complain, for sympathy is denied us if we do.

With man it is otherwise. He can with impunity express all, nay, more than he feels; court sympathy and obtain it, while at the same time poor neglected woman cannot be allowed to share in the many pursuits and pleasures which man has to occupy his time; of course he does not need to be pitied, unless it be for his vices and excesses.

You will recollect I spoke to you relative to visiting me oftener than twice a week. It is now the only pleasure I receive, when every one else is unkind to me, to have my dear Frank to tell all my feelings, who will listen patiently and then pity me. And it is indeed a pleasure to sit for hours and work for you and think of you: not as I think of the rest of the world, but to really feel grateful. These to me are enviable feelings, aye, ones which I could not be induced to relinquish for anything which I can now recollect. You must reply to me soon at length.   Your devoted, HELEN.[18]

There is a genuineness about this letter; it departs from Helen's routine bid for sympathy for unfortunate victimhood. Here she asserts that men in general are insensitive to women. They claim the limelight, talk a lot to gain women's sympathy, and then exclude women from their own pleasures. Frank, however, is an exception; he listens and pities, she claims, and this is why he is special.

But her suspicions were not imaginary. It appears that Robinson wrote to announce he had something to tell her and at the same time wished for more independence. Her sarcasm was quick:

Dear Frank.—You certainly were extremely kind in selecting language to express yourself in your last note, which I have just received. What in the name of *Heaven* can you have to say! why is it requisite that you should leave me in such painul [*sic*] suspense? Whoever for a moment wished to question your being independent; you shall be as much so as you like, act as saucy as you like, but you will oblige me particularly, if you will not use that word as a signature to me, and the tone in which your notes are written, must be less harsh, until you are convinced I deserve them otherwise. I felt very independent until I saw your note.   FIREFLY.[19]

The signature "Firefly" suggests a flashing yet small anger. Her next began with cold formality, using the clerk's real name in the salutation:

Tuesday morning.
     Mr. R. P. Robinson: If you think it requisite that I should remain longer in this most painful suspense, you must pardon me for saying that I think differently. If you were placed in my situation (with all your independence) you would ere this have demanded an explanation. I parted with you on Friday last at the confectionary, wtihout [*sic*] any feeling of hostility, and you (apparently) as kindly disposed as ever, and then on Saturday to receive that most inexplicable of all notes; commencing with your accustomed "Dear Nell." You also sent me the book I want and what construction am I to put upon all this? Why pay me the same attentions if I am no longer worthy of them? as I must infer from the tenor of your note. If I have in aught wronged you, who so fit to make you reparation as myself; and I now request an understanding, and as a gentleman you cannot withhold it.
     I do not ask you to fix upon any time, nor do I ask you to come here if disagreeable to you. But I certainly do ask a note before this night from you, in which you will mention a time and a place when I may see you, and you will find me punctual. If you ever liked me you will not deny me this. With all this inquietude upon my mind, I cannot sleep, for I am laboring under that illness which maketh sick the heart—hope deferred. Let me for Heaven's sake hear from you soon, and believe me now as ever, Truly your own, Nell.[20]

Perplexity and anger are what Jewett experiences: Robinson is re-
treating while still giving her a gift. The "tenor" of his note is that she is
no longer quite so beloved, and Helen is hurt and wonders what she has
done to deserve this sudden distancing.

A final two-part note in this set finally names their problem: Richard's
involvement with another woman. Helen got up at half past six one
Thursday morning to attempt a rapprochement via a letter. She communicated overwhelming sadness in language not contrived for literary
effect; this is no longer an accomplished prostitute trying to maintain or
repair a business relationship. Her business, of course, is not set aside,
for her opening sentence refers to a customer known to them both who
has just left in the early morning after spending the night in her bed—her
sexual behavior with other men is evidently unproblematic for their relationship. But his behavior is, and she is taking him to task on the grounds
that he owes her something ("a proper sense of what is due"):

Half-Past 6 Thursday Morning
———— has just left me, and Heaven only can be my witness
what a painful rush of feelings I am now trying to contend with—
feelings, which I hope, and from my heart too, my dearest Frank,
may never be yours. I am very sure I have not merited such treatment, for never since the commencement of our acquaintance here,
I had the slightest concealment from you, and I do not hesitate to
say it was wrong in you to take advantage of it. Although you may
have yielded to a temporary infatuation, (perhaps an involuntary
one) now I think you are effectually awake to a proper sense of
what is not only due to yourself, but to your friends.

As I continue writing I find myself shedding tears, which has
produced a convulsion of feeling too painful to be borne, yet women
seem in some degree born for weeping, and as I find it relieves me,
why should I strive to restrain or repress them? but when I think of
you as the only being on earth I really love, I feel the more inclined
to weep. You may, but do not think me sadly selfish for intruding
my thoughts upon you now, when I am aware of the nature of those
which must at present occupy your attention. Alas! you know not
what it costs me to reproach you, but I have never since I have
known you, had but one hope, one wish, which is that long after
you had ceased to see me, you would think of me as not utterly
beneath the herd with whom I have been obliged to associate. But a
truce to this, which must be as painful to hear as to relate, if you
could read my heart while I write you, you would pity me, and yet

strange as it may appear to you, I would not have you pity, it seems so very like contempt. You are not aware what an effort it has cost me to tame my language and curb my thoughts, and triumph over the madness which is lurking at my heart; then indeed, you would not despise, though you might dislike me.

A second part of the letter, penned in the afternoon, offers him forgiveness:

Thursday afternoon.

I had fancied that I had become cool and collected, but upon reflection my heart is full to bursting, that another should have been preferred to me, when you have so often assured me that you loved no one else, and I think every one with me must acknowledge the singular and powerful force with which a girl innocent in herself clings to the belief of innocence in her lover; and so firm a reluctance to think that where we love there can be that which we would not esteem. But my dearest Frank, I had pictured you out as an image all divine (by the way I refer to you in one of my late letters in which you find what I said relative to discovering your faults with smoked glass). In you I found high, generous, noble, independent feelings, such as I had never before met with. A woman should perhaps blush to make the avowal, but I saw and loved you, and my life became a new object, and when I say that I loved you truly, devotedly, disinterestedly, and still do, I only speak the truth, and you can yet be to me all that I in my fondness have wished you were. You cannot be ignorant of the power you possess over me, and you must not betray it; I should not say you must not, but rather why, why, have you done so? I have ransacked and reransacked my memory, and cannot tax myself in any one instance since our reconciliation of having deceived you, and from that I derive consolation. But I am weak and can write no more, and I long to cast myself into some illimitable waste and flee on forever.

But my dearest Richard all you have done is forgiven, as completely as I hope you have forgotten the cause of it, and but for your urgent request, you should never have had this scrawl, which was written under the influence of disappointed feelings.
HELEN.[21]

Extraordinary language in the context of prostitution: "a girl innocent in herself" believing her lover to be innocent as well and crushed to find out he is not. In her mind, their love transcended her other sexual liaisons, occupying a different realm. Setting Robinson apart might be expected in a prostitute who kept her heart from other customers, but Jewett typically drew her many clients into a circle of friendship and romance. In this letter Helen discloses a deeper set of feelings, bordering on dependency, for an idealized Robinson. He had truly hurt her.

A glimpse of what had happened in August emerges in the grand jury proceedings of April 18, 1836, a week after Jewett's murder, when a group of women came forward to attest to Robinson's unfaithfulness to Jewett. Witness 24 was Hester Preston, an eighteen-year-old who lived at 55 Leonard Street with Ann Welden, who said that Frank Rivers had "visited her for some time." Witness 25, Julia Brown, confirmed that Rivers visited Preston "about a year ago"; he then visited Adelia Phantom, who lived at Brown's brothel on Chapel Street. In August, Brown revealed, "he sedused [*sic*] a young girl" at a house at 171 Reade Street. The keeper of that house, Elizabeth Stewart, appeared next, and the telegraphic deposition says: "a little girl came to board with her—paid 6 dollars a week—gave him a Night Key—staid about 3 weeks, a girl about 17 years old—came there from school—and said she was married to Douglass [a false name used by Robinson]. Imogene Chancellor was her name—her aunt came after her and said she ran away with Douglass—gave her several Dresses and Books." Julia Brown, who knew both Jewett and Robinson, added that "F. Rivers told her if any woman exposed him he would blow out her brains—last August this took place." Robinson's threat probably arose from fear of his other liaison with Chancellor getting back to Jewett. A threat as dire as this sounds extreme; but Robinson had his volatile side, and he was right to expect that Jewett would be devastated to learn about Imogene. Another witness before the grand jury, Newton Gilbert, also a clerk at Hoxie's store, reported enigmatically that Robinson "had some difficulty with a young lady but Mr. Hoxie did settle it."[22]

Letters later in August (the eighteenth, the twenty-second) show that the Chancellor episode was smoothed over or set aside surprisingly quickly. On August 18 Robinson named for Helen characters he called Mr. G., Mr. Grey, Mr. Wm. St. J—— Jr., W.G.; he seems to be asking her to take part in some kind of setup that involves accepting Mr. G. as a customer. Robinson feeds her names to drop with Mr. G., and cautions her to remember "his knife and pencil."[23] Sometime later, a short note from Helen mentions St. J. and also suggests the couple's mutual sexual attraction has been rekindled. "I beg you will wait to-night until half past eight, when I promise you my door shall be kept unlocked for you, and you shall have all the fun you anticipate."[24] The mysterious Cashier figures in a number of letters from August through November. "I am aware how *dis-*

agreeable it would be to you to encounter Cashier, who sent me word he was coming to my house early this evening," Helen wrote. Or, "This evening the cashier intends calling upon me. I tell you this because I am aware with how much reluctance you would meet him at my house." In another letter, Helen wrote, "I should also write Cashier if I knew whether it would do or not, but you will tell me and I can apprise him of my return on Monday." And another: "I did tell you that Mr. G. was coming, but— on Tuesday evening early. I cannot imagine why you wish to know so particularly about Mr. G. Your request alarms me, and I beg you may assign some reason for it."[25] And finally, Robinson reveals Cashier and Mr. G. are different names for the same person:

> Dear Nelly, I intended coming up to your house last night, but someting [*sic*] transpired which compelled me to stay away. I———, importer, overheard Cashier M.G. say, "they would watch the house till they found out who it was." I am the one they want to find out, and was afraid last night to call on you. It was late when I learnt this—too late to write you. I will meet you at the Park to-night early—our old rendezvous. If you have not hinted W.C.R.'s name to them, substitute Read Gordon's.[26]

There is a plot afoot here, but its details are hazy. It might be an embezzlement scheme, involving goods or cash, where a cashier is watching or auditing a business establishment; or possibly the "house" refers to Jewett's house, which is why Robinson cannot visit her. His reluctance probably has to do with some complicated scheme involving Helen, who is taking direction from Robinson in dropping names to someone. In another note, Robinson writes, "I do not know whether I may be at the Park to-night or not, but I cannot come to your house. . . . Am I lost then? Touch lightly, or a reaction may blow you to heaven high. Feel no apprehension—I mean nought." The nefarious scheme clearly gave Robinson a case of nerves. In his mercurial mind, Helen can blow him and herself to high heaven—a dangerous thought which he quickly retracts.

In mid-November the couple fought again, and this time the rupture can be followed only through three letters from Robinson. (Only one is dated; the other two are grouped here by inference.)

> Friday evening, 7 o'clock.
> My Dearest Nelly—Agreeable to promise, I write you the first opportunity I have, though it is a bitter cold night to send Thomas to your house, but I wanted to hear how you are.

You was offended Wednesday evening at my language. I do not wonder that you were. It was harsh—very harsh, but I could not help it. No one can love you more than I do, dear Nelly; yet how strange, whenever I meet you I cannot treat you even with respect. You must think it very strange that I profess to love you so much and yet always treat you so harshly. Yet I have told you over and over again, that loving you as I do and not being able to see you, it makes me most crazy, and I have no control over my feelings, but Nelly you must forgive me. I hope to God it will not be always thus, and when you are again in the same situation as when I first became acquainted with you, I shall endeavor, by the most assiduous attention and kindness, to recover part of that affection and regard, which I believe you once felt for me, and which I know I have forfeited by my unjust behavior.

For one thing, dearest Nelly, I can never reward you sufficiently. You have promised me your miniature; what can I give you in return? Nothing but my repeated vows of unutterable affection. But I will always wear it next my heart, and forever guard it as a sacred treasure.

I know my letters cannot be very interesting to you, Nell; they are full of oh! how I love you and a piece of other nonsense, exactly what they all write you. They all call you dearest Nelly, so do I. I suppose you think us all alike.

But Nelly, for God's sake, don't forget me. I shall see you again Sunday at 1 o'clock, until that time I shall count the hours. Tell Thomas how you are to-night. I envy him the pleasure of seeing you to-night, if it is but for a moment. It makes me laugh to hear him give a description of you, your house, how snugly situated it is, &c. He thinks a good deal of you, is always talking about how neat you are, &c. But I must close.   FRANK.[27]

This sounds at first perusal like an unproblematic love letter. The *National Police Gazette* printed it with the subheading "Master Frank in his first ardor," as though it were early romantic sweet talk. But an undercurrent of fear runs through it; Robinson has exploded at Helen and senses her pulling away. Yet she has promised him her miniature, and he chooses this moment of pleading to remind her of her promise. He even attempts to flatter her by claiming that his letter carrier, Thomas, finds her attractive too.

Robinson's pleading did not work to reengage Helen. In this next letter, things had deteriorated for him.

Thursday morning.

My Dearest Nelly—I little expected when I hurried from the store last evening, and almost run to your house, that I might see you the sooner, to meet with such a reception—and the more I think of it, the more am I surprised. Instead of asking me how I was, and appearing glad to see me, you say, "What did you come up here for, to put me to the *trouble* of going up stairs?" My mind was made up in a moment not to trouble you, but as I walked out, and after I had got out, I could hear your *loud laugh*. I was not always thus, Nelly. There was a time when the *trouble* of going upstairs was compensated by the pleasure my visit occasioned you, but I have recently had occasion to think that you have got tired of me, and that I am now in your estimation placed on a par with all the others. I know I have treated you harshly now and then, but I always suffered for it. Lately I had resolved to treat you kindly, and hoped that nothing would again mar my feelings towards you. 'Tis useless for me to tell you how I love you, for you now make it an object of sport. Nelly, if you have ceased to love me, for God's sake tell me so—if you still love me, why did you drive me from you last evening? You saw I was going. You might have even asked me to stop—but my exit only occasioned mirth for you. You may say you did it only for fun. If that was fun to you, it was cruelty to me—do you think I am entirely devoid of feeling that I can be driven from your door, by you, and not feel it, and sensibly too? I have suffered for you, Helen, not bodily suffering, that is nothing—I have often set for hours and thought of you, until my heart has nearly broken. You think it strange that apparently such an inanimate thing as I am could even be moved by you or anything else. But Nell you are not the only person in the world who can conceal their feelings. I have acknowledged that I have often suffered intensely by allowing myself to think of you so; I will never acknowledge so much again. By God, I love you, but unless I am loved in return as *much* as ever, I never shall enjoy myself with you as I have done. I never can bear to have your love for me diminished *one atom*.

You must excuse my writing you with a pencil, for I have no chance to do otherwise. For God sake let me know *soon* the cause of your treating me as you did last night, and when I can again visit you without being of too much *trouble* to you.   From one who loves you, FRANK.[28]

This letter shows that Helen retained some measure of independence from Robinson; she could challenge his presumption in calling on her, term his upstairs visits "trouble," and laugh at his embarrassed exit. And he responded to her rejection with fury, revealing a hurt and temperamental personality. His style of anger here is to command her to continue to love him as much as ever, or otherwise—in an oddly self-centered threat—he cannot enjoy her as he once did.

The last of the three letters of this presumed set was written November 14 and is the same one the district attorney read into the trial record. Robinson proposes he and Helen cut all ties. He addresses her as Maria G. Benson, thinking that is her true name, just as Helen called him Richard in her more serious notes; aliases fall away when they want to speak from the heart—or appear to speak from the heart. Robinson thinks Helen has lost all love for him, despite her prior assurances, and that she now has or is about to plunge him into "ruin and disgrace," and further, she no longer counts him a gentleman. It is a most histrionic letter; Frank ardently wishes either for death or transfiguration:

> Miss Maria—I think our intimacy is now old enough for both of us to speak plain. I am glad you used the expression in your note of yesterday—"And as long as you pursue a gentlemanly course of conduct, &c. &c." I dont know on what footing I stand with you. Any deviation from the line of conduct which you think I ought to pursue, and I am blown. All your *professions*, *oaths* and *assurances* are set aside to accommodate your new feelings towards me. Even this very letter will be used as a witness against me, to avenge a fancied insult received at my hands. Poor Frank, has indeed, a thousand insurmountable difficulties to encounter. Bandied about like a *dog*, who as he becomes useless is cast aside, no longer worthy of a single thought, except to be *cursed*. No sooner extricated from one difficulty than he is plunged into ruin and disgrace by one who he had confidence in; one who professed attachment more sincere than any other, who swore to be true and faithful, and let *all others* be false, she would be my friend till death parted us. Oh! has it come to this, and she the first to forsake me, whom I so ardently endeavored to gain her lasting regard and love; then are *all* vows false, or Frank is indeed altered. He has but two wishes left, either of which he would embrace, and thank his Heavenly Father *with all the ardor of his soul, death,* or a complete alteration, and make me what I once was—'tis strange, yet 'tis true.
>
> After reflecting on our situation all night, I arose this morning feverish and almost undecided, and so ill as to be able to attend to but a portion of my business of the day. *I have,* however, come to this conclusion, that it is best for us both to dissolve all connexion.

I hope you will coincide in this opinion; for you well know, that our meetings are far from being as sweet and as pleasant as they once were, and moreover I concluded from the terms of your last note, that you would not regret such a step. I am afraid it will be the only way for me to pursue a gentlemanly course of conduct; in *my opinion*, my conduct the last time I was at your house, was far from being gentlemanly or respectful. I behaved myself as I should never do again, let the circumstances be what they might, even if I had to prevent it by never putting my foot in your house again. I was very sorry for it, and now can beg your pardon. I have done to you, as I have never done to anybody else, (in the case where other gentlemen are concerned). This I hope will be forgiven, as there is no harm done, and let the circumstances justify the act. H—— as we are about to part, allow me to tell you my genuine sentiments.—I have always made it a point to study your character and *disposition*; I admired *it more than any other female I ever knew,* and so deep an impression has it made on my heart, that never will the name and kindness of Maria G. Benson be forgotten by me. *But for the present, we must be as strangers.* I shall call on you tonight to return the miniature, and then ask you to part with that which is no longer welcome. That you should think I would use subterfuge to obtain the cursed picture, wounded my feelings to the quick: for God knows, I *am not*, nor ever was as mean as that. *Your note of Wednesday I never received that I am aware of.* I would not insult you by leaving you to infer that another will receive my visits, for "pius" I shall remain. Nelly, I have only to say, do not betray me; but forget me, I am no longer worthy of you.

> *Me ex memoria amitte et ero tuus servus,*
>   Respectfully, Frank

14 Nov. 1835,
Helen Jewett, 128 Duane St.[29]

No doubt what interested the prosecuting attorneys was Robinson's reference to Helen's ability to disgrace and betray him. The letter also showed an angry Robinson admitting that he had abused her.[30] Hugh Maxwell, Robinson's lawyer, said "the obvious intent . . . was to show, that he had, at some distant period, entertained malignant feelings towards the deceased, and had, on one or two occasions, threatened her with injury."[31] But, Maxwell argued, the letter was too vague to sustain the weight of such an interpretation and too distant in time to bear on the murder.

The third major quarrel occurred in December, once again over Robinson's suspected infidelity. The odd twist this time, however, was that Robinson deliberately provoked Helen's jealousy. Helen took a trip to Philadelphia in early December, and a few notes she wrote right before leaving make it clear that the two were at least back on speaking terms in the weeks since November 14, although Robinson was not very responsive. Several times she asked him to return her green ring and postponed her leaving to hear from him. She wrote to him that a man called Crockett, first encountered on her June trip to Philadelphia and met again when he visited New York, had invited her to visit him: he "has written for me, and in leaving I consult my interest which you have ever wished me to do."[32] As usual, Jewett assumed her client relationships lay outside the emotional calculus of this couple. But there is a brisk or chilly tone in her announcement of the trip.

Helen took the train to Philadelphia around December 10. This was the coldest winter of the entire first half of the nineteenth century, and her letter to Robinson is one of the few in the entire set to comment on the weather. "I begin to thaw out from the excessive freezing," she wrote him.

> The day, as you know was extremely cold, so much ice in the Delaware as to render it impossible for any boat to take the passengers, therefore, we had to make the journey all the way on the railroad, and then had to cross from Camden in a small ferry boat, without any cabin or fire, and when we arrived, we were nearly perished from the cold, and but for the kindness and attention of a gentleman whom I met in the car, I never should have got along.

It was so like Helen to remind Robinson that she encountered gentlemen eager to assist her. At the end of her letter, Helen described the state of their relationship, now characterized as a fast friendship:

> Take good care of yourself, as you know you have many, very many friends who would be pained to learn that any ill had befallen you. You also know how dear you are to me, and though it can never be in my power to requite all your kindness and though I sometimes forget to acknowledge it, I can never cease to remember, and I cannot sufficiently regret that anything has occurred to render you less fond of me than when first you knew me. I am sure we shall ever continue friends, for I have never intentionally wronged you, and you have made me promise that I never will, and I shall religiously keep it with you, and you, I am sure, will never again pain

me for asking for your miniature, for heaven only can be my witness what pleasureable [*sic*] feelings it excites, while gazing upon it
and recuring [*sic*] to the kind and generous manner with which you
gave it me.[33]

A slight distance pervades the letter. Helen professes strong feelings
for him still, especially when gazing at his miniature, but she does not
proclaim her love. With regret she surmises that Robinson's ardor has
diminished, but she promises lifelong friendship and assures him she will
never wrong him. Her claim that she has never *intentionally* wronged him
suggests that unintentionally she once did, maybe leading to the November blowup, for she pairs her promise with one extracted from him, to
never again ask for his picture back, another feature of the November
incident.

While Helen was away, Robinson went to Mary Berry's house on
Duane Street and attempted to set up a date with another girl, Hannah
Blisset. This was a deliberate and blatant insult to Jewett, and it had the
expected effect. Mary Berry instantly wrote to Helen about his breach of
brothel etiquette:

New York, December 14th, 1835
    Dear Helen—An incident which took place last evening, obliges
me to write to you this morning, to give you a little information.
Last evening about seven o'clock, Bill Easy and Mr. Cook called to
the house. I had a fire made in your room so they went up stairs
and sat there some time. Bill Easy appears rather melancholy at
your absence. He thought he would send you a letter, so he gave it
to Hannah to carry to you, but as Hannah is not going to Philadelphia until next Monday, the letter shall be sent with this.
    Now I shall commence with a more important subject. Your
Frank came about nine o'clock, enquired for Hannah and said he
should see her. She was then up-stairs with a gentleman. I asked
her down stairs, but judge my surprise when he told me he wanted
to remain with her. I told him he should not but he tried to insist
upon so doing, but I again told him I would not suffer such a thing.
I asked him in my front room. Hannah came in so I should hear
what passed. He wanted Hannah to consent then, or to meet him
next Thursday night at the theatre; I waited to hear her reply. She,
in a very ladylike and candid manner, told him *she would not*, and
rejected his offer with becoming dignity, so he went away just as he
came. He had another gentleman with him.

Bill Easy is very anxious to see you. I wish you to come home as soon as possible, be assured all things shall be right until you return.[34]

Helen's insistence on fidelity from Robinson was obviously a standard of conduct shared and enforced by the other women in her household. In attempting to pay court to another girl, Robinson was certainly making a statement. Tellingly, he managed to do it with Mrs. Berry and another gentleman as witnesses. This breach of etiquette was so serious that Mrs. Berry suggested Helen return home right away, and she did. (Was she also annoyed to learn Marston and Cook were allowed to moon about in her room during her absence?) She came back and wrote Frank curtly:

Tuesday afternoon
    I have returned to town, and wish to see you this evening with-out fail. I am back thus soon on your account, so you will please sacrifice an hour of your time on mine. It may be for your interest to accede to this request. Yours, &c., HELEN.[35]

In suggesting it may be in his interest to answer her summons, Helen implies she has something on him. Robinson was full of apology:

Wednesday afternoon
    My Dearest Nell—Forgive me, forgive me! Though things may look against me, I can easily explain, and, as I think, to your satis-faction. Your language is cruel—bitter, but I can forgive it on the ground of the apparent cause you have for it. I will be at your house to-night at eight without fail. Yours ever, FRANK.[36]

Robinson deliberately waited a day to reply to Jewett's peremptory summons. A glimpse of him biding his time comes from a letter by George Marston written that same Wednesday to Helen. "I was taking a lunch and a glass of porter at Clark & Brown's with Frank . . . and it was then he informed me you had got back. I supposed he had been to see you but he said he had not. Ah, Helen may I hope that—but never mind now. Yours, W.E." Bill Easy and Frank were friends, but Bill hoped to edge out his rival for Helen's affections. This same note is the one where Bill praised Helen's "beautiful letter" from Philadelphia, declared his love for her, and slyly slipped in a jab at Frank's attentions to Hannah Blisset: "I am not so fond of change as a certain gentleman named Frank of my acquaintance."[37] Marston had been upstairs in Helen's room the evening

Frank made his call, and he no doubt heard the story from the upset Mary Berry.

On December 26 Frank wrote Helen again; he had tried to visit her on Duane Street but Mrs. Berry turned him away. Frank writes as though it pains him that Helen's affections are otherwise engaged with George and she is cooling off to him, but in reality he is still gently pushing her away:

> December 26, 1835
>
> Dear Nelly—You have maintained silence longer than I expected; you know that I never shall go into *that* house again, therefore I could not come to you, but expected you would tell me where I could see you, as you said the last time we met that you wished to see me for an hour or so particularly. However, in the society of ——————, 'tis not strange that I am forgotten. So ardent an admirer, and one who is your best friend, should not be neglected for one who is not worthy of a single kind wish or thought from you. By my conduct since my acquaintance with you, I have forfeited every claim to your confidence or friendship. I am a broken merchant; I must earn my reputation anew as well as he his fortune. You have done me injustice but once, when you believed what Mrs. B. stated in her letter. *You might and ought* to have disbelieved it, from the conversation we had previous to your departure from Philadelphia. Still I don't know that you can be blamed, for I once deceived you and others sadly. *But my* days of deception are over and I hope we can at least be friends. Monday night perhaps you will be at the Park, and then I shall see you. *Burn this if you please.* I hope you had a merry Christmas.
>
> Respectfully, your ob't servant, FRANK.
>
> P.S. *Whenever* you send me a letter through the Postoffice direct Box 1628, which I think will not be intercepted. F.[38]

Robinson commits a lie in this letter: he denies Mrs. B.'s bad report of him. But he is not begging Helen to take him back; he is merely asking that they still be friends. The postscript and the command to burn the note reveal a concern to keep this letter from falling into the wrong hands; possibly it is his bald lie that he does not want others to see, as well as his admission of "days of deception" in the past. Helen's reply to this (or to another note about the same time no longer extant) shows she is still clinging to Robinson and seems not to see how manipulative he is:

> My dear Frank—You are perfectly aware of the disappointment I felt at not seeing you, also my anxiety to do so, but dearest, you

know I can forgive you anything. I think your account will be quite square when we meet tonight. I am at loss to know what you mean by "if Mrs. Berry will admit you," for Heaven's sake tell me, for if you have been refused, I will vacate the premises immediately. True I have seen St. John, but what you mean by Frank Robinson, I cannot imagine. I am ill, I mean sick, sick at heart, and you do not know how unhappy I shall be until I see you.   Ever your own, Nelly. What I have to tell you can be told to-night.[39]

In the grand jury proceedings, Mrs. Berry testified that she barred Frank from visiting her house "because he made quarrels and was under age."[40] (He was eighteen.) Since she obviously had not barred him during the six months previous to December, she invoked this new excuse of age simply to add weight to her view of him as a troublemaker.

It is hard to establish facts from these several dozen letters. Each one, taken alone, reveals very little, and it is little wonder that the prosecution so quickly abandoned its effort to introduce any into the trial. Put in context, though, the letters bring us closer to understanding the bond between these two extraordinary young people. They both lived on—indeed, thrived on living on—an emotional edge. Both experienced an intensity of feelings, not merely romantic or sexual longing, but dark, moody, depressive feelings as well, that they both enjoyed giving vent to. If Robinson was involved in some shady scheme, and Helen insisted he follow right conduct or she would "blow" (expose) him, neither one was content just to leave it at that. They seem deliberately and extravagantly overwrought. Robinson declared all vows are false, he is a cursed dog, and death is preferable to life as he leads it. Miniatures will be returned, they will be as strangers to each other. Their histrionics were worthy of melodrama. Perhaps these two habitués of the theater took their cues for conducting the business of life from the make-believe world of the stage.

Their literary talents are also much in evidence. Not only could these two—he eighteen, she twenty-two—flourish subjunctive verbs and construct complicated clauses and subclauses in their sentences. They reached for metaphor (not always successfully), employed a rich vocabulary, sustaining a tone or a mood at unusual length. They both could be clever, suspenseful, teasing. Writing such letters took time—as well as dexterity with the quill pen and its repeated dips into ink pots. They proclaimed themselves to be a couple in love, at least at the summer of their meeting, yet they did not spend hours and days together because both had other jobs that claimed their time and kept them apart. So they wrote letters. But such an exchange was not simply a way of staying in touch; it was a way of managing one's face and disposition, to construct a lover persona to attract the other, to fashion an identity as a basis for intimacy. It was a way of composing oneself. Helen's formulaic scripts with clients made her adept at all this. She understood the power of her letters to draw men in, make them blush, and arouse their sexual and protective longings. She knew well how to manipulate men through epistolary exchanges. In Richard P. Robinson, she had finally met her equal.

Blowing Up

I N J A N U A R Y 1 8 3 6 , Helen Jewett moved out of Mary Berry's house on Duane Street and took up lodgings four blocks north on Franklin Street right off Broadway, at a house run by a Mrs. Cunningham. Her move was likely a retreat, both from Mary Berry, who now scorned Robinson for being quarrelsome and barred him from her house, and from Robinson himself, whose deceitful ways were increasingly apparent to her. She moved without notifying him, and on January 12 he wrote her a heated, bitter, turbulent letter. From January to April, their relationship ran onto increasingly rocky ground.

January 12.

Dear Nelly—Thinking you had entirely forgotten me, I think it high time to enquire what has become of you. Hearing you had left Mrs. B's, I am astonished that you don't inform me. *Is it* that the name of Frank has no power to please you longer; is it *true* that you have made up your mind to forget me; TO DENOUNCE ME, to those you *most* sacredly promised not to? Am I not then *debased* enough when I deserve to be forgotten by you, but that you must go still further and betray me? Nelly, Nelly, *pause* ere you go further; think of how we were once situated, and if you can convince yourself that you are acting a *noble* part in cutting my throat, *go on, is all I have to say.* My course will be short and sweet! No *bitter, bitter* as well you know. Since our acquaintance commenced, what an eventful one. Can you look back on it without pleasure *and pain; I cannot.*   FRANK.[1]

The heavy emphasizing of words indicates an intense emotional reaction to her withdrawal. The district attorney did not enter this letter as evidence at the trial, perhaps because a witness asked about the handwriting rejected it as Robinson's. (Joseph Hoxie and his clerk Newton Gilbert offered their opinions under oath as they examined the letters; mostly they equivocated that they could not be sure any item was Robinson's hand.) This January 12 letter clearly reveals that Helen had the power not only to reject him, but also to betray him and in effect (in his dramatic terms) cut his throat. He begged her not to, but his real message was a threat: Go ahead, and see what the bitter outcome may be.

Helen promptly made a conciliatory reply:

Wednesday, 1 o'clock

My Dearest Frank—I have not forgotten you believe me, I am very desirous of seeing you, and cannot tell what you mean by sending me an unsealed note and your expressions relative to blowing you, which you have my word, that I will never under any circumstances do, and whatever you may *learn* from *others*, you will find that inviolable. I have only time to spare to tell you that I will meet you tonight at eight o'clock on the corner of Chapel and Franklin, by Tom Rielly's Hotel. Be punctual. Yours ever.[2]

She had moved without informing him, as a way to gain distance on him, but now his heated note pulled her back into his orbit, forcing her to deny any plan to denounce him. Her note implies that someone else was in on their secret, some *other* one who knew what Jewett knew and had perhaps hinted to Robinson that she planned to betray him. Jewett offered to meet Robinson but in public, at a street corner near her new residence. Perhaps she realized a private meeting might be too risky, given the explosive tone of his letter. She sought to defuse his anger, but she also snatched an opportunity to chastise him for failing to seal his note: she can be counted on to be careful, she implies, while he cannot.

Three more letters between late January and mid-February map out their rocky efforts to reconcile. Robinson teetered from loving concern to apologies for brutishness, with an uncharacteristic theme of jealousy surfacing as well. Helen's reply to the jealous remark showed her keeping an emotional distance:

Monday afternoon

My Dear Nelly—I have only a few moments to write you that I am well. This is the first moment I have had any kind of a chance to write you since I last saw you. We are taking account of stock, which accounts for my being so unusually busy. I was in hopes that I should have had a letter from you this afternoon, but have not yet received any. I hope the reason is not because you are too ill to write. Nelly, for God's sake, write me soon and tell me how you are getting along! It is hard to me to know that you are sick, and not be able to assist you—not to see you, and even not to hear from you. But if it is too much of an effort for you to write, I beg of you not to . . . I had not rather hear from you than have you make yourself sick by overexerting yourself to gratify me. . . .

I wish I could see you this evening, Nelly; but it cannot be. By heavens! you are in my thoughts day and night all the time. If I knew you thought half as much of me as I do of you, it seems as though I should be most happy. But, Nelly, you must not forget me, though I do treat you cold sometimes—do not be angry with me. I know you think me a strange being, yet cold and insensible as I sometimes appear, I *have* feelings over which I have no control, and which, if trifled with in any way, would make me unhappy and almost crazy.

I am called away; excuse me and the one thousand and one mistakes.   Forever yours, FRANK.[3]

Editor George Wilkes placed this letter among the earliest between the couple, and Robinson's anxiety over a possible illness and his claim of constant thoughts of her certainly sound of a piece with the opening weeks of their new love in summer 1835. But the address was to Franklin Street, where she lived from January to mid-March 1836, and the reference to taking inventory also suggests a January date. Possibly, then, this is a disingenuous note: Robinson loudly proclaims romantic feelings—yet he cannot find the time to see her. More significantly, he refers to episodes of uncontrolled feelings, as he had in earlier letters, but here they sound even more chilling. What appears to be a cold and insensible exterior, he hints, masks a potential for blind rage—if trifled with, he can be made crazy. The tender love letter echoing sentiments of early romance actually delivers an ominous warning.

A second letter dates from January or February, for it refers to *Norman Leslie*, a new play which drew rave reviews and crowds to the Bowery Theatre night after night between January 11 and February 7. (Based on a recently published book by Theodore Fay of the *New-York Mirror*, *Norman Leslie* told the story of a 1799 New York murder of a young girl whose lover was arrested for the crime. Scenes in the play showed the lover lodged in Bridewell and then facing trial in a City Hall courtroom, a preview of what Robinson would experience in a few months' time.)[4] Robinson again apologizes for his despondency:

Friday Evening.

Dearest Nelly—Your letter was received at 2 o'clock, and I thank you for it. You were right in thinking me unhappy last evening. If I had not been, believe me I should not have treated you as I did. I know I did not treat you as I ought, I knew it at the time, yet I could not help it. Did you ever know me to appear happy a whole evening when with you at the theatre? I don't believe you have, at any rate, not lately. I have told you often, I believe, that when I am with you, I want to be alone, where no one can see us. Can you think it is in my power to sit at your side a whole evening, "however much I may want to," your friend—watching you, and you him, and feel happy? Those who do not feel as interested in you as I do, might, but Nelly, I *cannot*, I cannot sit with you in the presence of one who has, and may again purchase you as his; do you really think I can? I again repeat I cannot, I cannot. I am glad to see you; yet I am never more unhappy than when with you at the theatre. Never for one moment think that I would have you offend for *me*, or that I am angry with you for having such a friend, for it is not so. I am glad you have such a friend although it is the means of keeping me from you. But I must shorten my letter for I have not much time to write you, as we are about shutting up.

. . . To-morrow evening I go to the Bowery, to see Normand [*sic*] Leslie. Sunday afternoon I shall come to see you, which ought to be more pleasant. I am much better to-day than I have been for some time. This letter will go into the office to-night, but the Postoffice department is managed so bunglingly, I don't suppose you will get it under a week.

Goodbye Nelly.   FRANK.[5]

The jealousy here is oddly expressed. Repeatedly Robinson protests that he cannot bear to sit with her at the theater with another man, watching her watch him, knowing he purchases her for sex. Yet he also claims to be glad that she has this special friend, and he wishes not to offend him! Possibly there is heavy sarcasm clinging to the well-wishing part that we moderns find hard to credit. Yet in Jewett's world, her clients seemed agreeable to her terms. Though smitten by her, Attree and Marston understood full well there would be others, not just as sex partners but as close friends. And even in the initial heady phase of love,

Robinson never before lodged a protest about her other clients. He had given no signs of being a possessive lover. Why now?

In what may well have been a reply to this note, Jewett wrote to Frank: "I hasten to undeceive you as to the supposition that in the society of Mr. E. [Easy] or any other gentleman, that you could be forgotten. He treats me well, but not more kindly than you, and you do me injustice when you think that I retain any animosity for your having once deceived me."[6] Her note is marked by formal politeness and an effort to defuse jealousy.

A set of undated letters suggests that a new estrangement set in between February and early April. Ten notes by Jewett invite Robinson to contact her about some piece of information she has to share with him, and Robinson finally replies. Hers grow increasingly impatient: "If you do not drop in and see me to-night, I shall not readily forgive you, as I shall be so cruelly disappointed, beside I have something to tell you which from any one else you would never give credence to."[7] "I have waited long enough in all conscience for you to come up to my house without being solicited, and I must now try to draw some signs of animation from you on my own account. I wish an answer by the bearer of this, as I wish to consult you relative to going New Orleans."[8] (Possibly she was giving thought to joining Attree there, in February.) "I saw you to-day, and to-night you must call upon me, for I have something very particular indeed to communicate, which may interest you more than you are aware of. If you cannot come up to my house, say when and where I shall meet you, and I will do so at any place you choose, at any rate you must give me an answer, I know that you are watched, I also know—but never mind I will tell you when we meet."[9] "I want to see you to-morrow afternoon or evening very much, as I have something urgent to say to you. I know you are strictly virtuous now, but I have no designs upon you, in that way, I assure you."[10] "Unkind, ungenerous Frank, to remain away from me so long . . . I do not think I merit such treatment from you . . . I am unhappy this morning, really unhappy."[11] "It is in your power to decide whether or not I longer remain thus unhappy. I never expected that you would desert me quite, in this manner, and if it is the case that you have done so, I should certainly learn it from no one but yourself. . . . I told you in my last letter that I had a communication to make that affected you, and you have not paid the slightest attention to it."[12] "My dear Frank, what in the name of wonder can have kept you so long from me; I am not conscious of having done anything which might offend you, and yet you do not seem to consider it of the slightest consequence, whether I am relieved of the most intolerable suspense, or remain in ignorance of your feelings towards me. On Saturday last I wrote you a note, which you have not yet replied to, and I am sure I do not deserve to be treated so cavalierly, and I must see you before another night has elapsed or I shall be half crazy, beside which I have something very particular to say to you, which I cannot well postpone."[13] "If, my dearest Frank, you have ever tolerated for one day the painful suspense I yesterday endured, then you will pardon me for writing you a harsh, cold letter . . . I feel amazingly like blowing you up, if I dared—not with powder."[14] The hint that Robinson was being watched, that Helen had information to deliver to him, perhaps from Cashier, and that in anger she felt like exposing him, "blowing" him up: all this suggests a subplot of something like embezzlement by Robinson.

Her patience wearing out, Jewett made one last urgent appeal:

Thursday evening, 7 o'clock.

My Dear Frank—You have passed your promise by two nights, and yet you have not thought proper to send me a single line, even in the shape of an excuse. Do you think I will endure this. Shall I who have rejected abundance for your sake, sit contented under treatment which seems invented for my mortification; nay, for my destruction. Pause, Frank, pause, ere you drive me to madness. Come to see me to-night or to-morrow night, if you do not receive this before 12 o'clock [midnight]. Come and see me and tell me how we may renew the sweetness of our earlier acquaintance, and forget all our past unhappiness in future joy. Slight me no more. Trample on me no further. Even the worm will turn under the heel. You have known how I have loved, do not, oh do not provoke the experiment of seeing how I can hate. But in hate or in love, Your HELEN.[15]

Robinson's answer came swiftly, the next day:

Friday morning, half-past one.

I did not get your note till one o'clock, so that will excuse my not having come to you at once. It so happens that I cannot come till Saturday night. I cannot explain the reason why, on paper, but try and be satisfied it is a good one, until I can assure you of it in person. I shall come about nine o'clock, and I wish you would let me in yourself. I shall see Gilbert to-morrow, and will accomplish what we were speaking of, without fail. I have read your note with pain, I ought to say displeasure; nay, anger. Women are never so foolish as when they threaten. You are never so foolish as when you threaten me. Keep quiet until I come on Saturday night, and then we will see if we cannot be better friends hereafter. Do not tell any person I shall come. Yours ———[16]

Undated notes in an unconfirmed hand would never stand as evidence in a criminal proceeding. Yet these last two sound like the prologue to the weekend of April 9, when Helen Jewett was murdered. The sweet and all-consuming love of 1835 had degenerated into mutual threats and recriminations in 1836. Robinson veered between chilly reserve and open anger, and Jewett from cautious mollifying to begging him to return with promises of important information, threats to expose him, or unrealistic hopes of renewing the romance. This was an unaccustomed role for Jewett to take with a man, but then nothing about this relationship had conformed to her usual practice of her trade. When Robinson first turned from her in August with the girl in Reade Street, she was desolate. When he exploded at her in November, she laughed him off but then took him back. When he staged his insult with Hannah Blisset in December, she rushed back from Philadelphia to reprimand him. She moved from one brothel to another without telling him, but still she took him back, despite his repeated ugly moods. She then tenaciously tried to hang on to him, even when his interest had clearly waned. The two seemed locked in a kind of struggle, each with plenty of other options, but neither able to break away from the relationship. So confident with other men, Jewett seemed insecure and vulnerable in the face of Robinson's moody and domineering personality.

On March 18, Helen Jewett returned to Rosina Townsend's brothel on Thomas Street, where she had lived for much of 1834. She already knew at least Elizabeth Salters and Caroline Stewart, two of the girls resident there.[17] Six more girls lived at the double house under Townsend's care; several testified at the grand jury proceedings, but only two, Salters and Emma French, who had material facts about the evening of April 9, testified at the trial in June.[18] Townsend was of course the star witness, and Helen's black servant girl, Sarah Dunscombe, also offered important testimony. The attorneys confined themselves to questions meant to establish the presence of the accused at the scene: time of day, clothing worn, entrances and exits. But from such narrow questions emerges a picture of Helen's three-week residency at 41 Thomas.

Mrs. Townsend asserted that Robinson had visited Jewett perhaps six or eight times over the three-week period, usually in the evenings but once on a Sunday afternoon. Helen's flurry of letters must have succeeded in commanding the clerk's presence. Their visits gave no sign of rancor; Mrs. Townsend knew of no disputes between them. She had talked to

Robinson once in her parlor (evidence that she knew his voice); and on another occasion "he was once in my room in company with Ellen Jewett and three southern gentlemen." No lawyerly follow-up question explored what the five people were doing.[19]

Helen saw other men, too, of course. On the three previous Saturdays, George Marston had spent the evening with her; he was known in the house as her regular Saturday-night customer. Marston had also visited her for fifteen or twenty minutes (by his own account) the Friday night before the murder. In assessing Robinson's standing with Jewett, Mrs. Townsend allowed that "there was a Gentleman that visited her oftener than Def't."—probably Marston.[20] Robinson's roommate, James Tew, also patronized Jewett occasionally, as he admitted and Townsend and Elizabeth Salters confirmed. Odder still, Tew and Robinson passed themselves off as cousins, and both went by the name of Frank Rivers. They even dressed alike, reported Elizabeth Salters.

Salters was a more important witness than any of the lawyers realized. Under questioning intended to establish that she knew the defendant, Salters revealed she had been intimate with both Frank Riverses. She had even entertained both in her room once, as Emma French also attested. Her sexual relationship with Robinson had begun in February, seven weeks before the murder, and before Jewett moved to Thomas Street. "I have more than once seen the prisoner with his clothes off," she declared. But Salters had not told Jewett that either Frank Rivers had been her customer, and apparently neither did any of the other brothel women. "There was no ill feeling between Ellen Jewett and me because of Frank Rivers coming to visit me. I never said anything to her about visiting me. I thought that she had the most right to him, as I understood from her that she had known him intimately for a long time."[21]

Was it coincidence that in March Helen Jewett had chosen to relocate to the very Thomas Street brothel where her dear Frank was seeing another woman? Probably so; she had lived there before, among some of the same people, and according to trial testimony she got along well with all the residents—"she was a favorite amongst all the girls, and I never knew or heard of her having a quarrel with any one in the house," said Salters, a sentiment the servant Sarah Dunscombe echoed.[22] Salters testified she had not seen Robinson arrive the night of the murder, and, she volunteered, she had not seen him at all for two weeks. It sounds as though she deliberately kept out of the way during his six or eight visits to Thomas Street, perhaps as a courtesy to Jewett, or perhaps out of regard for Robinson, who knew Jewett did not take betrayal lightly. Robinson also took pains to avoid encountering someone at 41 Thomas. Not only did he conceal his face upon entry the night of the murder, but, according to Townsend, he habitually pulled his cloak up "to avoid being seen by other visitors," the madam surmised. But likely he was warding off an awkward meeting with Helen and Salters. Indeed, the invention of a second Frank Rivers sounds like a clever contrivance meant to account for possible slips of the tongue by Salters, Emma French, or Rosina Townsend. Tew testified to the coroner's jury that he first accompanied Robinson to the Thomas Street house on March 23, just five days after Jewett moved in. Perhaps the two visited Elizabeth Salters and established an interchangeable identity that might prove useful in the event Jewett overheard talk of prior visits by a Frank Rivers.

The lawyers missed all this, but the interchangeable identity did surface in connection with the murder. At the early moment in the trial when Rosina Townsend said, "There were two visitors at my house who called themselves Frank Rivers," a loud hissing and clapping burst out in the courtroom, "evidently from the friends and partisans of the unfortunate prisoner," wrote one reporter. The commotion reminded the jury that confusion over identity was central to the case.[23]

When asked about friction between the couple, Townsend, Salters, and French all mentioned a significant event about ten days before the murder, around March 31. To the coroner's jury the day after the murder, Rosina said, "Only about 10 days ago Deceased told Witness that Frank Rivers had Returned her letters and wanted her to Return or destroy them, and the Deceased told Witness that prisoner was agoeing to get married." French reported, "Don't know of any dispute between deceased and prisoner, but deceased said she had went and got some Letters from him, belonging to her about 10 days since." And Salters: "Prisoner and Deceased had a little dispute about some letters about 10 days since, as deceased informed witness." Not one of these witnesses was asked during the trial in June about this dispute; the lawyers attributed little significance to it, especially since the letters, unspecific and undated, proved to be of little value to the prosecution. But the quarrel over letters does hint at yet another stormy moment and perhaps dramatic ending to the rocky relationship between Robinson and Jewett. Jewett's allegedly telling Rosina Townsend that Robinson was to marry seems on the face of it hard to credit, for her lover was only nineteen years old that April 9 and in no financial position to take on a wife. Only a passionate love and/or an unplanned pregnancy could have driven a nineteen-year-old clerk into matrimony in Jacksonian America, where most men of the business classes were well into their twenties before they took such a step. Robinson *might* have told Jewett about an impending marriage just to make a decisive break with her; or she might have used it as a plausible excuse for some other explanation she did not want to reveal to Townsend. In any event, by the time of the trial, lawyers for neither the defense nor prosecution were interested in pursuing the grounds of the troubled relationship between the accused and the murder victim.

In the late afternoon of Saturday, April 9, Jewett and Elizabeth Salters went out together for a walk down Broadway. Jewett carried a letter and a book destined for an address on Pearl Street—probably a gift for Marston, who worked at David Felt's stationery store at number 245—which she gave to a porter to deliver. On Broadway near the multistoried emporium called A. T. Stewart's, the biggest and newest department store in New York, Jewett met Edward Strong, a young clerk at Stewart's, who had also seen her briefly earlier in the day. Strong followed Salters and Jewett back to Thomas Street, at a little distance, and then went up to her room. It was now between five and six in the early evening, and Sarah Dunscombe was on duty there, preparing the room for the evening.

Dunscombe came to Thomas Street every morning from eight to nine and every evening from five to seven. She fetched water and wood, changed the bed, and usually helped Jewett dress for her evening entertainments. (Corsets, stays, eyelet closures, buttons, pinned-on ruffles, collars, and sleeves: dressing in the 1830s really did require an extra pair of hands, as did hairdressing, with sleeked coiffures and over-the-ear corkscrew curls, the whole perhaps ornamented by a jewel pendant dangling over the forehead.) Dunscombe had brought hickory wood from the cellar and had started a fire in the fireplace by the time Jewett and Strong arrived. Strong sat on a chair near the head of the bed and leaned his shoulders and head on the bed; Helen sat in his lap. Dunscombe reported they talked, but she could not catch what they said. She busied herself with bringing a pitcher of water and clean clothes into the room; the three of them acted as though there was nothing very unusual about a servant bustling around while a prostitute entertained a client in the same room. Evidently, however, Jewett told Dunscombe she could leave early, so the young woman went back to her mother's on Franklin Street. Both Dunscombe and Strong agreed on these details in their testimony to the grand jury and at the trial, but Dunscombe was clearly rattled to be in court. She confessed to being frightened: "I have never spoken to any one but my mother about this, and she told me to tell nothing but the truth."[24]

Dunscombe's testimony was relevant on two counts. First, she told the grand jury that the form and hair color of the man in Jewett's room Saturday resembled Robinson's, a point she later retracted at the trial. And, she further testified, while dusting Helen's room Friday morning, she admired a miniature in a Moroccan-leather case, an item she had sometimes seen Helen wear around her neck. Jewett informed her it was a portrait of Robinson. The servant dusted it and put it in a bureau drawer.[25]

Jewett expected Robinson to visit that Saturday evening—or so she told Townsend, Salter, and French "at tea table," around seven o'clock. Saturday night was Bill Easy's usual night, and Helen was concerned enough that he might come that she directed Rosina not to admit him. (Bill, however, never came; maybe Helen had asked him not to, in their short interview Friday night or in her note on Saturday, but not being sure he would honor her request, she advised vigilance at the door.) Sometime between nine and nine-thirty, Rosina answered a knock at the locked front door. A voice asked for Miss Jewett, and to make certain it was not Bill, Rosina asked the man to repeat his request. Then she opened the door. Immediately the guest drew his cloak up over his face, leaving only his eyes visible. A soft cap covered his head. There stood Frank Rivers, his face seen plainly if fleetingly, illuminated by a globe lamp hanging behind her in the entryway. Emma French stood in the doorway of her first-floor room, opposite Rosina's, and as he entered she also thought she recognized the man known as Frank Rivers. The man moved down the hall to the parlor at the back; Rosina followed and then passed him, opening the partly closed door to tell Helen that Frank had arrived. By that time, the man had turned back to the double staircase and had started up the right-hand flight, which joined the left stairs at a landing, one house having been made from two separate dwellings only three years earlier. Helen went up the stairs, met him at the landing, plucked on his cloak, and said, "My dear Frank, I am glad you have come." From then until near eleven, Helen and her guest remained in her second-floor room.

James Tew and Rodman Moulton showed up shortly after nine-thirty and talked in the hallway for a quarter hour with Elizabeth Salters, who told them Frank Rivers was upstairs with Helen. Tew and Moulton had taken tea with Robinson in the early evening at their Dey Street boardinghouse, run by Moulton's mother. Charles Tyrrell, another young boarder, joined them for a walk up Broadway in the chilly April evening air. They split into two groups at the foot of City Hall Park, across from the American Museum, and Tyrrell and Robinson continued on together, walking down Beekman Street east of the park. Tyrrell left Robinson there sometime between eight and nine. Robinson said he was going to go to the Clinton Hotel (on the corner of Beekman and Nassau), "but to my certain knowledge he did not go there," Tyrrell said at the trial (perhaps because that is where Tyrrell went). Robinson was in a very cheerful mood, his friend said, bantering about its being his birthday. Tyrrell remembered that he wore a dark cloth cloak, trimmed with a velvet collar and facings.[26]

Between ten and eleven, Helen went downstairs to collect repaired gaiter boots a shoe man delivered at the front door. Emma French witnessed this brief appearance and reported Helen was still dressed in the evening clothes she had been wearing in the parlor. How remarkable that New York shoe men made deliveries, and so late on a Saturday night! Curious, too, that French summoned Helen to receive her boots when she knew she was with a customer. Perhaps Helen had to pay the man on the spot and Emma would not cover it for her.

At about eleven, Helen emerged from her room wearing nightclothes. She asked for champagne, and Rosina, realizing there was none in the cupboard, volunteered to get a bottle from the basement. She carried a tray bearing two glasses and the bottle up to Helen's room. Helen invited her to have a glass herself, but Rosina declined. She stood in the doorway talking to Helen for a few minutes and observed the guest lying in bed, with the covers up to his shoulders. The bed was a French sleigh bed, standing opposite the door, its curved mahogany footboard facing the doorway. Rosina could see the back of Frank Rivers's head and a bit of his face on the side. He reclined on his left elbow and was reading a book or a paper, she said, with a candle for light right in front of him on the pillow or on a small bedside table. Rosina left. She was the last resident of the house to see Helen Jewett alive.

Rosina had her own guest for the night, a man named Charles Humphrey, who arrived just before eleven. At a quarter past twelve, she locked the front door from the inside, taking the key into her room where her boarders knew to get it if a guest had to leave. Then she and her guest went to bed. And how many beds do you have in your room? a defense attorney asked her at the trial; "But one," she replied. In such small ways the lawyers managed to hint at a brothel's true business without raising indelicate questions about sexual services. Seven customers were in the brothel that night: Humphrey, Frank Rivers with Helen, Thomas P. Waters and another man with Maria Stevens, a "gentleman" with Caroline Steward, a "friend" up on the third floor with Amelia Elliot, and James Ashley, who arrived at three in the morning to see Elizabeth Salters. Just a quarter hour into his appointment, Ashley would be rudely interrupted.[27]

Robinson and Jewett did not drink much of the champagne, for the mostly full bottle was still on her mantel the next morning. (Rosina and Elizabeth Salters both told the grand jury that Helen was not an "intemperate" girl, and Salters added that she had never seen her intoxicated.) If they engaged in sex that night, it probably occurred just before or after the call for champagne, since neither was dressed when Rosina took the wine up. They then either fell asleep, or talked in bed, the one warm place in a chilly room; winter was not through with New York yet. Other women in the house had gone to bed between ten and twelve. Salters said she went to sleep around ten-thirty, waking up briefly around eleven when she heard someone call for champagne. She was taking the opportunity to get some sleep before her middle-of-the-night appointment arrived. It was something of a slow night, Rosina said, and in any event the house customarily shut down at midnight. With servants showing up as early as eight in the morning to do the rooms and empty the chamber pots, this brothel kept regular hours.

And it surely *was* Robinson in her room. Rosina and Emma French both recognized him when he came, and Jewett called him Frank as she went up the stairs with him. When Rosina saw him in bed at eleven, she noticed a small balding patch at the back of his head, something she had not seen before because he usually wore a cap, and she made a mental note to ask Helen about it the next day. By the time of the trial, nearly two months later, Robinson had shaved his head and was wearing a wig, rendering Rosina's bald-spot identification moot. But she had also recognized the side of his face and was quite sure it was Richard P. Robinson whom she saw in Jewett's bed. Jewett certainly knew who her guest was. It would have required an elaborate and convoluted story to explain why she would harbor some other man in her room and pretend to Rosina it was Frank Rivers, and no one tried to advance such a story at the trial. But a defense attorney is not obliged to present alternative accounts. Punching a convincing hole in the prosecution's story is enough.

Presumably the couple slept for a time; at least, no one in the house heard any noise. The wall between Jewett's bed and Maria Stevens's room was especially thick. Entertaining two men at once, she might not have heard anything anyway, and she had little to contribute to the coroner's jury or the grand jury. Before the end of May she died in Mary Gallagher's brothel, of a cold or flulike disease. Her sudden death gave rise to speculations in the press that she knew too much, that she held the secret to the case. But to the grand jury she had simply said that she had never met Frank Rivers and had lived at Thomas Street for only a year. The *Herald* reported that Maria got up in the night to fix a window shutter banging in the wind but heard no sound from the next room.[28]

Sometime between eleven at night and three in the morning, Robinson killed Jewett with a hatchet blow to the forehead. Three gashes marked her brow, two from light blows delivering cuts and contusions and a third so fierce that it embedded a piece of her skull into her brain. In his autopsy report, Dr. Rogers concluded that she died quickly and "without a struggle"; "the blow was unexpected," he wrote. Her body lay on its back and left side, the right forehead facing up, "the countenance composed as if in sleep." Presumably Rogers concluded there was no struggle on better grounds than her composed countenance and sleeplike position;

the autopsy report was silent about defensive wounds, usually found on the arms and hands of a victim warding off blows, so probably there were none.[29]

The report duly noted the brown skin, crisp and parchmentlike, of the left arm, one side of the lower right leg, and part of her back. The body and limbs were stiff; rigor mortis had set in by the time of the nine o'clock autopsy. Rogers and his assistant found nothing in the thoracic cavity and the abdomen that struck them as significant. "The stomach was partially filled with food," the men noted. They attended carefully to the uterus and found it "labouring under an old disease," probably scarring or old adhesions from pelvic inflammatory disease, a condition undoubtedly common to someone who had frequent sex with multiple partners. The adhesions probably had diminished her odds of getting pregnant.

The autopsy report was quickly passed over at the trial; it established the cause of death, but apparently no one called on Dr. Rogers's medical expertise to sharpen an understanding of the circumstances of the murder. But there were details that yield information to a modern forensic analysis. First, Rogers noted "a quantity of blood on the bed whereon her head lay." If he meant there was a nontrivial amount, Jewett bled after the blows; her heart pumped after the hatchet smashed into her forehead, and her death was not instantaneous. When Rogers opened her chest, "a considerable quantity of blood was discharged." He drew no conclusion from this. But the presence of blood, subcutaneous or pooled in the thoracic cavity, implies she suffered a traumatic blow to the chest as well, either from being struck hard or from being held down. No ribs were reported broken—but neither were they noted to be unbroken, and the force of the autopsy itself might have obscured any undisplaced fractures. Dr. Rogers's report suggests three possible scenarios. First, the killer delivered a light blow, waking Jewett and causing her to sit up; he then aggressively pushed her down and struck twice more, finally with enough force to kill her. Second, the first blow or two could have caused convulsions, frightening the killer into thinking that forceful action was needed to restrain the body while another blow was administered. Or finally: he held her down, awake or asleep, maybe by straddling her and pinning her arms with his knees, and then dispatched her with three quick hatchet strokes, each stronger than the last until he achieved the right degree of force.[30]

However Helen was killed, it was accomplished quickly, deliberately, efficiently. There was no sign of overkill, the savage multiple blows or mutilation of extreme rage or lust killing. And the murder was premeditated. Robinson brought the hatchet with him—it did not belong to Jewett or to the Thomas Street brothel. In a final act of destructive rationality, the killer lighted the bedside candle, probably from the fire-

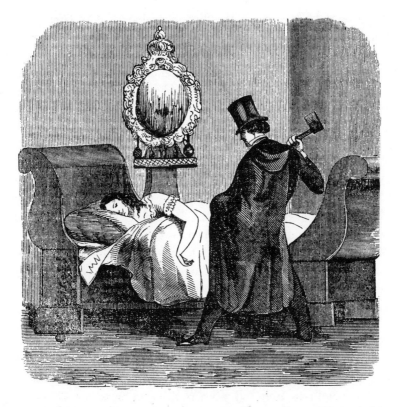

The moment of murder as depicted by an artist for George Wilkes's Lives
of Helen Jewett and Richard P. Robinson, *1849. Robinson is shown fully
clothed and improbably hatted; he was said to have worn a cap that night.*

place embers, and set it in the bed, intending to ignite his victim, her
room, indeed the entire brothel, in order to conceal his crime. Just four
months earlier, in December 1835, many blocks of downtown New York
had burned to the ground, and periodic fires consumed buildings and
lives, so the idea of an obliterating arson was easy to summon. Expecting
a fire to consume the Thomas Street brothel and everyone in it may be
what emboldened him to wake Rosina for the key. Rosina sleepily told the
departing man to "get your woman to let you out," forcing Robinson to
leave by the back door into the yard, where tall fences obstructed his
escape. Expecting a conflagration to destroy evidence of his deed would
also explain why he did not bother to remove his letters from Helen's
room. The miniature, however, was an object he valued. Sarah Dunscombe had put the tiny portrait of a ruddy-cheeked lad in Jewett's
drawer Friday morning. On Sunday, the police found it, in its green
leather cover, among Robinson's belongings on Dey Street.

Robinson did not count on the three o'clock arrival at Thomas Street of James Ashley. Since Ashley was expected, Rosina was prepared to rouse up and let him in. Once up and about, she noticed the globe lamp out of place in the parlor and the open back door, and soon after she discovered the smoke in Jewett's upstairs room. (Ashley, headed for Elizabeth Salters's room, was perhaps too preoccupied to notice the smoke. If he smelled it at all, perhaps he figured someone's fireplace was still burning, although burning wool and wood smell markedly different.) The sleigh bed's bedding had burned long enough to brown the skin on diverse parts of Jewett's body, but not so long that the bed was full aflame. Probably her left arm was behind her torso—it, her back, and her right leg were the areas burned, suggesting the fire was set in blankets behind her and had not yet engulfed the whole bed.

The hatchet found near the back fence of the brothel yard had earth on its blade; an early morning rain had washed it clean of visible blood. A common wood-handled hatchet worth twenty-five cents, its blade had been manufactured in Connecticut and the handle added by a New York firm. Some 2,500 such hatchets were produced in 1834, the owner of the New York firm that stamped its name on the handles testified at the trial, and they were sold all over the city. The porter in Hoxie's store used such a hatchet to open boxes and crates. James Wells said he had last seen the store's hatchet on the Wednesday before the murder, but he did not miss it until the following Monday morning, when he could not find it. At both the grand jury and the trial, Wells positively identified the hatchet found at the brothel as the one from Hoxie's store, "from the dark marks that are upon it, and from its being blunted in a particular way." Robinson had worked at the store until five-thirty on Saturday, Wells said, and he was "very cheerful and lively that afternoon."[31]

The hatchet was found with a string attached to it. (A few witnesses from the police watch did not remember the string, giving rise to doubts that Robinson's attorneys grandly exploited.) A matching short string was tied to a tassel on a closure on the cloak, found abandoned beyond fences in the neighboring yard in the path of the killer's probable escape. The police reasoned that Robinson had tied the hatchet under his cloak, so that he could appear freehanded with the weapon concealed. Yet his housemate Charles Tyrrell had seen him don the cloak on Dey Street and was certain no hatchet was hidden beneath it then. Tyrrell said he left Robinson on Beekman Street between eight and nine, plenty of time for Robinson to walk south to Maiden Lane, acquire the hatchet from the store, tie it in place, and hurry the half mile north to reach the Thomas Street brothel around nine-thirty, Rosina's most specific guess about when he had knocked on the door. The prosecution tried to establish that

Robinson had a key to the store, but their only witness on that point, the younger Joseph Hoxie, who clerked with Robinson, offered ambiguous testimony. The porter, Wells, had one key, and head clerk, Newton Gilbert, usually had the other key, which he sometimes gave to Robinson. But when Gilbert was on the stand later, unaccountably no attorney asked him who had the key that weekend. (Instead, they grilled him about handwriting and the letters. Maybe they surmised he would report he had the key, and they preferred not to put that before the jury.)

There seems little doubt that Robinson wore the cloak that night. When first asked about it the morning of the murder, he denied owning it, and strictly speaking, he did not. The cloak belonged to a friend named William Gray, a young man from Ohio Robinson had roomed with in 1835.[32] Gray gave him the cloak as security for a loan a few months earlier. It had a velvet collar and facings, fancy frog closures down the front made of black silk cording, and decorative tassels also of black silk cording along the edges. Elizabeth Salters could link the particular cloak with Robinson, for a tassel had come off in February during a sleigh ride (a fact also confirmed by Charles Tyrrell, who was on the ride), and she had noticed it when he visited her. A short time later, the tassel was sewn on again (possibly by an obliging Helen Jewett, living over on Franklin Street), and Robinson showed off the workmanship to Elizabeth. When she examined the cloak found in the yard, it had the same resewn tassel—now with the string attached. Robinson's friends—Tyrrell, Tew, and the younger Hoxie—all agreed he had a similar coat, but they declined to swear positively it was the same one. It took a woman's eye, a woman's knowledge of sewing, to identify the one idiosyncratic feature that made it Robinson's cloak and his alone. Whether her affirmative stood up to the young men's doubt was a matter for the jury to decide.

Robinson's cloak and pantaloons came in for inspection at the trial, but no interest was evinced in the rest of his clothing. When arrested Sunday morning, he no longer had a cloak with velvet collar and tassels in his possession. He pulled on blue pantaloons after he got out of bed, and police officer Brink noticed a spot or smear of white on one leg. Townsend's back fence had recently been whitewashed; but the porter from Hoxie's store, James Wells, reported that on the Saturday of the murder some pillars at the store had been painted, providing an alternate explanation for the white smudge. (The pants were not offered as an exhibit.)

And no one considered whether bloodstains marked the killer's clothes; the forensics of blood splatter were in infancy then. Yet surely a murderer wielding a short-handled hatchet would be splashed by his victim's blood. In all likelihood Robinson was naked in bed—unless we presume Jewett kept sets of men's nightclothes for her clients. After delivering the fatal blows, he probably wiped or washed any blood splatter off, using water Sarah Dunscombe supplied to the room and tossing the bloody washcloth or handkerchief into the fireplace. He then dressed in his street clothes, put on the cloak, took up the lamp—and the hatchet, in case he met someone face-to-face unexpectedly—and crept down the stairs. Once in the backyard, he abandoned the hatchet, no longer necessary for his own protection and an encumbrance on a city street in the night hour. Losing the cloak, however, was a serious mistake.

Helen Jewett's body slowly roasted in bed until Rosina sounded the alarm. Then it was doused with pots of water, as frantic women and night watchmen worked to extinguish the fire. Next, concerned neighboring women like Mary Gallagher and Mary Berry came to bewail their poor departed friend. Robinson himself was led to her bedside between eight and nine on Sunday morning; he betrayed no trace of emotion at a scene he had left just five or six hours earlier. (No one watched to see if her wound bled fresh blood.) Around nine the body was moved to the floor where the doctors Rogers and Kassam probed her broken skull and sliced her open from sternum to pelvis. Magistrate Oliver Lownds arrived to take her private papers into custody, followed by the mayor of New York, Cornelius Lawrence, come to view the chamber of horrors and to register his sanctimonious and marketable concern over the foul and shocking deed. An engraving artist showed up and sketched the scene as he imagined it looked moments after the murder, employing a little mental gymnastics to return the body to a sleeping position in bed. In the midday, lines of men and boys from the neighborhood traipsed through to view the mangled corpse, and at four in the afternoon, editor James Gordon Bennett conducted his tour of the scene, described in intimate detail for twenty thousand readers of Monday's *New York Herald*. "The perfect figure—the exquisite limbs—the fine face—the full arms—the beautiful bust—all—all surpassing in every respect the Venus de Medicis."

On Monday Helen Jewett was buried in St. John's Burying Ground, about a mile north of Thomas Street. Bounded by Leroy, Clarkson, Hudson, and Varick (now Seventh Avenue) Streets, the cemetery was associated with St. John's Episcopal Church to the south on Varick. It was the only Episcopal burying ground in active use in the city since an 1831 edict closing off new interments in the overfilled churchyards of Trinity and St. Paul's. Someone—Rosina Townsend? William Wilder? John R. Livingston? Mayor Lawrence?—approached the rector of St. John's on Sunday or Monday to arrange a plot for the murdered prostitute, paying six dollars for the privilege of Christian burial. The Trinity Parish monthly "Report of Interments" listed Ellen Jewett, a widowed woman, age twenty-three, born in Maine, living on Thomas Street, with cause of death "Homicide."[33] The decision to designate her as a widow (the alternate check-off columns were "Girls, Mar. Women, Single Wom'n") must have occasioned a pause in the conversation, as the gravesite broker pondered the choices. Jewett was not a girl or a married woman; and "single woman" probably sounded too virginal. So widow it was.

St. John's Burying Ground became Hudson Park in the 1890s, and in turning the land over to the city the parish advertised widely for anyone with loved ones to reclaim and rebury the bodies interred there; few did. The remaining thousands of bodies and hundreds of monuments were turned under the soil, covered by a formal French park graced with a belvedere overlooking a reflecting pool. The park was renamed James J. Walker Park in the 1940s, in honor of a beloved New York mayor who lived in an 1860s brownstone on Leroy Street across from the site. In 1972, a backhoe transforming the park into a playground ripped into underground crypts that had long been forgotten.[34]

But Helen Jewett did not meet that backhoe. She was not in Walker Park, nor Hudson Park, nor St. John's Burying Ground, not for long anyway. Four nights after her burial, medical students went at her grave with spades and pickaxes, removed her body in a bag, and carted it off for dissection at the College of Physicians and Surgeons on Barclay Street. A short time later, the *Herald* reported, her "elegant and classic skeleton" hung in a cabinet at the medical school.[35]

CHAPTER FOURTEEN

Overconfident Youth

ROBINSON WAS FORMALLY arrested on Sunday at the Thomas Street brothel, the scene of the crime, to which detectives Brink and Noble had taken him earlier that morning from his boardinghouse on Dey Street. By early afternoon he was committed to Bridewell in City Hall Park. The large crowd that quickly assembled outside his jail window showed that Jewett's murder tapped into a deep reservoir of emotions, and Robinson played to them by calling out "I am innocent, and I shall prove it tomorrow." By nightfall his employer, Joseph Hoxie, had hired Ogden Hoffman, one of the city's foremost trial lawyers, to defend him. Hoxie had chosen well, for Hoffman's client was from then on shrewdly silent.[1]

Opinion in the city quickly divided into two camps. After a few days of cautious and neutral reporting, most of the press seemed to conclude that the police had the right man. The circumstantial evidence against Robinson appeared overwhelming, and then the sensational revelation of his private writings only seemed to seal his fate. Wrote William Stanley, editor of the *Transcript*, on April 14:

> The excitement in the public mind in reference to this monstrous affair, continues to be unabated; and, notwithstanding the puny and purchased efforts of a ricketty, tottering print—notorious only for its easy access to petit bribery, and as being the most corrupt, profligate, and contemptible concern that was ever yet palmed upon any community—to produce an impression that other persons than Robinson have been the perpetrators of the foul assassi-

nation; yet the general conviction, from the evidence already before the public, is, (and we record it with regret,) that he alone is the guilty individual, and that his hands only are stained with the blood of Ellen Jewett.

Bennett of the *Herald* was the corrupt and profligate editor Stanley had in mind, for Bennett had cast doubts on Rosina Townsend's story and published a trumped-up, preposterous letter of confession. As Robinson's lone partisan, Bennett offered flimsy excuses and alternative hypotheses, serving mainly to distinguish his paper from the rest and to stir interest in the murder to a fever pitch. And it worked: combined circulation of the three major penny papers topped fifty thousand by mid-April. A fourth daily penny paper joined the market; its editor, William Newell, issued the *Ladies Morning Star* with the promise that it would cover crime but eschew lurid details, as befitted a readership of ladies.[2]

Bennett's strategy was predicated on knowing that some of the public would support Robinson. As he surmised, a large pro-Robinson sentiment mushroomed up in the days and weeks following the April murder. Young men of the clerking class made him their hero. They harassed the women of Thomas Street, they formed "Robinsonian Juntos" and imitated his trademark dandy clothes, and they hissed and booed at public meetings called to pontificate on the sins of prostitution. The evidence against their hero was strong but still largely circumstantial, giving them grounds to let loose with gender and class animosity. Simply put, they judged Robinson to be of higher worth than a prostitute. Could such a promising young man, they wondered, really be put at risk of hanging for murdering a lowly prostitute? The *Sun* published a letter signed "Veritas," who claimed to be Robinson's friend and a brothel patron "who has held familiar intercourse with that unfortunate girl." Disparaging Jewett as immoral and ugly, the writer concluded, "I am sorry to see so young a person [Robinson] sacrificed for ridding the city of so great a disgrace to her sex." The *Sun*'s editor, Benjamin Day, was quick to condemn the writer's hypocrisy and to challenge his assertion that Jewett deserved to die.[3] However, not all papers were so morally fastidious. A paper in Albany, New York, the *Microscope*, pursued Veritas's line of thinking: "If Robinson is in town, and has a spare hatchet, we would direct him to a sink of pollution in our neighborhood where he might do the public some service in his line."[4]

Rosina Townsend received anonymous threatening letters warning she would suffer "a fate similar to the melancholy and untoward one which befel the unfortunate Ellen Jewett" if she offered testimony against Robinson; one warned she would not live three days after the trial.[5]

Rosina handed the death threats over to the district attorney, and the police posted a guard at her house. When the grand jury met on April 18 and 19, crowds hooted and jeered Rosina and the other prostitutes who testified as they entered the court chambers. Several who testified indicated they had already left 41 Thomas Street for new and safer quarters elsewhere in the Fifth Ward.

Her business ruined, Rosina scheduled an auction of her furniture the day after her grand jury testimony. Anticipating the possibility of trouble at the auction, she hired two police officers (Dennis Brink was one) to stand guard during the sale. The *Herald* reported that the buyers were mostly young men, and they shelled out up to four times what the expensive furnishings had originally cost. Some buyers might have been seeking sentimental souvenirs to memorialize Jewett, but others were after a ghoulish talisman signifying sex and murder. At one point, the *Herald* editor reported, someone called out "Come, boys, let's have some relic of departed worth" and proceeded to hack up the footboard of Jewett's charred sleigh bedstead. Members of the crowd accepted the splinters "as meekly, but joyously, as would a wearied pilgrim a portion of the true cross," according to Bennett.[6] Possibly this was a respectful eucharistic scene; more likely, it was morbid fascination run amok.

The now vacant brothel became the site of spirited high jinks. On at least two occasions in early May, news of ghost sightings electrified the credulous and drew a carousing throng of fifty to one hundred people to the narrow confines of Thomas Street. The ghost of a young woman "with blood upon her face and hair streaming" was seen to glide past the street windows "as if on wings." Some reported seeing a hatchet floating around her. Ten days later, some claimed to see a woman in the window chased by a man with a hatchet poised as if to strike her.[7] How—or even whether—this hoax was perpetrated matters less than the glimpse it provides of crowd involvement in the Jewett murder. Jewett's sympathizers might well have wished to congregate at her death site to honor or marvel over her last moments. But this late-night gathering sounds more like spectators enjoying themselves at an impromptu street theater—the more especially, since the spectral show was reported only in the *Herald* and not any other newspapers.

Robinson-style coats and caps were another expression of sympathy with the young man under arrest. Some months after the crime, a broadside posted in the streets described the uniform for a "Robinsonian Junto" or club: a plum-colored dress coat with black velvet collar, black neck scarf, and floppy cap like the one Robinson wore throughout his trial.[8]

A series of quickly produced lithographs, marketed in late April and May, evinced the magnetic appeal of the murder and the partisanship of public reaction. Four prints featuring Jewett were prepared by artists and sold in bookshops and stalls along Broadway. Engraver and buyer together expressed their ardor for Jewett by turning her likeness into an object of contemplation, something that could be hung on a wall and used, like an icon, to stimulate admiration or fantasy. Jewett herself had expected to elicit a similar reaction when she loaned out her portrait miniature to particular male friends as a token of affection. But in place of the miniature's one-of-a-kind intimacy, mass-produced lithographs made Jewett's image available to anyone for a modest price. Jewett, post-mortem, became a pinup.[9]

One picture showed a pert and lively Helen out on the street, dressed in her trademark green silk dress, wearing gloves, a scarf, a brooch, a hat with a long lace veil, and carrying a parasol and a handkerchief. (See page 21.) A sealed letter in hand, she is presumably on her way to the post office. Her large dark eyes connect boldly with the viewer, and her playful smile suggests confidence and spirit. This picture of a vivacious, accomplished girl, richly dressed and not in the least resembling a loathsome bawd, captured the essence of the "worthy victim" theme that Jewett's supporters promoted in newspaper and pamphlet accounts. The artist, Alfred Hoffy, emphasized the big eyes and impossibly tiny hands and feet that were the hallmarks of refined feminine beauty in Jewett's era. But there is something undeniably smug and self-confident about her expression, registering a departure from demure femininity. "From an original Painting taken from Life," claimed the print publisher, H. R. Robinson—no relation to the accused—so her expression here may well be exactly the one Jewett herself chose when her portrait miniature, now lost, was painted.[10]

Two other pictures depicted Jewett's body in solemn repose. Bennett of the *Herald* predicted that one sketch in preparation would rival the *Ariadne* by New York artist John Vanderlyn—a cynically tasteless remark, for the mythic Ariadne napped peacefully in a meadow, inviting the viewer to gaze at her full-length nudity, whereas Jewett's real body—bludgeoned, burned, and eviscerated—surely caused the artist, Alfred Hoffy, to avert his eyes. The *Herald* trumpeted:

A View of the Scene of Murder.—An artist has taken a sketch of the beautiful form of Ellen Jewett, reposing in the embrace of death, like another Ariadne. . . . If correctly drawn, it will as far exceed Venus de Medicis, as nature always excells art.[11]

A day later, print seller H. R. Robinson offered for sale a picture showing Jewett dead in her bed, shoulders, breasts, and nipples exposed, filmy

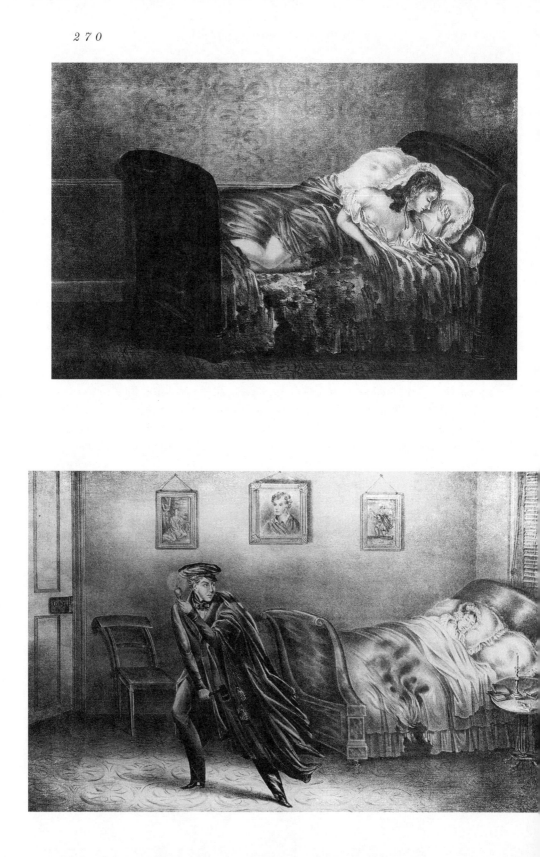

OPPOSITE TOP: Ellen Jewett, *by Alfred M. Hoffy, April 1836. This is the picture Bennett compared to Vanderlyn's* Ariadne.

OPPOSITE BOTTOM: The Innocent Boy, *by Alfred M. Hoffy, 1836, showing Robinson slinking away from the crime scene with the hatchet and a small globe lamp in his hands.*

LEFT TOP: Richard P. Robinson, Taken from the Miniature, *by A. E. Baker, April 1836.*

LEFT BOTTOM: Richard P. Robinson. Taken from life as he appeared in the Court of Oyer and Terminer, on his arraignment, *May 1836.*

and burned blankets barely covering her hips, naked legs visible from midthigh to midcalf.[12] Hand coloring rendered the bedsheets purple, the pillows light blue, the walls and rug green, and the bedstead brown; the print was only nine by thirteen and a half inches, sharply diminished from Vanderlyn's life-size painting. Bennett's promise that this would rival in eroticism the completely nude *Ariadne* was not met. But it was undeniably intended to be an erotic picture. No blood, no gashes, and certainly no incisions marred Jewett's peaceful slumber. The caption undid the work of Dr. Rogers by turning back the clock: "A correct likeness & representation of this unfortunate female, taken in the spot very shortly after she had become the victim of a foul and barbarous murder and her bedclothes had been set fire to on the night of the 9th of April 1836, in New York."[13] The *Sun* took note of the lithograph too: "It is sufficiently indecent to render it attractive to persons of depraved tastes, but as to being a likeness of Ellen Jewett, those who have seen her say that H. R. Robinson has murdered her far more barbarously than Richard P. Robinson did."[14]

Hoffy produced another crime-scene picture showing Richard P. Robinson stealing away from Jewett, who was lying in bed primly attired in nightgown and nightcap and covered to the shoulders with blankets. Only Robinson's leaving the scene, hatchet in hand, conveys the clue that the body in bed is a corpse. Robinson carries a very small lamp, and he wears the tasseled cloak that—if his—proved his guilt in many minds. If this picture did not overtly eroticize Jewett, displaying a woman in bed was itself an uncustomary intrusion into an intimate scene. The artist's accomplishment was to provide a window into the heart of the mystery, depicting the moment that proved Robinson had indeed committed the crime. It was a picture that could be conjured only in imagination, encouraging voyeuristic fantasies of the actual killing, which in the picture's scheme has taken place just minutes earlier.[15]

A lithographer on Wall Street named Alfred E. Baker produced a fourth picture of Jewett said to be based on her miniature; only the record of its copyright registration remains. (It may well have been the basis for a pirated print of Jewett, also said to be from her miniature, that decorated the cover of the totally fictional Boston-published story of Ellen Jewett; see page 224.)[16] A companion poster of Robinson, measuring eight by twelve inches, was issued by the same Alfred Baker, titled *Taken from the Miniature . . . the Supposed Murderer of Ellen Jewett*. In this version, Robinson appears as a cherubic lad with bee-stung lips and large, dreamy eyes looking off to the side and upward, suggesting either a coy femininity—or a short stature. Another Robinson print accompanied his arraignment for trial in late May. H. R. Robinson commissioned the artist Edward W. Clay to sketch the defendant "from life" as he appeared in court on May 25. In this full-length portrait, the slender youth wears a tight frock coat and pants, a ribbon bow tie, and heeled boots, and he carries his floppy cap at his side. His babylike face, smooth and androgynous, registers a sort of composure—not fear, not confidence, but some blank mental space in between, as if the subject's mind were quite dissociated from the hubbub of the murder trial.

In a free-ranging interview after the trial, Robinson was asked if he had seen any of the lithographs. "Yes," he replied,

> and how d——d innocent they make me look! I should take myself for one of the babes in the woods. I look as harmless as an infant Jesus. If that be a correct copy of my countenance, Ogden Hoffman ought to be thrown over the Bar for not setting up idiotcy in my defence. My face would have furnished an irresistible argument to any jury. In trying to make me look innocent, the artist has made me look foolish. I do'nt like to be Caspar Hauserized in this way. As for Helen, poor thing, she looks so brazen in the print, as Mary Magdalene; whereas, in truth, she was a fine intellectual looking woman. They say these caricatures are put up at the windows of the print shops and hawked about the country by vagabond boys? Never mind. The romancers may yet make us the Eloise and Abelard of the Age.[17]

(Kaspar Hauser was a German adolescent of the 1820s who had spent much of his childhood in a cage deprived of all human contact up to age seventeen; not a wild child, Hauser was a gentle and lovable soul in a state of arrested development. The narrative of his life had been published in Boston in 1833, which is how Robinson could know of it.)[18]

Robinson spurned his innocent representation, but his lawyer capitalized on it, although not by pleading idiocy for his client. During the trial, Hoffman repeatedly referred to the youth as "the innocent boy" or "the poor boy," and the appellation stuck. (A cartoon showed Robinson from behind, sitting at the bar of the courtroom with his lawyers, his narrow-shouldered coat emblazoned with the label "Innocent Boy." See page 313.) Probably he truly had a soft-faced, childish look younger than his nineteen years, which these lithographs emphasized for the mystery it added to the unfolding murder case (the commingling of innocence with guilt) and also because it enhanced Robinson's appeal as a dandy.

A popular masculine style of the 1830s, dandyism drew its inspiration from the aristocratic and aesthetic ideals supposed to be typified by Lord Byron, Beau Brummell, and their circle; the Parisian flaneur was a similar type. In New York and in the European capitals, some young men played the dandy by affecting colorful clothing, sloped shoulders, tiny boots, curled heads, and effeminate visages and gestures. So the lithographs of an angelic Robinson and his bee-stung lips might have been pin-ups as well, objects of erotic contemplation for a more specialized market. New York dandies occupied a sexually ambiguous space. No commentator (at least not in print) directly impugned Robinson's masculinity or raised any doubts about his ardent love for Helen Jewett. (The *New York Journal of Commerce* came close when it described Robinson as having a "feminine cast" and being "fashionably appareled" at his late-May arraignment.)[19] But a few hinted more directly that dandies as a class operated on a somewhat different set of sexual assumptions. A humorous pocket guide to New York City published in 1837 by a co-editor of the *Transcript* devoted a short chapter to dandies, right after a chapter on "rogues." Dandies, author Asa Greene wrote, numbered three thousand in New York, about 1 percent of the population. Greene's taxonomy included "chained dandies," with watch chain about the neck; "switched dandies," who carried a certain style of cane; and "quizzing glass dandies," marked by their monocles. "Ladies don't like them," Greene wrote, predicting they would therefore die out. For Greene, "dandy" was code for "homosexual."[20]

Beyond dandified clothing, threatening letters, and souvenir hunting, Robinson's supporters found another means of proclaiming their views. They seized the opportunity to disrupt moral reform meetings, called in the wake of the Jewett murder to lecture youth on chastity and prostitution.

Moral reform was one of the more controversial strains of social activism to arise in a decade suffused with radical movements of various kinds. Linked by outlook and membership to both temperance and anti-slavery, organized moral reform surfaced in New York in 1831, when the Magdalen Society was formed, the first of five associations dedicated to the problems of illicit sex. The New York Female Benevolent Society followed in 1832, the Seventh Commandment Society in 1833, the New York Female Moral Reform Society in 1834, and the American Moral Reform Society in 1836. Such unprecedented attention to the evil of licentiousness arose partly from the demographics of 1830s New York. Fears of sexual sin surged as the population grew, fears apparently justified by the increasing visibility and public acceptance of prostitution. The burst of attention to sex as sin also drew enormous strength from an evangelical crusade of vast proportions that engulfed a large segment of American Protestantism in the 1820s and 1830s, called the Second Great Awakening. Spouting a powerful message of religious reform and perfectionism, the five moral reform groups emerged from a Presbyterianism energetically awakened to sin and suffering by the Reverend Charles G. Finney's evangelistic crusade of 1830 to 1831 in New York City.

Why five groups instead of one? They all considered prostitutes the victims of male licentiousness, the central cause of illicit sex. But each group took a somewhat different stance on how to combat sexual sin, and they fought with each other, as siblings often do. The statistics-collecting Reverend John McDowall headed the Magdalen group, and he fearlessly roamed the rough Five Points area and the genteel Fifth Ward, accosting fallen women to give them Bibles and religious tracts. He prayed over their souls in the streets, in their houses, and sometimes over their beds, with the aim of reclaiming the women for Christ, which was probably easier than reclaiming them for respectable marriage and motherhood. McDowall's bold tactics finally brought him down. Critics within his own denomination charged that his publication, *McDowall's Journal*, was little more than a road map for the dissipated, a tour guide to the brothels. His accounts of girls' sexual stories were challenged as lurid encouragements to depravity. In 1835 fellow Presbyterians subjected him to a church trial in which he lost his ministry; he died soon after. The Benevolent Society of 1832, composed of Presbyterian women who had initially supported McDowall, turned away from his street ministry and opened a halfway house to prepare reformed prostitutes for employment in domestic service. But their labors never benefited more than a handful of penitents.

In sharp contrast, the Seventh Commandment Society, formed in 1833, made no attempt to rehabilitate fallen women. This group consisted entirely of men, most of them clerics concerned about adultery and fornication, as well as abolition and temperance.[21] Their monthly newspaper, the *Journal of Public Morals*, contented itself with vague, general statements about the moral deterioration of society.[22] The attacks on Reverend McDowall had shown the dangers of specificity when it came to opposing the sex trade. No brothel tours or halfway houses for these circumspect reformers; the entire program of the Seventh Commandment group consisted of an effort to convince ministers to overcome their squeamishness and preach to their congregations against sexual sin. The group remained timid, and by late 1834 it was moribund and no longer publishing about licentiousness. But it would spring back to life in the immediate wake of Jewett's murder.

McDowall's confrontational style was taken up in 1834 by the New York Female Moral Reform Society, which also bought his newspaper and subscription list and renamed it the *Advocate of Moral Reform*. Nearly all wives or close associates of the Seventh Commandment ministers, in their first issue of the *Advocate* in January 1835, the society's directors announced their intention of zeroing in on the sin of licentiousness, "for the sole reason, that the *men will not do it*. . . . Show us the man, or the body of men, that will do it, and we females, will gladly retire from this self-denying field, leaving it in better hands."[23] But their immediate experience was that men (their own husbands and ministers!) had lacked the courage to take on sexual sin. In contrast to the Female Benevolent Society, the Moral Reform women had little interest in reclaiming profligate females.[24] Their principal aim was to shame lustful men and to educate respectable women about the error of accepting libertines into the bosom of a family. They took on all manner of sexual threats to women— unescorted travel, seduction, courtship, novel reading, and the theater. The *Advocate* reached many hundreds of towns across the Northeast; by 1836 some four hundred towns from Maine to Michigan had established auxiliary societies. The crusade against male sexual predators drew large numbers of women throughout the northern states. Durham, Connecticut, Robinson's tiny home village, registered its local auxiliary in June 1836; the town's sudden and unsought fame in connection with the murder no doubt motivated the group's formation. And up in Maine, the news of Jewett's murder drove membership in the Hallowell Moral Reform group to seventy members.[25]

Curiously, the Female Moral Reformers made no original contribution to the debate over the murder of Helen Jewett. They publicized the crime, naturally, since the murder of a prostitute so perfectly fulfilled their warnings about the wages of sin. But they contented themselves with verbatim reprints from the *New York Sun*, withholding any special female perspective on Jewett's death. (The one exception: after printing the *Sun*'s transcript of the trial, which consumed the entire eight-page issue of the June 15 *Advocate*, they added an item of their own highlighting Mrs. Moulton, keeper of Robinson's boardinghouse, a person completely ignored by the court and by every other commentator on the case. The Moral Reform women wondered what kind of a "strange and reprehensible" mother she could be; did she know or care what her son and young boarders were doing?)[26] The reformers certainly were not inclined to see Jewett as the worthy victim portrayed by the *Herald* or the pamphlet literature; fallen women fell beyond earthly rescue. Instead, they ceded the initiative to their husbands in a revitalized Seventh Commandment Society, suspending publication of the *Advocate* for an issue in May so that the men could write and distribute the revived *Journal of Public Morals*, using the women's circulation list, which now numbered over twenty thousand subscribers nationwide.[27] Possibly the sense of crisis calling for action is what made the women step back; for evangelical women, convening public meetings was men's work.

Having nearly faded away in 1834, the Seventh Commandment men reassembled the week of April 11 to establish a Men's Moral Reform Society. "Such was the excitement attending the recent horrid murder in

Thomas Street, and so obvious was it to every one that something ought to be done to check the increasing licentiousness of the city, that it was deemed expedient for this object to call a public meeting," they explained. Placards and handbills issued forth announcing that on April 15, just five days after Jewett's murder, a moral reform meeting would occur at the Chatham Street Chapel on Chatham Square, above City Hall Park, a large church where the Reverend Charles G. Finney and other Presbyterians regularly held forth. Until 1832 the chapel had actually been a theater run by Thomas Hamblin, manager of the Bowery Theatre, so it was commodious enough to seat a large crowd.[28] Over 1,500 people came to the meeting.

Irony was not the strong suit of the moral reformers, but surely the irony of holding their meeting in a former theater, site of sin and sexual pollution, was not lost on them. The massive gray stone walls, hard wooden pews, and stained-glass windows of Trinity Church or St. Paul's might have discouraged rowdyism. But the Chatham's gaslit stage and cushioned seats arranged in boxes and tiers apparently encouraged the attendance that evening of a distinctly unchurchlike crowd that soon reverted to the raucous behavior characteristic of playgoers. To some extent, the Men's Moral Reformers foresaw problems: "It was apprehended that 'certain lewd fellows of the baser sort' might be disposed to make disturbances, therefore it was thought prudent to change the exercises from addresses, which had been expected, to a regular sermon" calculated to draw on as much customary deference as possible.[29] This was the only subtle allusion to any disturbance at the meeting that made its way into the published account in the *Journal of Public Morals*. The *New York Herald* wrote with obvious relish:

> Several long-visaged gentlemen with long coats made long speeches and longer prayers. They proposed that the ladies should reject every suitor who had not their certificates of good behavior. Tired of cant and hypocrisy, the audience began to groan, hiss, hoot, holloa, and fling torpedoes about like hailstones. Several females fled. A general row took place. The front lamps were broken.[30]

Nevertheless, the Men's Moral Reformers were not entirely displeased with the outcome. A constitution for the new society gained some ninety-six signatures that evening and chartered the group on the course of gathering the statistics of sin, the uniquely masculine approach to social ills ("more proper for a society of gentlemen than of ladies," they asserted). They made a bid for national status by renaming themselves the American Moral Reform Society. The Jewett murder appeared to have done what several years of female agitation over sexual sin had not been able to accomplish: it spurred male reformers to reorder their priorities and promise to give licentiousness the same attention they gave to drink and slavery.[31]

What analysis did the male reformers bring to bear on the murder of a prostitute? Unwilling to defend either Jewett or Robinson, since both were partners in profligacy, the female reformers had declined to engage with the case. The sermons of the Reverend W. C. Brownlee, a vice president of the organization, represented the views of the male reformers. Reverend Brownlee lectured twice on the Jewett murder, on April 24 and again on June 12, after the trial. At well-publicized evening meetings sponsored by the Men's Moral Reform group, Brownlee condemned Jewett as a "miserable, execrable being . . . leprous in soul and body." Robinson, in contrast, was a lost innocent who succumbed to temptations offered by "that class of our salesmen, who, to beguile young merchants, introduce them to the numerous sinks of iniquity."[32] The Reverend Brownlee blamed the corruption of youth on avaricious employers: "He laid much of the sin at the doors of the wholesale merchants who encourage their salesmen to accompany their customers to the theatres and brothels to induce them to purchase largely."[33] So completely did he exonerate Robinson in his April 24 lecture that an informant for the *Sun* sarcastically reported Brownlee virtually "acquitted" the accused. It was the police, who tolerated and patronized houses of prostitution and who therefore had Jewett's blood on their hands, the minister told an attentive overflow crowd at his Carmine Street church.[34] In short, the Men's Moral Reform group basically sided with the unfortunate young men of New York, sucked into temptations sanctioned by the police and the mercantile elite.

What all these open meetings showed was that large crowds were eager to listen to addresses on the Jewett murder—crowds that contained a wide variety of opinions about prostitution and Jewett. The Men's Moral Reformers professed to be glad to get ninety-six signatures endorsing their group that night of the first mass meeting. But, significantly, an additional 1,400 people present left without joining up, and some of them had hissed and thrown projectiles at the stage, seizing a moment of intense public agitation over sex to thumb their noses at moralists and publicly flout the conventional pieties and standards of behavior. "Lewd fellows of the baser sort" were emboldened to claim their day in the sun.

The Female Moral Reformers avoided taking a stand on the Jewett murder, but they did not succeed in escaping its consequences. In fact, they were accused of encouraging the licentiousness that contributed to Jewett's death. Like McDowall before them, they were charged with being immoral reformers, obsessed with sex and delighted to revel in lurid narratives of seduction. What is the cause of the spread of sexual immorality, so nakedly revealed in "the recent case of young Robinson and his associates," the *New York Commercial Advertiser* pointedly asked. Look to the Moral Reform ladies and their "moral quackery," the editor answered. These respectable women were "so blinded by their fanaticism as to forget the delicacy and reserve of their sex." How could they imagine, the *Commercial Advertiser* complained, that teaching children about lewdness and prostitution would do anything but stimulate and encourage that very evil? The *Advocate of Moral Reform*, it charged, abounded "in loathsome details, which, we venture to assert, would not have been openly read in the drawing room of Rosina Townsend!" Here was a striking assertion indeed: that prostitutes like Jewett and Townsend had more ladylike delicacy than the Female Moral Reformers!

The *Advertiser* further berated the male moral reformers' open meetings, led by "young men and almost beardless boys," inappropriately discussing prostitution and vice, "entering into details of the most revolting description and filling the minds of young and old with ideas that they had never before entertained, and associations of the very existence of which they were previously and happily ignorant."[35] The *New-York Transcript* congratulated the *Commercial Advertiser* for its editorial and elaborated on a parallel theme, the corruption of women. "The mischief done to the female part of society by McDowall's infamous publications, is incalculable," said the editor. "If the mind . . . is accustomed to investigate the details of depravity, there is no security for the preservation of innocence, no safe-guard to purity of heart and soul, no reasonable assurance that that shrinking and instinctive modesty, which is the charm and strength of womanhood, will not be tarnished, and become a matter of convenience, a mask, and a pretence."[36] Women should not even think about depravity, even in the service of working to improve morals; feminine modesty required ignorance.

Just how innocent and ignorant were the young clerks of New York? Robinson's image as a respectable young man came apart five days after the murder when editors got a glimpse of a diary the police confiscated from the youth's room on Dey Street. Even Bennett had to admit that the Robinson of the diary was corrupt, but he soberly reminded his readers that a depraved character alone was insufficient grounds for convicting a man of murder. The diary was smart and rude, the *Sun* reported; it covered the months from June 1834 to the present, and it carried a rather peculiar threat (or promise?) on the cover: "Whoever shall pry unbidden into the secrets of this book, will violate the whole of the ten commandments."[37] Such an inscription functioned as a commonplace adolescent warning: Keep out, secret diary. But it also suggested that a reader would himself be corrupted merely by reading it. The warning revealed a diarist grandly engaged in fantasies of power and contagion.

The editors of the *Sun* and the *Transcript* owed their reading of the diary to an uncircumspect clerk at the Police Office. After hesitating over whether it would prejudice the murder case, both papers published very brief excerpts. Bennett apparently did not get to see the diary, so he took the high ground and righteously criticized his rival editors for printing prejudicial material.[38] In fact his competitors' revelations were so narrow and limited as to suggest that the editors did not see passages—if there were any—that bore on the Robinson-Jewett relationship.

The diary excerpts were enough to reveal a Robinson of self-conscious duplicity. Entries bragged that the writer "carried an old head between his young shoulders" and was routinely "credited with more honesty and innocence than he was entitled to," especially in his dealings with women. Most disconcerting of all was Robinson's vulgar contempt for his employer, Joseph Hoxie. "Cursed be he twice, and all his family, forever," he snarled, in a complaint about his paltry annual salary of sixty dollars. The clerk's vengefulness "not only astonished but also severely shocked some of his most sincere and true friends," reported the *Sun*. If Hoxie himself was shocked, he did not let on publicly; nor, on the other hand, did he rush to protest that Robinson had understated the salary. Most full-time clerks earned several hundred dollars a year; sixty dollars, or barely more than a dollar a week, was an amazingly low salary even for a beginning clerk, and Robinson had worked for Hoxie for two years.[39]

Even worse, the diary opened with a highly unusual dedication, which the *Sun* identified as a quotation from Lord Byron's *Manfred*: "When these eyes shall be closed in death, the heiress of this book is my mother." Literary allusion aside, what manner of son would bequeath a private diary recording irreverent and corrupt ideas to his mother? The *Sun* assumed that a profligate young man would hide his shameful acts most of all from a mother, yet here was Robinson claiming he would thrust his corruption in her face.[40]

The *Transcript* editors pronounced the diary fragments "appalling and astounding":

> In one part of his diary, he says;—"Most youths at seventeen or eighteen years of age take a pride in boasting of their amours, of their dissipations, and of their wild exploits; I have, however, no taste for such exposures. If I had, I could mention things that would make my old granny, and even wiser folks, stare, notwithstanding that I am young, and look very innocent."[41]

Was it his dissoluteness that troubled the *Transcript* most, or Robinson's unusual and unsettling claim that he preferred to keep silent about his exploits instead of boasting of them to male friends? Male camaraderie over amours, no matter how conceited or exaggerated, at least functioned as a boundary setter of sorts. For a young man to keep mum about sexual adventures implied a deeper depravity, beyond the approval of unrestrained clerks in the city. In addition to sexual depravity, the *Transcript* intoned, the diary revealed his profligacy. "Not only does it [the diary] show that he has been for a considerable time past squandering large sums of money, but it also exposes a course of vice which but few, of the most depraved individuals even, ever indulge in."[42] Naturally this provoked curiosity about where Robinson got such sums to spend on his spectacularly low salary of sixty dollars per annum.

A diary detailing Robinson's reprehensible secret life gave even James Gordon Bennett pause. But the *Herald*'s editor remained fastidious about Robinson's rights. The state of his morals should not permit jumping to the conclusion that the youth had committed the murder. "Robinson's private life appears to have been, so far as the female sex was concerned, licentious in the extreme," Bennett conceded. "Yet he has not been sunk in pollution lower than hundreds of his age and sex and at this day, still moving in respectable society, smiled upon by the virtuous; adorned by the beautiful and desired by the witty and accomplished."[43] A scoundrel, maybe, but a scoundrel with lots of company; whether he was guilty of murder was yet to be ascertained.

Neither Robinson's lawyer nor any police official protested the publication of quotations from Robinson's diary or contested their accuracy. Robinson's lawyers were simply unaccustomed to factoring in press coverage, especially since the penny press with its pretrial crime coverage was a new force in public life. Hoffman chose to ignore it, probably calculating that its popular readership would be unlikely to show up in the jury box. Juries in New York City were not drawn from the population at large but from lists submitted by aldermen containing the names of the leading male citizens of each ward. Hoffman probably thought he could safely disregard the penny press and still give his client a good defense. Attempts at managing, or "spinning," the news lay in the future.

Within weeks of the murder, a pamphlet purporting to be an earlier section of Robinson's diary appeared in bookstores and stalls. The title page bore no author or publisher, although the *Philadelphia Ledger* helpfully noted that copies could be obtained from Sackett and Branch, printers in New York. (The lithographers hustled to copyright their works to prevent theft, but none of the Jewett pamphlets was entered under copyright protection. Copyrighting required merely strolling to the federal

District Court in Manhattan, filling out a form, and paying a small fee. The form required names—of author, of publisher—and perhaps that was the sticking point, the desire to maintain anonymity.) The printed diary of Robinson first appeared under the name "Francis P. Robinson," corrected in subsequent printings to "Richard P. Robinson."[44] ("Francis" was the name the *Sun* printed in its early coverage of the murder, assuming "Frank" to be Robinson's nickname.) The entries covered October and November 1833, the months immediately preceding Robinson's arrival in New York City. These dates are consistent with Hoxie's trial testimony. Robinson had worked for him for two years, he said, and he had known him for four years, an allusion to the family connection forged by Hannah Hoxie's marriage to James Robinson, Richard's cousin.

Was this printed diary extract authentic? George Templeton Strong, a son in a well-to-do merchant's family living on Greenwich Street who himself kept a long-running diary, wrote on June 11 that he had purchased a copy of the pamphlet "which the loafers are hawking about the streets." He pronounced this one bogus: "No more his diary than it is mine."[45] Strong was sixteen, exactly Robinson's age in 1833. In sharp contrast with the youthful Strong's dutiful daily record of weather, social calls, business news, and cheerful gossip, Robinson's printed diary presented a tangle of nihilistic, negative, and arrogant observations—little wonder Strong found the document hard to credit. The Robinson revealed in the diary extract, its anonymous publisher emphasized,

> has an astonishing insight into human nature—a depth and grasp of observation uncommon to men of maturer age. No person, perhaps, ever relied more entirely upon the resources of his own mind than he. He seems to have adopted no opinions upon the credit of great names. He scanned every measure—he analyzed every character that came under his notice. . . . There seems to be nothing in nature destitute of interest to him. And yet there is little in his appearance or conversation indicative of strong character. He seems to have lived within himself.[46]

Four reasons favor the authenticity of the diary. None is sufficient in itself, but the weight of them together makes it more probable than not that Robinson wrote it. First, the 1833 extract matched the character and description of the 1834 to 1836 diary seen by the editors of the *Sun* and the *Transcript*: snappy, rude, egotistic. Second, it echoes themes from the Robinson-Jewett correspondence about day-night mental states and parallels as well some rather sharply worded letters Robinson wrote that surfaced a dozen years after the trial. If a printer fabricated this 1833 diary, he somehow hit upon a few distinctive attitudes not publicly associated with Robinson in 1836. Third, and most convincing, the pamphlet moves through three phases of successively smaller type. Up to page 17, the extracts are of a usual print size; from page 17 to 21, the print is smaller, and from 21 to 24 it approaches the microscopic. Cheap pamphlets of the era came in three basic lengths of sixteen, twenty-four, and thirty-six pages, a standard governed by type layout and ways of cutting and folding large sheets of paper to make pages. A printer had to carefully estimate how many pages would be required to set a text in one size of type. A too short text was not a big problem, and cheap pamphlets frequently had a blank page or two at the end. But one that was too long might have to undergo editing to make it fit. An author could easily have tailored and trimmed the entries of a bogus diary to fit the printer's specifications. In this case, it is evident that the printer was trying to squeeze an unedited document into the space he had available by progressively shrinking the type.

The fourth reason for thinking the diary was genuine is that it is unspecific in detail and telegraphic in content. A writer intent on forging a document displaying Robinson's evil or murderous character would likely have done a better job. Recall the bogus letter Bennett printed in the *Herald*. Going to the heart of the matter, it crisply ascribed the murder to a different person. This pamphlet diary remains vague and elusive. It never says enough to convince the reader Robinson could be capable of murder. True, the pamphlet might have been an exceptionally skillful forgery. What weighs against authenticity was the *Sun*'s report that the diary the police found began in 1834. Conceivably, though, police magistrate Oliver Lownds recovered two volumes from the Dey Street room, and only the one bearing on Robinson's New York life was glimpsed by the press.

The printer's preface offered justification for putting the diary extracts before the public. As the chief suspect, Robinson formed "a legitimate area of inquiry." (And certainly the newspapers were not giving him or his character much play.) Further, the thrilling story was a tragedy as well as a romance that if rightly told "will do more to guard the footsteps of the young than all the fictions of the stage, or the homilies of the pulpit." True stories of sinful youth and seduced girls were educational, schooling youth in the hard lessons of life. The preface promoted Jewett as a gifted woman exceptional in beauty and intelligence, brought to a tragic "career of guilt" through the work of a heartless villain, her original seducer who started her on the path to prostitution. Robinson was said to be of strict Calvinist stock, so rigidly disciplined in religion that his acute mental training led him to become a "consummate scoundrel" and one "much addicted to novel reading."[47] And yet no particular evidence suggested he would become a murderer, the printer allowed. The fearful part of Robinson's story was precisely that it could happen to any young man like him:

> Robinson's history, previous to his late unfortunate intimacy with Helen Jewett, was very much like the history of thousands of other young men, similarly educated, who have left behind them the restraints of home, and waded in the dissipation of cities. . . . In short, thousands who think of Robinson only as a murderer, may find in his earlier history a fearful resemblance to their own.[48]

The October and November 1833 entries of the diary place Robinson somewhere other than his hometown, Durham, yet not yet in New York. Each diary entry is a short self-contained essay, sometimes about an event of daily life, or about politics, or a shrewd observation of a social custom. Three examples give the flavor of the pamphlet:

Oct. 6, 1833

    I am almost sick this evening; have just returned from the races, having won, let me see, twenty-seven dollars. This is the last day of the races; the day on which they run out all the dregs and draw off the equestrian settlings, the spavined, the ring-boned, the stifled, the blind, lame and halt. Friend P. advises me not to bet; he gives me so much advice that, in fact, it would require more wisdom to profit by it than to live without it; his system of morals is like J. R.'s patent dog churn, which was a most excellent machine only it required three hands to tend it. I shall not attempt to cleanse my inner man particularly, being well convinced that, if I shake the devil out of me, there will be nothing left. G. pretends to be a moralist and a philosopher; but what better is a moralist than a stoic; or a philosopher than an hypothesis maker, and a wretched squatter on the wilderness of conjecture?

Oct. 11th

    Had an argument with Mr. M. on the question of the utility of Sunday schools; he is perfect master of the church and state cant. Forsooth, he considers the institution dangerous to liberty, &c. For my part, I believe it is doing good. It tears up a great deal of ignorance by the roots, and is at war with priestcraft. It is good policy, in carrying a point against an obstinate adversary, to seem to yield; for by this means he is generally disarmed. To convince an obstinate and conceited man, it is sometimes necessary to throw arguments around him and within his reach, which, though he may not observe it, really go to sustain the opinions you wish him to embrace; and then, by attacking him in some weak point, compel him to lay hold of your strong arguments for defence; which, regarding as his own he will examine and view favorably; and, before he is aware of it, make them the frame of the very conclusion you wish him to adopt. Some of the best reasoners are little skilled in changing men's opinions. Conviction is one thing—persuasion another.

Oct. 14th

Had an interview with Miss D. She is perfectly enchanting. Her splendor is not dimmed by a single speck of vanity or affectation. She takes no pains to show her handsome little feet. You see no mincing and trying to look lovely. I wish I could appropriate her. She is aided by art to be sure; but that is right; so is the painted girl of the forest. How does art differ from affectation? Art is a transparent covering of nature—affectation, an *opaque*. Art is consistent with natural grace and ease—; affectation is not. The former adorns—; the latter deforms natures. If Miss D. * * * *

Here follows a long dissertation, which however interesting, I [the printer] shall take the liberty to suppress.

Many of the entries consist of aphorisms and one-line jokes. The author bounces from topic to topic; Miss D. and other young women come under scrutiny, and various young men are chided for being wicked, stupid, or "a profound ass."

Nov. 12.

Why should I be angry at a fellow like S.? There are some men of whom God only requires that they shall do no harm. He has but two ideas in his head, and those two are not breeders. I should despise myself if I believed I were jealous of him. What a beauty he is! I wish I could hire him to let me take his picture for a pair of dog-irons. I wonder whether he belongs to the human species or is from Tennessee? And yet the girl seemed to countenance the wretch's addresses. What whimsical fools women are!

There is a strand of brief commentary running through several entries about the author's sense of being different from others:

Nov. 12th. I think my death would not increase the sale of crape in this town. How little I should be missed here; how much less in the world!

Nov. 14th. Is it uncommon for men to distrust their own sanity of mind? I believe not. I speak from my own experience. Thoughts and feelings in which we indulge without aversion in the evening, often fill our minds with disgust when we reflect on them in the morning.

Nov. 23rd. This world wears more ruffle than shirt. I have often felt, (when shaving, for instance) a sudden and almost ungovernable desire to commit suicide. And yet I had as keen a relish for life as ever. I feel a kind of horrible delight in thus poising myself in imagination, over the dark gulf of eternity. There may be danger of increasing this excitement to such a degree as to induce insanity and suicide. Perhaps curiosity as often causes suicide, as misanthropy. My good old father would call it a temptation of the devil.

[Undated—an early entry in New York City.] Just returned from a visit at the Insane Hospital. What chaos of mind is there! But is any person perfectly sane? No. I grant that the madness of the maniac is more peculiar, and less popular, and therefore less apparent; but probably not more real than mine. No mind is strictly sane while under the undue influences of any passion; for passion always distorts the intellectual vision. We are, perhaps, generally more sane in the morning than in the evening. How many sanguine projects we form in the evening, which we reject as foolish or visionary the next morning? This results from the different states of our minds. In the morning the mind is calm, and reason vigorous and imagination asleep; but at night the passions are up. They love late hours. Sometimes, at the dead hour of midnight, a thought is roused up from the deep caverns of the mind, like a startled maniac, which all the energy of reason can scarcely re-cage![49]

These are worrisome entries, the kind that would alarm a middle-class parent of our own day into seeking psychiatric help for a child. The Jekyll-Hyde theme of day and night, of calm and passion, of frightening night fears, also appears in Robinson's correspondence with Jewett. The flirtations with suicide and mania seem not to draw their energy from anger or despondence, but to arise out of curiosity, of "horrible delight" in contemplating the abyss of eternity—or insanity.

Robinson's parent does appear several times in this diary, most fully when the youth received a letter which he copied into the diary. The diarist Robinson wrote on Oct. 14, "I have spent this day in castle-building, New-York plans, &c." On November 5 he inserted into the diary a letter received from his father, who wrote:

I dislike the idea of your going to New York to reside; nor will I attempt to disguise the reasons. I fear that your moral character may suffer. You will there be ensnared by a thousand temptations which I fear you have not strength of principle to resist. I know your self-confidence; but I also know your weakness, my son. Even where you are, I tremble for you. Indeed, indeed, you are, I fear, a child of the devil!

The diarist then elaborated his reaction with sarcasm and wit:

My old father little knows the strength of my character. So I am not to be risked in a city! Forsooth the carriages would run over me! Indeed! indeed! I think I had best be taken back to the nursery! But the danger arises from my being a child of the devil. Really the old man gives himself a hard name—I dislike such paternity.[50]

This is the sort of cleverness that made George Templeton Strong doubt that the diary was genuine. But Strong had not yet seen a set of letters Robinson wrote in jail and passed to William D. Gray, a friend also in Bellevue awaiting trial on charges of theft. Gray was the original owner of the tasseled cloak and holder of a series of smart, sly letters from Robinson that were splashed all over the newspapers in mid-July.

The police moved Robinson to Bellevue after the grand jury indicted him on April 20. Built in 1811, Bellevue included a three-story almshouse, a three-story workhouse, and a two-story prison grouped together on a site near Kips Bay along the East River at Twenty-eighth Street. The prison housed about 150 prisoners awaiting trial, plus another 150 female convicts lodged there because the state prison at Sing-Sing did not accept women. The building was small but somehow commodious enough to allow each woman her own cell.[51] Robinson also rated a single cell and commanded a steady supply of cigars, coffee, and reading matter, mainly novels and newspapers. James Gordon Bennett of the *Herald* tried to visit him in mid-May, but the keeper of Bellevue Prison, Daniel Lyons, informed him that Robinson's attorney Ogden Hoffman had forbidden unapproved guests. Bennett did learn that a male friend from Connecticut had visited Robinson, as had his father and uncle. Lyons also told him that a "Miss Norris, the young lady to whom he was engaged, was there, and had spent some time with him." Bennett did not explain who Miss Norris might be. As Lyons informed Bennett, Robinson

> has been quite moderate lately. As his trial approaches, his great flow of good spirits decreases, but his firmness remains unshaken. He amuses himself with smoking and reading. . . . Mr. Lyons says his deportment generally, is perfectly correct, and if he does occasionally exhibit a little exuberance of spirit, it is pardonable.[52]

But Hoffman's rule forbidding guests was not in effect a bit earlier than Bennett's visit. About a week after Robinson's arrest a young lady (whose name was unknown to Daniel Lyons when he testified at the trial) visited him and was heard to remark, "Richard, how thin your hair is getting behind!" Lyons also noticed the bald spot. A Bellevue doctor was sent for to evaluate the rapid hair loss, said to be copious. Next a barber appeared and shaved the head. At trial, Lyons reported he was very upset to learn of the shaving, because he was sure lawyer Hoffman would be angry to find his client's appearance modified in any way. Hoffman was angry, Lyons said, and ordered tighter security.[53]

But that order did not prevent another visit, also not authorized by Hoffman. A grocer named Robert Furlong presented himself at Bellevue perhaps two weeks after the murder and asked Lyons for permission to see the prisoner. He told Lyons he had read a description of Robinson in a penny paper (probably the *Herald*, describing Robinson's miniature) and wondered if it was the same young man he had seen in his store the night of the murder. Lyons continued:

> When he saw Robinson, he went up to him, and reminded him that he knew him; said that he had seen him in his store on the Saturday night before the murder, and remembered his buying half a dollar's worth of cigars. Robinson said that he remembered it, and he thanked Mr. Furlong for the trouble he had taken in his behalf, for the purpose of identifying him, and for his good wishes.

Furlong's own testimony was rather more specific:

> Burnham, one of the keepers, was present when I first went there, and I told him that my object in wishing to see Robinson was mere curiosity, to ascertain whether or not I knew him. Burnham went up with me to the cell, and he called him out. When he came out, I

said to Burnham, "now let us see whether he will speak to me," and
as soon as he came out of the cell he came up to me, shook hands,
and said, "how do you do Furlong?"[54]

As it happens, Henry Burnham had an acquaintance with Furlong of
seven or eight years' standing, and this no doubt eased Furlong's entry
into the jail. Burnham's memory of the meeting filled in a few details:

> Went with him to Robinson's cell. Robinson was laid down and as
> soon as he went in, he got up. Furlong said to him how do you do
> Mr. Robinson, and he answered how do you do, sir, and shook
> hands with him. Furlong then told him that he thought he had seen
> him in his store on the Saturday before the murder. Robinson
> replied that if he had anything to say he had better speak to his
> counsel. Nothing further of any importance was said by either of
> them.[55]

Furlong paid a second visit to Bellevue about four weeks later, again to
check his visual memory, he claimed. By this time he had contacted
Joseph Hoxie, who urged him to contact Ogden Hoffman. As Furlong testified, "I did see him, and told him the whole story. No one ever told me
that my testimony would be very material in this case. I did not know that
I should be called upon as a witness until lately. I did not know it until just
as I was going out of town, and then Hoffman requested me to remain in
the city, saying that I should be wanted. I afterwards received a subpoena
to attend this trial."[56]

Bennett was barred from seeing Robinson, but Furlong was admitted
on the say-so of his acquaintance Henry Burnham. His quick identification of Robinson was then conveyed to an indifferent-sounding Hoffman,
on the grocer's own initiative; or so went Furlong's testimony. The timid
Furlong was not even certain he would be called to testify until he got his
eleventh-hour subpoena. But when Hoffman opened the case for the
defense, Furlong was the witness he called first to the stand. Cast in the
leading role in the drama at the City Hall courtroom, Furlong provided
Robinson's alibi for part of Saturday night, and he played to a highly
receptive audience. Gentleman Philip Hone, once mayor of New York,
attended the trial and assessed the large gallery of spectators:

> There appears to be a fellow-feeling in the audience; I was sur-
> rounded by young men, about his own age, apparently clerks like
> him, who appeared to be thoroughly initiated into the arcana of
> such houses as Mrs. Rosanna Townsend's. They knew the wretched

female inmates as they were brought up to testify, and joked with each other in a manner illy comporting with the solemnity of the occasion.[57]

Robinson supporters jammed the courtroom and cheered loudly at Furlong's testimony. The room seated nearly a thousand, and thousands more young men attempted to gain entry. Clearly this murder touched a nerve, and youthful men most of all pressed forward, eager to witness the spectacle much as they flocked to theatrical productions. Here was a chance to learn more about the lurid details of the world of illicit sex, to stare at beautiful prostitutes grilled on the stand, to relive the blows of the midnight assassin, and to root for one of their own kind, a promising nineteen-year-old boy whose youthful indiscretions could not really be made to hurt him, or so the sympathetic audience hoped.

One group of young men with a very particular interest in the murder of Jewett and trial of Robinson also convened in solidarity during the trial. Nathan Weston and Joseph Williams, rooming together at Harvard Law School, welcomed three guests on about June 3 or 4 for a week: brothers Daniel and George Melville Weston came down from Maine, accompanied by George Robinson, the twenty-two-year-old editor of the *Augusta Age*. This was a reunion whose mere date establishes its certain purpose: to follow the trial and its aftermath in the local Massachusetts papers and to provide space for the boys to unburden themselves of whatever personal emotions had surfaced in what must surely have been a terrible and painful episode. Letters to mothers would never be used to convey how these young men felt about Dorcas Doyen / Helen Jewett, and the surviving letters written by the mothers (Paulina Cony Weston, Sarah Cony Williams) make it quite clear that this was a family determined to drop a veil of silence around the whole affair. Face-to-face discussions in Harvard student lodgings at least allowed for a managed release of pent-up anxieties and fears.[58] Even with the savaging of Jewett's character that these five young men had perpetrated in the *Boston Post* and the *Augusta Age*, serving to defend their family's reputation, it remains an open question whether they finally rooted for Robinson or mourned Jewett in that room in Harvard Yard. She, after all, was the one they had grown up with for five years along the banks of the Kennebec River.

CHAPTER FIFTEEN

Trial in June

ICHARD P. ROBINSON'S trial for murder opened on a "wet and boisterous" Thursday morning in early June. A crowd estimated at six thousand persons waited to surge into the courtroom on the southeast corner of the second floor of New York's City Hall when its doors opened at ten in the morning. Packing the marble staircase and the downstairs lobby, the eager spectators spilled out into the windy rain falling in the park outside. Judge Ogden Edwards presided at the bench of the court of Oyer and Terminer, assisted by four city aldermen.

The trial was unusually long by contemporary standards—five days, encompassing eleven or twelve hours a day for the first four days and stretching to fourteen hours the final day. The marathon sessions ensured that the jury kept a tight focus on the details of the case. A daily half-hour recess at three provided the only break in the strenuous drama; on the last day, the recess extended to an hour and a half while the lawyers prepared their closing arguments. (The record is silent about how and when the principal players ate food or managed toilet breaks, beyond the once-daily half-hour recess.) Twenty reporters from newspapers in New York and Philadelphia bent their efforts to capture the testimony as best they could, racing to meet the next day's deadlines. No official transcripts of trials were made in the 1830s. Court-employed scribes typically made brief notes on such preparatory events as coroner and grand jury testimony and depositions—but trials themselves were like theatrical productions, events to be heard and judged by the jury on standards of performance. The effort to capture the proceedings verbatim arose not from conviction that exact wording mattered in any judicial sense, but from the demands of the market. The intense public interest in Robinson's trial inspired an abundance of commercial publishers each to create a script of the dramatic proceedings, so thousands outside the courtroom could vicariously experience the trial.[1]

Judge Edwards, fifty-five, usually headed a Superior Circuit Court which met in New York City in alternate months. The court of Oyer and Terminer met infrequently, and different judges were at risk for assignment to it, as needed; this time it was Judge Edwards's turn. The court handled only serious criminal cases, amounting to seven in all of 1836: three cases of murder, two of manslaughter, one arson, and one conspiracy trial, the latter a landmark labor case involving twenty journeymen tailors charged with price-fixing and conspiring to strike and presided over by Judge Edwards.[2] The judge had convicted the tailors in late May, but they awaited sentencing, a difficult decision Judge Edwards was postponing until after the Robinson case. Some of the strong passions over the murder case intermingled with similarly strong passions still hanging over the tailors' case. So Judge Edwards found himself a controversial figure even before he gaveled the Robinson case into session.

Ogden Edwards was a major figure in legal circles in New York in the 1830s. Family connections furthered his career. His grandfather was the brilliant Congregational minister Jonathan Edwards, whose religious labors in the pulpit of Northampton, Massachusetts, in the mid-eighteenth century helped shape the intellectual forces of the First Great Awakening. The judge's father, Pierpont Edwards, also a lawyer, represented Connecticut at one of the historic Continental Congresses of Revolutionary days and then became a federal judge. Ogden Edwards started his career in 1807 serving as judge of New York's Surrogate Court; in the 1810s he sat in the state legislature, and he served in the state's Constitutional Convention of 1821. In the 1820s he was counsel for the corporation of New York, and then he became Circuit Court judge for nearly twenty years. In 1846, he was a Whig candidate for governor. His brother, Henry Edwards, was annually elected governor of Connecticut for five terms in the 1830s, where it is possible, indeed likely, that his path crossed with Richard Robinson's father, then serving in Connecticut's legislature.[3]

Judge Ogden Edwards shared a first name and distant heritage with Ogden Hoffman, Robinson's celebrated attorney. A common ancestor named John Ogden in seventeenth-century New Jersey furnished the surname, carried on until it reached fifth-cousin women descendants in the Revolutionary era who married (one to Nicolas Hoffman, one to Pierpont Edwards) and bequeathed their surnames as first names to sons and grandsons.[4] It is not at all clear that Edwards and Hoffman acknowledged or even realized their family connection, or that it made the least difference in the trial. The confraternity of lawyers and judges throughout America was growing rapidly in the Jacksonian years, but as demonstrated by these two, highly successful lawyers typically came from old first families with superior access to legal training, so it is not really surprising to find cross-linkages in their family trees.

Ogden Hoffman, forty-three, had a silver tongue. Every nineteenth-century tribute to him marveled at his expressiveness: he "captivated all by his wit and his wonderful eloquence; his voice was music from the note of a lute to the blast of a bugle."[5] "In criminal cases, he was infinitely the superior of any man at the bar . . . [due to] his perfect knowledge of criminal law—his deep insight into the springs of human action—his solid sense, combined with his surpassing eloquence."[6] Able to build compelling and highly pathetic stories, sometimes out of mere wisps of circumstantial evidence, Hoffman had mastered the art of appealing to a jury. So dazzling were his oratorical powers that his two- and three-hour summary arguments caused spellbound reporters to throw aside their pens and listen in awe.[7] In an otherwise ordinary trial involving a woman charged with fraud, the *Transcript* reported that the crowd witnessing Hoffman's closing argument "paid tribute in tears to its potency and influence," interrupting his "forensic oratory" with "loud and indecorous tokens of admiration and applause."[8] Said an 1890s biographical compendium of the bench-and-bar variety, "He was probably the most consummate criminal lawyer that America has produced. He was polished, suave and courteous, and never resorted to bullying or browbeating witnesses."[9]

The son of a prominent judge and adroit lawyer, Josiah Ogden Hoffman, Ogden Hoffman graduated from Columbia University, served as an officer in the navy, and saw combat in the War of 1812. Following the war, he began practicing law, eventually joining Hugh Maxwell in a partnership that spanned many years. His love of language manifested itself not only in the courtroom, but in his mastery of English literature and his leading role in a debating society good enough to charge admission. From 1829 to 1835 Hoffman served as the city's district attorney, providing him a lot of practice in persuading juries.[10] He was the D.A. in the courtroom when Helen Jewett and John Boyd had their legal dispute in 1835. Six months before the murder, he had returned to private practice, and many speculated on how different things might have been if the mellifluous Hoffman had still been the district attorney instead of the neophyte Thomas Phoenix. In 1836 and again in 1838 Hoffman won election to the U.S. House of Representatives, and then he was appointed a district attorney for the United States. At the end of his career he was the attorney general for the state of New York. These were all highly distinguished

posts, reflecting the faith friends and voters had in his considerable intellectual and rhetorical skills. And yet Hoffman was not known to be a
hardworking, hard-driving man; he succeeded by his wits. He had a reputation for enjoying a very active social life with a wide circle of friends.
And, despite his eminence, he died utterly poor, a condition his obituary
attributed to his "generous and indolent" nature. "He was a notoriously
lazy man and an extravagantly high liver," a Massachusetts lawyer
lamented, "but for which he would have won a still more brilliant and
extended fame."[11]

Hoffman's defense of Robinson was assisted by two other able lawyers,
his partner Hugh Maxwell and William Price. Maxwell, forty-nine and a
Scot by birth, attended Columbia, read law, and for two decades prior to
1829 served as New York's district attorney.[12] Price, fifty and English by
birth, also attended Columbia. Price and Maxwell had neighboring offices
in 1827 when the disagreeable Anne Royall—the ungracious tourist at
the Westons' in Augusta—paid them a visit. Her sketch of the two "petti-
foggers," "P****" and "M******," contrasts sharply with the flattering
portraits drawn in the bench-and-bar directories:

> M. is a great tall gangling fellow, with a sly countenance, slipery
> tongue and slip slop gate; his face is fair, long and brazen, his age
> may be about 26 years. [Maxwell was actually thirty-nine.] This
> Pill Garlic keeps his office next door to his friend and ally Mr. P.,
> for the better convenience of co-operating in the very laudable and
> gentlemanly purpose of making war upon the unfortunate, and
> sporting with the tears of the widow and the orphans. P. is not so
> tall as M. but older and more robust. His face is like no other
> man's; in shape it is hexigonical, full, and a deadly pale. His coun-
> tenance is that of a thorough-paced assassin; the same treacherous
> smile with which the savage enjoys the tortures and writhings of
> the victim enveloped in flames marks his marble lip.[13]

Anne Royall clearly had little sympathy for lawyers as a class, but maybe
she had a flash of intuition about Price. Ten years after the Robinson
trial, driven by "a resistless despair" and a "heart ossified with melancholy forebodings," Price committed suicide in a pistol gallery on Canal
Street.[14] Mrs. Royall would no doubt have liked the high-living, silver-
tongued Hoffman better—although maybe not much.

The state's case against Robinson was presented by District Attorney
Thomas Phoenix assisted by Robert H. Morris, who noted during the trial
that he had been brought in to help Phoenix on account of the D.A.'s
unsound "state of health." Neither man appears in any of several legal

directories of the period. Morris later became city recorder and then mayor for four years in the 1840s; Phoenix left the D.A.'s office in less than two years and then vanished from notice.[15] Clearly this team was outmatched by the defense lawyers in skill and experience.

Judge Edwards's packed courtroom required repeated reminders to be quiet on the first morning of the trial, but the trial started close to the scheduled hour of ten. On the second day, an even greater throng assembled, reaching over six thousand by eight in the morning. The vast and unruly crowd broke railings when it surged into the courtroom at ten, prompting Judge Edwards to order the sheriff to call on fifty extra marshals to clear the building. Finally order was restored, and the trial resumed at noon. To prevent further delays, the police worked out a crowd-control plan. But each day, nearly one thousand people squeezed into seats in the courtroom, almost all of them men. Luckily, load-bearing floor joists proved equal to the task.[16]

Escorted by Daniel Lyons, the keeper of the Bellevue Prison, Robinson arrived punctually each day. He wore a new blue suit and a curly light brown wig to conceal his close-cropped skull. The reporters scrutinized his face for telltale signs of emotion, but Robinson remained composed, walking with a steady step to his place at a table in front of the bar near the jury box.[17] Only a constant twirling and dangling of his trademark cloth cap in his hands gave outward sign to his inner state. His employer, Joseph Hoxie, his father, and his uncle Alsen Parmelee sat behind him. Standing while the charges against him were read, he evinced no apparent anxiety or fear.

Selecting the jury took five hours of the first day, and protocol required that Robinson stand before the prospective jurors for the entire proceeding. Fifty-nine men had been summoned for duty, chosen from a citywide juror list composed of substantial and respectable male citizens and periodically revised by each ward's tax assessor. (Members of volunteer fire companies were exempted.)[18] Only twenty-one of the fifty-nine summoned showed up, the rest evidently preferring twenty-five-dollar fines rather than risking prying questions about their acquaintance with brothel life and clerks like Robinson. Seven of the twenty-one made it onto the jury, while four were dismissed for cause, and ten were excused on preemptory challenge by the defense; the prosecution challenged no one.[19] One of the men excused for cause was Joseph W. Harper, printer, one of four brothers of the enterprising Harper Brothers publishing firm, who volunteered that he could not serve because he was "distantly related by marriage" to the defendant. (The massive 1910 Spelman family genealogy that gives the Robinson lineage and collateral branches back to 1640 fails to disclose a connection to Joseph Harper's wife, so maybe Harper meant *really* distant, or maybe he was just trying his best to get excused.)[20]

With only seven jurors seated and the panel exhausted, the judge resorted to "talesmen," an ancient practice under British and American law. Normally such candidates were drafted at random from in or about the court. But in this case, Judge Edwards decided it would be unwise to draw from the huge and hardly disinterested crowd at hand. So he sent court officers to round up talesmen from nearby streets and stores. After several more hours of winnowing, Edwards came up with a jury of twelve white men: four merchants, a coal dealer, two grocers, an insurance company secretary, a clothier, a fancy-goods storekeeper, a shoemaker, and a druggist.[21] After the trial some critics charged that the call for talesmen landed young clerks just like Robinson on the jury. An extended humorous dialogue printed in the June 10 *Transcript* had one young blade approvingly report that "the counsel for the prisoner knew what they were about. They knew that a jury of youngerly men would not be too hard upon a poor young fellow, for being caught in a scrape which any gallant young man might be caught in." In a more serious vein, a mercantile paper that overcame its antipathy for sordid news to cover the Robinson trial charged that "great difficulty was found in obtaining a jury. Men were objected to who perhaps had never been objected to for any act of responsibility before, and only after a delay of several hours had taken place, was the jury completed. *It was a jury of young men!*"[22]

But in fact the jury was composed overwhelmingly of established businessmen and retailers. Eleven of the twelve were listed in Longworth's 1837 city directory, so they were not the clerks or boardinghouse boys whose lack of householder status would have excluded them. Of course, we have seen how Longworth the enumerator sometimes elevated households into respectability, as with Frank Berry the tailor. And with five of the members selected in a nonrandom process involving court officers procuring men from nearby streets and stores, jury stacking was at least a distinct possibility. Moreover, in an era far less insistent on furnishing proof of identity than our own, whether the men in the jury box were really who they said they were was not easy to establish. Merchants might be well known to the public, but their clerks were not. One man's showing up in the place of another was known to happen. In 1835 a young man answered for his father at a jury trial at City Hall and apparently saw nothing wrong with his deception, since he and his father shared the same name. Jurors, he reported, got paid only twelve and a half cents a day for their trouble, and his father deemed it a waste of time to go. Other jurors evidently shared his opinion, for on the wall in the jury room someone had scribbled "The laborer worthy of his hire: 12½ cents" along with "Eleven stubborn men against one easy fellow."[23] The citizen's chore of jury duty has rarely been smooth or uncomplicated.

Once the twelve men were seated, the indictment of one count of willful and deliberate murder was read. Robinson remained still; "not a feature faltered—not a muscle was agitated." The court broke for its first half-hour recess, and eight police officers were assigned to guard the jury in seclusion. At three-thirty, the court reconvened, but the crowd took longer to settle down as more men sought standing room in the audience.[24]

District Attorney Phoenix gave a very brief opening statement of his case against the accused and called Rosina Townsend to the stand, where she sat for the next five hours under direct and cross-examination. (She and the other women witnesses awaited their turn to testify in the grand jury room in the building behind City Hall and were escorted to and fro by police officers.) Phoenix took her through the same testimony she had given in earlier depositions—about admitting Robinson to the house between nine and ten, seeing him in Helen's room at eleven, and then the discovery of the murder and fire at three in the morning. Hugh Maxwell's cross-examination attempted to produce inconsistencies and confusions, but she stuck to her story, even when the spectators erupted in a noisy show of hostility toward her. Her revelation that there were two Frank Riverses provoked such a prolonged response that the judge threatened the most boisterous young men in the audience with contempt of court. At another point in her testimony, Rosina asked for a glass of water, and a while later "the same glass with some water was handed to one of the jurors"—evidently an unexceptional custom of sharing cups—"and he declined drinking from it, and asked the officer for another glass." In a city where everyone used cups shared in common to drink from public wells and backyard cisterns, this juror was making an emphatic state-ment about how he felt about Rosina Townsend, as no newspaper scribe failed to notice.

Rosina was excused at half past eight at night, and Phoenix next began questioning a series of official witnesses to link Robinson to the crime through circumstantial evidence. Dr. David L. Rogers briefly reviewed the cause of death, looked at the hatchet, and said its blade was consistent with the wounds, and then a watchman named Richard Eldridge described finding the hatchet and the cloak the morning of the murder and the layout of the house, yard, and block to show how the killer made his escape. The defense attorneys tried their best to cloud things: Could the hatchet have been put there at dawn by a girl in the house? Pos-sible but improbable, Eldridge said. The court adjourned at ten and the jury was committed to its police guard for the night.

The trial resumed the next morning following the two-hour delay occasioned by the near riot of onlookers scrambling for seats in the courtroom. The parade of prosecution witnesses continued. Coroner William Schureman described his initial examination of the hatchet and cloak, watch captain George Noble and constable Dennis Brink recounted the arrest of Robinson. The defense held Brink's feet to the fire. Did he play cards with prostitutes? Hoffman asked. Visit 41 Thomas on his own? Adjudicate disputes between prostitutes? No, Brink insisted, but Hoffman persisted, drawing on his own recent experience as D.A. to connect Brink to the prostitute world. He accused Brink of interceding with the D.A. on behalf of Mary Berry and Rosina Townsend, and although Brink denied it, Hoffman's status as the former D.A. surely gave his questions credibility in the minds of jurors. Hoffman even dredged up the 1835 case between Jewett and John Boyd, to insinuate that Brink had sided with Jewett in that episode. The fierce and lengthy effort to discredit Brink by suggesting he was a friend of prostitutes underscores Brink's importance to the prosecution. Brink was the source of two of the most damaging pieces of information against Robinson that the jury heard. When he went to Dey Street to question Robinson, before telling him about the murder, Brink had asked the clerk if he owned a blue cloth cloak or a dark cloak of any kind, and Robinson had said no, while a host of later witnesses had to say yes. And further, on the afternoon of April 10, he had searched Robinson's boardinghouse room and found in the bureau the same miniature that Sarah Dunscombe had dusted in Jewett's room on April 8. Yet the prosecutors listened in silence to Hoffman's methodical badgering of their witness.

The prosecution pushed on. Witnesses offered conflicting testimony about pieces of string found both on the hatchet and on a tassel of the cloak. The prosecution wanted to show that Robinson concealed the weapon inside the cloak when he went to Thomas Street the night of the murder. The defense made hay out of conflicting testimony over whether the string was actually attached to the hatchet and tassel when they were found or added later, in an attempt to frame Robinson, in a conspiracy fomented by women in the brothel determined to pin the crime on the clerk. Charles Tyrrell, Robinson's night-walking companion on April 9, identified the cloak as the one Robinson was wearing at eight that night, as did Elizabeth Salters, who knew about the resewn tassel. The cross-examination of Salters brought out other facets of life at 41 Thomas—for example, Salters's visits from both Frank Riverses and Jewett's jewelry, last seen by Salters in Mrs. Townsend's hands. Hugh Maxwell was skillfully planting in the minds of jurors seeds of other motives for the murder.

The prosecution then called the porter from Hoxie's store who identified the hatchet as one he used often for opening crates. On cross-examination, the defense elicited the information that the Hoxie store was being painted on the fatal Saturday—a possible source of the white smudge on Robinson's pants that Brink and Noble had described. The porter also characterized Robinson's demeanor late Saturday at the store as "cheerful and lively."

Emma French was the last major witness of the second day. (Her real name, she had said at the grand jury hearing, was Ophelia Bowles, a name right out of a twentieth-century romance novel. But Ophelia chose a work alias with a sophisticated Gallic flair.) She too put Robinson's arrival at nine-thirty and that of the boot repairman between ten and eleven. As it had done in cross-examining Salters, the defense sought to ferret out rivalries at Thomas Street and also tested French's memory of what happened at critical moments. The trial had been humdrum so far: District Attorney Phoenix laid out his circumstantial case piece by piece, and the defense seized opportunities to uncover confusion over the evidence or introduce hints of discord among the witnesses. Curiously, almost nothing had been said about either Jewett or Robinson—their characters, their personalities, their relationship. Phoenix made no attempt to introduce Jewett to the jury or to make them feel sympathy for her. Nor did he examine Robinson's character or motives. Construing his job narrowly, he aimed to tie the hatchet and cloak to the murder and then to the defendant.

Saturday, June 4, brought more "wretched weather," but this did not deter large crowds from gathering once again in City Hall Park. This time the constables had sealed off the building and restricted all other business in City Hall, so that only select groups—witnesses, lawyers, and reporters—could enter the courtroom. Robinson arrived, still with a "firm, calm, and composed appearance," Joseph Hoxie still at his side. (Newspaper accounts fail to mention his father or uncle.)

Phoenix resumed his plodding course. Calling the servant Sarah Dunscombe to the stand, he asked her to recount dusting the miniature of Robinson Friday morning and her observation of a client's visit to Jewett very early on that Saturday evening. (This was Edward Strong, the young clerk Jewett met on the street that late afternoon; his testimony soon corroborated Dunscombe's account.) Maxwell and Hoffman alternated in interrogating Dunscombe, a strategy designed to heighten pressure on the timid young woman. They emphasized how she had confused Strong with Robinson when she appeared before the grand jury. Their pressure served to make her testimony carry even less weight than would normally be credited to someone who was young, black, and female. Dunscombe bravely held her ground, however, attributing her earlier mistake to fright and to her inexperience in speaking with the kind of authority a courtroom required: "I was never brought up [in court] before to swear against any one."[25]

Next, the clerk Joseph Hoxie, who worked alongside Robinson in his uncle's store, came forward. One of the papers had noted that the prosecution had had to subpoena young Hoxie and the other clerk, Newton Gilbert. On the stand, Hoxie remained uncooperative. Phoenix asked him to identify Robinson's handwriting in a letter, and he could not swear it was his: "I am acquainted with his handwriting only in some measure." Phoenix probed further; Hoxie worked for eight months alongside Robinson and had observed him copying business letters, but still felt uncertain. Maxwell was quick to object, since the witness had said he was not competent to judge the hand, and the judge sustained the objection. For the prosecution, Morris veered in the direction of establishing whether Robinson had a key to the store, a piece of evidence crucial to understanding how Robinson came to possess the hatchet the Saturday night of the murder. Hoxie equivocated here too. Maybe Newton Gilbert knew about the key, he said. But Gilbert was never asked what he knew.

By asking about handwriting, Morris and Phoenix were trying to lay the groundwork for introducing the correspondence between Robinson and Jewett. Young Hoxie was no help, so they tried a different angle: they called a porter, William Van Ness, who described being hired by Jewett to deliver letters to Robinson (and incidentally described the line of men at the murder scene viewing the corpse). But the defense objected that a prostitute could write any man without his knowledge or involvement: "Every man living was liable to receive letters from a prostitute, who thought proper to address him." No real correspondence had been established, they argued, and when the judge sustained their objection, Van Ness left the stand. Then William's brother Samuel Van Ness, also a porter, swore he had taken letters and even book-shaped packages from Robinson to Jewett, both at Thomas Street and at Mrs. Berry's on Duane Street. When he was asked to identify a folded-up letter with the address on it, the defense objected on the grounds that it could not be proven that there actually had been a letter inside the folded paper when the delivery was made. For once overruling a defense objection, Judge Edwards allowed Morris to continue with Van Ness, who thought possibly this letter was one or like one he had delivered. The defense declined to cross-examine him.

To build a case for the importance of the correspondence, Phoenix called Oliver Lownds, the police magistrate, who reviewed the hatchet and cloak evidence and described items he found in Jewett's room. Among them were a watch, a chain, and rings, sequestered by the coroner—jewelry theft was thus not a motive for the crime—as well as letters and papers that he took home and read. He had not inspected Robinson's room, Lownds said, but he did open locked trunks and a chest of drawers brought by Brink to the Police Office from Dey Street. Among the contents he found a wallet stuffed with large numbers of bills of exchange made out to the elder Joseph Hoxie. Such bills were roughly the equivalent of modern-day bank checks, written orders by one person to pay a specific sum to another. In the free-flowing, credit-crazy economy of Jacksonian America, bills of exchange could be cashed by third parties (like third-party checks today). They were also subject to the same kinds of discounting as bank notes and other money substitutes in an inflationary economy where the ultimate worth of a piece of paper—whether bank note or bill of exchange—could not be known with certainty. At the grand jury hearing, the clerk Newton Gilbert had at first declared he "never knew R. to have money," but perhaps on being told about the wallet, he shifted to saying "but it was reported R. had money to discount Notes with."[26] Phoenix failed to pursue the tantalizing incongruity of a wallet stuffed with bills of exchange in the keeping of an impecunious Robinson. In cross-examination, Maxwell led Lownds off on a line of questioning about fences and exit routes, so boring and seemingly immaterial that reporters stopped taking notes. The shrewd defense attorney did not wish to remind the jury of the fat wallet in the possession of a lowly clerk.

Phoenix pushed on toward the recess hour, recalling Elizabeth Salters and then neighboring madam Mary Gallagher to talk about the handkerchief found under Jewett's pillow. Hoffman seized the occasion to ask Salters about the other Frank Rivers: Was he at the brothel that night, who let him in and out and when? What sort of cloak did *he* wear? At Phoenix's request, James Tew, Robinson's roommate, stood up in the courtroom, and Salters affirmed he was the other Rivers. Finally George Marston took the stand. The D.A. established that he was Bill Easy, that he usually visited Jewett on Saturdays but not on the night of the murder, and that he gave her the handkerchief as well as other items to sew and wash for him. That his handkerchief was under her pillow thus was reduced to a commonplace and trivial occurrence, for other items of his laundry might well have lain about the room too. Marston was also drawn out on Jewett's large wardrobe and rich jewels. The defense subjected Bill Easy to perfunctory questioning. In Marston's case, as in that of Newton Gilbert, it shunned the opportunity to cast suspicion onto other young men. The court took its customary (and single) short recess in the midafternoon.

When testimony resumed late Saturday afternoon, the prosecution faced uncooperative witnesses and frustrating rulings from the judge that seemed to close off promising avenues of inquiry. Robert Morris called the elder Joseph Hoxie and asked about the terms of Robinson's employment. Maxwell quickly objected to a question about salary, claiming it had "no bearing upon the case," an opinion the judge shared. In one of the few such moments in the trial, the prosecution approached the bench apparently to argue for being allowed to pursue the question. No doubt Morris was trying to establish that a badly paid clerk in possession of a fistful of bills of exchange belonging to his boss may have been an embezzler. Perhaps the fat wallet, or Jewett's knowing of it, represented a motive for murder. But Morris was not allowed to make his point. Nor did he ask Hoxie straight out if he had any reason to suspect Robinson of financial misconduct, since no groundwork for such a question had been laid.

Instead Morris focused on the issue of Robinson's handwriting. Hoxie told how he promoted his young employee from underclerk to assistant bookkeeper to clerk and had seen him copy letters and knew his hand. But when Morris handed him a manuscript book (said by reporters to be Robinson's diary), Hoxie faltered: "I dare not swear it is . . . I cannot see any writing that I could venture to swear positively was his." A business hand differed from a personal, informal one, Hoxie suggested. He believed some of the writing might be Robinson's, but he could not swear to it. Morris next handed him fifteen letters, signed "Richard P. Robinson" and found in Jewett's room; and of these, Hoxie would only venture that one might be in Robinson's hand. Perhaps Hoxie had scruples about what he could affirm under oath; perhaps the handwriting of the emotion-laden letters differed markedly from the business hand of his clerk. Perhaps he was hedging or lying. Morris gave up.

Phoenix then brought forward a surprise witness, Frederick W. Gourgons, a clerk in the store of Dr. Chabert, the self-styled "Fire King," who owned an apothecary store on Broadway. Chabert the Fire King was a medical huckster, quack, and charlatan who advertised spectacles of the believe-it-or-not variety in the penny press. His clerk, Gourgons, had appeared on the list of witnesses Phoenix compiled for the grand jury hearing in April, but he did not appear or give testimony then. Called to the witness stand, Gourgons reported that Dr. Chabert frequently saw and treated prostitutes in the back room of his store. An apothecary shop receipt made out to "Mr. Douglas" and found in Robinson's trunk had led the police to Chabert. Gourgons remembered Robinson visiting Dr. Chabert's back room on several occasions under the name "Douglas." His most recent visit, Gourgons said, had been sometime in early April, when Douglas came after dark and asked for arsenic for killing rats, he said. Gourgons refused: "We are always in the habit of refusing to sell arsenic to strangers." (Accounts of Gourgon's testimony vary; the *Sun*, for instance, reported that Gourgons told Douglas that the store did not carry arsenic. And some reporters put the event the Saturday of the murder, while others heard it as the previous Saturday.)

This was startling testimony. No newspaper in town had gotten wind of the arsenic story. Gourgons was nearly certain Douglas and Robinson were the same man, although the defendant was pointed out to him for the first time only after he had arrived in court to testify. Why the D.A. failed to determine beforehand whether Gourgons could identify Douglas as Robinson is puzzling. It suggests that Phoenix did not decide to use Gourgons until the trial was under way. In any case, Gourgons proved easy pickings for the skillful Maxwell, who flustered him by pounding on his verbal mistakes:

> I meant to say when I said that I did not know the prisoner, and asked persons where he was, that I did not know where he was seated. (Mr. Maxwell here gave the witness one of the most severe cross-examinations that ever emanated from counsel, completely confounding and confusing him, and closing in some impassioned remarks which led to loud and uproarious plaudits from the audience. The Judge put a stop to this uproar and the counsel took his seat.)[27]

Phoenix tried to repair the damage done to his witness's credibility, but to no avail. That reporters got Gourgons's direct testimony confused (about which Saturday it was, or what Gourgons replied to Douglas) does suggest that the apothecary clerk was not very clear in expressing himself, which opened him to the attack he experienced. The next witness he had meant to corroborate Gourgons's testimony was not yet available, so he turned to Newton Gilbert, a clerk in Hoxie's store. Phoenix reverted to the handwriting question, and Gilbert confidently declared he knew Robinson's hand well from seeing it in the store for two years. About the diary he was less equivocal than Hoxie, but still of little help to the prosecution. "I do not believe that it is all in his hand writing; I do not think it is; it resembles his hand writing very much." Of the writing on the title page, he recognized Robinson's hand only in "New-York, June, 1834." So in the courtroom, not a word was uttered of the title-page sentence that had shocked the penny press editors in April: "Whoever shall pry unbidden into the secrets of this book, will violate the whole of the ten commandments."[28] Gilbert turned the diary page by page and marked twelve leaves he thought were in Robinson's hand. The rest "he could not positively and unequivocally recognize to be in the hand writing of the pris-

oner, although, he said, they resembled it very much." This tentative identification did not give Phoenix much to work with. If Gilbert marked the
twelve pages as shrewdly as he appraised the title page, he probably tied
fairly innocuous passages to his fellow clerk. His testimony was very limited; after examining the diary, he was handed the letters, only eight of
which he felt secure in saying were Robinson's. Gilbert had only a vague
memory of a dark cloth cloak Robinson had back in February or March.
His memory failed him so convincingly that Phoenix neglected to ask him
who had the key to the store that Saturday night. Predictably, the defense
declined to cross-examine him, preferring to leave him a vague presence
for the jury to overlook. If Newton Gilbert and Richard P. Robinson had
been rivals for Helen Jewett, or rivals (or partners) in some business
scheme—was Gilbert "Mr. G.," the Cashier of the letters?—no sign of
rivalry emerged in the trial.

Now Gourgons's corroborating witness arrived in court: Elizabeth
Stewart kept a house of assignation at 171 Reade Street. As soon as she
said Robinson had come "to see me about a room that he wanted," Price
objected. Phoenix explained that he merely intended to use Stewart to
show that Robinson went by the name of "Douglas." But of course he and
the defense lawyers knew full well that Elizabeth Stewart and several
other women had told the grand jury about Robinson, alias Douglas, renting a room for Imogene (or Emma) Chancellor, a very young girl he had
seduced and discarded. In April, this line of testimony had led to Julia
Brown's recounting of Robinson's dramatic threat to blow out the brains
of any woman who exposed him. Robinson's lawyers did not want the jury
to hear this, so they effectively blocked the line of inquiry leading up to it.
Gourgons's testimony was inadmissible, they argued, because

> the circumstance of the prisoner's attempting to obtain poison for
> the purpose of killing Ellen Jewett, or any other woman, was not
> proper evidence under this indictment—in which the date, the
> hour, the weapon and death were specifically charged—and that
> therefore any evidence in corroboration of it could not be received.

The judge agreed, forcing Morris and Phoenix to abandon the entire
effort. Jewett was killed with a hatchet, so whether the accused had tried
to buy arsenic that very evening of the murder was immaterial. Price's
exact words—"killing Ellen Jewett, or any other woman"—might simply
have been part of his rhetorical style, a way of emphasizing that the
specifics of *this* crime were at issue: Jewett with the hatchet in the
brothel; not any victim with arsenic anywhere. But after the trial, Robin-

son's opponents seized on his lawyer's very words as a slip of the tongue, a hint that perhaps Robinson *had* killed another woman, Emma Chancellor, alleged to be missing and maybe dead from a murder lawyers knew of and were trying to keep secret.

Frustrated in attempts to establish handwriting samples as Robinson's or to link the accused to murderous threats and actions, the prosecution proposed reading aloud to the jury the letters Gilbert had identified as Robinson's. Hoffman objected, but even before he had finished his objection, Phoenix broke in ("with a magnanimity for which he is justly distinguished") and withdrew the request, expressing "some doubt as to the legality of their admission as testimony." The D.A.'s critics found Phoenix's surrender inexplicable and astonishing. On the face of it, it was, given all the time he and Morris had invested seeking to establish the letters as Robinson's. But the critics did not know how little the letters actually contributed to an understanding of motive in the murder. The eight identified as written in Robinson's hand may have been of little value in terms of their contents. Since the prosecution did not see fit to explore the relationship between Jewett and Robinson, the jury had no context in which to evaluate the letters. Perceiving this, Phoenix probably decided that reading the eight notes was worse than *not* reading them. By implying a motive buried within their contents, mysterious letters mysteriously withheld from the jury might in the end carry far more weight than letters read out in the courtroom. Phoenix immediately rested the prosecution's case.

Hours had gone by since the three o'clock recess, hours in which the jury listened to uncooperative witnesses, heard a snatch of incomprehensible testimony about arsenic, and watched while letters were dangled in front of them only to be snatched back by a high-minded D.A. who appeared to value the rules of evidence above convicting the defendant. Hours more lay ahead on this Saturday. With nary a break, Ogden Hoffman opened for the defense, "in one of those brilliant, eloquent and fervent effusions, which in the career of his long and extensive practice have acquired for him an imperishable celebrity, and a never-dying fame." So enraptured were reporters that they merely summarized his talk instead of getting his remarks down word for word, as they had for those of witnesses. Hoffman's preview of the case attacked the character of the prosecution witnesses. His client suffered the misfortune of being an obscure young man who had dined alone at an oyster bar late in the evening of the murder. His obscurity meant that no witness could place him there, Hoffman said. The scurrilous newspapers of the city had excited prejudice against his client, Hoffman complained, but his client would be shown to be innocent, he promised, by a witness providing an alibi the night of the murder and discrediting the testimony of the women of the brothel. Immediately, he called Robert Furlong to the stand.

Like Gourgons the apothecary clerk, Furlong was a surprise witness to the jury and crowd. The newspapers had never heard any word about Robinson's whereabouts on the night of the murder, except the statements of the women at 41 Thomas who said he was there. At both the coroner's jury and the grand jury hearings, Robinson had declined to answer any questions at all, as was his right. The sudden news that his lawyers would establish an alibi must have immeasurably heightened the drama of that long Saturday in court.

Robert Furlong, thirty-three, owned a small family grocery at the corner of Nassau and Cedar.[29] At Hoffman's urging, he told how Robinson came into his store at about nine-thirty on April 9, bought a bundle of twenty-five cigars, lighted one, and smoked it while sitting on a barrel. For some part of the time, he read the *Evening Post*. He teasingly dropped cigar ashes on the napping store porter. Just as a clock struck ten, Furlong said, Robinson opened his watch and checked the time, and Furlong did the same with his pocket watch, both calibrating to the clock. Robinson smoked a second cigar while Furlong's porter moved barrels from the sidewalk into the store, a task he performed every Saturday in preparation for the Sunday closing. Robinson left about ten-fifteen, Furlong said, saying as he went, "I believe I'll go home, I am tired."

On Monday morning, a boy in his store read aloud a newspaper account of Jewett's death and Robinson's arrest, but Furlong made no connection between the story and the unnamed young man who bought cigars from him. But within a few more days when his regular customer, who usually came by about twenty times in a month, had not returned, Furlong became curious. He also knew his customer worked nearby on Maiden Lane, where Hoxie's store was located. An article in a penny paper describing Robinson (probably the *Herald* for April 13 that characterized the miniature) piqued his curiosity—could the clerk arrested for murder be his regular cigar customer? Knowing a guard at Bellevue made it easy to go see for himself. Robinson greeted him by name, he testified, and Furlong was satisfied it was the man he had seen often in his store. Furlong even confirmed that the watch Robinson wore at the trial was the same watch he remembered from the night of the murder. The D.A.'s cross-examination may actually have served to implant Robinson's alibi more deeply in jurors' minds. As Phoenix asked for more details, Furlong eagerly supplied them—Robinson wore a coat, not a cloak, and he commented on the weather. The D.A. could not catch him out, even with questions about the two Bellevue visits. As the clock approached ten, the defense put the merchant Joseph Hoxie back on the stand to say he had given Robinson the watch in question several months earlier. Court adjourned, and twenty-two guards were assigned to the jury during the Sunday recess.

By this time the trial had already gone on far longer than most trials, and the long hours were no doubt taking a toll on all participants. When the court reconvened Monday morning, the melodrama of Saturday's testimony drew even greater crowds.

> Each day's progress in this interesting trial seems but to increase the interest and excitement which have existed in the public mind since its commencement, and the gates of the City hall were again surrounded yesterday by a dense and anxious multitude, rendered still more dense and numerous by the expectation that the twenty journeymen tailors who were convicted a few days since of conspiracy, would be arraigned for sentence.[30]

The Monday flow of defense witnesses was steady, rapid, and confusing—as Hoffman intended. The strategy of the defense was not to produce a different script of what happened the night of the murder, beyond the time-bound alibi of Furlong for forty-five minutes Saturday evening. The defense neither had to account for Robinson's evening, nor account for the murder. Rather, the lawyers' task was to discredit the prosecution's version of events, a narrative largely based on the testimony of Rosina Townsend, Elizabeth Salters, and Emma French. The defense called to the stand various watchmen who on April 10 had responded to the alarm from the brothel. One of them contradicted small but significant details in Rosina Townsend's testimony, claiming Rosina had been heard to say that she would not recognize Frank Rivers on the street if she saw him. Another defense tactic was to implicate Maria Stevens in the crime, whose room adjoined Jewett's. Only a thin wall separated the two rooms, a watchman said. Only Maria knew where Frank Rivers lived. Aside from Jewett, only Maria, of the women present at Thomas Street that evening, had died a sudden death herself. Clearly, she had known too much and had met an untimely end, the defense implied.

At the defense's behest, Rodman Moulton, Robinson's fellow boarder, swore that he and Robinson had been at the Park Theatre the entire evening of Thursday, April 7, when Sarah Dunscombe and Rosina Townsend thought he might have paid his penultimate visit to the brothel. The defense then called the stage manager to verify the Park Theatre's bill and the duration of the shows. Under cross-examination by Phoenix, Moulton admitted he had seen Robinson wear a cloak with velvet facings and tassels and had even been on the sleigh ride with him when a tassel came off. But when shown the cloak in evidence, he hesitated; it was similar in appearance, "but he would not positively swear that it was the same."[31] James Tew came forward to swear to his roommate's alibi in the early hours of the morning. He told of waking up between one and two and finding Robinson next to him in bed; sharing beds was a perfectly common practice in the nineteenth century. When Tew woke again between three and four, Robinson was still there. He recounted the Saturday evening walk with Robinson, Moulton, and Tyrrell, his brief visit to the brothel exclusively for a chat, and waking up in the morning to the police knock on the door. He, Robinson, and Moulton had made plans to go horseback riding early Sunday morning, Tew said, but when he got up at daybreak and saw the rain, he conferred with Robinson, and they both returned to bed, only to be roused an hour or so later by Brink and Noble.

Cross-examination of Tew was rigorous. Phoenix asked repeatedly about the white marks on Robinson's pants, whether the cloak was there in the morning, and whether there were cigars in the room. Tew probably had heard Furlong's testimony on Saturday night, since he was in the audience earlier on Saturday when Salters identified him as the second Frank Rivers, but still he blundered. He had the "impression that Robinson had a quantity of cigars in his room" on Saturday evening. Then realizing the implication—why would Robinson buy twenty-five more that night at Furlong's?—he backtracked. There was a box of cigars, Tew explained, but Robinson shared it with Moulton, and he could not say whether it was full or empty. Tew claimed not to be familiar with Robinson's handwriting, and as to a diary, he was remarkably evasive: "Cannot exactly say whether Robinson kept a journal or not."[32] Unless Robinson wrote all his entries during work hours at Hoxie's store, or at tables in oyster bars, Tew's statement reached the limits of the credible. Seeing where the prosecutor's inquiry was leading, Maxwell objected: Had they not agreed to drop the letters and papers found in Robinson's trunk? And Phoenix again graciously conceded. "Rather than they should think that their client had not had a fair trial . . . he would forego any interrogations in reference to those matters." Again, Phoenix played the gentleman and let the letters go.

Late in the day on Monday, the defense rested its case. The prosecution opened rebuttal by calling the keeper of Bellevue Prison, Daniel Lyons, to try to chip away at Furlong's testimony. In the course of Lyons's remarks, the story of Robinson's unknown female visitor who commented on the youth's hair loss emerged, but no particular importance was attached to it. Henry Burnham, the jailer who admitted Furlong to Bellevue, was also called, but nothing damaging to Furlong came

up. In keeping with legal customs of the day, a juror directly asked Burnham a question. What was his opinion of Furlong's word? He had known
him seven or eight years, the jailer replied, and "never knew anything of
him but good." His purpose in asking, the juror elaborated, "was merely
to satisfy some of the jurors who did not know Mr. Furlong as well as some
of the others." This astonishing aside reveals the chasm between legal
practice then and now. Few if any district attorneys today would seat a
jury containing members who were friends or acquaintances of the
defense's star witness. But at Robinson's trial, apparently several jurors
knew Robert Furlong personally. Two were grocers, after all, and three
others were merchants with stores on Pearl or Maiden Lane within a few
blocks of Furlong's grocery. Furlong apparently enjoyed a good reputation among them.

Realizing this may have alarmed Phoenix. For as his next move he
took back his surrender over the letters and proposed to read four
acknowledged to be in Robinson's hand, two from August 1835, one from
November, and one undated. This may have been a feint. Of the large set
of letters the *National Police Gazette* published in 1849, two of Robinson's
were dated in August, and neither bears on the murder. (See chapter 12.)
It is hard to see how Phoenix could have induced jurors to read into them
a motive for killing Jewett.[33] But Phoenix pressed his demand, and Hoffman objected—only to find that the court overruled his objection, an outcome that, according to the trial transcripts, had so far happened only
twice before. Maybe the prosecutor had finally aroused Judge Edwards's
curiosity.

Maxwell joined the fray. Moving beyond the legal reasons Hoffman
had given for the inadmissibility of the letters, Maxwell added that

> the obvious intent of submitting them as evidence against the pris-
> oner was to show, that he had, at some distant period, entertained
> malignant feelings towards the deceased, and had, on one or two
> occasions, threatened her with injury. The learned counsel said
> that if such threats and such letters had not been written immedi-
> ately antecedent to the murder, they ought not to be made use of to
> prejudice the minds of the jury against the unfortunate accused.

But Phoenix persisted, all the while claiming that "he did so with feelings towards the unhappy prisoner at the bar, far from being harsh,
unfriendly, or unkind." It was his duty as the D.A. for the people to pursue this, he insisted. He suggested letting the judge and his assistants
read the letters first to decide if they were fully or partially admissible, or
if irrelevant parts might be withheld, since people unconnected to the case

were named (which was true for the August 18 letter). So Edwards got to see the letters. The lawyers made final arguments, Hoffman reminding the judge that since the defense was not attempting to prove their client's good character, the prosecution could not present evidence of his bad character. In the end, the judge ruled the letters inadmissible, and the court adjourned for the night at nine-fifteen.

The final day, the trial resumed where it had left off the evening before. Phoenix reopened the question of the letters. One, he said, contained evidence connected to "material evidence" already presented, and he wished that one to be read. The defense finally acquiesced, on condition that no other letters be admitted, and so Robinson's letter of November 14, 1835, was read aloud by Phoenix and then passed to the reporters to copy. This was the letter expressing Robinson's desire to break off the relationship with Jewett and get her to return the valued miniature. Robinson accused Helen of forsaking him and of planning to plunge him into "ruin and disgrace." He apologized for some unstated bad behavior and ended dramatically: "Do not betray me; but forget me, I am no longer worthy of you." Once it was read, there was no further discussion of the letter, no meaning attached to it, no construction put upon it—all this would presumably await the closing arguments.

The rest of the morning was devoted to matters of detail. A courthouse employee (the crier of the court) revealed that he knew from inspection that 41 Thomas had been two houses once, with a brick wall separating Jewett's and Stevens's rooms. Dr. Rogers returned to say he thought he saw blood on the hatchet the morning of the murder. A fire insurance agent called by the defense disclosed that Townsend had recently raised her insurance on the furniture of 41 Thomas Street to $3,500. The jury likely assumed that this was a very large sum compared with other house-holders' coverage, but it was not out of keeping with Townsend's personal property tax assessment. Hoxie confirmed that his store had been recently painted, and the manufacturer of the hatchet said he had sold 2,500 such tools in New York since 1834. And there, at about noon, the testimony ended.

The real courtroom drama now began. In trials of the 1830s, the eagerly awaited theater came not in the patient accumulation of evidence from witnesses but in the lawyers' closing speeches, where the evidence was sifted, weighed, and interpreted. Courtroom dramas of film and television have reversed the aesthetics of trial performance. The brilliant line of lawyerly questioning that elicits an important truth or a known lie from a witness is now usually the dramatic pivot of trial as entertainment. In contrast, effective closing arguments by actor-lawyers are short and pithy, meant to focus the jury and audience on the essence of a case.

Lawyers in real-time trials no doubt give closing arguments that are longer than the paragraph or two allotted on television shows, but in important trials that themselves become fodder for television coverage as news, the same condensation effect shrinks the closing statement down to compact form when it is reported to the world beyond the courtroom. We no longer inhabit the world of Daniel Webster, where oratorical genius held audiences in thrall for hours at a time.

The apportioning of time at the trial further suggests the vast difference between then and now. Robinson's trial stretched over 5 days, or 56.5 hours, not counting recesses. Five hours went to jury selection, 41 hours to prosecution and defense questioning, but 10.5 hours, or nearly 20 percent of the whole, were devoted to the closing arguments. Each of the five lawyers spoke, Hoffman alone taking three hours, and under the guise of instructions to the jury Judge Edwards gave a long speech of his own. And then the jury phase of the trial required only 15 minutes.

Several papers complained that it proved very hard to take the closing speeches down. The give-and-take of testimony was far easier, since only the answers and not the questions were being transcribed, and witnesses who spoke reluctantly or timidly probably also spoke slowly. But speeches, with all their power of emotion, their train of argument, their rhetorical flourishes, and their direct engagement with the listener, were far more difficult to capture on paper. As the *Newburyport Daily Herald* lamented, regarding Hoffman's three-hour speech,

> if we were to present our readers with every word he uttered, we could by no means do him the justice he deserves, or thereby afford the reader even a faint idea of the incomparably noble and lofty strain of eloquence with which it was delivered, or of that extremely pathetic and emphatically energetic manner in which he at times worked on the feeling of his auditors till nearly all eyes were moist; and here we must stop, or our own feelings attendant on its bare recollection will lead us away, to attempt to describe that which surpasses description. In fine, we hesitate not to say it was as great a masterpiece of eloquence as was ever delivered at the Bar.[34]

And this was a paper that fiercely disagreed with Hoffman's position! Another paper, the *New York Commercial Advertiser*, explained that its reporter "had to stop writing, to give all his attention to the mere act of listening" to Hoffman's "uninterrupted, unfailing stream" of eloquence. Hoffman clearly had a gift for manipulating his listeners.

Other papers published "extra" editions with all the closing statements; the *New-York Transcript* bragged that it had sold fifteen thousand copies of its first extra of the trial transcript in one day, and two days later an extra with the closing speeches was on sale.[35] One publisher turned the set of closing statements into a twenty-four-page small-print pamphlet titled *Murder Most Foul* (a famous line from *Hamlet* often used to head-line murder reportage). The cover carried crude woodcuts of a well-dressed Robinson and Jewett ogling each other with half-closed eyes and below it a half-dressed Jewett on her deathbed.

Price opened for the defense. No direct proof linked Robinson to the crime, he emphasized. True, Robinson kept bad company, but Price appealed to the jury to see the clerk as one of them: "Gentlemen is he from one of yourselves—does he seem like an old convict that would go into a house and commit murder and arson." Why would he foolishly leave the hatchet and cloak behind? What motive could he possibly have—plun-der of her jewels? Price insisted that Townsend's debased status rendered her word worthless; she was little better than a criminal herself, murder-ing the souls of beautiful girls and breaking the hearts of their grieving parents. Since a court could not take any convicted criminal's word, why should it take Townsend's? When it came to Jewett's killer, it was as rea-sonable to presume that Rosina Townsend "be the one," a statement greeted with great applause in the courtroom. Furlong's testimony was "conclusive," he argued; "he came here without knowing the prisoner or his people, in behalf of the young man."[36]

Morris countered for the prosecution. His two-hour speech, inter-rupted by lunch, rehearsed the circumstantial evidence based on the hatchet and the cloak. Morris had been called into this trial to assist the D.A., Phoenix, who was ailing in some unspecified way. But unfortunately Morris was outclassed in this trial, in over his head. His speech wandered through the evidence without apparent purpose, often repeating conflict-ing viewpoints without declaring which the prosecution favored. He elabo-rately deferred to the good judgment of the jury: "Gentlemen, if you think the prisoner is innocent you have a right to acquit him . . . if the cloak was not his, he is not guilty. If it was his, he still may not be guilty." Still, in his slow and rambling way he eventually arrived at an essential observation: there was no way to account for the circumstantial evidence of hatchet, cloak, and miniature, if Robinson was innocent, without resorting to a conspiracy theory of improbable proportions. Morris again read Robin-son's November 14 letter to elucidate a motive. Robinson feared betrayal and ruin at the hands of Jewett, Morris said. There was "an evident secret here, that she had a knowledge that she could betray . . . a secret that operated on his standing in life." As to Furlong, he was honest but confused and mistaken. If Robinson frequently visited Furlong's store, how could the grocer be so sure he had done so the night of the murder?

The Trial of R. P. Robinson, *by J. T. Bowen, 1836. Robinson is labeled, on his back, "The Innocent Boy." The cartoonist disapproves of the verdict; he shows Justice as a female figure behind the judge, shielding her eyes. The judge holds a balance in his right hand, in which three men's names (Furlong, Hoxie, and an illegible third) outweigh many more women's names. Most of the men in the jury box appear to be extremely youthful.*

According to Tyrrell, at eight Robinson was wearing the cloak. What had he done with it, if he appeared in a coat at Furlong's at nine-thirty? Tew's testimony about the time Robinson came home was suspect; he had not looked at a clock, and when he asked Robinson what time he came in, Robinson lied. Robinson probably came in after the murder, and his arrival was what woke Tew up between three and four; Robinson only pretended to be asleep. This cool young man had only one moment of "trepidation"—after the murder, when he dropped both the hatchet and cloak. Morris ended on a magnanimous note, inviting the jury to acquit if they could "account for the cloak, hatchet and miniature without believing that the prisoner participated in carrying them there" or even if they had "doubt" about it. But otherwise they must convict, "no matter what your own feeling."[37] This was an oddly tentative summation for a prosecutor bent on showing a skeptical jury that the evidence against the accused was overwhelming. Morris must have had doubts of his own.

Ogden Hoffman rose and established his "poor boy" theme in his first sentence. Throughout he called Robinson "the boy." He too was generous to his opponents. The police had not acted improperly toward his client, and the district attorney had shown "great magnanimity; he felt that the District Attorney should act as a mediator between the prisoner and the people." He skillfully redirected the jury's hostility to the real culprit who had "brought this prosecution": Rosina Townsend. "It is her who has sworn against him; it is she who would erect a gallows for that man; it is she who would send him to an early grave. . . . There is a foul conspiracy in this matter, and the whole in that house have combined."

Hoffman tore Rosina's testimony apart. He suggested that Dennis Brink told her that Robinson's hair was falling out as he sat in jail, inspiring her to concoct her story of the bald spot she claimed to notice at Thomas Street, when in fact his hair had fallen out from worry only following his arrest. Rosina swore to the time Robinson arrived the night of the murder, and French and Salters confirmed it; this indicated there was "a deep and a damnable perjury between them."

> I am not going to say that a prostitute's oath is not legal in a court of justice, but I am going to say that eminent judges have held it very doubtful as to the credit that should belong to it. Can a juror go with his oath based on the polluted declarations of a common prostitute. Does she care for human life; she who has seen victims every day in her house, who has seen with pleasure, the plague spot on his cheek and knew that corruption was doing its work. What was it to Rosina Townsend that a father's hopes lay buried there? what was it to Rosina Townsend, that a mother's hopes are destroyed?

Hoffman asked why neither the man in Rosina's bed nor the man who arrived at three in the morning was produced at trial. They might have corroborated Rosina's story—or maybe not, he implied. Maybe Rosina's crass motive was to collect fire insurance. The fire in the bed had been extinguished just in time, because of course Rosina would not intend to burn down the whole building, and her fire insurance covered the damage to Jewett's room.

Dunscombe's testimony was harder to discredit, but Hoffman insisted she was unreliable and had been "tampered with" by Townsend. Why would the women conspire to frame Robinson? "God knows who he had offended in that house. God knows who he had deserted and taken up with another," a clear reference to the evidence that Robinson had visited Salters first and then Jewett.

A woman's pride once wounded, a woman never forgets—a prostitute, when once her pride is injured, will pursue her victim to the
grave. . . . Salters has sworn that she had no feelings of unkind-
ness at being deserted, but do you believe her? It is contrary to
woman's character, to bear such a thing without feelings of
revenge.

How could this boy commit this crime? Hoffman asked. He showed no
guilt the next day. No "long aspirations" of fearful breathing woke his bed
partner Tew in the night, no beardless cheek blanched when the police
knocked the next morning. Furlong's testimony stood unimpeached by
any other witness, and he was known to the jury as an honest man. And as
for the letter of November 14, Robinson composed it partly from his own
feelings "and part from a novel"—Hoffman's way of discounting the sentiments expressed in it. The lawyer did divulge that Robinson "felt love
and passion for that woman," an admission that actually served to enno-
ble the clerk's character. The secret he begged Jewett not to betray, Hoffman averred, was the secret of his immoral life with prostitutes. If there
was any other secret, why did the prosecution not bring it out?
    Hoffman took a short break for "refreshments" and then launched in
again. There were hatchets identical to the murder weapon all over New
York. That a tassel had been resewn to the cloak had been sworn to only
by a prostitute of doubtful word. And what had happened to the cloak
between eight, when Tyrrell saw it, and nine-thirty, when Furlong did not?
Here Hoffman probably astonished the room by saying that Robinson
could have gone to the brothel during that time, leaving the cloak to have
the tassel sewn on again. Had not Marston testified that Jewett performed sewing jobs? Hoffman must have been very confident about the
jury to have ventured such a potentially dangerous hypothesis; or else he
simply made a mistake in implying that Robinson might indeed have visited Thomas Street the night of the murder. He quickly shifted gears by
focusing on Marston for a moment. Did Marston's handkerchief under
Jewett's pillow point to Marston as the killer? No, it was merely circumstantial evidence, which could easily have been planted there by Rosina
Townsend—just as she might have planted Robinson's cloak. Hoffman
offered a stirring peroration about Robinson's poor sick mother "that
doats on him," who might die if her boy is convicted, and whose father
would live a blighted life.

But gentlemen, you will not allow it; you will not come the stern
executioner, you will come the messenger of peace; you will wipe the
tears away from their eyes, they will say our son has been lost but

is found; but, if that verdict shall be—death—I cannot answer for the result. May God, in his mercy, guide you in your decision.[38]

At eight-thirty Hugh Maxwell had his turn, and he kept it short and focused on the rules and limitations of circumstantial evidence. He read from Blackstone and reminded the jurors that a conviction required that all reasonable doubt be allayed; while a chain of circumstantial evidence might be "probable ground for presuming guilt," it could not support a conviction.[39]

It was now nine in the evening, and Thomas Phoenix finally rose to speak. He expressed sympathy with the jury but reminded jurors of their duty to convict in a case of premeditated murder. "I have come to the conclusion that the person who owned the cloak and hatchet was the one that committed the murder. I wish I could think that the prisoner at the bar had not committed the murder. I would be the first man to throw the shield around him." But he is guilty, Phoenix declared.

Phoenix reviewed Rosina's testimony. He re-created the scene of Robinson creeping downstairs and out the back door after the murder, dropping the hatchet and cloak as he fled. If the fire had fully consumed Jewett's body, the murder would have gone undetected, and he would have been safe. But the store porter swore the hatchet was Hoxie's, and witnesses saw Robinson wearing the cloak that night.

Phoenix next attacked Hoffman's picture of the innocent young man who manifested no sign of guilt. Far from being evidence in his favor, Phoenix ventured, Robinson's composure was unnatural and deeply troubling. He was "an extraordinary young man," Phoenix said, who showed no strong emotion upon learning of the murder or seeing the corpse.

She whom he had been so long in intimacy with, with whom he had been but a few hours before probably mingling his caresses! Why, gentlemen, even a dog would have howled forth his lamentations. . . . Will it be told that this was coolness! It looks like a man who had made up his mind to the act! . . . His appearance in this case seemed unnatural, and the next thing to his manner would have been to eat a portion of her flesh and drink a portion of her blood. No wonder there is an excitement in this community.

With this vivid image, Phoenix took off the gloves and proclaimed Robinson a monster. Knowing the audience's sympathies lay with Robinson, and having had over fifty hours to take his measure of the jury, perhaps he decided there was little point in maintaining the pretense of civility now. Calling Robinson a vampire was unlikely to impress the jury, but maybe Phoenix was reaching beyond it to the court of public opinion.

Phoenix was more circumspect about the Furlong testimony. Furlong was simply mistaken about the night of Robinson's visit, and the proof was that until Furlong visited the jail on his own initiative, Robinson had not mentioned having been at the grocer's to anyone. "Gentlemen, he has a tongue in his head, he can, as you have found, write a very superior letter; could employ counsel, and yet, on the morning of his arrest could say not a word of where he had been on the previous night." Phoenix was on a roll now. How did Robinson know about the handkerchief under the pillow when he talked to Mrs. Gallagher? Was it at all credible that Mrs. Townsend would murder Jewett just to set her house on fire and collect the insurance? What secret did Jewett hold over Robinson? Read the letter in the jury room, Phoenix advised, "and the more you read it the more you will find there was a cause for murder. You will find in it a threat, and that he crouched as no man of spirit should crouch to a prostitute, because she professed a secret which he was afraid would be exposed." The secret—Phoenix was sailing along—was something ruled inadmissible. "Suppose I could have shewn to you another offence." But of course he could say no more along this line, because Gourgons and Elizabeth Stewart had not been allowed to testify about the alias "Douglas." Phoenix did his best to hint there was some explosive secret he was prevented from naming. The secret could not simply have been his immoral life, said Phoenix, because he went to the theater and out in public with Jewett, and Hoffman himself had called the relationship "only a little peccadillo."[40]

Judge Edwards took the final hour, from eleven to just past midnight, to sum up the case and instruct the jury. He began by reminding them that to convict they had to agree "beyond all reasonable doubt" that Robinson was guilty. He told them they had to weigh the character of the witnesses—and then he told them how much those characters weighed. The prostitutes "are not to be entitled to credit unless their testimony is corroborated by others, drawn from better sources. . . . Testimony derived wholly from persons of this description, without other testimony, is not to be received." In siding with Hoffman on this issue, Edwards had in effect just directed the jury's verdict to acquittal. But he did not stop there. As if thinking out loud, the judge meandered on at length about the cloak and the timing of Robinson's movements that evening. Probably he went to the brothel earlier in the evening and left the cloak, the judge concluded, picking up the dangerous speculation Hoffman had inadvertently introduced in his closing speech. Perhaps he had taken the hatchet as well, since any young man was well advised to go armed to brothels. Then he went to Furlong's store, leaving the weapon at Thomas Street where anyone could have used it. As for the miniature, the judge directed that Sarah Dunscombe's testimony about seeing it on Friday was to be disregarded. Frightened and mistaken, she was not a credible witness, and besides, "she is attendant on that stew," meaning she shared in the brothel's polluted status and her character was thereby reduced. If Robinson had wanted his miniature back, he merely had to ask Jewett for it, for "she seemed to feel much affection towards him." (Jewett's feelings about anything, including Robinson, had in fact never arisen in the trial until Edwards raised them.) The letter had been written months earlier and thus was of no account. The judge concluded by telling the jury to be calm and firm, to attend to honorable witnesses but not improper people, to convict if they felt it was beyond reasonable doubt, but to acquit and "not immolate an innocent victim."[41]

At close to half-past midnight, the case went to the jury, which asked before leaving the room "if the court would remain in session" while they were out. Yes, said the judge. Clearly a quick verdict was anticipated. Various reports placed the jury's deliberation at anywhere from eight to fifteen minutes. When the "not-guilty" decision was announced, the "court-house rung with loud and reiterated plaudits, which the officers were for sometime unable to suppress."[42] The newsmen reported that Robinson sat down and burst into tears, and then left the room on the arms of Hoxie and his father.

Years later a rumor took hold that Hoxie had paid off a juror. The story was first reported in 1874 in a book on famous New York crimes and was repeated in popular accounts of crime ever since.[43] On the face of it, it seems an unlikely story, and hardly necessary as an explanation of the jury's swift verdict. Once Judge Edwards had so narrowly instructed jurors, their not-guilty verdict was virtually certain. A story about a payoff to the judge would seem more plausible.

Judge Edwards's sympathies obviously lay with the defense. He sustained defense objections repeatedly, forbade prosecution witnesses from reporting hearsay conversations but allowed the defense to do the same, and allowed Hoffman to grill Dennis Brink, the police officer, about seemingly irrelevant things. He prevented all but one of the letters from being read at the trial. True, he had the D.A.'s willing acquiescence. A joke making the rounds in New York a week after the trial had Robinson winning because he had six lawyers: How do you figure? Well, came the reply, there was Price, Maxwell, and Hoffman, and Judge Edwards, Phoenix, and Morris.[44]

Judge Edwards required no bribe to make him well disposed toward the defense. Just by sitting beside the prisoner, Robinson's aged father reminded the judge that a member of a venerable Connecticut family was on trial. Ties of friendship between the governor of Connecticut—the judge's brother—and Robinson's father may also have strengthened this inclination. Moreover, the judge was no stranger to the libertine's life. His father, Pierpont Edwards, was and remains widely regarded as the original for the rake Major Peter Sanford in *The Coquette*, Hannah Webster Foster's best-selling seduction novel of 1796, which enjoyed steady readership for many decades in the nineteenth century and a burst of eight separate editions in the 1820s alone.[45] And Pierpont's first cousin was none other than Aaron Burr, Thomas Jefferson's notorious vice president known for political intrigue, dueling, and a reputation with ladies. A ladies' man par excellence well into his nonagenarian years, Burr was no stranger to the world of prostitutes and the games of seduction and conquest. He died three months after the trial, attended by his devoted cousin Judge Ogden Edwards.[46] None of this makes Judge Edwards a rake, but he surely knew and understood the world of male sexual privilege that young Robinson had chosen to join.

Robert Furlong's testimony was absolutely crucial to the defense. If he was right about where Robinson was from nine-thirty to ten-fifteen that night, then Rosina Townsend was wrong. In the judge's view, Furlong's reputation for probity and his unchallenged testimony meant that he had to be right. The prosecution did not even try to bring his story into doubt. And neither prosecution nor defense sought to substantiate Furlong's testimony by bringing to the stand the porter in whose face Robinson had flicked his cigar ash. (Reporters got hold of him quickly after the trial, of course.)[47] Could Furlong have been bribed? The *New-York Transcript* claimed that a witness "whose testimony had considerable weight with the jury"—probably Furlong—was heard boasting in the days after the trial that "it was neck and neck with me and Rosina Townsend. But I was determined not to be outsworn by a wh———e."[48]

Furlong enjoyed his moment of fame, but it was brief indeed. His grocery failed in 1837, he took up heavy drinking, and in August 1838 he threw himself off a ship in the Atlantic four days out of New York. Many took his death as a guilt-driven suicide.[49]

A sense of guilt did not haunt Ogden Hoffman. Winning his client's acquittal considerably enhanced his own reputation. The bench-and-bar directories portray the trial of Robinson as one of Hoffman's finest professional moments. His closing speech, recalled an 1870 biographical sketch, was "one of those brilliant, eloquent, and fervid effusions, which in the career of his large and extensive practice, gave him imperishable celebrity, and never-dying fame."[50]

Still, the great man's conscience was not entirely at ease. A lawyer who later lost a case against him reported that Hoffman consoled him with a reminder that a victory for a guilty client was not always really a victory:

> Mr. Evarts, said he, though you conducted this case in a manner highly creditable to you, and though it may not be agreeable to you to know that your efforts have been defeated, let me say to you, that it is the most fortunate circumstance in the result of the trial to you. I was, some years ago, the counsel for a criminal accused of a great crime. The result of my effort secured his acquittal. I gained in professional repute, but I have ever been sensible, though my own conscience suggests nothing to reproach myself with, that the sober sense of the community had taken some umbrage at that result.[51]

CHAPTER SIXTEEN

The Great Unhung

H AD RICHARD ROBINSON been found guilty, it is likely
that the Jewett murder would quickly have faded from memory, taking its place alongside a number of similarly lurid
crimes that have agitated or mystified the public for a brief time before
attaining obscurity. But the unexpected acquittal deprived the case of a
sense of closure. It entered the limbo where unsolved mysteries linger,
tantalizing public memory. Commentators rushed to decry a miscarriage
of justice, creating enough controversy and speculation to keep fiction
writers busy in the century to come. No fewer than five novels based on
the case were published, each ingeniously working out a different solution
to the crime.[1] A few members of the reading public wrote to newspapers
asking them to discontinue coverage of the sordid and tiresome story.
Others constructed conspiracy theories involving bribed jurors and secret
prominent brothel habitués to account for what they saw as an enormous
miscarriage of justice. Newspapers that had devoted all their columns to
the trial pondered the outcome for another week. The less restrained
penny papers stretched their posttrial coverage over several weeks, offering editorials that sifted through the evidence and, in a few cases, multipart series (the *Sun*, the *Ladies Morning Star*, and the *Transcript*) setting
forth what went wrong. A few papers outside New York weighed in with
lengthy analyses: the *Philadelphia Ledger* and the *Newburyport Daily
Herald* (in George P. Marston's hometown) devoted considerable space to
the aftermath of the trial. A few papers, like the *New York Commercial
Advertiser*, defended the verdict. James Gordon Bennett of the *Herald*,

ever the maverick, still held out for the possibility that Robinson might in fact be innocent. (But even Bennett changed his mind in July, when new information about Robinson came to light.)

The crime and the trial shocked and titillated, to be sure, but the verdict opened a fissure running deeper than media sensationalism. The perplexity over the acquittal exposed to view the raw dynamics of class and sex privilege in American society.

Male privilege of course was hardly new in 1836; it was as old as civilization, and it was built into the ways that most men and women thought about who has power and authority, whose word counts more, and who is more highly valued. Its cultural embeddedness gave it force and substance—and also rendered it largely invisible. Male privilege pervaded society and went unremarked because it was taken for granted. Many in June of 1836 took it for granted here too and wished to get the Jewett trial off the public stage.[2] Robinson's acquittal was discomfiting precisely because for a short moment the veil over male privilege was lifted up and its workings exposed to view. Compelling circumstantial evidence indicated that Robinson had murdered Helen Jewett, but he was acquitted anyway. The grocer Robert Furlong's sketchy and tardy alibi and the vague recollections of Robinson's young male friends counted for more, in the end, than the vivid and detailed testimony of four women, Rosina Townsend, Elizabeth Salters, Emma French, and Sarah Dunscombe. The men's testimony even overrode the evidence of cloak, hatchet, and miniature. Judge Edwards's instructions to the jury laid bare the terms of power between men and women—or, more precisely, women of questionable character.

Before the trial, most New York papers had assumed Robinson guilty of killing Jewett. His rapid acquittal stunned them. Not that they all disagreed with the verdict as a legal outcome; many papers concluded the verdict was legally correct because of the judge's instruction to discount the women's words. But others raised questions about the district attorney's strategy. Why had he failed to anticipate that the prostitutes' testimony needed bolstering? Why had he not called the male visitors at 41 Thomas to the stand to corroborate the women's testimony? Who were those visitors? Was the D.A. perhaps protecting important people? If the women were of bad character, rendering their sworn testimony doubtful, what then could be said about men who frequented brothels, like James Tew, whose testimony was critical to Robinson's defense? Were they not partners in illicit sex and thus equally doubtful?

The police knew the identities of some of the men in the brothel; the prostitutes had named three in the grand jury hearing. James M. Ashley, who arrived close to three in the morning, could have confirmed Rosina Townsend's account of the light in the parlor and the open back door. Charles Humphrey, the man in Townsend's bed, might have confirmed her reports of answering knocks and inspecting the back door. He could also have provided Rosina with an alibi, undermining the insinuation that she might have been the murderer. But Thomas Phoenix, the district attorney, claimed otherwise. Responding to harsh criticism of his conduct of the case, he arranged for an article to be published in one of the most staid of the mercantile journals. Phoenix argued that the men were not crucial witnesses. Two were "genteel men" from out of town who got away without being identified, he claimed; two were local "merchants of respectability," and another was a clerk. The man with Rosina, Phoenix explained, was one of the merchants, "a single man of good business standing, and with the exception of the cloud that this might throw around his good name, one that stands well with his fellow men." He had no real evidence to give, Phoenix said, and the man begged to be spared. And while he could have vouched for Rosina's innocence, that was not the issue at trial.[3]

The clerk, Phoenix reported, could "state nothing as to the facts further than that the alarm was given and that he fled . . . terrified at the sound of fire and murder that prevailed. He was of respectable connexions, and plead with tears, not to be brought on the stand, as it would he said, destroy him in the estimation of his employer and his friends." The last known man, according to the district attorney, was the young merchant Rosina let in at three, and Phoenix conceded that he could have "testified to seeing the lamp in the back room, and hearing Mrs. T give the alarm of fire and of murder a few minutes after he came in and went to Elizabeth Salter's chamber." Phoenix claimed that he tried to subpoena this man, but he had left the city, and an officer sent to his presumed upstate destination could not find him.

The men's names were never printed in any newspapers, although several editors threatened to reveal them. Mentioned in the closed grand jury hearings and listed on the D.A.'s list of potential witnesses, Charles Humphrey, James Ashley, and Thomas P. Waters successfully begged Phoenix's sympathy and avoided public identification. Waters was no mere clerk; he had enough standing to be listed in several city directories as an agent working for the Washington Line Canal Boats on lower Broadway. Ashley was a single man, aged twenty-seven, in the dry-goods business. He had come to work in New York City in the early 1830s, and he would not marry until 1840, when he was thirty-one; a brother who was a minister officiated at his wedding.[4] Charles Humphrey remains a mystery. The *Sun* alleged that the man in Rosina's bed was a respectable merchant who lived near City Hall, yet still he was not subpoenaed to testify.[5] No Charles Humphrey appeared in the city directories, but Horatio Humphreys, a merchant on nearby Broadway, was the complainant in the case of stolen silk goods fenced to Rosina Townsend in June 1835, and possibly Horatio employed a relative named Charles.[6]

Thomas Phoenix further justified his court performance by claiming that he really expected the evidence of the cloak, hatchet, miniature, and white-paint smudge on the pants to prove decisive and to carry the case. He claimed not to have anticipated the judge's adverse ruling on the admissibility of the letters and diary, which hinted at secrets Helen held over Robinson. Now that the trial was over, Phoenix was free to make the letters public, but he chose to quote only one:

> This letter commences by asserting that Helen was in possession of a very important secret in relation to him, and he puts interrogatories to her as to whether she will betray him. Will you expose me to the world, he says, *will you cut my throat*. If you persist in what you threaten, I know my course. It shall be short and sweet—no, not sweet—*bitter! bitter!*

This was obviously the most pointed letter Phoenix had. Although it was one of the only dated letters in the set, he still did not divulge its date. January 12 was three months before the murder, and an Ogden Hoffman–like reply might well have been that, as threats go, it was too insubstantial and too distant in time to bear directly on the April murder. And this was the best poor Phoenix could muster to substantiate motive for Jewett's murder; little wonder that he did not try very hard to introduce the letters as evidence.

Phoenix further complained that the lithographs of Jewett and Robinson undermined his case. They appeared "in the windows of all our print shops, and in every public place where people would allow them to remain. These pictured Robinson as a very modest youth, one apparently incapable of crimes, and Helen, on the other hand, as a coarse looking brazen eyed shrew, that would do any thing."[7] This was a telling reading of the representation showing Jewett in her green silk dress with letter in hand. (She was dead in the two other extant lithographs, hardly capable of projecting brazenness.) Jewett did have an audacious, knowing smile in this print, but to infer from her confident face that she "would do any thing"—surely a sexual innuendo—was a leap betraying the D.A.'s own censure of Jewett as an immodest, loose woman. He may not have tried to win the jury's sympathy for the murder victim because he had none himself.

The *Newburyport Daily Herald* followed the Robinson trial closely, spurred by George P. Marston's status as a local boy. It was essential to condemn the acquittal in order to deflect any challenge to the innocence of the Marston youth; already, in the wildly speculative atmosphere right after the trial, a Boston paper had suggested that Bill Easy might be the killer. (Young Marston was no doubt oblivious to the cloud of suspicion that threatened, however distantly, to envelop him. He returned to New York in mid-August for a while, but perhaps he found it uncomfortable to remain there, for by the fall of 1836 he had moved to the infant settlement of Chicago, and a year after that he was starting a new life in a small town in Wisconsin.)[8] Ever loyal, the *Daily Herald* reprinted Phoenix's exculpatory excuses and then denounced them in an adjacent column:

> A more lame and impotent apology for glaring favoritism or utter imbecility, was never, in our opinion, sent to press. It would seem from his own confession, that charity for the seniority and respectable standing (was it not for the long purses) of some individuals, who were not willing to bear the shame of testifying in this case, led him to dispense with evidence which could not have failed to convict the criminal.[9]

The Newburyport paper next quoted the *Boston Courier*'s reaction to Phoenix's "benevolent feelings" for the gentlemen in the house:

> Here we have a merchant, affianced, engaged to be married . . . in the mean time, he frequents the most noted brothel in the city, and is in bed with a common strumpet, while a murder is committed in her house. The district attorney knows the fact, and has the power to summon the profligate debauchee into court as a witness; but is swayed from that course—a course dictated by every principle of justice, and probably required by a solemn oath of office—by his "BENEVOLENT FEELINGS." . . . What right has Mr. Phenix, as a public prosecutor, to allow compassion for such an unprincipled fellow to interfere with his official duties? Benevolence to the female to whom this adulterer was "affianced?" What sort of benevolence is that which, by screening the rascal from exposure, throws him into a matrimonial connexion with an innocent and lovely woman, reeking from the stews, with pollution and filth of

body and mind enough to entail misery and disease upon a whole generation? Benevolent feelings indeed! Was it a sister or daughter of Mr. Phenix to whom this "respectable" merchant was "affianced"?[10]

Except for the *New York Herald* and the *Commercial Advertiser*, newspapers everywhere denounced the verdict. The *Albany Evening Journal* (a Whig paper edited by Thurlow Weed) termed it "a mockery of justice." The women's testimony was consistent and corroborated, Weed wrote, while Hoffman's "poor boy" was really "the habitual, practised, profligate associate of prostitutes" who tried to buy poison and whose wallet was "gorged with bills of exchange, stolen from his employer." The prostitutes were actually "less guilty and more entitled to sympathy and forbearance."[11]

The *Middletown Advocate*, published in Connecticut just a few miles up the turnpike from Durham, Robinson's hometown, felt obliged to be somewhat more circumspect in condemning the trial, but it did publish a letter intended "to provoke discussion and thought" from a local gentleman "too elevated to be motivated by unworthy reasons" who contemplated the role bad character played in the credibility of witnesses:

> I am not exactly prepared to say that Robinson's acquittal was wrong, though till some other person can be pointed out as the probable murderer, I shall consider him as guilty. The court obviously leaned towards him, and I think ruled out improperly an important part of the evidence, and too highly impeached others. It is my maxim that the company that a man voluntarily keeps, are always good witnesses against *him*, though they may be poor, or good for nothing, against others. . . . This is the principle of rogues being allowed and induced to turn state's witnesses. Without them, the most shocking crimes must very often go unpunished. It is the same with the inmates and frequenters of brothels. Those who haunt such places ought to be liable to all the difficulties into which they may be brought by their companions in vice. If they cannot be competent witnesses, every crime committed in such a place is almost sure to escape the law.[12]

The Middletown gentleman accused New Yorkers of being so tolerant of brothels that they simply failed to recognize the corruption of Robinson. "They do not seem to have considered his character as soiled by his infamous connexion, so as to become a suitable candidate for every crime, and therefore treated him as if he had harmlessly fallen into bad company. Here is the mistake. He and his associates were equally culpable, and from the length of the intimacy, of equally depraved habits." This worthy (but anonymous) citizen of Middletown probably knew the Robinson family and offered his sympathies:

> No one more sincerely sympathises with his connexions than I do, and perhaps no one has a greater pity for him, yet my sympathetic feelings can never so far run away with my judgment and love of justice, as to treat him like the innocent victim of an unforeseen misfortune. He it is that has brought all their griefs upon them, and he has no right to make use of them and their feelings, as a shield to protect his dissolute conduct from the strictest public scrutiny. It is a duty to exhibit him as a beacon, to warn all the licentious youth of their extreme criminality and danger.

Though papers denounced the verdict of acquittal, isolated reports of spontaneous reactions to the trial registered substantial animosity toward prostitutes. A militia training on the common at Salem, Massachusetts, on the eve of July 4 reportedly practiced shooting at a target consisting of a life-size representation or effigy of Rosina Townsend.[13] Salemites apparently accepted Judge Edwards's and Ogden Hoffman's cynical view that Townsend was the real embodiment of evil in the murder case, and in their masculine enthusiasm they emptied their guns in the mockery of blowing the brothel keeper to pieces. A paper in Albany, New York, recounted that a Robinson look-alike drew a curious and appreciative crowd:

> A fidgetty, good looking sort of chap, who appeared to be burdened with his own thoughts, put up at the Mansion house the other day, and passed for young Robinson. It got abroad that the young R. was actually at the Mansion house, and hundreds flocked there to look upon the uneasy gentleman, who appeared to be sitting upon thistles, while he *enjoyed* a greater notoriety probably than ever fell to his lot before. A mob stood gaping around, while more *affable* dupes were pressing forward to shake hands with him. The prettiest hoax that has been played here in a long time.[14]

The Albany impersonation may have been an intentional hoax or a momentary case of mistaken identity, but the crowd's desire to greet Robinson and shake his hand reveals an instant public willingness to make a celebrity of the acquitted killer.

Two penny newspapers, the *New York Sun* and the *Philadelphia Public*

Ledger, published in installments detailed analyses of the crime and the trial. The *Sun* dredged up the porter in Furlong's store, a Mr. McDermott, who said he did not remember seeing Robinson the night of April 9.[15] The *Sun* claimed that a Mr. Kyle, associated with the Park Theatre, had also visited the prisoner at Bellevue and was prepared to swear falsely that Robinson was with him between nine and ten at the Shakespeare Refectory on Park Row, an eatery catering to the theater crowd. Worse still, the *Sun* alleged that the D.A. was aware of Kyle's effort to falsify an alibi but still failed to challenge the defense in the remarkably similar Furlong story.

Both the *Sun* and the *Ledger* zeroed in on the question of motive, the great missing element of the trial. Benjamin Day, writing in the *Sun*, and Russell Jarvis, the author of the *Ledger* series, both believed the Emma Chancellor story represented the truth suppressed. (Jarvis was a lawyer-turned-journalist who worked on papers in Washington and Philadelphia in the 1820s to 1830s.) Day and Jarvis drew on grand jury testimony (or possibly, in the case of the *Sun*, directly from witnesses like Elizabeth Stewart and Julia Brown, whose comments enlarged on what was recorded at the grand jury hearings) to disclose that Robinson had seduced and kept a young woman, who, they now alleged, was missing. Robinson, they asserted, threatened to kill anyone who revealed "the reckless and profuse expenditure in which he indulged, and which many of them well knew he could only sustain by peculation." He frequently made presents of bolts of cloth to his various prostitute friends, they said, and he was often armed with a pistol which he put under the pillow when he slept at brothels. Day of the *Sun* concluded that Robinson, armed, dangerous, and up to his neck in embezzlement, had done away with Emma Chancellor, and *this* horrible murder was the secret that Helen Jewett knew and held over him.[16]

The *Ledger* echoed all these ideas in its seven-part series, published about a week after the *Sun*'s and obviously partly derived from it (although with a few embellishments: Robinson, Jarvis claimed, always traveled about with a dirk, a small dagger). Both editors said the proof positive of Robinson's guilt came from Hester Preston, a prostitute to whom Jewett had confided the secret of Emma Chancellor's murder. Further proof resided in the words of the defense attorney William Price at the trial, when he said that the attempt to purchase poison, to kill Jewett, "or any other woman," was irrelevant. Price as much as admitted that another woman had died by Robinson's hand, these editors concluded.

Such a dramatic revelation had great appeal. It supplied the missing motive, it contributed to a picture of Robinson as a fiend even worse than first presumed, and it made it sound like the entire legal system—defense, prosecution, and judge alike—had conspired to protect an evil one of their own kind. When George Wilkes came to write his fictional version of the Jewett murder for the *National Police Gazette* in 1848 to 1849, he made the Emma Chancellor story the pivot of the plot, the dark secret that at last explained what drove Robinson to kill Jewett.

Compelling as it was, it did not quite add up. Hester Preston did not come forward to elaborate her tale. She had in fact appeared at the grand jury in April, along with Julia Brown and Elizabeth Stewart, and her role then was very minor. She merely explained that in 1835 Frank Rivers had been a client of hers for a time. She gave her address as 55 Leonard Street, Ann Welden's brothel, but she had been "on the town" only two years, so her stay at Welden's did not overlap with Jewett's. She testified that she "only saw Ellen Jewett at the theatre," which if true does not make it sound like they shared a relationship close enough to permit sharing such deep secrets. And given Jewett's propensity for jealousy, it does not seem likely she would be such intimate friends with someone her dear Frank also saw or had seen. Moreover, if Hester Preston did have any knowledge that Robinson had committed another murder, and he was now free on acquittal of Jewett's death, she was very imprudent to share her secret with the *Sun* editors, lest she become a third victim of his rage. In any case, in late June, subsequent to the appearance of the *Sun* series, police officers arrested her and six other young women, all residents of the brothel at 55 Leonard Street, on a disorderly conduct charge. Preston was sentenced to thirty days at hard labor.[17] Perhaps a die-hard conspiracy fanatic might conclude that Preston's incarceration was retribution by the police for sharing her alleged secrets with the *Sun*; but no editor in June of 1836 reached that conclusion. Preston was merely mentioned in the *Sun* and the *Ledger* editorials, and no one followed up on the allegation, tried to interview her, or expressed the least concern when she was incarcerated in late June. The Police Office columns that recorded her sentencing did not even link her to the Jewett case.

The *New York Herald* was quick to discredit the *Sun*'s devious subplot of fiendish murders: Emma E. Chancellor "is still alive," Bennett wrote, living at a different house on Reade Street.[18] This wasn't just Bennett's typical perversity; the editors of the *Transcript* also claimed to have tracked her down:

> The girl Emma Chancellor—the *chère amie* and protegé of the young miscreant Robinson—has, since the flight of the latter from the city, seduced into actual marriage, an amiable, unsuspicious,

and "good natured" young man, with whom she is now living in Brooklyn, of which city he has for a considerable time past been a resident.[19]

Probably the best test of the Emma Chancellor story is one no newspaper attempted in 1836, because they really had not fathomed much about Jewett's personality or relationship with Robinson. Would Jewett have continued seeing Robinson, in February and March of 1836 imploring him repeatedly to reopen their relationship, if she thought he had murdered another lover? She knew he had dark moods, and she tolerated some degree of cruel treatment, as we know from his frequent apologies for misbehavior. But if she had certain knowledge that he was capable of murder, it seems most unlikely that she would have subjected herself to the risk of becoming his next victim. Her anger with him flared over jealousies of the heart; she was ready to break with him in December 1835 merely for asking to visit with Hannah Blisset while she was in Philadelphia. It is clear that she did know some secret about him, as early as November, yet almost certainly this had to do with embezzlements from Hoxie or others, nefarious money schemes that seemed to involve another man (Cashier). She had known about the romance with Chancellor back in August, and it made her deeply unhappy. But the couple seems to have put it behind them, Helen occasionally remarking on the time when he had been unfaithful to her. Robinson learned from that episode that Helen demanded fidelity, so he took precautions to keep from her his other amours and exploits (for example, with Elizabeth Salters and Hester Preston). For him to have murdered another lover—and for her to know about it and still continue with him—strains belief.

And yet there were other women. Of Miss Norris, the mysterious woman who visited Robinson in jail, we know next to nothing. Editor Bennett claimed this was an alias for Emma Chancellor, still alive and waiting for her lover. Bennett breezily predicted Chancellor/Norris and Robinson would take off for Texas shortly, and "after the lapse of a few years, he may yet return to Washington a member of Congress from some of the new states beyond the Mississippi. Who can tell?"[20] The joke here rested on the absurdity of the transformative powers of western wilds, turning the rejects and failures of the East into statesmen in the West (in the celebrated mode of Davy Crockett and Sam Houston, two congressmen from Tennessee). Miss Norris might have been Emma, or any of several other women—for example, another prostitute or even a Hoxie daughter. (Hoxie, forty-one, had five daughters, two of whom were old enough to marry in 1837 and 1838.)[21]

Miss Norris was not the only woman who visited Robinson in jail. While in Bellevue, he employed a servant woman named Margaret Fields. Apparently this was a customary practice; she probably brought him his cigars, extra food, reading material, and clean clothes. She also surreptitiously carried letters between his cell and that of William D. Gray, his friend, onetime roommate, and original owner of the famous cloak, awaiting trial since mid-May on theft charges.[22] Gray and Robinson had boarded together for most of 1835 at 31 Maiden Lane, and for two or three weeks Gray had overlapped with Robinson at 42 Dey Street, the Moultons' boardinghouse, according to the *New York Sun*.[23] When Gray, age twenty, appeared before a judge in early July, the police found in his pockets five letters from Robinson. On July 13 and 14 they were printed in the *Transcript* and the *Herald*. Gray began the exchange, but Robinson was careful to destroy those Gray sent. Why Gray was not similarly cautious is an interesting question; he kept the letters and walked into court with them in his pocket. He could have shredded them, chewed them up, burned them with matches used to light cigars, or given them to the servant to carry away. But he chose not to, later telling the *Sun* that he had kept them as "mementoes of a man he assumed was doomed." Robinson wrote to his friend:

> To W.D.G.—I have waited a couple of days to ascertain your charges. The turnkeys don't like to talk to me about it, but I have learned that you are confined as a witness to appear against me. Now, Bill, all that I can say is, bear down upon me as lightly as possible, for God knows there is already such a mass of evidence (and a greater part false) against me that many a heart stouter than mine would sink in despair. So you and Emma must quarrel to keep your hands in, eh? Comforts such as this place affords are around me, and I hope you are not destitute. Destroy this, as I have your's and be careful. Your's, Jhn. Johnson's Son.

Even to Gray, Robinson maintained his innocence. He was wrong about Gray's being put on the stand; it is not clear when or from whom District Attorney Phoenix learned that Gray was the actual owner of the cloak, and in any event who owned it did not much matter to events of April 9. But Robinson thought it possible Gray would be called to testify, maybe to some aspect of his relationship with Jewett. The reference to Emma is clarified in the next letter. She was Gray's new bride, Mary Jane Stevenson, whom he married in January 1836, according to a marriage notice in the *Herald*. Robinson called her Em (M) or Emma for short, probably for loose disguise.[24] (Signing the letter John Johnson's son was further subterfuge.)

17th [May]—Grey [*sic*]—I received your's yesterday morning, but have not felt in a good humor till this afternoon. I cant say much, I'm interrupted continually. My trial [the arraignment, actually] takes place next Tuesday, so say the papers. I think they show me favor by putting mine down No. 1; anyway, I thank God the time is near at hand. And so you say you are going to knock off with sweet Em. Let me make a bargain with you, *it will not be the first one of the kind I have made;* supposing you part with her, you'll want to marry another before long, this you can't do without great danger. *Let you be where you will*, you must recollect you have a very *severe* father-in-law, from what I've heard—when wronged, he's unforgiving; now if I understand you, you want to abandon her; this you, for your own security, ought not to do, without a reason. You probably know, that while all were free to come and go, I was a lodger with her one night. I don't want to wound your feelings, but become the willing tool to assist you, as I have others, "sick of their bargain." If I have mistaken your sentiments, I humbly beg pardon, and plead in my defence, "par avis etrayed." My interference [*sic*] is simply this. You must know then, in the first place, I expect to get cleared; well, when I am cleared, and at liberty, just let me seduce your wife, and if your inclinations are fell intent [*sic*], she has no further claim on you. She will not be the first married woman, who has felt my persuasive powers; "how can you," they all say, and * * *. Like a trained Race Horse, she must be in fine order now, and I would (with all respect for your feelings,) like to * * * * *. But mind ye, I dont do it without your permission and wish, as I have plenty of them who are but too willing, and, poor sweet creatures, they come to see me most every day; they now and then drag their husbands along, so as to keep up appearances. Sweet devils, how I love them. Be careful you destroy all my notes you have or may receive, for if discovered, it will injure us both very much. Bennett was here Sunday, but the tell-tale could'nt see your humble servant. Harlaam, Jno. Johnson's Son.

The asterisks were inserted by the newspapers reprinting the letters. Presumably Robinson's original language was unprintably frank and descriptive of what an experienced "Race Horse" could now provide in the way of sex. His casual offer to seduce Gray's wife to facilitate his friend's divorce or abandonment of her, coupled with his admission that he had slept with her before Gray married her, points up the unrestrained sexual culture to which these young men belonged. It seems unlikely that Mary Ann Stevenson was a prostitute, if she had a severe father and a family that cared enough to insert her marriage notice in the *Herald*. Yet she had consented to intercourse with Robinson and then married Gray, and Robinson was confident of his powers to seduce her again. Conceivably, Robinson was exaggerating his sexual conquest, although it would be unusual, to say the least, to brag about such exploits to the husband of the woman he had seduced. Moreover, Robinson the diarist had written that he did not parade his sexual adventures before other friends, and in this case it appears he was informing his good friend Gray for the first time of his early visit with "sweet Em." Gray's possibly anxious reply asked Robinson to elaborate on when and where he had slept with her.

> Grey [*sic*]—My stay with Em, was before the time that I met you and her at the Park. And it was in Church street, what number I know not; why didn't you tell me the name of her who lives at ———— Howard street? I fancy she knows me, and if you write me again before our servant leaves (which is to-day,) tell me her name. I am nervous to-day, and my writing is crow's marks. I don't believe we can keep up our correspondence any longer, for the time before trial is so short, I don't think it best to trust another servant; we've trusted one, and I guess she will say nothing. I've given her some change, and you had better a few fips if you have any, and if you have an opportunity, which I have not, tell her she must keep dark, when she is out. 21st. Yours. C.C.

(Fips were "fippenny bits," five-penny coins of Spanish origin in circulation in the Jacksonian era.) Robinson was probably bragging extravagantly when he claimed that "sweet creatures"—enamoured women whom he had already seduced—came to see him almost daily, some accompanied by their ignorant husbands. But the jail keeper Lyons did testify at the trial that it was during a visit by a woman that he first noticed Robinson's thinning hair, and no lawyer thought it remarkable that he had such a visitor.

Attached to this third note found in Gray's pocket was a list of three men and their bank accounts, which the newspapers presented as if it were a postscript from Robinson to Gray. The *Transcript* printed it with the comment that "there can be no doubt of the object intended to be accomplished therefrom."[25] In a way that must have been transparent to men familiar with banking practices of the 1830s, this postscript appeared to refer to a scheme to bilk or fraudulently obtain money from the accounts in question.[26]

After Robinson's arraignment on May 24, he wrote Gray again:

> Gray—There is no doubt but my trial will come on this week. Your Em. might have been at the court room; the ladies wore all veils; I distinguished none *but the devilish old hag*. What makes you think you are not to be a witness? tell me; and what are the reports respecting us conjointly. You asked me in your last note per our 1st servant if I will assist you? In case I get clear, my dear fellow, to my utmost, and now I've ascertained that that same servant is a damning deceitful lying bitch. Whether she has or will blab us I know not, but in case she does, *we'll deny it to the last and be d——d to her*. In place of rewards she'll get her bellyfull of something *not so agreeable* for her pains.
>
> Sunday 29, 1836

Here was vigorous language expressing anger toward the servant woman and threatening assault, possibly sexual assault because of the reference to giving her a bellyful of something. (The *Herald* chose to replace "bitch" with five asterisks, but the *Transcript* did not cut it.) This is a Robinson consistent with the caustic diary and the threats alleged by Julia Brown and others, a Robinson wearing the midnight face hinted at in the Jewett correspondence. Robinson imagines Gray is a pal, with whom he can banter about raping a "deceitful lying bitch" and about giving black eyes to Gray's wife:

> W.D.G.—My pen is so poor, I can't use it. It is worn off one side, like a crab. In my last note I perfectly recollect using the word "conjointly." I see, however, you understood me and set me right. But the idea of partnership in keeping *Her*, is laughable. Gramercy! I liked to have split a laughing when I read it. And you gave *her* black eyes! Haven't these folks mistaken one girl for another? Does my journal edify you? Whether Mrs. Potter will be a witness or not, I can't say—Mrs. M. probably will. It is no sign that you are not a witness because you didn't go down last week; only those, I believe, were subpoened whom they wished to give *recognizances*. They will try to injure my "*caracter*." Don't be caught napping. *My trial commences tomorrow, Thursday*. Saturday night I'll be either free or *crazy*; and as soon afterwards I will pay you a visit as I possibly can. It's lucky it's cold, or how the court room

would smell tomorrow. When do you have the doctors come to see you? They are with me a good deal, smoking and drinking, and a real clever merry set. It's about dinner time, and I shall have to break off sudden, as soon as I hear the doors begin to open. One of the Doctors has just left me, and gone for a couple of bottles of porter—will be back in five minutes or less. I am very busy today, fixing to go down tomorrow, and writing and poking names out of my sleepy head. Done 1 June.

OLD PORT

Don't tell Jewell of our correspondence.

Robinson wrote this on the eve of his trial, which began Thursday, June 2. He walked into the City Hall courtroom to all appearances composed and unruffled, but underneath that exterior he was frenetic and more than a little manic—yet still capable of being charming. The Bellevue doctors who shaved his head and studied him for signs of disease also found him an agreeable drinking and smoking companion. Maybe they were seeking to bolster his courage with bottles of dark beer against the next day's ordeal. Robinson anticipated that the trial would only take three days, after which he would be "free or crazy." He still claimed to Gray that he was innocent—Em with her two black eyes was the victimized woman, not Helen Jewett, Robinson implied—an astonishing sentiment in view of Jewett's death. He referred to the printed version of his journal; maybe the doctors or the servant woman brought him a copy, and he assumed Gray had seen it too. His offhand remark reveals little about authorship, but it is perhaps significant that he termed it "my journal" while neither denying it was his nor undercutting it with a sarcastic comment. The reference to Mrs. Potter is a mystery; Mrs. M. is likely Mrs. Moulton. Robinson clearly anticipated an attack on his character, and his boarding-house keeper, who figured, after a fashion, in loco parentis, might have shed light on his nocturnal activities. But neither the prosecution nor the defense entered into a discussion of his character. (The final post-script refers to a member of the Chichester Gang, Joseph Jewell, imprisoned and awaiting trial for a brawl that had ended in the killing of a city watchman.)

William D. Gray saved these five notes, written over a space of about two weeks. He told the *Sun* he destroyed a few others, as "unfit for the eyes of any one," so he was obviously not hesitant to demonize his onetime friend now by implying he had written shockingly worse things.[27] If Gray really entertained any distant hope of using these notes to bargain with authorities to mitigate the charges against him, he was mistaken. If anything, in demonstrating his connection to the fiendish Robinson, he convicted himself of guilt by association. Gray was speedily convicted of theft: an employer who hired him as a bookkeeper had accused him of collecting and then pocketing debts owed the store. Gray admitted he had dunned creditors of his boss's store and appropriated about $117, but he pledged that his father would pay it all back. On an unrelated count, he was accused and found guilty of stealing an expensive coat (worth $32) and a cloth cap ($3.50) from a man staying at a hotel; he had been caught with the pawn ticket for the goods in his pocket.[28] Gray read a heartfelt if pathetic appeal to the judge, invoking his reputable father near Zanesville, Ohio, who had trusted him with his little brother in the big city and was willing to make good his debts. He characterized his downward spiral as a very recent descent into pleasure-loving vices, following twelve months of exemplary behavior. (He omitted to mention that he roomed with Robinson for all of those twelve months, if his account to the *Sun* about living on Maiden Lane with the Connecticut clerk held true.) He begged to be allowed to return to Ohio; and, curiously, he never mentioned his wife or recent marriage. Gray's appeal for mercy was unsuccessful. The judge sentenced him to five years in Sing-Sing prison, a stiff sentence indeed.[29]

The notes found in Gray's pocket created an instant sensation in the press. No handwriting witnesses confirmed they were penned by Robinson, but no one questioned their authenticity. The public dissatisfied with the acquittal was eager to brand Robinson a wretch and scoundrel fully capable of committing terrible deeds. What particularly substantiated his depravity was his plot to seduce Gray's wife "by collusion with her husband": "This fact is sufficient to prove him capable of murder, or any other crime," declared the *Philadelphia Public Ledger* on July 12. The *Boston Herald* called him "a monster of profligacy, a fiend in human shape."[30] At long last, James Gordon Bennett reversed his opinion about the verdict, and even Joseph Hoxie withdrew his support. Wrote Bennett in the *Herald*, "Mr. Hoxie believes now, since the developements [*sic*] made by Grey, that Robinson was guilty of murder and arson, and that if Maxwell or Hoffman had been public prosecutor, he would have been convicted."[31]

The *Public Ledger* called for impeachments of Judge Edwards and Phoenix, the D.A. The *Transcript* in New York reported that a petition calling for Edwards's resignation was making the rounds, charging the judge with "physical incapacity" for his rulings in the trial of Robinson; it was garnering many signatures, including those of "distinguised laymen and lawyers."[32] Nothing came of these efforts, but they were signs of intense public discontent with the trial's outcome.

By mid-July, Robinson had left New York. The papers reported he had returned to his parents in Durham, which finally aroused some interest in the "respectable" Robinson family. Were they stricken by discovering a monster in their midst? The *Public Ledger* further explored the meaning of "respectable." The Robinsons enjoyed a "basic competency," the editors said, the nineteenth-century phrase for having achieved a fully adequate economic status; and the father had some "notoriety among village politicians," a belittling reference to his membership in the state legislature. But inquiries revealed that neighbors now judged the family less than fully wedded to "sound moral and religious sentiments." In fact, "the family are noted in their neighborhood for opposition to religion and religious institutions," the *Ledger* reported. (The neighborhood gossips conveniently failed to recall the role the unpleasant Reverend Smith played in driving many Durhamites away from Congregational Calvinism.) As evidence of the Robinsons' contrary ways, one informant pointed to the time the senior Robinson had been approached for a donation to the Sunday-school fund, and he allegedly snarled back, "I would sooner see my children go to the brothel." The *Ledger* had the sense to suspend belief about this statement, but the editors concluded that it at least showed something about how the Robinsons were viewed in town—but newly viewed, of course, against the backdrop of the national sensation over their unconvicted, brothel-going, murderous boy.[33]

An enterprising writer collared Robinson in Durham in July for a long interview he published in a twenty-four-page pamphlet titled *Robinson Down Stream; Containing Conversations with the "GREAT UNHUNG."*[34] The anonymous writer (and apparently onetime friend of the clerk's) guaranteed the public that the interview was published with Robinson's consent and was nearly verbatim, having been taken down on the spot. (In the text, Robinson suggested that the author's profits on the publication should cancel a debt he owed the author.) The interview reveals a Robinson unrestrained in grandiosity, bravado, and arrogance, embroidering his remarks with evasions and lies. The interviewer's first question, "Have you as much pride as ever, Robinson?" produced a self-dramatizing reply that played off the themes of disguise, deception, and playacting:

No. I have run my career. I have nothing more to hope from the patronage of this hypocritical world. I have no desire to flatter it. Mankind! I love ye not. I will no longer pretend to see you as you would seem to others. I know your disguise; I have worn it—I know your arts; I have practiced them—I know the trickery of the stage; I have myself been behind the curtains—examined the scenes, scrutinized the tinselled wardrobes—sneered at the elements of a thunderstorm, and convivialized in the green-room. I can unmask one half of New York and uncloak the other. I know that city, web and woof, male and female, from the East river to the North, and from Castle Garden to Washington Place. I have not only surveyed its length and breadth, but sounded, also, its depth, even from La Fayette Place down to Corlear's Hook.[35]

Egotism suffused his replies. Did his conscience trouble him? "Not a bit. . . . Did it appear in Court that Helen was murdered by me? . . . Think you I would have thus ruined my brilliant prospects?" On his new-found celebrity, he commented, "What entitles me to be gazed at as the young lion of the day? I fear I am unworthy of such universal admiration. What great action have I performed, that the eyes of all mankind should be thus turned upon me! Indeed I am honored over-much. My modesty is burdened." When the interviewer reminded him that the public basically viewed him as "worse than a savage," he snapped back, "The public is a d——d, long eared ass."

Robinson evaded questions about the murder and trial, insisting that only a "bungler" would use a dull hatchet "to cut up the girl"—"I would sooner use a jack knife," an oddly engaged reply from a man protesting his innocence. Furlong, he granted, "has an excellent memory, much better than mine." Evidently Robinson felt free to cloak himself in the double-jeopardy rule; knowing that he could not be tried a second time, he took small and clever liberties with his answers. The Furlong alibi, he joked, proved the value of cigars: "Smoking may kill other folks, but it keeps me alive," and from there he launched into an explanation of precisely how to open and light a cigar. "I like to see things done exactly right—for example, the tying of a cravat or the folding of a letter."[36]

The interviewer ventured to ask if Helen loved him. In an answer echoing his boasts to Gray, Robinson revealed his inflated sense of sexual attraction:

How could she help it? Half the women in New York were in love with me. Somehow I pass for "a marvellous proper man." I can go back to Gotham and marry an heiress. But out upon matrimony, say I. I am not fond of cold ham.[37]

To be restrained by marriage was to be doomed to metaphorical leftovers. He expressed regret he was not back in New York, away from the boredom of Connecticut, "a very stupid little state." Ducking the question of where he got the money for his extravagant life, he protested that it was not hard to come by: "When you need five dollars, why beg it, or borrow it or get it in any of forty ways."

When asked about New York prostitutes, Robinson remarked that "some of them surpass all other women I have ever known, in beauty; but above all, in eloquence. They can tell piteous tales of their wrongs and sufferings,—tricks of the trade, tho',—tricks of the trade, I do assure you."[38] So Robinson could see through Jewett's calculated tales of seduction and woe. Evidently he had come to understand how her invented stories enticed clients into genuinely caring for her and desiring her sexually. Perhaps he himself had been similarly entrapped back in June of 1835. But now, after her murder—a murder he committed—he condemned her eloquent bids for sympathy as nothing more than a trick of the prostitute's trade.

The interviewer returned to the elements of the trial. "Look me in the eye, if you can, and deny that you dropped the cloak there yourself," he commanded, but the evasive Robinson said, "Deny! why should I deny—or confess?" The questioner pressed on: Why did the clerk deny to Officer Brink that he owned the tasseled cloak when he was arrested? "It was none of Brink's business to inquire into the state of my wardrobe. I told him a lie because it was natural. Neither clerks nor merchants, in New York, scruple to lie. Lying is their vocation—'tis too common to be considered even an accomplishment. Would you hang up a poor counter-jumper for lying? If all the liars in New York were killed, there would be few people left for mourners." Admitting to lying, he took refuge in the disingenuous claim that all New Yorkers lie. Not content to stop there, his description of the corruption of the rogues of New York mushroomed out of control in sentence after sentence, leading him finally to assert that being locked up in jail kept the "rascally world" away from *him*. Whether he meant this absurd claim seriously or as a joke is hard to say. But the interviewer continued to press for statements about the murder, and soon Robinson reached the point when a confused and defensive criminal blurts out something incriminating:

> I have nothing more to say about it. My conscience does not hurt me. Don't report, now, that I confess myself guilty.—look like a criminal, &c. I don't confess any thing at all. They can't prove that I ever saw Helen. It might have been somebody else. There was a dark passage—nor that the hatchet—was'nt I at Furlong's till—I deny the whole affair—handkerchief, miniature, letters, cloak and all. (Robinson said other things in this connection, which the writer is unable to quote correctly.)[39]

But the interviewer failed to trip him up, and Robinson regained his composure, switching topics to flourish a letter just received from Mrs. S.

in sensuous New York: "Oh! I would give worlds to be with her again for a single hour." He then suddenly announced his intention to go to Texas and "join the devoted band of desperadoes."[40] The fall of the Alamo in March of 1836 had drawn hundreds of young recruits to the defense of Texas, a disputed territory between Louisiana and Mexico. News of battles at San Jacinto and Bexar filled the papers in the spring and summer of 1836, and promises of free land to new settlers lured thousands more Americans to East Texas. Robinson proposed to join them and was acquiring appropriate gear, including shirts, blankets, boots, a gun, a compass, a tinderbox, and matches, which caused the interviewer to comment shrewdly that he was "a person of more forecast than I had supposed." Robinson hoped to join the Texas army, under a new name, he said. "I have been Richard the fourth long enough for my interest and safety. The world has somehow got a grudge against me."[41] Self-imposed exile to a rough land beyond the United States borders seemed an appropriately grand gesture for this theatrical young man.

Apart from the questions and answers, the interviewer offered his own assessment of Robinson's mental state, based on two days of close observation as they fished together on the Quinipiac River in Durham. Robinson was in "good spirits": "He seems to be constitutionally happy" and exhibited no remorse. "I asked him one day whether he ever really loved Helen Jewett? He replied, 'sort of' "—a rather tepid and circumspect response. The interviewer was clearly troubled that Robinson did not conform to contemporary expectations about how guilt eats away at the heart and eventually seeks relief through "disclosure of the soul's secrets." His prolonged contact with Robinson allowed the author to observe that "he was generally much more reserved in the morning than in the evening," but overall his health was excellent. Most amazingly, he seemed to show no ill effects of a life of urban debauchery, two months' imprisonment in jail, and the grueling trial. His untroubled mind, said the writer, resulted from Robinson's "total want of moral perception."[42] It was as if he were missing his moral compass altogether.

When the New York papers called him a fiend, they implied a demonic immorality, a willful disregard for right and a deliberate embracing of wrong. But the assessment his old acquaintance made in the course of a fishing trip along the banks of a small Connecticut river probably came closer to the truth. Robinson was not immoral; he was amoral, unfeeling, unable to experience remorse or even sorrow over the death of Helen Jewett—or over much of anything at all. Modern crime literature has offered up the concept of the psychopathic criminal, the amoral, introspective, narcissistic, obsessive personality, a disordered character that has entered popular consciousness in the late twentieth century via journalistic treatments of notorious crimes and crime movies. A precise clinical definition of "psychopath" has proved elusive, but in its broadest mass-market stereotype—the remorseless and manipulative killer—there is more than a faint echo of Richard P. Robinson.[43]

In late July Robinson departed for Texas. The concluding part of *Robinson Down Stream* consisted of a long letter, said to have been copied from a journal the acquitted young man kept and brought back to Connecticut by his traveling companion, a Mr. E. Much of it is a travelogue describing his journey along the Erie Canal ("Clinton's ditch") to a lake steamer, and then down through the Scioto Valley on canal boats past Indian mounds to the Ohio River, where the steamboat *Tuscarora* carried Robinson and Mr. E. on to New Orleans. In one passage Robinson recounted sitting on the upper deck of the boat as night fell, looking at the emerging stars and wondering, in an elevated literary style:

> Where am I? Am I not he who lately produced such a sensation in the City of New York? Why am I wandering through these Western climes: What seek I here? Alas! I am tired of notoriety—I would fain shun the public—I am sick of popularity. . . . Like Byron, I have drained the bowl of dissipation to its dregs—I have felt the intoxication of fame, and am now about to become a martyr to the cause of liberty.

In his grandiose reverie, Robinson imagined that the New York episode was a bad dream—"Brink, Bellevue, Furlong, hatchet, Helen, Hoffman," all fading from his mind as the boat raced on to New Orleans at top speed in the dark. He tried out a different explanation on himself: "Left New York, it is true, partly on account of a slight misunderstanding with my ladye love, a 'daughter' of a wealthy broker in Thomas street, sign of the 'Red Ram.' "[44] His sense of humor had not left him, nor his propensity for flights of fancy.

The Mr. E. who brought this long letter back to Connecticut elaborated on the trip with Robinson in the last three pages of *Robinson Down Stream*. On the steamboat, "the murder of Helen Jewett was a very common topic of conversation amongst the passengers," he reported. Robinson would join these conversations "with perfect coolness" and present an evaluation of the trial without ever revealing his identity. He "compared the testimony and weighed probabilities with great apparent candor—said that considering the vagueness and contradictions of the evidence—the bad character of the female witnesses for the prosecutions—but above all the youth and well known probity of the accused, he, for his part, felt entirely satisfied with the verdict of the Jury." This slight young man of nineteen demonstrated an uncanny ability to act and dissemble, to play the con artist. Lying came easily to him; in conversations about the Jewett case with utter strangers he boldly plumped for his own probity while completely misrepresenting himself.

He was also a cheerful and entertaining companion. Mr. E. observed him "saying gentle things to every girl" encountered on the trip, whether fellow passenger or hotel maid. E. also listened while Robinson "enumerated twenty-three females with whom he had been on the most intimate terms in New-York; fourteen of whom were married"—yet another instance of Robinson's self-aggrandizing claims of sexual prowess, this time exceeding in number and detail his earlier recorded boasts. He freely talked about the murder to E., never admitting a shred of guilt. And E. confessed that he had found Robinson a most agreeable traveling partner. "I parted from him very reluctantly" at New Orleans, where Robinson boarded a boat for Galveston, Texas, intending to enlist in the army of the Empire of the South West and live forever in Texas, "where the brand of Cain is honorable," he declared to E.—at last some sort of admission of guilt. His parting words offered one last occasion for dramatic fanfare, which E. dutifully recorded: "I go, tell those who call me friend, never more to return. If I have sinned with an high hand, God alone knows it. Man, if he will can defy all but the scrutiny of Heaven. The past is sealed. It is even to me, as a dead letter. But the future is open. . . . Tell them— tell all—that I go into exile with all the firmness of a martyr—Farewell."[45]

It is a bit of a strain to imagine such a grandiloquent speech delivered to an audience of one on the gangplank of the ship bound for Galveston, as it took on passengers at a New Orleans landing along the Mississippi River. Yet martyrdom for liberty was indeed the immediate course of action the new Texas immigrant seized on. On August 7, 1836, within a day or days of his arrival in Texas, Richard Robinson had enlisted for two years or the duration of the war with Mexico, in Company C of the First Regiment of the Texas Army, commanded by Lieutenant Colonel Henry Millard. Robinson's newfound patriotic ardor quickly evaporated: the muster records show he was almost immediately discharged. Six other men discharged from that same company in August have reasons listed next to their names: four were deserters, one was disabled, and one court-martialed. No reason is entered for Robinson's discharge.[46] Much as he liked a properly tied cravat or a ritually lit cigar, this young man was not really army material, ready to submit to military discipline, as Lieutenant Colonel Millard may have perceived. Or perhaps the Jewett murder story had reached even faraway Texas, and Millard wanted no part of such a young man and his ill-gotten celebrity.

By August 15, 1836, just one week after the aborted enlistment, Robinson appeared in Nacogdoches. The East Texas town had swelled with many hundreds of newcomers in 1835 to 1836, flooding to Texas on account of the war with Mexico. True to form, the nineteen-year-old Robinson immediately thrust himself into the center of the swirl of town doings. On the day of his arrival, he witnessed, with his signature, a deed of sale. Twice more in his first week in town he witnessed other deeds and contracts, repeating this four more times in the remaining months of 1836. Surely he relished these little legal rituals. Putting his name to official documents established him as a man of integrity, a man whose signature to other men's binding agreements counted, a man whose very act of witnessing acknowledged his probity, dependability, and reliability. His act of inscribing also accomplished the major feat of changing his identity: all of the legal documents were signed "Richard Parmalee."[47] He had taken his mother's maiden name, which was also his own middle name, changing the central vowel from *e* to *a* (either by choice or by the caprice of nineteenth-century spelling). Expressive flourishes added substance to his new identity.

Robinson, the celebrated "Great Unhung," the talk of steamboat passengers on the Mississippi and the subject of unending newspaper verbiage nationwide, slipped into an obscurity of his own choosing as the young and ingratiating Parmalee, eager to help regularize the contractual relations of his new fellow townsmen.

CHAPTER SEVENTEEN

Texas

N ACOGDOCHES was one of six Texas mission pueblos settled by the Spanish in the 1720s on the remnants of a once-thriving Caddo Indian village, located a few miles north of the Angelina River in the gently rolling and wooded hill country of East Texas. Sixty miles overland from the Sabine River, the border with Louisiana, Nacogdoches lies about 150 miles north of Galveston Bay, the gateway for the earliest immigrants to Texas. By the 1820s, American expatriates had begun arriving in sufficient numbers to attempt a strike for independence from Mexico. The abortive Fredonia Revolt of 1827 to 1828 centered on Nacogdoches. In the early 1830s, leading men of the coming independence movement—Stephen F. Austin, Davy Crockett, Sam Houston—traveled through and stayed in Nacogdoches; Houston lived there for a time in 1832.[1] By 1840, when the town had become part of the Republic of Texas, its population was just under a thousand.

A Virginian passed through Nacogdoches in February 1836 and again in 1837, and his observations from his two journeys bracket the arrival not only of Robinson but that of many other Americans drawn by the prospect of colonizing this big area west of the United States, wresting it away from Mexico, turning it into a glorious, independent country called Texas, and not incidentally acquiring 640-acre headrights of free land. "I was really surprised that so shabby a looking place could assemble so many good looking, well dressed, and well-behaved women," said Colonel William Fairfax Gray in 1836; he found the old settlers of Nacogdoches full of "hospitality and unaffected kindness." But returning a year later, he reported that "the new race [of settlers] are adventurers, sharpers, and many of them blacklegs." The older settlers feared the new and put locks on their doors. The adventurers and sharpers, Gray claimed, had occupied all the town offices.[2] Amos Andrew Parker of New Hampshire, who visited Texas in 1835, confronted the legend that Texas settlers were "a set of robbers and murderers": yes, people fled to Texas to escape the law in America, and there were billiard rooms and racetracks in every town, he wrote, but despite that Texas was safer than many realized.[3] In 1836 an Ohio visitor found the settlers "composed of a class who had been unfortunate in life," rough and unprincipled.[4]

Robinson might have stepped straight from the pages of Gray and Parker. By 1837 he had become the proprietor of a saloon with a billiard room, and in 1838 he took office as the deputy clerk of the court. Both jobs required his very considerable skills in penmanship, honed in the years clerking for Hoxie and the months writing to Jewett. The saloon account book survives, recording daily transactions with named patrons who bought crackers, candles, cigars, bottles of claret, and—for more immediate pleasure—"glasses," cards, and games at the billiard table. His business partner was Rodolph von Roeder, a recent German immigrant, and the establishment likely was on or very near the plaza that defines the center of Nacogdoches.[5] By 1838 the account book included sales of clothing and personal items—combs, flannel shirts, gloves, boots, threads, yards of cloth. Robinson also noted purchases he made against the store's till: for a jacket run up by a local tailor (and regular tavern customer), for a bookcase, and for paper, steel pens, quills, India rubber, blotting paper, sealing wax, and black and red ink Robinson bought when he was elected clerk of the court. (This connoisseur of the art of writing made sure to charge his work-related expenses against the Nacogdoches County Treasury.) With his partner Roeder, the city boy purchased a farm, or rather some property the account book referred to as "Spring Farm," an enterprise that also entailed buying lumber, shingles, chisels, and an ax. (The partners appear to have sold it within a few months in favor of concentrating their efforts on the store/saloon.)[6] Robinson bought and sold other town lots and properties in the 1830s and early 1840s. And in a bid for male camaraderie and good fellowship, he joined the local Masonic Lodge in early 1839 and served as recording secretary for several years. For a time the lodge met at his house.[7]

In the summer of 1837, within his first year in Nacogdoches, Robinson was called to testify in a murder case. The court's minute book is sketchy: one man was accused of shooting another three times, and the victim died a few days later. The witness list contained the names of six men, five of them regulars at Robinson's tavern (as was the alleged killer), so possibly the murder occurred in or near the establishment. In less than a day, the accused was acquitted. Here was a moment when Robinson must have relived—and perhaps even revealed—his own experience as a defendant in a murder trial. The acquitted man continued to frequent his bar, so the opportunity for conversation and shared confidences was ever present.[8]

There were other possible confidants as well. Adolphus Sterne was a German Jew who had arrived in Nacogdoches in the 1820s. Robinson met him almost immediately in 1836; he was one of the parties to several contracts newcomer "Parmalee" had witnessed that year. Sterne's diary, which he kept sporadically from 1839 to 1851, mentions Parmalee many times. Although nearly two decades his senior, Sterne was clearly fond of the younger man. On April 9, 1842, on Robinson's twenty-fifth birthday—and the sixth anniversary of the murder of Helen Jewett—Sterne, Parmalee, and a third man went fishing in a stream about twelve miles southwest of town. The April weather was "very fine," and the quiet activity in an isolated spot in the woods of East Texas offered a propitious moment to memorialize the anniversary, if Robinson were capable of reflecting sentimentally or remorsefully on the past. But Sterne's diary carries no hint of confidences revealed or of memories indulged or confessed. Instead, the trip was a fiasco. The horses ran off and could not be found until dark, at which point the men were forced to camp overnight "in the Swamp." They were "nearly eat up with Black gnats & musquitoes, never passed a more wretched night—so much for pleasure," wrote Sterne.[9]

Sterne's fondness for Robinson extended to Robinson's brother James, who arrived in Nacogdoches in 1851. James had been eight at the time of his brother's trial; in 1851 he was twenty-three. Sterne first met James on a trip to the East Coast in early 1851, when he conducted some business for Richard Parmalee and also visited the Robinson family in Durham. So he knew his friend's real name and had met his parents and siblings; quite possibly he knew the entire story of Robinson's past. Two of Robinson's younger sisters, Cynthia and Emma, came to live in Nacogdoches in the 1840s with their Connecticut husbands. Sterne's diary also notes that Parmalee traveled to Connecticut between May and August in 1851 and visited New York City in June or July. Even though he had changed his name, by 1850 Richard Parmalee Robinson was apparently making no big secret of parts of his past to his friends in Texas.[10]

Robinson was also very close to Archibald Hotchkiss, another older man who worked as an agent for the Galveston Bay and Texas Land Company and farmed near Nacogdoches. Forty-one when Robinson met him, Hotchkiss appeared in the saloon ledger every couple of days for much of

1837, running up a tab for games and glasses. Although one of the older settlers—he had come to Texas in the early 1830s from upstate New York—he was at heart a sharper and an adventurer. The traveling Colonel Gray of Virginia first met him in New Orleans in 1835 and spent an evening over drinks hearing Hotchkiss tell tall tales about his life. Hotchkiss bragged about his West Point education, the nineteen battles and skirmishes he fought during the War of 1812—including one where he was left for dead on the battlefield under a carpet of bodies—and his seven years of exploits in Mexico and South America.[11] Hotchkiss liked to talk; he liked to drink; he liked to embroider the truth. (In reality, his war service amounted to a brief stint in the Cayuga County, New York, militia, and he spent most of the 1820s in Montgomery, Alabama, not in South America.)[12] Hotchkiss also liked young Parmalee; possibly he saw a version of himself in the charming young newcomer. In 1837 Hotchkiss had a seventeen-year-old daughter, Attala, and a nineteen-year-old son, Rinaldo. (The exotic names lent credence to his Mexican saga, no doubt.) Within a year of meeting Robinson, Attala married a rich Kentucky planter's son, acquiring in the bargain several families of slaves. The Kentuckian died in 1844, leaving her with two young children, and in September 1845 she became Mrs. Richard Parmalee, making Richard the master of a score of slaves on a farm three miles from the center of Nacogdoches. Richard was twenty-eight, Attala twenty-five, when they married. The union produced no children.

A third friend who knew Robinson's true name was Bennett Blake, a prominent judge and lawyer who settled in Nacogdoches in 1835. Blake signed an affidavit in 1875 attesting that he had known Parmalee well, knew his handwriting, and knew that he and Richard P. Robinson were the same man.[13] (The occasion for the affidavit seems to have been a real estate transaction Robinson signed in 1838, maybe in a forgetful moment signing his true name.) Sterne's diary noted trips Blake and Parmalee made to other towns in East Texas. Years later, Blake's son, Robert B. Blake, became a noted collector of East Texas history and the source for a persistent story that Richard Parmalee kept a pamphlet about the Jewett murder on his parlor table in Nacogdoches.

To someone in town—Sterne, Hotchkiss, Blake, or maybe many more—Robinson did confide his story, or, rather, a modified version of the story. For in the second or third decade of the twentieth century, a Nacogdoches historian named Lois Foster Blount committed it to paper. "The Man Who Came Back," her twelve–half-page typescript, tells the story of a pariah who rebuilt an honorable life in Texas.[14] Helen Jewett, the employee of a haberdashery in New York, had been his lover and had "sacrificed her honor to his unfulfilled promises," wrote Blount. Learning that

Robinson was courting another girl, Jewett "threatened to expose him to her rival" unless he promised to marry her. He did promise, but "that night Helen was killed." A tassel ripped from a distinctive cloak was found on the picket fence behind Jewett's house. Only two men in town owned such a cloak, and Robinson's was the one with the tassel missing! The hatchet used in the murder was traced to a grocery store owned by Hoxie where Robinson worked (but so did other clerks). Arrested, tried, and acquitted, Robinson was ostracized by a "wrought up" public opinion, so he moved to Texas to make a clean start.

Blount captured the reverberations of a Nacogdoches legend repeated over three or four generations. Its self-serving features echo the story Robinson must have told on himself. Most notably, it avoided any admission—any simple declarative sentence—that Robinson committed the crime; he was the murderer only by inference. The story equivocated on the hatchet and the cloak, the two key pieces of circumstantial evidence. Many grocery clerks had access to the hatchet; instead of one cloak owned by two men (William Gray and Robinson), the story invented two cloaks. Hoxie's name survived the oral transmission in one piece, but he had been made into a grocer, a blend with Furlong. And Jewett's career as a prostitute was entirely obscured. Some of these errors no doubt arose from repeated retellings. But some sound like distortions Robinson introduced from his first telling of the story in Texas. How very like him to imagine that his trouble with Jewett stemmed entirely from his having two lady loves jealous of each other. Concealing Jewett's true profession by turning her into a shopgirl made it easier to sustain the illusion of a jealous and demanding lover—for what person, even among the morally limber freethinkers of early Texas, would believe a highly paid prostitute would fall in love with a client and insist on his absolute fidelity?

Lois Blount's brief typescript continued Robinson's story into Texas, where he became a model citizen under a new name. "He was particularly fond of young men, and never tired of giving them good advice." The friendly townsfolk welcomed him; "they liked his looks," Blount wrote, without elaborating on what that might mean—probably personal magnetism. When he wanted to, Robinson could be a charmer, an attractive mixture of sociable acuity and boyish good looks. He joined a military expedition under General Thomas Rusk, Blount reported, that rode against the Cherokee Indians in the summer of 1839, and during a battle Parmalee maimed his right hand when a musket exploded. This was true; Robinson was a volunteer in this short-lived campaign, and he somehow injured his right hand. For months after July 1839, the month of the raid on the Cherokee near Tyler, Texas, his clerking job was taken over by the deputy clerk. Friends in the Masonic Lodge sent a get-well delegation to his house.[15] When Robinson resumed clerking, a surprisingly skillful ambidextrous talent flowered: he wrote a beautiful left-slanting cursive with his left hand.

The final anecdote in Blount's narrative was pure legend, the kind of beguiling episode that animated the whole story and made it memorable in Nacogdoches's oral tradition. In it the rehabilitated pariah honorably confronted his past. Blount related that Parmalee owned and operated a stage line running through Nacogdoches, from Natchitoches in the east, along Louisiana's Red River, to Crockett, thirty miles to the west. In September 1845, a passenger on the stage chanced to leave behind a pamphlet on the Helen Jewett murder. The driver gave it to Parmalee, who assumed it was "the work of an enemy," a deliberate attempt to make his past catch up with him. On the eve of marrying Mrs. Attala Hotchkiss Phillips, Parmalee straightaway went to her and gave her the pamphlet: "Take it and read it," he allegedly announced, "and whatever decision you reach in regard to me, will be satisfactory to me." Of course she determined to stay with him, and they were married that very month.

Could this conceivably have happened? Not as Blount reported. All but two of the many Jewett pamphlets were published in 1836; one came out in 1837 (Thomas Armstrong's *A Letter from Richard P. Robinson*), followed by George Wilkes's *Police Gazette* novella in 1849. An 1836 pamphlet left by accident on a Texas stagecoach in 1845 would have been a worn and tattered tract indeed. Joseph H. Ingraham's popular dime novel *Frank Rivers* came out in 1843, but its intricate plot exonerated Rivers, and, besides, it never implicated Robinson or Parmalee by name, so it would not have been automatically linked to Parmalee in Texas. Still more damaging to Blount's version of the story, Robinson did not run a stagecoach line in Nacogdoches until 1851, six years after his marriage date. Still, Blount's story resonates with the other tradition, credited to Robert and Bennett Blake, that Robinson always kept a Jewett pamphlet on his parlor table. Common to both stories is the assertion that Robinson's wife knew of his past, his indictment for murder, and his sensational acquittal. What Attala thought of it all can only be imagined.

If Robinson did flaunt a Jewett pamphlet under the nose of his wife, stepdaughters, and parlor guests, it most likely was the 1837 latecomer to the flurry of cheap publications. All the 1836 pamphlets condemned Jewett's killer and made Helen into as near a paragon of virtue as a prostitute could be; Wilkes's 1849 novella made Robinson out to be the blackest of villains. But in 1837 a pro-Robinson entry attempted to rehabilitate "the Great Unhung." This sixteen-page pamphlet took the form of a letter from Robinson, living in "banishment" under a new name and addressed to a childhood schoolfellow named Thomas Armstrong. Armstrong now told his old friends and the reading public the truth about the night of the murder.[16]

The Armstrong pamphlet is an ingenious fake, written by someone who had carefully reviewed the trial transcripts and news reports of 1836. Entwining inventions with trial testimony, it told the story of Emma T. (now a terrible young woman, standing in the place of Emma Chancellor) and the good-hearted Ellen Jewett, for whom Robinson truly cared. But then he met Sophia, a virtuous woman, with whom he fell deeply in love, necessitating a clean break with Jewett. The crux of this version was that Robinson slipped in the brothel front door unseen by any woman of the house as Ellen let out her nine o'clock visitor. Still in Ellen's room at eleven, when Rosina delivered champagne, he left the house by the back door at one, losing his cloak on the way. Ellen had borrowed the hatchet a few days earlier to break up her firewood, the implausible assumption being that if Ellen bought her own hatchet, the other girls would want to borrow it all the time. She preferred Richard bring her one on the sly. (This author did not know that the maid Sarah Dunscombe tended Jewett's fires.) The Robinson of the Armstrong pamphlet did not know who killed Jewett; the strong implication was that it was a woman of the house.

If ever a murder pamphlet could have graced the Parmalee family parlor table, this was the one. Robinson would have enjoyed this version, which so completely cleared him and even made him into an honorable young man but for his youthful weakness for a pretty face. Internal evidence easily undermines its authenticity. Helen is called Ellen, the relationship is said to have lasted more than two years, the author has Ellen living on Reade Street with Emma T., and so on. There was no Armstrong family in all of Durham's long but tidy and contained history and so no schoolchum Thomas Armstrong. What the pamphlet mainly shows is that interest in the case had not subsided a year after the murder. Authors like the bogus Armstrong could expect readers still to be familiar with the intricate details surrounding the night of April 9, 1836. The writer acted under the same challenge that motivated the fictional accounts of the murder by Ingraham, Wilkes, and others far into the twentieth century: the intellectual puzzle of fitting the main points of evidence into a distinctive plot.

Richard Parmalee Robinson apparently lived out a quiet life in Nacogdoches. He retained his elected post as clerk of the County Court throughout the 1840s, keeping the books of wills, deeds, and criminal dockets in his neat left hand. The saloon account book continues sporadically into the mid-1840s, but at some point he either sold the business or stopped keeping records of games and glasses. He shows up in deeds periodically in the 1840s, buying and selling lands in small towns around the county. About five months before his marriage to Attala in 1845, Parmalee purchased a house and lot on the southwest corner of Main and North, and this became his town house. (The lot is the site of the modern Nacogdoches County Court House.) The marriage brought him a farm and lands about three miles out of town to the southwest, as well as the mastership of over twenty slaves, most of them women and children, making him one of the largest slave owners in the county. Robinson appears in tax lists, the Texas census of 1847, and finally the Free Schedule of the 1850 U.S. Census, where his occupation was listed as clerk of the District Court and his estate valued at $16,700, making him one of the wealthiest ten men in town. The slave schedule of the U.S. Census counted sixteen slaves on his farm in 1850: seven adults and nine children. In 1851 he went into business with his brother-in-law, Daniel B. Coe (married to Cynthia Robinson Coe, both from Durham, Connecticut), running a livery stable and a stagecoach line.[17] The arrival of the railroad in the mid-1850s posed a serious challenge to his business.

Only once in all his years in Texas did Parmalee get in trouble with the law. In September 1846 he was indicted for assault and battery against one Frederick A. Wingfield, a Nacogdoches resident who had arrived in town in 1835. The warrant indicates that Wingfield fought back and beat up Parmalee, but since Parmalee had started it, he was the one prosecuted. The cause of the fight remains unknown. Parmalee pleaded guilty and was fined thirty-three and a third cents—a very trivial judgment indeed.[18]

There is no record of his getting in any trouble over women; except for his marriage, there is no evidence of any involvement with women, for that matter, but such involvements rarely show up in public records until they run afoul of the law. For his first nine years in Texas, he remained a bachelor; to presume he was celibate all that time would be to assume a state of affairs quite at variance with his reputed activities in New York City. Many young women, both single and married, socialized with men at occasional balls and parties. Adolphus Sterne's diary describes an all-night ball marking the sixth anniversary of Texas's independence, in March 1842. Another ball in town in January 1843 was attended by Mrs. Attala Phillips, then twenty-two, who left the party early after announcing she was "tired of frolics" and eventually stayed the night at the Sterne house.[19] Mr. Phillips missed the ball and was either three miles out at the farm with the slaves or away on a business trip—precisely the kind of opportunity the New York City Robinson would surely have known how to exploit. But that is merely a wisp, a hint of possibility. There is really no way to know how or whether he kept his seductive skills with women in top form. Evidently no Texas husband or father came after him. A few Spanish and Mexican families remained in Nacogdoches in the late 1830s, and as the black population grew in the 1840s another group of exploitable women increased. Nacogdoches contained 1,589 white males, 1,328 white females, 1,228 slaves, and 27 free persons of color in the 1847 census. Possibly Parmalee changed his sexual proclivities when he changed his name, and went into a period of prolonged abstinence. But it does not seem likely.

Occasionally in the 1840s the Jewett case gained notice in newspapers around the country. In 1841 a paper in Columbus, Georgia, carried the news that Robinson had gone to Texas and there "lost his right arm—the arm with which he planted a hatchet into the forehead of a frail, but to him an unoffending girl." Justice denied in the courtroom was partially delivered "in a fight with the Mexicans," the paper exulted, and the murderous right arm "has been cleft from his shoulder."[20] In 1848, a story made the rounds claiming that the notorious Richard P. Robinson, killer of Helen Jewett, had died after spending the preceding dozen years as a reclusive proprietor of a small drugstore in West Florida. Unspecified letters found in the dead man's possession suggested the link, but his fellow townsmen had nonetheless found him a quite likable and fully moral citizen. "He had sought to escape from the relentless persecutions of an uncharitable and unforgiving world, and that, buried here in the most humble obscurity, he was striving to live down the bitter past, by an even and exemplary life."[21] The evidently appealing message was that nineteenth-century men, fiends included, could start over in a new town and count on neighborly support.

When the West Florida story reached the *New Orleans Crescent*, a paper in a city frequented by travelers from East Texas, that journal took the trouble to set the facts right. Robinson was not dead, it proclaimed. He had gone to Texas and fought at the battle of San Jacinto (one of only two clear errors in this account: Robinson was in jail in New York when that battle occurred) and then in the Cherokee campaign with General Rusk, where he was wounded and lost the use of his right arm. Yet he still could write, "expeditiously too," in a beautiful left hand—the informants to the *Crescent* here proved their familiarity with the man. Robinson had changed his name to "Parmlee" and had amassed a comfortable fortune as he approached the age of forty (actually thirty-one). He was married to "an interesting lady of respectable family" and had two children. "His manners are somewhat reserved, taciturn, and haughty; but, from our information, he is well liked by the neighbors. He does not particularly shun conversation on the shocking topic which has given such notoriety to his name. He, of course, avows himself innocent—as a jury has declared him."[22]

On several occasions, Parmalee traveled East to visit his family and possibly to arrange for his stagecoach purchases. His elderly father died in 1848, his younger brother Henry in 1850. Siblings Emma, James, and Cynthia had all relocated to Nacogdoches by the early 1850s; James died there in 1855, and the sisters later moved on. The formerly celebrated villain returned to New York City several times perhaps to revisit his old haunts. His lawyer, Ogden Hoffman, recalled that he appeared in his office one day in New York about 1853, announced that he was living in Texas and doing well. He assured Hoffman yet again that he was innocent of the murder of Helen Jewett.[23]

On one such trip in 1855, Richard P. Robinson suddenly took sick and died. Several passengers came down with yellow fever on the Ohio River steamboat he was on. When the boat docked at Louisville on August 3, Robinson, dangerously ill, was carried off and installed in the Galt House, a local hotel. Two doctors examined him and pronounced that his disease was not yellow fever, but an unidentifiable and possibly fatal inflammation of the brain and stomach. His case was "hopeless," they said, and the proprietor of the Galt House engaged an elderly black woman to attend him over several days. She reported that in his final hours her patient was delirious, ranting and raving and speaking often of a Helen Jewett in ways that made her assume Jewett was his wife. Clearly this woman, probably illiterate, did not know about the notorious murder case of the 1830s. Finally her patient asked for the hotel proprietor, but by the time he arrived, Robinson could no longer speak. He died a half hour later, on August 8.[24]

News of his death was spread by the proprietor, John Raine. His letter carrying the particulars first appeared in the *New Haven Palladium* of August 18. The *Palladium* probably got the Raine letter from Robinson relatives in Durham, and from New Haven the news quickly spread, reaching the *New York Times* on August 25 and looping back to the *Louisville Journal* on August 28. Raine explained that although Parmalee had been traveling alone, some other Texans staying at the Galt House somehow knew that he was the famous Richard P. Robinson. The nurse's report that Robinson had called out Jewett's name might have alerted the proprietor's curiosity. That Texans not in his company should have known who Robinson was is an odd coincidence. The whole story of Robinson's last hours, especially the dramatic deathbed rantings about Jewett, sounds suspiciously concocted.

Concocted or not, it was a fitting end to the sensational murder of Helen Jewett. The Great Unhung had avoided the gallows, and those who had followed the case twenty years earlier could savor its deeply romantic ending: Robinson died with Jewett tormenting his inflamed and fevered mind. If John Raine made the story up, he was clever to attribute it to a slave woman, someone the reading public would assume was ignorant of the case and therefore unable to invent such a satisfying ending to an extraordinary story.

Robinson's body was shipped back to Nacogdoches. The Masonic brothers at the local lodge buried his remains in December 1855, more than three months after he died in Louisville. The last words said at graveside were perfectly in keeping with Robinson's lifelong penchant for reinventing himself: "In him we beheld the valiant soldier of the Republic, and the enterprising citizen of the State, and while his friends admired a character noble and firm of purpose, the blessings of the poor rewarded the beneficence of his charity."[25]

Epilogue

WHO WAS HELEN JEWETT? Was she an innocent (or at least admirable) victim, or was she an evil temptress whose fate was fitting and maybe even preordained? How could such a respectable, personable, and promising youth as Robinson be capable of a monstrous homicide? The crime both horrified and confounded an avid public. Premeditated murders were rare, stonewalling defendants even rarer, and the acquittal in the face of abundant circumstantial evidence against the accused left the door open to decades of speculation.

The case touched a nerve in Jacksonian America, a nerve already exposed and sensitive to the issue of the moral supervision of youth. The unprecedented geographic mobility of the American population of the 1820s and 1830s propelled not only adults but adolescents away from home. Stage roads, canals, steamboats on the rivers, and short-line railroads carried youthful male job seekers away from their families and into rapidly growing urban areas, where they landed not in surrogate families provided by the older master-apprenticeship system but in urban boardinghouses, like Mrs. Moulton's, that provided little more than bed space for the thousands of clerks training in the new commercial establishments. Girls too left home in the 1830s in numbers unimaginable by the customs of earlier generations, attracted to boarding schools, textile mills, or to jobs as domestic servants or shopgirls in the larger towns and cities. No matter how much benevolent mill owners or school preceptors assured parents that their daughters would be closely watched, there was always the possibility of slippage in these systems of supervision, which could be evaded once the watchful eye of the parent was no longer close by.

Many feared that girls might either willfully or ignorantly depart from protective custody and wind up among the growing prostitute population, ruined and doomed.

The story of Dorcas Doyen's entry into the world of prostitution gave form to the anxiety of moralists uneasy over new customs of adolescent training in America. The fear of unsupervised youth was the fear of illicit sexuality. The many versions of Jewett's life and death added force and weight to a cultural prescription about the importance of female virginity, a prescription renewed and invigorated in the early decades of the nineteenth century, serving to tighten up a considerably more relaxed sexual regime of the late eighteenth century. Here—apparently—was an accomplished, lovely, and innocent young girl, seduced, ruined, and abandoned to a life of degradation by some thoughtless and selfish young man of the business class. This was ideal grist for the moralists' mill. Her fated punishment was the worst imaginable: prostitution and then death. Jewett's history seemed to provide a real-life and therefore powerful version of the archetypal seduction story, so useful for instructing youth of both sexes about the evils of illicit sex. Several of the pamphlets published about Jewett explicitly argued that her story was a "beacon to youth." Judge Weston closed his April 20 letter to William Wilder and James Gordon Bennett with that very thought: "I very sincerely hope that the catastrophe, cruel as it was, may not be without its moral uses."

Of course none of her contemporaries realized that Jewett herself had embellished and perhaps even fabricated her life story in order to conform to the seduction fictions of the day. (No one, that is, except possibly Robinson, who remarked in his interview in the *Robinson Down Stream* pamphlet that prostitutes' "piteous tales" were mere "tricks of the trade.") On the surface, moralists intended seduction stories to scare young women into vigilance, to teach them to guard their sexual treasure against unscrupulous men. Jewett's use of them reveals an altogether different purpose: seduction narratives bolstered male egos, encouraged men to assert sexual mastery over women, and allowed women the latitude to exhibit sexual energy on their own, under the guise of its being unlocked from slumber by a thrilling man. In this way, an ethic of passionlessness for women, the pervasive belief that good women could not possibly be sexual aggressors, was rendered consistent with some acknowledgment of the power of romance and desire in the hearts of women.

In truth, an underlying contradiction lay at the heart of all seduction stories: the moralistic tale of sexual danger could so easily slide over into an immoral recipe for how to engage the passions. A reader could pity and identify with the victim in such stories—or study the moves of the rake.

The Female Moral Reformers had certainly come under fire for publishing tragic tales of seduction (in their journal, the *Advocate of Moral Reform*) that to some seemed lurid and inflammatory and therefore a cause, not a cure, of immorality. The press coverage of the Jewett murder balanced along the same thin line. Merely to recount Jewett's fall from virtue (as William Attree had in his column) or describe the circumstances of her murder risked conjuring up in readers' minds erotic mental images. (James Gordon Bennett's descriptions of Jewett's naked corpse, followed by Alfred Hoffy's lithograph of the scene, were deliberately over the top, of course, encouraging indecent thoughts among their readers and viewers.)

The moral reformers recognized this dilemma; true-life seduction stories were instructive, they argued, but the novels dangerously glamorized sexual sin, and Jewett's life story in some sense confirmed this. She had been indulged with romantic reading, from Sir Walter Scott to Edward Bulwer-Lytton to the very devil himself, Lord Byron, and look what happened to her. Probably there was more than a little truth to this view. Jewett was by all accounts an avid reader from childhood onward. Reading gave her an idea of life beyond the confines of small Maine towns like Farmington and Temple, beyond the confines of servitude in the Westons' home in Augusta. Medieval Scottish heroines and Persian princesses vivified her imagination. No longer content to be a servant, nor even content with the prospects of ordinary marriage to a man of her social station, Jewett developed inappropriate ambitions to lead an exciting life of adventure. She read fictions, she enjoyed a cameo role as a perfect little lady in Anne Royall's *Black Book*, and she discussed books with an early romantic friend in private walks in the Kennebec fresh air. Later, after she left Augusta, she fictionalized her own early life in her various accounts of her fall from innocence, and she created fictional personae in an epistolary style to engage probably scores of young men in pursuit of her unconventional career as a prostitute selling romantic fantasy as well as sex. She was her own self-made character, and all but the final stage of her literary career was under her own control. That final stage came after her death, when she truly passed over the line into fiction and became a tragic but exciting figure rendered in pamphlets, stories, and short novels. The works by Joseph H. Ingraham (*Frank Rivers, or, The Dangers of the Town*, 1843) and George Wilkes (*The Lives of Helen Jewett and Richard P. Robinson*, 1849) were racy reading indeed, the 1840s version of soft-core pornography intended to arouse readers' prurient interests. This was a startling outcome from a childhood of dangerous reading that even the moral reformers could not have predicted.

If Jewett's character became a work of cheap romantic fiction, her body helped define an aesthetic of erotic death, as her nude remains moved from a voluptuous marblelike statue, to a pinup corpse, and finally to a cadaver stolen from the grave by medical students, dissected, and boiled up into a macabre skeletal trophy hanging in a medical cabinet. Her final faux-corporeal appearance was as a life-size wax figure in a waxworks exhibit of famous murderers, victims, and pirates that traveled the East Coast circuit in the late 1830s. When it appeared at Union Hall in Boston, one newspaper commented that "Ellen is beautiful and the silks and jewels in which she is arrayed, are well calculated to set off her lovely form to advantage. Any person who wishes to contrast triumphant vice with betrayed innocence, will have an excellent opportunity by observing the countenances of Miss Ellen Jewett and Sarah Maria Cornell, which are here placed in close proximity." (Cornell was seduced and murdered by the Reverend Ephraim Avery in a celebrated Massachusetts case in 1833.) Another review of the exhibit praised the accurate portrayal of Robinson and Jewett, adding that Jewett's dress and ornaments cost "a cool hundred." A waxworks show allowed spectators to peer into the faces of vice and evil, to savor the repulsive and the grotesque buried in the human heart, and then to walk away from it. The virtuous would be confirmed in the normality of their everyday life, and potential transgressors chastened. "We hope the young men will visit this scene" ran another testimonial to the exhibit. "It is a solemn one. It furnishes an awful warning to transgressors."[1] Nathaniel Hawthorne visited the exhibit and pronounced the Jewett figure "very pretty," drawing close scrutiny from "decent-looking girls and women." In contrast, the Robinson figure was "awkward and stiff, it being difficult to stuff a figure to look like a gentleman," he surmised.[2]

Hawthorne did not comment on Robinson's countenance or expression. Acquitted at trial, Robinson remained a mystery man throughout the rest of his life. After the publication of his letters to William Gray in July 1836, public opinion turned against him, and there was even talk in New York of trying him again for arson, to get around the double-jeopardy rule. The overwhelming circumstantial evidence, joined now by the news that Robinson's character as shown by the Gray letters was thoroughly depraved, blackened his name indelibly. Yet when he died, the *New York Times* ran a two-day recapitulation of the case in which it cautiously ventured that the verdict might well have been the correct one and that the suspicions cast on Rosina Townsend might have had some basis in fact. Novels written about the case either worked out elaborate scenarios to show how someone else did it—a bad Bowdoin boy named Hart Grange in Ingraham's 1843 book, or Maria Stevens in the 1982 fictionalized treatment by Raymond Paul—or else they gave Robinson a substantial and believable motive in the form of the prior murder of Emma Chancellor, as in Wilkes's *Police Gazette* novel of 1849, a murder which Robinson feared Jewett would expose to view. What this suggests is that Robinson's action in murdering Jewett remained incomprehensible; only by adding new elements to the story could it be made to make sense.

Yet surely he did kill her, and the explanation for it lies buried and implicit in their extraordinary correspondence and in the other interviews and letters Robinson left to the world after his trial. These were two very unusual and talented young people. They somehow found each other, in a city of more than 270,000 people. Starting out as prostitute and client, roles they each knew well from ample prior experience, they quickly found that the relationship deepened, perhaps unexpectedly. Early on, Robinson confided hints about his midnight terrors; Jewett implored him to visit more often, to stay the night. Their correspondence cemented their emotional bond, as they came to see and admire each other's rich interior life (hers romantic, his grandiose about his "brilliant prospects"). He did not merely admire her literary talents, as other clients did, he matched her and engaged her mind and heart, making her think she had at last met her true love. Besides a definite flair for writing, they had a number of things in common. Each could be cheerful and charming, highly skilled at sociable exchanges, but each was liable to be theatrical or moody at times. They admired the refinements of gentility, and at the same time they relished the rawer, darker, exciting world of illicit sex and petty embezzlement. And each could be deceitful, lying, and manipulative.

The normally remote and caustic Robinson could not handle such an intense relationship for long. He fancied himself a seducer of women, a man who challenged the virtue of women, single and married alike, and who, besting his conquests, moved on from one to the next. Deep involvement was not his style, nor was it something for which he was prepared. To meet a young woman so much like himself must have at first brought him the excitement of discovery but soon the fear of exposure—of his carefully concealed inner life of turmoil and hatred. Her clinging to him must have bothered him too. Apparently he was used to using anger to get his way, leading to ugly scenes between them. (Anger too was manifest in his comment to Julia Brown that he would blow out the brains of any woman who exposed him.) But Jewett forgave him these episodes; she even forgave his affair with Emma Chancellor in August, weeping over his infidelity but hanging on to him nonetheless. A smart, assertive young woman able to snap back at British officers and take a rich merchant's son to court, she had somehow grown dependent on him, although not so subordinate that she could not on occasion still ridicule him and laugh him out of her house, as happened in November. From December and the provocative attempt to injure Jewett by asking Hannah Blisset for sex, until April, their relationship was rocky, mercurial, and distressed. Jewett wrote often to demand that he visit her; busy with other women, he spaced out his visits or ignored her for stretches of time. She grew impatient and irritable, he grew distant and cool, building a facade to screen out her obsessive demands. Finally he broke with her, in the meeting ten days before the murder when they agreed to a mutual return of letters. Yet still she pestered him, insisting he come to her, hinting she would expose his embezzlements, threatening him with intense hatred in place of devoted love.

So he decided to kill her, a calculated move that would free him from what had become an oppressive emotional burden. He—and the whole theatergoing town—had seen the play *Norman Leslie* at the Bowery in the winter of early 1836; Jewett had recently read the book. The play fictionalized a notorious New York City murder nearly forty years earlier, in which a young man, "tired of his bargain" (as Robinson had written to Gray), killed his fiancée and threw her body down a well—and won acquittal with the help of brilliant lawyers Alexander Hamilton and Aaron Burr. In Robinson's universe, he was a sun around which all else orbited; it must have made sense to him to solve his problem in the fashion of Norman Leslie. He wrote Jewett he would come on Saturday and she should tell no one; he was cheerful at work all day, optimistic about his prospects. Telling his friends he was going to the Clinton Hotel, he went to 41 Thomas instead, the hatchet under his cloak and his cloak concealing his face. The fire he set was put out in short order; the hatchet and cloak he dropped as he ran were traced to him. He had blundered, yet still he was acquitted. Richard Robinson must have figured that he was unaccountably—or maybe deservedly—lucky. He had gotten away with murder.

N O T E S

• ONE •
SNOW IN APRIL

1. The unusually late winter was reported in newspapers. One New York diarist recorded that snow stayed on the ground for three months that season, until early Apr., which remained unseasonably cold; Dr. James MacDonald, Diary, Apr. 1836, New-York Historical Society. Another diarist noted that Apr. 7 was cold and icy, while Apr. 9 was the first day of the year warm enough not to require a fire, and on the tenth it rained all day; *The Diary of Michael Floy Jr., Bowery Village, 1833–1837*, ed. Richard Albert Edward Brooks (New Haven, Conn.: Yale University Press, 1941), 229. See David M. Ludlum, "1835–36: The Standout Winter of the First Half of the Nineteenth Century," *Early American Winters II, 1821–1870* (Boston: American Meteorology Society, 1968). I thank John Kobar of the National Climatic Data Center for this citation.

David Brion Davis presented the first brief scholarly treatment of the Jewett murder in a chapter in his book *Homicide in American Fiction, 1798–1860: A Study in Social Values* (Ithaca, N.Y.: Cornell University Press, 1957), 161–70. Two studies of the history of prostitution devote attention to Jewett: Timothy J. Gilfoyle, *City of Eros: New York City, Prostitution, and the Commercialization of Sex, 1790–1920* (New York: W. W. Norton, 1992), 92–99; and Marilynn Wood Hill, *Their Sisters' Keepers: Prostitution in New York City, 1830–1870* (Berkeley: University of California Press, 1993), 9–16, 34–36, 150–51, 257–66, 272–80, 297–304. Other scholarly works have studied the Jewett murder in the context of the history of journalism and the rise of sensationalism in the news: Oliver Carlson, *The Man Who Made News: James Gordon Bennett* (New York: Duell, Sloan and Pearce, 1942), 143–67; James L. Crouthamel, "James Gordon Bennett, the New York *Herald,* and the Development of Newspaper Sensationalism," *New York History* 54 (July 1973), 294–316; David Ray Papke, *Framing the Criminal: Crime, Cultural Work and the Loss of Critical Perspective, 1830–1900* (Hamden, Conn.: Archon Books, 1987), 41–43; Dan Schiller, *Objectivity and the News: The Public and the Rise of Commercial Journalism* (Philadelphia: University of Pennsylvania Press, 1981), 57–65; John D. Stevens, *Sensationalism and the New York Press* (New York: Columbia University Press, 1991); and Andie Tucher, *Froth and Scum: Truth, Beauty, Goodness, and the Ax Murder in America's*

First Mass Medium (Chapel Hill: University of North Carolina Press, 1994), 1–96. See also Patricia Cline Cohen, "The Helen Jewett Murder: Violence, Gender, and Sexual Licentiousness in Antebellum America," *National Women's Studies Association Journal* 2 (Summer 1990), 374–89; Patricia Cline Cohen, "Unregulated Youth: Masculinity and Murder in the 1830s City," *Radical History Review* 52 (Winter 1992), 33–52; and Patricia Cline Cohen, "The Mystery of Helen Jewett: Romantic Fiction and the Eroticization of Violence," *Legal Studies Forum* 17 (1993), 133–45. For a recent cultural studies interpretation of another antebellum urban murder, see Amy Gilman Srebnick, *The Mysterious Death of Mary Rogers: Sex and Culture in Nineteenth-Century New York* (New York: Oxford University Press, 1995).

2. This account of the discovery of the murder draws on four episodes of sworn testimony: the coroner's inquest of Apr. 10, taken down Sunday morning at the scene of the crime; an unlabeled and truncated transcript of testimony taken Apr. 16 at the Police Office; the proceedings of the grand jury on Apr. 18 and 19, where twenty-eight witnesses were heard; and the trial in the court of Oyer and Terminer, June 2–6. Manuscript transcripts of the first three events are filed in the District Attorney's Indictment Papers, *People vs. Richard P. Robinson*, Apr. 9, 1836, Municipal Archives on Chambers Street, New York City. The final trial transcript was taken down by court reporters for local newspapers. I have used a pamphlet version, *The Trial of Richard P. Robinson, Before the Court of Oyer and Terminer on the 2nd of June, 1836, for the Murder of Ellen Jewett, on the Night of the 9th of April, 1836* (New York, [1849]). George Wilkes, editor of the *National Police Gazette*, prepared this pamphlet based on newspaper versions of 1836. I have read at least six distinct transcripts printed in various newspapers; reporters caught slightly different wordings and nuances of the testimony. The most detailed and probably most accurate transcript, containing significant nuggets not in the 1849 pamphlet, appeared in the *New York Commercial Advertiser*, June 3–7, 1836. Rosina Townsend's testimony does not vary in any significant detail over all these versions of the discovery of the crime. Information in these opening paragraphs that came from parties other than Rosina Townsend derives from sworn trial testimony that was unchallenged or undisputed.

3. Warrant of *Rosina Townsend vs. William W. Kenny, Andrew Lane, and Edward Falkner*, Aug. 2, 1833, Police Court Papers, box 7446, Municipal Archives.

4. This was watchman Peter Collyer; noted in trial transcript in the *New-York Transcript*, June 7, 1836.

5. James F. Richardson, *The New York Police: Colonial Times to 1901* (New York: Oxford University Press, 1970), 23–42; James F. Richardson, *Urban Police in the United States* (Port Washington, N.Y.: Kennikat Press, 1974), 22–23.

6. Time was still reckoned by local sun time in 1836. Noon, defined as the time when the sun was at its apex, or directly overhead, divided the day into two equal parts. Thus on April 10, 1836, sunrise came at 5:32 and sunset at 6:28, according to almanacs figured for New York. Clocks and watches of 1836, insofar as they were accurate timepieces, kept mean time, not sun time. Because the earth's orbit is elliptical and because the earth tilts on its axis, true noon does not come every twenty-four hours exactly, whereas on a clock it does. Hence people had to set and reset their timepieces, perhaps weekly, to correspond to sun time. They could do this by checking an almanac at sunset, by reading a sundial, or by listening for a local bell tower whose ringer was abiding sun time. A well-attended clock would thus rarely be more than a few minutes out of synchrony with someone else's well-attended clock. By the early 1840s, the eastern United States switched to mean time for formal reckoning of time. Michael O'Malley, *Keeping Watch: A History of American Time* (New York: Viking, 1990).

7. Allan Stanley Horlick, *Country Boys and Merchant Princes: The Social Control of Young Men in New York* (Lewisburg, Pa.: Bucknell University Press, 1975); Walter Barrett [Joseph A. Scoville], *The Old Merchants of New York City*, 4 vols. (New York: Carleton,

1863–69), gives many individual stories of the social origins of merchants of the midcentury, most of whom got their start in clerkships in the 1820s to 1840s.

8. Horlick, *Country Boys*, 25–26; Elizabeth Blackmar, *Manhattan for Rent, 1785–1850* (Ithaca, N.Y.: Cornell University Press, 1989); Paul E. Johnson, *A Shopkeeper's Millennium: Society and Revivals in Rochester, New York, 1815–1837* (New York: Hill and Wang, 1978); Mary P. Ryan, *Cradle of the Middle Class: The Family in Oneida County, New York, 1790–1865* (Cambridge, Eng., and New York: Cambridge University Press, 1981).

9. The group was the General Society of Mechanics and Tradesmen of the City of New-York, founded in 1792. Its *Charter and By Laws* (New York, 1839) lists Hoxie as a member from 1831 on. On the library, see *Annals of the General Society of Mechanics and Tradesmen of the City of New-York, from 1785–1880*, ed. Thomas Earle and Charles T. Congdon (New York: The Society, 1882), 97; and *Catalogue of the Apprentices Library in New York* (New York, 1860). In 1860 the library had five titles by J. H. Ingraham, the Maine novelist who wrote racy fiction in the 1840s; it did not own Ingraham's *Frank Rivers, or, the Dangers of the Town* (Boston: E. P. Williams, 1843), a fictional reworking of the Jewett story. See also Sean Wilentz, *Chants Democratic: New York City and the Rise of the American Working Class, 1788–1850* (New York: Oxford University Press, 1984), 38–40.

10. Testimony of Mary Gallagher, *Trial of Richard P. Robinson*, 12; *New-York Transcript*, June 6, 1836.

11. David D. Hall, *Worlds of Wonder, Days of Judgment: Popular Religious Belief in Early New England* (New York: Knopf, 1989), 176–77; and Karen Halttunen, *Murder Most Foul: The Killer and the American Gothic Imagination* (Cambridge, Mass.: Harvard University Press, 1998).

12. *New York Sun*, Apr. 11, 1836.

13. Obituary of David L. Rogers, *Medical Register of New York, New Jersey, and Connecticut* (New York, 1878), 16:187–89. I thank Robert C. Davis of Case Western Reserve University for his help in tracking New York physicians of the period.

14. Dr. David L. Rogers, autopsy report, *People vs. Robinson*, Apr. 9, 1836, District Attorney's Indictment Papers.

15. Coroner's inquest, Apr. 10, 1836, *People vs. Robinson*, District Attorney's Indictment Papers.

16. *New York Evening Post*, Apr. 11, 1836.

17. Coroner's inquest, Apr. 10, 1836.

18. *New York Herald*, Apr. 11, 1836.

19. The porter testified at the trial that he had carried letters between Jewett and Robinson. Another would-be witness to this grisly tour was George Thompson, author of erotic literature in the 1840s (for example, *Venus in Boston: A Romance of City Life* [New York, 1849]). In his autobiography, Thompson claimed that he grew up on Thomas Street, and though a mere lad of twelve, he joined the line of spectators filing through the death scene that Sunday; *My Life: Or the Adventures of Geo. Thompson, Being the Autobiography of an Author* (Boston, 1854), 6–8. Thompson, writing under the pseudonym "Paul de Kock," wrote about the Jewett murder accurately but briefly, but I doubt that he personally viewed the corpse. His autobiography places him at five or six major crime scenes between 1836 and 1850; like a fly on the wall, he just happened to be nearby. Van Ness's casual testimony about the neighborhood viewing of the corpse suggests that such public spectacle was not an unusual practice.

20. *New York Herald*, Apr. 11, 1836, reprinted Apr. 12, 1836.

21. Ibid., Apr. 12, 1836.

22. Ibid., Apr. 11, 12, and 13, and brief back-page note on the "parcel of papers" found in the room, Apr. 14, 1836. "A fig for Justice Lownds, he may be as stiff as he pleases," bragged Bennett, but he never did print any further letters in the *Herald*. At the

trial, Officer Dennis Brink reported that the police removed from Jewett's room two trunks containing books, clothing, albums, and the letters; *New York Commercial Advertiser*, June 4, 1836.

23. *New York Herald,* Apr. 14, 1836.

24. Ibid., Apr. 13, 1836.

25. Ibid., Apr. 14, 1836.

26. The *New York Herald* for Apr. 14 called the snowfall of Apr. 13 the 127th snowstorm of the season. A diarist recorded that the snow fell thickly all day on the thirteenth, but it had entirely disappeared on the fourteenth; *Diary of Michael Floy Jr.*, 229.

• TWO •

SENSATIONAL NEWS

1. Annual Bill of Mortality, reported in Edwin Williams, *New-York Annual Register for the Year of our Lord 1836* (New York: E. Williams, 1836), 322. On capital trials, see the directory *New-York As It Is, in 1837: Containing a General Description of the City of New-York, List of Officers, Public Institutions, and Other Useful Information* (New York: J. Disturnell, 1837), 40. On the long-term trend in murder statistics, see Eric Monkkonen, "New York City Homicides," *Social Science History* 19 (Summer 1995), 201–14.

2. New York's Municipal Archives hold many large and dusty boxes of warrants sworn out in Police Court by citizens protesting the often violent or threatening behavior of others from the late 1820s to the 1840s. Without a police force to call on, individuals had to bring complaints on their own, and those numbers rose dramatically in the 1830s. On Police Office figures, Richardson, *New York Police,* 26. In 1834, there were 8,717 complaints brought; in 1835, the number was 10,168; "Police Statistics," *New-York Transcript*, Feb. 18, 1836.

3. Coroner's inquests were convened nearly daily to determine the identity and cause of death of a body; the vast majority of the cases were perfectly routine. Abandoned infants were nearly always classified as stillborn. The inquest records are on microfilm at the Municipal Archives. The official Bills of Mortality for the city, listed in Williams's *New-York Annual Register* for 1836, reported 474 stillborn infant deaths for the preceding year, but only one case charged as infanticide; 322. Coroner Schureman earned his salary by collecting fees on each inquest, and the *New-York Transcript* (May 4, 1836) reported that his annual income was over $3,400 in 1835, a princely sum.

4. Testimony of Lownds, *Trial of Richard P. Robinson*, 12.

5. Gilfoyle, *City of Eros*, 104.

6. *New York Herald*, Apr. 12, 1836. The issue of Apr. 11, 1836, containing Bennett's "Visit to the Scene," was completely sold out; day-old copies of the Apr. 11 issue sold for a shilling, well above the newsboy price of one penny, so Bennett reprinted it all on Apr. 12. The microfilm edition of the *New York Herald* lacks the Apr. 11 issue and all issues of Apr. 16 to 23. The New-York Historical Society has the full set of the original papers for all of April.

7. *History of Middlesex County, Connecticut, with Biographical Sketches of Its Prominent Men* (New York: J. B. Beers, 1884), 269. The years of his terms were 1820, 1822, 1826, 1827, 1830, 1831, 1834, 1837.

8. *New-York Transcript*, Apr. 12, 1836.

9. *New York Sun*, Apr. 13, 1836.

10. Isaac Clark Pray, *Memoirs of James Gordon Bennett and his Times, by a Journalist* (New York: Stringer and Townsend, 1855); James L. Crouthamel, *Bennett's New York Herald and the Rise of the Popular Press* (Syracuse, N.Y.: Syracuse University Press, 1989); Crouthamel, "James Gordon Bennett," 294–316; Michael Schudson, *Discovering the News: A Social History of American Newspapers* (New York: Basic Books, 1978); Dan Schiller, *Objectivity and the News*; Willard Grosvenor Bleyer, *Main Currents in the History*

of American Journalism (Boston and New York: Houghton Mifflin, 1927); Frank Luther Mott, *American Journalism: A History, 1690–1960*, 3rd ed. (New York: Macmillan, 1962); Frederic Hudson, *Journalism in the United States, from 1690–1872* (New York: Harper and Brothers, 1873); Carlson, *Man Who Made News*; Alexander Saxton, "The Jacksonian Press," in *The Rise and Fall of the White Republic: Class Politics and Mass Culture in Nineteenth-Century America* (New York and London: Verso, 1990), 95–108; Gerald J. Baldasty, *The Commercialization of News in the Nineteenth Century* (Madison: University of Wisconsin Press, 1992); and Tucher, *Froth and Scum*, 1–96.

11. On crime chapbooks, see Daniel A. Cohen, *Pillars of Salt, Monuments of Grace: New England Crime Literature and the Origins of American Popular Culture, 1674–1860* (New York: Oxford University Press, 1993); David Papke, *Framing the Criminal*, 19–32. On sexualized victims, see Halttunen, *Murder Most Foul*. Daniel Cohen argues that the eroticized female victim as a crime genre dates from an 1801 Massachusetts murder; "The Beautiful Female Murder Victim: Literary Genres and Courtship Practices in the Origins of a Cultural Motif, 1590–1850," *Journal of Social History* 31 (Winter 1997), 277–306.

12. *New-York Transcript*, Apr. 13, 1836.

13. *New York Sun*, Apr. 11, 1836.

14. Barrett, in *Old Merchants*, 2:114–18, judged Hoxie deficient in business skills: " 'Profit and loss,' was an account he could not rightly understand." See "Joseph Hoxie," in *Appleton's Cyclopaedia of American Biography*, ed. James Grant Wilson and John Fiske (New York: D. Appleton, 1887–89), 3:288. Hoxie's school attracted boarding students from outside the city; the Long Island artist William Sidney Mount attended in the early 1820s; Mary Bartlett Cowdrey and Hermann Warner Williams Jr., *William Sidney Mount, 1807–1868, an American Painter* (New York: Columbia University Press for the Metropolitan Museum of Art, 1944), 2. See also Wilentz, *Chants Democratic*, 202, 207n, 263n, 281. Wilentz describes Hoxie as an "evangelical master artisan," but Hoxie seems not to have had an artisanal skill. A decade after his store failed, Hoxie tried business again, going into partnership with the lawyer Hugh Maxwell in a fire insurance company; and in 1864 President Abraham Lincoln appointed him an Internal Revenue collector, a payoff for Hoxie's decades of work in the Whig and Republican Parties. See also Leslie Ray Hoxie, *The Hoxie Family: Three Centuries in America* (Ukiah, Ore.: L. R. Hoxie, 1950), 65; this family history lists only his four younger children. James P. Maher, *Index to Marriages and Deaths in the New York Herald, 1835–1855* (Baltimore: Genealogical Publishing Co., 1987), 195, notes the marriages of the two oldest Hoxie daughters, in 1837 and 1838. For benevolent activities, see the General Society of Mechanics and Tradesmen of the City of New-York, *Charter and By Laws*, 49. For his city political activities, see Leo Hershkowitz, *New York City, 1834–1840: A Study in Local Politics* (Ann Arbor, Mich.: University Microfilms, 1974), 20, 54, 85, 91, 131, 176, 162, 173, 505, 509, 512.

15. *New York Sun*, Apr. 13, 1836.

16. Ibid., Apr. 15, 1836.

17. *New York Herald*, Apr. 15, 1836.

18. For circulation figures for many of the 1830s papers, see Bleyer, *Main Currents*, 154–84.

19. This version surfaced first in the *New York Sun*, Apr. 12, 1836 (Tuesday). It was repeated in the *New York Star*, Mordecai Noah's paper; it was reprinted widely, most fully in the bimonthly, nationally distributed *Advocate of Moral Reform* (Apr. 15, 1836), 64, a female-edited newspaper published by the New York Female Moral Reform Society.

20. *New-York Transcript*, June 30, 1834, reprinted in the *New-York Transcript* of Apr. 12, 1836. The merchant's son's name was given in the earlier version, John Laverty, whose father, Henry, was partner in the firm of Laverty and Gantley at 173 Pearl Street as well as on the board of directors of the Commercial Bank; Henry Laverty appeared on a

list of the 150 richest New Yorkers in 1820, for having an assessment of personal property worth over twenty thousand dollars. The reprinted article in the *Transcript* kindly omitted young Laverty's name, leaving long dashes in its place. Disturnell, *New-York As It Is*, 125. The list of rich New Yorkers appears in a later edition of Disturnell's work, *New York As It Was and As It Is* (New York: D. Van Nostrand, 1876), 38–40.

21. Bennett's first "Visit to the Scene" took place on Sunday and was described in Monday's newspaper, Apr. 11. A second visit occurred on Tuesday the twelfth, with Bennett accompanied by William Wilder. On Wednesday the thirteenth he reported further in the *Herald* on the contents of Helen's room, observations based either on his Sunday visit or on the visit on the twelfth. On the fourteenth he explicitly described his entry to the house on the twelfth, with Wilder at his side, and mentioned a brief conversation that ensued with Mrs. Townsend. And on Saturday the sixteenth, he printed a transcript of what appears to be a verbatim interview with the brothel keeper, at which Wilder was also present. This might have been a third visit to the scene, on Thursday or Friday, or it might have been a late and more elaborate report of the already noted conversation on Tuesday the twelfth. The latter seems more likely, since Mrs. Townsend was greatly annoyed by Bennett's printed conversation, and she complained to the police authorities that she had not spoken to Bennett at all. He and Wilder came to her house, she said, and only Wilder spoke to her, about raising a monument to Helen. Townsend's denial was reported in the *New York Sun*, Apr. 18, 1836 (Monday).

22. Mitchell Stephens, *A History of News: From the Drum to the Satellite* (New York: Viking, 1988), 242–47.

23. Among others gingerly covering the "horrid murder": *Paris (Maine) Oxford Democrat*, Apr. 26 and May 3, 1836; *Natchez (Miss.) Daily Courier*, May 12 and 13, 1836; *Columbus Ohio State Journal*, May 7 and 14, 1836; *Newport (R.I.) Mercury*, Apr. 16, 20, and 23, 1836. On newspaper exchanges, see Richard R. John, *Spreading the News: The American Postal System from Franklin to Morse* (Cambridge, Mass.: Harvard University Press, 1995), 154–55; and Richard B. Kielbowicz, *News in the Mail: The Press, Post Office, and Public Information, 1700–1860s* (Westport, Conn.: Greenwood Press, 1989), 51–80.

24. *Philadelphia Gazette and Commercial Intelligencer*, reprinted in *New York Evening Post*, Apr. 23, 1836.

25. *Boston Post*, Apr. 16, 1836.

• T H R E E •

A SELF-MADE WOMAN

1. Sarah Cony Williams to Joseph Williams, Apr. 16, 1836, Reuel Williams Papers, box 21, folder 9, Maine Historical Society, Portland.

2. James W. North, *The History of Augusta, from the Earliest Settlement to the Present Time* (Augusta, Maine: Clapp and North, 1870), 504–5; William Willis, *A History of the Law, the Courts, and the Lawyers of Maine, From Its First Colonization to the Early Part of the Present Century* (Portland, Maine: Bailey and Noyes, 1863), 510–17.

3. The *Herald* of Apr. 28, 1836, identifies Wilder as the sender of the letter. Bennett's second visit to the brothel, described in the *Herald* of Apr. 14, mentions being accompanied by "a young man acquainted with the lady mistress"; the *New York Sun* (Apr. 18, 1836) revealed this accomplice to be Wilder, a "pettifogger" and "occasional visitor to her [Townsend's] house." William H. Wilder appears on a list of attorneys in Williams, *New-York Annual Register*, 410; he was not listed in *Longworth's American Almanac, New York Register and City Directory* (New York: T. Longworth, 1836). The *New-York Transcript* of Dec. 29 and 30, 1835, identified him as a lawyer with offices on Chambers Street in connection with a case involving sixteen sailors from the U.S.S. *Constitution* charged with mutinous behavior.

4. The oldest son, Nathan, age twenty-three, was at Harvard studying law, rooming

with his cousin, Joseph Williams; and the second son, Daniel, twenty-one, had recently arrived home from a trip. The others were still in residence with the judge, including his eldest child, Catharine, then twenty-six years old, divorced, and living at home. For family news of the comings and goings of that week, see Sarah Cony Williams (sister to Mrs. Weston) to her son Joseph Williams, Apr. 16, 1836, Reuel Williams Papers, box 21, folder 9, Maine Historical Society.

5. *Portland Eastern Argus*, Apr. 22, 1836; *New York Herald*, Apr. 28, 1836.

6. *New York Herald*, Apr. 28, 1836.

7. On the Cony Academy founding: North, *History of Augusta*, 422–23. Catharine attended Cony Academy in 1824; a poem she wrote while a student there is in the Melville Weston Fuller Papers, box 2, Library of Congress, Washington, D.C.

8. *Boston Post*, Apr. 26, 1836; *Massachusetts (Worcester) Spy*, May 4, 1836; *Maine (Winthrop) Farmer and Journal of the Useful Arts*, May 6, 1836; *Paris (Maine) Oxford Democrat*, May 3, 1836; *Philadelphia Public Ledger*, Apr. 30, 1836.

9. *Authentic Biography of the late Helen Jewett, A Girl of the Town, by a Gentleman fully acquainted with her History* (New York, 1836); *The Life of Ellen Jewett; Illustrative of her Adventures with Very Important Incidents, From Her Seduction to the Period of her Murder, Together with Various Extracts from her Journal, Correspondence, and Poetical Effusions* (New York, 1836); and *A Sketch of the Life of Miss Helen Jewett, Who Was Murdered in the City of New York, on Saturday Evening, April 9, 1836, with a Portrait Copied from her Miniature* (Boston, 1836). All were anonymously authored; see chapter 5 for an analysis of these pamphlets.

10. *Boston Daily Advocate*, Apr. 18, 1836.

11. *Authentic Biography*, 16.

12. *Augusta Age*, Apr. 20, 1836.

13. Attree's reputation was summarized in his nickname: Oily Attree. See "Gallery of Rascalities and Notorieties," *New York Sunday Flash*, Sept. 12, 1841. On the genre of the seduction novel, see Cathy N. Davidson, *Revolution and the Word: The Rise of the Novel in America* (New York: Oxford University Press, 1986), 83–109.

14. Letter from "Wandering Willie," reprinted in the *New York Herald*, Apr. 13, 1836. Editor James G. Bennett likely obtained this letter from the police, who let him leaf through a large set of letters found in Jewett's room after the murder. Horace Greeley, another young journalist in town, wrote a friend in mid-May: "You enquire—Who is the Wandering Willie of Bennett? I presume he is a scribbler of whom you have heard little or nothing. His name is Wm. H. Attree a Londoner by birth, and a Public, Law and Speech Reporter by profession, but known here as a shrewd, active and unprincipled penny-a-liner, mainly for the small dailies. He was just starting for Louisville and Nashville by way of Niagara when I last saw him." Greeley to B. F. Ransom, May 9, 1836, Greeley Papers, New York Public Library; I thank Andie Tucher for bringing this reference to my attention. Tucher argues that Bennett made up the Wandering Willie letter he printed on Apr. 13, as a slur against a rival newspaperman and as part of the general hokum she attributes to Bennett; Tucher, *Froth and Scum*, 214n. I acknowledge that Bennett and the editors of the *Sun* fabricated some joking letters about each other a week later in the case, but on the whole, Bennett was far more accurate in his reportage than the *Transcript* or the *Sun*. Also, it would be uncharacteristic to skewer a rival who was not around to enjoy the joke. Attree was in Texas in Apr.; he left for the West in Dec., and his return was not soon anticipated. While no letters signed "Wandering Willie" appear on a list of Jewett's letters logged in by the district attorney before the trial, two such letters were with the set when it was loaned to George Wilkes, editor of the *National Police Gazette*, in 1849. Wilkes printed two signed with that appellation, and those two further clarify that Attree had a sexual relationship with Jewett. See chapter 11 for confirming evidence that Wandering Willie, aka Attree, was Jewett's lover.

15. A search of Kennebec County Probate Court, Letters of Guardianship and Wills

and Settlements, for the period 1818–1830 failed to yield any evidence that Weston had any legal obligation to John Doyen for Dorcas.

16. See letters of Sarah B. Williams and Paulina Cony Williams from Saugus to relatives in Augusta, May 17, 1823, July 2, 1823, Aug. 27, 1823, and Sept. 30, 1823, in the Reuel Williams Papers, box 17, file 10, Maine Historical Society.

17. Jane Porter, *The Scottish Chiefs, A Romance in Five Volumes* (London: Longman, Hurst, Rees, and Orme, 1810). The novel was reprinted in America sixteen times up to 1831, by presses in New York, Philadelphia, Hartford, Conn., Exeter, N.H., and Brattleboro, Vt., according to the *National Union Catalog*. It was a popular novel and probably easily available to Dorcas Doyen. It remained popular throughout the nineteenth century, issued in thirteen more editions into the 1850s and an additional sixty times up until 1934.

18. *Farmington (Maine) Town and Vital Records,* vol. 21, *Marriages, 1818–1851*, 12, for the marriage record of John Doyen and Lydia Dutton, July 20, 1823. Lydia Dutton was born in Farmington in Mar. 1800; *Surname Index* (microfiche), Church of Latter-day Saints. John Doyen's birth year, 1784, is noted in his father's Revolutionary War pension record; Jacob Doyen, record W. 27513, petition of Mercy Hibbert, May 1, 1843.

19. North, *History of Augusta*, 422–23.

20. Advertisement, *Maine Patriot and State Gazette,* Apr. 2 and 9, 1828. Tuition was given as four dollars to seven dollars per quarter, with no explanation for the variation in the price.

21. *Farmington (Maine) Town and Vital Records,* vol. 20, *Births, 1749–1874*, 43. This family record group for John and Sally Doyen lists Nancy Doyen, born in Avon, Sept. 18, 1807; Daniel Tuck Doyen, born in Farmington, Sept. 28, 1810; and Dorcas Doyen, born in Temple, Oct. 18, 1813. The *Temple Vital Records* book does not include a birth record for Dorcas.

22. The 1830 U.S. Census lists the Doyen families of Francis, Israel, and two Samuels, the latter a great-uncle and the others second cousins of Dorcas, in the Somerset County towns of Anson, Avon, Milburn, and Canaan.

23. George Wilkes, *The Lives of Helen Jewett and Richard P. Robinson* (New York, 1849), 10; first serialized in the *National Police Gazette* in 1848 to 1849.

24. Samuel Jones Spalding, *The Spalding Memorial: A Genealogical History of Edward Spalding of Virginia and Massachusetts Bay, and His Descendants* (1872; reprint, Chicago: American Publishers' Association, 1897), 307.

25. There were three other banks in Augusta in 1836, each with one cashier: sixty-nine-year-old George Crosby of the Augusta Bank, Silas Leonard of the newly founded Granite Bank, and Asa Redington of the Citizens Bank. Henry D. Kingsbury and Simeon L. Deyo, *Illustrated History of Kennebec County, Maine: 1625–1799–1892* (New York: H. W. Blake, 1892), 440–41; *Augusta Centennial Souvenir*, pamphlet (Augusta, Maine: *Daily Kennebec Journal*, 1897), 8.

26. On Ira Berry's association with the *Eastern Argus* and the *Augusta Age*, see Kingsbury and Deyo, *Illustrated History*, 243, and North, *History of Augusta*, 522.

27. *The Maine Justice: Containing the Laws Relative to the Powers and Duties of the Justices of the Peace*, 3rd ed. (Hallowell, Maine: 1835), 71–72.

28. Frank Luther Mott, *American Journalism: A History, 1690–1960*, 3rd ed. (New York: Macmillan, 1962), 217.

29. This altered story most likely appeared in the Apr. 16 issue of the *Courier*, no copies of which exist. The *Eastern Argus* repeated the slander by publishing the letter of complaint.

30. Horace Bridge's full name was "Horatio," but his family and friends all called him Horace. For the letter by "M***" and Berry's editorial comment, see *Eastern Argus*, Apr. 19, 1836. On Horace/Horatio, see Jane Williams to her brother Joseph Williams, May 12, 1836, Reuel Williams Papers, box 21, folder 9, Maine Historical Society. Jane

wrote: "Horace is the same creature as ever—only a little older—he is going to take rooms in his father's house." The father, James Bridge, had died in 1834, and before 1837 Horatio had settled into the family mansion along the shore of the Kennebec River. See Horatio Bridge, *Personal Recollections of Nathaniel Hawthorne* (London: J. R. Osgood, McIlvaine, 1893), 70–71. The manuscript censuses of Augusta and Hallowell for both 1830 and 1840 yield no other surnames that start with a *B* and end in an *e*.

31. On the *Kennebec Journal* and Luther Severance, see North, *History of Augusta*, 448–49, 600–4. In the 1840s, Severance served two terms in the U.S. House of Representatives.

32. *Kennebec Journal*, Apr. 20, 1836.

33. One town historian described the arrangement as the *Age* "absorbing" the *Patriot*. Kingsbury and Deyo, *Illustrated History*, 243.

34. North, *History of Augusta*, 521–22. The seven bachelors were Aurelius Chandler, James Dickman, Harlow Spaulding, James Bradbury, George Robinson, William R. Smith, and George M. Weston. The *Patriot*'s first editor, in 1827, had been Aurelius Chandler, age nineteen, and its initial publisher was James Dickman. Dickman sold the paper to the twenty-six-year-old Spaulding in May of 1830, and Chandler's early death in Dec. 1830 brought James Bradbury into partnership with Spaulding. Bradbury was a law student in his midtwenties and a Bowdoin College classmate of Horatio Bridge. (Bradbury later served a term in the United States Senate in the late 1840s.) The *Patriot* folded completely in 1831 and was reincarnated six months later as the *Age*. Initially, the two Portland men, Ira Berry and Frank O. J. Smith, were editor and publisher; Smith had been editor of the *Portland Eastern Argus*, and Berry would return to be the editor of it after 1834; he was the editor in 1836 when the Jewett story broke. Berry replaced Smith with the nineteen-year-old George Robinson as editor in 1832. Robinson was also a law student, studying in the office of Reuel Williams, prominent Augusta attorney and brother-in-law of Judge Weston. Robinson soon sold his share to Edmund T. Bridge, age thirty-three, married, son of the wealthy lawyer James Bridge and older brother of Horatio Bridge. In 1834 Bridge and Berry sold out to a printer from Saco, Maine, named William J. Condon, who only kept the paper a year. In 1835, George Robinson and William R. Smith bought it and soon thereafter brought in George Melville Weston, third son of Nathan Weston. In 1840, Weston became the editor in chief, a position he held for four years.

35. *Augusta Age*, Apr. 20, 1836.

36. *Eastern Argus*, Apr. 21, 1836.

37. *Augusta Age*, Apr. 20, 1836.

38. *Boston Post*, Apr. 13, 14, 15, and 16, 1836; its editor was Charles Gordon Greene.

39. Sarah Cony Williams to Joseph Williams, Apr. 16, 1836, Reuel Williams Papers, box 21, folder 9, Maine Historical Society. Harvard Law School in 1835 to 1836 had fifty-two students: twenty-one from Massachusetts, eleven from Maine, and a scattering of two or three from six other states down to South Carolina. Professors included Charles Sumner, Simon Greenleaf, and Joseph Story, who had just left the U.S. Supreme Court to return to teaching. Joseph Williams had also attended Harvard for a B.A. degree, in the class of 1834. Charles Warren, *History of the Harvard Law School and of the Early Legal Conditions in America* (New York: Lewis, 1908), 1:495, 501; 3:13, 14.

40. Joseph Williams got his law degree in 1837 from Harvard and subsequently practiced law in Augusta. In the 1850s he was a member of the Maine State Senate, and when the governor resigned in 1857, Joseph, as president of the Senate, stepped into the governorship for nearly a year. North, *History of Augusta*, 962–63.

41. *Boston Daily Advocate*, Apr. 18, 1836.

42. The article was picked up by other papers and reprinted; see, for example, the *Middletown (Conn.) Sentinel and Witness*, Apr. 27, 1836, where I first saw it. This was early in my research, and I did not yet realize its significance as a genuine insider view of

the Weston household. Two years later, I came to that realization and backtracked to the *Boston Daily Advocate*. Without that reprinting, it is likely I would have overlooked the *Advocate* altogether. I thank Doreen D. McCabe of the Connecticut Historical Society for typing the entire *Sentinel and Witness* article and sending it to me.

43. Joseph Williams to Sarah Cony Williams, May 14 and June 10, 1836; Reuel Williams Papers, box 21, folder 9, Maine Historical Society. The two letters of Paulina Cony Weston are to Mrs. William Dewey of Philadelphia, who until recently had lived on the same block as the Westons in Augusta. The letters, dated June 2 and Sept. 28, 1836, make no mention of Jewett, even though the first was written right on the eve of the murder trial in New York. Paulina Weston apologizes for not seeing more of Mr. Dewey, who had been visiting Augusta that week, on the grounds that the Westons had been very busy with two sick grandchildren, Catharine's many music scholars, and "gentlemen every evening to consult about Law." Weston to Dewey, Melville Weston Fuller Papers, box 2, Library of Congress.

44. *Philadelphia Public Ledger*, Apr. 30, 1836.

45. *New York Herald*, Apr. 25, 1836. The *Age* did not include Weston's name anywhere in the paper, and the chief editors' names would not have meant anything to Bennett.

• FOUR •
NEW YORK'S SEX TRADE

1. *New-York As It Is*, 20.

2. The major historical works on nineteenth-century American prostitution are Gilfoyle, *City of Eros*; Hill, *Their Sisters' Keepers*; Barbara Meil Hobson, *Uneasy Virtue: The Politics of Prostitution and the American Reform Tradition* (New York: Basic Books, 1987); Christine Stansell, *City of Women: Sex and Class in New York, 1789–1860* (New York: Knopf, 1986); Anne M. Butler, *Daughters of Joy, Sisters of Misery: Prostitutes in the American West, 1865–1890* (Urbana: University of Illinois Press, 1985); Ruth Rosen, *The Lost Sisterhood: Prostitution in America, 1900–1918* (Baltimore: Johns Hopkins University Press, 1982); Larry Whiteaker, "Moral Reform and Prostitution in New York City, 1830–1860" (Ph.D. diss., Princeton University, 1980).

3. John Robert McDowall, *Magdalen Facts* (New York, 1832).

4. *Orthodox Bubbles, Or a Review of the "First Annual Report of the Executive Committee of the New York Magdalen Society"* (Boston, 1831), 24.

5. Hill, *Their Sisters' Keepers*, 27, 343.

6. A taxonomy of identities is listed by Abigail Solomon-Godeau, "The Legs of the Countess," *October* 39 (Winter 1986), 99. See also Alain Corbin, *Women for Hire: Prostitution and Sexuality in France after 1850*, trans. Alan Sheridan (Cambridge, Mass.: Harvard University Press, 1990); Charles Bernheimer, *Figures of Ill Repute: Representing Prostitution in Nineteenth-Century France* (Cambridge, Mass.: Harvard University Press, 1989); Jann Matlock, *Scenes of Seduction: Prostitution, Hysteria, and Reading Difference in Nineteenth-Century France* (New York: Columbia University Press, 1994).

7. *Oxford English Dictionary*, s.v. "town."

8. The legal basis of prostitution is covered in Hill, *Their Sisters' Keepers*, 116–18, 126–29; Gilfoyle, *City of Eros*, 139; Whiteaker, "Moral Reform," 285–90; Lawrence M. Friedman, *Crime and Punishment in American History* (New York: Basic Books, 1993), 224.

9. Hill, *Their Sisters' Keepers*, 120; data are from 1849 to 1856.

10. Whiteaker, "Moral Reform," 285–86.

11. *Journal of Public Morals*, Oct. 1, 1836.

12. *New York Herald*, Apr. 15, 1836.

13. *Journal of Public Morals*, Oct. 1, 1836.

14. Faye E. Dudden, *Women in the American Theatre: Actresses and Audiences, 1790–1870* (New Haven: Yale University Press, 1994), 105–7.

15. Claudia D. Johnson, "That Guilty Third Tier: Prostitution in Nineteenth-Century American Theaters," *American Quarterly* 27 (Dec. 1975), 575–84.

16. Dudden, *Women in the American Theatre*; Richard Butsch, "Bowery B'hoys and Matinee Ladies: The Re-Gendering of Nineteenth-Century American Theater Audiences," *American Quarterly*, 46, no. 3 (Sept. 1994), 374–405; Bruce A. McConachie, *Melodramatic Formations: American Theatre and Society, 1820–1870* (Iowa City: University of Iowa Press, 1992); Lawrence Levine, *Highbrow/Lowbrow: The Emergence of Cultural Hierarchy in America* (Cambridge, Mass.: Harvard University Press, 1988); Theodore Shank, "The Bowery Theater, 1826–1836" (Ph.D. diss., Stanford University, 1956).

17. Shank, "Bowery Theater," 193, quoting the unpublished minutes for 1829 of the New York Association, a group that called for the Elizabeth Street privies.

18. Gilfoyle maps the geography of prostitution by decade; *City of Eros*, 29–49.

19. The theater, rebuilt, burned again two years later; a wall of the brothel at 55 Leonard collapsed, and a woman inside was killed. Julia Brown then purchased the house and rebuilt the business quickly. Kenneth Holcomb Dunshee, *As You Pass By* (New York: Hastings House, 1952), 201–3.

20. *Diary of William Dunlap, 1766–1839: The Memoirs of a Dramatist, Theatrical Manager, Painter, Critic, Novelist, and Historian* (New York: New-York Historical Society, 1930), 3:596, 605. The daily health broadsides confirm that the Fifth Ward and the more squalid Five Points areas were especially hard hit by the epidemic. One bill dated July 18 listed new cases located at 39½ Thomas Street, a brothel soon to be conjoined with number 41 next door in a double house; broadside from the Museum of the City of New York, July 18, 1832, in Louis Auchincloss, ed., *The Hone and Strong Diaries of Old Manhattan* (New York: Abbeville Press, 1989), 24.

21. Charles E. Rosenberg, *The Cholera Years: The United States in 1832, 1849, and 1866* (Chicago: University of Chicago Press, 1962), 13–39.

22. Wilkes, *Lives of Helen Jewett*, 44, 45.

23. These books were named in a court case when two destruction-bent bullies of the Chichester Gang, Thomas Reeves and George Rice, invaded Welden's house in March 1835 and slashed these items into pieces with a large knife; *New York Sun*, Mar. 3, 1835.

24. New York Records of Assessment, Fifth Ward, 1831–35, Municipal Archives.

25. Richard L. Bushman, *The Refinement of America: Persons, Houses, Cities* (New York: Knopf, 1992), 70.

26. [Harrison Gray Buchanan], *Asmodeus; or, Legends of New York; Being a Complete Expose of the Mysteries, Vices, and Doings, as Exhibited by the Fashionable Circles of New York* (New York: John D. Munson, 1848), 9–20.

27. Welden was listed at the address in Longworth's *City Directory* up until the 1837–38 volume. She disappeared from the personal property tax list in 1835, when no occupant was listed under the property owner's name.

28. A. Butt Ender, *Prostitution Exposed: Or, A Moral Reform Directory*, 5th ed. (New York, 1839), 6. The pseudonymous author chose a name with double meaning, for the Butt Enders were a company of firemen. I am grateful to Barbara Cohen, owner of New York Bound Bookshop in New York City, for allowing me to examine this booklet.

29. Julia Brown ran the house from late 1839 into the mid-1840s. Records of Assessment, Fifth Ward, 1842.

30. *The Sporting Whip*, Jan. 28 and Mar. 4, 1843. "Walk About Town" was a regular feature column that visited and rated the brothels.

31. Gilfoyle, *City of Eros*, 78 and appendix 2; Paul A. Gilje, *The Road to Mobocracy: Popular Disorder in New York City, 1763–1834* (Chapel Hill: University of North Carolina Press, 1987), 237.

32. Warrant of *Rosina Townsend vs. William W. Kenny, Andrew Lane, and Edward Falkner,* Aug. 2, 1833, Police Court Papers, box 7446, Municipal Archives.

33. Warrants of *Julia Brown vs. James Jarvis and Peter Crosby,* Mar. 24, 1834, and *Brown vs. Robert S. Davis, John Maynes, and Matthew Greene,* Apr. 25, 1834, Police Court Papers, box 7446, Municipal Archives.

34. Deposition of Eliza Ludlow, Mar. 2, 1836, in John Chichester and Coon Gainer, District Attorney's Indictment Papers, Apr. 8, 1836, Municipal Archives.

35. A guide to brothels published in 1839, three years after this incident at Eliza Ludlow's house, identified Miss Ludlow of Greene Street as the constant paramour and "chere amie of a celebrated and handsome Levite." If true in 1836, the deliberate insult Chichester's men delivered that night might have included an element of anti-Semitism. Butt Ender, *Prostitution Exposed,* 15.

36. On the rise of the professional police force in 1845 and its relation to crackdowns on prostitution, see Srebnick, *The Mysterious Death of Mary Rogers,* 96–97. On the rise of the pimp system, see Gilfoyle, *City of Eros,* 90–91. On prostitutes in police courts, see George G. Foster, *New York Naked* (New York: Robert M. DeWitt, 1850), 157. On banishing prostitutes from New York theaters, see Dudden, *Women in the American Theatre,* 79.

37. *Ohio State Journal,* May 14, 1836. Two literary gentlemen did write brief essays about Jewett: Willis Gaylord Clark, in the *Knickerbocker,* May 1836, 544–45; and Theodore Fay, in the *New-York Mirror,* Apr. 30, 1836, 348–50. Jewett had subscribed to both of these periodicals.

• FIVE •

ACCLAIM FOR A WOMAN OF SPUNK

1. The latter two pamphlets are listed in Thomas M. McDade, *The Annals of Murder: A Bibliography of Books and Pamphlets on American Murders from Colonial Times to 1900* (Norman: University of Oklahoma Press, 1961); *Authentic Biography* is not.

2. *The Private History of Helen Jewett, Embellished with Six Engravings and Illustrated with Portions of her Correspondence and Poetical Productions; Ellen Jewett, or, The Victim of Seduction;* and *Sketch of the Life of Miss Ellen Jewett (By One who Knew Her).* The first of these missing pamphlets was advertised in the *New York Herald* on Apr. 20 for a week. The second was promised in a blurb at the end of the published pamphlet *Life of Ellen Jewett.* The third is a title listed in McDade's bibliography of crime pamphlets and said to be located at New York's Association of the Bar Library; but that association now has no record of it. McDade listed it as a twelve-page pamphlet published in New York, so it cannot be a copy of the Boston *Sketch of the Life,* which was twenty-four pages long.

3. Even though Attree was in Texas at the time of the murder, his compatriots at the *New-York Transcript* probably knew of his ongoing friendship with the young woman, making them generally more attentive in their coverage of her murder.

4. *Authentic Biography,* preface.

5. Ibid., 3, 4, 5.

6. Bonnie G. Smith, "History and Genius: The Narcotic, Erotic, and Baroque life of Germaine de Staël," *French Historical Studies* 19 (Fall 1996), 1059–81.

7. *Authentic Biography,* 9–10.

8. Ibid., 9.

9. Samuel Flagg Bemis, "The Scuffle in the Rotunda: A Footnote to the Presidency of John Quincy Adams and to the History of Duelling," *Massachusetts Historical Society Proceedings* 71 (1953–57), 156–66. The journalist who pulled the nose was Russell Jarvis, then a partner of Duff Green on the *U.S. Telegraph.* In June 1836 Jarvis prepared a long analysis of the Jewett murder case for the *Philadelphia Public Ledger,* discussed in chapter 16. On nose tweaking, see Kenneth S. Greenberg, "The Nose, the Lie, and the Duel in the Antebellum South," *American Historical Review* 95, no. 1 (Feb. 1990), 57–74.

10. *New-York Transcript*, June 30, 1834.

11. Ibid., Apr. 12, 1836.

12. When George Wilkes came to write about this incident, he added many of his fictional embellishments to give the story a greater verisimilitude—for instance, that Burke used pearl-handled scissors to cut the dresses and that he strangled a canary belonging to Jewett. However, one item was probably not fiction: Wilkes reported that the respectable (but unnamed) friend of Burke's who vouched for him in court was the "editor of a celebrated weekly magazine." George Morris, thirty years old in 1832, was indeed the editor of the weekly *New-York Mirror* throughout the 1830s, and a member of the august circle of New York writers and intellectuals that included Theodore Fay, Nathaniel P. Willis, Fitz-Greene Halleck, and William Cullen Bryant. The *Dictionary of American Biography* (New York: Charles Scribner's Sons, 1934) notes that he went by the title of "General" Morris due to vaunted service in the state militia.

13. *Authentic Biography*, 9.

14. Ibid., 10.

15. *New York Sun*, June 28, 1834. The *Sun* did not run this item in its Police Office column, but instead entered it with the regular news in the far left column of page 2.

16. *New-York Transcript*, Mar. 13 and 14, 1835.

17. Ibid., Feb. 26, 1835.

18. *New York Sun*, Feb. 26, 1835.

19. Cases involving John Boyd: *John Gill vs. John Boyd*, District Attorney's Indictment Papers, Mar. 14, 1834, and General Sessions, Apr. 7, 1834; *John Boyd vs. James O'Brien, John Gill, and Samuel McMullen*, District Attorney's Indictment Papers, May 16, 1834, and General Sessions, May 16, 1834; *Elizabeth Jeffries vs. Al Hamilton, John Chichester, and John Boyd*, General Sessions, May 7, 1835; *People vs. John Chichester, John Boyd, and Benjamin S. Penniman*, General Sessions, May 11, 1835; and *Michael Riordan vs. John Boyd*, General Sessions, Mar. 9, 1836.

20. *New York Sun*, June 8, 9, and 12, 1835. Thurlow Weed, editor of the *Albany Journal* (Spencer's parents resided in Albany), condemned the *Sun's* police reports for being exaggerated: Attree's reports are "so extravagantly embellished and exaggerated as almost to defy identity, and are very frequently unfounded." Reprinted in the *Sun*, June 5, 1835. In July 1835 Attree visited Massachusetts to cover a Fourth of July oration by the governor, Edward Everett, in Salem. Attree wore his weapons inside his coat, but they were discovered by guards as he aggressively pushed his way toward the front of the rally. Attree was saved from arrest when several New Yorkers attending the celebration identified him as a newspaperman; later in the day Governor Everett invited him to sit at the head table for the meal. Edward Everett, Diary, entries for July 4–9, 1835, Edward Everett Papers, folder 147, reel 36, Massachusetts History Society, Boston.

• SIX •

THE BROTHEL BUSINESS

1. *Eliphalet Wheeler vs. Ann Welden and Ellen Jewett*, Jan. 19, 1833, Watch Returns Docket, reel 23, item 3384, Municipal Archives.

2. *Ann Welden vs. Joseph Watson, James O'Brien, and a third unknown man*, May 20, 1833; *Welden vs. Peter Cote*, Oct. 25, 1833, Police Court Papers, box 7445, Municipal Archives.

3. *Ellen Jewett vs. Ann Welden*, Apr. 20, 1833, Watch Returns Docket, reel 23, item 3044; *Jewett vs. Welden*, Apr. 22, 1833, Police Court Papers, box 7445, Municipal Archives.

4. Wilkes, *Lives of Helen Jewett*, 56.

5. *Authentic Biography*, 7.

6. Ibid.

7. Ibid., 7, 8.

8. For very similar formulations, see two letters of Helen to Richard P. Robinson, June 20, 1835, and one undated, in *National Police Gazette*, Apr. 28, 1849, reprinted in chapter 12.

9. Testimony of Rosina Townsend, *Trial of Richard P. Robinson*, 3.

10. "David L. Rogers," *Medical Register of New York, New Jersey, and Connecticut,* 16:187–89. Dr. Rogers studied under Dr. Valentine Mott of the New York College of Physicians and Surgeons, the foremost anatomist and body snatcher of his time in early New York. Suzanne M. Shultz, *Body Snatching: The Robbing of Graves for the Education of Physicians in Early Nineteenth-Century America* (Jefferson, N.C.: McFarland, 1992), 8, 35, 49. On Valentine Mott, see *Autobiography of Samuel D. Gross, MD . . . Emeritus Professor of Surgery in the Jefferson Medical College of Philadelphia, With Sketches of his Contemporaries,* edited by his sons (Philadelphia: G. Barrie, 1887), 2:308–9. Dr. Rogers was not above participating in the humorous culture of the penny press papers. The *Sun* and the *Herald* had a sharp rivalry in 1835 to 1836, first over the "Moon Hoax," when the *Sun* claimed astronomical observations had verified inhabitants on the moon, and then the "Joice Heth Hoax," in which an old black woman was alleged to be 160 years old. The *Sun* announced she had died and sold tickets to 1,500 people—or so reported Bennett in the *Herald*—to watch Dr. Rogers of Chambers Street dissect her body. Bennett accused Rogers of being party to both hoaxes. *New York Herald*, Feb. 27 and 29 and Mar. 2, 1836.

11. Testimony of George Marston, *Trial of Richard P. Robinson*, 12.

12. A June 20, 1836, article on dress in the *Ladies Morning Star*, a short-lived penny paper, complained, "There is a remarkable impropriety and want of taste in the dress of people in this city. All dress as fashionably and expensively as they can, without regard to their calling." Silks in the kitchen, printed challis over the washtub: this complaint focused on inappropriate blurring of class distinctions in dress.

13. Testimony of George Marston, *Trial of Richard P. Robinson*, 12.

14. Testimony of Elizabeth Salters (twelve dollars a week for room and board), Ophelia Bowles (twelve dollars a week), Maria Stevens ("pays different prices for board"), Hester Preston (five dollars and three dollars "at a time"), Grand Jury Proceedings, Apr. 18, 1836, *People vs. Robinson*, District Attorney's Indictment Papers, Municipal Archives.

15. Testimony of Sarah Dunscombe, *Trial of Richard P. Robinson*, 10.

16. Asa Greene, *A Glance at New York: Embracing the City Government, Theatres, Hotels, Churches, Mobs, Monopolies, Learned Professions, Newspapers, Rogues, Dandies, Fires and Firemen, Water and Other Liquids, &c. &c.* (New York: A. Greene, 1837), listed typical prices in the city; the elegant Astor House, for example, charged $2.50 a night for room and meals. On travel costs, see John Mason Peck, *A New Guide for Emigrants to the West* (Boston: Gould, Kendall and Lincoln, 1836), 373–74, quoted in Seymour Dunbar, *A History of Travel in America* (New York: Tudor, 1937), 799–800.

17. On clerks and journeymen's salaries, see editorial, *New-York Transcript*, Feb. 24, 1836. Hershkowitz lists the daily wage demands, ranging from $1.50 to $2.50, of building-trades workers and other skilled laborers according to Mar. 1836 newspaper stories; employers argued the demands were too high; Hershkowitz, *New York City, 1834–1840*, 153–54.

18. Bill Easy to Helen, Tuesday evening, n.d., *National Police Gazette*, May 26, 1849.

19. "City Clerks," *Advocate of Moral Reform*, Mar. 1, 1836, 33–34. The reformers argued that the clerks fed a "torrent of pollution," and employers should "warn them of the hidden dangers of the city."

20. Testimony of Elizabeth Salters, *Trial of Richard P. Robinson*, 11.

21. Deposition of Rosina Townsend, Grand Jury Proceedings, Apr. 18, 1836, *People vs. Robinson*, in District Attorney's Indictment Papers; testimony of Rosina Townsend, *Trial of Richard P. Robinson*, 3. Townsend's brothel career can be traced in successive New York tax assessment records; the data are abstracted in Gilfoyle, *City of Eros*, 318–19. On

Henry Beekman, see Longworth's *City Directory* for 1827–1828. The Beekmans were a large, wealthy Dutch family, active in New York politics in the mid-eighteenth century. Henry Beekman was listed as one of the 150 richest men in New York City in 1820 for having over twenty thousand dollars in assessed personal wealth; Disturnell, *New York As It Was*, 38–40. The mother of the Livingston sons—John, Robert, Edward—was a Beekman.

22. Antiblack riots over a week in July 1834 targeted black residences on Centre, Leonard, Orange, Cross, Anthony, and Mulberry Streets, an area just north and east of Thomas Street on the other side of Broadway. Twenty houses were heavily damaged, and an African Methodist Episcopal church on Leonard Street was also wrecked. Paul Owen Weinbaum, *Mobs and Demagogues: The New York Response to Collective Violence in the Early Nineteenth Century* (Ann Arbor, Mich.: UMI Research Press, 1979), 46.

23. Early-nineteenth-century censuses listed only the name of the head of the household and then charted the other inhabitants by sex, race, and broad age categories. As shown by the Thomas Street listing, the federally mandated age categories for blacks and whites were different. Whites were grouped by five-year intervals up to age twenty and then by ten-year intervals, probably because it was assumed whites could report their ages with some degree of accuracy. Blacks were classed into much broader groupings of a dozen or more years, as if specificity of age were less available or less important. Having different classification systems impeded direct comparisons of age structures between whites and blacks.

24. *Horatio Humphreys vs. Ann Williams*, June 4, 1835, Police Court Papers, box 7447, Municipal Archives.

25. On John R. Livingston's extensive brothel holdings, see Gilfoyle, *City of Eros*, 43–44, 317–20.

26. Tax assessment records show real property ownership and indicate when structures were first built on lots; they also note names of renters and their personal property assessments. See microfilms of the Record of Assessments, Fifth Ward, 1808–36, Municipal Archives. For ownership transfers, see the *New York City Real Property Index* (microfiche), records for block 144, lot 24. Livingston bought the property later numbered 41 Thomas in 1816 from Catharine Cox; *Real Property Index*, liber 115, 599. His executors sold it in 1853 after his death for $10,400; *Real Property Index*, liber 642, 163. Conveyance records are stored on microfilm at the Office of the City Register, Surrogate Court Building.

27. Testimony of Silas Bedell ("Cyrus Beadle" in other transcripts), *Trial of Richard P. Robinson*, 21. On house construction and skylights, see the early fire insurance maps issued by William Perris, *Atlas of New York City*, vol. 3 (1853), plate 33. On the garden description, see the *New York Herald*, Apr. 20, 1836. The Perris maps show that a narrow alley, measuring two and a half to three feet wide, separated number 41 from number 43; it opened into the backyard of number 43. It appears on the Perris map, dated 1852, and on another undated map from the mid-1840s (estimated date based on owners' names on the property; map microfilm, Record of Assessments, Fifth Ward, Municipal Archives, New York); it seems highly likely that the alley was there in 1836 as well. It would have served as a horse entry or as a service alley for deliveries to the rear of the house at number 43. In theory, someone could have exited Jewett's bedroom by dropping out of her back window (on the south wall) onto the roof of the piazza that ran across the two back parlor rooms. From there, a very nimble person could possibly have jumped into the neighboring alley—a fall of at least ten to twelve feet—and exited onto Thomas Street. This possible escape route was never mentioned in the trial. The open back parlor door, plus the location of the hatchet and cloak, powerfully focused attention on surface routes over yards and fences.

By the 1850s, the backyards of the three Livingston properties on Thomas Street contained nonbrick outbuildings of varying sizes, possibly barns or sheds. In 1870, the last

year the houses appeared on fire insurance maps, the first floor of each three-story building was in use as a store, with number 41 marked as a "special hazard" property, meaning
that combustible materials were stored or sold there (according to the legend: candles,
liquor, soap, perfume, or paint). The backyard of number 41 now contained a five-story
brick building, roughly twenty by thirty-two feet, probably a warehouse. The fire atlas of
1875 shows a completely new five-story brick building occupying the entire double lot of
number 41, with a large skylight covering the back half-dozen feet of the structure. A late-
nineteenth-century brick building of five stories currently occupies the site, very possibly
the same one erected in the early 1870s. It is numbered 84 Thomas, and it appears to be
part warehouse, part commercial use, with some possible residential use as well. William
Perris, *Insurance Maps of the City of New York* (New York: Perris and Browne, 1870), plate
8, and (1875), plate 8.

28. *New York Herald*, Apr. 13, 1836.

29. *People v. Mary Wall*, July 13, 1830, District Attorney's Papers, Municipal
Archives. I thank Timothy Gilfoyle for sending me this reference very early in my
research.

30. Martin Bruegel, "Unrest: Manorial Society and the Market in the Hudson Valley,
1780–1850," *Journal of American History* 82, no. 4 (Mar. 1996), 1393–1424. In the
1790s John R. Livingston had 160 tenants, many of them quite discontented.

31. Clarence Winthrop Bowen, ed., *The History of the Centennial Celebration of the
Inauguration of George Washington As First President of the United States* (New York: D.
Appleton, 1892), 42.

32. George Dangerfield, *Chancellor Robert R. Livingston of New York, 1746–1813*
(New York: Harcourt, Brace, 1960), 112.

33. Dangerfield, *Chancellor Robert R. Livingston*, 128; *Public Papers of George Clin-
ton, First Governor of New York* (Albany, N.Y.: J. B. Lyon, 1902), 4:427–29; Lorna
Skaaren, "John R. Livingston and the American Revolution," in *The Livingston Legacy:
Three Centuries of American History*, ed. Richard C. Woles and Andrea Zimmerman
(Annandale-on-Hudson, N.Y.: Bard College, 1987), 150–61; Anne Hume Livingston,
*Nancy Shippen, Her Journal Book: The International Romance of a Young Lady of Fashion
of Colonial Philadelphia with Letters to Her and About Her*, ed. Ethel Armes (Philadelphia
and London: J. B. Lippincott, 1935), 249, 265.

34. Dangerfield, *Chancellor Robert R. Livingston*, 113, 246. See also Patricia Joan
Gordon, "The Livingstons of New York, 1675–1860: Kinship and Class" (Ph.D. diss.,
Columbia University, 1959), 244, for letter of John to Robert in 1783 on his speculations
in government securities. Chancellor Robert Livingston veered into the emerging Republican Party in the 1790s and opposed Alexander Hamilton's various schemes for funding
the national debt that stood to make John a lot of money.

35. Dangerfield, *Chancellor Robert R. Livingston*, 416. Dangerfield characterized
John Livingston as a man who always drove a hard bargain.

36. Letters of John R. Livingston, Robert R. Livingston Papers, reels 4 and 5, New-
York Historical Society. Other sources on the Livingston family rarely contain more than
a paragraph or two about John R. Livingston. Gordon's dissertation has good material on
his financial wheelings and dealings; "The Livingstons," 223–27. See also Cynthia A.
Kierner, "Family Values, Family Business: Work and Kinship in Colonial New York," *Mid-
America* 71, no. 2 (Apr.–July 1989), 55–64; Joseph Livingston Delafield, *Chancellor
Robert R. Livingston of New York and His Family* (Albany, N.Y.: J. B. Lyon, 1911),
313–56; Clare Brandt, *An American Aristocracy: The Livingstons* (Garden City, N.Y.:
Doubleday, 1986), 113, 125, 146, 157–58; Clare Brandt and Arthur Kelley, *A Livingston
Genealogy* (Rhinebeck, N.Y.: Order of Colonial Lords of Manors in America, 1982);
Thomas Streatfield Clarkson, *A Biographical History of Clermont, or Livingston Manor:
Before and During the War for Independence, with a Sketch of the First Steam Navigation of*

Fulton and Livingston (Clermont, N.Y., 1869), 25, 156; Florence Van Rensselaer, comp., *The Livingston Family in America and Its Scottish Origins* (New York and Richmond, Va.: William Byrd Press, 1949), 87, 100–1, 132. A brothel guide published in 1839 in New York provides a slender clue to Livingston's nonbusiness brothel involvement: a madam named Sal Harvey of Reade Street was identified as the onetime mistress of "——— Livingston." Harvey gained notoriety in her day for allegedly urinating from the balcony of the third tier of the Park Theatre onto the crowded pit below. Butt Ender, *Prostitution Exposed*, 14.

37. *Journal of Public Morals*, May 1, 1836, in an article on 41 Thomas Street suggested that brothel mirrors were known to cost as much as five hundred dollars and even seven hundred dollars. The expense derived from the cost of quicksilver used to coat the glass and the difficulty of achieving an unmarred, unbroken coating over a very large area. For a contemporary description of the complexity of mirror making, see G. A. Siddons, *The Cabinet Maker's Guide, or Rules and Instructions in the Art of Varnishing, Drying, Staining, Japanning, Polishing, Lackering, and Beautifying Wood, Ivory, Tortoiseshell & Metal* (Concord, N.H.: Jacob B. Morse, 1827).

38. It is of course possible that the painting in the brothel was an amateur's copy of the well-known Vanderlyn work, made by a student artist during the years when the original was on exhibit at the Academy. One copy is known to have existed in 1839; it appeared in an exhibition by the Apollo Association, a successor to and rival group of the Academy, and then disappeared from sight. A second copy, dated by canvas marks to 1842, is now owned by the New York State Historical Association in Cooperstown, New York, so that is ruled out. The original Vanderlyn is in the Hartford Atheneum in Connecticut.

Vanderlyn undertook the subject of Jane McCrea on commission to illustrate a book-length poem by the Connecticut poet Joel Barlow (titled *The Columbiad*), which included a long section on the Jane McCrea story as an American tragedy. Barlow found Vanderlyn's price too high and refused to buy the painting. Instead, steamboat inventor Robert Fulton, business partner of the Livingston brothers, purchased it in Paris and then donated it to the American Academy of Art, of which Robert Livingston was then president. The work appears in exhibition catalogs of 1816, 1826, and 1827. The Academy moved from Chambers Street in 1831 and reopened in a much smaller building on Barclay, and many pictures went into storage in those years. A fire in 1837 destroyed some of the upper rooms in that building, and in 1841 the remaining holdings of the Academy were auctioned off. See Mary Bartlett Cowdrey, *American Academy of Fine Arts and American Art Union: Introduction, 1816–1852, Collections of the New-York Historical Society*, vol. 76 (New York: New-York Historical Society, 1953); Louise Hunt Averill, "John Vanderlyn, American Painter, 1775–1852" (Ph.D. diss., Yale University, 1949), 150–52; David M. Lubin, *Picturing a Nation: Art and Social Change in Nineteenth-Century America* (New Haven, Conn.: Yale University Press, 1994), chapter 1; Marius Schoonmaker, *John Vanderlyn, Artist, 1775–1852. A Biography* (Kingston, N.Y.: Senate House Association, 1950); Kathleen H. Pritchard, "John Vanderlyn and the Massacre of Jane McCrea," *Art Quarterly* 49 (Winter 1949), 361–66; Samuel Y. Edgerton Jr., "The Murder of Jane McCrea: The Tragedy of an American *Tableau d'Histoire*," *Art Bulletin* 47, no. 4 (Dec. 1965), 481–92.

39. June Namias, *White Captives: Gender and Ethnicity on the American Frontier* (Chapel Hill: University of North Carolina Press, 1993), 117–44.

40. *New York Herald*, Apr. 14, 1836.

41. Vanderlyn to John R. Murray, 1809, quoted in Lillian B. Miller, "John Vanderlyn and the Business of Art," *New York History* 32 (Jan. 1951), 36.

42. On the sale to Durand: David M. Lubin, "*Ariadne* and the Indians: Vanderlyn's Neoclassical Princess, Racial Seduction, and the Melodrama of Abandonment," *Smithsonian Studies in American Art*, 3, no. 2 (Spring 1989), 6.

43. *New York Herald*, Apr. 19, 1836.

44. For the souvenir hucksterism, see Edgerton, "Murder of Jane McCrea."

45. My reading of the McCrea legend is much indebted to June Namias's chapter in her book *White Captives*, 117–44.

• SEVEN •

EPISTOLARY ENTICEMENT

1. "African Schools," in *New-York As It Is*, 57.

2. Deposition of John A. Spencer, Mar. 11, 1835, in *John Boyd vs. Mary Berry, Frank Berry, and Helen Jewett*, Apr. 14, 1835, District Attorney's Indictment Papers, Municipal Archives.

3. Record of Assessments, Fifth Ward, 1832, 1833, Municipal Archives.

4. *New York Sun*, quoted in the *Advocate of Moral Reform*, Jan. 1, 1836, 1–2. The *Sun*'s Police Office column featured Berry's gaming and fleecing habits.

5. Only two serious crimes under early American law were directly chargeable to a married woman whether or not her husband abetted her: treason and running a brothel. See Linda K. Kerber, "A Constitutional Right to Be Treated Like American Ladies: Women and the Obligations of Citizenship," in *U.S. History and Women's History: New Feminist Essays*, ed. Linda K. Kerber, Alice Kessler-Harris, and Kathryn Kish Sklar (Chapel Hill: University of North Carolina Press, 1995), 22.

6. Thomas Longworth and his father, David, produced New York City directories from the early 1800s until 1841. They acknowledged that collecting householder data was difficult because residents preferred to stay anonymous: canvassing, Thomas later wrote, is like "pulling teeth without the use of ether"; "City Directories," *The Encyclopedia of New York City*, ed. Kenneth T. Jackson (New Haven, Conn.: Yale University Press, 1995), 230. Longworth cleverly did double duty in signing on as census enumerator for the Fifth Ward in 1830; it allowed him to accumulate and verify his directory data while he counted heads for the federal government. The official printed census schedules made no provision to record addresses, instead simply numbering households sequentially. But on the manuscript schedules prepared by Longworth, the street names and individual house numbers are penned in the left margin of each page.

7. *Flash*, June 23, 1842.

8. *Sunday Flash*, Sept. 12, 1841. "Scorpion," "Startle," and "Sly," eds., were pseudonyms for William J. Snelling, George Wilkes, and George Wooldridge. Another similar racy paper, the *True Flash*, edited by Sly in late 1841, refers to "Scorpion Snelling" and "Startle Wilkes" in its columns; see Dec. 4, 1841. "Flash," used by all three papers, was slang for the language and style of sporting men of the brothel world. It could be used as a noun, as in these titles, or more often as an adjective—"a flash man," "a flash dresser"; it suggested deception or sham.

9. *Charles M. Locke vs. Francis Berry*, July 13, Aug. 19, and Sept. 5, 1835, Police Court Papers, box 7447, Municipal Archives.

10. *Advocate of Moral Reform*, Jan. 1836, 1–2. The *New York Sun* of Nov. 19, 1835, reported that Berry showed up in court with a lawyer on a three-hundred-dollar swindling charge and was about to skip town. On the twentieth the paper reported that a displeased Berry, "a common black-leg," visited the newspaper office with his lawyer, said to be "one of the first counsellors of the city," to complain. Frank Berry did leave New York for a time. Mary Berry wrote Jewett in Dec.: "You wanted to know if Mr. Berry was home. He is not, but this morning while sitting at the breakfast table a letter was handed to me. On opening it I found it was from Mr. B. He merely wrote a few words, stating that he wanted fifty dollars. He is in Washington. If he should happen to come on to Philadelphia [where Jewett was], I wish you to see him and talk with him about his extravagance, &c. He spends faster than I can make, whenever he gets loose." Berry to Jewett, Dec. 12, 1835, *National Police Gazette*, May 5, 1849.

11. J. to Helen, Thursday, n.d., *National Police Gazette*, June 2, 1849.

12. Edward to Helen, May 4 and 13 [1834], *National Police Gazette*, June 2, 1849.

13. Helen to Robinson [sometime in summer 1835, from internal evidence], *National Police Gazette*, Apr. 28, 1849.

14. Both letters from Edward appear on the list of letters logged into the D.A.'s office in 1836. No last name for Edward appears on that list, whereas for most of the others the surname is given, which means that Edward did not sign his last name on the actual letters. *People vs. Robinson*, Apr. 10, 1836, District Attorney's Indictment Papers, Municipal Archives.

15. T.C. to Helen, Feb. 26, 1834, *National Police Gazette*, May 26, 1849.

16. "Cambaceres" to Helen, n.d., *National Police Gazette*, May 26, 1849. The *Magnolia, or Literary Tablet*, was published in Hudson, New York, in 1833–1834. Alternatively, the item here was a periodical gift book, *The Magnolia*, published in New York City in 1836, 1839, 1843, 1844, and 1846.

17. Frederick to Helen, n.d.; J.J.A.S. to Helen, Dec. 4, 1835, *National Police Gazette*, May 26, 1849. The issues of May 26 and June 2 printed similar letters that had been saved by Jewett, from men who signed as Stanhope, Archibald, Bob, William, Pupil H., N.J., Charlie H., and Robert.

18. W. E. [Bill Easy] to Helen, Wednesday [Dec. 1835], *National Police Gazette*, Apr. 28, 1849.

19. John P——y to Helen, Nov. 9, 1834, *National Police Gazette*, June 2, 1849; Charles Ch——r to Miss H.J., June 22 and Oct. 3, 1834, *National Police Gazette*, May 26 and June 2, 1849. The D.A.'s log of letters identifies the last name as Chandler.

20. Robinson to Jewett, Aug. 18, 1835, *National Police Gazette*, May 26, 1849.

21. On letter-writing manuals, see Karen Lystra, *Searching the Heart: Women, Men and Romantic Love in Nineteenth-Century America* (New York: Oxford University Press, 1989), chapter 1; Karen Halttunen, *Confidence Men and Painted Women: A Study of Middle-Class Culture in America, 1830–1870* (New Haven, Conn.: Yale University Press, 1982), 119–21; and Roger Chartier, Alain Boureau, and Cécile Dauphin, *Correspondence: Models of Letter-Writing from the Middle Ages to the Nineteenth Century*, trans. Christopher Woodall (Cambridge, Eng.: Polity Press, 1997), 112–57.

22. *New York Herald*, Apr. 12, 1836.

23. John, *Spreading the News*, 164–66; *New York Evening Post*, Aug. 18, 1835.

24. Schoonmaker, *John Vanderlyn*, 355.

25. Helen to Richard Robinson, Wednesday, n.d., *National Police Gazette*, May 26, 1849.

26. Pupil H. to Helen, Aug., n.d., *National Police Gazette*, June 2, 1849.

27. M.G.B. [Maria G. Benson] to Frank [probably early Dec. 1835], *National Police Gazette*, June 9, 1849.

28. Frank to Nelly, Dec. 26, 1835, *National Police Gazette*, May 12, 1849.

29. Frank to Nelly, Friday evening [internal evidence suggests Jan. or Feb. 1836], *National Police Gazette*, May 19, 1849.

30. Nelly to Robinson, Tuesday, n.d., *National Police Gazette*, June 9, 1849; and Nell to Frank, Wednesday morning, n.d., *National Police Gazette*, June 9, 1849.

31. Frank to Nelly, Friday evening [early 1836], *National Police Gazette*, May 19, 1849.

32. Testimony of William Van Ness, *Trial of Richard P. Robinson*, 10–11.

33. John E. Morris, *The Felt Genealogy: A Record of the Descendants of George Felt of Casco Bay* (Hartford, Conn.: Case, Lockwood and Brainard, 1893), 155.

34. Wm. E. [George Marston] to Helen, Wednesday noon [probably Dec. 1835], *National Police Gazette*, May 12, 1849.

35. M.G.B. [Maria G. Benson] to Robinson, n.d., *National Police Gazette*, Apr. 28, 1849.

36. Helen to Richard, Tuesday, n.d., *National Police Gazette*, May 26, 1849.

37. Frank to Helen Jewett, n.d., *National Police Gazette*, June 9, 1849.

38. Wm. E. to Nelly, Sunday morning, n.d., *National Police Gazette*, May 12, 1849.

39. Wandering Willie to Helen, Dec. 2 [but misdated by the printer, probably for a date between the twentieth and twenty-ninth, because the letter makes reference to the New York fire of Dec. 16], 1835, *National Police Gazette*, June 2, 1849.

40. G.B.M. to Helen, Monday evening, n.d., *National Police Gazette*, Apr. 28, 1849.

41. Ibid.

42. Stanhope to Helen, n.d., *National Police Gazette*, May 26, 1849.

43. W.E. [Bill Easy] to Helen, Wednesday noon, *National Police Gazette*, May 12, 1849.

44. Testimony of Charles Tyrrell, *Trial of Richard P. Robinson*, 8.

45. Bob to Helen, Aug. 1, 1835, *National Police Gazette*, June 2, 1849.

46. W.E. to Helen, Tuesday evening, n.d., *National Police Gazette*, May 26, 1849.

47. Wm. E. to Nelly, Sunday morning, n.d., *National Police Gazette*, May 12, 1849.

48. Testimony of George Marston, *Trial of Richard P. Robinson*, 12.

• EIGHT •
A SERVANT GIRL IN MAINE

1. Anne Royall, *The Black Book: or, A Continuation of Travels, in the United States* (Washington City, D.C.: Anne Royall, 1828–29), 2:269.

2. North, *History of Augusta*, 501–5; Willis, *History of the Law*, 510–17; John Livingston, "Hon. Nathan Weston, LL.D." in *Biographical Sketches of Eminent American Lawyers, Now Living*, part 2 (New York: Apr. and May 1852), 283–89. The population of Hallowell in 1784 was 629; North, *History of Augusta*, 189.

3. North, *History of Augusta*, 47–49.

4. Hallowell–Augusta was the town of midwife Martha Ballard; Laurel Thatcher Ulrich, *A Midwife's Tale: The Life of Martha Ballard, Based on Her Diary, 1785–1812* (New York: Knopf, 1990).

5. North, *History of Augusta*, 1–10, 79–91.

6. Alan Taylor, *Liberty Men and Great Proprietors: The Revolutionary Settlement on the Maine Frontier, 1760–1820* (Chapel Hill, N.C.: University of North Carolina Press, 1990); James S. Leamon, *Revolution Downeast: The War for American Independence in Maine* (Amherst: University of Massachusetts Press, 1993), 191–92.

7. North, *History of Augusta*, 501.

8. Livingston, "Hon. Nathan Weston," 284.

9. North, *History of Augusta*, 502. Mrs. Cheever was the sister of the Reverend Aaron Bancroft of Worcester, Massachusetts, and the aunt of George Bancroft, the nineteenth-century historian. Aaron and Elizabeth Bancroft grew up in Reading, Massachusetts, the same town the senior Nathan Weston was born in. Possibly Nathan and Elizabeth knew each other as children, before their first marriages took them in separate directions.

10. Willis, *History of the Law*, 445–61; North, *History of Augusta*, 511–15. The Reuel Williams Papers, 1799–1897, at the Maine Historical Society, contain much material on real estate deals and property litigation.

11. Governor Gerry passed over two or three more senior men who had hoped for the appointment; indeed, precisely because partisans for the senior men politicized the appointment process, the governor chose a relative newcomer. Weston had met Governor Gerry briefly at some point and made a good impression on him. More critically, Weston's new status as son-in-law to Daniel Cony—well connected in Federalist circles in Boston—helped ease the taint of being the son of a Jeffersonian Republican. North, *History of Augusta*, 503.

12. Ibid., 430.

13. Ulrich, *Midwife's Tale*, 256–58.

14. North, *History of Augusta*, 170–73, 836–37; 970–73; Willard L. King, *Melville Weston Fuller: Chief Justice of the United States, 1888–1910* (New York: Macmillan, 1950), 1–17. Dr. Cony's brief diary is in Charles Elventon Nash, *A History of Augusta; First Settlements and Early Days as a Town* (Augusta, Maine: Nash and Son, 1904).

15. North, *History of Augusta*, 222–23; Kingsbury and Deyo, *Illustrated History*, 412. An article on "Literary Institutions" in Maine in the Portland *Eastern Argus* noted that the Cony Academy had started with a donation of over three thousand dollars from its founder; in 1829 it had real and personal property valued at nearly ten thousand dollars and a library of 1,200 volumes; *Eastern Argus*, Feb. 3, 1829.

16. N. F. Carter, *History of Pembroke, N.H., 1730–1895* (Concord, N.H.: Republican Press Association, 1895), 1:20.

17. The land is marked out on an 1892 town map as "F. Doyne, 1788, First Settler," at the north end of Pembroke Street. *Town and City Atlas of the State of New Hampshire* (Boston: D. H. Hurd, 1892), 40.

18. Nathaniel Bouton, *The History of Concord* (Concord, N.H.: Berning W. Sanborn, 1856), 565. A footnote to this Shute family legend notes that Dawen soon settled in Pembroke. The family names of "Doyenne," "Doyne," and "Chiout" appear in the records of the Huguenot churches in Dublin; see J. J. Digges la Touche, ed., *Registers of the French Conformed Churches of St. Patrick and St. Mary, Dublin*, vol. 7 of *The Publications of the Huguenot Society of London* (Dublin: A. Thom, 1893), 17, 112, 245.

19. Otis G. Hammond, ed., *Probate Records of the Province of New Hampshire, 1635–1771* (Concord, N.H.: Rumford Printing, 1907–1941), 9:303, will of Nathaniel Abbott of Concord. Rebecca Abbott had acquired a second last name, Merrill, by the time she married Jacob Doyen, so she was probably a young widow. The Doyen family genealogy in New Hampshire is in Carter, *History of Pembroke*, 2:70–72.

20. Carter, *History of Pembroke*, 1:126; Isaac W. Hammond, ed., *Town Papers: Documents Relating to Towns in New Hampshire* (Concord, N.H.: P. B. Cogswell, 1882–84), 13:160, 161, 166.

21. The service record is reported in Jacob Doyen's 1818 Revolutionary War pension application, record 27513, National Archives. His service claim is corroborated by documents in Isaac W. Hammond, ed., *Rolls and Documents Relating to Soldiers in the Revolutionary War* (Manchester, N.H.: John B. Clarke, 1886–89), 1:604, 3:83, 240, 516, 789, 790. A fuller account of his regiment's activities comes from *Frederic Kidder's History of the First New Hampshire Regiment in the War of the Revolution, with a New Introduction by Richard F. Upton* (Hampton, N.H.: Peter E. Randall, 1973), 36–53. I am grateful to Wayne Bodle for bringing this reference to my attention. Samuel Doyen also filed a pension claim in the nineteenth century, asserting he was a wagon master in the Continental Army, but it was turned down by the government because he could not substantiate his service record; Revolutionary War Pensions, record 4832. Given Samuel's later propensity to lie about his holdings and status, it would not be surprising if he knowingly filed a false pension claim. As late as the 1850s, his heirs were still badgering the government about the denied claim.

22. The estate of Jacob Doyen was inventoried in 1799 and consisted of twenty-one acres of land, wearing apparel, a chest of drawers, an old wheel, a saw, a gun, two pitchforks, an auger, a compass, a small amount of old pewter, and three books, all told valued at $529.47. The real property ($508) had to be sold to pay off his creditors, and after the administrative expenses of probate were deducted, the five surviving heirs were left with a total of $148.97. *Rockingham County Probate Records, 1799–1800* (microfilm) 77, 185, 272, 330, New England Historic Genealogical Society, Boston.

23. Carter, *History of Pembroke*, 1:70–72. Nathaniel and Francis, twins born in 1767 and brothers to Jacob and Samuel, stayed behind in New Hampshire. Nathaniel lived out his life there and had a family of daughters; Francis moved to Maine in the early nine-

teenth century. In 1812 Jacob Doyen quitclaimed land to a Francis Doyen in Temple; Kennebec County Conveyance Records, Deed Records, liber 18, 192. And in 1845 "old Mr. Francis Doyen died," according to the *Temple Vital Records Book, 1773–1891* (microfilm), reels 572, 58, Maine State Library. Jacob had no son named Francis, and any son of Samuel's would not have been over fifty-five or sixty in 1845. The twin Francis would have been almost eighty in 1845.

24. *Vassalboro Town Records*, 1771–1847, 128. The Doyens are only mentioned once, in connection with the 1800 census, in Alma Pierce Robbins, *This History of Vassalborough, Maine, 1771–1971* (1971), 50. On the humorous use of the hog reeve title, see Ulrich, *Midwife's Tale*, 160; and Edward H. Cook Jr., *The Fathers of the Towns: Leadership and Community Structure in Eighteenth-Century New England* (Baltimore: Johns Hopkins University Press, 1976), 218, n.14.

25. *Hallowell Town Records*, Augusta City Hall, manuscript record book transcribed from the original in 1814 by the town clerk, 102–7; the warrants of 1791–92 are summarized in Nash, *History of Augusta*, 535.

26. Extensive records of cases of the local and temporary poor can be traced in the Letters of Guardianship, Kennebec County Probate Court. Vol. 16 covers the years 1817–29.

27. North, *History of Augusta*, 232; and *Last Words and Dying Speech of Edmund Fortis, A Negro Man* (Exeter, N.H., 1795). Fortis, a runaway slave from Virginia, was in his midthirties when he came to Maine and married a Hallowell woman. Fortis fulfilled the conventions of the confession pamphlet by describing his life in Hallowell as one of continual drinking, stealing, and gaming, wickedness he continued in Vassalboro, culminating in the rape and murder of a fourteen-year-old white girl in the fall of 1794. Fortis's confession notes how he morally bested the lawyer assigned by Kennebec County to represent him—possibly Bridge or Cony—in the early 1790s. The lawyer advised him to plead not guilty, but, true to the conventions of Puritan murder confessions, Fortis dreamed of angels, singing birds, and representations of heaven, and then told the lawyer that he could not lie to God.

28. Spalding, *Spalding Memorial*, 92, yields only one Dorcas Spaulding of the roughly right age: a woman born in 1744 in Plainfield, New Hampshire. If this is the same person, Dorcas Spaulding was forty-eight when she was warned out of Hallowell.

29. [Nathan Weston], "Reminiscences of Early Times," *Kennebec Journal*, Oct. 23, 1851.

30. *Court of Common Pleas, Kennebec County*, Sept. 1799, case 62, 1:350. Daniel Cony was one of the three presiding judges in this court.

31. Ibid., June 1800, case 29, 1:347.

32. Ibid., Dec. 1804, case 334, 4:167.

33. Kennebec County Conveyance Records, *Deeds, 1790–1820*, liber 6, 260, 373.

34. Louise Helen Coburn, *Skowhegan on the Kennebec* (Skowhegan, Maine: Independent Press, 1974), 1:193; and J. W. Hanson, *A History of the Old Towns, Norridgewock and Canaan* (Boston: J. W. Hanson, 1849). Skowhegan is eight miles west of Canaan; before 1823, they were the same town, called Canaan.

35. A. J. Coolidge and J. B. Mansfield, *History and Description of New England: Maine* (Boston: A. J. Coolidge, 1860), 42–43, 322–23.

36. "Temple Settlers," taken from a map of Temple in the Franklin County Registry of Deeds and Town Plans, May 1807, listed in typescript in Dorothy Wirth, ed., *Maine Cemetery Records*, 2–5, in the New England Historic Genealogical Society. About forty names are on this list; one cluster includes Benjamin Abbott, Thomas Russell, Samuel Tuck, and Zebulon True, indicating contiguous properties for families that figure in the Dorcas Doyen story.

37. *Temple Vital Records, 1773–1891* (microfilm), reel 572, 9, Maine State Library. The children were John (1784), Benjamin (1794), Joel (1796), Jeremiah (1798), Samuel

(1800), Rachel (1803), and Abbott (1805). Jacob was twenty-five when his first son was born and was forty-six at the birth of the last. A son of Jeremiah Doyen married in 1865 and reported on the vital records marriage form that his father had been born in Temple. Since Jacob, Mercy, and the children were in Vassalboro in the 1800 census, the report on the marriage form must be an error. *Maine Vital Records to 1892* (microfilm), reel 36, marriage of Dennis Doyen, 1865.

38. *Farmington Town and Vital Records, Births, 1749–1874*, 20:43.

39. Daniel Scott Smith, "Continuity and Discontinuity in Puritan Naming: Massachusetts, 1771," *William and Mary Quarterly* 51, no. 1 (Jan. 1994), 67–91.

40. John Doyen appeared on a muster list for Sept. of 1814, at a critical juncture in the War of 1812 when British ships threatened to invade the coast of Maine. Ill-practiced militia units sprang up everywhere, but only relatively few were actually moved to defend the coast, and Doyen's artillery group was not among them. Doyen played soldier for four days and then returned home to Temple, having never left Farmington. Francis Gould Butler, *A History of Farmington, Franklin Co., Maine* (Farmington, Maine: Knowlton, McLeary, 1885), 122.

41. Ethel Colby Conant, comp., *The Vital Records of Augusta, Maine, to the Year 1892* (Auburn, Maine: Maine Historical Society, 1933–34), was based on a variety of sources, mainly church records and family Bibles, the kind of sources least likely to capture any Doyens. Some town clerks in Maine kept rather complete records of births, deaths, and marriages, but the Augusta clerk was unfortunately not one of them.

42. Kennebec County Conveyance Records, Grantors, liber 43, 30; liber 44, 127–28, 128–29.

43. Prices prevailing during the Malta War of 1812, when farmers hoped to buy their disputed rural properties for a dollar an acre but often were forced to pay triple and quadruple the amount to the men who held legal title; see Taylor, *Liberty Men*, 227, 233.

44. North, *History of Augusta*, 847.

45. Faye E. Dudden, *Serving Women: Household Service in Nineteenth-Century America* (Middletown, Conn.: Wesleyan University Press, 1983), 12–27.

46. *Farmington Vital Records, Marriages 1818–1851*, 21:12. No death or burial record has been found for Sally Doyen, but death records were not always kept in Maine in those years. Likewise, I find no record of Lydia Doyen's death. But John married a third time, for the U.S. Census of 1850 shows the shoemaker John, sixty-seven, of Avon, living with a wife named Betsy, fifty-three. A tombstone in the Avon cemetery records that Betsy, wife of John Doyen, died at age sixty. Dorothy Wirth, comp., "Forty Five Cemeteries of Franklin County, Maine, copied in 1959" (typescript, Boston: New England Historic Genealogical Society), 2:64. John must have died soon after, since he does not appear in the 1860 census for Maine. No tombstone marked his grave in Avon.

47. E.L. (a cousin) to Paulina Williams, Nov. 18, 1831, Reuel Williams Papers, box 17, file 11, Maine Historical Society, Portland.

48. Daniel Williams to Abigail Williams, Augusta, Apr. 22, 1822, Reuel Williams Papers, box 17, file 10, Maine Historical Society. Daniel and Abigail were siblings of Reuel.

49. North, *History of Augusta*, 423–24.

50. On the Dillingham genealogy, see North, *History of Augusta*, 847; and George Thomas Little, *Genealogical and Family History of the State of Maine* (New York: Lewis Historical Publishing, 1909), 4:2106.

51. The *Boston Post*, Apr. 18, 1836, stressed that Jewett was employed with the Westons up to age eighteen and that she strained at the bit to be able to leave upon reaching the age of majority.

52. Sarah Williams to Paulina Williams Jones, Nov. 2, 1836, Reuel Williams Papers, box 17, file 11, Maine Historical Society.

53. *Maine Patriot and State Gazette*, Apr. 2, 1828.

54. On Daniel Weston's visiting a relative named Samuel in Farmington, see Sarah B. Williams to Reuel Williams, July 22, 1825, Reuel Williams Papers, box 17, file 10, Maine Historical Society.

55. Revolutionary War Pension record of Jacob Doyen, record 27513, National Archives.

56. 1820 U.S. Census, Canaan, Somerset County. The Canaan schedule was copied neatly in alphabetical order, but Jacob Doyen's household appeared at the very end of the list, suggesting that the census marshal remedied an oversight and added it belatedly. An 1849 local history of the Canaan region identified the brothers Jacob and Samuel Doyen as among the earliest inhabitants of Skowhegan, a town formed in 1823 out of the western end of Canaan; Hanson, *A History of the Old Towns, Norridgewock and Canaan*, 303.

57. If Jacob abandoned Mercy before 1820, it is possible that she developed her relationship with her second husband much earlier than 1830, and only waited to marry him when she learned of Jacob Doyen's death in 1830. To complicate matters further, the *Augusta Vital Records* show a marriage record for a Jacob Doyen in 1829, to yet another widow, Mrs. Betsey Ratcliffe. Augusta is about four miles south of Belgrade, the town where Jacob supposedly died in 1829, according to one widow.

58. *Portland Eastern Argus*, Oct. 2, 1827, reprinted from the *Salem* (Mass.) *Observer*. The editor of the *Argus* described his own encounter with Mrs. Royall in early September 1827: She entered his office and announced, "I suppose, Sir, you must know whom I am?" Of course, replied the editor; she was "a little, short, snug-built sharp-eyed lady, who looks just as if she were ready to give you place on her black list. Without a doubt, she will receive the most courteous attentions from our hospitable, good-natured, fun-loving citizens. Let them keep in mind, however, that her ladyship has a *black* book." By these means, only slightly disguised by a veneer of politeness, editors heralded her arrival to the public and in effect invited citizens to make fun of the older woman. *Eastern Argus*, Sept. 4, 1827.

59. Royall, *Black Book*, 2:269. Judge Weston was in fact forty-five.

60. Ibid. The abbreviated word in the text I take to be "vixen."

61. Ibid., 2:270.

62. Mrs. Weston was in no way implying that she had adopted Dorcas to raise as her own. Musty record books containing all the guardianship papers processed by the Kennebec County probate court in the 1820s confirm that no legal tie bound Dorcas to anyone—naturally enough, since her father was still alive and hence she was not in fact a legal orphan; Letters of Guardianship, Kennebec County Probate Court, vol. 16, 1817–1829. Old Judge Daniel Cony presided over this court. Had the Westons intended to adopt Dorcas, instead of taking her in as a servant or a foster child–servant, there surely would have been legal paperwork to document the deal. Pitt Dillingham took on temporary legal guardianship of minor children on several occasions, but there exists no paper trail linking Dorcas to him, nor would there have been if she were indentured as a servant girl; the guardianship contracts were a by-product of probate court. When Dillingham died in 1829, a Williams family woman wrote to another, "Mr. Dillingham is no more. . . . The widow and the orphan will miss his character." So Pitt Dillingham had a reputation for safeguarding orphans; taking in nine-year-old Dorcas Doyen is consistent with that reputation. Sarah L. Cony Williams to daughter Paulina Cony Williams, July 23, 1829, box 17, file 10, Reuel Williams Papers, Maine Historical Society.

63. Royall, *Black Book*, 2:270, 272.

64. *Maine Patriot and State Gazette*, Nov. 10, 1830.

65. Royall, *Black Book*, 2:272.

66. Ibid., 2:270. His Bowdoin classmates remembered Gage later as something of a washout in life. The college alumni files contain these four assessments from his classmates in later years: "He was possessed of kind feelings, but the intellectual faculties were not of high order"; "I have heard that he was far from correct in his morals—became sep-

arated, and if I do not err—divorced from his wife"; he has "wandered from place to place"; he "was through his own fault unsuccessful" (Franklin Gage, Class of 1827, Bowdoin Alumni File, Bowdoin College Library, New Brunswick, Maine). Gage trained as a doctor and went to Panama as a surgeon for the Panama Railroad Company; he died at age forty-three from a fever contracted in Central America.

67. Royall, *Black Book*, 2:273.

68. The tax list for 1828 assessed Reuel Williams for $109.82; the next seven highest taxpayers were James Bridge, $100.18; Daniel Cony, $83.38; Thomas W. Smith, $49.19; Bartholomew Nason, $46.21; Henry W. Fuller, $34.79; Joshua Gage, $31.50; and Nathan Weston Jr., $27.94. The modal tax assessment in town was in the range of $1 to $6. State, County, and Town Taxes in Augusta for 1828, Maine State Archives, Augusta.

69. Royall, *Black Book*, 2:274–75.

70. Catharine Weston Fuller to Paulina Williams Jones, her cousin, Nov. 3, 1834. Catharine urged Paulina, who lived near Boston, to bring her servant Ann with her to the Thanksgiving gathering: "Do bring Ann along—she will be sad to be left behind." Reuel Williams Papers, box 17, file 12, Maine Historical Society.

71. The paper, dating from 1804, was produced by the wallpaper firm of Joseph Dufour, in Mâcon, France, and designed by Jean Gabriel Charvet. This company made several panoramic papers; popular designs included the ancient world (Egypt, imperial Rome), inspired by Napoleon's campaign in Egypt. See John A. Cuadrado, "Art: 19th-Century French Wallpaper," *Architectural Digest* (Oct. 1995), 52:162–67. For the octagon parlor, see Emma Huntington Nason, *Old Hallowell on the Kennebec* (Augusta, Maine: Burleigh & Flint, 1909), 277; Joseph T. Beck, *Historical Notes on Augusta, Maine* (Farmington, Maine: Knowlton and McLeary Co., 1962), 2:9; and Richard D. Hathaway, *Sylvester Judd's New England* (University Park: Pennsylvania State University Press, 1981), 287. Hathaway notes the splendor of the house: a Brussels carpet with a pile so thick it was barely worn after a century; a piano; a painting of Daniel Cony by the famous artist Gilbert Stuart, mirrors from England, a mahogany wine cooler, a Japanese highboy, and of course the Polynesian wallpaper with dancing girls. (Sylvester Judd, a minor novelist, was a son-in-law of Reuel Williams.) When the Williams mansion was razed in 1947, the furnishings and carpets were sold to antiques dealers, and the Captain Cook wallpaper was removed to Historic Deerfield, Massachusetts, where it is now displayed in the Asa Stebbins House. The DeYoung Museum in San Francisco also exhibits a set of the 1804 Captain Cook paper; I thank Mary W. Cline for bringing this to my attention. Though very elaborate, requiring hundreds of carved blocks applied by hand, the French *papier peint* was not exorbitantly expensive, according to art historian John Cuadrado. Scenic wallpaper showing battles or famous monuments was often chosen for public rooms in taverns and inns. Cuadrado quotes an unidentified woman traveler who in 1838 observed American humor in action: "It seems to be an irresistible temptation to idle visitors to put speeches into the mouths of the painted personages; and such hangings are usually deformed with scribblings."

72. The presidential visit is noted in King, *Melville Weston Fuller*, 16. See also Reuel Williams to James K. Polk, July 1, 1847, Polk Papers, Library of Congress, reel 50. Hathaway notes that the Williamses maintained a guestbook, showing entries signed by President Polk, George Bancroft, and Josiah Quincy, president of Harvard College. The guestbook in 1981 was in the possession of John T. G. Nichols of Marblehead, Massachusetts; Hathaway, *Sylvester Judd's New England*, 287.

73. Rudiger Joppien and Bernard Smith, *The Art of Captain Cook's Voyages* (Melbourne: Oxford University Press, 1985–1988), 3:216, discusses the fashion for South Seas art prints in the late eighteenth century. Also: Marshall David Sahlins, *How "Natives" Think: About Captain Cook, For Example* (Chicago: University of Chicago Press, 1995), and Gananath Obeyesekere, *The Apotheosis of Captain Cook: European Mythmaking in the Pacific* (Princeton, N.J.: Princeton University Press, 1992). The

French designer chose to portray Cook's discovery of Tahiti, not Cook's fatal voyage to Hawaii, which would have entailed a far more complicated story.

74. North, *History of Augusta*, 469–72.

75. Royall, *Black Book*, 2:277.

76. Paulina Williams to Aunt Helen Williams, Sept. 2, 1832, Reuel Williams Papers, box 17, file 11, Maine Historical Society.

77. *Maine Patriot and State Gazette*, Oct. 15, 1828.

78. *Maine Patriot and State Gazette*, Dec. 10, 1828. An early owner of a set of the *Black Book* annotated early chapters with sarcastic marginalia and ridicule; see the copy of the American Antiquarian Society in Worcester, Massachusetts.

• NINE •
READING AND IMAGINATION

1. The Lyceum's dues were a hefty twenty-dollar flat fee, augmented by quarterly payments of fifty cents per man, or twenty-five cents for those under age eighteen. North, *History of Augusta*, 459, 500; *Maine Patriot and State Gazette*, Nov. 19, 1828.

2. E.L. to Paulina C. Williams, Mar. 7, 1822, box 17, file 9; Sarah B. Williams to Helen Williams, May 17, July 2, and Sept. 30, 1823, and Aug. 13, 1826, box 17, file 10; Daniel Williams to Paulina Williams, Feb. 5, 1831; Catharine Weston Fuller to Paulina Williams Jones, Nov. 3, 1834, box 17, file 11; Reuel Williams Papers, Maine Historical Society.

3. The wedding is described in King, *Melville Weston Fuller*, 1–5. Dorcas Doyen may have been a quick study at religious learning, as Judge Weston said, but she never gained full membership in Reverend Tappan's Congregational church. Standards for authentic conversions were apparently quite rigorous. Mrs. Weston was admitted to full membership in 1812, but Judge Weston delayed until 1821, twelve years into his marriage; Catharine was twenty-two (in 1832) when she was admitted, and Daniel followed suit in 1834. The other Weston children—Nathan, George, Charles, and Louisa—never gained full membership. Church records of the First Church in Augusta, 1794–1830s; I thank the docents and minister of the United Church of Christ in Augusta for letting me examine their early record books.

Dorcas's churchgoing reputation penetrated the newspaper world of New York City; Isaac Pray, in his 1855 biography of James Gordon Bennett, reviewed the Jewett murder coverage in the press and in the process made reference to Jewett's attendance at church: "This unfortunate young woman . . . eight or ten years before, in the pride of youth and beauty, could be seen on Sunday taking her customary place in one of the most conspicuous pews in the broad aisle of the Rev. Mr. Tappan's church in Augusta, Maine." Pray, *Memoirs of James Gordon Bennett*, 209–10. Pray lived in Boston in 1836; it is not clear how he came to know this piece of information about Jewett and Tappan's church.

4. Dudden, *Serving Women*.

5. Davidson, *Revolution and the Word*; Mary Kelley, "Reading Women/Women Reading: The Making of Learned Women in Antebellum America," *Journal of American History* 83, no. 2 (Sept. 1996), 401–24; Kate Fleet, *The Woman Reader, 1837–1914* (Oxford: Clarendon Press, 1993); William J. Gilmore, *Elementary Literacy on the Eve of the Industrial Revolution: Trends in Rural New England, 1760–1830* (Worcester, Mass.: American Antiquarian Society, 1992); William J. Gilmore, *Reading Becomes a Necessity of Life: Material and Cultural Life in Rural New England, 1780–1835* (Knoxville: University of Tennessee Press, 1989); Ronald J. Zboray, *A Fictive People: Antebellum Economic Development and the American Reading Public* (New York: Oxford University Press, 1993). The quotation is from Sarah Pierce, commencement address at Litchfield Academy, Conn., Oct. 1818, quoted on p. 280 of Nina Baym, "At Home with History: History Books and

Women's Sphere Before the Civil War," *Proceedings of the American Antiquarian Society* 101, no. 2 (1992), 275–95.

6. Judge Weston's letter to the *New York Herald*, dated Apr. 20, 1836; see chapter 3.

7. *Maine Patriot and State Gazette*, Sept. 11, 1827, and Dec. 10, 1828.

8. One biographer of Royall has suggested that the relative paucity of copies extant of this bitter travelogue is explained by the fact that libeled acquaintances of Royall bought them up in order to destroy them; Sarah Harvey Porter, *The Life and Times of Anne Royall* (Cedar Rapids, Iowa: Torch Press Book Shop, 1909), 85. See also Bessie Rowland James, *Anne Royall's U.S.A.* (New Brunswick, N.J.: Rutgers University Press, 1972), and Alice S. Maxwell and Marion B. Dunlevy, *Virago! The Story of Anne Newport Royall (1769–1854)* (Jefferson, N.C.: McFarland, 1985).

9. Plays in the *Maine Patriot and State Gazette* advertisement of May 12, 1828: *The Hundred Pound Note*, by Richard Peake; *Brian Boroihme, or The Maid of Erin*, by James Sheridan Knowles; *XYZ, or The American Manager*, by George Colman; and *La Dame Blanche*, a French play. For their American play dates, see George C. D. Odell, *Annals of the New York Stage*, 4:273, 283, 299, 469.

10. In the decade 1826 to 1836, a total of ninety-two books were published by the two printers in Hallowell, none of them novels. Rosemary Maynard, "A Check List of Maine Imprints, 1826–1836, with a Historical Introduction" (master's thesis, Catholic University of America, 1951), 5.

11. A recent biographer of Hawthorne suggests *Fanshawe* was largely a confessional melodrama based on the Hawthorne and Bridge friendship; Edwin Haviland Miller, *Salem Is My Dwelling Place: A Life of Nathaniel Hawthorne* (Iowa City: University of Iowa Press, 1991), 77–84. Miller says only a thousand copies of the book were originally printed, and very few survive today. For the Bridge-Hawthorne friendship, see also Bridge, *Personal Recollections*. Another example of how Bridge aided his friend Hawthorne was Bridge's secret underwriting of the cost of Hawthorne's *Twice-Told Tales* with a Boston publisher, guaranteeing the doubtful publisher more than half the cost of the first printing of one thousand copies, if the book did not sell; *Personal Recollections*, 88–89.

12. Porter, *The Scottish Chiefs*, 3:48 for the quotation. I am grateful to Professor Peter Stoneley of the Queen's University of Belfast for bringing Jane Porter's novel to my attention.

13. The two editions printed in Exeter, N.H., were very small but fat volumes, measuring about three by five inches, small enough for a servant girl to fit into an apron pocket.

14. "Awful Shipwreck—Schooner Helen Mar," *New York Herald*, May 19, 1836. On the steamboat, see William M. Lytle and Forrest R. Holdcamper, eds., *Merchant Steam Vessels of the United States, 1790–1868* (Staten Island: Steamship Historical Society of America; distributed by University of Baltimore Press, 1975), 93. The steamer *Helen Mar* was ported at Cincinnati; it exploded near Peoria, Illinois, on June 1, 1836, and two were killed. (Two later steam vessels took the same name, one built in 1852 and one in 1863.) I have been unable to determine the date of origin of the Maine schooner.

15. Helen Jewett to Richard P. Robinson [probably from summer 1835], *National Police Gazette*, Apr. 28, 1849.

16. *New York Herald*, Apr. 13, 1836.

17. Sarah B. Williams to Helen Williams, Aug. 13, 1826, Saugus, Mass., Reuel Williams Papers, box 17, file 10, Maine Historical Society.

18. There were adult speakers as well, with the more customary (and probably long-winded) exhortations about how to lead a good life; in 1833 Judge Nathan Weston, a trustee of Bowdoin, gave the main speech when son Nathan graduated, but since his speech was not a graded exercise like the students', the Bowdoin College archives did not preserve it. Only the students with poor records suffered the indignity of not being allowed

to read commencement addresses; in the class of 1825, Horatio Bridge, Nathaniel Hawthorne, and two of their college chums were the ones singled out for this exemplary treatment; Bridge, *Personal Recollections*, 46–47.

19. Nathan Weston, commencement speech, 1833, Bowdoin College Archives, New Brunswick, Maine.

20. Oliver Ditson to Catharine Weston Fuller, July 2, 1840, Melville Weston Fuller Papers, box 2, Library of Congress.

21. Daniel Weston and George M. Weston, commencement speeches, 1834, Bowdoin College Archives.

22. *Journals of Ralph Waldo Emerson*, ed. Edward Waldo Emerson and Waldo Emerson Forbes (Boston: Houghton Mifflin, 1909–14), 6:393, entry for May 10, 1843, and 6:388, entry for Apr. 17, 1843.

23. Caroline Sturgis to Ralph Waldo Emerson, Apr. 23, 1843, letter 341, Tappan Collection, Houghton Library, Harvard University, Cambridge, Mass. I much appreciate the assistance of Professor Charles Capper, who brought these letters to my attention.

24. Court-martial of Charles Weston, July 25, 1842, Records of General Courts-Martial and Courts of Inquiry of the Navy Department, reel 48, case 834, National Archives. Judge Nathan Weston came to New York City to act as his son's attorney in the court-martial. Weston was found guilty of seditious language and desertion, but the court also acknowledged there was some foundation for his characterization of the captain of the *Warren* and his two first officers as drunken petty tyrants who abused the crew. The officers were court-martialed too; two of them were dismissed from the navy and the third acquitted. Abel Upshur, the secretary of the navy in 1842, added his own note to the end of the lengthy file, expressing regret that young Charles had been cashiered: "The truth is, the *Warren* will long be memorable for her last cruise. There is scarcely one of her officers willing to remain in service. It would be well for the navy, if all of them would go out together."

25. *Maine Patriot and State Gazette*, Oct. 31, 1827.

26. Ibid., Nov. 27, 1827.

27. Ibid., Nov. 14, 1827, reprinted from the *Albany Microcosm*, and Jan. 16, 1828, reprinted from the *Philadelphia Souvenir*.

28. "Matrimony," *Maine Patriot and State Gazette*, May 21, 1828, reprinted from the *Philadelphia Album*.

29. "Love's Memories," *Maine Patriot and State Gazette*, May 7, 1828.

30. North, *History of Augusta*, 485, and chapter 3 of this book. James Dickman was the publisher of the paper, meaning he fronted the money for it. But it is possible that he also contributed pieces of writing. Dickman's birth date is not known, but he had been involved in publishing Maine papers in other towns since 1824, so he was conceivably four or more years older than Chandler and thus in a somewhat more mature state to reflect on the joys and sorrows of unchecked love.

31. *Maine Patriot and State Gazette*, Feb. 16, 1828.

32. Ibid., July 30, 1828.

33. Ibid., June 3, 1829.

34. Ibid., Feb. 16, 1828.

35. Ibid., Jan. 2, 1828 (on dress); Sept. 17, 1828 (on the seraglio); Jan. 16, 1828 (on "be easy"); Oct. 1, 1828 (on flirtation); and Jan. 16, 1828 (on Black Sal).

36. Ibid., Aug. 13, 1828.

37. North, *History of Augusta*, 532.

38. *Maine Patriot and State Gazette*, Feb. 25, 1829.

39. Michael Grossberg, *Governing the Hearth: Law and the Family in Nineteenth-Century America* (Chapel Hill: University of North Carolina Press, 1985), 31–63.

40. *Maine Patriot and State Gazette*, Sept. 17, 1828; *American Advocate*, Sept. 19, 1828.

41. John Todd, *The Student's Manual* (Boston: W. Pierce, 1835); quoted and reviewed in the *Journal of Public Morals*, May 1, 1836, a New York–based moral reform periodical. On the Reverend Todd, see G. J. Barker-Benfield, *The Horrors of the Half-Known Life: Male Attitudes Toward Women and Sexuality in Nineteenth-Century America* (New York: Harper and Row, 1976), 135–224.

42. *Journal of Public Morals*, May 1, 1836.

43. *Advocate of Moral Reform*, July 1, 1836, 93.

44. Wilkes, *Lives of Helen Jewett*, 6.

45. On the racy literature of the 1830s and 1840s, see David S. Reynolds, *Beneath the American Renaissance: The Subversive Imagination in the Age of Emerson and Melville* (Cambridge, Mass.: Harvard University Press, 1988), 169–224.

· TEN ·

TRACING SEDUCTION

1. Sarah B. Williams to Aunt Helen Williams, Sept. 30, 1823, April 20, 1828; Sarah Cony Williams to Reuel Williams, Feb. 16, 1826, box 17, folder 10; Daniel Williams to Paulina Williams, Feb. 5, 1831, box 17, folder 11; Jane Williams to Joseph Williams, May 12, 1836, box 21, folder 9; and Catharine Weston Fuller to Paulina Williams Jones, Nov. 5, 1834, box 17, folder 12, Reuel Williams Papers, Maine Historical Society.

2. *The American Notebooks: The Centenary Edition of the Works of Nathaniel Hawthorne*, ed. Claude M. Simpson (Columbus: Ohio State University Press, 1972), 8:44, 59–60, entries for July 11 and 26, 1837.

3. Hawthorne had an earlier crush on a servant girl when he was in college that set tongues wagging in Brunswick; apparently Augusta's Nancy was part of a pattern. Town gossip had it that Hawthorne was enamored of a beautiful girl who answered the door at Professor Cleaveland's house, near Hawthorne's, on Federal Street. George Thomas Little, "Hawthorne's *Fanshawe* and Bowdoin's Past," in *Under the Bowdoin Pines: A Second Collection of Short Stories of Life at Bowdoin College Written by Bowdoin Men*, ed. John Clair Minot (Augusta, Maine: Kennebec Journal Print, 1907), 102–9.

4. In the winter and spring of 1836, Hawthorne lived in Boston and edited the *American Magazine of Useful and Entertaining Knowledge*. Bridge wrote him from a vacation in Havana, Cuba, in late February, and the next extant letter was the one sent from Augusta on May 14, where Bridge mentions "Helen J———." (The published letter does not indicate whether the abbreviation was done by Bridge himself or by Hawthorne's son Julian, the editor of this collection.) The paragraph in which Bridge mentions Jewett is all about women, morals, and wickedness, an ongoing topic between the two men. "I shall try your advice with regard to the women some time when I am away from here, though I shall make a poor hand of it most certainly," wrote Bridge. The nature of the advice is unclear, except that it was something to be done away from home base. At the letter's end, Bridge asks Hawthorne to check with a Boston tailor about sending his clothes to Augusta, evidence that Bridge visited Boston on his way home from Havana. Thus it is very possible the two together watched the murder story unfold in the Boston newspapers in mid-Apr. and discussed it. Julian Hawthorne, *Nathaniel Hawthorne and His Wife: A Biography* (Boston: Houghton Mifflin, 1884), 1:133–37.

5. Judge Weston's letter to the *New York Herald*, Apr. 20, 1836; printings discussed in chapter 3.

6. An unmarried girl or woman of any age made pregnant through seduction had further legal remedies open to her, in both the eighteenth and nineteenth centuries. She could initiate a paternity suit to obtain child support from a putative father, an action that first might require her to confess to fornication. Town leaders also pursued bastardy actions; they were interested parties because, failing paternal accountability, the town would be

liable for the maintenance of a pauper infant. Ulrich, *Midwife's Tale*, 134–61; Cornelia Hughes Dayton, *Women Before the Bar: Gender, Law, and Society in Connecticut, 1639–1789* (Chapel Hill: University of North Carolina Press, 1995), 157–230; Grossberg, *Governing the Hearth*, 31–63.

7. Jane E. Larson, " 'Women Understand So Little, They Call My Good Nature "Deceit" ': A Feminist Rethinking of Seduction," *Columbia Law Review* 93, no. 2 (Mar. 1993), 374–472; and Patricia Cline Cohen, "Suits and Suitors, Courts and Courtship: Sexual Seduction and the Law in Antebellum America" (paper delivered at the Berkshire Conference, Douglass College, New Brunswick, N.J., June 1990).

8. *Maine Reports: Reports of Cases Argued and Determined in the Supreme Judicial Court of the State of Maine*, ed. Simon Greenleaf (Hallowell, Maine: Goodale, Glazier and Co., 1828), 4:33–41, *Emery vs. Gowen*. Weston adjudicated one other seduction appeal, in June 1828, *Clough vs. Tenney* (1829), 5:445–49, and a bastardy case, *Dennett vs. Kneeland*, May 1830 (1831), 6:460–62.

9. *New York Commercial Advertiser*, Apr. 25, 1836.

10. Spaulding does not appear in the 1830 census for Augusta as an independent householder. Very likely he lived with his brother Calvin, two miles away in Hallowell, whose household in the census contained one male age twenty to thirty and one thirty to forty, in addition to four children, a woman twenty to thirty, and an older woman fifty to sixty.

11. Spalding, *Spalding Memorial*, 1872 ed., 216. For land records, see the Kennebec County Conveyance Records, Grantee and Grantor Indices, 1830–1840, Kennebec County Courthouse, Augusta, Maine. On Spaulding as bank cashier, see Kingsbury and Deyo, *Illustrated History,* 440–41; and "A Record of the Doings of the Stockholders of the Citizen's Bank, Act of Incorporation, June 1833," Maine Historical Society, showing Spaulding as owning five shares. The trail to the Brooklyn Navy Yard in the 1870s has proven a dead end. (A Horatio Spalding, age sixty, born in Maine, lived in Brooklyn in the 1870 census in a boardinghouse with other single men; Harlow would have been sixty-seven, but the name and age discrepancy might easily arise if the enumerator only spoke to one informant at the boardinghouse to collect the census data, instead of interviewing each person; U.S. Census, 1870, Third Ward, Brooklyn, household 781.) A search via the Soundex index to the federal census yielded no other possibilities.

12. Petition of Catharine Martin Fuller, May 10, 1833, Supreme Court Judicial Records, Kennebec County; photocopies of these documents are part of the Melville Weston Fuller Papers, Chicago Historical Society. The divorce is briefly discussed in King, *Melville Weston Fuller*, 10–11. Sidney, the only place specified in the warrant, is five miles north of Augusta.

13. Sarah B. Williams to Paulina Williams, Sept. 8, 1830, box 17, file 11, Reuel Williams Papers.

14. Melville Weston Fuller Papers, box 2, Library of Congress.

15. King, *Melville Weston Fuller*, 10–11.

16. Paulina Cony Weston to Melville Weston Fuller, Mar. 15, 1850, Apr. 18, 1850, box 1, folders 2 and 3, Melville Weston Fuller Papers, Chicago Historical Society.

17. Catharine Fuller Wadleigh to Melville W. Fuller, Mar. 21, 1852, Mar. 15, 1853, box 1, folder 3 and 5, Melville Weston Fuller Papers, Chicago Historical Society.

18. *Boston Daily Advocate*, Apr. 15, 16, 1836.

19. Jane Williams to Joseph Williams, May 12, 1836; Reuel Williams Papers, box 21, folder 9, Maine Historical Society.

20. Joseph H. Williams to his mother, Sarah Cony Williams, May 14, 1836, box 21, folder 9, Reuel Williams Papers, Maine Historical Society.

21. Nathan married Catherine B. Webster of Orono; the rift is implied in a letter by his mother, Paulina Cony Weston, to Mrs. William Dewey, Feb. 11, 1839, Melville Weston Fuller Papers, Library of Congress. Nathan Weston served in the war with Mexico

from 1846 to 1847 as a paymaster and suffered an injury in the line of duty. He served one term in the Maine state legislature, from 1849 to 1850, and in 1859 he moved to the Boston area. He married a second time, to a Miss Rogers of Newton, Massachusetts. He had three sons, probably all by the second wife, since they were born in the late 1850s and 1860s, when he was in his late forties. He died in Dorchester, Massachusetts, in 1887.

Daniel Weston, the judge's second son, trained for the law after graduating from Bowdoin in 1834. In the 1840s he turned his attention to religion and was ordained as an Episcopal deacon in 1851, serving at churches in Saco, Maine, and Stonington and Stratford, Connecticut. He earned a divinity degree in 1867 from Trinity College in Hartford. His wife, Mary North, was related to both the North family of Augusta and the Duane and Livingston families of the Hudson River Valley. She wrote many religious books; they married in 1842 and had six children, four of whom died in childhood. He died in 1903, lauded for "a lifetime of pure living."

George Melville Weston, the third son, became a newspaperman. After college he trained for the bar, passing it in 1837, while he wrote for the *Augusta Age*. Twice he served as attorney for Kennebec County (in 1839 and 1842), serving at the same time as editor of the *Age* (from 1840 to 1844). He moved to Bangor, Maine, in the late 1840s, and then was appointed a commissioner to process claims of Maine citizens under the Ashburton Treaty of 1855 with Canada. In Washington he became the editor of a free-soil newspaper, the *National Republican*; later he wrote tracts on the federal monetary system and served as librarian for the U.S. Senate. He married first in 1838 to Ruth Roberts, who soon died; he married a second time in 1841 and had two children; he died in 1887. The Bowdoin College archives has a collection of classmates' recollections of early graduates, one of whom reported that George Melville Weston was "a man of decided ability,—but errotic"—presumably a mistake for "erratic," but still, an arresting evaluation; recollection by T. W. Chandler, Bowdoin College Archives. On the Weston descendants: "Hon. Nathan Weston of Augusta, Maine," *New England Historical and Genealogical Register* 1 (1847), 278–79, and 29 (1876), 224; North, *History of Augusta*, 955–56; Kingsbury and Deyo, *Illustrated History*, 311, 339; *History of Penobscot County, Maine* (Cleveland: Williams, Chase and Co., 1882), 223; "Obituaries," *Boston Transcript*, Feb. 12, 1887, and Nov. 14, 1889; *The Churchman*, Apr. 11, 1903.

22. Catharine Fuller Wadleigh to Melville Weston Fuller, Mar. 21, 1852, box 1, folder 3, Melville Weston Fuller Papers, Chicago Historical Society.

23. Wilkes, *Lives of Helen Jewett*, 8.

24. Ibid., 7.

25. Ibid., 10.

26. The consul was George W. Hubbell. He wrote superiors in Washington, D.C., in Apr. of 1825 that he was leaving Manila on account of ill health, for a cooler climate, and no other American citizens were present to act in his place. In late 1827 Hubbell was in New York when he was reappointed to the post; he submitted his first annual report from the field in 1829. *Dispatches from UC Consuls in Manila, Philippines, 1817–1899*, National Archives Microfilm, T43.

27. Sumner's uncle was Jacob A. Russell; this very strange land deal of 1822 is discussed in chapter 8. Kennebec County Conveyance Records, Kennebec County Courthouse, liber 44, 127–28.

28. On "black Jerusha," Sarah B. Williams to Helen Williams, Aug. 13, 1826, box 17, file 10, Reuel Williams Papers, Maine Historical Society. Jerusha appears not to have been a member of the two black families that lived next door to the Westons in Augusta. Women of the extended Foye and Lewis families were named Betsy, Lucy, Durinda, Lydia, Clemena, Rhodie, and Sally. See *Vital Records of Augusta, Maine, to the Year 1892*.

29. Hawthorne, *American Notebooks*, 8:58–59.

30. The editor was Daniel C. Colesworthy, who published the *Juvenile Reformer*, the only moral reform newspaper in Maine. Colesworthy claimed that "the first judge" of "the

County of S." (which could only be Somerset) "was universally known to be a visitor of females of loose character. . . . Another judge of the same bench was under the necessity of falling on his knees, and asking the forgiveness of his wife, for having had unlawful intercourse with another woman. His wife was a minister's daughter." Yet a third judge, a man of great property in the state, had left his wife and lived now with a black woman, with whom he had had children; worse yet, Colesworthy charged, he had sold two of them south for slaves! *Portland (Maine) Juvenile Reformer and Sabbath School Instructor*, Mar. 30, 1836, 180.

31. Dudden, *Serving Women*, 214–17. Dudden suggests that Americans, unlike Europeans, were more open to the possibility of marriage between servant and employer, and this expectation operated as a brake on employer seductions, for a man might be held accountable by being pressured into marriage. On the other hand, she quotes Dr. Elizabeth Blackwell, who worked at a female asylum in Philadelphia in the late 1840s and observed that "a large proportion" of the former servants now on the syphilitic ward had been seduced by their employers.

32. Willis, *History of the Law*, 510–17.

33. Royall, *Black Book*, 2:235–38.

34. In most cities, a local newspaper printed a monthly list of addressees of federal mail not yet picked up; unclaimed mail was reported only once in the listing, so that each month's list was of recent mail; *Eastern Argus*, Feb. 3, 1832. Private conveyance of mail was quite common, because it was fast and cheap. But it did require that an actual address be put on the outside of the letter, to direct the carrier where to go. Public mail service was necessary if two correspondents did not have go-betweens and frequent visitors, or if one correspondent could not comfortably commit the recipient's address to paper. The *Maine Patriot and State Gazette* printed an unclaimed mail list, and Dorcas Doyen appeared in it once, in the Jan. 6, 1830, issue. (Harlow Spaulding was on the same list, but he appeared with some frequency. Was he merely slow to pick up business mail, or gone from town on trips? Or were these unwelcome personal letters he chose to ignore for stretches at a time? On July 21, 1830, Spaulding had eight unclaimed letters awaiting him.) I found no other mail listings for Doyen in the Augusta, Portland, or Boston papers, under any of her many aliases. In New York City, the *New York Times* for Jan. 30, 1836, listed an unclaimed letter for Miss Helen Jewett.

35. Hawthorne was moved by the scene that unfolded before him that evening. The man came to Barker's Mansion House inquiring for Mary Ann Russell. The crowd of men recognized her to be one of several prostitutes who just three days before had been thrown out of the Mansion House by the proprietor and a constable. They greeted the stranger with ridicule and mirth, while the unfortunate man had to pretend to be too simple to get their cruel jokes. For a tip, the black man led the husband to his wife; Hawthorne's calling him a pimp thus might have overstated the case considerably. Hawthorne wrote, "I would have given considerable to witness his meeting with his wife. On the whole there was a moral picturesqueness in the contrasts of this scene—a man moved as deeply as his nature would admit, in the midst of hardened, gibing spectators, heartless towards him. It is worth thinking over and studying out." After an intervening passage on the servant Nancy doing laundry with naked arms, Hawthorne ruminated further on sexual infidelity: "Query—in relation to the man's prostitute-wife—how much desire and resolution of doing her duty by her husband can a wife retain, while injuring him in what is deemed the most essential point." Hawthorne, *American Notebooks*, 8:58–60.

36. George W. Stanley was the sheriff of Kennebec County and Jesse Jewett was the deputy sheriff in the 1830s; North, *History of Augusta*, 559, 892. Possibly there is a connection to the names Dorcas chose.

37. Wilkes depicts Dorcas's descent into prostitution as an accident: a nice older woman meets the runaway girl on the street and offers her a home. Only slowly does Dor-

cas realize the nature of the establishment she is in, and only slowly does she succumb to the habits of it, again only because of honest emotions when the bank cashier (in Wilkes's story, said to be from Portland) shows up as a customer, and her genuine love for him transforms her from a resisting prisoner of the madam into a grateful, eager, and responsive lover. Wilkes provides many details, specific names, newsworthy events such as a murder (of poor hapless Sumner, who shows up unexpectedly and fights with George Benson, a wealthy Portland professional man now keeping Jewett as his own trinket), none of which can be verified in any Portland sources. Wilkes briskly moves Dorcas to Boston, now under the name of "Helen Mar," where she is robbed on the streets and is taken in by a prominent family who live on Park Street, and who themselves are taken in by her story explaining her momentarily unprotected status, even though she comes from an excellent family. Wilkes dishes out a familiar story of false identities, blackmail, and a fall from grace just at the point when Dorcas, now Helen Mar, is about to be married into a very respectable Boston family. The instrument of evildoing is a courtesan named Suze Bryant, nicknamed Lil' Belt; and oddly enough, this is the only fact in his entire story anchored in reality, for in the 1840s there was a well-known prostitute in Boston of that name, as Wilkes would have known from the racy newspapers he worked on in the early 1840s. Otherwise, Wilkes is quite mistaken at key points. For example, the wealthy Park Street family sounds plausible enough until it is remembered that Park Street was only one block long, bordering the Boston Common, and filled with commercial and institutional properties—stores and churches. No wealthy merchant's family would have had such an address. The likely explanation is that George Wilkes had never been to Boston.

38. *Munjoy Hill, Historic Guide* (Portland, Maine: Greater Portland Landmarks, n.d.), 1–3; Writers' Program of Work Projects Administration in the state of Maine, *Portland City Guide* (Portland, Maine: Forest City Printing, 1940), 274.

39. *Eastern Argus*, Nov. 11, 1825, reprinted in Richard Hofstadter and Michael Wallace, eds., *American Violence: A Documentary History* (New York: Knopf, 1970), 447–50.

40. *Eastern Argus*, Aug. 21, 1827. A longer article in May of 1829 reported in some detail about a half-dozen young men aged twelve to twenty-five hauled into Municipal Court for riotous and disorderly conduct. They had been part of a crowd of thirty to forty boys who had harassed three young women returning home from an evening lecture on the "Christian Connexion." The men used obscene, rude, and insulting language and threatened to beat up several good-hearted men who came to the rescue of the girls. "Nothing but the respect we feel for their parents and friends prevents us from publishing their names," the paper said, suggesting that the parents of these boys were respectable citizens who had reputations that could be injured. What can be done about these gangs? the editor of the *Eastern Argus* wondered. They gather in "squads" at street corners, notably on Sunday nights, and insult passersby, especially "unprotected females." They are "in training for the gallows" and "in open defiance of decency," and worse, they attract mere children and apprentices to admire their vicious ways. A letter to the editor published two months later reiterated these points about crowds of boys, elaborating further that serious vandalism was a major concern, along with the threats to women. The boys—"men in size"—were hanging out on corners, "filling up our pumps with rubbish," defacing doors and windows, and insulting females. *Eastern Argus*, May 1, 1829, July 3, 1829.

41. No copies of the *Courier* for 1830 have become available to me, but a card-file index of its contents in the Portland (Maine) Public Library documents a continuing concern for street violence and brothel contestations: *Daily Courier*, June 9, notice of raids in Mount Joy Hill area and dispersal of brothel inmates; June 23, on gangs of boys; June 25, on arrival of two new girls from Boston bound for brothels; July 13, letter to the editor on promenading girls; Aug. 4, a letter from a girl on Mount Joy Hill defending her brothel life, and an item on the corner gangs; Aug. 20, a letter attacking the patrons of Mount Joy Hill; Aug. 20, an editorial on the brothels; and May 30, 1832, news of an official raid on

Mount Joy Hill conducted by the mayor, the city council, the city marshal, and constables. See the Jordan Index in the Portland Public Library's Special Collections and Local History Room.

42. *Sketch of the Life of Miss Ellen Jewett, Apr. 9, 1836*, 18–19.

43. Daniel Scott Smith and Michael S. Hindus, "Premarital Pregnancy in America, 1640–1971: An Overview and Interpretation," *Journal of Interdisciplinary History* 5 (1974–75), 537–70; David H. Flaherty, "Law and the Enforcement of Morals in Early America," *Perspectives in American History* 5 (1971), 203–53; Cissie Fairchilds, "Female Sexual Attitudes and the Rise of Illegitimacy: A Case Study," *Journal of Interdisciplinary History* 3 (1977–78), 627–67; Robert A. Gross, *The Minutemen and Their World* (New York: Hill and Wang, 1976); P. E. H. Hair, "Bridal Pregnancy in Rural England in Earlier Centuries," *Population Studies* 20 (Nov. 1966), 233–43; Peter Laslett et al., eds., *Bastardy and Its Comparative History: Studies in the History of Illegitimacy and Marital Nonconformism in Britain, France, Germany, Sweden, North America, Jamaica, and Japan* (Cambridge, Mass.: Harvard University Press, 1980); Mary Beth Norton, *Liberty's Daughters: The Revolutionary Experience of American Women, 1750–1800* (Boston: Little, Brown, 1980); G. R. Quaife, *Wanton Wenches and Wayward Wives: Peasants and Illicit Sex in Early Seventeenth-Century England* (New Brunswick: Rutgers University Press, 1979); Keith Thomas, "The Double Standard," *Journal of the History of Ideas* 20 (1959), 195–216; Roger Thompson, *Sex in Middlesex: Popular Mores in a Massachusetts County, 1649–1699* (Amherst: University of Massachusetts Press, 1986). Two recent dissertations examine the class and racial dimensions of illicit sex, the first in Philadelphia and the second in North Carolina: Clare Lyons, "Sex Among the 'Rabble': Gender Transitions in the Age of Revolution, 1750–1830" (Ph.D. diss., Yale University, 1996), and Kirsten Fischer, "Dangerous Liaisons: The Politics of Illicit Sex in Colonial North Carolina" (Ph.D. diss., Duke University, 1995).

44. Ulrich, *Midwife's Tale*, 151–56.

45. Bastardy suits remained uncommon, probably because most unwed mothers avoided suit if they could possibly support the child themselves, with help from parents, since legal action entailed a preliminary confession of fornication and a fine, as well as intrusive publicity.

46. In one revealing and probably not very unusual Maine case, Ruth Greene, a town selectman's daughter, became pregnant in 1806 by Samuel Fessenden, a young Dartmouth student spending a short stint teaching school in her small town. Fessenden consulted his equally youthful friend Daniel Webster, who advised him not to marry. Fessenden returned to college; Webster was godfather to the child; and Fessenden's mother took the day-old infant and raised him for six years, at which point Fessenden married another woman and reclaimed the child. Ruth Greene suffered no apparent detriment to her prospects; she soon after made a respectable marriage. The person who internalized the most shame from this event was the boy himself, Samuel Pitt Fessenden, who came of age and gained public notice as a leading U.S. senator in the mid-nineteenth century. In a climate far less forgiving about sexual indiscretions, he felt highly sensitive about his bastard birth. His first biographer (his son) neatly sidestepped the story altogether; Francis Fessenden, *The Life and Public Service of William Pitt Fessenden* (Boston and New York: Houghton Mifflin, 1907), 1:1–2. A modern biographer notes his lifelong humiliation; Charles A. Jellison, *Fessenden of Maine: Civil War Senator* (Syracuse, N.Y.: Syracuse University Press, 1962), 3–5.

47. For an instructive comparison with another society tolerant of premarital sex, see George Alter, *Family and the Female Life Course: The Women of Verviers, Belgium, 1849–1880* (Madison: University of Wisconsin Press, 1988), 112–20.

48. See genealogies of the Fuller, Weston, Bridge, North, Cony, Williams, Vose, and Nason families of Augusta, in the appendix to North, *History of Augusta*. Only one single

case of bastardy appears in the Kennebec County Court Records in the 1820s, and it was resolved in favor of the man. Joanna Smith, single woman of Augusta, brought her charges against John Crosby before the Court of Common Pleas in 1826. (Joanna lived alone, four households away from John Doyen [Dawen] in the 1820 Augusta census, so she was probably a young adult woman in 1826. John Crosby was probably related to the George Crosby family that owned a store and several properties around Augusta.) She testified that she and Crosby had sex "at a place near his dwelling house" on a June day in 1825, and now she wanted him to support her son. A jury found Crosby not guilty; Kennebec County Court of Common Pleas, Records, book 6 (1826), case 152, 43.

49. Ellen K. Rothman, *Hands and Hearts: A History of Courtship in America* (New York: Basic Books, 1984), 3–84.

50. Davidson, *Revolution and the Word*; Elizabeth Lee Barnes, "A Revolution in Feeling: The Politics of Seduction in American Sentimental Fiction, 1789–1856" (Ph.D. diss., University of California at Santa Barbara, 1991); Elizabeth Hardwick, *Seduction and Betrayal: Women and Literature* (New York: Random House, 1974); Jan Lewis, "The Republican Wife: Virtue and Seduction in the Early Republic," *William and Mary Quarterly*, 3rd ser., 44 (1987), 689–721.

51. Nancy F. Cott, "Passionlessness: An Interpretation of Victorian Sexual Ideology, 1790–1850," *Signs: A Journal of Women in Culture and Society* 4 (1978), 219–36; Estelle B. Freedman and John D'Emilio, *Intimate Matters: A History of Sexuality in America* (New York: Harper and Row, 1988). A major problem with the literature on the emergence of passionlessness is that it fails to control for women's age and instead presumes that particular constructions of female sexuality that are shared by a culture—for example, white middle-class bourgeois culture—apply equally to all ages of women within that culture. Studies of sex delinquency for girls in the twentieth century suggest that age matters greatly; Ruth H. Alexander, *The Girl Problem: Female Sexual Delinquency in New York, 1900–1930* (Ithaca, N.Y.: Cornell University Press, 1995); Regina Kunzel, *Fallen Women, Problem Girls: Unmarried Mothers and the Professionalization of Social Work, 1890–1945* (New Haven, Conn.: Yale University Press, 1993); Mary Odem, *Delinquent Daughters: Protecting and Policing Adolescent Female Sexuality in the United States, 1885–1920* (Chapel Hill: University of North Carolina Press, 1995).

• ELEVEN •

ADOLESCENT CLERKS

1. Joel Hawes, *Lectures to Young Men on the Formation of Character* (Hartford, Conn.: Cooke, 1829); William Alcott, *A Young Man's Guide* (1833); Jared Bell Waterbury, *Considerations for Young Men* (New York, 1832); John Todd, *The Student's Manual* (1836); Sylvester Graham, *A Lecture to Young Men on Chastity; Specially Intended for the Serious Consideration of Young Men and Parents* (1833; reprint, Boston: George W. Light, 1837). The genre of advice to young men is discussed by Horlick, *Country Boys and Merchant Princes*. See also Stephen Nissenbaum, *Sex, Diet, and Debility in Jacksonian America: Sylvester Graham and Health Reform* (Westport, Conn.: Greenwood Press, 1980); and Robert H. Abzug, *Cosmos Crumbling: American Reform and the Religious Imagination* (New York: Oxford University Press, 1994), especially chapter 7.

2. Alcott, quoted in Ronald G. Walters, ed., *Primers for Prudery: Sexual Advice to Victorian America* (Englewood Cliffs, N.J.: Prentice-Hall, 1974), 35.

3. *New York Herald*, Apr. 11, 1836. On Apr. 20, Bennett added that Robinson was the only son of a second wife, which was not accurate.

4. *New-York Transcript*, Apr. 12, 1836.

5. *New York Sun*, Apr. 11, 1836.

6. *Philadelphia Public Ledger*, Apr. 15 and Aug. 3, 1836. The *Public Ledger* had just

begun publication on Mar. 25, 1836. Its three editors, A. B. Abell, Azariah Simmons, and William Swain, were all New York printers who had worked with Benjamin Day on the *Sun* in 1833 to 1836.

7. On the many stagecoaches, see David Nelson Camp, *Recollections of a Long and Active Life* (Concord, N.H.: Rumford Press, 1917), 2–6. Camp was born in Durham in 1820 and was thus three years younger than Richard Robinson.

8. A rendition of the history and location of each old house in Durham is found in William Chauncey Fowler, *History of Durham, Connecticut, From the First Grant of Land in 1662 to 1866* (Hartford, Conn.: Hartford, Wiley, Waterman and Eaton, 1866), 204–5, on the Robinson cluster of houses. The U.S. Census of 1830 also helps re-create a household map. Numbers of land sales can be counted in alphabetized file cards of conveyance records, Durham Town Hall, Conn. I thank Marjorie Hatch, town clerk, for making these available to me.

9. Asher Robinson, a first cousin of Richard P. Robinson—but nearly three decades older than the young man—was the town clerk of Durham from 1830 to 1843; apparently the Robinson family did not get turned out of office in associated shame; *History of Middlesex County*, 269–70.

10. Fannie Colley Williams Barbour, *Spelman Genealogy* (New York: Frank Allaben Genealogical Company, 1910), 166–67.

11. Robinson's lawyer, Ogden Hoffman, commented in his closing remarks at the trial that the mother was too sick to travel to New York; *Murder Most Foul: A Synopsis of the Speeches on the Trial of Robinson for the Murder of Ellen Jewett* (New York: R. H. Elton, 1836), 17.

12. Fowler, *History of Durham*, 168–69. E. Anthony Rotundo, "Boy Culture: Middle-Class Boyhood in Nineteenth-Century America," in *Meanings for Manhood: Constructions of Masculinity in Victorian America*, ed. Mark C. Carnes and Clyde Griffen (Chicago: University of Chicago Press, 1990), 15–36.

13. School descriptions of the 1820s are from Camp, *Recollections*, 4–6.

14. Fowler, *History of Durham*, 103–5.

15. Greater Middletown Preservation Trust, "The History and Architecture of Durham, Connecticut, An Architectural Historical Survey," typescript in binder (Durham, Conn.: Durham Public Library, n.d.), 29.

16. Congregational Church Records, 1799–1832, ministry of Reverend David Smith, Durham, Conn.

17. *History of Middlesex County*, 212.

18. *Boston Illuminator*, July 27, 1836, 153; the editor was Joseph A. Whitmarsh.

19. The Green Street mansion was in use in the 1990s as a funeral home; it is now number 35. I thank Todd C. Woodworth, coproprietor of the funeral home, for sending me material on the Marston family and for allowing me to tour the property. Mary Gilman Marston, comp., *George White Marston: A Family Chronicle* (n.p.: W. Ritchie Press, 1956), 1:8–11; John J. Currier, *History of Newburyport, Massachusetts, 1764–1909* (Newburyport, Mass.: John J. Currier, 1901), 1:190–91, 681; 2:149, 165–67, 280, 287, 414, 601.

20. *Newburyport Daily Herald*, Sept. 26, 1834.

21. Ibid., Sept. 1, 1834.

22. Eliza Amelia White Peabody to Mary Jane Williams, Oct. 1834, Everett-Peabody Papers, Massachusetts Historical Society, Boston.

23. This is the family story, handed down to his granddaughter, who compiled the family biography; see Marston, *George White Marston*, 1:11. Among Stephen Marston's seven ships, two were named *Minerva* and *Venus*. For ship lists, see "Ship Registers of the District of Newburyport, 1789–1870, Compiled from the Newburyport Customs House Records, Now in the Possession of the Essex Institute," *Essex Institute Historical Collections* 70 (1934), 186; 71 (1935), 89, 94, 171, 269, 275.

24. Marston, *George White Marston*, 1:11.

25. Mary White Marston to William Marston, Apr. 1835, in Marston, *George White Marston*, 1:11–15.

26. Dartmouth College, Records of the Faculty, Sept. 30, 1841, May 30 and Nov. 13, 1843. I am grateful to college archivists Kenneth C. Cramer and Barbara Krieger for sending me material from the Dartmouth Archives.

27. Marston, *George White Marston*, 1:21.

28. Ibid., 1:24.

29. Eliza Amelia Peabody to Judge Stephen Marston, July 13, 1836. Peabody was the judge's niece. Marston, *George White Marston*, 1:15–16. Peabody's extensive correspondence from the 1820s to 1840s is held by the Massachusetts Historical Society, which describes the collection as a "virtual diary" because of the regular frequency of the letters. Unfortunately, there is a complete break in the letters from Apr. to Sept. 1836.

30. *Boston Daily Advocate*, June 6, 1836.

31. George P. Marston to Stephen Marston, Aug. 15, 1836, in Marston, *George White Marston*, 1:17–18.

32. G.B.M. to Helen, Monday evening, n.d., *National Police Gazette*, Apr. 28, 1849. Wilkes only printed six letters by Bill Easy in his serial; the district attorney logs list nineteen found in Jewett's room. Five of the six were signed "W.E."; this one was signed with Marston's initials, with the *P* mistaken for a *B*, perhaps by the *Gazette*'s typesetter.

33. W.E. to Nelly, n.d., *National Police Gazette*, May 12, 1849.

34. *New York Herald*, Nov. 20 and 21, 1849.

35. "Oily Attree," *Sunday Flash*, Sept. 12 and 19, 1841. George Wilkes, then twenty-one, was one of the paper's editors.

36. Attree was a witness in this case, in which a printer for the *Courier and Enquirer* named John H. Potts sued the editors of the *Sun*, Benjamin Day and George Wisner, for libel for calling him a "drunken fellow." The *New-York Transcript* covered the case in detail in its issue of May 22, 1835; printers, compositors, and editors testified. In 1835, Attree's binge days still lay ahead.

37. Wandering Willie to Helen, Louisville, Dec. 2, 1835 [date a misprint, because the letter refers to the great fire in New York City of Dec. 16], *National Police Gazette*, June 2, 1849. In the letter, Attree mentions visiting a brother in Louisville, married, with five children, several slaves, and an estate worth $70,000. In the subsequent letter he refers to "a supply of physic" acquired from the brother. According to the "Oily Attree" profile in the *Sunday Flash*, Attree claimed to be named "Petit" on his ship voyage to America. The 1830 and 1850 censuses of Louisville list William F. Pettitt, apothecary, born England around 1796, in a household of ten in 1830 that included two slaves, four small children, and two young men, in addition to the husband and wife. By 1850 Pettitt was a very successful merchant in town, worth $100,000. English vital records indexed by the Mormons show a large number of Petits in the Brighton Parish registers around 1800. Detailed genealogical checks like this are what provide confidence that the letters George Wilkes printed in the *National Police Gazette* in 1849 were not fabrications.

38. Wandering Willie to Helen, Velasco Brazos de Dios, Texas, Jan. 27, 1836, *National Police Gazette*, May 26, 1849. Confirmation that Attree was in Texas at this time comes from a Feb. 10 issue of the *New-York Transcript*, which carried a plea from W.H.A., "travelling correspondent," for "all who love liberty" to come to Texas to fight. Attree said he had met with independence leaders Sam Houston and Stephen Austin, who needed men quickly. Pay, rations, and 640 acres of land would go to each volunteer. Attree further claimed that Texas was safe for women and children and reported that he was traveling near San Felipe with a group of four men, seven women under age twenty-five, thirteen children, and assorted dogs. It would seem that he and the solitary "Ellen" were in fact not alone together. *New-York Transcript*, Feb. 10, 1836.

• TWELVE •

LOVE LETTERS AND LIES

1. *New York Herald*, Apr. 13, 1836.

2. Ibid., Apr. 19, 1836.

3. Ibid., probably Apr. 20, 1836, reprinted in *Philadelphia Public Ledger*, Apr. 22, 1836.

4. Wilkes, *Lives of Helen Jewett*, 115.

5. "I found out yesterday in looking over my letters that I had kept one of yours unintentionally, and of course you will not misconstrue my motives in sending it you." Helen wrote this to Robinson in an undated letter that was written either on Oct. 24 or Nov. 30, 1835, a determination based on her reference to a play she planned to attend that night; *National Police Gazette*, June 9, 1849.

6. H. to My dear Friend, June 17, 1835, *National Police Gazette*, Apr. 28, 1849, reprinted June 2, 1849.

7. On Hamblin's love life, see Dudden, *Women in the American Theatre*, 56–74. On Jewett's letter to Hamblin, see Wilkes, *Lives of Helen Jewett*, 54. For further details of Hamblin's association with brothel keeper Mary Gallagher, said to be the mother of his daughter Missouri Miller, see "Oily Attree," *Sunday Flash*, Sept. 19, 1841.

8. Helen to Richard, June 20, 1835, *National Police Gazette*, Apr. 28, 1849.

9. Helen to Richard P. Robinson, n.d., *National Police Gazette*, Apr. 28, 1849.

10. Described in the *New York Herald*, Apr. 13, 1836. It was a round painting (rather than oval or rectangular, the most common shapes) on ivory encased in a green cover. The object was found in Robinson's room after the murder and was logged into the district attorney's file, along with Robinson's journal. Neither miniature nor original journal can now be located. On typical miniature prices, see Frederick W. Coburn, "Thomas Bailey Lawson (1807–1888), Portrait Painter of Newburyport and Lowell, Massachusetts, and His Register of Portraits Made Between 1833 and 1887," *Essex Institute Historical Collection* 84 (Jan. 1948), 29–63; a miniaturist's account book (1828–64), folder 3, John Wood Dodge Papers, Archives of American Art, National Portrait Gallery, Smithsonian Institution, Washington, D.C.; and Harry B. Wehle, *American Miniaturists, 1730–1850* (New York: Doubleday, Page, 1927), 58–59. Both Lawson and Dodge worked in New York City in the early 1830s, Dodge first on Franklin Street and then on Pearl Street very near Marston's store. The records of neither show commissions to Jewett or Robinson. Other New York miniaturists and portrait painters in business in the mid-1830s include Thomas S. Cumings at 38 Reade; Asher Durand at 82 Duane; James Herring at 389 Broadway; Charles Ingham at 61 Franklin; Henry Inman at 18 Walker; Rembrandt Peale on Barclay Street; Nathaniel Rogers on Cortlandt at Broadway; R. Burling at 205 Hudson; and Mrs. Folsom at 66 Beekman. All of these addresses were within a mile of Jewett's various brothel houses in the Fifth Ward; "Classified Mercantile Directory," *New-York As It Is*, 16, 89. I entertain hopes that the miniatures both of Jewett and Robinson still exist, unidentified in some private collection. I thank Dale T. Johnson, Research Associate of the Metropolitan Museum of Art in New York, for checking in that collection for me.

11. Helen to R. P. Robinson, n.d., *National Police Gazette*, Apr. 28, 1849.

12. Robinson to Helen, n.d., *National Police Gazette*, May 26, 1849. The same letter was also printed in the Apr. 28 issue, with minor word changes and the entire middle section about the "bark" of life and his dark moods omitted.

13. Helen to Richard, July 24, 1836, *National Police Gazette*, June 9, 1849.

14. Helen to Richard P. Robinson, Monday, two o'clock, n.d., *National Police Gazette*, Apr. 28, 1849.

15. Helen to Frank, four o'clock, n.d., *National Police Gazette*, Apr. 28, reprinted May 26, 1849.

16. Frank to Helen, Tuesday morning, *National Police Gazette*, April 28, 1849.

17. Rosina Townsend, *Trial of Richard P. Robinson*, 3.

18. Helen, Monday evening, *National Police Gazette*, Apr. 28, 1849.

19. Firefly to Frank, Friday, n.d., *National Police Gazette*, May 12, 1849.

20. Nell to R. P. Robinson, n.d., *National Police Gazette*, May 19, 1849.

21. Helen Jewett to Frank Rivers, n.d., *National Police Gazette*, May 19, 1849.

22. Depositions of Hester Preston, Julia Brown, Elizabeth Stewart, and Newton Gilbert, Grand Jury Proceedings, Apr. 18, 1836, in *People vs. Robinson*, Apr. 10, 1836, District Attorney's Indictment Papers, Municipal Archives, New York.

23. Frank to Nelly, Aug. 18, 1835, *National Police Gazette*, May 26, 1849.

24. Helen to Frank, Tuesday, twelve o'clock, n.d., *National Police Gazette*, June 9, 1849.

25. Helen to Richard, Saturday the seventh [probably Nov. 7, 1835], and M.G.B. [Maria G. Benson] to Frank, Saturday [probably Dec. 5, 1835], *National Police Gazette*, June 9, 1849; Helen to Richard, Wednesday, n.d., and H. to Richard, n.d., *National Police Gazette*, May 26, 1849.

26. Frank to Nelly, n.d., *National Police Gazette*, May 26, 1849.

27. Frank to Nelly, Friday evening, seven o'clock, n.d., *National Police Gazette*, June 2, 1849.

28. Frank to Nelly, Thursday morning, n.d., *National Police Gazette*, May 12, 1849.

29. Frank to Maria, Nov. 14, 1835, *National Police Gazette*, Apr. 14, 1849. The Latin closing roughly translates as "Leave me out of your memory and I will be your servant."

30. The three other letters the prosecution wanted to include were said to be two dated in August and a third not dated. The only two dated August that were printed in the *National Police Gazette* were ones in which Robinson names men for Helen to contact in some unclear scheme. The D.A. stipulated that if he could read one particular letter, he would omit the names as immaterial. The defense then objected that this letter impugned Robinson's character, yet since his attorneys did not plan to argue for his good character, the letter hinting at bad character was not admissible. *Trial of Richard P. Robinson*, 20.

31. Hugh Maxwell, quoted in *Trial of Richard P. Robinson*, 20.

32. Helen to Richard, Monday, six o'clock [Dec. 7, 1835], *National Police Gazette*, June 9, 1849.

33. Helen to Richard, Sunday morning, ten o'clock [Dec. 13, 1835], *National Police Gazette*, June 9, 1849.

34. Mary Berry to Helen, Dec. 14, 1835, *National Police Gazette*, May 5, 1849.

35. Helen to Richard P. Robinson, Tuesday afternoon [probably Dec. 22, 1835], *National Police Gazette*, May 12, 1849.

36. Frank to Nell, Wednesday afternoon [Dec. 23, 1835], *National Police Gazette*, May 12, 1849.

37. W.E. to Helen, Wednesday noon [Dec. 23, 1835], *National Police Gazette*, May 12, 1849.

38. Frank to Nelly, Dec. 26, 1835, *National Police Gazette*, May 12, 1849.

39. Nelly to Frank, n.d., *National Police Gazette*, June 9, 1849.

40. Deposition of Mary Berry, Grand Jury Proceedings, Apr. 18–19, 1836, in *People vs. Robinson*, Apr. 10, 1836, District Attorney's Indictment Papers, Municipal Archives.

• THIRTEEN •
BLOWING UP

1. Frank to Nelly, Jan. 12, 1836, *National Police Gazette*, May 12, 1849.

2. Jewett to Rivers, Wednesday, n.d., *National Police Gazette*, May 12, 1849.

3. Frank to Nelly, Monday afternoon, n.d., *National Police Gazette*, Apr. 28, 1849.

4. The murdered girl was Juliana Sands, her fiancé, Levi Weeks. Weeks was acquitted with the help of a powerful legal defense team consisting of Alexander Hamilton,

Aaron Burr, and Brockholst Livington. In the novel by Fay, the Weeks character is the hero; he lives under a cloud of suspicion for several years after the murder, until the real killer is unmasked. In staging it as a play (with script by Louisa Medina), Thomas Hamblin of the Bowery assembled a huge cast; two hundred people crowded the stage in a carnival scene in the last act; Shank, "Bowery Theater," 420–22, 449; Odell, *Annals of the New York Stage,* 4:79–81. The play continued to run Feb. 8 to 26 on a variable schedule, alternating with other shows. It was staged once more, on Mar. 15, a Tuesday night. Rarely did New York theaters continue with the same show many nights in succession; theater patrons (prostitutes, for example) went to the theater often and expected to see different fare each time. Theodore Fay was a novelist and regular editor of the *New-York Mirror,* a literary magazine to which Jewett subscribed.

5. Frank to Nelly, Friday evening, n.d., *National Police Gazette,* May 19, 1849.

6. Nell to My Dear Frank, Monday, n.d., *National Police Gazette,* May 12, 1849.

7. Nell to Frank, Friday afternoon, n.d., *National Police Gazette,* June 9, 1849.

8. Helen to Richard, n.d., *National Police Gazette,* May 26, 1849.

9. Helen to Robinson, Friday, n.d., *National Police Gazette,* May 26, 1849.

10. Nell to Frank, Wednesday, n.d., *National Police Gazette,* June 9, 1849.

11. Helen to Frank, n.d., *National Police Gazette,* June 2, 1849.

12. Nelly to Frank, Tuesday, n.d., *National Police Gazette,* June 9, 1849.

13. Helen to Frank, Thursday evening, n.d., *National Police Gazette,* June 2, 1849.

14. Helen to Frank, Monday, n.d., *National Police Gazette,* June 9, 1849.

15. Helen to Frank, Thursday evening, n.d., *National Police Gazette,* June 23, 1849.

16. No names [Richard Robinson to Helen Jewett], Friday morning, n.d., *National Police Gazette,* June 23, 1849.

17. Salters, whose real name was Caroline Paris, had lived at Townsend's for only one year but said at the trial that she had known Jewett for about two years. Caroline Stewart said she had lived there for five or six years, so she would have known Helen in 1834.

18. The six deposed at the grand jury were Elizabeth Salters, Emma French, Caroline Stewart, Maria Stevens, Mary Jones, and Amelia Elliot.

19. Townsend's testimony from the grand jury, the coroner's jury, and the trial. Quotation is from *Trial of Richard P. Robinson,* 3.

20. Deposition of Rosina Townsend, Apr. 16, 1836, in *People vs. Robinson,* District Attorney's Indictment Papers, Municipal Archives.

21. Testimony of Elizabeth Salters, *Trial of Richard P. Robinson,* 9. Salters did not volunteer this relationship to either the coroner's jury or the grand jury.

22. Ibid., 8.

23. Testimony of Rosina Townsend, *Trial of Richard P. Robinson,* 3.

24. Testimony of Sarah Dunscombe and Edward Strong, Grand Jury Proceedings, Apr. 18, 1836, in *People vs. Robinson,* Apr. 10, 1836, District Attorney's Indictment Papers, Municipal Archives, and the *Trial of Richard P. Robinson,* 10–11.

25. Testimony of Sarah Dunscombe, affidavit signed Apr. 21, 1836 (after the grand jury), and *Trial of Richard P. Robinson,* 10.

26. Testimony of Rodman Moulton and Charles Tyrell, *Trial of Richard P. Robinson,* 8, 16–17.

27. At the grand jury each woman was asked about her client for the night. Both Waters and Ashley were listed on the docket as being present at the grand jury proceedings, although neither was called to testify. Humphrey was also named, but he was not listed on the docket.

28. *New York Herald,* Apr. 12, 1836. Bennett might have learned this in a conversation he had on Sunday, on his first tour of the brothel.

29. Rogers, autopsy report, District Attorney's Indictment Papers, Municipal Archives.

30. I am indebted to two forensic pathologists for their valuable observations on Dr.

Rogers's autopsy report: Dr. William R. Oliver of the U.S. Air Force and Dr. John D. Butts, Chief Medical Examiner of the state of North Carolina. I also thank Dr. Richard M. Levenson, pathologist at Carnegie Mellon University, for putting me in touch with these experts.

31. Testimony of James Wells and of Laban Jacobs, owner of the hatchet firm, *Trial of Richard P. Robinson*, 9, 21.

32. The *Philadelphia Public Ledger*, July 13, 1836, reported that Gray and Robinson roomed together at 31 Maiden Lane for thirteen months in 1835, and then again at the Dey Street house for two to three weeks until Gray moved out.

33. "Report of Interments in the Cemetery of Trinity Church," page for April 1836. I thank Marie Sauvé, Office of Parish Archives, Trinity Parish, New York, for sending the burial reports to me, along with a pamphlet published by Trinity Parish, "Churchyards of Trinity Parish, in the City of New York." St. John's Burying Ground is distinct from St. John's Park, a once elegant square below Canal Street across from St. John's Church on Varick Street. This latter site is now the exit of the Holland Tunnel from New Jersey.

34. Robert A. M. Stern, Gregory Gilmartin, and John Montague Massengate, *New York 1900: Metropolitan Architecture and Urbanism, 1890–1915* (New York: Rizzoli, 1983), 136–37; "Improvement of St. John's Park, New York City, Messr. Carrière & Hastings, Architects," *Architectural Review* 5 (Dec. 10, 1898), plate 88; "New York Unearths Cemeteries and Finds Politics," *New York Times*, May 23, 1993, 1. When the cemetery was plowed under in the 1890s, one church official estimated that while only eight hundred monuments and stones marked the surface, more than ten thousand bodies had been officially interred on the site; Felix Oldboy, *Walks in Our Churchyards* (1896), cited in Morgan Dix, *A History of the Parish of Trinity Church, in the City of New York* (New York: Putnam's, 1906), 4:195. I thank Mary Weavers Cline for her help in tracking the history of St. John's Park.

35. *New York Herald*, Apr. 16 and 19, 1836. A highly sentimentalized and fictionalized short story of Jewett's life and death written by Theodore Fay in the May 1836 *New-York Mirror* ends with her dissection in the medical school. Shultz, *Body Snatching*, 31–34, describes the preferred methods of the day for procuring fresh, usable bodies. Claude M. Heaton estimated that in the 1840s, some six hundred to seven hundred bodies a year were snatched in New York City, to supplement the cadavers purchased for five dollars each from Bellevue Almshouse; "Body Snatching in New York City," *New York State Journal of Medicine* 43 (1943): 1861–65. John C. Dalton, *History of the College of Physicians and Surgeons in the City of New York* (New York, 1888), 36, describes a stable on Park Street behind the college built to receive the bodies recovered from "noctural expeditions in the interest of the anatomical department." Dr. Valentine Mott of the College of Physicians and Surgeons was the foremost snatcher of his day; but at the time of Jewett's burial, he was in Europe. Mott built a large collection of medical curiosities which was cataloged in 1858. Numbering over a thousand items, the collection included bones, skeletons, and jars of organs taken from patients, murder victims, and not a few famous people, for example the alleged skull of Davy Crockett; but, alas, no Jewett bones are listed. (Item 714 was a lacerated cerebellum, undated and unidentified.) Mott's entire collection burned in a fire in the 1860s. See Valentine Mott, *Catalogue of the Surgical and Pathological Museum of Valentine Mott, MD, LLD, and of his Son, Alexander B. Mott, MD* (New York: William Taylor, 1858), 30, 74.

• FOURTEEN •
OVERCONFIDENT YOUTH

1. *New-York Transcript*, Apr. 11 and 13, 1836.

2. Combined circulation figure is from Bleyer, *Main Currents*, 181. Bleyer notes Newell's paper with its promise to be a literary and moral paper for women; *Main Cur-*

rents, 170. The American Antiquarian Society has fourteen issues of the *Ladies Morning Star*, scattered from May to Sept. 1836, concentrated in June when the editor wrote extensively on the case at the conclusion of the trial.

3. *New York Sun,* Apr. 19, 1836.

4. *Albany Microscope,* quoted disapprovingly in the *Philadelphia Public Ledger,* June 14, 1836.

5. *New-York Transcript,* Apr. 16, 1836.

6. *New York Herald,* Apr. 20, 1836. On Brink's standing guard at the auction, see his testimony in the *Trial of Richard P. Robinson,* 8.

7. *New York Herald,* May 2 and 16, 1836.

8. Ibid., Mar. 30, 1837.

9. On similar lithographs produced in France, see Abigail Solomon-Godeau and Beatrice Farwell, *The Image of Desire: Femininity, Modernity, and the Birth of Mass Culture in Nineteenth-Century France* (Santa Barbara, Calif.: University Art Museum Exhibition Catalogue, 1994), 1–15. Solomon-Godeau and Farwell argue that lithographs and early photographs of the nude moved away from classical artistic treatments of mythic figures presented in narrative contexts (like Vanderlyn's *Ariadne*) to showing simply the female nude as early pornography.

10. The lithograph was registered by printmaker H. R. Robinson in federal copyright books maintained by a District Court in Manhattan (the Southern District of New York), on May 24, 1836; Library of Congress, no. 128, 438. Alfred M. Hoffy, the artist, had migrated to New York from Germany in 1835, when he was forty-five. He left New York in 1838 for Philadelphia, where he had a long career as a lithographer. George C. Groce and David H. Wallace, *The New-York Historical Society's Dictionary of Artists in America, 1564–1860* (New Haven: Yale University Press, 1957), 321. For comparisons of conventional treatments of the female face in the 1830s, see illustrations in Dale T. Johnson, *American Portrait Miniatures in the Manney Collection* (New York: Metropolitan Museum of Art, 1990). Lithographs were pressed with black ink; watercolor came as a second hand-painted stage of production.

11. *New York Herald,* Apr. 14, 1836.

12. H. R. Robinson was a reputable businessman who commissioned and sold prints from his store on Cortlandt near Greenwich Street; but in 1842, he was arrested for selling obscene pictures and books, found stockpiled by the thousands in his back room. *People vs. H. R. Robinson,* Sept. 28, 1842, District Attorney's Indictment Papers, Municipal Archives. I am grateful to Timothy Gilfoyle for bringing this case to my attention. An expert on political cartooning of the period notes that the Hoffy nude of Jewett was "one of the most suggestive popular prints of the early nineteenth century"; Nancy Davison, "E. W. Clay: American Political Caricaturist of the Jacksonian Era" (Ph.D. diss., University of Michigan, 1980), 168–69.

13. Library of Congress federal copyright books, no. 92 (Apr. 18, 1836), 403.

14. *New York Sun,* Apr. 21, 1836.

15. This lithograph is owned by the New-York Historical Society, which credits it to Hoffy also, but dates it 1856. Perhaps Hoffy did this two decades later (but why?); more likely it is a dating mistake. The face resembles the Jewett face in the other bed scene, but details in the room are different. The figure of Robinson carries an extremely small globe lamp giving off an aura of light.

16. Everything else about the pamphlet *The Life of Ellen Jewett* (Boston, 1836) marks it as bogus, but the publisher may well have acquired a print of the Baker lithograph, now missing, and made his own copy onto a relief block of wood or metal in violation of copyright laws. I thank Georgia Barnhill, Curator of Graphic Arts at the American Antiquarian Society, for her help with the lithographic history of the Jewett case.

17. *Robinson Down Stream; Containing Conversations with the "GREAT UNHUNG," since his Acquittal; and an Account, by Robinson Himself, of his Travels from Connecticut to*

New-Orleans on his Way to Texas (New York, 1836), 15–16. This extraordinary document will be more fully mined and substantiated in chapter 16.

18. Paul Johann Anselm Ritter von Feuerbach, *Caspar Hauser, An Account of an Individual Kept in the Dungeon, Separated from all Communication with the World, From Early Childhood to About the Age of Seventeen,* trans. from the German, 2nd ed. (Boston: Allen and Ticknor, 1833). Over three thousand stories, books, novels, and movies have taken up the Hauser story since the boy was discovered (in 1829) and then murdered (in 1833) in Nuremberg. From the beginning of the mystery, there was speculation that the child was an heir to the throne in Baden. See Jeffrey Moussaieff Masson, trans. and ed., *The Lost Prince: The Unsolved Mystery of Kaspar Hauser* (New York: Simon and Schuster, 1996). That Robinson was familiar with the story indicates something of his reading habits and his participation in a culture of popular literature. On one level, his remark seemed to be about innocence: the childlike lithographic representation of him was parallel to the arrested development of the caged youth. But it is also possible that he identified with the story of Hauser on deeper levels: the isolated boy, cut off from human contact, who is really a prince.

19. *Philadelphia Public Ledger,* May 26, 1836, reprinted from the *Journal of Commerce.*

20. Asa Greene, *A Glance at New York* (New York, 1837), 79–83. Charles Bernheimer, *Figures of Ill Repute,* chapter 3, discusses the 1844 work by Jules Barbey D'Aurevilly, *Du Dandysme et de George Brummell,* which figured the dandy as a sphinxlike man of indeterminate sexuality who refused to become enmeshed in desire. John F. Kasson describes the "fashion-conscious dandy" of New York, aiming to be "conspicuous," and hints that critics of the dandy scorned the style as effeminate; *Rudeness and Civility: Manners in Nineteenth-Century Urban America* (New York: Hill and Wang, 1990), 117–23.

21. Its founders and associates included Dirck Lansing, Joshua Leavitt, William Goodell, Charles Grandison Finney, Beriah Green, Simeon Jocelyn, Henry Wright, and Theodore Weld.

22. Only a few known copies of this early paper survive; the largest set consists of nine issues running from Jan. 7 to Dec. 2, 1833, at Amherst College, Amherst, Mass.; I acknowledge the assistance of Floyd S. Merritt, Reference Librarian at Amherst, for supplying me with photocopies. The editors were William Goodell, S. P. Hines, and Charles W. Denison. The paper did not succeed, and it soon merged with another publication that some of the same men were already involved with, the *Emancipator,* an antislavery paper. The merged concerns were reflected in the new subjoined title, added in 1834: the *Emancipator and Journal of Public Morals.* The last page of the paper was now given over to columns of generalized complaint about "the sin of licentiousness" and "the atmosphere of pollution." The editor of the paper was the Reverend Charles W. Dennison. Others associated with the moral reform part were the Reverend Dirck C. Lansing, the Reverend Beriah Green, R. M. Chipman, and G. W. Blagdon.

23. Its first officers were Mrs. Charles G. Finney, Mrs. William Green, Mrs. John McComb, Mrs. Charles Hawkins, Mrs. Dirck Lansing, and Mrs. Joshua Levitt. Flora L. Northrup, *The Record of a Century, 1834–1934* (New York: American Female Guardian Society and Home for the Friendless, 1934), 16. Quote is from the first issue of the *Advocate of Moral Reform,* Jan. 1835, 1.

24. For a short time the group sponsored a missionary house on Waverly Place, which closed in mid-1836.

25. *Advocate of Moral Reform,* June 1, 1836, 73.

26. Ibid., June 15, 1836, 88.

27. Circulation figures cited in June 1, 1836, issue of the *Advocate of Moral Reform.* Not all of those subscriptions went to eager advocates of sexual purity; some seven hundred were sent gratis and unsolicited to various educational institutions such as Yale, Amherst, Brown, and Princeton.

28. *Journal of Public Morals*, May 1, 1836.

29. Ibid.

30. *New York Herald*, Apr. 16, 1836.

31. For a time the Jewett murder reinvigorated moral reform and pulled men back to a central role, but their attention did not last very long. The *Journal of Public Morals* continued to publish through August 1837, but then the organization and the journal dropped from sight. (Whiteaker, "Moral Reform," 217, gives that end date for the paper. Only four issues of it exist today, at the American Antiquarian Society: June 1, June 15, and Oct. 1, 1836, and Mar. 1, 1837. The Boston Public Library once had copies but can no longer locate them.) The initial enthusiasm it spawned did lead to male moral reform meetings called in places such as Portland, Maine, and Utica, New York, but these efforts were very short-lived. In contrast, the Female Moral Reformers continued to pursue their uniquely female approach to sexual sin: warning women, denouncing bad men, publishing anecdotal (not statistical) articles in the *Advocate of Moral Reform*. By 1841 they claimed to have fifty thousand members in 555 auxiliaries; *Advocate of Moral Reform*, June 1, 1841. In the 1840s, the women modified their tactics somewhat and gained interest in rescuing girls at risk for sexual ruination. They first sponsored urban employment bureaus to help country girls find decent domestic employment. Then in 1848 they established a home for "friendless and destitute girls" (only ones of good character) and changed their name to the American Female Reform and Guardian Society. The *Advocate* enjoyed a wide and long circulation up into the 1870s; its institution for homeless girls, located finally in the Bronx, survived into the early twentieth century; Northrup, *Record of a Century*.

32. *New-York Transcript*, June 14, 1836.

33. *Journal of Public Morals*, May 1, 1836.

34. *New York Sun*, Apr. 26, 1836.

35. *New York Commercial Advertiser*, reprinted in the weekly *Norwich (Conn.) Courier*, Aug. 17, 1836.

36. *New-York Transcript*, Aug. 10, 13, and 15, 1836.

37. *New York Sun*, Apr. 15, 1836.

38. Bennett named Resolvat Stevens, a clerk in Oliver Lownds's office, as the party who allowed the improper handling of the diary; *New York Herald*, Apr. 19, 1836.

39. In the wake of the Jewett murder, the *Philadelphia Public Ledger* editorialized about clerks' salaries. Clerks worked long hours, six days a week, and a typical low pay in that city was six hundred dollars per year. The *Ledger* linked low salaries with routine pilfering by underpaid employees. *Philadelphia Public Ledger*, July 11, 1836.

40. *New York Sun*, Apr. 15, 1836.

41. *New-York Transcript*, Apr. 16, 1836.

42. Ibid.

43. *New York Herald*, Apr. 20, 1836.

44. *A Sketch of the Life of Francis P. Robinson, the Alleged Murderer of Helen Jewett; Containing copious extracts from his Journal* (New York, 1836). The copy owned by the New-York Historical Society is a Francis P. Robinson version; the copy owned by the American Antiquarian Society appears to be typographically identical except for the name on the title page and a one-letter change on page 5, "F. P." to "R. P."

45. *Diary of George Templeton Strong*, ed. Allan Nevins and Milton Halsey Thomas (New York: Macmillan, 1952), 1:24, entry for June 11, 1836. Strong went on to speculate, as if the diary were genuine, "By the by, I wonder if ever I shall be placed in a predicament of the same sort—and shall have this scrawl brought up to be argued on by lawyers and commented on and explained by that glorious trio, the *Sun*, *Transcript*, and *Herald*?" Calling Robinson's trial for murder "a predicament" suggests that the young Strong was aligned with Robinson's supporters.

I have assigned the Robinson pamphlet diary to 1990s college students, and nearly to a person they have difficulty believing it to be the work of a sixteen-year-old boy, based (they report) on its syntax and vocabulary as well as its dark and sarcastic passages. But invariably a few students confess that it could be their own, even at that tender an age.

46. *Sketch of the Life*, 24.

47. Ibid., 4–6.

48. Ibid., 6.

49. The lunatic asylum in New York in 1834 was the Bloomingdale Asylum for the Insane, on a prospect 150 feet above the Hudson River, seven miles north of City Hall.

50. *Sketch of the Life*, 14–15.

51. The prison building measured one hundred by twenty-five feet, or five thousand square feet total. That came to only seventeen square feet per prisoner; the women's cells must have been tiny. In 1837, the city's Common Council investigated conditions at Bellevue and found them substandard; jail fever was rampant among the prisoners, vermin and dirty bedding among all the inmates. The prison at Blackwell's Island was ready to take males in late 1836, and in 1838 the Tombs, a new jail near City Hall, took the women convicts. Robert J. Carlisle, ed., *An Account of Bellevue Hospital: With a Catalogue of the Medical and Surgical Staff from 1836 to 1894* (New York: Society of the Alumni of Bellevue Hospital, 1893), 23, 37. For inmate statistics, see *New York As It Is,* 44–45.

52. *New York Herald*, May 16 and 17, 1836.

53. Testimony of Daniel Lyons, *Trial of Richard P. Robinson*, 19–20.

54. Testimony of Robert Furlong, *Trial of Richard P. Robinson*, 14.

55. Testimony of Henry Burnham, *Trial of Richard P. Robinson*, 20.

56. Testimony of Robert Furlong, *Trial of Richard P. Robinson*, 15.

57. *The Diary of Philip Hone, 1828–1851*, ed. Allan Nevins (New York: Dodd, Mead, 1936), 210–11.

58. While the Williams and Weston family letters for this period are sparse and individually quite uninformative, still, taken together they show a convergence of the five boys on Boston. Joseph wrote his mother in mid-May that he and Nathan were expecting Daniel Weston to visit soon, and Mrs. Weston's June 2 letter to her Philadelphia friend bragged that George Melville, the third son in the family, was about to make his first trip to Boston for a week to stay with Nathan. Finally, a letter from Joseph Williams confirmed that George had come, along with a friend, George Robinson (both Georges being writers for the *Augusta Age*). Joseph Williams to Sarah Cony Williams, May 14 and June 10, 1836, box 21, folder 9, Reuel Williams Papers; Paulina Cony Weston to Mrs. William Dewey, June 2, 1836, Melville Weston Fuller Papers, box 2, Library of Congress.

• FIFTEEN •

TRIAL IN JUNE

1. The twenty reporters probably worked together, or at least in groups, to get all the words down. Variants of the transcript were published in the *New-York Transcript*, the *Sun*, the *Herald*, the *Courier and Enquirer*, the *New York Commercial Advertiser*, the *New York Daily Advertiser*, and the *Journal of Commerce*. Many papers outside New York picked up the trial transcripts and reprinted them in part or in full: the *Philadelphia Public Ledger*, the *Norwich (Conn.) Courier*, the *Massachusetts (Worcester) Spy*, the *Boston Transcript*, the *Portland (Maine) Eastern Argus*, the *Augusta Age*, the *Albany Evening Journal*, the *Newburyport Daily Herald*, and the *New York Evening Post*.

2. The six trials are listed in *New York As It Is,* 40.

3. David McAdam et al., eds., *History of the Bench and Bar of New York*, 2 vols. (New York: New York History Co., 1897), 318–19.

4. William Ogden Wheeler, comp., *The Ogden Family in America, Elizabethtown Branch, and Their English Ancestry: John Ogden, the Pilgrim, and His Descendants,*

1640–1906, Their History, Biography & Genealogy (Philadelphia: Lippincott, 1907), 1:67–70, 84, 103, 185, 258.

5. McAdam, *History of the Bench and Bar*, 241.

6. L. B. Proctor, *The Bench and Bar of New-York, Containing Biographical Sketches of Eminent Judges, and Lawyers of the New-York Bar, Incidents of the Important Trials in Which They Were Engaged, and Anecdotes Connected with Their Professional, Political and Judicial Career* (New York: Diossy, 1870), 16.

7. "Ogden Hoffman," *Dictionary of American Biography*, edited by Allen Johnson et al. (New York: Scribners, 1928–1958), 5:115–17; *Appleton's Cyclopaedia*, 3:227; Ogden Hoffman Papers, New-York Historical Society; Proctor, *Bench and Bar of New-York*, 1–26. Hoffman came from a literary family; his half brother was Charles Fenno Hoffman, who wrote novels and edited the *Knickerbocker*, while a sister, Matilda Hoffman, was engaged to the author Washington Irving before her early death.

8. *New-York Transcript*, Jan. 18, 1836.

9. McAdam, *History of the Bench and Bar*, 359.

10. The most extensive biography of Hoffman appears in Proctor, *Bench and Bar of New-York*, 1–26.

11. Joseph H. Choate to his mother, 1856; quoted in "Ogden Hoffman," *Dictionary of American Biography*.

12. McAdam, *History of the Bench and Bar*, 415.

13. Royall, *Black Book*, 2:9.

14. Quotes from death notices in the *Knickerbocker Magazine* and the *New York Commercial Advertiser* in 1846, quoted in a brief profile of Price in *American State Trials: A Collection of the Important and Interesting Criminal Trials Which Have Taken Place in the United States, From the Beginning of Our Government to the Present Day* (St. Louis: Thomas Law Books, 1914–1936), 5:360.

15. *American State Trials*, 5:432. This volume wrongly says the D.A. was J. P. Phenix. On Phoenix's state of health, see Robert Morris, closing argument, *Murder Most Foul*, 6.

16. On the unruly crowd and the broken railings, see *Diary of Philip Hone*, 210. For estimates of crowd size, see *Trial of Richard P. Robinson*, 1, 5.

17. *New-York Transcript*, June 3, 1836.

18. John Guinther, *The Jury in America* (New York: Facts on File Publications, 1988), 47–48. Editorial on jury selection process, *New-York Transcript*, Aug. 25, 1836.

19. A grocer named Israel Cook on the official panel was dismissed on preemptory challenge. Either he or a son was in business in 1834 to 1835 with Robert Furlong, grocer, shortly to be the star witness for the defense; Longworth's *City Directory*, 1834–35. They were not in business the year before or after.

20. Barbour, *Spelman Genealogy*. Robinson did have some notable relations. A second cousin, Mary Jane Robinson, in 1832 married Robert Dale Owen, founder of the New Harmony utopian community in Indiana; and a fifth cousin, Laura Spelman (born in 1839), married the industrialist John D. Rockefeller in the 1860s.

21. The seven jurors seated from the jury list were Isaac Winslow, a lower Broadway merchant; Burtis Skidmore, who ran a coal yard with his brother at Washington and Franklin; Daniel Comstock, a grocer on South Street; Joseph M. Imlay, a dry-goods merchant on Pearl Street; Perry Jewett, a Walnut Street grocer; James S. Schermerhorn, secretary to the Ocean Insurance Company; and Edward D. Boker, a clothier on Water Street. The five talesmen were Iziah Bull (also spelled "Jireh" and "Gerah" in different transcripts), identified as a Fourth Ward merchant (Jereh Bull, dealer in silks, had a store at 76 Maiden Lane and a home address on Pearl Street); Jeremiah R. Field, also a Fourth Ward merchant with a dry-goods store on Pearl Street; James C. Parsells, fancy storekeeper, listed as a stock manufacturer on Broadway near the City Hall; Caleb (or "Select" in some papers) Waterbury, shoemaker (a Seleck Waterbury had a shoe store on Grand);

and finally John J. Mattrass, identified as a druggist of the Fifteenth Ward. "Mattrass" is the one name not found in the 1830 or 1840 census nor in any city directories.

22. Quoted in the *Newburyport Daily Herald*, June 13, 1836.

23. *Diary of Michael Floy Jr.,* 144–45.

24. In the pages that follow, all quotations (unless otherwise noted) are from *Trial of Richard P. Robinson,* the pamphlet published by George Wilkes in 1849.

25. Testimony of Sarah Dunscombe, *Trial of Richard P. Robinson*, 10.

26. Deposition of Newton Gilbert, Grand Jury Proceedings, Apr. 18, 1836.

27. *Trial of Richard P. Robinson*, 13.

28. *New York Sun*, Apr. 15, 1836.

29. Furlong testified that he apprenticed under Miles Hitchcock, a well-known merchant in the downtown area. Hitchcock ran a grocery for many years at Nassau and Liberty in an old, small house dating from Revolutionary days that backed up to the famous landmark the Sugar House on Liberty Street, a five-story stone building used as a prison by the British during the war. Furlong was married in July 1834 in Rye, New York, to Nancy Jane Park, and a daughter was born in 1835, making him a fairly new father at the time of the trial. "Furlong," Surname Index, Church of the Latter-day Saints, New York. On Hitchcock's store: "Letter from Laurie Todd, Being Scraps from his Note Book for 1799" (letter to the editor), *New-York Mirror*, Feb. 1835, 261.

30. *Trial of Richard P. Robinson*, 15.

31. Testimony of Rodman Moulton, *Trial of Richard P. Robinson*, 17.

32. Testimony of James Tew, *Trial of Richard P. Robinson*, 18.

33. It remains possible that there were two other letters of August 1835 that got separated from the full set, maybe as a result of this moment in the trial. The D.A. mentioned fifteen letters by Robinson when he questioned Hoxie and seventeen when he interrogated Newton Gilbert. The police log of June 1836 only numbers nine from Robinson, but George Wilkes printed fifteen in the *National Police Gazette*. Possibly, then, there were two missing letters containing more explicit evidence on the relationship.

34. *Newburyport Daily Herald*, June 14, 1836.

35. *New-York Transcript*, June 6 and 8, 1836.

36. *Murder Most Foul*, 3–6.

37. Ibid., 6–11.

38. Ibid., 12–17.

39. Ibid., 17; *Trial of Richard P. Robinson*, 22.

40. *Murder Most Foul*, 17–21.

41. Ibid., 21–24.

42. *Trial of Richard P. Robinson*, 22.

43. Charles Sutton, *The New York Tombs; Its Secrets and Its Mysteries* (New York: United States Publishing Company, 1874), 97–135; the bribery charge is on 133–34.

44. "A Reason for the Acquittal of Robinson," *New-York Transcript*, June 15, 1836.

45. Hannah Webster Foster, *The Coquette; Or, The History of Eliza Wharton. A Novel, Founded on Fact* (1796); Davidson, *Revolution and the Word,* 140–50. One joking boast about Edwards told by friends in his lifetime was that "Pierpont Edwards, it is said, was so vain upon this point [of sexual gallantry], that when unjustly charged with the parentage of a child, he could not find it in his heart to deny the soft impeachment, and would pay the sum demanded rather than lose the compliment." This claim says little about Edwards's actual behavior but much about upper-class male camaraderie around sexual indiscretions. James Parton, *The Life and Times of Aaron Burr*, 2 vols. (Boston: Houghton, Osgood, 1880), 301.

46. Parton, *Aaron Burr*, 300–8, 328. Judge Edwards visited the ailing Burr often in the months from June to Sept. 1836.

47. *Ladies Morning Star*, June 18, 1836. The editor, William Newell, ran several long editorials on "Reflections on the Late Trial." He claimed the porter would have testified

that Robinson was there the Saturday before, and that it was another man on April 9 who dropped ashes on his face. Newell insisted this information was available to Phoenix and he failed to use it.

48. *New-York Transcript*, June 11, 1836.

49. The *New York Herald* of Dec. 15 and 18, 1838, reported the story. Furlong, despite his marriage to a "respectable" woman from Rye, New York, and his "interesting" family, fell in with bad characters after the trial and became a drinker. He jumped or fell overboard after a three-day brandy binge. James Gordon Bennett reported that other newspapers were claiming this as a "suicide by impulse of conscience." But Furlong made no dramatic confessions. His grocery had already disappeared from Longworth's directory in the edition sold in June 1838. Nancy Furlong, widow of Robert, appears in 1840 as a milliner. See also Philip Hone's diary entry for Dec. 14, 1838.

50. Proctor, *Bench and Bar of New-York*, 14.

51. Ibid., 17.

• SIXTEEN •

THE GREAT UNHUNG

1. The first fiction in print was a full-length dime novel by the prolific fiction writer Joseph Holt Ingraham, *Frank Rivers, or, the Dangers of the Town* (Boston, 1843, and several New York editions, 1844). Remarkably, Ingraham actually grew up in Augusta, Maine; his father lived not far from the Westons' house in the 1830 census. He was born in 1809 and left town in 1826 to ship out to sea; after a two-year voyage to Argentina, he returned home and matriculated at Yale College but was thrown out for misconduct in 1829. He lived in Augusta from 1829 to 1830, years when he could conceivably have gotten to know Dorcas Doyen; he left in the fall of 1830 (as did she), he bound for Natchez. He was in New York at various times in the 1830s and then lived most of his adulthood in Mississippi. In his fictional rendition, Frank Rivers was a nice New York lad who fell in love with the prostitute Jewett, a vengeful woman who pulled him into her spiderweb as she did all her clients, in retribution for an early seduction in Maine by a Bowdoin student. Her real killer, wrote Ingraham, was that Bowdoin student, now about to marry the daughter of the governor of Maine. Ingraham portrays Rivers innocently visiting Jewett that Saturday, leaving his cloak for her to mend and his hatchet so she could cut her firewood. But later that evening the evil Bowdoin student shows up and kills her in a rage, angry over her threats to expose his immoral ways to the governor's daughter. The killer then flees the country for Europe. Nothing in Ingraham's story suggests he had any insider's knowledge of Dorcas Doyen, either in Maine or New York. See Robert W. Weathersby II, *J. H. Ingraham* (Boston: Twayne, 1980). Weathersby has suggested this story "goes against type" compared with the scores of other dime novels Ingraham wrote, in that it failed to produce a happy ending where all loose ends are tied up; personal communication from Weathersby.

The second novel, *Lives of Helen Jewett*, by George Wilkes, appeared as a serial in his *National Police Gazette* and then was issued in several yellow-cover paperback editions. The 1880s crime publishing house of Philadelphia, Barclay's, reprinted it in both English and German in the late nineteenth century with updated pictures reflecting 1880s standards of beauty. Wilkes adhered to the skeleton of the story revealed by the trial and by Jewett's letters and constructed a novel embellished with dialogue, motive, and fully fictional characters mixed in with the principals. More than any other author who turned his hand to this story, Wilkes played up the sexual dimension of Jewett's prostitute life.

The third novel appeared in the 1930s: Manuel Komroff, *A New York Tempest* (New York: Coward-McCann, 1932). Komroff (a onetime and fourth-rate author) leaned on the Wilkes version, shifting names around to seemingly fictionalize the story (Robinson became Benson, for example, and Hoxie was transformed into the real New York businessman and reformer Arthur Tappan). If there were a prize for ruining a rather engaging story, it would go to Komroff for his 430-page clunker.

Gore Vidal produced the fourth fictional and very lively treatment. He used the Jewett story as a minor backdrop in his historical novel *Burr* (New York: Ballantine Books, 1973), the story of Aaron Burr situated in 1830s New York with flashbacks to earlier vital moments in Burr's career. Vidal's narrator, a young and fully fictional newspaperman who writes for the *Evening Post*, visits Rosina Townsend's parlor and develops a love relationship with Helen Jewett. Near the end of the book, he is arrested, mistakenly, for her murder, but then Richard Robinson is swiftly arrested, tried, and acquitted. Vidal's afterword explains that his characters are nearly all true to life, including Jewett and Townsend. Vidal inserts Edward Livingston into his story and comments on his own residential connection to the Livingston family, Edward having lived near the author's own home in Dutchess County. What Vidal did not realize, in all probability, was that the Livingston brother—John R.—who built Vidal's home along the Hudson River, was so centrally implicated in the story of Helen Jewett.

Finally, the late Raymond Paul, novelist and professor at Montclair State College in New Jersey, published *The Thomas Street Horror: An Historical Novel of Murder* (New York: Ballantine Books, 1982), an elaborate reconstruction of the crime that exonerated Robinson and implicated Maria Stevens, the prostitute in the room next door who had died precipitously in late May. Paul's book succeeds in being quite a page-turner, and his grounding in the published accounts of the murder case (by the *Herald* and the *Sun*) is very solid.

2. The *New-York Transcript* on June 14, 1836, printed one letter from a reader asking to stop his subscription because of the unending attention to the trial; the editors declared they had gotten many such letters, but they planned to disregard the advice. The *New York Sun*, June 20, 1836, announced that if subscribers disagreed with them, they were welcome to quit buying: "If five thousand of them should stop in a week, it would be nothing to us; it would not for a moment influence us to swerve from a course which we believed to be right"; The *Philadelphia Public Ledger* also fielded letters from readers insisting Robinson was innocent; see letter of S.F.W., June 13, 1836.

3. *New York Times*, July 11, 1836, reprinted in the *Newburyport Daily Herald*, July 15, 1836. The *Ladies Morning Star* alleged that Townsend's bed companion had been subpoenaed and was in the courtroom during the trial, but the D.A. failed to call him to testify.

4. Francis Bacon Trowbridge, *Ashley Genealogy* (New Haven: 1896), 226. James Morgan Ashley was born in 1809 in Sandy Hill, New York; he and his wife both died in the 1849 cholera epidemic in New York. Letters to his mother existed in 1890, kept by Mrs. Charles Sidney Adams of Winthrop, Massachusetts. Trowbridge wrote: "While as a business man he was eminently successful in his latter years, he had had reverses earlier that only his persistence and fortitude could overcome. But it is as the husband and father, within the inner circle of the man's life, that we find his true character. He was a most honorable and kindly man, and greatly beloved by family and friends. These letters to his mother are touching and beautiful in their description of his home and family."

5. *New York Sun*, June 14, 1836.

6. *People vs. Ann Williams*, District Attorney's Indictment Papers, June 1835. Charles Humphrey was also the name of a very well known New Yorker of 1836, an Ithaca lawyer and civic leader who had served in the U.S. Congress and who for several years up through 1836 was Speaker of the New York state assembly in Albany. The Honorable Charles Humphrey could not have been in the brothel on April 9 because he introduced a petition in the assembly that morning; *Albany Evening Journal*, Apr. 11, 1836. With the ice on the Hudson blocking boats, travelers were forced to go by land, and the trip required two overnights, according to James Gordon Bennett, who was in Albany covering the sessions on the state banking crisis in late Mar. 1836; *New York Herald*, Mar. 25, 1836.

The Honorable Charles Humphrey did have a son named Charles, born around 1818 to 1820—too young to have been the adult (placed variously at age twenty-five or forty by women at the grand jury hearing) in Rosina's bed. Thomas W. Burns, *Initial Ithacans: Comprising Sketches and Portraits of the Forty-Four Presidents of the Village of Ithaca (1821–1888) and the First Eight Mayors (1888–1903)* (Ithaca, N.Y., 1904), 16–18.

7. *New York Times*, reprinted in *Newburyport Daily Herald*, July 15, 1836.

8. In 1836, Chicago was a frontier town just starting to grow extremely rapidly around old Fort Dearborn, at the junction of the Chicago River and Lake Michigan. George P. Marston first became a schoolteacher, but he soon quit that and took up clerking duties in a clothing store in the center of the new town, activities documented in a letter he wrote his father in August 1837. George, nineteen, was undecided about his course in life. In 1838 his father bought 640 acres of land in Jefferson County, Wisconsin, for George to farm. For a decade he struggled to earn a living; a family legend reports that one year his entire crop of wheat brought him five dollars on the Milwaukee market, which he impulsively spent in its entirety in a shop that sold oysters at five dollars a plate. Perhaps the luxury oysters, imported at great expense to the prairies of Wisconsin, reminded him of the daily diet he had heedlessly enjoyed during his New York years frequenting oyster bars with Richard Robinson; Marston, *George White Marston*, 1:19–21, 59. An 1879 history of Jefferson County reports that George was the defendant in the first jury trial ever held in the county seat Fort Atkinson, Marston's new home. The plaintiff, Mary Bennett, "sued him for the amount of a wash bill, and the hearing of the facts was had at the house of Charles Rockwell, first Justice of the Peace." George was clearly learning that some women expected to be paid in cash for performing personal domestic services; *History of Jefferson County, Wisconsin* (Chicago, 1879), 500.

By 1849 George was thirty and ready to marry. He bought the Fort Atkinson farm from his father and secured a marriage agreement with a sixth cousin, Harriet Marston of Oxford, N.H. The couple married in October 1849 in Oxford, just as the *National Police Gazette*'s serial on Helen Jewett was finishing its yearlong run. George and his bride appear in the U.S. Census for Jefferson County, childless but with an eighteen-year-old English girl living with them. Marston's total wealth was reported as $7,000, which was enough to rank them as the second-richest household in the village of Fort Atkinson. In the 1860 enumeration, George and Harriet had three children; George was now a merchant, with $32,500 in real estate and $10,000 in personal wealth; by 1870, his total worth was $45,000, making him the richest man by far in his town. In 1871 the family relocated to San Diego, California, where Marston became a leader in the new city's growing mercantile community. He opened a store, which later became Marston's department store; and by the 1880s his son, George White Marston, was well on his way to establishing his role as one of the premier town fathers of San Diego. I thank Gregg Hennessey of San Diego, who is preparing a biography of George White Marston, for his generous sharing of research notes with me over the years. See Gregg R. Hennessey, "George White Marston and Conservative Reform in San Diego," *Journal of San Diego History* 32 (Fall 1986), 230–53.

In San Diego in 1873, George P. Marston again became involved with a woman who had been a prostitute, this time to rescue her. Sing Yee was a young Chinese woman forced into prostitution by a Chinese gang in Los Angeles. She escaped and joined the Marston household, marrying their servant Ah Quock. The Marstons gave them a wedding at the family's Presbyterian church. But gang members came after Sing Yee, kidnapped her, and took her back to Los Angeles. Marston sent his son, George W., after the woman; as the *San Diego Union* phrased it, the elder Marston was "by no means the person to permit such an iniquitous deed to be consummated without resistance." The woman was saved from her "life of infamy" and restored to service and protection in the Marston household. *San Diego Union*, July 13, 15, and 17, 1873; and *Los Angeles Daily Star*, July 15, 1873.

George P. Marston died in 1877; a lengthy tribute to him in the *San Diego Union* of

Sept. 23, 1877, outlined his distinguished career but omitted to mention that he had ever lived in New York City.

9. *Newburyport Daily Herald*, July 15, 1836.

10. *Boston Courier*, quoted in the *Newburyport Daily Herald*, July 15, 1836.

11. *Albany Evening Journal*, June 10, 1836.

12. *Middletown Advocate*, quoted in the *Newburyport Daily Herald*, June 21, 1836.

13. *Philadelphia Public Ledger*, July 4, 1836.

14. *Albany Microscope*, reprinted in the *Philadelphia Public Ledger*, June 15, 1836.

15. *New York Sun*, June 10, 1836.

16. Ibid., June 14, 1836.

17. *New-York Transcript*, June 22, 1836. The paper named three of the women: Mary Lamont, Esther Preston, and Eliza Bailie. I have found no record of the arrest in the boxes of Police Office warrants for that month. The *Herald* of June 22 covered the same story in greater depth, reporting that 53 Leonard Street (a mistake for number 55, where Helen once lived in 1832 under Ann Welden's housekeeping) was raided and seven women sent to Bellevue. Mrs. Welden was away and avoided arrest, the *Herald* reported; five of the women were freed on bail provided by young men, "mechanics just starting in business." The remaining two drew ninety-day sentences, according to the *Herald*. "This house which was formerly the resort of all the gay and fashionable youths of the city, where rioting, debauchery and drunkenness held uncontrolable sway, is now desolate. . . . Several more descents upon houses of similar character, and in the immediate neighborhood, are in contemplation." Coming two weeks after the Robinson trial, stepped-up sweeps of elegant brothels look like a police reaction to public attention to vice.

18. *New York Herald*, June 15, 1836.

19. *New-York Transcript*, July 29, 1836.

20. *New York Herald*, June 15, 1836.

21. Eliza Hoxie married John Sutphen Jr., son of a New York merchant, in 1837; Delia Hoxie married William L. Mitchill in 1838; *Index to Marriages and Deaths in the New York Herald, 1835–1855*, 195. It remains possible that these two young women were Hoxie nieces. The Hoxie family genealogy lists only four children of Joseph and his wife, Eliza Blossom: Maria S., Nathaniel B., Josephine, and Elsie. Maria married in 1847 to Henry Norris, and Nathaniel married a year later in 1848; the family history gives only this son's birth date, in 1825. Eliza and Delia might have been older siblings somehow missed by the family history (although typically it is younger children most often overlooked in such compilations); if they were Joseph's daughters, they would have to have been born before 1820 to be of marriageable age in 1837 and 1838. Joseph Hoxie was born in 1795, but his marriage date is unknown. Eliza and Delia are not listed in the Hoxie genealogy as sisters of the nephew Joseph who clerked in the store with Robinson; Hoxie, *The Hoxie Family*, 65. George Wilkes's fictional rendering of 1848 to 1849 conjured a romance between Robinson and his employer's daughter as one cause of the break between Robinson and Jewett. Wilkes, *Lives of Helen Jewett*, 100.

22. Margaret Fields's role was described by Gray in a letter printed in the *New York Herald*, July 18, 1836. Gray further said that Fields herself was committed to Bellevue for thirty days after the letters were discovered, although it is nowhere stated what she was charged with.

23. *New York Sun*, reprinted in the *Philadelphia Public Ledger*, July 13, 1836.

24. The marriage notice appeared in the *Herald* for Jan. 21, 1836; *Index to Marriages and Deaths in the Herald*, 52. The D.A.'s list of potential witnesses, scrawled on the front page of the coroner's inquest file, included "Wm Gray," at Stewart's store on Broadway, and "Mary Ann Gray," 89 Sixteenth Street.

25. *New-York Transcript*, July 14, 1836.

26. "Isaac Ballard, No. 14 Ferry street, keeps his cash account in the Tradesman's Bank, and the Manufacturing Bank, does most in L. M.'s Bank. Andrew Cobb, 31 Ferry

street, keeps his account in the Mechanics Bank, Phenix Bank, and Leather Manufacturer's Bank. Johnathan Thorne, 14 Jacob street, keeps his account in the Phenix Bank
and Merchants' Exchange Bank." *New-York Transcript*, July 13, 1836.

27. *New York Sun*, reprinted in *Philadelphia Public Ledger*, July 13, 1836.

28. *Bradley Brown vs. William D. Gray, Richard M. Lansing vs. Gray*, July 7, 1836,
District Attorney's Indictment Papers, Municipal Archives.

29. Gray's speech was printed in the *Herald* on July 18, 1836. The Police Office column in the same issue describes his sentencing.

30. *Boston Herald*, quoted in the *Philadelphia Public Ledger*, July 20, 1836.

31. *New York Herald*, July 19, 1836.

32. *Philadelphia Public Ledger*, July 12, 1836; *New-York Transcript*, July 23, 1836.

33. *Philadelphia Public Ledger*, Aug. 3, 1836.

34. *Robinson Down Stream*. The inside cover boldly claimed "copyright secured," but
no record of this pamphlet appears in the Library of Congress federal copyright records
for the district of southern New York. The interviewer demonstrated a combative but still
friendly attitude toward Robinson. They exchanged comments about particular Connecticut girls, so very possibly the author was an acquaintance who lived in Durham. Yet he
published the booklet in New York.

35. Ibid., 3.

36. Ibid., 4, 5.

37. Ibid., 5.

38. Ibid., 7.

39. Ibid., 10.

40. Ibid., 11.

41. Ibid., 15.

42. Ibid., 12–13.

43. Jane Caputi, *The Age of Sex Crime* (Bowling Green, Ohio: Bowling Green State
University Press, 1987), 109–10; Deborah Cameron and Elizabeth Frazer, *The Lust to
Kill: A Feminist Investigation of Sexual Murder* (New York: New York University Press,
1987), 69–119. Caputi writes that psychopaths often present a normal exterior, but then
goes on to list attributes that, while not instantly indicative of murderous tendencies,
hardly sound like a coherent cluster of fully normal personality traits: beguiling, guiltless,
manipulating, cynical, egocentric, unempathetic, restless, unperturbed. Cameron and
Frazer deplore the often-circular definition of "psychopath" as a person capable of committing horrific crimes. They demonstrate that the clinical profile varies in different coun-
tries and that the character traits commonly associated with the term are not well
explained as causal factors. As with "fiend" in the nineteenth century, "psychopath" and
its cousin "sociopath" convey a sense of the utter separation between normal people and
murderers. Their book aims to situate sexual murders in the realm of power and politics in
society and in the way masculinity configures sexual desire and violence. See also Jane
Caputi, "The Sexual Politics of Murder," *Gender & Society* 3 (Dec. 1989), 437–56, which
discusses modern-day murderers Joel Steinberg and Ted Bundy. For a cultural studies
approach to the meaning of murder, see Charles R. Acland, *Youth, Murder, Spectacle: The
Cultural Politics of "Youth in Crisis"* (Boulder, San Francisco, and Oxford: Westview
Press, 1995), a book-length analysis of the New York "preppy murder" case of 1988 studied through a Stuart Hall/moral-panic framework. Two other recent books address the
features of modern murders that make some riveting and compelling to a public eager to
hear horrible details: Wendy Lesser, *Pictures at an Execution* (Cambridge, Mass.: Harvard
University Press, 1993), and Joel Black, *The Aesthetics of Murder: A Study in Romantic
Literature and Contemporary Culture* (Baltimore: Johns Hopkins Press, 1991). Serial
killers constitute a different genre, there being almost no examples before the trendsetting
Jack the Ripper of the 1880s; see Judith R. Walkowitz, "Jack the Ripper and the Myth of
Male Violence," *Feminist Studies* 8 (Fall 1982), 542–74.

44. *Robinson Down Stream*, 19.

45. Ibid., 22–24.

46. *Muster Rolls of the Texas Revolution* (Austin, Tex.: Daughters of the Texas Revolution, 1986), 146.

47. Deeds of Aug. 15, 16, and 18; Nov. 6, 26, and 28; Dec. 23, 1836 (microfilm); packet E, reel 1003756, Nacogdoches Archives. I thank Linda Cheves Nicklas, Director of the East Texas Research Center at Stephen F. Austin State University, for sharing her file on Richard P. Robinson with me and for help with Nacogdoches history. Nicklas prepared the entry on Robinson for the *New Handbook of Texas* (Austin: Texas Historical Association, 1996), 5:6265.

• SEVENTEEN •

TEXAS

1. Archie P. McDonald, ed., *Nacogdoches, Wilderness Outpost to Modern City, 1779–1979* (Burnet, Tex.: Eakin Press, 1980); Nugent E. Brown, *The Book of Nacogdoches County, Texas* (Houston, 1927); Archie P. McDonald and Bill Murchison, *Nacogdoches Past and Present: A Legacy of Texas Pride* (Odessa, Tex., 1986). Stephen F. Austin came to Texas heading a large migration of Americans to settle land his father, Moses Austin, had been granted by the Spanish government before Mexico won its independence from Spain in 1821. Moses Austin was a native of Durham, Conn., and a contemporary of Richard P. Robinson's father; he lived in a house on Broad Street in the heart of Durham. But he left Durham in the 1780s, at the age of fifteen, and never returned. David B. Gracy II, *Moses Austin: His Life* (San Antonio, Tex.: Trinity University Press, 1987), 9–17.

2. William Fairfax Gray, *From Virginia to Texas, 1835. Diary of Col. Wm. F. Gray, Giving Details of his Journey to Texas and Return in 1835–36 and Second Journey to Texas in 1837* (Houston: Fletcher Young Publishing Co., 1965), 94, 224.

3. Amos Andrew Parker, *Trip to the West and Texas, Comprising a Journey of Eight Thousand Miles, through New York, Michigan, Illinois, Missouri, Louisiana, Texas, 1834–35* (Concord, N.H., 1835; reprint, Austin, Tex.: Pemberton Press, 1968), 208–9. See also Edward Stiff, *The Texan Emigrant: Being a Narrative of the Adventures of the Author in Texas* (Cincinnati: G. Conclin, 1840; reprint, 1968), 119–21.

4. David B. Edward, *The History of Texas; or, The Emigrant's, Farmer's, and Politician's Guide to the Character, Climate, Soil, and Productions of that Country* (Cincinnati: J. A. James, 1836), 177.

5. Possibly Robinson's saloon was located in the Old Stone Fort, the oldest building in Nacogdoches, built in 1780 on the northeast corner of the central square of town. The fort was removed in 1902 and reconstructed on the campus of Stephen F. Austin University. Current tourist literature from the fort lists its many functions over the years, including public building, grocery store, candy store, and saloon.

6. *Parmalee and Roeder Journal*, East Texas Research Center. The account book starts in Mar. 1837 and continues into the mid-1840s with some gaps. The entries for the jacket and bookcase appear on Aug. 7, 1838; the writing materials span several entries from Sept. 1839 into 1841. Spring Farm entries appear in Sept. 1837. The clothing entries are in Oct. 1838. Deed activity in the county record books suggests that Roeder and Robinson bought the farm property in summer of 1837 and then sold it in November. Robinson was involved in a number of land sales in and around Nacogdoches in the late 1830s and 1840s. In 1838 he collected his 640-acre headright near the town. Tax lists from 1840 and 1847 indicate that he held property in other rural areas of East Texas as well. By the 1850s, when his estate was probated, he owned over 11,000 acres of land in East Texas.

7. Archie P. McDonald, *By Early Candlelight: The Story of Old Milam* (Fort Worth, Tex.: Masonic Home Press, 1967), 44–47.

8. Minutes of the District Court of Nacogdoches County, Book A, transcribed by Emma Barrett Reeves (1981), *Texas vs. David Milton Shropshire,* Aug. 20, 1837, 9–11.

9. Archie P. McDonald, ed., *Hurrah for Texas: The Diary of Adolphus Sterne, 1838–1851* (Waco, Tex.: Texan Press, 1969), 91.

10. McDonald, *Hurrah for Texas,* 205, 211, 218, 229, 231, 235, 236.

11. Gray, *From Virginia to Texas, 1835,* 73.

12. Mary Smith Fay, *War of 1812 Veterans in Texas* (New Orleans: Polyanthos Press, 1979), 161–62.

13. Bennett Blake Papers, box 7, folder 16, East Texas Research Center, Nacogdoches.

14. "The Man Who Came Back," Lois Foster Blount Papers, box 10, folder 7, East Texas Research Center, Nacogdoches. Blount was on the faculty at Stephen F. Austin University in Nacogdoches in the early twentieth century and was also a director of the East Texas Collection, to which she contributed thirty-five boxes of materials. This typescript is undated, but it refers at the start to an Oklahoma gubernatorial candidate who wrote a book called *Beating Back,* about a comeback from criminal activity; Alphonso Jennings's *Beating Back* was published in 1914 (New York: D. Appleton, 1914).

15. Minutes of the Milam Lodge, Aug. 19, 1839: "A suggestion made by Bro. Sterne to appoint a committee to wait on Bro. Parmalee to ascertain if he stands in need of any assistance." Robert B. Blake Collection, vol. 37, 68, East Texas Research Center. On the Cherokee wars, see Dorman H. Winfrey, *Battles of Texas* (Waco, Tex.: Texan Press, 1967), 81–100. The Nacogdoches volunteers under General Thomas J. Rusk went after the Cherokee in the first two weeks of July 1839, along with two other large contingents of Texans. Only two days of fighting occurred, between nine hundred Texans and about seven hundred to nine hundred Indians. In all, two Texans were killed and thirty wounded (Robinson probably counted among them); about a hundred Cherokee were killed or wounded.

16. *A Letter from Richard P. Robinson, as Connected with the Murder of Ellen Jewett, Sent in a Letter to His Friend, Thomas Armstrong, with a Defence of the Jury* (New York, 1837, and Providence, R.I., 1837).

17. Letters to and from J. S. Abbott of Concord, New Hampshire, document the purchase of the two passenger coaches and a hack. Letters of Oct. 7 and Dec. 10, 1851, Crossland, box 4, folder 1, Burton Collection, East Texas Research Center. I am indebted to Linda Nicklas, Director of the Center, for sharing these documents with me. Parmalee's probate inventory of 1855 includes a blue fourteen-passenger coach and eighteen horses, listed as stabled at his stagecoach stops along this route. The inventory also mentions a blacksmith shop, a town lot and stable, a rifle and a shotgun, an iron safe, a gold watch, and various household furnishings. Record of Inventory, Book B, Estate of Richard Parmalee, 117–18, 123, 130–32. No slaves are entered in his inventory; probably Attala retained title to the slaves throughout their marriage. In the 1850 census she is listed with him, but separately credited as being worth $4,000. About a year after Parmalee's probate, Attala became legal guardian of an estate of six slaves, worth $3,650, belonging to her minor daughter Catherine Phillips. Sept. 29, 1856, Inventory Book B, p. 146.

18. Nacogdoches County Criminal Docket, Book B, Sept. 25, 1846, 53, East Texas Research Center. Wingfield came to Nacogdoches in 1835 from Virginia. He was not a tavern regular.

19. McDonald, *Hurrah for Texas,* 83, 139.

20. *Columbus (Georgia) Inquirer,* Jan. 13, 1841. I thank Thomas Baker of the University of North Carolina, Chapel Hill, for sending me this reference.

21. *Albany Weekly Argus,* Feb. 26, 1848; *Syracuse Weekly Star,* Mar. 4, 1848; reprinted from the *New York Tribune,* n.d.

22. *New Orleans Crescent,* reprinted in the *National Police Gazette,* Mar. 25, 1848. George Wilkes, the editor of the *National Police Gazette,* added a correction about Robin-

son's age. Just six months later, Wilkes started running his serial on the lives of Jewett and Robinson.

23. "The Ellen Jewett Tragedy," *New York Times*, Aug. 29, 1855.

24. "Interesting Particulars on the Death of Richard P. Robinson," *New York Times*, Aug. 25, 1855.

25. Minute Books of Milam Lodge 2, Robert B. Blake Collection, vol. 37, East Texas Research Center. My thanks to Linda Nicklas for providing me with this document.

• EPILOGUE •

1. *Life and Conversations of Richard P. Robinson, the Supposed Murderer of Ellen Jewett, with an Account of his Trial, Together with an Account of the Life of Ellen Jewett* (New Haven, Conn., 1840). Quotes on the waxworks show from the *Boston Wanderer*, the *Boston Traveller*, and the *Boston Trumpet* are on the back inside cover.

2. Hawthorne, *American Notebooks*, 8:176–78.

ACKNOWLEDGMENTS

I first came across the Helen Jewett murder case in 1988, while I was working at
the American Antiquarian Society in Worcester, Massachusetts, on another project, a study of women and sexual danger in public. One of my research strategies
was to read through the society's vast collection of crime pamphlets from the
early national period, calling out from the stacks all titles that included a
woman's name. One day, three of the Jewett pamphlets were delivered to my car-
rel, and I was instantly captivated by the mysterious and clashing narratives they
produced over this young murder victim's identity. In a sense, my own introduction to the story exactly replicated what newspaper readers in New York City in
April 1836 experienced. Within a day I located the pamphlet represented to be
several months of Richard Robinson's diary, a remarkable document so unlike
any young man's diary I had ever encountered from the period that I became
determined to learn whatever I could about this strange young couple. The Antiquarian Society's incomparable set of early-nineteenth-century newspapers
allowed me to indulge my fantasy of being a member of the reading public of Jewett's day, turning the pages of New York's penny and mercantile papers (the originals, not microfilm) to follow the daily progress of the case. A third major
collection in the Antiquarian Society, their large holding of nineteenth-century
county and local history records, answered my need to play detective. Before
long, I had the Weston family of Maine and all their collateral relatives staked
out; finding the Doyens took rather longer. I am very grateful to the Antiquarian
Society for inviting me to spend a year there, funded by the National Endowment
for the Humanities. Members of the staff have continued to be unfailingly helpful, and I thank John B. Hench, Joanne D. Chaison, Georgia B. Barnhill, Nancy
Burkett, Marcus McCorison, Ellen Dunlap, Dennis Leary, Thomas G. Knoles,
Marie Lamoroux, and the late Joyce Ann Tracy.

My sister, Mary Weavers Cline, has had a long-standing fascination with the history and architecture of old New York City, so when she started getting daily e-mail from me in 1988 about the Jewett murder story, she suggested we meet in New York to walk the streets of the old Fifth Ward. She had worked for many years in a building between Thomas and Worth Streets, down the block from the site of the murder, and knew the neighborhood well. She showed me the few remaining antebellum buildings tucked in between late-nineteenth- and early-twentieth-century commercial structures, and I took her to the Municipal Archives on Chambers Street, where we pored over the manuscript depositions of the coroner and grand jury hearings that indicted Richard Robinson for murder, filed in the District Attorney's Indictment Papers. Mary has been a constant source of advice and encouragement, supplying me with pictures of old Manhattan to help me visualize the period, listening to me describe my discoveries, and finally reading the entire manuscript as it moved to completion.

I've made many trips since to the Municipal Archives, rich with records of tax assessments, old maps, police court warrants, and arrest dockets. Kenneth Cobb, the director, was ever helpful. He supplied me with plastic gloves to wear while going through boxes of warrants, dusty from age, and he engaged in a special search of the storage rooms for the hatchet, portrait miniatures, Robinson diary, and cache of ninety letters held by the District Attorney during the trial. But all that turned up from that era was a dirk from some other murder case. The material evidence relating to the Robinson trial has disappeared—probably borrowed by George Wilkes in 1848 and never returned. I still hope that the miniatures exist somewhere, since they are objects of evident artistic value that I imagine would more likely be saved than tossed out.

In the course of research I visited many archives and libraries and incurred debts of gratitude. In New York they include the New York Public Library and the New-York Historical Society; the latter has the largest concentration of Jewett pamphlets, as well as the *New York Herald* in hard copy. In Augusta, Maine, I worked at the Maine State Library and adjoining Maine State Archives, as well as the Fort Western Museum, where Jeffrey Zimmerman was particularly helpful. I thank archivist Nicholas Noyes of the Maine Historical Society in Portland for permission to quote from the Reuel Williams Papers. It was there that I learned about the Captain Cook wallpaper and its removal to Historic Deerfield. I found much of use at the Bowdoin College Special Collections and in the local history collections of the Portland (Maine) and Newburyport (Massachusetts) Public Libraries. In Boston, I thank the Massachusetts Historical Society and especially Virginia Hay Smith, who kindly sent me copies of the Amelia Peabody letters of 1836 in advance of my trip there. The Boston Public Library proved a great source of New England newspapers on microfilm, and the New England Historic Genealogical Society was a gold mine of local history materials; microfilms of probate records and of the 1798 federal tax were especially useful. The Connecticut Historical Society in Hartford was the source of one pamphlet about Robinson not available elsewhere.

The Library of Congress's manuscript collections include Chief Justice Melville Weston Fuller's papers; a secondary collection on the judge is held by the

Chicago Historical Society. I thank archivist Ralph Pugh in Chicago for sending me photocopies of Weston family letters from the 1830s and particularly the divorce papers of Catharine Weston Fuller, which are not included in the Library of Congress collection.

I twice visited the East Texas Research Center at the Stephen F. Austin State University in Nacogdoches. I offer special thanks to the center's director, Linda Cheves Nicklas, herself the local expert on Robinson's life in Texas; she graciously shared her personal Parmalee file with me. I also thank Archie P. McDonald, professor at Stephen F. Austin University, for corresponding with me in 1988 and sharing his vast knowledge of Nacogdoches.

Closer to home in California, the Bancroft Library at UC–Berkeley and the Sutro Library in San Francisco proved invaluable. And I thank the interlibrary loan staff of UC–Santa Barbara's Davidson Library for their efforts in acquiring distant materials in the periods when I could not travel to archives.

Long-distance aid from interested archivists was often forthcoming in this project. I thank Marie Sauvé and Phyllis Barr of the Parish Archives of Trinity Church in the City of New York, Kenneth C. Cramer and Barbara Krieger of the Dartmouth College Library, Elsa Meyers of the New Jersey Historical Society, and James P. Danky of the State Historical Society of Wisconsin.

I am grateful to Deborah Bershad of New York City, who gave me an impromptu but full tour of the second-floor courtrooms, back rooms (once jury rooms), and attic spaces of City Hall, where Robinson's trial was held. Not many 1830s structures remain in lower Manhattan; I profited greatly from a detailed tour of the Merchant's House Museum on Fourth Street, a row house built in 1832 and kept in the same family for nearly a century. It approximates the milieu and probably even the decor of Jewett's residence on Thomas Street.

On my many trips to Boston, I stayed with my friends Carol Axelrod and Ed de Franceschi in Brookline, who turned over their attic floor to me for days and weeks at a time. I started writing this book at their house on one of those trips; now that this long project is at last done, I will have to dream up new projects in New England to continue visiting them.

A yearlong grant in 1994 to 1995, funded by the National Endowment for the Humanities, took me to the National Humanities Center in North Carolina, where a central part of the book was written. I thank the staff and especially Kent Mulliken, the assistant director, who by chance or design brought two other scholars working on early American crime together with me in that year's set of fellows. Daily lunches with Karen Halttunen and Robert Ferguson generated interesting conversations about murders and spectacular trials; I especially thank Karen for allowing me to read her manuscript on early American murder. Charles Capper, also a fellow that year, provided important assistance in fleshing out the literary pretensions of some of the Weston family members. Dr. Richard Levenson, a pathologist then at Duke University, assisted me with forensic questions. Linda Kerber, Mary Beth Norton, Helen L. Horowitz, and Laurel Thatcher Ulrich helped make that fellowship year possible by writing letters of support for me, and I thank them.

I have a bigger debt to Laurel, since we share early Hallowell/Augusta as a research arena. Laurel generously provided research materials as well as Augusta travel tips. She gave me her copy of an 1838 map of Augusta once her book was finished, and she hosted me in Durham, New Hampshire, on one of my trips to Maine.

Other colleagues shared work in progress with me and sent materials relating to Jewett my way. They include Timothy Gilfoyle, who alerted me to New York's land conveyance records and the brothel ownership of John R. Livingston, among other things; Amy Gilman Srebnick, whose research on the Mary Rogers murder dovetailed with mine; Gregg R. Hennessey, who helped with Marston family history; Dan Schiller and Michael Schudson, who answered journalism questions; Andie Tucher, whose enthusiasm for the Jewett case matches my own; Richard Johns, invaluable on post office history; Robert C. Davis, who sent me material on New York physicians; Clare Brandt, a source on the Livingston family; and Martha Burns, who located a Jewett pamphlet at Brown University for me. Specific guidance from art historians about John Vanderlyn's painting of Jane McCrea came from Carrie Rebora, William H. Gerdts, Lillian Miller, and Wendell Tripp. Dottie McLaren produced the Maine map in chapter 8.

I've delivered papers on the Jewett murder at various meetings, and I thank these friends for useful comments and suggestions on these early essays: Daniel A. Cohen, Elliot Gorn, Eric Monkkonen, David Papke, Alan Taylor, Eric Lott, Mark Carnes, Angela Woollacott, Carroll Pursell, and Kathleen Brown.

Students and friends have helped in many ways, as sounding boards for ideas and as researchers and fact checkers: they include Stacey Robertson, Betsy Homsher, Clare Lyons, Kirsten Hawkins, Elizabeth Debrulle, and Lee Stone, who was the first to read the manuscript straight through as a kind of unofficial continuity editor. Karen Gundersen, my assistant in the dean's office at UC–Santa Barbara, assembled multiple copies of the manuscript on several occasions under the gun of deadlines; she also read it with enthusiasm while she collated, which helped reassure me that I had not lost the inherent interest and mystery of the Jewett story in a mass of overresearched details.

I owe a special debt of gratitude to Jane N. Garrett, my editor at Knopf, whose patience and support helped nurture this project through to completion. My family has also been very patient over the years. My parents, Laura and Jack Cline, never stopped asking when the project would be done; each has read parts of the manuscript and offered excellent editorial advice. My in-laws, Helen and Harry Cohen, hosted me on many research trips to New York City. When I first told Helen about my discovery of the Jewett murder, she instantly put in my hands *The Thomas Street Horror: An Historical Novel of Murder*, the 1982 historical fiction by Raymond Paul, from whom she had taken courses at Montclair State University. Serendipity in research no longer surprises me, but it does please me greatly. My husband, Ben, and my sons, Daniel and Jeremy, have provided the support and encouragement so necessary to the completion of a long-term project. They are even more happy than I, if possible, that the book is finally finished.

TRADER JOE'S

TRADER JOE'S COMPANY
2217 SOUTH SHORE CENTER
ALAMEDA, CA 94501
(510) 769-5450
STORE 109

% MILK- 1/2 GALLON	1.79
SLICED WHITE MUSHROOMS	1.39
NORI MAKI RICE CRACKER	1.69
=NC JUICE HANSENS APPLE FILTE	1.99
5% ANGUS GROUND BEEF	4.18

SUBTOTAL	$11.04
TOTAL	$11.04
DEBIT	$11.04

36@@@@@@@@@@6011
PURCHASE
SWIPED
AUTH# 00000000
12-08-2004 05:11PM
REFERENCE #:   0010019010

ITEMS 5   B., Kris
12-08-2004 05:11PM   0109 01 0092 7271

THANK YOU FOR SHOPPING AT
TRADER JOE'S
YOUR UNIQUE GROCERY STORE

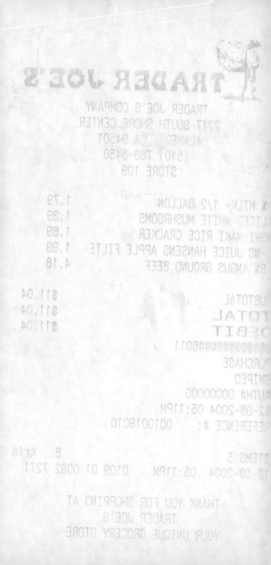

A NOTE ON THE TYPE

THIS BOOK WAS SET IN DE VINNE, AN AMERICAN TYPEFACE THAT IS ACTUALLY A
RECUTTING BY GUSTAV SCHROEDER OF FRENCH ELZEVIR. IT WAS INTRODUCED
BY THE CENTRAL TYPE FOUNDRY OF ST. LOUIS IN 1889. NAMED IN HONOR OF
THEODORE LOW DE VINNE, WHOSE NINE-STORY PLANT, CALLED THE FORTRESS,
WAS THE FIRST BUILDING IN NEW YORK CITY ERECTED EXPRESSLY FOR
PRINTING, THE TYPE HAS A DELICATE QUALITY OBTAINED BY THE CONTRAST
BETWEEN THE THICK AND THIN PARTS OF LETTERS. AN ENORMOUSLY POPULAR
TYPE DURING THE EARLY PART OF THIS CENTURY, DE VINNE COMBINES EASY
READABILITY WITH A NOSTALGIC FEELING.

COMPOSED BY NORTH MARKET STREET GRAPHICS,
LANCASTER, PENNSYLVANIA

PRINTED AND BOUND BY QUEBECOR PRINTING,
MARTINSBURG, WEST VIRGINIA

DESIGNED BY IRIS WEINSTEIN